CONFLICTS IN AMERICAN HISTORY

THE CIVIL WAR ERA
1861–1865

Volume III

Volume I. The Colonial and Revolutionary Eras: 1492–1783

Volume II. The Early Republic Era: 1783–1860

Volume III. The Civil War Era: 1861–1865

Volume IV. The Reconstruction Era: 1865–1877

Volume V. The Gilded Age, Progressive Era, and World War I: 1877–1920

Volume VI. The Roaring Twenties, Great Depression, and World War II: 1920–1945

Volume VII. The Postwar and Civil Rights Era: 1945–1973

Volume VIII. Toward the Twenty-First Century: 1974–Present; and Index

CONFLICTS IN AMERICAN HISTORY

THE CIVIL WAR ERA
1861–1865

Volume III

edited by
Edward J. Blum
San Diego State University
and
Brian L. Johnson
Johnson C. Smith University

A Bruccoli Clark Layman Book

Facts On File
An imprint of Infobase Publishing

Conflicts in American History, Volume III: The Civil War Era: 1861–1865

Edited by Edward J. Blum and Brian L. Johnson

EDITORIAL DIRECTOR
Richard Layman
SERIES EDITORS
Sally Evans
James F. Tidd Jr.

Copyright © 2010 by Bruccoli Clark Layman, Inc.

All rights reserved. No part of this book may be reproduced or utilized in any form or by any means, electronic or mechanical, including photocopying, recording, or by any information storage or retrieval systems, without permission in writing from the publisher. For information contact:

Facts On File, Inc.
An imprint of Infobase Publishing, Inc.
132 West 31st Street
New York NY 10001

Library of Congress Cataloging-in-Publication Data

Conflicts in American history : a documentary encyclopedia.
   p. cm.
   Each volume has a different editor.
   "A Bruccoli Clark Layman book."
   Includes bibliographical references and index.
   ISBN 978-0-8160-7093-0 (8-Volume set) — ISBN 978-0-8160-7094-7 (Volume 1) — ISBN 978-0-8160-7095-4 (Volume 2) — ISBN 978 0 8160 7096 1 (Volume 3) — ISBN 978-0-8160-7097-8 (Volume 4) — ISBN 978-0-8160-7098-5 (Volume 5) — ISBN 978-0-8160-7099-2 (Volume 6) — ISBN 978-0-8160-7100-5 (Volume 7) — ISBN 978-0-8160-7101-2 (Volume 8) 1. United States—History—Encyclopedias, Juvenile.
   E174.C655 2010
   973.003—dc22
                          2009047715

Facts On File books are available at special discounts when purchased in bulk quantities for businesses, associations, institutions, or sales promotions. Please call our Special Sales Department in New York at (212) 967-8800 or (800) 322-8755.

You can find Facts On File on the World Wide Web at http://www.factsonfile.com

Text design by James Scotto-Lavino
Composition by Manley, Inc.
Cover printed by Sheridan Books, Ann Arbor, MI
Book printed and bound by Sheridan Books, Ann Arbor, MI
Date printed: August 2010
Printed in the United States of America

10 9 8 7 6 5 4 3 2 1

This book is printed on acid-free paper.

CONTENTS

Foreword ... ix
Introduction ... xi
List of Contributors ... xv
Chronology ... xvii

1 The Rise of Abolitionism and the Conflict over Slavery ... 1
    Introduction ... 1
    Chronology ... 8
    Documents ... 11
        1. Pennsylvania Act for the Gradual Abolition of Slavery ... 11
        2. Instructions in the Quock Walker Case ... 14
        3. *Notes on the State of Virginia* ... 14
        4. Abolition of the Atlantic Slave Trade by U.S. Congress ... 15
        5. *Appeal to the Coloured Citizens of the World* ... 19
        6. From the First Issue of *The Liberator* ... 21
        7. "Civil Disobedience" ... 23
        8. What to the Slave Is the Fourth of July? ... 24
        9. Review of *Uncle Tom's Cabin* ... 27
        10. "Negro Slavery," from *Sociology for the South: Or the Failure of Free Society* ... 35
    Bibliography ... 38

2 Dred Scott: The Constitution, Slavery, and the Future of America ... 40
    Introduction ... 40
    Chronology ... 46
    Documents ... 48
        1. Selections from the Constitution ... 48
        2. Congressional Action on Slavery in the Territories ... 49
        3. *Scott v. Sandford* ... 51
        4. Benjamin Curtis's Dissenting Opinion ... 56
        5. Abraham Lincoln's Speech on the Dred Scott Decision ... 61
        6. Abraham Lincoln's Debate with Stephen A. Douglas ... 63
    Bibliography ... 64

3 Antebellum Compromises ... 66
    Introduction ... 66
    Chronology ... 71
    Documents ... 73
        1. James Tallmadge Jr.'s Proposed Amendment ... 73
        2. Failed Amendments Prohibiting Slavery, August 8, 1846, and March 3, 1847 ... 73
        3. John C. Calhoun's Resolutions ... 74
        4. James K. Polk's Address to Congress ... 74
        5. Federal Fugitive Slave Laws ... 75
        6. Henry Clay's Last Major Speech on Compromise Resolutions ... 76
        7. Calhoun Defends the Rights of the South ... 80
        8. Speech by Daniel Webster ... 84
        9. Kansas-Nebraska Act ... 89
    Bibliography ... 90

4 The Secession Crisis ... 92
    Introduction ... 92
    Chronology ... 96
    Documents ... 97
        1. Letter from James M. Mason ... 97
        2. A Moderate Stance on Secession ... 97
        3. President James Buchanan's Opinion of Secession ... 98
        4. John Parker Hale Opposes Secession ... 100
        5. Southern Manifesto ... 102
        6. Ordinance of Secession ... 102
        7. Split Sentiments ... 103
        8. Another Declaration of Independence ... 103
        9. Crittenden Compromise ... 106

10. Alexander H. Stephens's Speech at the Secession Convention	108
11. The Fate of Fort Sumter	109
12. Lincoln's Inaugural Address	112
Bibliography	113

5 Armed Conflict: Logistics, Strategy, and the Experience of Battle — 115

Introduction — 115
Chronology — 119
Documents — 121
1. Call for Troops — 121
2. McClellan v. Lincoln — 121
3. A Vengeful President — 122
4. Lee's Resignation — 124
5. Campaign Life — 124
6. Shiloh — 125
7. Clash of the Ironclads — 132
8. Upcoming Battle — 133
9. Moving North — 137
10. Gettysburg — 137
11. Quantrill's Raiders — 142
12. Grisly Sights — 143
13. Blockade Runners — 144
14. Attack on All Fronts — 145
15. War Is Hell — 155
16. Columbia Is Burning — 160
17. Appomattox — 161
Bibliography — 161

6 African Americans in the Military: Contrabands, Freemen, and Women — 163

Introduction — 163
Chronology — 168
Documents — 170
1. Our Historic Development—Shall It Be Superceded by a War of Races? — 170
2. The Late Election — 171
3. Lincoln's Reply to Henry Raymond — 172
4. Letter from Jacob Dodson — 172
5. Lincoln's Letter to Orville H. Browning — 172
6. Letter from William Scott — 173
7. John Boston's Letter — 174
8. Sambo's Right to Be Kilt — 175
9. The Diary of Salmon P. Chase — 175
10. Negro Soldiers on Duty — 177
11. C. B. Wilder's Testimony — 177
12. Letter from Elias Strunke — 178
13. Harriet Tubman — 179
14. Lincoln's Letter to His Critics — 180
15. Letter from James Henry Gooding — 182
16. The Ovation for the Black Regiment — 183
17. Letter from Colonel C. T. Trowbridge — 184
Bibliography — 184

7 Violent Abolitionism: John Brown and the Raid on Harpers Ferry — 186

Introduction — 186
Chronology — 190
Documents — 193
1. Letter from John Brown to His Brother — 193
2. Words of Advice — 194
3. Eyewitness Testimony — 195
4. Provisional Constitution and Ordinances for the People of the United States — 197
5. John Brown's Testimony — 203
6. Last Address of John Brown to the Virginia Court — 206
7. Captain John Brown Not Insane — 207
8. Letters from Prison — 209
9. Brown of Osawatomie — 214
10. Nat Turner's Rebellion — 215
Bibliography — 216

8 Temperance: Religion, Politics, and Ethnic Groups — 218

Introduction — 218
Chronology — 225
Documents — 226
1. Catholic Temperance Association — 226
2. Celebrating Temperance — 227
3. The Prohibitory Liquor Law of Maine — 228
4. Letter from the New Jersey Sons of Temperance — 233
5. Minutes of the Proceedings of the Ten Islands Baptist Association — 234
6. The Temple of Honor — 237
7. "O, Come and Sign the Pledge" — 240
8. A Man of Unique Methods — 241
9. Two Methods of Reform — 242
10. Frances Willard — 243
Bibliography — 244

9 Religion in the Age of Slavery — 246

Introduction — 246
Chronology — 251
Documents — 252
1. The Martyr — 252
2. *Sketches of Slave Life* — 256
3. "The 'Infidelity' of Abolitionism" — 258
4. "The Bible Argument" — 262
5. *Religious Instruction of the Negroes* — 269

    6. "The Battle Hymn of the Republic" — 273
    7. The Twenty-Ninth Anniversary of the American Anti-Slavery Society — 274
    8. Abraham Lincoln's Second Inaugural Address — 276
    9. "Ecclesiastical Equality of Negroes" — 277
    10. *Army Life in a Black Regiment* — 279
  Bibliography — 282

10 The Emancipation Proclamation: Slavery, the Civil War, and Abraham Lincoln — 285

  Introduction — 285
  Chronology — 290
  Documents — 291
    1. An Early Look at Slavery — 291
    2. Lincoln's First Inaugural Address — 291
    3. Abraham Lincoln to John C. Frémont — 292
    4. Appeal to the Border States — 293
    5. A New Plan for Emancipation — 295
    6. Life outside the United States — 295
    7. Abraham Lincoln to Horace Greeley — 296
    8. The First Draft — 297
    9. An Appeal to Many — 298
    10. Strategic Advantages — 299
    11. Dissenting Opinions — 300
    12. "Enslaving the Whites to Free the Blacks" — 301
    13. The Emancipation Proclamation — 303
    14. Freedom to Slaves! — 304
    15. A Soldier's Opinion — 305
  Bibliography — 305

Appendix — 307

  1: The Confederate Constitution — 309
  2: Abraham Lincoln's Proclamation on the Wade-Davis Bill — 317
  3: The Wade-Davis Manifesto — 317

Biographies — 319

  James Black — 319
  John Brown — 319
  John C. Calhoun — 320
  Henry Clay — 320
  Benjamin Curtis — 320
  William Earl Dodge — 321
  Stephen Arnold Douglas — 321
  Frederick Douglass — 322
  Neal Dow — 322
  Nathan Bedford Forrest — 323
  William Lloyd Garrison — 323
  Ulysses S. Grant — 324
  Charles Colcock Jones — 325
  Abraham Lincoln — 325
  Robert H. Milroy — 326
  Wendell Phillips — 326
  James K. Polk — 327
  Robert Barnwell Rhett — 327
  Franklin B. Sanborn — 328
  Dred Scott — 328
  Philip H. Sheridan — 329
  Robert Smalls — 329
  Edwin M. Stanton — 330
  Alexander H. Stephens — 330
  Eliza Daniel Stewart — 331
  Harriet Beecher Stowe — 331
  Roger Brooke Taney — 331
  Harriet Tubman — 332
  St. George Tucker — 332
  Henry McNeal Turner — 333
  Daniel Webster — 334
  John Greenleaf Whittier — 334
  William Wilberforce — 334
  Frances Willard — 335
  William Lowndes Yancey — 335

General Bibliography — 337
Index — 343

FOREWORD

> In times of danger we are driven to the written record by a pressing need to find answers to the riddle of today. We need to know what kind of firm ground other men, belonging to generations before us, have found to stand on. In spite of changing conditions of life they were not very different from ourselves, their thoughts were the grandfathers of our thoughts, they managed to meet situations as difficult as those we have to face.... We need to know how they did it.
>
> John Dos Passos,
> *The Ground We Stand On* (1941)

How we got where we are; how we became the people we are; how we became the nation we are: that is the concern of history, and we study it most confidently by an enlightened examination of the evidence left behind. *Conflicts in American History: A Documentary Encyclopedia* is a set of eight volumes, organized chronologically, that present a written record in American history contextualized by means of background essays, timelines, and short biographies of key figures. The organizing rationale of this reference work is that the political, social, military, moral, and cultural struggles that have influenced American life and shaped American values are best understood by analyzing primary documents and learning about the people who created them. An effort has been made to present documents that represent a diverse range of viewpoints so that users may come to their own conclusions about the viability of the arguments of the day. A broad assortment of materials is presented, including speeches, letters, editorials, songs, poems, diaries, laws, public documents, memoirs, magazine and newspaper articles; graphic materials, such as political cartoons, posters, advertisements, broadsides, tables, charts, and maps are also employed.

Every era in American history has been marked by conflicts in which people have fought passionately for what they believed in. These conflicts define America, and our understanding of them colors our national identity. Yet, standard interpretations that reveal cultural biases are frequently subject to challenge. Thus, increasingly history is being taught through primary documents, and document-based questions (DBQs), featured prominently in the National History Standards and Social Studies curricula, are routinely included on standardized tests and AP history exams. Such emphasis is eminently sound, though it presents daunting challenges, requiring students to have a command of the social, cultural, and historical contexts in which documents were created. To understand the words of the past, one must first understand what they meant to the people who first used them. Context is a necessary complement to the study of primary documents.

This encyclopedia provides students with both a selection of the documents that have shaped our nation and with the tools they require to read and interpret them. Blending primary and secondary material, *Conflicts in American History* adopts the standard set by the National Center for History in the Schools, encouraging students "to raise questions and to marshal solid evidence in support of their answers; to go beyond the facts presented in their textbooks and examine the historical record for themselves; to consult documents, journals, diaries, artifacts, historic sites, works of art, quantitative data, and other evidence from the past, and to do so imaginatively—taking into account the historical context in which these records were created and comparing the multiple points of view of those on the scene at the time."

As *Conflicts in American History* is broad in its coverage of national concerns, it is necessary to choose defining conflicts within different aspects of American life. Conflicts treated in each volume have been selected to represent the topical categories identified by the College Board for the curriculum in AP History:

    Political Institutions, Behavior, and Public Policy;
    Social Change and Cultural and Intellectual Developments;
    Diplomacy and International Relations; and
    Economic Developments.

The goal of *Conflicts in American History* is to suggest to students the richness and the complexity of historical study: What has happened when individuals were faced with sets of circumstances that required deliberation, interpretation, and finally action in matters that have determined the course of our development as a nation? The answers reveal the social, moral and intellectual currents that make us who we are today.

Richard Layman

INTRODUCTION

The Civil War was the great turning point of American history. It was the moment when the contradictions of America's founding were settled with blood. The nation could no longer remain half slave and half free, and four years of titanic conflict settled the score. The bloodiest battle on American soil, the Civil War was the result of a multitude of events working against one other. Fundamental disagreements in social, political, and economic policy pushed the country into war in 1861 and worked to reshape American life. Driven by the sectionalism that had begun to debilitate the federal government by the mid to late nineteenth century, the conflicts of the war and the following period of Reconstruction influenced the development of the distinct regions of the North, the South, and the West.

After several decades of wrangling over the future of slavery in the United States, the nation began splintering in late 1860. By April 1861 two rival governments squared off against one another. In the four-year war that followed, roughly six hundred thousand Americans lost their lives. The schism pitted section against section, church against church, friend against friend, neighbor against neighbor, brother against brother, and sister against sister. Death tolls rose far above those of all previous American war casualties.

The third volume of Conflicts in American History examines the historical conflicts surrounding the Civil War, focusing particularly on the relationship of each conflict to the causes and outcome of the war. In general, historians agree that the central issue was the future of slavery in the western territories. But slavery had existed for hundreds of years in North America; there had been threats of disunion before; there had been deep divisions over slavery before; there had been nullified laws before; and there had been showdowns between the federal government and state governments before. Why in 1861 did war break out? Scholars point to the rise of militant abolitionism, the failure of congressional compromises, and the rise of the new Republican Party. Conflict stood at the heart of these issues.

The Dred Scott decision (1857), in which the Supreme Court declared that African Americans had no right to federal citizenship, agitated abolitionists and fueled the coming war. In the meantime, the increased violence of the period preceding the Civil War—such as that in Bleeding Kansas (1854–1859; a small-scale civil war between abolitionists and proslavery forces over the legality of slavery in Kansas), and that exemplified in John Brown's raid on Harpers Ferry, Virginia (1859)—signaled the growing divide between abolitionists in the North and proslavery ideologues in the South and contributed to the sectional animosity that led to war. The struggle was further affected by the economic development distinct to each region: in the North the move toward a manufacturing society influenced the development of infrastructure, while in the South the dependence on cotton and tobacco as cash crops prolonged the slave trade and the legality of slavery.

Elections and other legal issues (such as the status of slaves in each region) often were decided by a system of compromise that challenged the essence of the political process and, perhaps more important, influenced the interpretation of U.S. law. Through sectional compromises such as the Missouri Compromise of 1820, the Compromise of 1850, and the Kansas-Nebraska Act of 1854, Congress played an essential role, not only in the development of U.S. law and in the fate of slavery, but also in the related division of the Union.

The Republican Party, formed in the early 1850s, came to replace the Whig Party as the main opposition to the Democratic Party and then won the presidency in 1860. Abraham Lincoln, the Republican candidate who became the sixteenth U.S. president, had promised he would not abolish slavery in the states where it already existed but would stand against it expanding into the western territories, a platform that elicited mass support among Northern whites. Considering Lincoln's position on slavery, it is curious that Southern whites reacted to his election by leaving the Union and forming the Confederate States of America.

The Civil War, in large part, involved three theaters of combat: the western frontier; the land battles in the East, principally between Washington D.C., and Richmond, Virginia; and the sea battles along the eastern seaboard. Historians debate which was most vital to the war effort. Was it the frontier West and the Mississippi River where Ulysses Grant and William Sherman devised their tactics of "hard war"? Was it the capturing or protecting of each nation's capital—Washington D.C., and Richmond, Virginia—only one hundred miles apart? Was it the Union blockade that curtailed Confederate imports and exports?

New technology was instrumental in shaping the war, as were generals, politicians, and tactics. With the breechloading rifle and the minié ball, soldiers could now shoot farther, more accurately, and more rapidly. These advancements, coupled with older strategies of war that tended to lump soldiers together, resulted in carnage of epic proportions. The death tolls, sometimes reaching more than three thousand in one day, were not bested until the Gatling gun and trench warfare of World War I killed millions half a century later.

Before, during, and after the Civil War, internal conflict was as troubling as the war itself. White Southerners divided against one another in the new Confederate States of America. Confederate women seemed at first to support the struggle, but over time they encouraged their men to leave the army. Enslaved African Americans navigated the contours of war, leaving plantations when they could, protecting their masters and mistresses when necessary, and seeking their own freedom. Northern whites debated battle tactics and political strategies, while the Emancipation Proclamation inspired both accolades and rioting in that region.

The military struggle could not be separated from these internal political and social conflicts. The Confederate government and peoples struggled to reconcile their commitment to states' rights with the necessity of wartime centralization. Georgia governor Joseph Brown often declined when asked to send troops to aid General Robert E. Lee in Virginia; Brown's argument, in favor of states' rights, suggested that Georgians should take care of Georgia, and Virginians should take care of Virginia. By the end of the war it seemed clear that the Confederacy would lose, and Southern politicians began to consider arming and emancipating slaves to aid the war effort. In the North, Republicans and Democrats debated wartime policies while President Lincoln and the Republican-dominated Congress moved toward a policy of emancipation.

Coming well after thousands of African Americans had taken to the road during the war and shown up at Union military units and forts, the Emancipation Proclamation, issued on January 1, 1863, freed relatively few slaves. Contemporary scholars question whether white political leaders in the North initiated emancipation, or if Lincoln's Proclamation was influenced by the sheer number of African Americans in the South. Union general George B. McClellan followed a policy of returning slaves to their masters, but other Union military men, such as Benjamin Butler, held on to the runaways and declared them "contraband of war," effectively transferring them from private property to federal property.

It is often forgotten that the Emancipation Proclamation articulated a strategy of employing African Americans in the U.S. military. By the end of the war, almost two hundred thousand African Americans had served in the army and navy. Their willingness to fight and die for the Union led some Northern whites to rethink their overarching racist attitudes, and postwar legislation, such as the three Reconstruction Amendments (Thirteenth, Fourteenth, and Fifteenth) and various civil rights bills, was supported largely because of the military efforts of these black men.

A remaining question considers whether steps could have been taken either by President Lincoln or by his predecessor, President James Buchanan, to prevent the Civil War. Since Southern states did not secede from the Union as a group, it is important to ask whether President Buchanan and Congress could have stalled the secession crisis. This volume probes a series of conflicts in American culture, society, and religion in the middle of the nineteenth century. Essays examine the various religious responses to slavery, sectionalism, and war from Southern whites, Northern whites, and African Americans. Although it was not until after the Civil War that Americans hotly debated Charles Darwin's evolutionary theory and its religious implications, Darwinism fueled one of the main religious conflicts of the late nineteenth century, and so a study of Darwin's *On the Origin of Species,* first published in 1859, is included. In the realm of social reform, particularly in terms of temperance, conflict resides at the intersection of American religion and politics.

From the battlefields to the bars, from the homes of presidents to the houses of worship, from the lives of common soldiers to the exploits of extraordinary intellectuals, the era of the Civil War and Reconstruction was an exhilarating time in American history. It was full of triumph and tragedy, of mighty moves forward and terrible suffering. It was a moment replete with conflicts, many of which live with us today.

Edward J. Blum
Brian L. Johnson

LIST OF CONTRIBUTORS

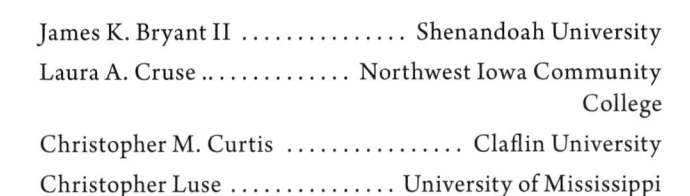

James K. Bryant II .... Shenandoah University
Laura A. Cruse .... Northwest Iowa Community College
Christopher M. Curtis .... Claflin University
Christopher Luse .... University of Mississippi

Francis MacDonnell .... Southern Virginia University
Jonathan A. Noyalas..... Lord Fairfax Community College
Christina Proenza-Coles .... Virginia State University
Anthony J. Scotti Jr. .... Midlands Technical College
Zoe Trodd .... Harvard University

CHRONOLOGY

1737
Benjamin Lay publishes Quaker antislavery essay.

1754–1763
Seven Years War (French and Indian War) encourages the growth of antislavery sentiment among Quakers.

1765–1769
William Blackstone's *Commentaries on the Laws of England* are published.

1769
Granville Sharp publishes *A Representation of the injustice and the dangerous tendency of tolerating slavery; or of admitting the least claim of private property in the persons of men.*

1772
Somerset v. Stewart. English legal ruling holding that slavery violates natural law and "is so odious that nothing can be suffered to support it but positive law."

1774
The Continental Congress resolves to prohibit further slave importations at its first meeting.

1775
Virginia's Colonial governor, John Murray, Lord Dunmore, issues a proclamation guaranteeing the freedom of slaves who run away from masters engaged in rebellion against the Crown.

1776
July 4: The Second Continental Congress approves the Declaration of Independence. Supporters and opponents of the Dred Scott decision later debate whether this document is meant to include blacks within its claims that "all men are created equal," endowed with the inalienable rights of "life, liberty, and the pursuit of happiness."

1777
Vermont state constitution prohibits slavery.

1780
Pennsylvania adopts plan for gradual emancipation.

1782
Virginia passes law allowing for the private manumission of slaves.

1783
Treaty of Paris signals the formal end of the American Revolution. The treaty stipulates that the British army must return runaway slaves to the United States. The refusal of some states to repay British loans prevents the return of the former slaves.

British courts decide Zong Case, an insurance claim for the loss of 131 slaves thrown from a Liverpool slave ship in 1781. Publicity fosters antislavery sentiment.

Quock Walker case determines that slavery is unconstitutional in Massachusetts.

1787
July 13: The Congress under the Articles of Confederation passes the Northwest Ordinance, banning slavery in territories north and west of the Ohio River (later Indiana, Ohio, Illinois, Michigan, and Wisconsin).

U.S. Constitutional Convention meeting in Philadelphia agrees to prohibit legislation outlawing the slave trade for twenty years.

1788
June 21: The U.S. Constitution is ratified with the inclusion of a fugitive-slave clause.

State legislatures in Connecticut, New York, and Massachusetts pass laws prohibiting their citizens from participating in the slave trade.

1789
Olaudah Equiano's autobiography published.

1790
May 26: Congress approves the Southwest Ordinance, allowing for the organization of this territory with slavery. These lands will eventually make up the future state of Tennessee. From the beginnings of the republic some territories were declared forbidden to slavery, while other territories tolerated the institution. From its creation the nation admitted both free states (Vermont, 1791) and slave states (Kentucky, 1792).

1791
Sierra Leone Company chartered to establish a colony in West Africa for freedmen.

Initial Wilberforce bill to abolish slave trade defeated by a vote of 163 to 88.

1793
Upper Canada (British colony) enacts a gradual emancipation law.

1794
France outlaws slavery in all colonies and extends equal rights of citizenship to freedmen.

1799
New York adopts plan of gradual emancipation.

1800
In Philadelphia, free blacks petition Congress to repeal the 1793 Fugitive Slave Act.

May 9: John Brown is born in Torrington, Connecticut. His father, a strict Calvinist, believes slavery to be a sin against God.

August 30: Gabriel Prosser's plan to lead Virginia slaves in rebellion is revealed; the rebellion is prevented when a deluge delayed the planned initial attack, and an informer alerted authorities.

October 7: Gabriel Prosser is hanged.

1803
April 30: Final agreement of the Louisiana Purchase treaty is negotiated between the United States and France.

October 21: Louisiana Purchase treaty is ratified by the U.S. Senate, and the territory is declared a possession of the United States of America.

October 31: U.S. Congress establishes a territorial government for Louisiana.

1804
March 26: U.S. Congress passes an act that divides Louisiana into two territories: Territory of Orleans (Lower Louisiana below the southern border of Arkansas) and District of Louisiana (encompassing the territory including Arkansas north). The latter "district" is under administrative control of the Indiana Territory.

1805
March 3: U.S. Congress passes an act creating the Territory of Louisiana from the District of Louisiana, separating it from the Indiana Territory, and establishing territorial government.

June: The Brown family joins the westward migration of New Englanders and moves to Hudson, Ohio, a town eventually known for its strong abolitionist views.

1808
The United States abolishes the Atlantic slave trade.

1812
April 30: Territory of Orleans admitted into the Union as Louisiana, the eighteenth state.

June 4: Territory of Louisiana becomes Territory of Missouri.

June 18: The United States declares war on Great Britain, starting the War of 1812.

1814
December 24: American and British representatives sign the Treaty of Ghent, ending the War of 1812.

1815
January 8: General Andrew Jackson's forces, unaware of the Treaty of Ghent, defeat British forces at the Battle of New Orleans.

February 16: The United States ratifies the Treaty of Ghent.

1816
December 21: The American Colonization Society is founded in Washington, D.C. Supported by leading clergymen, the society's mission is to send freed blacks back to Africa.

The African Methodist Episcopal (AME) Church is founded in Philadelphia. It is the first independent African American denomination in America.

1817

James Forten leads three thousand blacks in a Philadelphia protest meeting against colonization.

1818

December 3: Illinois is admitted to the Union as a free state.

1819

February 13: The U.S. House of Representatives takes up consideration of enabling the people of Missouri Territory to form a state government. Representative James Tallmadge Jr. of New York proposes an amendment restricting new slaves from being brought into Missouri, emancipating slaves currently residing in Missouri by age twenty-five, and declaring free those born in Missouri after it is admitted into the Union. House adjourns without taking any further action.

February 17: Bill to admit Missouri to statehood with slavery restrictions passes the House. The U.S. Senate passes the Missouri bill without the slavery restrictions.

March 2: House takes up the Senate's version of the Missouri bill to admit. The House refuses to strike out the slavery-restrictions clause. Without concurrence of both Houses of Congress, the bill is dropped.

December 14: Alabama is admitted to the Union as the twenty-second state.

1820

January 3: The U.S. House of Representatives passes a bill admitting Maine (formerly a part of Massachusetts) into the Union.

February 16: The U.S. Senate takes up consideration of admitting Missouri into the Union by attaching it as an amendment to the bill admitting Maine into the Union. Senator Jesse B. Thomas of Illinois proposes a compromise amendment in three parts: 1.) allow Missouri to draft a constitution without slavery restrictions; 2.) admit Maine, a state that prohibits slavery, as a free state to achieve sectional balance; 3.) prohibit slavery from the area existing north of the 36° 30' line and allow slavery south of the line in the remaining parts of the original Louisiana Purchase Territory.

March 2: Both Houses of Congress passes the Maine-Missouri bill.

March 6: The Maine bill with the Missouri admission and slavery amendments are signed into law by President James Monroe, completing the "First Missouri Compromise."

March 15: Maine is admitted as the twenty-third state in the Union.

June 21: John Brown marries Dianthe Lusk in Hudson, Ohio.

September 27: Missouri drafts its constitution and includes a clause deeming it a duty of the state legislature "[t]o prevent free negroes and mulattoes from coming to, and settling in, this state, under any pretext whatsoever...." (Shoemaker, 1916, p. 335)

November 14: Proposed Missouri constitution taken up by the U.S. Senate and referred to the appropriate committee.

American Colonization Society sends a group of ninety-one emigrants to establish a colony in Liberia.

1821

February 12: A House select committee chaired by Henry Clay of Kentucky offers a resolution to admit Missouri, provided that its state legislature does not enact laws barring any description of U.S. citizens or those to become U.S. citizens from residing in the state. This resolution is defeated in the House.

February 23: The House appoints Clay to head another select committee to work with a corresponding Senate committee to resolve the Missouri crisis.

March 2: Both Houses of Congress approve the admission of Missouri.

June: The Missouri state legislature approves of the Congressional measure, but stipulates that Congress does not have the right to bind a state.

July 25: Brown's first child and namesake, John Brown Jr., is born in Hudson, Ohio.

August 10: Missouri is admitted as the twenty-fourth state in the Union, completing the "Second Missouri Compromise."

The Republic of Liberia in West Africa is established as a refuge for freed American slaves. In 1847 this becomes the independent nation of Liberia.

Benjamin Lundy begins publishing *The Genius of Universal Emancipation*.

1822

June 22: Citing Old Testament verses calling for God's vengeance against slave owners, Denmark Vesey attempts a slave revolt in Charleston, South Carolina. When the plot is uncovered, more than thirty-five blacks are executed, many of them members of the Charleston AME Church. Whites institute a wave of repression against independent black religious life; the AME church is outlawed.

American colony for freedmen is settled in Liberia.

1825

A fugitive slave and his wife appear at John Brown's house. Brown feeds and hides the pair.

Ralph Gurley begins publishing *The African Repository and Colonial Journal* for the American Colonization Society.

1826

John Brown and family move to Randolph, Pennsylvania, where Brown establishes a tannery.

Secretary of State Henry Clay asks the Canadian government to return escaped slaves, and Canada refuses.

1827

The first black-owned newspaper, *Freedom's Journal,* is published in New York.

1829

April: William Lloyd Garrison becomes coeditor of *The Genius of Universal Emancipation.*

August 10: White mobs attack black freedmen in Cincinnati, Ohio, and one thousand blacks leave for Canada.

September: David Walker's *Appeal to the Coloured Citizens of the World* published.

Methodist William Capers organizes the first formal domestic mission to the slaves in the South Carolina low country.

1831

January 1: William Lloyd Garrison begins publishing *The Liberator,* the first newspaper in the country to demand an immediate end to slavery.

August 22: Nat Turner leads a slave uprising in Southampton County, Virginia.

1832

August 10: Dianthe Brown dies of heart failure in New Richmond.

Slavery debated in the Virginia legislature. Gradual emancipation proposal voted down.

December: Thomas Roderick Dew publishes review of Virginia debate.

The New England Anti-Slavery Society is founded.

Charles Colcock Jones organizes the Association for the Religious Instruction of the Negroes of Liberty County, Georgia.

1833

July 11: John Brown marries seventeen-year-old Mary Day.

December 4: Garrison and sixty delegates found the American Anti-Slavery Society (AAS).

Dr. John Emerson brings Dred Scott with him to Fort Armstrong in the free state of Illinois. They remain there until May 1836.

Britain adopts an emancipation and apprenticeship plan that prepares eight hundred thousand slaves for freedom.

1835

October 21: A mob pursues Garrison through Boston and nearly lynches him.

The AAS begins mailing antislavery literature throughout the South, employing "moral suasion" to call upon slave owners to repent of the sin of slavery.

1836

January: During a period of extreme land speculation, Brown moves his family to Franklin Mills, Ohio, and borrows money to buy land.

In the case of *Rachael v. Walker*, a Missouri court frees a slave named Rachael brought by her army-officer owner to free territory at Fort Snelling in Wisconsin Territory (near modern-day St. Paul, Minnesota).

U.S. Congress adopts "Gag Rule" prohibiting the introduction of antislavery petitions.

1836 – 1838

Dred Scott resides at Fort Snelling in territory subject to the Missouri Compromise line's ban on slavery. He marries Harriet Robinson during this time in an official ceremony.

1837

November 7: Upon hearing that abolitionist newspaperman Elijah Lovejoy has been shot and killed in Illinois by a proslavery mob, Brown commits himself to working for the destruction of slavery.

John Brown is almost ruined financially by the Panic of 1837.

Abolitionist newspaper editor Elijah Lovejoy killed by a mob in Alton, Illinois.

The Presbyterian Church splits into the "Old School" and the "New School." The "Old School" faction denounces the increasing antislavery orientation of many Northern "New School" churches.

1838

Slavery officially ends in all British colonies.

1838 – 1840

After a five-month stay in Louisiana, Dred Scott and his wife return to Fort Snelling.

1839

The Spanish slave ship *Amistad*, carrying fifty-three slaves, is taken over in a mutiny by their leader, Cinque, who orders the two surviving whites to sail the ship to Africa. The ship is seized off the coast of Long Island, and the Africans are jailed.

1841

November 7: Slaves aboard the *Creole* en route from Virginia to New Orleans revolt and sail the ship to a British port in the Bahamas, where they are freed.

1843

December: Dred Scott's master, Dr. John Emerson, dies. He wills his slave property to his wife, Irene Emerson.

1844

April: The Baptist Church splits over slavery, with controversy centering on whether slave owners can be appointed missionaries.

May: The Methodist Church splits over slavery. In the general conference, Northern antislavery delegates protest Georgia bishop James O. Andrew's inheritance of a slave through marriage, asserting that Northern Methodists will not accept a slave-owning bishop.

1845

March 1: The United States through a joint resolution of Congress annexes the independent "Lone Star Republic" of Texas.

April: The Southern Baptist Convention is formed in Atlanta, Georgia.

The Methodist Episcopal Church, South, is founded in Louisville, Kentucky.

May: Frederick Douglass publishes his *Narrative of the Life of Frederick Douglass, An American Slave.*

July 25: General Zachary Taylor lands a force of U.S. troops at Corpus Christi, Texas.

December 29: Texas becomes the twenty-eighth state of the Union and the fifteenth slave state.

1846

April 6: In a bid to gain their freedom, Dred and Harriet Scott bring suit against Mrs. Irene Emerson in a St. Louis court.

May 13: The United States declares war on Mexico.

August 8: Representative David Wilmot of Pennsylvania introduces his amendment to a special appropriation bill outlawing slavery in any territory that might be acquired from Mexico in the war. This amendment becomes commonly known as the "Wilmot Proviso," and the House passes the bill with Wilmot's Amendment.

August 10: The special appropriation bill with the attached Wilmot Proviso dies in the Senate.

Gerritt Smith sells land to Brown in North Elba, New York, where John Brown will live on and off, among a small community of freed slaves, until his death.

1846 – 1848

The Mexican-American War brings vast new territories in the Southwest under American control, reviving tensions between pro- and antislavery forces. In the House of Representatives, David Wilmot (D, Pa.) proposes that any territories acquired as a result of the war must prohibit slavery. The Wilmot Proviso passes the House on a purely sectional vote but dies in the Senate.

1847

February 19: Senator John C. Calhoun of South Carolina submits resolutions to the Senate guaranteeing constitutional protections for slavery.

March 3: Representative David Wilmot of Pennsylvania makes a second attempt to attach the Wilmot Proviso to an appropriation bill that is passed by the House.

December: Frederick Douglass founds the *North Star* in Rochester, New York. The paper is dedicated to immediate abolitionism and black rights based on the inherent equality of all children of God.

Dred Scott loses his first trial due to a technicality when he fails to provide evidence showing he is owned by Irene Emerson.

Liberia declared an independent nation.

1848

February 2: The Treaty of Guadeloupe-Hidalgo between the United States and Mexico ends the Mexican War.

December 5: President James K. Polk, in his final Annual Message to Congress, advocates extending the Missouri Compromise Line to the Pacific Ocean to settle growing sectional tensions.

1849

Henry David Thoreau publishes "Civil Disobedience."

1850

January: Henry Clay introduces the Compromise of 1850, which admits California as a free state and Texas as a slave state.

February 5–6: Senator Henry Clay of Kentucky makes his speech in the U.S. Senate in support of his Compromise Resolutions.

March 4: Senator John C. Calhoun of South Carolina makes his last speech (read by Senator James M. Mason of Virginia) against Clay's Compromise Resolutions.

March 7: Senator Daniel Webster of Massachusetts makes his "Seventh of March" speech in the U.S. Senate in support of Clay's Compromise Resolutions.

March 31: Senator John C. Calhoun of South Carolina dies in Washington, D.C.

July 9: President Zachary Taylor dies in Washington, D.C.

September 9: Clay's Compromise Resolutions admitting California into the Union as a free state; settlement of the Texas-New Mexico boundary issue and organization of New Mexico Territory; and the organization of the Utah Territory passes both houses of Congress.

September 16: Clay's Compromise Resolution on strengthening the federal fugitive slave law (Fugitive Slave Law of 1850) passes both houses of Congress.

September 18: The new Fugitive Slave Act is passed. This act allows slaveholders to retrieve slaves in Northern states and free territories without due process of law, prohibits anyone from helping fugitives, and requires government officials to assist in the retrieval of escaped slaves. Captured blacks are denied any legal power to prove their freedom. At Thanksgiving, Brown speaks on the Fugitive Slave Act to the congregation at his church.

September 20: Clay's Compromise Resolution abolishing the slave trade in the District of Columbia passes both houses of Congress.

Fall: Congress passes a series of laws commonly referred to as the Compromise of 1850, averting a potential breakdown of the Union. The Compromise does the following:
- admits California as a free state;
- prohibits Congress from interfering with the interstate slave trade;
- bans the slave trade, but preserves slavery, in the District of Columbia;
- agrees to accept the debt of the state of Texas in exchange for concessions and an agreement on the New Mexico boundary;
- promises a new tough fugitive-slave law; and
- accepts the New Mexico and Utah Territories without reference to slavery.

(Because most of the Utah Territory and some portions of the New Mexico Territory fall above 36°30' latitude, this last element of the Compromise preserves the possibility of slavery in lands north of the Missouri Compromise.)

A jury in St. Louis finds Dred Scott a free man. Mrs. Irene Emerson, widow of Scott's former master, appeals the decision.

The Independent Order of Good Templars, a temperance organization that includes elements of secrecy such as a handshake and ritual, is founded.

1851

June 2: The first of a series of state prohibition laws called "Maine Laws" is passed, thanks to the efforts of the mayor of Portland, Neal Dow.

December: The Supreme Court rules in *Strader v. Graham*. The case involves slave musicians from Kentucky who traveled to Ohio and later escaped to Canada. The Kentucky court determines that "a slave returning voluntarily with his master from a free State, is still a slave by the laws of his own country." In a unanimous decision, the Supreme Court endorsed the Kentucky court's decision. This ruling embraced the doctrine of reversion, which held that when a slave left a free state and returned to a slave state, his status was determined by the laws of the latter rather than of the former.

Brown establishes the United States League of Gileadites, a black self-defense organization. Senator Charles Sumner meets with Brown and the Gileadites.

1852

March 22: The Missouri Supreme Court in a 2–1 decision rules in favor of Mrs. Emerson, arguing that when Scott returned to Missouri he fell subject to Missouri law.

March: Harriet Beecher Stowe publishes *Uncle Tom's Cabin*. Stowe's novel becomes a literary phenomenon, selling three hundred thousand copies in less than a year. Stowe creates the character of Uncle Tom as a Christlike martyr, the perfect pious Christian destroyed by the evil of slavery.

June 2: Senator Henry Clay of Kentucky dies in Washington, D.C.

October 24: Daniel Webster dies in Marshfield, Massachusetts.

George Frederick Holmes and other defenders of slavery publish criticisms of Stowe.

George Schneider begins a brewery in St. Louis, Missouri, that will later become the Anheuser-Busch Brewing Company.

Vermont, Massachusetts, and Rhode Island adopt versions of the Maine Law. Minnesota Territory passes a short-lived prohibition law.

The New York State Women's Temperance Society is formed after The Sons of Temperance refuse a request by Susan B. Anthony to address the Sons.

1853

The Scotts appeal the ruling in the Missouri Supreme Court and file suit in federal court in St. Louis. Presiding judge Robert Wells determines that Scott qualifies as a citizen for purposes of bringing suit even if he does not qualify under the comity clause of the Constitution: ". . . the Citizens of each State shall be entitled to all Privileges and Immunities of Citizens of different states."

John Brown, now living with his family in Akron, Ohio, becomes involved with the Underground Railroad.

Michigan passes "Maine Law" prohibition.

1854

May 30: Congress passes the Kansas-Nebraska Act, opening up the Kansas and Nebraska Territories to slavery on the basis of popular sovereignty, nullifying the Missouri Compromise line.

June 2: Fifty thousand people in Boston watch Anthony Burns, a fugitive slave, taken in shackles to a ship.

July 4: Garrison publicly burns a copy of the U.S. Constitution.

Judge Wells advises the jury to rule against Dred Scott on the principle that Missouri law ought to determine the outcome of the case.

October: Brown's unmarried sons, Owen, Frederick, and Salmon, leave for Kansas Territory in the wake of the Kansas-Nebraska Bill.

December 30. Dred Scott's family files an appeal to the Supreme Court.

George Fitzhugh publishes *Sociology for the South.*

Elizabeth Cady Stanton asks the New York legislature to support prohibition and to pass divorce laws that will allow women to separate from intemperate husbands.

The Carson League, a citizens-action group in Maine, is formed to seek out evidence of violations of the Maine Prohibition law, under the liberal "search-and-seizure" clause of the law. In their records of October 1854 the organization boasts having contributed to twenty-five convictions for violations of the Maine Law as a result of evidence they obtained during raids.

Connecticut passes "Maine Law" prohibition.

The Republican Party is founded, due to the dissolution of the Whig Party and the weakening of other third parties.

The Massachusetts Supreme Court rules the search-and-seizure provisions of its Maine Law to be unconstitutional.

1855

April 21: The Lager Beer Riot in Chicago results in one death and sixty arrests as a result of the German and Irish reaction to the mayor's Nativist-motivated decision to close saloons on Sundays.

June 2: The Portland Rum Riot occurs when citizens gather at city hall in Portland, Maine, upon hearing rumors that a stash of alcohol is being stored there. Neal Dow, mayor of Portland, calls in the militia, which fires into the crowd, killing one man and injuring another seven.

June: Brown decides to follow his sons to Kansas and leaves Mary and their children behind at North Elba.

December 7: Brown and four of his sons help defend Lawrence, Kansas, during the Wakarusa War.

Prohibition laws, modeled after Maine Law, are passed in New York, Indiana, Delaware, Iowa, Nebraska, and New Hampshire.

1856

February 11: Opening arguments in the Dred Scott case are presented before the Supreme Court.

May 22: Senator Charles Sumner of Massachusetts is almost caned to death on the floor of the Senate in Washington, D.C., by Congressman Preston Brooks of South Carolina, after delivering an antislavery speech titled "The Crime against Kansas."

May 24: Brown directs his men in the murder of five proslavery settlers at Pottawatomie Creek.

June 2: At the Battle of Black Jack in southeastern Douglas County, Brown defeats Henry Clay Pate.

August 30: Brown fights at the Battle of Osawatomie, where his second son, Frederick, is killed.

The New York Supreme Court strikes down the search-and-seizure clause of its prohibition law.

1857

March 4: A supporter of the majority decision in the Dred Scott case, President James Buchanan is inaugurated. In his address he looks forward to a decision from the Court that will help clarify when territorial legislatures might address the issue of slavery in the territories.

March 6: Chief Justice Roger B. Taney announces the Supreme Court's decision in *Dred Scott v. Sandford*, declaring that Scott, a black slave whose master moved him into free territory, could not sue for his freedom in federal court because only whites could be citizens of the United States. Taney declares that Congress has no right to legislate for the territories, ultimately making the Missouri Compromise and the Compromise of 1850 unconstitutional. With a Southern majority, it also ruled that slaveholders have the right to take slaves into free territory; and that Congress has no power to prevent slavery in the territories.

March 12: John Brown tells a Concord audience that he hates violence but accepts it as God's will.

George Fitzhugh publishes *Cannibals All! Or, Slaves without Masters*.

1858

February 22: Brown meets with Gerrit Smith and Franklin Sanborn in Peterboro, New York, and outlines a plan to raid Harpers Ferry.

May 8: Brown's Constitutional Convention of the Oppressed People of the United States is held in Chatham, Ontario, Canada. Brown produces and presents his Provisional Constitution for government in a slave-free nation, and plans his Harpers Ferry raid.

June 16: At Springfield, Illinois, senatorial candidate Abraham Lincoln gives his "House Divided" speech at the close of the Republican state convention.

August–October: In the Illinois Senate race, Lincoln and Stephen Douglas engage in a series of debates focusing on the issue of slavery in the territories, paying special attention to the Dred Scott decision.

September 17: Dred Scott dies after briefly enjoying freedom.

December 20–21: Brown leads a raid on two proslavery homesteads in Missouri, confiscates property, and liberates eleven slaves. He then travels for eighty-two days, covering more than one thousand miles, to escort the slaves along the Underground Railroad to Canada.

December: Democratic Party Convention, meeting in Charleston, South Carolina, splinters over issues involving the candidacy of Stephen Douglas and slavery in the territories.

Congress rejects Kansas's proslavery Lecompton Constitution.

1859

January: In response to Brown's Missouri raid, President Buchanan offers a $250 reward for his capture.

Mid March: Brown reaches Detroit and moves the slaves into Canada.

July 3: Brown arrives at Harpers Ferry and rents a farm five miles away. His men slowly gather.

October 16: Brown and his men capture the armory at Harpers Ferry. They take as hostages some local militia leaders, including Colonel Lewis W. Washington, a grandnephew of George Washington.

October 17: At 7:00 A.M. the local railroad conductor at Harpers Ferry alerts railroad officials to the situation. Officials telegraph President Buchanan and local militia move on Harpers Ferry. Several of Brown's men are killed, and at nightfall Brown ignores demands for his surrender. Lieutenant Colonel Robert E. Lee and Lieutenant J. E. B. Stuart arrive.

October 18: At dawn, Lee's marines break into the engine house. Lieutenant Israel Green attacks Brown with the dress sword he brought by mistake, then hits Brown over the head with the sword's handle and knocks him unconscious.

October 25–November 2: Brown goes on trial at Charlestown.

December 2: Brown is hanged for murder, treason, and conspiracy to incite a slave insurrection and is buried at North Elba.

1860

The Democrats split into Northern and Southern wings over the question of slavery in the territories. Southerners insist on a slave-code-protecting institution; Douglas Democrats defend popular sovereignty.

November 6: Abraham Lincoln, the Republican candidate, defeats Democrats John Breckenridge and Stephen Douglas, as well as Constitutional Union candidate John Bell, in the presidential election of 1860.

December 3: President James Buchanan delivers his fourth annual message to a joint session of Congress.

Buchanan condemns secession as unconstitutional, but points out that the federal government does not have the authority to coerce a state back into the Union.

December 18: Kentucky senator John J. Crittenden proposes compromise in an attempt to avoid secession and civil war.

December 20: South Carolina approves an ordinance of secession, severing political ties with the United States.

Henry David Thoreau publishes "A Plea for Captain John Brown" in support of the martyred hero.

1861

January 9: Mississippi's secession convention passes ordinance of secession by a vote of 84 to 15.

January 10: Florida's secession convention approves secession ordinance by a vote of 62 to 7.

January 11: Alabama's secession convention approves secession by a margin of 61 to 39.

January 19: Despite the caution urged by Alexander H. Stephens, Georgia's secession convention agrees to sever its bond with the Union by a vote of 208 to 89.

January 26: Louisiana's secession convention approves secession by a vote of 113 to 17.

February 4: The six seceded states of South Carolina, Mississippi, Louisiana, Alabama, Georgia, and Florida begin meeting in Montgomery, Alabama, to form the Confederate States of America.

The Washington Peace Conference, urged by Virginia's legislature, meets in Washington, D.C. None of the seceded states attend.

February 9: Jefferson Davis is chosen as the provisional president of the Confederate States of America. Alexander H. Stephens is elected vice president.

February 23: A statewide referendum in Texas favors secession by a vote of 46,153 to 14,747.

March 4: President Abraham Lincoln is inaugurated as the sixteenth president of the United States. During his inaugural address Lincoln informs the country that he will uphold the Fugitive Slave Law and not eliminate slavery in states where it already exists; he announces that he will prevent slavery's extension into the territories in an attempt to avoid civil war. By this time, seven Deep South states have seceded from the Union.

March 15: Secretary of State William H. Seward urges President Abraham Lincoln not to supply and reinforce Fort Sumter in Charleston Harbor.

April 12: 4:30 A.M. Confederate forces, under the command of General P. G. T. Beauregard, open fire on Fort Sumter, commanded by Major Robert Anderson, in Charleston Harbor, South Carolina, ushering in the Civil War.

April 15: President Abraham Lincoln issues a call for seventy-five thousand volunteers to enlist for three months of service to help suppress the rebellion in the South.

April 17: Virginia's secession convention approves ordinance of secession by a vote of 88 to 55.

April 19: Lincoln issues a blockade against Southern ports. Although its legality and effectiveness were in question for a variety of reasons, the blockade reduced the ability of the South to trade and obtain resources.

April 20: Robert E. Lee resigns his commission in the U.S. Army and accepts command of the forces of his home state of Virginia.

May 6: Tennessee secedes from the Union.

May 7: The secession convention of Arkansas approves secession by a vote of 69 to 1.

May 20: North Carolina's secession convention unanimously approves its ordinance of secession, becoming the last state to secede from the Union and join the Confederacy.

May 24: General Benjamin Butler declares fugitive slaves at Fort Monroe, Virginia, "contraband" and puts them to work for the Union with pay.

July 21: Battle of Bull Run/Manassas. Expectations of a limited conflict are shattered by the military defeat of General Irvin McDowell's Union forces twenty-five miles south of Washington, D.C.

July 27: Lincoln replaces McDowell by appointing George D. McClellan as Commander of the Department of the Potomac. Three months later McClellan is named commander of all Union forces, replacing the aging Winfield Scott.

August 6: Congress passes the First Confiscation Act, which states that any person laboring "under the laws of any State" (that is, a slave state) for a Confederate supporter shall be discharged from their labor.

August 30: General John C. Frémont, commanding Union forces in Missouri, declares martial law and emancipates all slaves held by rebels in the state. Lincoln modifies this declaration to adhere to the Confiscation Act passed on August 6, 1861.

September 2: President Abraham Lincoln orders General John C. Frémont to rescind his order of August

30, 1861, in an attempt to reassure border slave states that he has no plans to abolish slavery.

September 11: Lincoln revokes the proclamation of General Frémont authorizing emancipation as a matter of military necessity in Missouri.

September 21: Navy secretary Gideon Wells authorizes recruiters to enlist former slaves in the Union navy.

November 8: The U.S. Navy seizes Confederate envoys James Mason and John Slidell, creating an international diplomatic crisis between Britain and the United States.

November: The Christian Commission, an organization of Northern evangelicals dedicated to supplying soldiers with chaplains, religious tracts, food, and medical supplies, is founded by the Young Men's Christian Association as an alternative to the Unitarian-dominated Sanitary Commission, which has been performing the same functions in support of the war effort.

December 10: Charles Colcock Jones delivers the inaugural address at the first meeting of the Presbyterian Church in the Confederate States of America, in Augusta, Georgia. The Old School Presbyterians split when Northern members force a resolution pledging support for the Union war effort and denouncing secession.

1862

February 16: Fort Donelson falls to Ulysses S. Grant, marking the first major victory for the Union.

February: "The Battle Hymn of the Republic" is published. Written by abolitionist Julia Ward Howe after hearing soldiers sing "John Brown's Body," the song is an excellent example of the use of millennial religious symbols dedicating the nation to the cause of freedom.

March 6: President Lincoln recommends compensated emancipation.

March 8–9: After sinking two Union ships, the Confederate ironclad *Merrimac* battles the Union's ironclad *Monitor* to a draw, effectively ending the utility of wooden ships in battle.

March–July: Peninsula Campaign. McClellan attempts to flank Confederate forces around Richmond by making an amphibious assault up the Virginia Peninsula. The attack quickly loses momentum, and Union forces retreat after the Seven Days' Battles.

April 3: General David Hunter begins to recruit black soldiers in South Carolina on his own authority after his request for permission has gone unanswered.

April 6–7: Battle of Shiloh. Confederates surprise Grant's unprepared forces, resulting in twenty-three thousand fatalities, more than the total in all previous American wars combined.

April 10: Congress adopts a plan for gradual compensated emancipation.

April 16: President Lincoln signs a bill abolishing slavery in the District of Columbia.

April 25: Naval forces under David Farragut capture New Orleans for the Union.

May 9: Union general David Hunter declares that slaves in Georgia, Florida, and South Carolina are free.

May 19: President Abraham Lincoln, who was not notified of General Hunter's plan, nullifies the general's emancipation edict and urges border states to embrace gradual, compensated emancipation and colonization.

June 25–July 1: Seven Days' Battles. Lee launches a series of counterattacks against McClellan's larger army, pushing the conservative Union general to a withdrawal and ending the Peninsula Campaign.

June–August: Senator James H. Lane begins to recruit the First Kansas Colored Volunteer Infantry, making Kansas the first state to officially recruit and train military units comprised of black soldiers.

July 12: Lincoln meets with Congressional representatives from the border states (Kentucky, Missouri, Delaware, and Maryland) to encourage them to accept compensated emancipation from the federal government. The states refuse.

July 13: During a carriage ride to the funeral of one of Secretary of War Edwin M. Stanton's infant sons Lincoln announces to Secretary of State William Seward and Secretary of the Navy Gideon Welles that he intends to issue a proclamation of swift emancipation.

July 17: Congress passes the Second Confiscation Act declaring that all slaves of Confederate sympathizers are to be set free.

July 22: Lincoln meets with his cabinet and offers his plans for a proclamation of emancipation. Lincoln accepts the advice of Secretary of State William Seward to delay the announcement to the public until Union armies have a military success.

August 14: At a meeting at the White House, President Lincoln urges a group of African American leaders to consider colonization, since African Americans will confront hardships in every region of the country regardless of when slavery is abolished.

August 22: General Butler incorporates several Louisiana Native Guard units of free black soldiers into Union forces and musters the first official all-black forces in the Union army.

August 25: After having withheld permission, the War Department authorizes Hunter's recruitment of black soldiers in the South Carolina Sea Islands.

August 29–30: Second Battle of Bull Run. Stonewall Jackson and James Longstreet defeat the Union Army of Virginia, forcing its commander John Pope to retreat to Washington, D.C.

September 5: Hoping to capitalize on his momentum, Lee launches an offensive campaign through Maryland in hopes of forcing the Union to surrender.

September 17: Union general George B. McClellan engages Confederate general Robert E. Lee at the Battle of Antietam in Maryland. McClellan fails to exploit his tactical advantage to destroy Lee's army, but his forces are able to halt Lee's offensive and end the threat of Confederate invasion. Although regarded as a tactical draw, Lee withdraws his troops from the battlefield, leaving McClellan with control of the field and the impression of a Union victory. The conflict's twenty-three thousand casualties make September 17 the bloodiest day in American history.

September 22: With the "victory" at Antietam, President Lincoln issues his preliminary Emancipation Proclamation, announcing that an official Emancipation Proclamation will take effect January 1, 1863.

October 28: In the first use of black troops in combat during the Civil War, the First Kansas Colored Volunteer Infantry fight at Island Mound, Missouri.

November 5: Citing his repeated failure to exploit his tactical advantages, Lincoln replaces McClellan with Ambrose Burnside in hopes of a more aggressive command strategy.

December 1: Lincoln offers a compensated emancipation plan to Congress for the areas not affected by the Emancipation Proclamation, which included the Border States (Maryland, Kentucky, Missouri, and Delaware) and areas under Union occupation.

December 13: Lee defeats the larger Union force under Burnside at Fredericksburg, Virginia. The battle causes another Union offensive to end in retreat and leads to Burnside's removal a month later.

December 23: Protesting the use of black soldiers, Jefferson Davis issues a proclamation ordering that black Union soldiers captured by Confederate troops are not to be treated as prisoners of war but remanded to Confederate state authorities and that their white officers will be executed.

The 1862 Internal Revenue Act taxes distilled and malt liquors and requires that retail distributors of alcoholic beverages purchase a federal liquor license. This measure is designed to generate revenue for the federal government to offset the costs of the Civil War. The measure is opposed by temperance reformers as a compromise of principle.

Thirty-seven breweries from New York form an association that in 1864 will become the United States' Brewers Association as a response to the new federal tax on distilled and malt liquor.

1863

January 1: President Lincoln issues his final Emancipation Proclamation. Union general Robert H. Milroy occupies Winchester, Virginia, and becomes the first to actively enforce Lincoln's measure. He also announces the Union's intention to enlist black soldiers and sailors.

January 26: Ambrose Burnside is replaced as Commander of the Army of the Potomac by Joseph "Fighting Joe" Hooker.

March 26: Adjutant General of the Army Lorenzo Thomas begins a large-scale effort to raise and administer black troops in the Mississippi Valley.

May 2: Stonewall Jackson is mortally wounded during the Confederate victory over Hooker's forces in the Battle of Chancellorsville. Lee is able to defeat the much larger Union force by dividing his army and attacking Hooker at several points. Lee once again seeks to seize his momentum by invading the North. Hooker moves to intercept Lee in Pennsylvania but is replaced by George Meade on June 28.

May 22: The Bureau of Colored Troops is established.

May 27: The Louisiana Native Guards play a vital role in the assault on Port Hudson, Louisiana.

June 7: The First Mississippi Volunteers of African Descent soldiers repel a Confederate attack at Milliken's Bend, Louisiana.

July 1–3: Union victory at Gettysburg, Pennsylvania. Lee's army is forced to retreat from his invasion of the North after three days of intense fighting that result in 50,000 casualties. The final day of fighting culminates in a massive charge of 12,500 Confederate soldiers under George Pickett. The attack is repulsed by Union soldiers and artillery, forcing Lee to withdraw his depleted forces back to Virginia.

July 4: Union forces under Ulysses S. Grant capture Vicksburg, Mississippi, the last Confederate garrison on the Mississippi River. This victory gives the Union control of the river and strengthens Grant's reputation as an effective general.

July 13–16: Draft riots throughout New York City reveal the latent racism of many Northerners as they attack African Americans and burn down an orphanage for black children. The draft riots also reveal frustration with provisions allowing middle- and upper-class draftees to hire a substitute, thus avoiding service.

July 18: The Fifty-fourth Massachusetts spearheads an assault on Fort Wagner, South Carolina.

July 30: Lincoln's Order of Retaliation states that Union soldiers, black or white, are entitled to equal protection if captured by the enemy. The order threatens retaliation for Confederates who enslave or kill black prisoners of war.

September 19–20: The most significant defeat of Union forces in the West occurs in the Battle of Chickamauga, along the Tennessee-Georgia border. Although the Union advance was halted, the "victory" proved costly to the Confederacy, as they suffered more casualties than did the Union forces.

October 3: The War Department orders full-scale recruitment of black soldiers in Maryland, Missouri, and Tennessee, with compensation to loyal owners.

November 19: Lincoln delivers his Gettysburg Address at the dedication of the National Cemetery in Gettysburg, Pennsylvania.

November 23–25: A Confederate siege on the Union-controlled city of Chattanooga is repulsed by Union forces under Grant. The victory effectively ends Confederate control in Tennessee and allows the Union the opportunity to invade the Deep South.

Rhode Island repeals prohibition.

1864

March 12: Grant becomes general in chief of the Union army.

April 8: The Senate approves the Thirteenth Amendment, abolishing slavery in the United States and its territories. The amendment fails to garner the two-thirds vote needed in the House of Representatives, delaying the amendment until after the election of 1864.

April 12: Confederate troops massacre black soldiers at Fort Pillow, Tennessee.

May 6–20: Both sides suffer heavy casualties during the Wilderness Campaign and Battle of Spotsylvania, but Grant continues to advance toward Richmond. Grant orders William T. Sherman to command forces in the West, beginning the Atlanta Campaign.

June 3: Grant orders a futile assault against fortified Confederate forces at Cold Harbor.

June 15: Following the bloody battles in May, Grant and Robert E. Lee's forces begin what will become a nine-month battle of attrition around the city of Petersburg, Virginia.

Congress equalizes the pay of black and white soldiers.

U.S. Colored Troops (USCT) Eighteenth Corps help to capture and secure regions around Petersburg, the supplier of the Confederate capital, Richmond, initiating the longest siege in American history.

June: The National Union Convention (Republicans) convenes in Baltimore and renominates Lincoln, issuing a platform that includes a constitutional amendment that will abolish slavery. Andrew Johnson, a Democrat from Tennessee, serves as Lincoln's running mate.

July 8: Lincoln pocket vetoes the Wade-Davis Bill, which is the Congressional vision for Reconstruction. (The bill requires readmitted states to abolish slavery and for 50 percent of the electorate to swear an "ironclad oath" that they have never taken up arms against the Union.)

July 30: USCT Ninth Corps divisions fight at the Battle of the Crater in Petersburg.

September 1: Federal forces under Sherman occupy the city of Atlanta after a series of battles.

September 29: Black soldiers are crucial to the success of the Battle of New Market Heights near Richmond. Fourteen black soldiers later receive the Medal of Honor for this battle.

October 12: Chief Justice Roger B. Taney dies. Lincoln replaces Taney with his former secretary of treasury, Salmon P. Chase.

November 8: Lincoln is reelected as president, largely owing to the recent military success of Union forces.

November 15: After burning most of the city of Atlanta, Sherman begins his notorious March to the Sea. Within five weeks Sherman's forces waged total warfare on the Southern countryside, burning fields and destroying livestock before capturing the seaport city of Savannah, Georgia.

December 6: Lincoln urges Congress to again take up a constitutional amendment to abolish slavery.

December 15: USCT regiments help to achieve victory at the Battle of Nashville, Tennessee.

1865

January 31: The Thirteenth Amendment, abolishing the institution of slavery in the United States, passes Congress.

February 1: The Thirteenth Amendment is sent to the states for ratification, after passing both houses of Congress and being signed by Lincoln.

March 4: President Abraham Lincoln delivers his Second Inaugural Address.

March 23: The Confederate War Department issues an order to recruit enslaved men as soldiers starting in April and to emancipate them upon completion of loyal service.

April 2–4: After Union forces under Philip H. Sheridan defeat George Pickett's forces at Five Forks, Grant's forces are able to break through Confederate lines and take the city of Richmond without a fight.

April 9: Confederate general Robert E. Lee surrenders to Union general Ulysses S. Grant at Appomattox Court House, Virginia, effectively ending major military operations in the "Eastern Theater." Black troops are present at the surrender.

April 11: Lincoln offers a public address in response to Lee's surrender, offering his plans for Reconstruction and African American suffrage.

April 14: Actor and Confederate sympathizer John Wilkes Booth assassinates President Abraham Lincoln during a performance of *Our American Cousin* at Ford's Theater in Washington, D.C.

May 12: The 62nd U.S. Colored Infantry fight in the final battle of the Civil War at Palmito Ranch, Texas.

December 18: The Thirteenth Amendment is ratified, solidifying President Lincoln's promise of emancipation.

The National Temperance Society and Publication House is formed in Saratoga, New York.

Massachusetts creates a state constabulary to enforce the Prohibition Law of 1855.

1865–1877

Throughout Reconstruction, the Southern churches undergo a profound change. Hundreds of thousands of African Americans leave white churches to form their own congregations. Missionaries, both African American and Caucasian, come from the North to assist in the reorganization of the South.

1866

January: Senator Lyman Trumbull (R, Ill.) introduces two bills to Congress, the Freedmen's Bureau Bill and the Civil Rights Bill.

1867

March 7: Senator John Brooks Henderson of Missouri introduces Senate Resolution Number 8, which is later modified and introduced as the Fifteenth Amendment.

Maine creates a state police force to enforce prohibition.

Pennsylvania's legislature bans sale of liquor on Sunday.

Germans in Pittsburgh gather to weaken liquor-license restrictions. Germans in Kansas organize to oppose temperance advances. Iowans form a political group called the "People's Party" to successfully fight against prohibition.

1868

July 28: The Fourteenth Amendment is ratified. The amendment defines in clear language American citizenship, abolishing discriminatory categories for men on the basis of race.

Henry McNeal Turner, along with every other black representative, is expelled from the Georgia legislature.

1869

A new prohibition law is passed in Massachusetts.

The Prohibition Party is formed.

1872

Prohibition Party candidate James Black polls 5,608 votes in the presidential election.

Southerners leave the Sons of Temperance to found the United Friends of Temperance, a whites-only temperance society.

1873

The Women's Crusade takes place from December to spring 1874 in response to an exhortation by Dio Lewis, an itinerant temperance speaker, for women to march on saloons and urge liquor sellers to destroy their stock.

1874

November: The Women's Christian Temperance Union is founded by women who leave the Templars to create a women-only organization, following the demonstration of female influence for temperance enforcement during the Women's Crusade.

1875

Massachusetts Prohibition law of 1869 is repealed.

1876

November 12: The Red Shirts, a white terrorist organization, effectively "redeems" the state of South Carolina by suppressing black votes. The terrorist activities ensure Democratic victories in the state elections.

The Supreme Court rules in *United States v. Reese* that the Fifteenth Amendment did not guarantee the right to vote to anyone but simply prevented the states from giving "preference" to one voter over another. In *United States v. Cruikshank* the court rules in favor of Ku Klux Klan defendants who were accused of storming a political meeting in Louisiana and murdering one hundred blacks trying to hold a rally for the vote.

~ 1 ~

The Rise of Abolitionism and the Conflict over Slavery

The American Civil War (1861–1865) represented the culmination of an ideological conflict over slavery. The eleven states of the Southern Confederacy seceded from the federal Union in a desperate effort to preserve slavery; their subsequent defeat, however, ensured its destruction. In the wake of the Union's military victory in 1865, the ratification of the Thirteenth Amendment formally abolished slavery in the United States. Although the institution persisted for another two decades in Cuba and Brazil, its abolition in the American South signaled its end as an accepted form of agricultural labor in a modern economy and, correspondingly, as a lawful form of personal status in a modern society. Historically speaking, the abolition of slavery occurred quickly. At the close of the eighteenth century, slavery showed no signs of weakening—indeed, it was difficult to imagine the modern economy without it. A mere four decades later, however, the Southern United States remained the only modern economy that depended principally upon slave labor. Thus, the end of slavery in the American South also marked the end of a historical era that had begun with the voyages of Columbus; an era that simultaneously was characterized by the widespread enslavement, dispersal, and transplantation of West African peoples to the shores of the Americas, as well as by the growing popular acceptance of modern conceptions of individual rights and liberty.

Slavery has existed in many cultures and many eras. Yet, the history of slavery in the Americas was made unique because of two fundamental circumstances arising from its African origins. First, the Atlantic slave trade reflected the development of a comprehensive system designed to enslave, deport, and redistribute people across continents on a grand scale. From the sixteenth to the nineteenth centuries approximately twelve to fourteen million people were enslaved and transported far from home, with virtually no opportunities of ever returning. The upheaval wrought by this process sundered traditional bonds of family, kinship, clan, linguistic, and national identity. The result was that slavery in the Americas was imbued with a specific dimension of racial identity that distinguished it from other historical circumstances of slavery. In the Americas, slaves were defined by their race. Second, the enslavement of African peoples emerged as an integral part of the triangular system of transatlantic trade that commercially connected the peoples of Africa, the Americas, and Europe. This commercial network fostered the growth and sustained the settlement of European colonies in the Americas for four centuries. African slavery developed to meet the labor needs of the agricultural production of commodity crops grown for exchange in a world market.

Historians have long noted that the framework of the modern capitalist economy was built upon the backs of enslaved laborers. At the same time, though, the ideological principles of this capitalist marketplace, with their emphasis on individual agency and autonomy, gave rise to the unorthodox idea that slavery was repugnant to the natural human condition of freedom. These ideas, coupled with an increasingly popular, evangelical

Benjamin Lundy (Ohio Historical Society)

Christian belief in salvation as an individual experience and Enlightenment notions of universal rights and liberty, contributed heavily to the historical development of an international antislavery movement that ultimately proved responsible for bringing about the end of slavery. Although the ambiguities of the master-slave relation had always been a cause for anxiety and required some justification, the emergence of an international abolitionist movement in the eighteenth century placed the religious, legal, and economic institutions that traditionally condoned slavery under a scrutiny heretofore unseen. Abolitionists raised a new question of whether slavery was reconcilable with human progress and, in so doing, required those who defended slavery to create a rival ideology that placed slavery at the cornerstone of human progress.

Despite the centuries-long existence of human bondage, this modern proslavery ideology was essentially reactionary. It demanded a sensible conservatism in the face of the tumultuous social changes wrought by industrialization and warned against upsetting the delicate social order upon which progress was grounded. Proslavery theorists characterized the arguments of the abolitionists as offering an idealistic vision of unrestrained liberty, which could only end in anarchy, chaos, and the undoing of modern progress. The conflict that arose between abolitionist and proslavery forces was thus a battle over the appropriate ideal of human progress. It was waged with vigor across the Atlantic world throughout the last decades of the eighteenth century and the first half of the nineteenth. The triumph of abolition during the American Civil War marked the conclusive settlement of this conflict and ultimately resolved the debate over whether there was a place for slavery in the modern world.

Initially, the locus of this international antislavery movement was composed of an influential group of merchants and lawyers in Great Britain. Notably, many of the individuals belonged to dissenting religious communities whose messages of evangelical reform were preached widely throughout Great Britain, as well as in the British colonies in North America and the West Indies. The Society of Friends, commonly known as the Quakers, has long been considered as particularly influential in the development of the antislavery movement. As early as 1737 Benjamin Lay published an essay characterizing slavery as a "notorious sin," the practice of which contradicted a truly Christian lifestyle; his work was published in Britain, but the teachings extended to the colonies as well. Similar to many early antislavery essayists, Lay focused on redeeming the soul of the slaveholder. Nevertheless, many Quakers rejected Lay's teachings and continued to own slaves as well as participate as carriers and merchants in the Atlantic slave trade. A theological crisis generated by the pressures placed upon Pennsylvania Quakers to renounce pledges of pacifism during the Seven Years' War (1756–1763) focused renewed attention on personal belief and behavior. A revitalized commitment to pacifism fostered the growth of antislavery sentiments and practices as well. This attitude of "Quaker renaissance" was captured in the writings of Pennsylvanian Anthony Benezet and disseminated among Quaker communities on both sides of the Atlantic. Thereafter, the Society of Friends assumed the vanguard of the international antislavery movement and remained in the forefront for nearly five decades. Quakers did not stand alone, however; other evangelical Christians, especially Methodists, contributed generously to the advancement of the antislavery cause.

Complementing the religious community's argument against slavery, many influential eighteenth-century British lawyers and judges considered slavery antithetical to the natural ideas of liberty embodied in the English common law. William Blackstone, in part of his magisterial four-volume *Commentaries on the Laws of England,* explicitly repudiated the natural-law theory of slavery advanced centuries before by the Roman jurist, Justinian. In 1769, Granville Sharp, an eccentric abolitionist, published an antislavery book, *A Representation of the injustice and the dangerous tendency of tolerating slavery; or of admitting the least claim of private property in the persons of men,* which was grounded in legal research and refuted previous judicial opinions suggesting that the English common law supported slavery. The most significant episode in the development of British antislavery jurisprudence occurred in 1772, however, when William Murray, first Earl of Mansfield, then chief justice for the Court of the King's Bench, delivered his ruling in the *Somerset* case. The case involved James Somerset, a slave owned by Charles Steuart, a British customs officer serving in the Virginia colony since 1741 (Steuart purchased Somerset in 1749). In 1769, Steuart returned to Britain, accompanied by Somerset. While in Britain, Somerset managed to escape; he was eventually recaptured and confined onboard a ship while awaiting transportation and sale back into slavery in Jamaica. While confined, his cause was taken up by Sharp, who obtained a writ of habeas corpus from the court in order to determine Somerset's status. Somerset was represented by Francis Hargrave, a young lawyer who argued that although colonial laws permitted slavery, no such laws existed in England. The case was debated for more than six months before the bench, as well as in the court of public opinion, before it was decided that Somerset must be released. In announcing the ruling for the court, Mansfield famously commented that slavery was "so odious, that nothing can be suffered to support it, but positive law." The proceedings of the case were published in many newspapers on both sides of the Atlantic, and they generated a vigorous pamphlet debate as well. Yet, Mansfield's carefully constructed decision was limited in scope to the specific matters of James Somerset. It did not free any other slaves in England and thus merely perpetuated long-standing tensions between slavery and English common law.

Despite these strong antislavery pronouncements within the religious and legal communities, the earliest organized efforts at abolition in Great Britain concentrated less on ending slavery than on simply bringing about an end to the Atlantic slave trade. In 1787 Thomas Clarkson and William Wilberforce—a member of Parliament—joined with Sharp and leading antislavery Quakers to form the Society for Effectuating the Abolition of the Slave Trade. The Society was essentially an expansion of a Quaker antislavery committee, but the interdenominational membership gave it a political voice; Quakers, as nonconformists, were not allowed to hold seats in Parliament. Now, however, Wilberforce emerged as the parliamentary leader for the society and orchestrated its legislative agenda. The society organized public lectures, rallies protesting the slave trade, and petition drives and facilitated the publication of former slave Olaudah Equiano's autobiography, which detailed the conditions of the "Middle Passage."

In 1791 Wilberforce introduced the first bill to abolish the slave trade in the House of Commons, but it was soundly defeated. His proposed legislation encountered strong opposition from Caribbean sugar planters and other commercial groups with an economic interest in continuing the slave trade. These defenders of slavery argued that abolition of the slave trade would necessarily bring about the end of slavery itself, a strategy to which many of the abolitionists aspired, and which many of those vested in the Atlantic economy feared. Despite sustained opposition, however, Wilberforce persisted in arguing against the slave trade for two decades until, in 1807, Parliament outlawed it and even authorized its suppression by the British Navy.

The tumultuous events of the French Revolution also stymied popular support for the antislavery cause. Initially, the revolutionary fervor to strike down the monarchy and other forms of social rank promoted the discussion of antislavery agendas in the Estates General and, later, in the National Assembly. As was the case in Britain, however, antislavery petitions and legislation encountered staunch opposition from representatives of the commercial and sugar plantation interests. But unlike elsewhere, the ideas embodied in the Declaration of the Rights of Man spread far beyond the halls of the assembly and into the Caribbean sugar fields. In 1790, an uprising of mulattos demanding the rights of citizenship in the French colony of St. Domingue had to be suppressed by force. A year later, a slave insurrection erupted in the northern regions of the colony inaugurating years of civil war that would lead to the creation of an independent Haitian republic in 1804. Toussaint L'Ouverture, a former slave, emerged as the leader of this independence movement. Other insurrections occurred on the French island of Guadeloupe. In 1794, at the height of Jacobin rule and the Reign of Terror in France, and inspired by events on St. Domingue, the National Convention abolished slavery throughout the French Empire. Abolition did not last long, however; a policy of retrenchment developed under the Bonaparte regime that eventually led to the reestablishment of slavery throughout France's Caribbean colonies. Only Haitian independence prevented the reestablishment of slavery. The consequences of the French experience on the international antislavery movement were severe. In the immediate aftermath of the French and Haitian Revolutions, the antislavery cause was associated with their most brutal and violent phases, and abolition was perceived henceforth as a recipe for racial warfare.

Although closely connected with the international movement in many respects, antislavery activities developed along a somewhat different path in North America. Unlike the sugar-producing islands of the Caribbean, where a high mortality rate and a limited demand for female slaves inhibited reproduction, slave communities in North America were successfully reproducing their population by the earliest decades of the eighteenth century. Accordingly, the demand for importing slaves diminished throughout the century and slowly was replaced by anxiety over the increasingly disproportionate racial balance in the mainland British colonies. As early as 1701, Virginia planters petitioned the Crown to suspend the slave trade because of a growing concern over the number of African slaves in their communities. This anxiety was exacerbated by the Stono Slave Rebellion in South Carolina in 1739, when a group of slaves and free blacks from the South Carolina low country rose up in armed rebellion, killed twenty to twenty-five white residents, attempted to capture the lieutenant governor, and began to make their way to freedom in the Spanish colony of Florida. The uprising was quickly and violently suppressed, but concerns about controlling the growing slave population persisted. Fears of a "Black Majority" encouraged many North American slaveholders, including Thomas Jefferson and George Mason, to ally themselves with the antislavery cause on the issue of abolishing the slave trade, but they did so in order to restrict importation of more slaves. With the onset of the American Revolution, the Continental Congress passed resolutions banning the further importation of slaves into the colonies, and in the wake of independence, nearly every state enacted legislation to suspend or inhibit the importation of slaves through the Atlantic trade. In 1787, during the Constitutional Convention in Philadelphia, an alliance between some antislavery and proslavery delegates contributed to a general consensus calling for the slave trade to be outlawed by the federal government. Delegates from Connecticut, Rhode Island, and Georgia dissented however, on the grounds that the abolition of the slave trade would adversely affect their economies. By threatening to withdraw their support for the new constitution, these delegates forced a compromise to be struck that prohibited Congress from restricting the international trade for two decades. A tacit assumption remained that Congress would do so once the prohibition elapsed, and indeed, it did outlaw the Atlantic slave trade in 1808.

Associating the American Revolution with the cause of universal liberty also contributed to fostering antislavery sentiments beyond a mere critique of the slave trade in North America. Slavery itself was challenged as a legitimate institution, although considerable ambivalence remained. Tensions between arguments for liberty and the existence of slavery were evident from the outset of the conflict. Samuel Johnson, a British critic of the American insurgency, famously asked, "Why is it that we hear the loudest yelps for liberty among the drivers of negroes?" (Fox-Genovese and Genovese 2005, 34). Such notable patriots as George Washington, Benjamin Franklin, John Hancock, Henry Laurens, and Thomas Jefferson were all slaveholders or commercially involved in the Atlantic slave trade. The question of slavery quickly emerged in the politics of the conflict as well. At the outset of the Revolution, Virginia governor John Murray, Lord Dunmore, offered freedom to any slaves who took up arms against their rebellious masters, while the New York legislature made a similar offer to slaves who enlisted in the militia to fight against the British. Early in the war, in 1777, a separatist group in upstate New York seeking to form an independent Commonwealth of Vermont drafted a constitution that expressly outlawed slavery. In general, though, those enslaved seemed to prefer their chances with the British. During the course of the hostilities, several hundred slaves ran away and sought refuge with British forces. These freedmen were temporarily given refuge in Nova Scotia before being resettled by the British in Sierra Leone, where they established a community at Freetown in 1787.

Faced with immediate questions of liberty, independence, and republican citizenship, many of the newly founded state governments grappled with the question of slavery. Pennsylvania became the first state to abolish it, by enacting a program for gradual emancipation in 1780. The Pennsylvania statute was replete with declarations of universal liberty, thanking God for deliverance from British tyranny and, in gratitude, extending that same liberty to those enslaved. Three years later, the Massachusetts Supreme Court determined slavery to be contrary to the declarations of liberty and equality in the state constitution through a series of judicial decisions collectively known as the Quock Walker case. New York began debating abolition two years later, but it took until 1799 to pass a plan of gradual emancipation similar to the Pennsylvania model. Connecticut, Rhode Island, and New Jersey also passed similar legislation during the period. Significantly, the rhetoric of liberty in North America transcended independence, as in evidence of the fact that the British colony of Upper Canada also passed a gradual emancipation act in 1793, a full forty years before slavery would be abolished elsewhere in the empire.

Such state-sponsored emancipation plans were confined to the Northern states during the Revolutionary period, but antislavery sentiment permeated the Southern states as well. Virginia jurist St. George Tucker expanded upon Blackstone's critique of Justinian to demonstrate how slavery was inconsistent with both republican government and natural law. However, much of the purportedly antislavery legislation in the South revealed more ambivalence. For example, in 1782 Virginia passed a manumission law giving slave owners the exclusive power to emancipate their slaves by deed or will. Previously, the legislature or the county courts had to sanction manumissions. On the surface, then, this act made manumission much easier, and indeed several Virginians engaged in this practice as a means of freeing their slaves. But the manumission act also confirmed the absolute ownership rights of the master over his slaves and reified the authority of the slave owner. Other states enacted private manumission legislation during this period as well and, coupled with gradual emancipation plans, defined North American antislavery activities of the late eighteenth and early nineteenth centuries.

A larger population of freedmen was a consequence of these liberalized emancipation policies and fostered the development of plans to resettle emancipated persons in areas lying outside the boundaries of the United States. In December 1816 the American Colonization Society (ACS) was organized by Charles Fenton Mercer and Presbyterian minister Robert Finley. The ACS was composed of several prominent national leaders and dedicated to establishing a colony for freedmen in West Africa. The plan was similar to the British colony established in Sierra Leone. In 1820, the ACS sent a small group of emigrants to plant a settlement in Liberia, but it took two years to become permanent. Emigration of freedmen continued for the next five decades, with the ACS funding approximately thirteen thousand freedmen and -women to settle in the colony. As was the case with the abolition of the Atlantic slave trade, colonization acted to bridge the interests of both antislavery and proslavery individuals. A number of ACS leaders were themselves owners of slaves, and the colonization movement eventually received its severest criticism from abolitionists such as William Lloyd Garrison, who contended that the removal of freed people was designed merely to perpetuate slavery.

Correspondent with the emergence of the colonization movement during the second and third decades of the nineteenth century, significant changes occurred within the antislavery movement in both Britain and the United States, marking a new phase of the antislavery movement. This new phase was distinguished by its calls for the immediate abolition of slavery. The persistence of slavery in the Caribbean despite the abolition of the slave trade discouraged British antislavery activists, who now sought a more immediate solution. Accordingly, Wilberforce again led the crusade in Parliament—this time he hoped to abolish slavery in the British colonies. In this second crusade Wilberforce was supported by a favorable attitude toward reform in Great Britain as well as by the recognition that two of the assumptions that had informed the abolition of the slave trade had proved to be fallacies. The first of these assumptions was that the end of the slave trade would adversely affect the sugar economy; it did not. The second held that by removing the supply source for new laborers would improve the material and spiritual conditions of those already enslaved; it did not. West Indian slaves remained in a wretched and desperate condition. Britons were reminded of this condition by the particularly violent and devastating "Baptist" slave revolt that occurred in Jamaica. Following the reform of Parliament in 1832, that body overwhelmingly passed the Abolition of Slavery Act the following year as part of a larger program of legal and social reform. It was a gradual emancipation plan that paid £20 million in compensation to the planters, freed all children in bondage less than six years of age, and consigned all others to a six-year apprenticeship program that demanded they work for their owners for forty hours a week without compensation. Still, the act was hailed as a victory for the antislavery cause. The apprenticeship system continued to be subjected to criticism, however, and the efforts of those who persisted brought about the ultimate end of slavery in the British colonies in 1838.

In the United States, debates over the expansion of slavery into the federal territories acted as the primary catalyst for the rise of an immediate abolitionist movement. State constitutional discussions and referenda over the expansion of slavery in Alabama, Illinois, Mississippi, Arkansas, and ultimately Missouri shattered the myth that slavery was a dying institution. The alluring prosperity offered by the growing cotton economy informed many of these debates. The specific question of slavery in Missouri gained national focus when antislavery congressmen protested the state's admission to the Union without an agreement to prohibit slavery. Proslavery proponents responded with an array of arguments; most significantly, they contended that Missouri's admission as a slave state would enable the diffusion of the South's slave population and thus expedite emancipation processes. After more than a year of debate, middle ground was reached; the famed Missouri Compromise admitted Missouri as a slave state in 1820 but prohibited further expansion of slavery north of 36° 30′ degrees latitude through the territories of the Louisiana Purchase.

Many antislavery activists considered the Missouri Compromise an intolerable endorsement of slavery by the U.S. government. They believed that slavery, if given any room to grow, would expand and prosper. Accordingly, the Missouri question reinvigorated the antislavery movement in the United States. A number of states formed antislavery societies over the course of the next decade, and many antislavery periodicals and newspapers appeared. In 1821 Benjamin Lundy began publishing *The Genius of Universal Emancipation*, an abolitionist periodical based in Mount Pleasant, Ohio. Lundy remained committed to a gradualist approach but sought the complete dismantling of the system of slavery. In 1828 Lundy met William Lloyd Garrison, a Massachusetts journalist who had spent his early years writing in support of temperance for various reform newspapers. Lundy offered Garrison a job at the *Genius of Universal Emancipation*, and Garrison, recently converted to the antislavery cause, began submitting editorials calling for the immediate abolition of slavery. Garrison's radical views created tension both with Lundy and in the Baltimore community (where the paper was then being published), and, after Garrison was arrested for libel, he and Lundy decided to part ways. Garrison returned to Boston, and in 1831 he launched *The Liberator*, a newspaper dedicated to bringing about the unconditional and immediate end to slavery. It quickly became the mouthpiece of the American abolition movement. Perhaps the most significant antislavery publication of the immediatist movement was a pamphlet published by David Walker, a Boston clothier who grew up in North Carolina as a free African American. In 1829 Walker published an appeal to the "Coloured Citizens of the World." In his *Appeal*, he called for the immediate abolition of slavery and justified the use of violence by slaves to attain their freedom. The pamphlet was widely circulated, especially in the South, despite serious efforts to suppress its circulation.

In 1833 Garrison joined with New York merchant Arthur Tappan to form the American Anti-Slavery Society. The Society was premised on the British model and, in addition to producing publications, they raised money, coordinated lectures, and sponsored public events to disseminate the abolitionist message. Prominent members of this organization included Lewis Tappan (Arthur's brother), Theodore Weld, Lydia Maria Child, Wendell Phillips, and, later, Frederick Douglass. Douglass and William Wells Brown, another former slave, often delivered lectures for the society, depicting the horrors of human bondage for a Northern audience otherwise unfamiliar with the details of slavery. The American Anti-Slavery Society was noted for its internecine squabbles; it split apart in 1840 over questions of Garrison's leadership, the appropriateness of violent tactics, the virtues of advocating for the rights of women, and the question of whether the society should organize politically. The separatists formed the Liberty Party and nominated James G. Birney, founder of the Kentucky Anti-Slavery Society, to run for president in the 1840 and 1844 elections. In 1848 the party joined with Conscience Whigs and antislavery Democrats to organize the Free-Soil Party. Despite the schism, the abolitionist movement continued to grow in numbers and in prominence during the decades of the 1830s and 1840s.

As abolitionist efforts increased, defenders of slavery responded to what they perceived as a direct threat to their way of life. The circulation of abolitionist pamphlets and literature proved particularly insidious to them, and a campaign to prevent the dissemination of these materials was organized across the South. Other proslavery activists adopted more-direct means of suppressing abolitionist literature by destroying abolitionist printing presses. In November 1837 a proslavery mob attacked a warehouse in Alton, Illinois, where Elijah Lovejoy kept his printing press and published his abolitionist newspaper the *Alton Observer*. Lovejoy was trapped in his warehouse and killed by an exchange of small-arms fire. In this instance, the proslavery contingent's efforts backfired, and Lovejoy became a martyr to both the abolitionist cause and the idea of a free press. The suppression campaign extended to the floor of the U.S. Congress as well with the enactment of the infamous "Gag Rule." The Gag Rule was enacted in May 1836 in response to the American Anti-Slavery Society's petition drive and prohibited the reading of any antislavery petitions in the

House of Representatives. It was renewed annually until 1844, when an opposition faction led by Congressman John Quincy Adams gathered sufficient votes to repeal it.

Not all proslavery efforts were directed at suppressing opinions. Proslavery theorists responded to the abolitionist challenge by composing sophisticated legal, economic, and scriptural justifications for the continuation of slavery. In December 1832, in the aftermath of Nat Turner's slave rebellion and an extended debate over emancipation in the Virginia legislature, William and Mary professor Thomas Roderick Dew published a seminal essay of the proslavery response. Dew detailed an extended legal and scriptural justification for the institution of slavery and criticized gradual emancipation and colonization efforts. Others followed Dew in defining the ideological foundations for slavery in the modern South. Nathaniel Beverley Tucker, son of antislavery jurist St. George Tucker, published a rebuttal to Blackstone's critique of Justinian's natural-law theory of slavery. Beverley Tucker sought to legitimate slavery as a necessity imposed by the natural order. South Carolina politician James Henry Hammond expanded upon Tucker's idea in articulating his belief that every society included a "mudsill class" that provided the essential labors for a society's subsistence. Scriptural justifications played an especially important role in refuting abolitionist claims about the immorality of slavery. A large number of Southern ministers published sermons defending slavery and characterizing the abolitionists as proponents of liberal theology. By 1845, both the Methodist and Baptist conventions had splintered into Northern and Southern branches because of the theological dispute over slavery. Increasingly, proslavery theorists articulated comprehensive social theories that placed the master-slave relation at the center of a harmonious society. George Fitzhugh, a Virginia lawyer, provided the most famous of these social theories in his treatise *Sociology for the South* (1854).

The Mexican War brought the question of slavery back to the forefront of national politics in the 1846. Many Northern abolitionists viewed the conflict as being ultimately motivated by a design to spread slavery into Texas and the Southwestern regions of the continent. Henry David Thoreau's famous essay "Civil Disobedience" (1849) was written to express this view and to explain his public protest against paying taxes to a government that supported slavery. Others of a less radical persuasion were unsettled by the potential consequences of the Mexican War as well. In August 1846, Pennsylvania congressman David Wilmot proposed amending an appropriations bill

Frederick Douglass; photograph taken by George K. Warren, circa 1879 (National Archives and Records Administration)

by adding to it the proviso that slavery would be forever barred from any lands ceded or acquired from Mexico. Although never enacted, the Wilmot Proviso inaugurated a debate for more than a decade over the question of how to conduct a program of national expansion in the midst of the debate over slavery. Several settlements were proposed and some even agreed upon, but none of them proved tenable. The Compromise of 1850 temporarily resolved the impasse that had grown up surrounding the question of the admission of California. One component of the compromise provisions, a stricter Fugitive Slave Act, fostered serious animosity among many Northerners who previously had considered slavery simply as a "Southern problem." This idea that slavery represented a problem of national proportions was articulated forcefully in Harriet Beecher Stowe's novel *Uncle Tom's Cabin* (1852). The popular novel elicited a number of critical responses from proslavery advocates, most notably one from George Frederick Holmes, which still stands as one of the most sophisticated commentaries of the proslavery argument. Southern reaction to the novel served only to confirm its appeal among Northern antislavery circles.

By the mid-1850s the conflict over slavery was no longer merely a war of words. Increasingly, it was a conflict that was being decided through the force of arms. From 1854 to 1856 armed combat raged across "Bleeding Kansas," a direct consequence of a political effort to decide the issue by democratic means. In such an environment, scriptural and legal arguments for or against slavery mattered much less than the tangible circumstances of family and community alliances on the ground. Both abolitionist and proslavery forces had successfully consolidated their "sides," and fewer Americans remained unaffiliated with one side or the other. Even the U.S. Supreme Court's pronouncement sanctioning the constitutionality of slavery in the 1857 opinion on the Dred Scott case engendered more controversy than it resolved. More violence erupted in October 1859 when abolitionist John Brown stormed the federal arsenal at Harpers Ferry, Virginia, with the hope of inciting a slave uprising. Brown's raid proved to be a mismanaged debacle that was doomed from its very inception. For Southern defenders of slavery, however, Brown's raid confirmed their darkest suspicions: abolitionists wanted to foster the terror of a genocidal slave insurrection throughout the South. In this light, the argument for secession became the dominant plank of the proslavery platform, and the argument that the political union between North and South could no longer be sustained grew in popularity. Henceforth, increasing numbers of Southerners believed that they could best defend the institution of slavery if they separated from the Union. The ideological divide fostered the Southern secession movement, which in turn set in motion a series of political and military actions leading to the Civil War and the ultimate resolution of the conflict over slavery.

Christopher M. Curtis

CHRONOLOGY

1737
Benjamin Lay publishes Quaker antislavery essay.

1754–1763
Seven Years War (French and Indian War) encourages the growth of antislavery sentiment among Quakers.

1765–1769
William Blackstone's *Commentaries on the Laws of England* are published.

1769
Granville Sharp publishes *A Representation of the injustice and the dangerous tendency of tolerating slavery; or of admitting the least claim of private property in the persons of men.*

1772
Lord Mansfield decides *Somerset* case, ruling that a slave could not be removed from England against his will.

1774
The Continental Congress resolves to prohibit further slave importations at its first meeting.

1775
Virginia's Colonial governor, John Murray, Lord Dunmore, issues a proclamation guaranteeing the freedom of slaves who run away from masters engaged in rebellion against the Crown.

1776
July 4: The Declaration of Independence is adopted.

1777
Vermont constitution prohibits slavery.

1780
Pennsylvania adopts plan for gradual emancipation.

1782
Virginia passes law allowing for the private manumission of slaves.

1783
Treaty of Paris signals the formal end of the American Revolution. The treaty stipulates that the British army must return runaway slaves to the United States. The refusal of some states to repay British loans prevents the return of the former slaves.

British courts decide *Zong* case, an insurance claim for the loss of 131 slaves thrown from a Liverpool slave ship in 1781. Publicity fosters antislavery sentiment.

Quock Walker case determines that slavery is unconstitutional in Massachusetts.

1787

Society for Effectuating the Abolition of the Slave Trade is formed in London.

U.S. Constitutional Convention meeting in Philadelphia agrees to prohibit legislation outlawing the slave trade for twenty years.

1788

Société des Amis des Noirs is formed in France.

State legislatures in Connecticut, New York, Massachusetts, and New York pass laws prohibiting their citizens from participating in the slave trade.

The U.S. Constitution is ratified.

1789

Olaudah Equiano's autobiography is published.

1791

St. Domingue slave revolt begins the Haitian Revolution (1791–1804).

Sierra Leone Company is chartered to establish a colony in West Africa for freedmen.

Initial Wilberforce bill to abolish slave trade is defeated by a vote of 163 to 88.

1793

Upper Canada (British colony) enacts a gradual emancipation law.

1794

France outlaws slavery in all colonies and extends equal rights of citizenship to freedmen.

1799

New York adopts a plan of gradual emancipation.

1800

Gabriel's Rebellion takes place in Richmond, Virginia.

1802

France restores slavery in West Indies colonies.

1807

Britain and the United States abolish the Atlantic slave trade.

1816

American Colonization Society is organized.

1818

Illinois state constitutional debates over slavery take place.

Arkansas Territory Enabling Act is passed in the U.S. Congress.

1819

Tallmadge Amendments prohibiting slavery in Illinois and Missouri constitutions are introduced into Congress.

Royal Navy Anti-Slave Trade Squadron patrols the coast of West Africa.

1820

Missouri Compromise is agreed upon, and Missouri is admitted as a slave state.

American Colonization Society sends a group of ninety-one emigrants to establish a colony in Liberia.

1821

Benjamin Lundy begins publishing *The Genius of Universal Emancipation*.

1822

July: Denmark Vesey leads a slave revolt in Charleston, South Carolina.

Illinois has further constitutional debates over slavery.

American colony for freedmen is settled in Liberia.

1823

London Anti-slavery Committee is organized.

1825

Ralph Gurley begins publishing *The African Repository and Colonial Journal* for the American Colonization Society.

1829

April: William Lloyd Garrison becomes coeditor of *The Genius of Universal Emancipation*.

September: David Walker's *Appeal to the Coloured Citizens of the World* published.

1831

January: Garrison publishes first edition of *The Liberator*.

August: Nat Turner slave revolt in Southampton, Virginia.

1831–1832

Slave revolt in Jamaica commences; becomes known as the "Baptist War."

1832

Slavery is debated in the Virginia legislature. The gradual emancipation proposal is voted down.

December: Thomas Roderick Dew publishes review of the Virginia debate.

1833
British Parliament passes Slavery Abolition Act.
American Anti-Slavery Society organized.

1834
Apprenticeship replaces slavery in British colonies.

1836
U.S. Congress adopts the "Gag Rule," prohibiting the introduction of antislavery petitions.

1837
Abolitionist newspaper editor Elijah Lovejoy is killed by a mob in Alton, Illinois.

1838
Slavery officially ends in all British colonies.

1844
The Methodist Episcopal General Conference divides over the question of slavery.

1845
Frederick Douglass publishes his *Narrative of the Life of Frederick Douglass: An American Slave*.
The Baptist Convention divides over the question of slavery. The Southern Baptist Convention is formed in Augusta, Georgia.

1846
August: Wilmot Proviso introduced to prohibit slavery in territories acquired from Mexico.

1846–1848
The Mexican War takes place.

1847
Frederick Douglass and Martin Delany begin publication of *The North Star* (1847–1851).
Liberia is declared an independent nation.

1849
Henry David Thoreau publishes "Civil Disobedience."

1850
The Fugitive Slave Act is passed as part of the Compromise of 1850.

1852
Harriet Beecher Stowe publishes *Uncle Tom's Cabin*.
George Frederick Holmes and other defenders of slavery publish criticisms of Stowe.

1854
July 4: Garrison publicly burns a copy of the U.S. Constitution.
George Fitzhugh publishes *Sociology for the South*.

1857
March 6: U.S. Supreme Court issues *Dred Scott* decision.
Fitzhugh publishes *Cannibals All! Or, Slaves without Masters*.

1859
October: John Brown launches an unsuccessful raid on Harpers Ferry, Virginia, hoping to incite slave insurrection.
December: Democratic Party Convention meeting in Charleston, South Carolina, splinters over issues involving the candidacy of Stephen Douglas and slavery in the territories.

1860
November: Abraham Lincoln elected president of the United States.
December: South Carolina secedes from the Union.
Henry David Thoreau publishes "A Plea for Captain John Brown" in support of the martyred hero.

1861
February: The Southern Confederacy is formed in Montgomery, Alabama.
March: Lincoln is inaugurated as president.
April: Fort Sumter surrenders; the American Civil War begins.

1862
September: Battle of Antietam. Lincoln issues the Emancipation Proclamation, freeing slaves in the geographical area of the rebellion.

1863
The Emancipation Proclamation goes into effect in the areas of rebellion.

1865
April–May: Confederate Armies surrender.
The Thirteenth Amendment abolishes slavery in United States.

DOCUMENTS

Document 1: PENNSYLVANIA ACT FOR THE GRADUAL ABOLITION OF SLAVERY

The Pennsylvania Act for the Gradual Abolition of Slavery (1780) became a model for legislative emancipation programs enacted in the wake of the American Revolution. Inspired by professions of liberty, its language illuminates the tensions arising from the natural liberty rhetoric of the American Revolution against the persistence of slavery. Controversially, though, the Pennsylvania Act allowed for the sale of slaves prior to their emancipation date and thus encouraged slave owners to sell their slaves in order to receive compensation prior to mandated emancipation. Accurate data concerning the number of slaves sold and the number actually emancipated remains undetermined, but most scholars believe that more Pennsylvania slaves were sold to the South than were freed. Irrespective of this fact, the Pennsylvania Act represents a clear statement against slavery by the people of that state and therefore should be considered as a fundamental episode in the emerging conflict between abolitionist and proslavery forces.

Section 1.

When we contemplate our abhorrence of that condition to which the arms and tyranny of Great Britain were exerted to reduce us; when we look back on the variety of dangers to which we have been exposed, and how miraculously our wants in many instances have been supplied, and our deliverances wrought, when even hope and human fortitude have become unequal to the conflict; we are unavoidably led to a serious and grateful fence of the manifold blessings which we have undeservedly received from the hand of that Being from whom every good and perfect gift cometh. Impressed with these ideas, we conceive that it is our duty, and we rejoice that it is in our power to extend a portion of that freedom to others, which hath been extended to us; and a release from that state of thralldom to which we ourselves were tyrannically doomed, and from which we have now every prospect of being delivered. It is not for us to enquire why, in the creation of mankind, the inhabitants of the several parts of the earth were distinguished by a difference in feature or complexion. It is sufficient to know that all are the work of an Almighty Hand. We find in the distribution of the human species, that the most fertile as well as the most barren parts of the earth are inhabited by men of complexions different from ours, and from each other; from whence we may reasonably, as well as religiously, infer, that He who placed them in their various situations, hath extended equally his care and protection to all, and that it becometh not us to counteract his mercies. We esteem it a peculiar blessing granted to us, that we are enabled this day to add one more step to universal civilization, by removing as much as possible the sorrows of those who have lived in undeserved bondage, and from which, by the assumed authority of the kings of Great Britain, no effectual, legal relief could be obtained. Weaned by a long course of experience from those narrower prejudices and partialities we had imbibed, we find our hearts enlarged with kindness and benevolence towards men of all conditions and nations; and we conceive ourselves at this particular period extraordinarily called upon, by the blessings which we have received, to manifest the sincerity of our profession, and to give a Substantial proof of our gratitude.

Section 2.

And whereas the condition of those persons who have heretofore been denominated Negro and Mulatto slaves, has been attended with circumstances which not only deprived them of the common blessings that they were by nature entitled to, but has cast them into the deepest afflictions, by an unnatural separation and sale of husband and wife from each other and from their children; an injury, the greatness of which can only be conceived by supposing that we were in the same unhappy case. In justice therefore to persons so unhappily circumstanced, and who, having no prospect before them whereon they may rest their sorrows and their hopes, have no reasonable inducement to render their service to society, which they otherwise might; and also in grateful commemoration of our own happy deliverance from that state of unconditional submission to which we were doomed by the tyranny of Britain.

Section 3.

Be it enacted, and it is hereby enacted, by the representatives of the freeman of the commonwealth of Pennsylvania, in general assembly met, and by the authority of the same, That all persons, as well Negroes and Mulattoes as others, who shall be born within this state from and after the passing of this act, shall not be deemed and considered as servants for life, or slaves; and that all servitude for life, or slavery of children, in consequence of the slavery of their mothers, in the case of all children born within this state, from and after the passing of this act as aforesaid, shall be, and hereby is utterly taken away, extinguished and for ever abolished.

Section 4.

Provided always, and be it further enacted by the authority aforesaid, That every Negro and Mulatto child born within this state after the passing of this act as aforesaid (who would, in case this act had not been made, have been born a servant for years, or life, or a slave) shall be deemed to be and shall be by virtue of this act the servant of such person or his or her assigns, who would in such case have been entitled to the service of such child, until such child shall attain unto the age of twenty eight years, in the manner and on the conditions whereon servants bound by indenture for four years are or may be retained and holden; and shall be liable to like correction and punishment, and entitled to like relief in case he or she be evilly treated by his or her master or mistress, and to like freedom dues and other privileges as servants bound by indenture for four years are or may be entitled, unless the person to whom the service of any such child shall belong shall abandon his or her claim to the fame; in which case the overseers of the poor of the city, township or district respectively, where such child shall be so abandoned, shall by indenture bind out every child so abandoned, as an apprentice for a time not exceeding the age herein before limited for the service of such children.

Section 5.

And be it further enacted by the authority aforesaid, That every person, who is or shall be the owner of any Negro or Mulatto slave or servant for life or till the age of thirty one years, now within this state, or his lawful attorney, shall on or before the said first day of November next deliver or claim to be delivered in writing to the clerk of the peace of the county, or to the clerk of the court of record of the city of Philadelphia, in which he or she shall respectively inhabit, the name and surname and occupation or profession of such owner, and the name of the county and township, district or ward wherein he or she resideth; and also the name and names of any such slave and slaves, and servant and servants for life or till the age of thirty one years, together with their ages and sexes severally and respectively set forth and annexed, by such person owned or statedly employed and then being within this state, in order to ascertain and distinguish the slaves and servants for life, and till the age of thirty one years, within this state, who shall be such on the said first day of November next, from all other persons ... and that no Negro or Mulatto, now within this state, shall from and after the said first day of November, be deemed a slave or servant for life, or till the age of thirty one years, unless his or her name shall be entered as aforesaid on such record, except such Negro and Mulatto slaves and servants as are herein after excepted; the said clerk to be entitled to a fee of two dollars for each slave or servant so entered as aforesaid from the treasurer of the county, to be allowed to him in his accounts.

Section 6.

Provided always, That any person, in whom the ownership or right to the service of any Negro or Mulatto shall be vested at the passing of this act, other than such as are herein before excepted, his or her heirs, executors, administrators and assigns, and all and every of them severally shall be liable to the overseers of the poor of the city, township or district to which any such Negro or Mulatto shall become chargeable, for such necessary expense, with costs of suit thereon, as such overseers may be put to, through the neglect of the owner, master or mistress of such Negro or Mulatto; notwithstanding the name and other descriptions of such Negro or Mulatto shall not be entered and recorded as aforesaid; unless his or her master or owner shall before such slave or servant attain his or her twenty eighth year execute and record in the proper county a deed or instrument, securing to such slave or servant his or her freedom.

Section 7.

And be it further enacted by the authority aforesaid, That the offences and crimes of Negroes and Mulattoes, as well slaves and servants as freemen, shall be enquired of, adjudged, corrected and punished in like manner as the offences and crimes of the other inhabitants of this state are and shall be enquired of, adjudged, corrected and punished, and not otherwise; except that a slave shall not be admitted to bear witness against a freeman.

Section 8.

And be it further enacted by the authority aforesaid, That in all cases wherein sentence of death shall be pronounced against a slave, the jury before whom he or she shall be tried, shall appraise and declare the value of such slave; and in case such sentence be executed, the court shall make an order on the state treasurer, payable to the owner for the same and for the costs of prosecution; but in case of remission or mitigation, for the costs only.

Section 9.

And be it further enacted by the authority aforesaid, That the reward for taking up runaway and absconding Negro and Mulatto slaves and servants, and the penalties for enticing away, dealing with, or harbouring, concealing or employing Negro and Mulatto slaves and servants, shall be the same, and shall be recovered in like manner as in case of servants bound for four years.

Section 10.

And be it further enacted by the authority aforesaid, That no man or woman of any nation or colour, except the Negroes or Mulattoes who shall be registered as aforesaid, shall at any time hereafter be deemed, adjudged, or holden within the territories of this commonwealth as slaves or servants for life, but as free men and free women; except the domestic slaves attending upon delegates in congress from the other American states, foreign ministers and consuls, and persons passing through or sojourning in this state, and not becoming resident therein; and seamen employed in ships not belonging to any inhabitant of this state, nor employed in any ship owned by any such inhabitant. Provided such domestic slaves be not aliened or sold to any inhabitants nor (except in the case of members of congress, foreign ministers and consuls) retained in this state longer than six months.

Section 11.

Provided always; And be it further enacted by the authority aforesaid, That this act or any thing in it contained shall not give any relief or shelter to any absconding or runaway Negro or Mulatto slave or servant, who has absented himself or shall absent himself from his or her owner, master or mistress residing in any other state or country, but such owner, master or mistress shall have like right and aid to demand, claim and take away his slave or servant, as he might have had in case this act had not been made: And that all Negro and Mulatto slaves now owned and heretofore resident in this state, who have absented themselves, or been clandestinely carried away, or who may be employed abroad as seamen and have not returned or been brought back to their owners, masters or mistresses, before the passing of this act, may within five years be registered as effectually as is ordered by this act concerning those who are now within the state, on producing such slave before any two justices of the peace, and satisfying the said justices by due proof of the former residence, absconding, taking away, or absence of such slaves as aforesaid; who thereupon shall direct and order the said slave to be entered on the record as aforesaid.

Section 12.

And whereas attempts may be made to evade this act, by introducing into this state Negroes and Mulattoes bound by covenant to serve for long and unreasonable terms of years, if the same be not prevented.

Section 13.

Be it therefore enacted by the authority aforesaid, That no covenant of personal servitude or apprenticeship whatsoever shall be valid or binding on a Negro or Mulatto for a longer time than seven years, unless such servant or apprentice were at the commencement of such servitude or apprenticeship under the age of twenty one years; in which case such Negro or Mulatto may be holden as a servant or apprentice respectively, according to the covenant, as the case shall be, until he or she shall attain the age of twenty eight years, but no longer.

Section 14.

And be it further enacted by the authority aforesaid, That an act of assembly of the province of Pennsylvania, passed in the year one thousand Seven hundred and five, intitled, "an Act for the trial of Negroes;" and another act of assembly of the said province, passed in the year one thousand seven hundred and twenty five, intitled, "An Act for the better regulating of Negroes in this province;" and another act of assembly of the said province, passed in the year one thousand seven hundred and sixty one, intitled, "An Act for laying a duty on Negro and Mulatto slaves imported into this province;" and also another act of assembly of the said province, passed in the year one thousand seven hundred and seventy three, intitled, "An Act making perpetual an Act laying a duty on Negro and Mulatto slaves imported into this province, and for laying an additional duty said slaves," shall be and are hereby repealed, annulled and made void.

JOHN BAYARD, SPEAKER
Enabled into a law at Philadelphia, on Wednesday,
the first day of March, A.D. 1780
Thomas Paine, clerk of the general assembly.

SOURCE:

The Avalon Project at Yale Law School: Documents in Law, History, and Diplomacy <http://www.yale.edu/lawweb/avalon/avalon.htm> [accessed May 15, 2007].

Document 2: INSTRUCTIONS IN THE QUOCK WALKER CASE

These instructions to the jury come from the April 1783 case of Commonwealth of Massachusetts v. Jennison—*the final appeal in a series of cases involving former slave Quock Walker and his one-time owner, Nathaniel Jennison. The case originally arose from a charge of assault and battery made by Walker against Jennison, following Jennison's attempt to recapture Walker and return him to slavery. At issue then was the legal status of Walker and his right to bring charges into court. The original court declared Walker to be a free man and thus capable of legal redress, on the basis that Jennison was aware that Walker's previous owner had promised him his freedom when he turned twenty-five years of age. This ruling eventually was overturned, however, by the appellate court, and the case was presented to the Massachusetts Supreme Court for final appeal. In the instructions to the jury, Chief Justice William Cushing held that the 1780 Massachusetts Constitution had implicitly granted rights that were incompatible with slavery, and the jury accordingly ruled that Jennison had assaulted a freeman.*

As to the doctrine of slavery and the right of Christians to hold Africans in perpetual servitude, and sell and treat them as we do our horses and cattle, that (it is true) has been heretofore countenanced by the Province Laws formerly, but nowhere is it expressly enacted or established. It has been a usage—a usage which took its origin from the practice of some of the European nations, and the regulations of British government respecting the then Colonies, for the benefit of trade and wealth. But whatever sentiments have formerly prevailed in this particular or slid in upon us by the example of others, a different idea has taken place with the people of America, more favorable to the natural rights of mankind, and to that natural, innate desire of Liberty, with which Heaven (without regard to color, complexion, or shape of noses—features) has inspired all the human race. And upon this ground our Constitution of Government, by which the people of this Commonwealth have solemnly bound themselves, sets out with declaring that all men are born free and equal—and that every subject is entitled to liberty, and to have it guarded by the laws, as well as life and property—and in short is totally repugnant to the idea of being born slaves. This being the case, I think the idea of slavery is inconsistent with our own conduct and Constitution; and there can be no such thing as perpetual servitude of a rational creature, unless his liberty is forfeited by some criminal conduct or given up by personal consent or contract.

SOURCE:

Letters and Documents Relating to Slavery in Massachusetts. Massachusetts Historical Society, Fifth Series, III (1877), pp. 401–402.

Document 3: NOTES ON THE STATE OF VIRGINIA

Author of the Declaration of Independence and owner of slaves, Thomas Jefferson wrote Notes on the State of Virginia *in 1785, which clearly demonstrates his ambivalence on the issue of slavery and suggests some limits to his antislavery leanings. Note that his initial lamentation about the "evil" of slavery refers to its pernicious effects upon the conduct of masters. This concern with an inability to "self-govern" reflects the problems that slavery posed to republican ideals of government in the wake of the American Revolution. Jefferson believed that the races were incompatible and that, even if emancipated, former slaves could never become American citizens. His emancipation schemes thus foundered on his commitment to compensatory payments to slave owners for the loss of their property and the prohibitive costs of removing freedmen from the United States. Still, Jefferson was convinced that an incongruity between republican liberty and slavery existed, and this belief marks his contrast with subsequent proslavery theorists such as Thomas Roderick Dew and George Fitzhugh, who considered slavery fundamental to the preservation of republican liberty.*

There must doubtless be an unhappy influence on the manners of our people produced by the existence of slavery among us. The whole commerce between master and slave is a perpetual exercise of the most boisterous passions, the most unremitting despotism on the one part, and degrading submissions on the other. Our children see this, and learn to imitate it; for man is an imitative animal. This quality is the germ of all education in him. From his cradle to his grave he is learning to do what he sees others do. If a parent could find no motive either in his philanthropy or his self love, for restraining the intemperance of passion towards his slave, it should always be a sufficient one that his child is present. But generally it is not sufficient. The parent storms, the child looks on, catches the lineaments of wrath, puts on the same airs in the circle of smaller slaves, gives a loose to the worst of passions, and thus nursed, educated, and daily exercised in tyranny, cannot but be stamped by it with odious peculiarities. The man must be a prodigy who can retain his manners and morals undepraved by such circumstances. And with what execration should the statesman be loaded, who, permitting one half the citizens thus to trample on the rights of the other, transforms those into despots, and these into enemies, destroys the morals of the one part, and the *amor patriae* [love of country] of the other. For if a slave can have a country in this world, it must be any other in preference to that in which he is born to live and labour for another; in which he must lock up the faculties of his nature, contribute as far as depends on his individual endeavours to the evanishment of the human race, or entail his own miserable condition on the endless generations proceeding from him. With the morals of the people, their industry also is destroyed. For in a warm climate, no man will labour for himself who can make another labour for him. This is so true, that of the proprietors of slaves a very small proportion indeed are ever seen to labour. And can the liberties of a nation be thought secure when we have removed their only firm basis, a conviction in the minds of the people that these liberties are of the gift of God? That they are not to be violated but with his wrath? Indeed I tremble for my country when I reflect that God is just: that his justice cannot sleep for ever: that considering numbers, nature and natural means only, a revolution of the wheel of fortune, an exchange of situation is among possible events: that it may become probable by supernatural interference! The Almighty has no attribute which can take side with us in such a contest.—But it is impossible to be temperate and to pursue this subject through the various considerations of policy, of morals, of history natural and civil. We must be contented to hope they will force their way into every one's mind. I think a change already perceptible, since the origin of the present revolution. The spirit of the master is abating, that of the slave rising from the dust, his condition mollifying, the way I hope preparing, under the auspices of heaven, for a total emancipation, and that this is disposed, in the order of events, to be with the consent of the masters, rather than by their extirpation.

SOURCE:

Thomas Jefferson. *Notes on the State of Virginia,* edited, with an introduction, by William Peden (Chapel Hill: University of North Carolina Press, 1992), pp. 162–163.

Document 4: **ABOLITION OF THE ATLANTIC SLAVE TRADE BY U.S. CONGRESS**

The abolition of the Atlantic slave trade by Congress on January 1, 1808, represented a key moment in the history of the antislavery movement. The federal legislation corresponded with the triumph of William Wilberforce's efforts in Parliament and the enactment of a similar law passed in Great Britain. The abolition of the slave trade by the two nations most heavily invested in it thus demonstrated the growing legitimacy of the antislavery crusade. Ambivalence persisted, however; many Southern representatives endorsed the abolition bill not because it was a step toward the abolition of slavery, but because it acted as a mechanism to limit the growing population of those of African descent in the South.

Indeed, the document prohibits the importation of African indentured servants and free laborers as well; because of this circumstance, it is something of a double-edged sword and could reasonably be considered a statement of immigration policy even as it is an indictment of the international slave trade. Nevertheless, the abolition of the slave trade in the United States and Great Britain represented a major triumph for the nascent antislavery movement.

An Act to Prohibit the Importation of Slaves into any Port or Place Within the Jurisdiction of the United States, From and After the First Day of January, in the Year of our Lord One Thousand Eight Hundred and Eight

Be it enacted by the Senate and House of Representatives of the United States of America in Congress assembled, That from and after the first day of January, one thousand eight hundred and eight, it shall not be lawful to import or bring into the United States or the territories thereof from any foreign kingdom, place, or country, any negro, mulatto, or person of colour, with intent to hold, sell, or dispose of such negro, mulatto, or person of colour, as a slave, or to be held to service or labour.

❖ ❖ ❖

Section 2.

And be it further enacted, That no citizen or citizens of the United States, or any other person, shall, from and after the first day of January, in the year of our Lord one thousand eight hundred and eight, for himself, or themselves, or any other person whatsoever, either as master, factor, or owner, build, fit, equip, load or otherwise prepare any ship or vessel, in any port or place within the jurisdiction of the United States, nor shall cause any ship or vessel to sail from any port or place within the same, for the purpose of procuring any negro, mulatto, or person of colour, from any foreign kingdom, place, or country, to be transported to any port or place whatsoever, within the jurisdiction of the United States, to be held, sold, or disposed of as slaves, or to be held to service or labour: and if any ship or vessel shall be so fitted out for the purpose aforesaid, or shall be caused to sail so as aforesaid, every such ship or vessel, her tackle, apparel, and furniture, shall be forfeited to the United States, and shall be liable to be seized, prosecuted, and condemned in any of the circuit courts or district courts, for the district where the said ship or vessel may be found or seized.

Section 3.

And be it further enacted, That all and every person so building, fitting out, equipping, loading, or otherwise preparing or sending away, any ship or vessel, knowing or intending that the same shall be employed in such trade or business, from and after the first day of January, one thousand eight hundred and eight, contrary to the true intent and meaning of this act, or any ways aiding or abetting therein, shall severally forfeit and pay twenty thousand dollars, one moiety thereof to the use of the United States, and the other moiety to the use of any person or persons who shall sue for and prosecute the same to effect.

Section 4.

And be it further enacted, If any citizen or citizens of the United States, or any person resident within the jurisdiction of the same, shall, from and after the first day of January, one thousand eight hundred and eight, take on board, receive or transport from any of the coasts or kingdoms of Africa, or from any other foreign kingdom, place, or country, any negro, mulatto, or person of colour, in any ship or vessel, for the purpose of selling them in any port or place within the jurisdiction of the United States as slaves, or to be held to service or labour, or shall be in any ways aiding or abetting therein, such citizen or citizens, or person, shall severally forfeit and pay five thousand dollars, one moiety thereof to the use of any person or persons who shall sue for and prosecute the same to effect; and every such ship or vessel in which such negro, mulatto, or person of colour, shall have been taken on board, received, or transported as aforesaid, her tackle, apparel, and furniture, and the goods and effects which shall be found on board the same, shall be forfeited to the United States, and shall be liable to be seized, prosecuted, and condemned in any of the circuit courts or district courts in the district where the said ship or vessel may be found or seized. And neither the importer, nor any person or persons claiming from or under him, shall hold any right or title whatsoever to any negro, mulatto, or person of colour, nor to the service or labour thereof, who may be imported or brought within the United States, or territories thereof, in violation of this law, but the same shall remain subject to any regulations not contravening the provisions of this act, which the legislatures of the several states or territories at any time hereafter may make, for disposing of any such negro, mulatto, or person of colour.

Section 5.

And be it further enacted, That if any citizen or citizens of the United States, or any other person resident within the jurisdiction of the same, shall, from and after the first day of January, one thousand eight hundred and eight, contrary to the true intent and meaning of this act, take on board any ship or vessel from any of the coasts or kingdoms of Africa, or from any other foreign kingdom, place, or country, any negro, mulatto, or person of colour, with intent to sell him, her, or them, for a slave, or slaves, or to be held to service or labour, and shall transport the same to any port or place within the jurisdiction of the United States, and there sell such negro, mulatto, or person of colour, so transported as aforesaid, for a slave, or to be held to service or labour, every such offender shall be deemed guilty of a high misdemeanor, and being thereof convicted before any court having competent jurisdiction, shall suffer imprisonment for not more than ten years nor less than five years, and be fined not exceeding ten thousand dollars, nor less than one thousand dollars.

Section 6.

And be it further enacted, That if any person or persons whatsoever, shall, from and after the first day of January, one thousand eight hundred and eight, purchase or sell any negro, mulatto, or person of colour, for a slave, or to be held to service or labour, who shall have been imported, or brought from any foreign kingdom, place, or country, or from the dominions of any foreign state, immediately adjoining to the United States, into any port or place within the jurisdiction of the United States, after the last day of December, one thousand eight hundred and seven, knowing at the time of such purchase or sale, such negro, mulatto or person of colour, was so brought within the jurisdiction of the United States, as aforesaid, such purchaser and seller shall severally forfeit and pay for every negro, mulatto, or person of colour, so purchased or sold as aforesaid, eight hundred dollars; one moiety thereof to the United States, and the other moiety to the use of any person or persons who shall sue for and prosecute the same to effect: Provided, that the aforesaid forfeiture shall not extend to the seller or purchaser of any negro, mulatto, or person of colour, who may be sold or disposed of in virtue of any regulation which may hereafter be made by any of the legislatures of the several states in that respect, in pursuance of this act, and the constitution of the United States.

Section 7.

And be it further enacted, That if any ship or vessel shall be found, from and after the first day of January, one thousand eight hundred and eight, in any river, port, bay, or harbor, or on the high seas, within the jurisdictional limits of the United States, or hovering on the coast thereof, having on board any negro, mulatto, or person of colour, for the purpose of selling them as slaves, or with intent to land the same, in any port or place within the jurisdiction of the United States, contrary to the prohibition of this act, every such ship or vessel, together with her tackle, apparel, and furniture, and the goods or effects which shall be found on board the same, shall be forfeited to the use of the United States, and may be seized, prosecuted, and condemned, in any court of the United States, having jurisdiction thereof. And it shall be lawful for the President of the United States, and he is hereby authorized, should he deem it expedient, to cause any of the armed vessels of the United States to be manned and employed to cruise on any part of the coast of the United States, or territories thereof, where he may judge attempts will be made to violate the provisions of this act, and to instruct and direct the commanders of armed vessels of the United States, to seize, take, and bring into any port of the United States all such ships or vessels, and moreover to seize, take, and bring into any port of the United States all ships or vessels of the United States, wheresoever found on the high seas, contravening the provisions of this act, to be proceeded against according to law, and the captain, master, or commander of every such ship or vessel, so found and seized as aforesaid, shall be deemed guilty of a high misdemeanor, and shall be liable to be prosecuted before any court of the United States, having jurisdiction thereof; and being thereof convicted, shall be fined not exceeding ten thousand dollars, and be imprisoned not less than two years, and not exceeding four years. And the proceeds of all ships and vessels, their tackle, apparel, and furniture, and the goods and effects on board of them, which shall be so seized, prosecuted and condemned, shall be divided equally between the United States and the officers and men who shall make such seizure, take, or bring the same into port for condemnation, whether such seizure be made by an armed vessel of the United States, or revenue cutters hereof, and the same shall be distributed in like manner, as is provided by law, for the distribution of prizes taken from an enemy: Provided, that the officers and men, to be entitled to one half of the proceeds aforesaid, shall safe keep every negro, mulatto, or person of colour, found on board of any ship or vessel so by them seized, taken, or brought into port for condemnation, and shall deliver every such negro, mulatto, or person of colour, to such person or persons as shall be appointed by the respective states, to receive the same, and if no such person or persons shall be appointed by the respective states, they shall deliver every such negro, mulatto, or person of colour, to the overseers of the poor of the port or place where such ship or vessel may be brought or found, and shall immediately transmit to the governor or chief magistrate of the state, an account of their proceedings, together with the number of such Negroes, mulattoes, or persons of colour, and a descriptive list of the same, that he may give directions respecting such Negroes, mulattoes, or persons of colour.

Section 8.

And be it further enacted, That no captain, master or commander of any ship or vessel, of less burthen than forty tons, shall, from and after the first day of January, one thousand eight hundred and eight, take on board and transport any negro, mulatto, or person of colour, to any port or place whatsoever, for the purpose of selling or disposing of the same as a slave, or with intent that the same may be sold or disposed of to be held to service or labour, on penalty of forfeiting for every such negro, mulatto, or person of colour, so taken on board and transported, as aforesaid, the sum of eight hundred dollars; one moiety thereof to the use of the United States, and the other moiety to any person or persons who shall sue for, and prosecute the same to effect: Provided however, That nothing in this section shall extend to prohibit the taking on board or transporting on any river, or inland bay of the sea, within the jurisdiction of the United States, any negro, mulatto, or person of colour, (not imported contrary to the provisions of this act) in any vessel or species of craft whatever.

Section 9.

And be it further enacted, That the captain, master, or commander of any ship or vessel of the burthen of forty tons or more, from and after the first day of January, one thousand eight hundred and eight, sailing coastwise, from any port in the United States, to any port or place within the jurisdiction of the same, having on board any negro, mulatto, or person of colour, for the purpose of transporting them to be sold or disposed of as slaves, or to be held to service or labour, shall, previous to the departure of such ship or vessel, make out and subscribe duplicate manifests of every such negro, mulatto, or person of colour, on board such ship or vessel, therein specifying the name and sex of each person, their age and stature, as near as may be, and the class to which they respectively belong, whether negro, mulatto, or person of colour, with the name and place of residence of every owner or shipper of the same, and shall deliver such manifests to the collector of the port, if there be one, otherwise to the surveyor, before whom the captain, master, or commander, together with the owner or shipper, shall severally swear or affirm to the best of their knowledge and belief, that the persons therein specified were not imported or brought into the United States, from and after the first day of January, one thousand eight hundred and eight, and that under the laws of the state, they are held to service or labour; whereupon the said collector or surveyor shall certify the same on the said manifests, one of which he shall return to the said captain, master, or commander, with a permit, specifying thereon the number, names, and general description of such persons, and authorizing him to proceed to the port of his destination. And if any ship or vessel, being laden and destined as aforesaid, shall depart from the port where she may then be, without the captain, master, or commander having first made out and subscribed duplicate manifests, of every negro, mulatto, and person of colour, on board such ship or vessel, as aforesaid, and without having previously delivered the same to the said collector or surveyor, and obtained a permit, in manner as herein required, or shall, previous to her arrival at the port of her destination, take on board any negro, mulatto, or person of colour, other than those specified in the manifests, as aforesaid, every such ship or vessel, together with her tackle, apparel and furniture, shall be forfeited to the use of the United States, and may be seized, prosecuted and condemned in any court of the United States having jurisdiction thereof; and the captain, master, or commander of every such ship or vessel, shall moreover forfeit, for every such negro, mulatto, or person of colour, so transported, or taken on board, contrary to the provisions of this act, the sum of one thousand dollars, one moiety thereof to the United States, and the other moiety to the use of any person or persons who shall sue for and prosecute the same to effect.

Section 10.

And be it further enacted, That the captain, master, or commander of every ship or vessel, of the burthen of forty tons or more, from and after the first day of January, one thousand eight hundred and eight, sailing coastwise, and having on board any negro, mulatto, or person of colour, to sell or dispose of as slaves, or to be held to service or labour, and arriving in any port within the jurisdiction of the United States, from any other port within the same, shall, previous to the unlading or putting on shore any of the persons aforesaid, or suffering them to go on shore, deliver to the collector, if there be one, or if not, to the surveyor residing at the port of her arrival, the manifest certified by the collector or surveyor of the port from whence she sailed, as is herein before directed, to the truth of which, before such officer, he shall swear or affirm, and if the collector or surveyor shall be satisfied therewith, he shall thereupon grant a permit for unlading or suffering such negro, mulatto, or person of colour, to be put on shore, and if the captain, master, or commander of any such ship or vessel being laden as aforesaid, shall neglect or refuse to deliver the manifest at the time and in the manner herein directed, or shall land or put on shore any negro, mulatto, or person of colour, for the purpose aforesaid, before he shall have delivered his manifest as aforesaid, and obtained a permit for that purpose, every such captain, master, or commander, shall forfeit and pay ten thousand dollars, one moiety thereof to the United States, the other moiety to the use of any person or persons who shall sue for and prosecute the same to effect. APPROVED, March 2, 1807.

Source:

The Avalon Project at Yale Law School: Documents in Law, History, and Diplomacy <http://www.yale.edu/lawweb/avalon/avalon.htm> [accessed May 15, 2007].

Document 5: Appeal to the Coloured Citizens of the World

David Walker's Appeal to the Coloured Citizens of the World *(1829) was an incendiary publication calling for active resistance and racial war to remove the yoke of slavery. Walker was born and raised in Wilmington, North Carolina, as a freeman. He traveled widely and settled in Boston as an adult, where he still felt the sting of racial discrimination while working as a clothing merchant in the port city. During the 1820s he contributed regularly to* Freedom's Journal, *the nation's first African American newspaper. In September 1829 he published the first of four articles in his "Appeal to the Coloured Citizens of the World." In 1830 Walker published his appeal in pamphlet form. He distributed it with the help of sailors on their way to Southern ports. He sewed several copies into the linings of the sailors' uniforms so that the pamphlets could escape detection. The essay was disseminated throughout the South. In response, proslavery advocates sought to restrict the individual movement of free black sailors in Southern ports and organized a movement to suppress the U.S. Postal Service from handling antislavery pamphlets.*

Preamble

My dearly beloved Brethren and Fellow Citizens:

Having traveled over a considerable portion of these United States, and having, in the course of my travels, taken the most accurate observations of things as they exist—the result of my observations has warranted the full and unshaken conviction, that we, (coloured people of these United States) are the most degraded, wretched, and abject set of beings that ever lived since the world began, and I pray God, that none like us ever may live again until time shall be no more. They tell us of the Israelites in Egypt, the Helots in Sparta, and of the Roman Slaves, which last, were made up from almost every nation under heaven, whose sufferings under those ancient and heathen nations were, in comparison with ours, under this enlightened and Christian nation, no more than a cypher—or in other words, those heathen nations of antiquity, had but little more among them than the name and form of slavery, while wretchedness and endless miseries were reserved, apparently in a phial, to be poured out upon our fathers, ourselves and our children by Christian Americans!

These positions, I shall endeavour, by the help of the Lord, to demonstrate in the course of this appeal, to the satisfaction of the most incredulous mind—and may God Almighty who is the father of our Lord Jesus Christ, open your hearts to understand and believe the truth.

The causes, my brethren, which produce our wretchedness and miseries, are so very numerous and aggravating, that I believe the pen only of a Josephus or a Plutarch, can well enumerate and explain them. Upon subjects, then, of such incomprehensible magnitude, so impenetrable, and so notorious, I shall be obliged to omit a large class of, and content myself with giving you an exposition of a few of those, which do indeed rage to such an alarming pitch, that they cannot but be a perpetual source of terror and dismay to every reflecting mind.

I am fully aware, in making this appeal to my much afflicted and suffering brethren, that I shall not only be assailed by those whose greatest earthly desires are, to keep us in abject ignorance and wretchedness, and who are of the firm conviction that heaven has designed us and our children to be slaves and beasts of burden to them and their children.—I say, I do not only expect to be held up to the public as an ignorant, impudent and restless disturber of the public peace, by such avaricious creatures, as well as a mover of insubordination—and perhaps put in prison or to death, for giving a superficial exposition of our miseries, and exposing tyrants. But I am persuaded, that many of my brethren, particularly those who are ignorantly in league with slave-holders or tyrants, who acquire their daily bread by the blood and sweat of their more ignorant brethren—and not a few of those too, who are too ignorant to see an inch beyond their noses, will rise up and call me cursed—Yea, the jealous ones among us will perhaps use more abject subtlety by affirming that this work is not worth perusing; that we are well situated and there is no use in trying to better our condition, for we cannot. I will ask one question here.—Can our condition be any worse?—Can it be more mean and abject? If there are any changes, will they not be for the better, though they may appear for the worse at first? Can they get us any lower? Where can they get us? They are afraid to treat us worse, for they know well, the day they do it they are gone. But against all accusations which may or can be preferred against me, I appeal to heaven for my motive in writing—who knows that my object is, if possible, to awaken in the breasts of my afflicted, degraded and slumbering brethren, a spirit of enquiry and investigation respecting our miseries and wretchedness in this Republican Land of Liberty!!!!!

The sources from which our miseries are derived and on which I shall comment, I shall not combine in one, but shall put them under distinct heads and expose them in their turn; in doing which, keeping truth on my side, and not departing from the strictest rules of morality, I shall endeavor to penetrate, search out, and lay them open for your inspection. If you cannot or will not profit by them, I shall have done my duty to you, my country and my God.

And as the inhuman system of slavery, is the source from which most of our miseries proceed, I shall begin with that curse to nations; which has spread terror and devastation through so many nations of antiquity, and which is raging to such a pitch at the present day in Spain and in Portugal. It had one tug in England, in France, and in the United States of America; yet the inhabitants thereof, do not learn wisdom, and erase it entirely from their dwellings and from all with whom they have to do. The fact is, the labor of slaves comes so cheap to the avaricious usurpers, and is (as they think) of such great utility to the country where it exists, that those who are actuated by sordid avarice only, overlook the evils, which will as sure as the Lord lives, follow after the good. In fact, they are so happy to keep in ignorance and degradation, and to receive the homage and the labor of the slaves, they forget that God rules in the armies of heaven and among the inhabitants of the earth, having his ears continually open to the cries, tears and groans of his oppressed people; and being a just and holy Being will at one day appear fully in behalf of the oppressed, and arrest the progress of the avaricious oppressors; for although the destruction of the oppressors God may not effect by the oppressed, yet the Lord our God will bring other destructions upon them—for not unfrequently will he cause them to rise up one against another, to be split and divided, and to oppress each other, and sometimes to open hostilities with sword in hand. Some may ask, what is the matter with this enlightened and happy people?—Some say it is the cause of political usurpers, tyrants, oppressors, &c. But has not the Lord an oppressed and suffering people among them? Does the Lord condescend to hear their cries and see their tears in consequence of oppression? Will he let the oppressors rest comfortably and happy always? Will he not cause the very children of the oppressors to rise up against them, and oftimes put them to death? "God works in many ways his wonders to perform."

I will not here speak of the destructions which the Lord brought upon Egypt, in consequence of the oppression and consequent groans of the oppressed—of the hundreds and thousands of Egyptians whom God hurled into the Red Sea for afflicting his people in their land—of the Lord's suffering people in Sparta or Lacedemon, the land of the truly famous Lycurgus—nor have I time to comment upon the cause which produced the fierceness with which Sylla usurped the title, and absolutely acted as dictator of the Roman people—the conspiracy of Cataline—the conspiracy against, and murder of Cæsar in the Senate house—the spirit with which Marc Antony made himself master of the commonwealth—his associating Octavius and Lipidus with himself in power,—their dividing the provinces of Rome among themselves—their attack and defeat on the plains of Philippi the last defenders of their liberty, (Brutus and Cassius)—the tyranny of Tiberius, and from him to the final overthrow of Constantinople by the Turkish Sultan, Mahomed II. A.D. 1453. I say, I shall not take up time to speak of the causes which produced so much wretchedness and massacre among those heathen nations, for I am aware that you know too well, that God is just, as well as merciful!—I shall call your attention a few moments to that Christian nation, the Spaniards, while I shall leave almost unnoticed that avaricious and cruel people, the Portuguese, among whom all true hearted Christians and lovers of Jesus Christ, must evidently see the judgments of God displayed. To show the judgments of God upon the Spaniards I shall occupy but little time, leaving a plenty of room for the candid and unprejudiced to reflect.

All persons who are acquainted with history, and particularly the Bible, who are not blinded by the God of this world, and are not actuated solely by avarice—who are able to lay aside prejudice long enough to view candidly and impartially, things as they were, are, and probably will be, who are willing to admit that God made man to serve him alone, and that man should have no other Lord or Lords but himself—that God Almighty is the sole proprietor or master of the whole human family, and will not on any consideration admit of a colleague, being unwilling to divide his glory with another.—And who can dispense with prejudice long enough to admit that we are men, notwithstanding our impriment noses and woolly heads, and believe that we feel for our fathers, mothers, wives and children as well as they do for theirs.—I say, all who are permitted to see and believe these things, can easily recognize the judgments of God among the Spaniards. Though others may lay the cause of the fierceness with which they cut each other's throats, to some other circumstances, yet they who believe that God is a God of justice, will believe that Slavery is the principal cause.

While the Spaniards are running about upon the field of battle cutting each other's throats, has not the Lord an afflicted and suffering people in the midst of them whose cries and groans in consequence of oppression are continually pouring into the ears of the God of justice? Would they not cease to cut each others throats if they could? But how can they? The very support which they draw from government to aid them in perpetrating such enormities, does it not arise in a great degree from the wretched victims of oppression among them? And yet they are calling for Peace!—Peace!! Will any peace be given unto them? Their destruction may indeed be procrastinated awhile, but can it continue long while they are oppressing the Lord's people? Has He not the hearts of all men in His hand? Will he suffer one part of his creatures to go on oppressing another like brutes always, with impunity? And yet those avaricious wretches are calling for Peace!!!! I declare it does appear to me, as though some nations think God is asleep, or that he made the Africans for nothing else but to dig their mines and work their farms, or they cannot believe history, sacred or profane. I ask every man who has a heart and is blessed with the privilege of believing—Is not God a God of justice to all his creatures? Do you say he is? Then if he gives peace and tranquility to tyrants, and permits them to keep our fathers, our mothers, ourselves and our children in eternal ignorance and wretchedness to support them and their families, would he be to us a God of justice? I ask O ye Christians!!! who hold us and our children, in the most abject ignorance and degradation, that ever a people were afflicted with since the world began—I say, if God gives you peace and tranquility, and suffers you thus to go on afflicting us and our children, who have never given you the least provocation,—Would he be to us a God of justice? If you will allow that we are men, who feel for each other, does not the blood of our fathers and of us their children, cry aloud to the Lord of Sabaoth against you, for the cruelties and murders with which you have, and do continue to afflict us. But it is time for me to close my remarks on the suburbs, just to enter more fully into the interior of this system of cruelty and oppression.

SOURCE:

Charles M. Wiltse, ed. *David Walker's Appeal in Four Articles: Together with a Preamble to the Coloured Citizens of the World* (New York: Hill & Wang, 1965).

Document 6: FROM THE FIRST ISSUE OF *THE LIBERATOR*

William Lloyd Garrison's inaugural issue of his newspaper The Liberator, *published January 1, 1831, set the tone for the campaign to immediately abolish slavery in the United States. His abolitionist message allowed for no compromise on the issue and came to dominate antislavery discussions over the next decades. It was a message of social revolution that readily aligned itself with other contempo-*

rary evangelical and utopian reform movements. His subscribers often involved themselves in the temperance crusade, workingmen's parties for just wages and land reform, and the nascent women's suffrage movement as well. Garrison thus imbued abolitionism with a more radical tinge, and in some cases alienated many people with antislavery sensibilities from the cause. Nevertheless, The Liberator *emerged as a banner for social reform and remained one of the most readily identifiable abolitionist newspapers through the end of the Civil War.*

To the Public

In the month of August, I issued proposals for publishing "THE LIBERATOR" in Washington city; but the enterprise, though hailed in different sections of the country, was palsied by public indifference. Since that time, the removal of the *Genius of Universal Emancipation* to the Seat of Government has rendered less imperious the establishment of a similar periodical in that quarter.

During my recent tour for the purpose of exciting the minds of the people by a series of discourses on the subject of slavery, every place that I visited gave fresh evidence of the fact, that a greater revolution in public sentiment was to be effected in the free states—*and particularly in New-England*—than at the south. I found contempt more bitter, opposition more active, detraction more relentless, prejudice more stubborn, and apathy more frozen, than among slave owners themselves. Of course, there were individual exceptions to the contrary. This state of things afflicted, but did not dishearten me. I determined, at every hazard, to lift up the standard of emancipation in the eyes of the nation, *within sight of Bunker Hill and in the birth place of liberty.* That standard is now unfurled; and long may it float, unhurt by the spoliations of time or the missiles of a desperate foe—yea, till every chain be broken, and every bondman set free! Let southern oppressors tremble—let their secret abettors tremble—let their northern apologists tremble—let all the enemies of the persecuted blacks tremble.

I deem the publication of my original Prospectus unnecessary, as it has obtained a wide circulation. The principles therein inculcated will be steadily pursued in this paper, excepting that I shall not array myself as the political partisan of any man. In defending the great cause of human rights, I wish to derive the assistance of all religions and of all parties.

Assenting to the "self-evident truth" maintained in the American Declaration of Independence, "that all men are created equal, and endowed by their Creator with certain inalienable rights—among which are life, liberty and the pursuit of happiness," I shall strenuously contend for the immediate enfranchisement of our slave population. In Park-street Church, on the Fourth of July, 1829, in an address on slavery, I unreflectingly assented to the popular but pernicious doctrine of gradual abolition. I seize this opportunity to make a full and unequivocal recantation, and thus publicly to ask pardon of my God, of my country, and of my brethren the poor slaves, for having uttered a sentiment so full of timidity, injustice and absurdity. A similar recantation, from my pen, was published in the *Genius of Universal Emancipation* at Baltimore, in September, 1829. My conscience is now satisfied.

I am aware, that many object to the severity of my language; but is there not cause for severity? I *will* be as harsh as truth, and as uncompromising as justice. On this subject, I do not wish to think, or speak, or write, with moderation. No! no! Tell a man whose house is on fire, to give a moderate alarm; tell him to moderately rescue his wife from the hand of the ravisher; tell the mother to gradually extricate her babe from the fire into which it has fallen;—but urge me not to use moderation in a cause like the present. I am in earnest—I will not equivocate—I will not excuse—I will not retreat a single inch—AND I WILL BE HEARD. The apathy of the people is enough to make every statue leap from its pedestal, and to hasten the resurrection of the dead.

It is pretended, that I am retarding the cause of emancipation by the coarseness of my invective, and the precipitancy of my measures. The *charge is not true.* On this question my influence,—humble as it is,—is felt at this moment to a considerable extent, and shall be felt in coming years—not perniciously, but beneficially—not as a curse, but as a blessing; and posterity will bear testimony that I was right. I desire to thank God, that he enables me to disregard "the fear of man which bringeth a snare," and to speak his truth in its simplicity and power. And here I close with this fresh dedication:

Oppression! I have seen thee, face to face,
And met thy cruel eye and cloudy brow;
But thy soul-withering glance I fear not now—
For dread to prouder feelings doth give place
Of deep abhorrence! Scorning the disgrace

Of slavish knees that at thy footstool bow,
I also kneel—but with far other vow
Do hail thee and thy hord of hirelings base:—
I swear, while life-blood warms my throbbing veins,
Still to oppose and thwart, with heart and hand,
Thy brutalising sway—till Afric's chains
Are burst, and Freedom rules the rescued land,—
Trampling Oppression and his iron rod:
Such is the vow I take—SO HELP ME GOD!

Source:

William Lloyd Garrison. *The Liberator,* January 1, 1831. Republished in William E. Cain, *William Lloyd Garrison and the Fight against Slavery: Selections from* The Liberator (Boston & New York: Bedford/St. Martin's Press, 1995), pp. 70–72.

Document 7: "Civil Disobedience"

"Civil Disobedience," Henry David Thoreau's most famous essay, resulted from his opposition to the Mexican War, which he believed was a conspiracy to extend slavery. He refused to pay the poll tax as a sign of his dissent and was sentenced to a night in jail for his protest. The essay, first published under the title "Resistance to Civil Government" in Elizabeth Peabody's journal Aesthetic Papers *in May 1849, achieved immediate popularity in the North. Thoreau's words reflect the particular historical context of the debate during the war but also emphasize the wider spirit of social reform embraced by many abolitionists.*

I heartily accept the motto,—"That government is best which governs least;" and I should like to see it acted up to more rapidly and systematically. Carried out, it finally amounts to this, which I also believe,—"That government is best which governs not at all;" and when men are prepared for it, that will be the kind of government which they will have. Government is at best but an expedient; but most governments are usually, and all governments are sometimes, inexpedient.... The government itself, which is only the mode which the people have chosen to execute their will, is equally liable to be abused and perverted before the people can act through it. Witness the present Mexican war, the work of comparatively a few individuals using the standing government as their tool; for, in the outset, the people would not have consented to this measure.

This American government,—what is it but a tradition, though a recent one, endeavoring to transmit itself unimpaired to posterity, but each instant losing some of its integrity? It has not the vitality and force of a single living man; for a single man can bend it to his will. It is a sort of wooden gun to the people themselves; and, if ever they should use it in earnest as a real one against each other, it will surely split. But it is not the less necessary for this; for the people must have some complicated machinery or other, and hear its din, to satisfy the idea of government which they have. Governments show thus how successfully men can be imposed on, even impose on themselves, for their own advantage....

But, to speak practically and as a citizen, unlike those who call themselves no-government men, I ask for, not at once no government, but *at once* a better government. Let every man make known what kind of government would command his respect, and that will be one step toward obtaining it.

After all, the practical reason why, when the power is once in the hands of the people, a majority are permitted, and for a long period continue, to rule, is not because they are most likely to be in the right, nor because this seems the fairest to the minority, but because they are physically the strongest. But a government in which the majority rule in all cases cannot be based on justice, even as far as men understand it....

How does it become a man to behave toward this American government to-day? I answer that he cannot without disgrace be associated with it. I cannot for an instant recognize that political organization as *my* government which is the *slave's* government also.

All men recognize the right of revolution; that is, the right to refuse allegiance to and to resist the government, when its tyranny or its inefficiency are great and unendurable. But almost all say that such is not the case now. But such was the case, they think, in the Revolution of '75. If one were to tell me that this was a bad government because it taxed certain foreign commodities brought to its ports, it is most probable that I should not make an ado about it, for I can do without them: all machines have their friction; and possibly this does enough good to counterbalance the evil. At any rate, it is a great evil to make a stir about it. But when the friction comes to have its machine, and oppression and robbery are organized, I say, let us not have such a machine any longer. In other words, when a sixth of the population of a nation which has undertaken to be a refuge for liberty are slaves, and a whole country is unjustly overrun and conquered by a foreign army, and subjected to military law, I think that it is not too soon for honest men to rebel and revolutionize. What makes this duty the more urgent is the fact, that the country so overrun is not our own, but ours is the invading army.... This people must cease to hold slaves, and to make war on Mexico, though it cost them their existence as a people.

Practically speaking, the opponents to a reform in Massachusetts are not a hundred thousand politicians at the South, but a hundred thousand merchants and farmers here, who are more interested in commerce and agriculture than they are in humanity, and are not prepared to do justice to the slave and to Mexico, *cost what it may*. I quarrel not with far-off foes, but with those who, near at home, co-operate with, and do the bidding of those far away, and without whom the latter would be harmless.... There are thousands who are *in opinion* opposed to slavery and to the war, who yet in effect do nothing to put an end to them; who, esteeming themselves children of Washington and Franklin, sit down with their hands in their pockets, and say that they know not what to do, and do nothing; who even postpone the question of freedom to the question of free-trade, and quietly read the prices—current along with the latest advices from Mexico, after dinner... They hesitate, and they regret, and sometimes they petition; but they do nothing in earnest and with effect. They will wait, well disposed for others to remedy the evil, that they may no longer have it to regret. At most, they give only a cheap vote ... I cast my vote, perchance, as I think right: but I am not vitally concerned that that right should prevail. I am willing to leave it to the majority. Its obligation, therefore, never exceeds that of expediency. Even voting *for the right* is *doing* nothing for it. It is only expressing to men feebly your desire that it should prevail. A wise man will not leave the right to the mercy of chance, nor wish to prevail through the power of the majority. There is but little virtue in the action of masses of men. When the majority shall at length vote for the abolition of slavery, it will be because they are indifferent to slavery, or because there is but little slavery left to be abolished by their vote.

SOURCE:

Henry David Thoreau. *Civil Disobedience and Other Essays* (New York: Dover, 1993), pp. 1–5.

Document 8: WHAT TO THE SLAVE IS THE FOURTH OF JULY?

Frederick Douglass delivered this famous speech to a meeting sponsored by the Rochester Ladies' Anti-Slavery Society on July 5, 1852. By this time Douglass was a well-known abolitionist and had published his autobiography, Narrative of the Life of Frederick Douglass *(1845), to popular acclaim in the North and in Great Britain. Anticipating Abraham Lincoln's Gettysburg Address by a decade, Douglass first honored the Declaration of Independence as the foundation of the principles of liberty and human equality, which he believed characterized the American Republic, and then used the opportunity to remind his audience that the scourge of slavery prevented the ideals of liberty and equality for all from being fully realized.*

Fellow Citizens, I am not wanting in respect for the fathers of this republic. The signers of the Declaration of Independence were brave men. They were great men, too—great enough to give frame to a great age. It does not often happen to a nation to raise, at one time, such a number of truly great men. The point from which I am compelled to view them is not, certainly, the most favorable; and yet I cannot contemplate their great deeds with less than admiration. They were statesmen, patriots and heroes, and for the good they did, and the principles they contended for, I will unite with you to honor their memory....

Fellow-citizens, pardon me, allow me to ask, why am I called upon to speak here to-day? What have I, or those I represent, to do with your national independence? Are the great principles of political freedom and of natural justice, embodied in that Declaration of Independence, extended to us? and am I, therefore, called upon to bring our humble offering to the national altar, and to confess the benefits and express devout gratitude for the blessings resulting from your independence to us?

Would to God, both for your sakes and ours, that an affirmative answer could be truthfully returned to these questions! Then would my task be light, and my burden easy and delightful. For who is there so cold, that a nation's sympathy could not warm him? Who so obdurate and dead to the claims of gratitude, that would not thankfully acknowledge such priceless benefits? Who so stolid and selfish, that would not give his voice to swell the hallelujahs of a nation's jubilee, when the chains of servitude had been torn from his limbs? I am not that man. In a case like that, the dumb might eloquently speak, and the "lame man leap as an hart."

But such is not the state of the case. I say it with a sad sense of the disparity between us. I am not included within the pale of glorious anniversary! Your high independence only reveals the immeasurable distance between us. The blessings in which you, this day, rejoice, are not enjoyed in common. The rich inheritance of justice, liberty, prosperity and independence, bequeathed by your fathers, is shared by you, not by me. The sunlight that brought light and healing to you, has brought stripes and death to me. This Fourth [of] July is yours, not mine. You may rejoice, I must mourn. To drag a man in fetters into the grand illuminated temple of liberty, and call upon him to join you in joyous anthems, were inhuman mockery and sacrilegious irony. Do you mean, citizens, to mock me, by asking me to speak to-day? If so, there is a parallel to your conduct. And let me warn you that it is dangerous to copy the example of a nation whose crimes, towering up to heaven, were thrown down by the breath of the Almighty, burying that nation in irrevocable ruin! I can to-day take up the plaintive lament of a peeled and woe-smitten people!

"By the rivers of Babylon, there we sat down. Yea! we wept when we remembered Zion. We hanged our harps upon the willows in the midst thereof. For there, they that carried us away captive, required of us a song; and they who wasted us required of us mirth, saying, Sing us one of the songs of Zion. How can we sing the Lord's song in a strange land? If I forget thee, O Jerusalem, let my right hand forget her cunning. If I do not remember thee, let my tongue cleave to the roof of my mouth."

Fellow-citizens, above your national, tumultuous joy, I hear the mournful wail of millions! whose chains, heavy and grievous yesterday, are, to-day, rendered more intolerable by the jubilee shouts that reach them. If I do forget, if I do not faithfully remember those bleeding children of sorrow this day, "may my right hand forget her cunning, and may my tongue cleave to the roof of my mouth!" To forget them, to pass lightly over their wrongs, and to chime in with the popular theme, would be treason most scandalous and shocking, and would make me a reproach before God and the world. My subject, then, fellow-citizens, is American slavery. I shall see this day and its popular characteristics from the slave's point of view. Standing there identified with the American bondman, making his wrongs mine, I do not hesitate to declare, with all my soul, that the character and conduct of this nation never looked blacker to me than on this 4th of July! Whether we turn to the declarations of the past, or to the professions of the present, the conduct of the nation seems equally hideous and revolting. America is false to the past, false to the present, and solemnly binds herself to be false to the future. Standing with God and the crushed and bleeding slave on this occasion, I will, in the name of humanity which is outraged, in the name of liberty which is fettered, in the name of the constitution and the Bible which are disregarded and trampled upon, dare to call in question and to denounce, with all the emphasis I can command, everything that serves to perpetuate slavery—the great sin and shame of America! "I will not equivocate; I will not excuse"; I will use the severest language I can command; and yet not one word shall escape me that any man, whose judgment is not blinded by prejudice, or who is not at heart a slaveholder, shall not confess to be right and just.

But I fancy I hear some one of my audience say, "It is just in this circumstance that you and your brother abolitionists fail to make a favorable impression on the public mind. Would you argue more, and denounce less; would you persuade more, and rebuke less; your cause would be much more likely to succeed." But, I submit, where all is plain there is nothing to be argued. What point in the anti-slavery creed would you have me argue? On what branch of the subject do the people of this country need light? Must I undertake to prove that the slave is a man? That point is conceded already. Nobody doubts it. The slaveholders themselves acknowledge it in the enactment of laws for their government. They acknowledge it when they punish disobedience on the part of the slave. There are seventy-two crimes in the State of Virginia which, if committed by a black man (no matter how ignorant he be), subject him to the punishment of death; while only two of the same crimes will subject a white man to the like punishment. What is this but the acknowledgment that the slave is a moral, intellectual, and responsible being? The manhood of the slave is conceded. It is admitted in the fact that Southern statute books are covered with enactments forbidding, under severe fines and penalties, the teaching of the slave to read or to write. When you can point to any such laws in reference to the beasts of the field, then I may consent to argue the manhood of the slave. When the dogs in your streets, when the fowls of the air, when the cattle on your hills, when the fish of the sea, and the reptiles that crawl, shall be unable to distinguish the slave from a brute, then will I argue with you that the slave is a man!

For the present, it is enough to affirm the equal manhood of the Negro race. Is it not astonishing that, while we are ploughing, planting, and reaping, using all kinds of mechanical tools, erecting houses, constructing bridges, building ships, working in metals of brass, iron, copper, silver and gold; that, while we are reading, writing and ciphering, acting as clerks, merchants and secretaries, having among us lawyers, doctors, ministers, poets, authors, editors, orators and teachers; that, while we are engaged in all manner of enterprises common to other men, digging gold in California, capturing the whale in the Pacific, feeding sheep and cattle on the hillside, living, moving, acting, thinking, planning, living in families as husbands, wives and children, and, above all, confessing and worshipping the Christian's God, and looking hopefully for life and immortality beyond the grave, we are called upon to prove that we are men!

Would you have me argue that man is entitled to liberty? that he is the rightful owner of his own body? You have already declared it. Must I argue the wrongfulness of slavery? Is that a question for Republicans? Is it to be settled by the rules of logic and argumentation, as a matter beset with great difficulty, involving a doubtful application of the principle of justice, hard to be understood? How should I look to-day, in the presence of Americans, dividing, and subdividing a discourse, to show that men have a natural right to freedom? speaking of it relatively and positively, negatively and affirmatively. To do so, would be to make myself ridiculous, and to offer an insult to your understanding. There is not a man beneath the canopy of heaven that does not know that slavery is wrong for him.

What, am I to argue that it is wrong to make men brutes, to rob them of their liberty, to work them without wages, to keep them ignorant of their relations to their fellow men, to beat them with sticks, to flay their flesh with the lash, to load their limbs with irons, to hunt them with dogs, to sell them at auction, to sunder their families, to knock out their teeth, to burn their flesh, to starve them into obedience and submission to their masters? Must I argue that a system thus marked with blood, and stained with pollution, is wrong? No! I will not. I have better employment for my time and strength than such arguments would imply.

What, then, remains to be argued? Is it that slavery is not divine; that God did not establish it; that our doctors of divinity are mistaken? There is blasphemy in the thought. That which is inhuman, cannot be divine! Who can reason on such a proposition? They that can, may; I cannot. The time for such argument is passed.

At a time like this, scorching irony, not convincing argument, is needed. O! had I the ability, and could reach the nation's ear, I would, to-day, pour out a fiery stream of biting ridicule, blasting reproach, withering sarcasm, and stern rebuke. For it is not light that is needed, but fire; it is not the gentle shower, but thunder. We need the storm, the whirlwind, and the earthquake. The feeling of the nation must be quickened; the conscience of the nation must be roused; the propriety of the nation must be startled; the hypocrisy of the nation must be exposed; and its crimes against God and man must be proclaimed and denounced.

What, to the American slave, is your 4th of July? I answer; a day that reveals to him, more than all other days in the year, the gross injustice and cruelty to which he is the constant victim. To him, your celebration is a sham; your boasted liberty, an unholy license; your national greatness, swelling vanity; your sounds of rejoicing are empty and heartless; your denunciation of tyrants, brass fronted impudence; your shouts of liberty and equality, hollow mockery; your prayers and hymns, your sermons and thanksgivings, with all your religious parade and solemnity, are, to him, mere bombast, fraud, deception, impiety, and hypocrisy—a thin veil to cover up crimes which would disgrace a nation of savages. There is not a nation on the earth guilty of practices more shocking and bloody than are the people of the United States, at this very hour.

Go where you may, search where you will, roam through all the monarchies and despotisms of the Old World, travel through South America, search out every abuse, and when you have found the last, lay your facts by the side of the everyday practices of this nation, and you will say with me, that, for revolting barbarity and shameless hypocrisy, America reigns without a rival....

Allow me to say, in conclusion, notwithstanding the dark picture I have this day presented, of the state of the nation, I do not despair of this country. There are forces in operation which must inevitably work the downfall of slavery. "The arm of the Lord is not shortened," and the doom of slavery is certain. I, therefore, leave off where I began, with hope. While drawing encouragement from "the Declaration of Independence," the great principles it contains, and the genius of American Institutions, my spirit is also cheered by the obvious tendencies of the age. Nations do not now stand in the same relation to each other that they did ages ago. No nation can now shut itself up from the surrounding world and trot round in the same old path of its fathers without interference. The time was when such could be done. Long established customs of hurtful character could formerly fence themselves in, and do their evil work with social impunity. Knowledge was then confined and enjoyed by the privileged few, and the multitude walked on in mental darkness. But a change has now come over the affairs of mankind. Walled cities and empires have become unfashionable. The arm of commerce has borne away the gates of the strong city. Intelligence is penetrating the darkest corners of the globe. It makes its pathway over and under the sea, as well as on the earth. Wind, steam, and lightning are its chartered agents. Oceans no longer divide, but link nations together. From Boston to London is now a holiday excursion. Space is comparatively annihilated.—Thoughts expressed on one side of the Atlantic are distinctly heard on the other. The far off and almost fabulous Pacific rolls in grandeur at our feet. The Celestial Empire, the mystery of ages, is being solved. The fiat of the Almighty, "Let there be Light," has not yet spent its force. No abuse, no outrage whether in taste, sport or avarice, can now hide itself from the all-pervading light. The iron shoe, and crippled foot of China must be seen in contrast with nature. Africa must rise and put on her yet unwoven garment. "Ethiopia shall stretch out her hand unto God." In the fervent aspirations of William Lloyd Garrison, I say, and let every heart join in saying it:

God speed the year of jubilee
The wide world o'er!
When from their galling chains set free,
Th' oppress'd shall vilely bend the knee,
And wear the yoke of tyranny
Like brutes no more.
That year will come, and freedom's reign,
To man his plundered rights again
Restore.

God speed the day when human blood
Shall cease to flow!
In every clime be understood,
The claims of human brotherhood,
And each return for evil, good,
Not blow for blow;
That day will come all feuds to end,
And change into a faithful friend
Each foe.

God speed the hour, the glorious hour,
When none on earth
Shall exercise a lordly power,
Nor in a tyrant's presence cower;
But to all manhood's stature tower,
By equal birth!
That hour will come, to each, to all,
And from his Prison-house, to thrall
Go forth.

Until that year, day, hour, arrive,
With head, and heart, and hand I'll strive,
To break the rod, and rend the gyve,
The spoiler of his prey deprive—
So witness Heaven!
And never from my chosen post,
Whate'er the peril or the cost,
Be driven.

SOURCE:

Philip S. Foner. *The Life and Writings of Frederick Douglass, Volume II Pre–Civil War Decade 1850–1860* (New York: International, 1954).

Document 9: REVIEW OF UNCLE TOM'S CABIN

George Frederick Holmes's review of Harriet Beecher Stowe's famous antislavery novel Uncle Tom's Cabin *(1852) in the December 1852* Southern Literary Messenger *provides one of the most sophisticated intellectual statements in defense of slavery. He critiques Stowe but also discusses the advent of the "social novel" that* Uncle Tom's Cabin *epitomized. Holmes acknowledged the sheer success and power of this literary form and lamented the inability of the Southern literary class to rival the popularity of Stowe. Ironically, his own review was written largely for other intellectuals and consequently reinforced the contrast with the vulgar sentimentalism of Stowe. Holmes's review, however, like George Fitzhugh's* Sociology for the South *(1854, Document 10) demonstrates complexity and erudition within the proslavery argument, layers that went well beyond simple racism. Nevertheless, the popular appeal of Stowe's novel proved insurmountable to Southern criticism and continued to influence many Northerners who had previously considered slavery a "Southern problem."*

This is a fiction—professedly a fiction; but, unlike other works of the same type, its purpose is not amusement, but proselytism. The romance was formerly employed to divert the leisure, recreate the fancy, and quicken the sympathies of successive generations, changing its complexion and enlarging the compass of its aims with the expanding tastes of different periods; but never forgetting that its main object was to kindle and purify the imagination, while fanning into a livelier flame the slumbering charities of the human heart. But, in these late and evil days, the novel, notwithstanding those earlier associations, has descended from its graceful and airy home, and assumed to itself a more vulgar mission, incompatible with its essence and alien to its original design. Engaging in the coarse conflicts of life, and mingling in the fumes and gross odours of political or polemical dissension, it has stained and tainted the robe of ideal purity with which it was of old adorned. Instead of remaining the ever welcome companion of an idle hour, which turned to profit by its sweet alchemy the loose moments devoted to intellectual reverie, it has entered upon a sterner career, and one which requires us to question the visitant before admitting it to our confidence or listening to its tale. Now-a-days, it frequently assumes both the stole of the philosopher and the cassock of the priest and exhibits strange contracts between its face and figure, and the garb in which they are enveloped. Sometimes, though rarely, we discover the fairy features of our former favorite under the new disguise, and are only amused by the quaint antics and grotesque *diablerie* which spring from the uncongenial union: but more commonly the airy phantom which flitted before our earlier fancy, is transmuted into an aged and haggard crone, who wears the mask, pads her shrivelled limbs, and clothes herself in a deceptive garb, that she may steal more securely into our unsuspicious favor, mumble her incantations before we recognise them as the song of Canidia, and distill into our ears the venom of her tongue, before any apprehension is awakened. In the one case we may imagine that we have before us Omphale in the arms of Hercules; in the other, it is the drunken Lais, proud of the conquests of her youth and beauty, and garnishing the silly tattle of her age with the shreds and patches she has preserved from her ancient association with Ariatippus. The one may still be a Venus, though bedecked with the casque and plumes of Minerva: the other is the veriest drab who ever pretended to sense or virtue, to modesty or religion.

The wide dissimilarity between these two classes of romancing missionaries renders it important for us to be on our guard, and should suggest the prudence of questioning at the threshold, these new votaries of fiction, that we may know whence they come, and to what end they visit us. We may tolerate the coquettish airs of the one; we must repel the disgusting and depraved seductions of the other. If they descend upon us like the angel visits of former dreams, bearing balm upon their wings, and bringing consolation in the afflictions or trials of life, by enlarging the range of our sympathies, and revealing to our eyes the pettiness of our own sorrows, murmurs, complaints, and difficulties, in comparison with the vast array of deeper agonies, more arduous struggles, and darker fortunes cumbered amongst the possible and probable contingencies of human life,—then, as in the days when they were still untainted with suspicion, let us bid them welcome, and receive or endure the philosophy which but little befits them, for the sake of the inspiration, the hope, or the resignation which they instill. But, if the emblems of fiction are assumed but to delude, if the stole which they wear is the robe of the Cynic, or their hood the cowl of the fanatic; if their mission is to produce discontent, to be the heralds of disorder and dissension, then, though their song be as sweet as the Syren's, and their skin as sleek and slimy and glistening as that of the serpent which tempted Eve, let us bid them avaunt! and repel them from our intimacy and from our dwellings, which their presence would contaminate. But, in either case, let us examine their nature before we extend to them our greetings, or reject them with disgust.

We have examined the production of Mrs. Harriet Beecher Stowe, which we purpose to review, and we discover it to belong to the latter class, and to be one of the most reprehensible specimens of the tribe. We own that we approach the criticism of the work with peculiar sensations of both reluctance and repugnance. We take no pleasure in the contact with either folly or vice; and we are unwilling to handle the scandalous libel in the manner in which it deserves to be treated, in consideration of its being the effusion of one of that sex, whose natural position entitles them to all forbearance and courtesy, and which, in all ordinary cases, should be shielded even from just severity, by that protecting mantle which the name and thought of woman cast over even the erring and offending members of the sex. But higher interests are involved; the rule that everyone bearing the name and appearance of a lady, should receive the delicate gallantry and considerate tenderness which are due to a lady, is not absolutely without exception. If she deliberately steps beyond the hallowed precincts—the enchanted circle—which encompasses her as with the halo of divinity, she has wantonly forfeited her privilege of immunity as she has irretrievably lost our regard, and the harshness which she may provoke is invited by her own folly and impropriety. We cannot accord to the termagant virago or the foul-mouthed hag the same deference that is rightfully due to the maiden purity of untainted innocence. Still, though the exception undoubtedly exists, and we might, without indecorum, consider that all claims to forbearance had been lost by Mrs. Stowe, we shall not avail ourselves of the full benefit of her forfeiture. We cannot take the critical lash into our hands with the same callous indifference, or with the same stern determination of venting our just indignation, that we might have done, had the penalty been required for "the lords of creation." We will endeavor, then, as far as possible, to forget Mrs. Harriet Beecher Stowe, and the individuality of her authorship, and will strive to concentrate our attention and our reprehension on her book, venturing only an aside at parting—a quotation from a work which it would be infamy to cite in connection with any other lady's name than her own....

We have said that *Uncle Tom's Cabin* is a fiction. It is a fiction throughout; a fiction in form; a fiction in its facts; a fiction in its representations and coloring; a fiction in its statements; a fiction in its sentiments; a fiction in its morals; a fiction in its religion; a fiction in its inferences; a fiction equally with regard to the subjects it is designed to expound, and with respect to the manner of their exposition. It is a fiction, not for the sake of more effectually communicating truth; but for the purpose of more effectually disseminating a slander. It is a fictitious or fanciful representation for the sake of producing fictitious or false impressions. Fiction is its form and falsehood is its end. When Aristotle assigned to poetry the precedence over history for its superior efficacy in instructing, refining, and ennobling mankind: when Bacon re-echoed the praise, and eulogised the works of the imagination, as seeking, by the universality and congeniality of ideal

truth, to correct and elevate the warped and imperfect examples of virtue furnished in human action, they certainly never anticipated that the realm of fiction would be degraded into the domain of falsehood, or that fiction would cease to be the means of inculcating truth for the sake of substituting itself as the ultimate aim in the place of truth. By the beneficent Providence of God, the mind of man has been so constituted that, amid all the frailties and illusions, the follies and the errors of fallen humanity, it can still conceive of virtue more enduring and undeviating, of justice more unswerving, of fortitude more constant and patient; and of charities more diffusive and ennobling than the trials, and difficulties, and obstacles of actual existence will permit to be exhibited. Fancy, as if lighted up by the radiance of the sun which gilded the landscapes of Eden, can revert to imagined possibilities of a higher, a holier, and a nobler existence, and recalling, as it were, the reminiscences of the days of purity and innocence, can strengthen our hearts and elevate our feelings, to resist the seductions of evil; when, without such aid, the imperishable relic of a better condition—we might too easily yield to the vanities, the vices, and the temptations of life. But the magic wand is broken—the priceless treasure lost—when, instead of limiting the play of the imagination to its legitimate employment, we turn it to unholy uses. Nay, it is degraded and stripped of its power of transmitting this baser life of ours into the semblance of a golden age, when we suffer its potency to be turned to opposite ends, and to be applied not to the revival of the latent image of ideal excellence, but to the dirty sorcery of party purposes and fanatical aims. The rod of Aaron, which blossomed in the desert, drew down day by day celestial food from heaven, and educed from the river rock the living waters, to quench the deadly thirst of the Israelites, was the same wand which brought the plagues of flies and frogs and locusts, famine and pestilence and death, over the populous valleys of the prolific Nile. So it is with fancy: the fiction, which is the hand-maiden of truth, may refresh our fainting spirits in the wilderness of life: the fiction, which ends in fiction and is the slave of falsehood, will spread a fatal blight where all was salubrious, and happy and prosperous before.

In *Uncle Tom's Cabin*, the vice of this depraved application of fiction and its desolating consequences, may be readily detected. Every fact is distorted, every incident discolored, in order to awaken rancorous hatred and malignant jealousies between the citizens of the same republic, the fellow countrymen whose interests and happiness are linked with the perpetuity of a common union, and with the prosperity of a common government. With the hope of expediting or achieving the attainment of a fanatical, and in great measure, merely speculative idea, of substituting the real thraldom of free labor for the imaginary hardships of slavery—the hydra of dissension is evoked by the diabolical spells of falsehood, misrepresentation, and conscious sophistry. What censure shall we pass upon a book, calculated, if not designed, to produce such a result? What condemnation upon an effort to revive all the evils of civil discord—to resuscitate all the dangers of disunion—allayed with such difficulty, and but recently lulled into partial quiescence by the efforts of the sages and the patriotic forbearance of the States of the Confederacy? What language shall we employ when such a scheme is presented, as the *beau ideal* of sublimated virtue, under the deceptive form of literary amusement, and is seriously offered as the recreation of our intellectual leisure?

We have neither the time nor the inclination [to] run methodically through the labyrinths of misrepresentation which constitute the details of this romance. It has obtained an unhappy notoriety, which would render the task as profitless as it would be ungrateful. The copy before us purports to belong to the ninety-fifth thousand already published in America; and we see that upwards of one hundred and fifty thousand have been issued in England. How rapid the circulation of error! How slow the program of truth! How easy the propagation of falsehood; how arduous the dissemination of its antidote! When in the course of a few short months, a quarter of a million of the readers of the English tongue manifest their readiness to welcome and their anxiety to believe a lie, it is useless for the injured party to disprove the false statement, as his disclaimers will be drowned by the clamors of the aggregated fanatics. The circumstances of the time; the distempered atmosphere of public sentiment, both at the North and beyond the Atlantic; the mawkish sensibilities and the imbecile ignorance of many within our own borders; the recent and still active agitation of the Slavery question in Congress and in the Presidential canvass; the frenzy of fanaticism and the fever of political intrigue, have all conspired to give a popularity and currency to the work at this particular moment, which its ability does not justify, and its purposes should forbid. Still, from whatever cause its multitudinous dispersion may arise, this of itself assures us both of the virulence of the venom and of the aptitude of the public mind both at the North and in England, to catch the contagion, and welcome the contamination. Hence, the necessity on the part of all those interested in the rights, the prosperity, the happiness and the integrity of the South, to accord to it a notice far beyond what its intrinsic merits or even vices might claim. But, as a bold, sweeping, unmitigated accusation against the Southern States, it cannot be suffered to pass entirely without challenge, nor can it be permitted to circulate without reprobation and repudiation. The consciousness of right, the dignity of our position, the knowledge of the inefficacy of our disclaimers, might prescribe unruffled contempt and unbroken silence, as the true mode of meeting the bald slanders and the forged accusations of mere fiction: but the purpose of the fiction—the intention of the libel is recognized, welcomed and applauded by myriads; and the numbers which swell the battalions of our adversaries render them dangerous, however contemptible the component units may be.

But, though we condescend to give more attention to *Uncle Tom's Cabin* than we think such a work or such an attack entitled to on its own score, we will not prolong our disagreeable duty so far as to follow it through all the mazes of its misrepresentation—through all the loathsome labyrinths of imaginary cruelty and crime, in which its prurient fancy loves to roam. So far as a false statement can be rectified by positive denial,—so far as misrepresentation can be corrected by direct, abundant, unquestionable proof of the error, this service has been already adequately rendered by the newspapers and periodical literature of the South. We have intimated our belief, that both the negation and the refutation are useless, for our adversaries are as deaf and as poisonous too, as the blind adder. But this service has already been fully rendered. It would, then, be a work of supererogation to repeat the profitless labor, to trace the separate threads of delusion which enter into the tissue of deception, and to exhibit the false dyes and the tangles of fiction which aid in the composition of the web. It would seem almost a hopeless waste of time to show how the truth which has been so scantily employed, has been prostituted to base uses, and made to minister to the general falsehood; how human sympathies have been operated on to encourage and sanctify most unholy practices: how every commandment of the decalogue and all the precepts of the Gospel have been violated in order to extend the sanctification of the higher-law, to every crime denounced and condemned by laws, human and divine. Unfortunately for the cause of the South, the evidence for or against her, is neither weighed nor regarded: the defence is rejected without consideration, and all slanders are cordially received, not because they are known or proved to be true, but because they are wished to be so; and harmonise with pre-conceived and malicious prejudices. We have not the ear of the court; our witnesses are distrusted and discredited, and in most cases, they are not even granted a hearing; but the case is presumed to be against us, and by a summary process a verdict of guilty is rendered, without any regard to the real merits of the cause, but in compliance with the fanatical complicity of the jurors. Why is this? And what is the court before which we are required to plead?

Assuredly, there is no necessity to convince the slave owners, or the residents in the Southern States, that the condition of society, the *status* of the slave, the incidents and accidents of slavery, the practices or even the rights of masters, are exhibited in a false light, and are falsely stated in *Uncle Tom's Cabin;* and that, by whatever jugglery or sorcery the result is obtained, the picture, with all its ostensible desire of truthful delineation, is distorted and discolored, and presents at one time a caricature, at another a total misrepresentation of things amongst us. It is not to Southern men that it is necessary to address any argument on a topic like this. They are already aware of the grossness of the slander by their own observation and experience. No, the tribunal to which our defence must be addressed, is the public sentiment of the North and of Europe. In both latitudes, the case is already prejudged and decided against us; in both, popular ignorance and popular fanaticism, and a servile press have predetermined the question. The special circumstances of the condition of society in both have led to the complete extinguishment of slavery, *eo nominee;* and what was dictated by pecuniary interest, and achieved by folly or accident, is believed to furnish the immutable canon for the action of all communities, and to constitute the valid criterion of a higher law, which shall promise all the blessings of redemption to those who vilify and malign their fellows for following the example of Abraham, Isaac and Jacob, and all the curses of damnation to those who are the innocent victims of the abuse. The ignorant and unreflecting outcry of those whose social condition is infinitely below that of our slaves, is eagerly caught up by the myriad serfs of the dominant cottonocracy; is re-echoed from all points of the horizon; and is believed to be the language of truth because it is the clamor of a multitude. A better class stimulates and repeats the defamation, because their interests are supposed to accord with the perpetuation of ignorance and the propagation of delusion on this subject; and because it is a cheap expenditure of philanthropy to melt in sentimental sorrow over remote and imaginary evils, while neglecting the ever present ills and pressing afflictions in their own vicinage. Such a tone of sentiment among both the educated and the illiterate classes in those communities where literature is a trade and the mercenary principles of Grub street constitute the morality of all intellectual avocations, generates a literary atmosphere which is fatal to the dissemination of unpopular truths, and which gives singular vitality and longevity to error, by pandering to the popular desire for its circulation and confirmation. In this manner, we may understand both the cause of the thousands of copies of *Uncle Tom's Cabin,* which have been sold at the North and in England, and also the extreme difficulty, not to say absolute impossibility, of securing a dispassionate hearing for our defence, or of introducing the antidote where the poison has spread. There is no obduracy so impracticable—no deafness so incurable—as that Pharisaical self-sanctification and half-conscious hypocrisy, which gilds its own deliberate delusions with the false colors of an extravagant morality, and denounces all dissent from its own fanatical prejudices, as callous vice and irremediable sin. The whole phalanx of Abolition literature, in all its phases and degrees, is fully imbued with this self-righteous spirit; and its influence, under all forms in fiction and in song—in sermon and in essay—in politics harangue as in newspaper twaddle is completely turned against us: and an aggregation of hostile tendencies is brought to bear upon us so as to deny to our complaints, our recriminations, or our apologies, either consideration or respect. The potency of literature, in this age of the world; when it embraces all manifestations of public or individual thought and feeling, and permeates, in streams, more or less diluted, all classes of society, can scarcely be misapprehended. But the illiberal, unjust, and unwise course of Southern communities, has deprived them of the aid of this potent protection, by excluding themselves and their views almost entirely from the domain of literature. The Southern population have checked and chilled all manifestations of literary aptitudes at the South; they have discouraged by blighting indifference, the efforts of such literary genius as they may have nurtured: they have underrated and disregarded all productions of Southern intellect; and now, when all the batteries of the literary republic are turned against them, and the torrent of literary censure threatens to unite with other agencies to overwhelm them, it is in vain that they cry in their dire necessity, "Help me, Cassius, or I sink." The voice of a home-born literature, which would have been efficient in their defence, is almost unheard, and, if uttered, is scarcely noticed beyond Mason and Dixon's line, because the Southern people have steadily refused to it that encouragement, both in the shape of material support and public favor, which is essential to its healthy development and assured existence, and which is imperatively required to give it respectability and influence abroad. Thus are we to explain the reason why the arguments and expositions of Southern sentiment on the subject of slavery, pass so entirely unheeded—why both its expostulations and denials are wholly disregarded, and its grave discussions contemptuously scorned and rejected without a moment's consideration....

It is a natural and inevitable consequence of this silly and fatal indifference to the high claims of a native and domestic literature, that the South is now left at the mercy of every witling and scribbler who panders to immediate profit or passing popularity, by harping on a string in unison with the prevailing fanaticism. It is a necessary result of the same long continued imprudence, that no defence can be heard, no refutation of vile slander regarded in the courts of literature, which comes from a land whose literary claims have been disparaged and crushed by its own blind recklessness and meanness. In *Uncle Tom's Cabin*, there is certainly neither extraordinary genius nor remarkable strength: the attack is unquestionably a weak one; there is only that semblance of genius which springs from intense fanaticism and an earnest purpose; and that plausibility which is due to concentrated energy and a narrow one-sided exposition of human afflictions: yet, though so slight be the merits of the book, the only criticism in reply which could pretend to any general efficiency in arresting the current of the virtual slander—and then by no means an adequate one—must be sought beyond the Atlantic, and gathered from the columns of the *London Times*. The South has benumbed the hearts and palsied the arms of her natural and willing defenders: she has dismantled her towers, and suppressed her fortresses of all efficient garrison, and she is now exposed, unarmed and unprotected, to all the treacherous stratagems and pitiless malice of her inveterate and interested enemies. She has invited and merited her own fate: she has wooed the slander which she is almost powerless to repel: she has offered a premium to vituperation and imposed a grave penalty on every attempt to redress the indignity to which she has subjected her citizens.

... But leaving this exceedingly vulnerable characteristic of *Uncle Tom's Cabin*, the argument of the work—for there is an argument even in successive dramatic pictures designed to produce a given effect, as well as in successive syllogisms designed to establish a special conclusion:—the argument of the work is, in plain and precise terms, that any organization of society—any social institution, which can by possibility result in such instances of individual misery, or generate such examples of individual cruelty as are exhibited in this fiction, must be criminal in itself, a violation of all the laws of Nature and of God, and ought to be universally condemned, and consequently immediately abolished. Unhappily, in all the replies to *Uncle Tom's Cabin* which have hitherto been attempted under the form of corresponding fiction, usually, we are sorry to say, by weak and incompetent persons, it has not been recognized with sufficient distinctness that the whole strength of the attack, as the whole gist of the argument, lies in this thesis. The formal rejoinders have consequently been directed to the wrong point: the real question has been mistaken; and the formal issue never joined. This explains the insufficiency of such counter representations as *Aunt Phillis's Cabin*, and similar apologies; and also that sense of insufficiency which they have not failed to produce. It is no valid refutation of the offensive fiction that slavery may be shown to present at times—no matter how frequently—a very different phase. This point was already guarded:—nay, it was already conceded in *Uncle Tom's Cabin*; and such a mode of replication consequently mistakes the subject of debate, and is entirely without force because directed against a post already surrendered. It may be doubted, indeed, whether an assault on a solemn interest, moral or social, conveyed under the garb of fiction, can ever be satisfactorily answered under a similar form. If it could be, it would be too trivial to be worthy of such an elaborate defence. If it be sufficiently important to demand a thorough reply, it is degrading to the serious character of the subject, it is trifling with the earnest and grave import of the question, to dress it up in the gewgaws and tawdry finery of a mere counter-irritant. Moreover, a reply in this shape too commonly necessitates such an adherence to the dramatic procedure and to the progression of sentiment adopted by the original work, that it places the replicant in a secondary position, and exhibits him in the false light of a mere imitator and plagiarist, by way of opposition, thus obviously yielding the vantage ground to the offender. If, however, the reply must be couched in the same form as the attack, the true picture to be delineated is not a mere representation of a real or imaginary state of beatitude enjoyed by fictitious slaves, but should be the portraiture of graver miseries, worse afflictions, and more horrible crimes familiar to the denizens of our

Northern Cities, and incident to the condition of those societies where the much lauded white labor prevails. But the main cause of failure in the replies which have been attempted, and whose inefficacy has been injurious to the interests of the South, has unquestionably been that the real thesis of *Uncle Tom's Cabin*, whence most of its dangers, its pernicious sophistry, and its wicked delusion proceed, has not been recognized with adequate clearness, and has not been refuted in a suitable manner. It is this thesis which we propose to examine.

The true and sufficient reply to this proposition is a very brief one. It is simply this, that the position is absolutely fatal to all human society—to all social organization, civilized or savage, whatever. It strikes at the very essence and existence of all community among men, it lays bare and roots up all the foundations of law, order and government. It is the very evangel of insubordination, sedition, and anarchy, and is promulgated in support of a cause worthy of the total ruin which it is calculated to produce. Pandemonium itself would be a paradise compared with what all society would become, if this apparently simple and plausible position were tenable, and action were accordingly regulated by it. Ate herself, hot from hell, could not produce more mischievous or incurable disorder than this little thesis, on which the whole insinuated argument of *Uncle Tom's Cabin* is founded, if this dogma were once generally or cordially received. In all periods of history—under all forms of government—under all the shifting phases of the social condition of man, instances of misery and barbarity equal to any depicted in this atrocious fiction, have been of constant recurrence, and, whatever changes may hereafter take place, unless the nature of man be also changed, they must continually recur until the very end of time. In thousands of instances, of almost daily occurrence, the affliction or the crime has sprung as directly from existing laws, manner, and institutions, as in the examples erroneously charged to the score of slavery in *Uncle Tom's Cabin*. But in all of them the real causes have been the innate frailties of humanity, the play of fortuitous circumstances, the native wickedness of particular individuals, and the inability of human wisdom or legislation to repress crime without incidentally ministering to occasional vices. If there be any latent truth in the dogma enforced by the nefarious calumnies of *Uncle Tom's Cabin,* it furnishes a stronger argument against all other departments of social organization than it does against slavery, as the records of our courts of justice and the inmates of our penitentiaries would testify. There is no felon who might not divest himself of his load of guilt, and extricate his neck from the halter, if such an argument was entitled to one moment's weight or consideration. In the complicated web of trials, difficulties and temptations, with which Providence in its wisdom has thought proper to intertwine the threads of human existence, an unbroken career of happiness or prosperity is not to be found. Every heart has its own sorrows,—every condition as every class its own perils and afflictions, and every individual his own bitter calamities to bewail. The very aptitude of this life for that state of probation which it was designed to be, depends upon the alternation and juxtaposition of weakness and virtue, of joy and misery, of gratifications and trials, of blessings and misfortunes, of adversity and prosperity. These varying shadows of our earthly career are due partly to the accidents by which we are surrounded, partly to the temper and conduct of our own hearts, but more than all to the concurrent or conflicting action of the members of the community among which our lot has been cast. The virtues of our neighbors may aid or encourage us, but their vices or their crimes may crush our hopes, ruin our fortunes, and entail irretrievable woe on our children as well as on ourselves. From this discord of fate it is our stern duty to educe the elements of our own career: beset with temptations, menaced by vicious intrigue, cheered by high examples or consoling counsel, but ever at the mercy of fortune, we must pursue our rough journey through the thorny paths of a world of trial. We cannot invent an Elysium or reclaim a Paradise: we can only turn to the utmost possible good the diverse conditions which encompass us around on all sides. It is only the insane hope of a frivolous and dreamy philanthropy to expect or wish that this order and variety of sublunary changes should be altered; as it is only the malignant hate of a splenetic and frenzied fanaticism which would venture to charge upon a particular institution, as its peculiar and characteristic vice, the common incidents of humanity in all times and under all its phases.

It is no distinctive feature of the servile condition that individual members of the class should suffer most poignantly in consequence of the crimes, the sins, the follies, or the thoughtlessness of others;—that children should be torn from their parents, husbands separated from their wives, and fathers rudely snatched away from their families. The same results, with concomitant infamy, are daily produced by the operation of all penal laws, and the same anguish and distress are thereby inflicted upon the helpless and innocent, yet such laws remain and must remain upon our statute books for the security and conservation of any social organization at all. The ordinary play of human interests, of human duties, of human necessities, and even of human ambition—unnoticed and commonplace as it may be conceived to be, produces scenes more terrible and agony more poignant and heart-rending than any attributed to slavery in *Uncle Tom's Cabin*. The temptations of worldly advancement, the hopes of temporary success, the lures of pecuniary gain, in every civilized or barbarous community throughout the world—in the deserts of Sahara as amid the snows of Greenland—in the streets of Boston and Lowell as in those of London, Manchester, and Paris, may and do exhibit a longer register of sadder results than even a treacherous imagination, or fiction on the hunt for falsehood has been able to rake up from the fraudulent annals of slavery in the present work. There is scarcely one revolution of a wheel in a Northern or European cotton-mill, which does not, in its immediate or remote effects, entail more misery on the poor and the suffering than all the incidents of servile misery gathered in the present work from the most suspicious and disreputable sources. The annual balance sheet of a Northern millionaire symbolizes infinitely greater agony and distress in the labouring or destitute classes than even the foul martyrdom of Uncle Tom. Are the laws of debtor and creditor—and the processes by which gain is squeezed from the life-blood of the indigent, more gentle;—or the hard, grasping, demoniac avarice of a yankee trader more merciful than the atrocious heart of that fiendish yankee, Simon Legree? Was the famine in Ireland productive of no calamities which might furnish a parallel to the scenes in *Uncle Tom's Cabin*? We would hazard even the assertion that the Australian emigration from Great Britain, and the California migration in our country—both impelled by the mere hope of sudden and extraordinary gains, have been attended with crimes and vices, sorrows, calamities and distresses far surpassing the imaginary ills of the slaves whose fictitious woes are so hypocritically bemoaned. But such are the incidents of life, and we would neither denounce nor revolutionize society, because such consequences were inseparable from its continuance.

It should be observed that the whole tenor of this pathetic tale derives most of its significance and colouring from a distorted representation or a false conception of the sentiments and feelings of the slave. It presupposes an identity of sensibilities between the races of the free and the negroes, whose cause it pretends to advocate. It takes advantage of this presumption, so unsuspiciously credited where slavery is unknown, to arouse sympathies for what might be grievous misery to the white man, but is none to the differently tempered black. Every man adapts himself and his feelings more or less to the circumstances of his condition: without this wise provision of nature life would be intolerable to most of us. Every race in like manner becomes habituated to the peculiar accidents of its particular class; even the Paria may be happy. Thus what would be insupportable to one race, or one order of society, constitutes no portion of the wretchedness of another. The joys and the sorrows of the slave are in harmony with his position, and are entirely dissimilar from what would make the happiness, or misery, of another class. It is therefore an entire fallacy, or a criminal perversion of truth, according to the motive of the writer, to attempt to test all situations by the same inflexible rules, and to bring to the judgment of the justice of slavery the prejudices and opinions which have been formed when all the characteristics of slavery are not known but imagined.

The proposition, then, which may be regarded as embodying the peculiar essence of *Uncle Tom's Cabin*, is a palpable fallacy, and inconsistent with all social organization. Granting, therefore, all that could be asked by our adversaries, it fails to furnish any proof whatever of either the iniquity or the enormity of slavery. If it was capable of proving any thing at all, it would prove a great deal too much. It would demonstrate that all order, law, government, society was a flagrant and unjustifiable violation of the rights, and mockery of the feelings of man and ought to be abated as a public nuisance. The hand of Ishmael would thus be raised against every man, and every man's hand against him. To this result, indeed, both the doctrines and practices of the higher-law agitators at the North, and as set forth in this portentous book of sin, unquestionably tend: and such a conclusion might naturally be anticipated from their sanctimonious professions. The fundamental position, then, of these dangerous and dirty little volumes is a deadly blow to all the interests and duties of humanity, and is utterly impotent to show any inherent vice in the institution of slavery which does not also appertain to all other institutions whatever. But we will not be content to rest here: we will go a good bow-shot beyond this refutation, though under no necessity to do so; and we maintain that the distinguishing characteristic of slavery is its tendency to produce effects exactly opposite to those laid to its charge; to diminish the amount of individual misery in the servile classes; to mitigate and alleviate all the ordinary sorrows of life; to protect the slaves against want as well as against material and mental suffering; to prevent the separation and dispersion of families; and to shield them from the frauds, the crimes, and the casualties of others, whether masters or fellow-slaves, in a more eminent degree than is attainable under any other organization of society, where slavery does not prevail. This is but a small portion of the peculiar advantages to the slaves themselves resulting from the institution of slavery, but these suffice for the present, and furnish a most overwhelming refutation of the philanthropic twaddle of this and similar publications.

Source:

George Frederick Holmes. Review of *Uncle Tom's Cabin*, *Southern Literary Messenger*, December 1852: 721–731. <http://quod.lib.umich.edu/cgi/t/text/text-idx?c=moajrnl&idno=acf2679.0018.012 > [accessed May 15, 2007].

Document 10: "Negro Slavery," from *Sociology for the South: Or the Failure of Free Society*

George Fitzhugh's 1854 treatise represents the incorporation of the proslavery argument into a larger, more comprehensive worldview that rejected the supposed progress of modern capitalism. Fitzhugh championed the personal relations of the traditional household, which included the master-slave relation, over the highly impersonal and atomistic social relations of the wage-labor economy. Fitzhugh, a Virginia planter and lawyer, has been treated as a controversial, even eccentric, individual in his defense of slavery as a means to social reform. But he stood in fundamental agreement with Abraham Lincoln in understanding that, by the 1850s, the Southern slave economy and the Northern wage-labor economy were no longer compatible under one common government. Fitzhugh thus attempted to reframe the argument from one that questioned the legitimacy of slavery in the American republic to one that challenged impersonal exploitation of capitalistic social relations in a self-governing society.

We have already stated that we should not attempt to introduce any new theories of government and of society, but merely try to justify old ones, so far as we could deduce such theories from ancient and almost universal practices. Now it has been the practice in all countries and in all ages, in some degree, to accommodate the amount and character of government control to the wants, intelligence, and moral capacities of the nations or individuals to be governed. A highly moral and intellectual people, like the free citizens of ancient Athens, are best governed by a democracy. For a less moral and intellectual one, a limited and constitutional monarchy will answer. For a people either very ignorant or very wicked, nothing short of military despotism will suffice. So among individuals, the most moral and well-informed members of society require no other government than law. They are capable of reading and understanding the law, and have sufficient self-control and virtuous disposition to obey it. Children cannot be governed by mere law; first, because they do not understand it, and secondly, because they are so much under the influence of impulse, passion and appetite, that they want sufficient self-control to be deterred or governed by the distant and doubtful penalties of the law. They must be constantly controlled by parents or guardians, whose will and orders shall stand in the place of law for them. Very wicked men must be put into penitentiaries; lunatics into asylums, and the most wild of them into straight jackets, just as the most wicked of the sane are manacled with irons; and idiots must have committees to govern and take care of them. Now, it is clear the Athenian democracy would not suit a negro nation, nor will the government of mere law suffice for the individual negro. He is but a grown up child, and must be governed as a child, not as a lunatic or criminal. The master occupies towards him the place of parent or guardian. We shall not dwell on this view, for no one will differ with us who thinks as we do of the negro's capacity, and we might argue till dooms-day, in vain, with those who have a high opinion of the negro's moral and intellectual capacity.

Secondly. The negro is improvident; will not lay up in summer for the wants of winter; will not accumulate in youth for the exigencies of age. He would become an insufferable burden to society. Society has the right to prevent this, and can only do so by subjecting him to domestic slavery.

In the last place, the negro race is inferior to the white race, and living in their midst, they would be far outstripped or outwitted in the chase of free competition. Gradual but certain extermination would be their fate. We presume the maddest abolitionist does not think the negro's providence of habits and money-making capacity at all to compare to those of the whites. This defect of character would alone justify enslaving him, if he is to remain here. In Africa or the West Indies, he would become idolatrous, savage and cannibal, or be devoured by savages and cannibals. At the North he would freeze or starve.

... [A]bolish negro slavery, and how much of slavery still remains? Soldiers and sailors in Europe enlist for life; here, for five years. Are they not slaves who have not only sold their liberties, but their lives also? And they are worse treated than domestic slaves. No domestic affection and self-interest extend their aegis over them. No kind mistress, like a guardian angel, provides for them in health, tends them in sickness, and soothes their dying pillow. Wellington at Waterloo was a slave. He was bound to obey, or would, like admiral Bying, have been shot for gross misconduct, and might not, like a common laborer, quit his work at any moment. He had sold his liberty, and might not resign without the consent of his master, the king. The common laborer may quit his work at any moment, whatever his contract; declare that liberty is an inalienable right, and leave his employer to redress by a useless suit for damages. The highest and most honorable position on earth was that of the slave Wellington; the lowest, that of the free man who cleaned his boots and fed his hounds. The African cannibal, caught, christianized and enslaved, is as much elevated by slavery as was Wellington. The kind of slavery is adapted to the men enslaved. Wives and apprentices are slaves; not in theory only, but often in fact. Children are slaves to their parents, guardians and teachers. Imprisoned culprits are slaves. Lunatics and idiots are slaves also. Three-fourths of free society are slaves, no better treated, when their wants and capacities are estimated, than negro slaves. The masters in free society, or slave society, if they perform properly their duties, have more cares and less liberty than the slaves themselves. "In the sweat of thy face shalt thou earn thy bread!" made all men slaves, and such all good men continue to be....

We have a further question to ask. If it be right and incumbent to subject children to the authority of parents and guardians, and idiots and lunatics to committees, would it not be equally right and incumbent to give the free negros masters, until at least they arrive at years of discretion, which very few ever did or will attain? What is the difference between the authority of a parent and of a master? Neither pay wages, and each is entitled to the services of those subject to him. The father may not sell his child forever, but may hire him out till he is twenty-one. The free negro's master may also be restrained from selling. Let him stand in loco parentis, and call him papa instead of master. Look closely into slavery, and you will see nothing so hideous in it; or if you do, you will find plenty of it at home in its most hideous form....

It is a common remark, that the grand and lasting architectural structures of antiquity were the results of slavery. The mighty and continued association of labor requisite to their construction, when mechanic art was so little advanced, and labor-saving processes unknown, could only have been brought about by a despotic authority, like that of the master over his slaves. It is, however, very remarkable, that whilst in taste and artistic skill the world seems to have been retrograding ever since the decay and abolition of feudalism, in mechanical invention and in great utilitarian operations requiring the wielding of immense capital and much labor, its progress has been unexampled. Is it because capital is more despotic in its authority over free laborers than Roman masters and feudal lords were over their slaves and vassals?

Free society has continued long enough to justify the attempt to generalize its phenomena, and calculate its moral and intellectual influences. It is obvious that, in whatever is purely utilitarian and material, it incites invention and stimulates industry. Benjamin Franklin, as a man and a philosopher, is the best exponent of the working of the system. His sentiments and his philosophy are low, selfish, atheistic and material. They tend directly to make man a mere "featherless biped," well-fed, well-clothed and comfortable, but regardless of his soul as "the beasts that perish."

Since the Reformation the world has as regularly been retrograding in whatever belongs to the departments of genius, taste and art, as it has been progressing in physical science and its application to mechanical construction. Mediaeval Italy rivalled if it did not surpass ancient Rome, in poetry, in sculpture, in painting, and many of the fine arts. Gothic architecture reared its monuments of skill and genius throughout Europe, till the 15th century; but Gothic architecture died with the Reformation. The age of Elizabeth was the Augustan age of England. The men who lived then acquired their sentiments in a world not yet deadened and vulgarized by puritanical cant and levelling demagoguism. Since then men have arisen who have been the fashion and the go for a season, but none have appeared whose names will descend to posterity. Liberty and equality made slower advances in France. The age of Louis XIV was the culminating point of French genius and art. It then shed but a flickering and lurid light. Frenchmen are servile copyists of Roman art, and Rome had no art of her own. She borrowed from Greece; distorted and deteriorated what she borrowed; and France imitates and falls below Roman distortions. The genius of Spain disappeared with Cervantes; and now the world seems to regard nothing as desirable except what will make money and what costs money. There is not a poet, an orator, a sculptor, or painter in the world. The tedious elaboration necessary to all the productions of high art would be ridiculed in this money-making, utilitarian charlatan age. Nothing now but what is gaudy and costly excites admiration. The public taste is debased.

But far the worst feature of modern civilization, which is the civilization of free society, remains to be exposed. Whilst labor-saving processes have probably lessened by one half, in the last century, the amount of work needed for comfortable support, the free laborer is compelled by capital and competition to work more than he ever did before, and is less comfortable. The organization of society cheats him of his earnings, and those earnings go to swell the vulgar pomp and pageantry of the ignorant millionaires, who are the only great of the present day. These reflections might seem, at first view, to have little connexion with negro slavery; but it is well for us of the South not to be deceived by the tinsel glare and glitter of free society, and to employ ourselves in doing our duty at home, and studying the past, rather than in insidious rivalry of the expensive pleasures and pursuits of men whose sentiments and whose aims are low, sensual and grovelling.

Human progress, consisting in moral and intellectual improvement, and there being no agreed and conventional standard weights or measures of moral and intellectual qualities and quantities, the question of progress can never be accurately decided. We maintain that man has not improved, because in all save the mechanic arts he reverts to the distant past for models to imitate, and he never imitates what he can excel.

We need never have white slaves in the South, because we have black ones. Our citizens, like those of Rome and Athens, are a privileged class. We should train and educate them to deserve the privileges and to perform the duties which society confers on them. Instead, by a low demagoguism depressing their self-respect by discourses on the equality of man, we had better excite their pride by reminding them that they do not fulfil the menial offices which white men do in other countries. Society does not feel the burden of providing for the few helpless paupers in the South. And we should recollect that here we have but half the people to educate, for half are negroes; whilst at the North they profess to educate all. It is in our power to spike this last gun of the abolitionists. We should educate all the poor. The abolitionists say that it is one of the necessary consequences of slavery that the poor are neglected. It was not so in Athens, and in Rome, and should not be so in the South. If we had less trade with and less dependence on the North, all our poor might be profitable and honorably employed in trades, professions and manufactures. Then we should have a rich and denser population. Yet we but marshal her in the way that she was going. The South is already aware of the necessity of a new policy, and has begun to act on it. Every day more and more is done for education, the mechanic arts, manufactures and internal improvements. We will soon be independent of the North.

We deem this peculiar question of negro slavery of very little importance. The issue is made throughout the world on the general subject of slavery in the abstract. The argument has commenced. One set of ideas will govern and control after awhile the civilized world. Slavery will everywhere be abolished, or everywhere be re-instituted. We think the opponents of practical, existing slavery, are estopped by their own admission; nay, that unconsciously, as socialists, they are the defenders and propagandists of slavery, and have furnished the only sound arguments on which its defence and justification can be rested. We have introduced the subject of negro slavery to afford us a better opportunity to disclaim the purpose of reducing the white man any where to the condition of negro slaves here. It would be very unwise and unscientific to govern white men as you would negroes. Every shade and variety of slavery has existed in the world. In some cases there has been much of legal regulation, much restraint of the master's authority; in others, none at all. The character of slavery necessary to protect the whites in Europe should be much milder than negro slavery, for slavery is only needed to protect the white man, whilst it is more necessary for the government of the negro even than for his protection. But even negro slavery should not be outlawed. We might and should have laws in Virginia, as in Louisiana, to make the master subject to presentment by the grand jury and to punishment, for any inhuman or improper treatment or neglect of his slave.

We abhor the doctrine of the "Types of Mankind;" first, because it is at war with scripture, which teaches us that the whole human race is descended from a common parentage; and, secondly, because it encourages and incites brutal masters to treat negroes, not as weak, ignorant and dependent brethren, but as wicked beasts, without the pale of humanity. The Southerner is the negro's friend, his only friend. Let no intermeddling abolitionist, no refined philosophy, dissolve this friendship.

SOURCE:

George Fitzhugh. *Sociology for the South: Or the Failure of Free Society.* The Gilder Lehrman Center for the Study of Slavery, Resistance, and Abolition (1854). <http://www.yale.edu/glc/archive/1057.htm > [accessed May 15, 2007].

BIBLIOGRAPHY

Aptheker, Herbert. *Abolitionism: A Revolutionary Movement.* Boston: Twayne, 1989. A provocative account that considers the radical nature of the abolitionist movement.

Brown, Christopher Leslie. *Moral Capital: Foundations of British Abolitionism.* Chapel Hill: University of North Carolina Press, 2006. A revisionist interpretation that considers the abolitionist movement in Britain arising from changing ideas of nationhood and empire in the aftermath of the American Revolution.

Cain, William E., ed. *William Lloyd Garrison and the Fight Against Slavery: Selections from* The Liberator. New York: Bedford/St. Martin's Press, 1994. A brief biography of Garrison and his abolitionist activities is accompanied by a number of excerpts from *The Liberator.*

Davis, David Brion. *The Problem of Slavery in Western Culture.* New York: Oxford University Press, 1966. Pulitzer Prize–winning study of the history of slavery and the contradictions it posed in various Western societies until the rise of the abolitionist movement in the 1770s. The study provides the intellectual background to demonstrate the historical uniqueness of the abolitionist movement.

———. *The Problem of Slavery in the Age of Revolution, 1770–1823.* Ithaca: Cornell University Press, 1975. A continuation of the previous study. It examines the conflict over slavery generated by the rise of the abolitionist movement. This study ends with the emergence of immediate abolitionism.

Eaton, Clement. *The Freedom-of-Thought Struggle in the Old South.* Revised edition. New York: Harper & Row, 1964. A classic study investigating the rise and influence of proslavery thought in the antebellum South.

Ericson, David F. *Debate over Slavery: Antislavery and Proslavery Liberalism in Antebellum America.* New York: New York University Press, 2000. A revisionist study that considers the debate over slavery as part of a larger debate over the meaning of liberalism. Ericson suggests that proslavery and antislavery activists had more in common than is generally thought.

Faust, Drew Gilpin. *The Ideology of Slavery: Proslavery Thought in the Antebellum South, 1830–1860.* Baton Rouge: Louisiana State University Press, 1981. This valuable study includes reprints of a number of significant proslavery essays.

Filler, Louis. *Crusade Against Slavery: Friends, Foes, and Reforms, 1820–1860.* Algonac, Mich.: Reference Publications, Inc., 1986. Examines individuals and their intellectual influences that informed the abolitionist movement.

Finkelman, Paul, ed. *Defending Slavery: Proslavery Thought in the Old South.* New York: Bedford/St. Martin's Press, 2003. Provides a summary of proslavery thought emphasizing continuity and its dominance in the American South. It includes excerpts of influential proslavery essays.

Fox-Genovese, Elizabeth, and Eugene Genovese. *The Mind of the Master Class: History and Faith in the Southern Slaveholders' Worldview.* New York: Cambridge University Press, 2005. The culmination of four decades of scholarly research and writings by two leading authorities of Southern slavery. They demonstrate how the Southern proslavery argument was incorporated into the religious and historical perspectives of the South's master class to serve as the foundation of their worldview in the face of modernity.

Harrold, Stanley. *The Abolitionists & the South, 1831–1861.* Lexington: University Press of Kentucky, 1995. Argues that the abolitionist movement was not confined only to the American North but existed in the South (especially the Upper South) as well and persisted until the Civil War muted dissent.

Jeffrey, Julie Roy. *The Great Silent Army of Abolitionism: Ordinary Women in the Antislavery Movement.* Chapel Hill: University of North Carolina Press, 1998. Examines the role of women in the abolitionist movement and connects their participation to larger causes of social reform, but not necessarily women's rights.

Jenkins, William Sumner. *The Pro-Slavery Argument in the Old South.* Chapel Hill: University of North Carolina Press, 1935. The classic study of the development and entrenchment of proslavery thought in the antebellum South.

Kraditor, Aileen S. *Means and Ends in American Abolitionism: Garrison and His Critics on Strategy and Tactics, 1834–1850.* New York: Pantheon, 1969. An influential examination of the struggles within the American abolitionist movement over such topics as the roles of religion, political parties, and women. Kraditor depicts the central conflict as one between radical action and the need to retain societal respectability.

Lerner, Gerda. *The Grimke Sisters from South Carolina: Pioneers for Women's Rights and Abolition.* Chapel Hill: University of North Carolina Press, 1967. A classic, sympathetic book that examines the roles of two protofeminist sisters in their embrace of antebellum social reforms and the leadership roles they assumed in reform movements.

McKivigan, John R., ed. *History of the American Abolitionist Movement,* 5 volumes. New York: Routledge, 1999. Each individual volume includes collections of significant scholarly essays and addresses a specific topic under the headings of religion, law, politics, reforms, and race.

——— and Mitchell Snay, eds. *Religion and the Antebellum Debate over Slavery.* Athens: University of Georgia Press, 1998. A collection of essays by leading scholars that examine aspects of the religious debate over slavery and the conditions of the evangelical schism.

Miller, William Lee. *Arguing about Slavery: John Quincy Adams and the Great Battle in the United States Congress*. New York: Knopf, 1998. A narrative account of Adams's battle in Congress to defeat the "gag rule."

Quarles, Benjamin. *Black Abolitionists*. New York: Da Capo, 1991. Emphasizes the importance of African American participation and leadership in the American abolitionist movement, especially after the publication of David Walker's *Appeal to the Colored Citizens of the World*.

Stewart, James Brewer. *Holy Warriors: The Abolitionists and American Slavery*. New York: Hill & Wang, 1976. Investigates the historical conditions leading to the emergence of abolitionism in the United States.

Tise, Larry E. *Proslavery: A History of the Defense of Slavery in America, 1701–1840*. Athens: University of Georgia Press, 1987. A detailed account of proslavery justifications in the Anglo American world from the beginning of the eighteenth century through the abolition of slavery in the British West Indies.

Walters, Ronald G. *The Antislavery Appeal: American Abolitionism after 1830*. Baltimore: Johns Hopkins University Press, 1978. An account of the political struggles within the antislavery movement.

Wolf, Eva Sheppard. *Race and Liberty in the New Nation: Emancipation in Virginia from the Revolution to Nat Turner's Rebellion*. Baton Rouge: Louisiana State University Press, 2006. Analyzes the many meanings of emancipation in the new American republic by using Virginia as a case study.

~ 2 ~

DRED SCOTT: THE CONSTITUTION, SLAVERY, AND THE FUTURE OF AMERICA

Americans should be familiar with the Dred Scott case, not merely for its considerable historical significance, but also for its potential to explain enduring problems with the role of the Supreme Court and the Constitution in contemporary life. Should the Court be restricted by the "original intent" of the Founding Fathers, or should it reach its decisions by attending to the general social values undergirding the Constitution? Does the Court have a duty to rule on deeply divisive political and moral issues about which there is no societal consensus? What are a citizen's options in a democracy when the Supreme Court renders a decision he considers immoral and unjust?

On March 6, 1857, Roger B. Taney, Chief Justice of the U.S. Supreme Court, rendered a final ruling in the case of *Dred Scott v. Sandford.* Taney's decision declared that black Americans, whether free or enslaved, were not citizens of the United States and consequently lacked access to the federal courts. The court majority also rejected the right of Congress to restrict slavery in the territories, overturning the Missouri Compromise of 1820 that had banned slavery in territories acquired through the Louisiana Purchase and north of 36°30′ latitude. Never before had the Court struck down a federal law of so much national consequence. Many Americans hoped that the Court's 7-2 decision would help allay sectional animosities surrounding the role of slavery in national life. By endorsing the right of slaveholders to bring their human property into all the territories, Chief Justice Taney appeared to settle one of the most divisive issues of the 1850s. Yet, no national reconciliation followed his ruling. Opponents of the verdict, drawing inspiration from the opinions of dissenting justices, rejected the majority opinion as illegitimate. Some critics of Taney, such as Republican Abraham Lincoln, even saw the ruling as a sign of a "slave power" conspiracy intent on thwarting the Founders' wishes to create a nation founded on principles of liberty and equality. The Dred Scott case highlights the conflicting views Americans held regarding the constitutionality of slavery and the role the institution should play in the nation's future.

The relationship of blacks to the Declaration of Independence was vigorously debated in the 1850s. In his majority opinion, Taney claimed that the language of the Declaration excluded African Americans, otherwise, "the conduct of the distinguished men who framed the Declaration would have been utterly and flagrantly inconsistent with the principles they asserted." He observed that at the time of the signing of the Declaration, all thirteen colonies legally sanctioned slavery, and blacks were viewed as "inferior" (Taney opinion). Taney found that neither the Declaration of Independence, drafted in 1776, nor the Constitution, drafted in 1787, conferred on blacks any rights. Historian David Potter perhaps best captured the ultimate significance of the Dred Scott case when he noted that it "converted the charter of freedom into a safeguard of slavery" (Potter, 293).

Abraham Lincoln, in contrast, asserted that the Founders meant to *include* blacks when they wrote that "all men are created equal" in their rights to "life, liberty, and the pursuit of happiness." He conceded that the signatories of the Declaration knew in 1776 that not all men enjoyed equality, but they "meant simply to declare the right" in order to enforce it as soon as practicable. Lincoln envisioned the Declaration as "a standard maxim for free men which should be familiar to all and revered by all; constantly looked to, and constantly labored for, and even though never perfectly attained, constantly approximated and thereby constantly spreading and deepening its influence, and augmenting the happiness and value of life to all people of all colors everywhere" (Lincoln's Speech on the Dred Scott Decision, June 26, 1857).

Although the word "slave" never appears in the Constitution, references to the institution occur in several places: Article 1, section 2, paragraph 3 counted slaves ("other persons") as three-fifths of a person for purposes of representation in the House of Representatives and for direct taxes; Article 1, section 9, paragraph 1 forbade any congressional action ending the African slave trade until 1808—at which time Congress did in fact outlaw the trade; and Article 4, section 2, paragraph 3 included a fugitive-slave law. As Americans in the 1850s worked to interpret the Constitution, they disagreed over whether it was hostile or friendly to the institution of slavery.

The language of the Constitution lent itself to many different interpretations. When Chief Justice Taney claimed that the fugitive-slave clause and the ban on ending the African slave trade proved that the Constitution was "not intended to confer on [blacks] or their posterity the blessings of liberty, or any of the personal rights provided for the citizen" (Taney opinion), he was giving voice to the proslavery agenda of the South. The opinions of many Northern Democrats, including the influential Illinois senator Stephen A. Douglas, differed. Douglas interpreted the Constitution as taking a neutral stance toward slavery, leaving the establishment or prohibition of the institution in the hands of popular white majorities. Many Republicans, including Abraham Lincoln, subscribed to a Constitution that disapproved of slavery. Lincoln imagined the Founders as physicians who found slavery so well established in the body politic that an effort to extract the "tumor" might have killed the fledgling Union. His metaphor assumed that the Founders sought to contain and limit slavery until it might at a future date be safely removed. A small percentage of Northern abolitionists went even further than Lincoln and read the Constitution's guarantee of a republican government (Article 4, section 4, paragraph 1) and of the Fifth Amendment prohibition on depriving citizens of

Portrait of Dred Scott, by Louis Schultze (Missouri Historical Society, St. Louis)

"life, liberty, or property" without due process as arguments against the legality of slavery.

Though addressing matters vital to the future of the entire nation and the meaning of liberty under the Constitution, the Dred Scott case emerged from the efforts of a single man to free himself, his wife, and his two children from the institution of slavery. This struggle, conducted with the help of white benefactors and antislavery lawyers, took eleven years to resolve as it moved from local Missouri courts, to the Missouri Supreme Court, and to federal circuit court, finally ending at the U.S. Supreme Court. After the Supreme Court's unfavorable ruling, Scott and his family remained slaves until May 1857, when a white friend acquired ownership of the family and set them free.

The Dred Scott case had its legal justification in the actions of Scott's second owner, Dr. John Emerson, an assistant surgeon in the U.S. Army. On multiple occasions Emerson brought Scott with him to free soil for extended stays. In December 1833, Emerson brought Scott to Fort Armstrong, Illinois, where the two resided until May 1836. When the military reassigned Emerson to Fort Snelling (near what is now St. Paul, Minnesota) in the Wisconsin territory, Scott accompanied him. This outpost was squarely located in territory subject to the line ban on slavery that had been established by the Missouri Compromise. Scott lived at Fort Snelling from May 1836 through the spring of 1838, and during this time, he married Harriet Robinson. (Except for five months in Louisiana with their owner Emerson, the Scotts stayed at Fort Snelling until May or June 1840.) Emerson eventually returned the Scotts to the South, and when he died in 1843, he left his slaves in the possession of his wife, Irene.

In April 1846 Scott and his wife, Harriet, sued in Missouri circuit court for their freedom. They had a strong case: precedents in multiple Missouri cases had liberated slaves brought to live in either a free state or a territory that outlawed slavery. (For example, in *Rachael v. Walker* [settled in 1836], courts freed a slave named Rachael who had been held in bondage by an army officer stationed at Fort Snelling, circumstances paralleling those of the Scott family.) However, Scott lost his initial suit on technical grounds when his lawyers failed to prove that he was owned by Mrs. Emerson. After a second trial led a jury to find in his favor, Mrs. Emerson appealed the decision to the Missouri Supreme Court.

In March 1852 Chief Justice William Scott overturned the lower court's ruling and returned Dred Scott to slavery. Breaking with established precedent, Judge Scott noted that Missouri had rendered earlier decisions for the sake of comity between the states. However, he charged, "a dark and fell spirit in relation to slavery" showed that it did not "behoove the state of Missouri to show the countenance to any measure which might gratify this spirit" (Scott quoted in Fehrenbacher, p. 264). Northern states such as Ohio had recently rejected prior laws granting slave owners liberal rights to transport their slaves through free soil. The judge turned to a recent decision, *Strader v. Graham,* in which the Supreme Court had appeared to sanction the doctrine of "reversion." Under this principle, slaves brought to free soil, but later returned to a slave state, fell back under the laws and jurisdiction of the slave state.

Dred Scott's lawyers next appealed to federal circuit court. At this time Mrs. Emerson had remarried, and she left legal matters in the hands of her brother, John A. Sandford, a merchant in New York City. Sandford's lawyers called for a "plea of abatement" in the case, asking for a halt to all judicial proceedings because Scott was not a citizen and hence lacked the standing to bring a suit. Justice Robert W. Wells disagreed and ruled that living in a state with the capacity to own property qualified one for access to the federal courts. Because Sandford resided in New York and the Scotts in Missouri, the case proceeded under Article 3, section 2 of the Constitution, which gives citizens of one state the right to sue those of another state in federal court. This trial began in May 1854 and ended when a jury following Judge Wells's instructions determined that the rules of comity gave precedence to Missouri law. Scott's lawyers appealed, and the case moved on to the highest court in the country.

The Supreme Court in 1857 was stacked against Dred Scott and his family. Five justices came from slave states and consistently supported Southern rights in their decisions. Two Northern members of the Court could fairly be described as "doughfaces"—Northern men with strong sympathies for the South. These seven justices, all appointed by Democratic presidents, supported the majority opinion in the Scott case. The remaining two members of the Court registered the dissents in the case: Benjamin Curtis, a conservative Whig, had supported the fugitive-slave law and, during the Civil War, opposed the Emancipation Proclamation. John McLean, who was seeking the Replication nomination at the time of the Scott case, was the sole strong antislavery justice.

The fact that each of the nine justices wrote his own concurring or dissenting opinion can make it hard to decipher the real meaning of what the Court said. Individual judges often made different arguments, focused on different facts, agreeing with one another on some findings, but disagreeing on others. For example, only three judges definitively rejected black citizenship; only six of nine repudiated the Missouri Compromise line; and seven held that under Missouri law, Scott remained a slave. Despite these variations, as historian Don Fehrenbacher writes: "There can be no doubt that Taney's opinion was accepted as the opinion of the Court by its critics as well as defenders" (Fehrenbacher, *The Dred Scott Case*, pp. 333–334).

Initially, the court appeared ready to offer a modest opinion that found against Scott while evading the larger questions about slavery in the territories and about black citizenship. Drawing on the *Strader* decision, Justice Samuel Nelson found that Scott's status turned entirely upon questions relevant to Missouri law, and concluded that once Scott returned from free soil to the state of Missouri, he reverted to his status as a slave. Justice Nelson's opinion suggested pro-Southern positions that the court might later adopt; he expressed doubts about the constitutionality of the Missouri Compromise and hinted that future court cases might expand the rights of slave owners traveling through free soil. For reasons still disputed, the majority of justices determined to confront the large questions before them, rather than following Nelson's more cautious approach.

In his decision denying blacks citizenship, Chief Justice Taney made frequent reference to the widespread discrimination and legal restrictions placed upon both free and enslaved blacks. In his view, at the time of the making of the Constitution, all blacks "were considered as a subordinate and inferior class of beings, who had been subjugated by the dominant race, and, whether emancipated or not, yet remained subject to their authority, and had no rights or privileges but such as those who held the power and the Government might choose to grant them" (Taney opinion). In an effort to get around the fact that several states had granted free blacks citizenship under the Articles of Confederation, Taney drew a distinction between state citizenship and national citizenship, holding that even if some states had given blacks citizenship rights at the time of their founding, this did not mean they had national citizenship.

In his dissent Justice Curtis noted that five states gave free Negroes citizenship at the time of the Constitution's ratification, rejected Taney's distinction between state and national citizenship, and pointed out that there was no language in the Constitution stripping free blacks of their previously established rights. The fact that blacks did not enjoy all political and civil rights did not mean that they possessed none at all. Both white women and minor children suffered considerable legal discrimination but were nonetheless viewed as citizens.

Nonetheless, until the ratification of the Fourteenth Amendment in 1868, the nature of citizenship remained ill defined. In 1857 black Americans faced extreme levels of discrimination. In the South during the antebellum period, white attitudes on slavery seemed to harden as the "peculiar institution" increasingly became defended as a positive good rather than simply a necessary evil. Southern legislatures made manumission more difficult and placed greater restrictions on free blacks. In the North, blacks encountered virulent racism. Ohio, Indiana, Illinois, and Iowa all passed laws aimed at prohibiting blacks from entering their states.

In its most radical action the Taney Court struck down the Missouri Compromise. From before the ratification of the Constitution until the final ruling in the Dred Scott case, federal legislators had repeatedly weighed in on the question of slavery in the territories, sometimes prohibiting and at other times sanctioning the institution. In 1787 the Congress under the Articles of Confederation banned slavery in the Northwest Territory—portions of unorganized lands that would later become Ohio, Indiana, Michigan, Illinois, and Wisconsin. A few years later the Southwest Ordinance left the territory that would become the state of Tennessee free to adopt slavery. In 1820 the Congress banned slavery above 36°30′ latitude as part of the Missouri Compromise. The Compromise of 1850 admitted California as a free state but left the status of slavery in the New Mexico and Utah Territories undetermined and thus potentially open to slavery. Most of the Utah Territory and some of the New Mexico Territory were north of the Missouri Compromise boundary. In 1854 Senator Stephen A. Douglas introduced the Kansas-Nebraska Act, legislation that effectively killed the Missouri Compromise line by leaving these territories free to embrace or reject slavery based on popular sovereignty.

In his ruling Taney determined that the federal prohibitions on slavery in the Missouri Compromise line read too much into the Constitution's stipulation that Congress might make "all needful rules and regulations" for the territories. These possessions, argued Taney, did not constitute colonies; the Constitution granted only a modest authority to Congress to help territories organize governments in preparation for future admission to the Union. Moreover, the Founders had meant the "needful rules" passage to apply only to the territories held at the time of the Constitution's ratification. (On this point Taney's argument appears historically unsound.) Finally, he applied the Fifth Amendment to the case, claiming that under the Bill of Rights, Congress could deny "no person" "life, liberty, or property" without due process of law. Taney saw slavery as a distinct kind of property given special status and protection under the Constitution. His ruling went even further, for not only was Congress banned from outlawing slavery, but also territorial legislatures were. Part of Taney's reasoning drew upon South Carolina senator John C. Calhoun's theory that the territories constituted the common property of the individual states, and as a result the national government could not act so as to discriminate against the slaveholding members of the Union.

Justice Curtis's dissent responded that the "needful rules and regulations" clause gave Congress very broad powers over the territories. He showed that from before the ratification of the Constitution until 1848, Congress had properly exercised its lawful authority and in "eight distinct instances . . . excluded slavery from the territory of the United States

Final judgment in the historic case of Dred Scott v. Sandford (National Archives)

and on six occasions recognized and continued" the institution. Thus, the ban on slavery in the territories rested on "the language of the constitution, and the long line of executive precedents under it" (Curtis). He dismissed Taney's claim that the Founders meant the territory clause to apply only to land then held by the nation. His dissent emphasized that Anglo-American jurisprudence long characterized slavery as a local, and not a national, institution. His decision was based on the Somerset Ruling, so named for James Somerset, a slave brought to England from America, who escaped and was recaptured on November 26, 1771. Somerset was forced onto a ship headed for Jamaica when Lord Mansfield, the Lord Chief Justice of England, ordered the ship's captain to bring Somerset before the court. Based on English law, which stated that a slave could not be forcibly sold to a foreign country because he or she had escaped, Mansfield discharged Somerset, thereby granting him his freedom. In sum, the removal of Scott to Illinois and the Wisconsin Territory and his residence therein made him a free man.

Curtis argued that once the Court had determined that Scott lacked citizenship it had no jurisdiction to rule on the question of the Missouri Compromise line. He found Taney's ruling on slavery in the territories as a *dictum*—an opinion delivered on a matter not directly before a court of law. Curtis repudiated the work of his colleagues: "I do not hold any opinion of this court, or any court, binding when expressed on a question not legitimately before it." Republican lawmakers and newspaper editors eagerly grasped at this line of reasoning as a way to justify their rejection of the Supreme Court decision without appearing to sanction an open break with the rule of law. Most scholars now reject Curtis's argument that Taney's ruling constituted dictum. They note that the Supreme Court has the right to offer multiple reasons for the decisions it reaches and that the question of Scott's citizenship was directly related to the legality of the Missouri Compromise line.

The Dred Scott decision infuriated members of the recently organized Republican Party, who saw the Court's Southern majority and its Northern allies as part of a militant conspiracy to make slavery a national, rather than a local, institution. The Republican Party was founded in the wake of the Whig Party's collapse in the early 1850s and unified around the issue of halting slavery's expansion into the territories. Republicans read the Court's ruling as a partisan attack lacking both legitimacy and constitutional standing. Many white Southerners hailed the decision as a validation of their view of the Constitution as a proslavery document. In the wake of the Scott case, Southerners grew emboldened in their demands for a slave code that protected the institution in all the territories, making a workable compromise solution with the Northern moderates ever more unlikely. Finally, the Court's verdict placed conservative Northern Democrats such as Stephen A. Douglas in an awkward position. Douglas championed "popular sovereignty" (in this context, the right of peoples in a territory to establish or prohibit slavery), but contradictorily supported the Dred Scott decision (wherein Taney expressly rejected the right of territorial legislatures to outlaw slavery). Douglas's effort to hold both positions, and even more important, his unwillingness to unequivocally endorse slavery in Kansas, alienated the Southern wing of his party.

Since its announcement in 1857, the Dred Scott decision has been widely denounced by legal scholars and historians. In *Dred Scott and the Problem of Constitutional Evil*, Marc Graber reviews the various perspectives of those critics who have condemned the decision. According to Graber, many hold that the Court erred by meddling in hotly contested political matters that ought to have been handled by the legislative and executive branches of government. Critics who support this view note that the Court should have crafted a narrow decision, along the lines set forth in Justice Nelson's opinion. Others contend that the failure of the Court was not in weighing in on matters better left to the political process, but in setting forth arguments that were "wrong"— that is, that fundamentally misunderstood the intentions of the Founders. These critics draw inspiration from Justice Curtis's dissent and point to the historical inaccuracies and breaks with judicial precedent as evidence that the Court's decision-making process was flawed. Finally, Graber's third group sees Taney and his supporters as failing to grasp the key animating principles behind the Constitution. According to this view, judges need not be enchained by the literal intentions of the Founding Fathers, but they should craft decisions reflective of the spirit of the Constitution. By this reckoning, the Dred Scott decision put the Constitution at odds with liberty and equality and behind the forces of tyranny and racism.

Graber dissents from much of the existing conventional wisdom surrounding the case. He posits that the Taney ruling, though morally deplorable, was legitimate within the political and legal framework of the Jacksonian period. Graber writes: "Virtually every state court that ruled on black citizenship before 1857 concluded that free persons of color were neither state nor American citizens" (Graber, 29). Graber defends the majority's ruling on the Missouri Compromise line, agreeing with Taney that "the limits on federal power in the territories and the rights protected by the due process clause better reflect the main lines of antebellum jurisprudence than those advanced by many prominent contemporary critics of Dred Scott" (Graber, 30). Graber concludes that the case does not console citizens with easy answers, but reminds us that all constitutions are inescapably fraught with provisions that "many people believe are inefficient, stupid, or evil" (Graber, 8).

The Founding Fathers did not share a single view about slavery and as a result, ambiguity and compromise characterized the revolutionary generation's handling of the issue in the late eighteenth century. The Constitution did indeed include explicit safeguards for slave property (as Justice Taney asserted) and early acts of Congress admitted new slave states outside the original thirteen colonies. Yet, the Revolutionary era also led to the outlawing of slavery in Northern states where it had previously existed, the prohibition of the institution in a number of newly acquired territories, and a softening in the upper South of the legal codes protecting the institution. Given the lack of consensus among the Founders on the subject of slavery and on its future in the United States, students should not find it surprising that in the 1850s well-read and powerful intellects interpreted the same documents and the same legislative history in very different ways. In the Dred Scott case, the Taney majority tried to resolve constitutional issues set aside by the Founders for future generations. The Court's proslavery findings did not offer a workable framework for national reconciliation.

Francis MacDonnell

CHRONOLOGY

1772

Somerset v. Stewart. English legal ruling holding that slavery violates natural law and "is so odious that nothing can be suffered to support it but positive law."

1776

The Second Continental Congress approves the Declaration of Independence. Supporters and opponents of the Dred Scott decision later debate whether this document is meant to include blacks within its claims that "all men are created equal," endowed with the inalienable rights of "life, liberty, and the pursuit of happiness."

1787

The Congress under the Articles of Confederation passes the Northwest Ordinance, banning slavery in territories north and west of the Ohio River (later Indiana, Ohio, Illinois, Michigan, and Wisconsin).

1788

The U.S. Constitution is ratified with the inclusion of a fugitive-slave clause.

1790

Congress approves the Southwest Ordinance, allowing for the organization of this territory with slavery. These lands will eventually make up the future state of Tennessee. From the beginnings of the republic some territories were declared forbidden to slavery, while other territories tolerated the institution. From its creation the nation admitted both free states (Vt., 1791) and slave states (Ky., 1792).

1818

Illinois is admitted to the Union as a free state.

1820

Congress passes the Missouri Compromise, banning slavery north of 36°30′ latitude. Maine is admitted to the Union as a free state, and Missouri is admitted as a slave state, thereby preserving the sectional balance of power in the U.S. Senate.

December 1833 – May 1836

Dr. John Emerson brings Dred Scott with him to Fort Armstrong in the free state of Illinois.

1836

In the case of *Rachael v. Walker,* a Missouri court frees a slave named Rachael brought by her army-officer owner to free territory at Fort Snelling in Wisconsin Territory (near modern-day St. Paul, Minnesota).

1836 – 1838

Dred Scott resides at Fort Snelling in territory subject to the Missouri Compromise line's ban on slavery. He marries Harriet Robinson during this time in an official ceremony.

1838 – 1840

After a five-month stay in Louisiana, Scott and his wife return to Fort Snelling.

1843

Dr. John Emerson dies. He wills his slave property to his wife, Irene Emerson.

1846

In a bid to gain their freedom, the Scotts bring suit against Mrs. Emerson in a St. Louis court.

1846 – 1848

The Mexican-American War brings vast new territories in the Southwest under American control, reviving tensions between pro- and antislavery forces. In the House of Representatives, David Wilmot (D, Pa.) proposes that any territories acquired as a result of the war must prohibit slavery. The Wilmot Proviso passes the House on a purely sectional vote but dies in the Senate.

1847

Scott loses his first trial due to a technicality when he fails to provide evidence showing he is owned by Irene Emerson.

1850

A jury in St. Louis finds Scott a free man. Mrs. Emerson appeals the decision.

Congress passes a series of laws commonly referred to as the Compromise of 1850, averting a potential breakdown of the Union. The Compromise does the following:
- admits California as a free state;
- prohibits Congress from interfering with the interstate slave trade;
- bans the slave trade, but preserves slavery, in the District of Columbia;
- agrees to accept the debt of the state of Texas in exchange for concessions and an agreement on the New Mexico boundary;
- promises a new tough fugitive-slave law; and
- accepts the New Mexico and Utah Territories without reference to slavery.

(Because most of the Utah Territory and some portions of the New Mexico Territory fall above 36° 30′ latitude, this last element of the Compromise preserves the possibility of slavery in lands north of the Missouri Compromise.)

1851

The Supreme Court rules in *Strader v. Graham*. The case involves slave musicians from Kentucky who traveled to Ohio and later escaped to Canada. The Kentucky court determines that "a slave returning voluntarily with his master from a free State, is still a slave by the laws of his own country." In a unanimous decision, the Supreme Court endorsed the Kentucky court's decision. This ruling embraced the doctrine of reversion, which held that when a slave left a free state and returned to a slave state, his status was determined by the laws of the latter rather than of the former.

1852

March 22: The Missouri Supreme Court in a 2–1 decision rules in favor of Mrs. Emerson, arguing that when Scott returned to Missouri he fell subject to Missouri law.

1853

The Scotts appeal the ruling in the Missouri Supreme Court and file suit in federal court in St. Louis. Presiding judge Robert Wells determines that Scott qualifies as a citizen for purposes of bringing suit even if he does not qualify under the comity clause of the Constitution: "the Citizens of each State shall be entitled to all Privileges and Immunities of Citizens of different states."

1854

Congress passes the Kansas-Nebraska Act, opening up the Kansas and Nebraska Territories to slavery on the basis of popular sovereignty, nullifying the Missouri Compromise line.

Judge Wells advises the jury to rule against Dred Scott on the principle that Missouri law ought to determine the outcome of the case. Scott's family files an appeal to the Supreme Court on December 30.

1856

The Dred Scott case is tried before the Supreme Court.

May: Proslavery forces attack the free-soil city of Lawrence, Kansas. In retaliation, abolitionist John Brown and his sons murder five men they believe to be tied to proslavery sentiment. The episode highlights ongoing civil conflict in Kansas.

1857

March 4: A supporter of the majority decision in the Dred Scott case, President James Buchanan is inaugurated. In his address he looks forward to a decision from the Court that will help clarify when territorial legislatures might address the issue of slavery in the territories.

March 6: Justice Taney announces the Dred Scott decision.

1858

Congress rejects Kansas's proslavery Lecompton Constitution.

August–October: In the Illinois Senate race, Lincoln and Douglas engage in a series of debates focusing on the issue of slavery in the territories, paying special attention to the Dred Scott decision.

September: Dred Scott dies after briefly enjoying freedom.

1860

The Democrats split into Northern and Southern wings over the question of slavery in the territories. Southerners insist on a slave-code-protecting institution; Douglas Democrats defend popular sovereignty. Abraham Lincoln is elected president.

1861

March 4: Lincoln is inaugurated. By this time, seven Deep South states have seceded from the Union.

1864

Chief Justice Taney dies. Lincoln replaces Taney with his former secretary of treasury, Salmon P. Chase.

1868

The Fourteenth Amendment is ratified. The amendment defines in clear language American citizenship, abolishing discriminatory categories for men on the basis of race.

DOCUMENTS

Document 1: SELECTIONS FROM THE CONSTITUTION

During the Revolutionary and Constitutional periods, slavery came under challenge in large parts of the new nation. Northern states outlawed the institution, usually through programs of gradual emancipation. In the upper South, many planters acknowledged slavery's violation of the most basic values of the American Revolution. States such as Virginia and Maryland liberalized manumission laws and entertained the possibility of future emancipation. In the lower South, however, the commitment to the institution remained intense. As a result of considerable disagreement among the Founders and a desire to hold together a Union of all thirteen states, the Constitution made concessions to slave interests. Nonetheless, the document's ambiguity about the institution led many principled Americans to disagree bitterly about the Founders' posture toward slavery.

Selections from the Constitution of the United States (1787)

A. KEY PASSAGES RELATING TO SLAVERY.

Article I.
Section 2.

Representatives and direct Taxes shall be apportioned among the several States which may be included within this Union, according to their respective Numbers, which shall be determined by adding to the whole Number of free Persons, including those bound to Service for a Term of Years, and excluding Indians not taxed, three fifths of all other Persons. The actual Enumeration shall be made within three Years after the first Meeting of the Congress of the United States, and within every subsequent Term of ten Years, in such Manner as they shall by Law direct.

Section 8.

To provide for calling forth the Militia to execute the Laws of the Union, suppress Insurrections and repel Invasions. . . .

Section 9.

The Migration or Importation of such Persons as any of the States now existing shall think proper to admit, shall not be prohibited by the Congress prior to the Year one thousand eight hundred and eight, but a Tax or duty may be imposed on such Importation, not exceeding ten dollars for each Person.

Article IV.
Section 2.

No Person held to Service or Labour in one State, under the Laws thereof, escaping into another, shall, in Consequence of any Law or Regulation therein, be discharged from such

Service or Labour, but shall be delivered up on Claim of the Party to whom such Service or Labour may be due.

B. CONGRESS, SLAVERY, AND THE TERRITORIES

Section 3.

New States may be admitted by the Congress into this Union; but no new State shall be formed or erected within the Jurisdiction of any other State; nor any State be formed by the Junction of two or more States, or Parts of States, without the Consent of the Legislatures of the States concerned as well as of the Congress.

The Congress shall have Power to dispose of and make all needful Rules and Regulations respecting the Territory or other Property belonging to the United States; and nothing in this Constitution shall be so construed as to Prejudice any Claims of the United States, or of any particular State.

Selections from the Bill of Rights, ratified 1791

AMENDMENT V

No person shall be held to answer for a capital or otherwise infamous crime, unless on presentment or indictment of a Grand Jury, except in cases arising in the land or naval forces, or in the Militia, when in actual service in time of war or public danger; nor shall any person be subject for the same offense to be twice put in jeopardy of life or limb; nor shall be compelled in a criminal case to be a witness against himself, nor be deprived of life, liberty, or property, without due process of law; nor shall private property be taken for public use, without just compensation.

C. THE COURTS AND THE CONSTITUTION

Article III.
Section 1.

The judicial Power of the United States shall be vested in one supreme Court, and in such inferior Courts as the Congress may from time to time ordain and establish....

Section 2.

The judicial Power shall extend to all Cases, in Law and Equity, arising under this Constitution, the Laws of the United States, and Treaties made, or which shall be made, under their Authority;—to all Cases affecting Ambassadors, other public Ministers and Consuls;—to all Cases of admiralty and maritime Jurisdiction;—to Controversies to which the United States shall be a Party;—to Controversies between two or more States;—between a State and Citizens of another State;—between Citizens of different States;—between Citizens of the same State claiming Lands under Grants of different States, and between a State, or the Citizens thereof, and foreign States, Citizens or Subjects.

In all Cases affecting Ambassadors, other public Ministers and Consuls, and those in which a State shall be Party, the supreme Court shall have original Jurisdiction. In all the other Cases before mentioned, the supreme Court shall have appellate Jurisdiction, both as to Law and Fact, with such Exceptions, and under such Regulations as the Congress shall make.

◆ ◆ ◆

Article VI.

This Constitution, and the Laws of the United States which shall be made in Pursuance thereof; and all Treaties made, or which shall be made, under the Authority of the United States, shall be the supreme Law of the Land; and the Judges in every State shall be bound thereby, any Thing in the Constitution or Laws of any State to the Contrary notwithstanding.

SOURCES:

The National Archives Experience, The Charters of Freedom, A New World Is at Hand, "Bill of Rights" <http://www.archives.gov/national-archives-experience/charters/bill_of_rights_transcript.html> [accessed December 31, 2007].

The National Archives Experience, The Charters of Freedom, A New World Is at Hand, "Declaration of Independence" <http://www.archives.gov/national-archives-experience/charters/declaration_transcript.html> [accessed December 30, 2007].

100 Milestone Documents, compiled by the National Archives of the United States: Constitution of the United States <http://www.ourdocuments.gov/index.php?flash=true&>[accessed June 21–July 9, 2007].

Document 2: CONGRESSIONAL ACTION ON SLAVERY IN THE TERRITORIES

From before the ratification of the Constitution in 1788 through the 1850s, American lawmakers repeatedly weighed in on the question of slavery's

existence in the territories, sometimes approving and sometimes forbidding its establishment. The Supreme Court's rejection of the Missouri Compromise line in the Dred Scott case (1857) divided the country. However, in the laws organizing New Mexico and Utah, Congress had already allowed for the possibility of slavery in areas north of the Missouri Compromise line. This decision evolved from a suggestion made by Kentucky senator Henry Clay; Clay's plan recommended that California enter the Union as a free state, while New Mexico and Utah's inhabitants would decide the issue of slavery themselves. In 1854 the Kansas-Nebraska Act expressly did away with the line, allowing people in the territories to decide the question of slavery on their own. Moreover, in both the Compromise of 1850 legislation and the Kansas-Nebraska Act, legislators invited a judicial resolution to the question of slavery in the territories, rather unheroically trying to throw the political hot potato of slavery into the laps of the justices on the Supreme Court.

Transcript of Northwest Ordinance (1787)

An Ordinance for the government of the Territory of the United States northwest of the River Ohio.

❖ ❖ ❖

Article VI.

There shall be neither slavery nor involuntary servitude in the said territory, otherwise than in the punishment of crimes whereof the party shall have been duly convicted: Provided, always, That any person escaping into the same, from whom labor or service is lawfully claimed in any one of the original States, such fugitive may be lawfully reclaimed and conveyed to the person claiming his or her labor or service as aforesaid.

Done by the United States, in Congress assembled, the 13th day of July, in the year of our Lord 1787, and of their sovereignty and independence the twelfth.

[Transcription courtesy of the Avalon Project at Yale Law School.]

Transcript of Missouri Compromise (1820)

An Act to authorize the people of the Missouri territory to form a constitution and state government, and for the admission of such state into the Union on an equal footing with the original states, and to prohibit slavery in certain territories.

Section 8.

And be it further enacted. That in all that territory ceded by France to the United States, under the name of Louisiana, which lies north of thirty-six degrees and thirty minutes north latitude, not included within the limits of the state, contemplated by this act, slavery and involuntary servitude, otherwise than in the punishment of crimes, whereof the parties shall have been duly convicted, shall be, and is hereby, forever prohibited: Provided always, That any person escaping into the same, from whom labour or service is lawfully claimed, in any state or territory of the United States, such fugitive may be lawfully reclaimed and conveyed to the person claiming his or her labour or service as aforesaid.

APPROVED, March 6, 1820.

Transcript of Compromise of 1850 (1850)

CLAY'S RESOLUTIONS–JANUARY 29, 1850

It being desirable, for the peace, concord, and harmony of the Union of these States, to settle and adjust amicably all existing questions of controversy between them arising out of the institution of slavery upon a fair, equitable and just basis....

❖ ❖ ❖

2. Resolved, That as slavery does not exist by law, and is not likely to be introduced into any of the territory acquired by the United States from the republic of Mexico, it is inexpedient for Congress to provide by law either for its introduction into, or exclusion from, any part of the said territory; and that appropriate territorial governments ought to be established by Congress in all of the said territory, not assigned as the boundaries of the proposed State of California, without the adoption of any restriction or condition on the subject of slavery.

APPROVED, September 9, 1850.

An Act . . . to establish a Territorial Government for New Mexico. [This provision was repeated in an Act to establish a Territorial Government for Utah (1850).]

Section 2.

And provided, further, That, when admitted as a State, the said Territory, or any portion of the same, shall be received into the Union, with or without slavery, as their constitution may prescribe at the time of their admission...

APPROVED, September 9, 1850.

An Act to Organize the Territories of Nebraska and Kansas (1854).

Section 19.

... and the same is hereby, created into a temporary government by the name of the Territory of Kansas; and when admitted as a State or States, the said Territory, or any portion of the same, shall be received into the Union with or without slavery, as their Constitution may prescribe at the time of their admission...

APPROVED, May 30, 1854.

SOURCES:

Northwest Ordinance (1787) <http://www.ourdocuments.gov/doc.php?doc=8&page=transcript> [accessed January 16, 2008].

Missouri Compromise (1820) http://www.ourdocuments.gov/doc.php?doc=22&page=transcript [accessed January 16, 2008].

Compromise of 1850 http://www.ourdocuments.gov/doc.php?doc=27&page=transcript> [accessed January 16, 2008].

Kansas-Nebraska Act (1854) [http://www.ourdocuments.gov/doc.php?doc=28&page=transcript> [accessed January 16, 2008].

Document 3: SCOTT V. SANDFORD

Chief Justice Roger Taney's decision of March 6, 1857, in the Dred Scott case offers a vision of the Constitution as a proslavery document. Taney decisively rejects the notion that blacks could ever become part of the American political community. He points to the racism animating federal and national law as evidence supporting his view. Taney's decision on slavery in the territories required an idiosyncratic reading of the "needful rules" clause in the Constitution. He held that this passage applied only to the Northwest Territories and not to any lands the nation acquired after the ratification of the Constitution. He also claimed that the language of the clause did not give Congress broad discretionary power in ruling the territories. In one of the most noted aspects of the opinion, Taney cites the Fifth Amendment assertion that no person can "be deprived of life, liberty, or property, without due process of law" as evidence that bans on slavery violated "due process" rights. Revisionist scholars have held that Taney's interpretation was constitutionally plausible within the context of the age in which he lived.

In the 2004 presidential debates, President George W. Bush asserted his intention to select justices to the Supreme Court who were "strict constructionists." He held that the Dred Scott decision was based on "personal opinion" and "not what the Constitution says."

Taney, C. J., Opinion of the Court Supreme Court of the United States

60 U.S. 393
Scott v. Sandford
Argued: — Decided:

Mr. Chief Justice Taney delivered the opinion of the court....

There are two leading questions presented by the record:

1. Had the Circuit Court of the United States jurisdiction to hear and determine the case between these parties? And

2. If it had jurisdiction, is the judgment it has given erroneous or not?...

The question is simply this: Can a negro whose ancestors were imported into this country, and sold as slaves, become a member of the political community formed and brought into existence by the Constitution of the United States, and as such become entitled to all the rights and privileges and immunities guaranteed to the citizen? One of which rights is the privilege of suing in a court of the United States in the cases specified in the Constitution?...

The words "people of the United States" and "citizens" are synonymous terms, and mean the same thing. They both describe the political body who, according to our republican institutions, form the sovereignty, and who hold the power and conduct the Government through their representatives. They are what we familiarly call the "sovereign people," and every citizen is one of this people and a constituent member of this sovereignty. The question before us is, whether the class of persons described in the plea in abatement compose a portion of this people, and are constituent members of this sovereignty? We think they are not, and that they are not included, and were not intended to be included, under the word "citizens" in the Constitution, and can therefore claim none of the rights and privileges which that instrument provides for and secures to citizens of the United States. On the contrary, they were at that time considered as a subordinate and inferior class of beings who had been subjugated by the dominant race, and, whether emancipated or not, yet remained subject to their authority, and had no rights or privileges but such as those who held the power and the government might choose to grant them....

In discussing this question, we must not confound the rights of citizenship which a State may confer within its own limits and the rights of citizenship as a member of the Union. It does not by any means follow, because he has all the rights and privileges of a citizen of a State, that he must be a citizen of the United States. He may have all the rights and privileges of the citizen of a State, and yet not be entitled to the rights and privileges of a citizen in any other State. For, previous to the adoption of the Constitution of the United States, every State had the undoubted right to confer on whomsoever it pleased the character of citizen, and to endow him with all its rights. But this character of course was confined to the boundaries of the State, and gave him no rights or privileges in other States beyond those secured to him by the laws of nations and the comity of States....

It is very clear, therefore, that no State can, by any act or law of its own, passed since the adoption of the Constitution, introduce a new member into the political community created by the Constitution of the United States. It cannot make him a member of this community by making him a member of its own. And for the same reason it cannot introduce any person or description of persons, who were not intended to be embraced in this new political family, which the Constitution brought into existence, but were intended to be excluded from it....

It becomes necessary, therefore, to determine who were citizens of the several States when the Constitution was adopted....

In the opinion of the court, the legislation and histories of the times, and the language used in the Declaration of Independence, show, that neither the class of persons who had been imported as slaves, nor their descendants, whether they had become free or not, were then acknowledged as a part of the people, nor intended to be included in the general words used in that memorable instrument.

It is difficult at this day to realize the state of public opinion in relation to that unfortunate race, which prevailed in the civilized and enlightened portions of the world at the time of the Declaration of Independence, and when the Constitution of the United States was framed and adopted. But the public history of every European nation displays it in a manner too plain to be mistaken.

They had for more than a century before been regarded as beings of an inferior order, and altogether unfit to associate with the white race, either in social or political relations; and so far inferior that they had no rights which the white man was bound to respect; and that the negro might justly and lawfully be reduced to slavery for his benefit....

And, accordingly, a negro of the African race was regarded by them as an article of property, and held, and bought and sold as such, in every one of the thirteen colonies which united in the Declaration of Independence, and afterwards formed the Constitution of the United States....

We refer to these historical facts for the purpose of showing the fixed opinions concerning that race, upon which the statesmen of that day spoke and acted. It is necessary to do this, in order to determine whether the general terms used in the Constitution of the United States, as to the rights of man and the rights of the people, was intended to include them, or to give to them or their posterity the benefit of any of its provisions.

The language of the Declaration of Independence is equally conclusive: ...

"We hold these truths to be self-evident: that all men are created equal; that they are endowed by their Creator with certain unalienable rights; that among them is life, liberty, and the pursuit of happiness; that to secure these rights, Governments are instituted, deriving their just powers from the consent of the governed."

The general words above quoted would seem to embrace the whole human family, and if they were used in a similar instrument at this day would be so understood. But it is too clear for dispute, that the enslaved African race were not intended to be included, and formed no part of the people who framed and adopted this declaration, for if the language, as understood in that day, would embrace them, the conduct of the distinguished men who framed the Declaration of Independence would have been utterly and flagrantly inconsistent with the principles they asserted; and instead of the sympathy of mankind, to which they so confidently appealed, they would have deserved and received universal rebuke and reprobation.

Yet the men who framed this declaration were great men—high in literary acquirements—high in their sense of honor, and incapable of asserting principles inconsistent with those on which they were acting. They perfectly understood the meaning of the language they used, and how it would be understood by others; and they knew that it would not in any part of the civilized world be supposed to embrace the negro race, which by common consent, had been excluded from civilized Governments and the family of nations, and doomed to slavery. They spoke and acted according to the then established doctrines and principles, and in the ordinary language of the day, and no one misunderstood them. The unhappy black race were separated from the white by indelible marks, and laws long before established, and were never thought of or spoken of except as property, and when the claims of the owner or the profit of the trader were supposed to need protection.

This state of public opinion had undergone no change when the Constitution was adopted, as is equally evident from its provisions and language....

But there are two clauses in the Constitution which point directly and specifically to the negro race as a separate class of persons, and show clearly that they were not regarded as a portion of the people or citizens of the Government then formed.

One of these clauses reserves to each of the thirteen States the right to import slaves until the year 1808, if it thinks proper. And the importation which it thus sanctions was unquestionably of persons of the race of which we are speaking, as the traffic in slaves in the United States had always been confined to them. And by the other provision the States pledge themselves to each other to maintain the right of property of the master, by delivering up to him any slave who may have escaped from his service, and be found within their respective territories. By the first above-mentioned clause, therefore, the right to purchase and hold this property is directly sanctioned and authorized for twenty years by the people who framed the Constitution. And by the second, they pledge themselves to maintain and uphold the right of the master in the manner specified, as long as the Government they then formed should endure. And these two provisions show, conclusively, that neither the description of persons therein referred to, nor their descendants, were embraced in any of the other provisions of the Constitution; for certainly these two clauses were not intended to confer on them or their posterity the blessings of liberty, or any of the personal rights so carefully provided for the citizen....

And if we turn to the legislation of the States where slavery had worn out, or measures taken for its speedy abolition, we shall find the same opinions and principles equally fixed and equally acted upon....

[Taney proceeds to reference several laws passed by New England states discriminating against free blacks.]

The legislation of the States therefore shows, in a manner not to be mistaken, the inferior and subject condition of that race at the time the Constitution was adopted, and long afterwards, throughout the thirteen States by which that instrument was framed; and it is hardly consistent with the respect due to these States, to suppose that they regarded at that time, as fellow-citizens and members of the sovereignty, a class of beings whom they had thus stigmatized; whom, as we are bound, out of respect to the State sovereignties, to assume they had deemed it just and necessary thus to stigmatize, and upon whom they had impressed such deep and enduring marks of inferiority and degradation; or, that when they met in convention to form the Constitution, they looked upon them as a portion of their constituents, or designed to include them in the provisions so carefully inserted for the security and protection of the liberties and rights of their citizens. It cannot be supposed that they intended to secure to them rights, and privileges, and rank, in the new political body throughout the Union, which every one of them denied within the limits of its own dominion. More especially, it cannot be believed that the large slaveholding States regarded them as included in the word citizens, or would have consented to a Constitution which might compel them to receive them in that character from another State. For if they were so received, and entitled to the privileges and immunities of citizens, it would exempt them from the operation of the special laws and from the police regulations which they considered to be necessary for their own safety. It would give to persons of the negro race, who were recognized as citizens in any one State of the Union, the right to enter every other State whenever they pleased, singly or in companies, without pass or passport, and without obstruction, to sojourn there as long as they pleased, to go where they pleased at every hour of the day or night without molestation, unless they committed some violation of law for which a white man would be punished; and it would give them the full liberty of speech in public and in private upon all subjects upon which its own citizens might speak; to hold public meetings upon political affairs, and to keep and carry arms wherever they went. And all of this would be done in the face of the subject race of the same color, both free and slaves, and inevitably producing discontent and insubordination among them, and endangering the peace and safety of the State....

No one, we presume, supposes that any change in public opinion or feeling, in relation to this unfortunate race, in the civilized nations of Europe or in this country, should induce the court to give to the words of the Constitution a more liberal construction in their favor than they were intended to bear when the instrument was framed and adopted. Such an argument would be altogether inadmissible in any tribunal called on to interpret it....

And, upon a full and careful consideration of the subject, the court is of opinion, that, upon the facts stated in the plea in abatement, Dred Scott was not a citizen of Missouri within the meaning of the Constitution of the United States, and not entitled as such to sue in its courts; and, consequently, that the Circuit Court had no jurisdiction of the case, and that the judgment on the plea in abatement is erroneous....

[Taney proceeds to discuss the question of slavery in the territories.]

In considering this part of the controversy, two questions arise: 1. Was he, together with his family, free in Missouri by reason of the stay in the territory of the United States hereinbefore mentioned? And, 2. If they were not, is Scott himself free by reason of his removal to Rock Island, in the State of Illinois, as stated in the above admissions?

We proceed to examine the first question.

The act of Congress, upon which the plaintiff relies, declares that slavery and involuntary servitude, except as a punishment for crime, shall be forever prohibited in all that part of the territory ceded by France, under the name of Louisiana, which lies north of thirty-six degrees thirty minutes north latitude, and not included within the limits of Missouri. And the difficulty which meets us at the threshold of this part of the inquiry is, whether Congress was authorised to pass this law under any of the powers granted to it by the Constitution; for if the authority is not given by that instrument, it is the duty of this court to declare it void and inoperative, and incapable of conferring freedom upon anyone who is held as a slave under the laws of any one of the States.

The counsel for the plaintiff has laid much stress upon that article in the Constitution which confers on Congress the power "to dispose of and make all needful rules and regulations respecting the territory or other property belonging to the United States;" but, in the judgment of the court, that provision has no bearing on the present controversy, and the power there given, whatever it may be, is confined, and was intended to be confined, to the territory which at that time belonged to, or was claimed by, the United States, and was within their boundaries as settled by the treaty with Great Britain, and can have no influence upon a territory afterwards acquired from a foreign Government. It was a special provision for a known and particular territory, and to meet a present emergency, and nothing more....

The words "needful rules and regulations" would seem, also, to have been cautiously used for some definite object. They are not the words usually employed by statesmen, when they mean to give the powers of sovereignty, or to establish a Government, or to authorise its establishment....

The words "rules and regulations" are usually employed in the Constitution in speaking of some particular specified power which it means to confer on the Government, and not, as we have seen, when granting general powers of legislation....

We do not mean, however, to question the power of Congress in this respect. The power to expand the territory of the United States by the admission of new States is plainly given; and in the construction of this power by all the departments of the Government, it has been held to authorize the acquisition of territory, not fit for admission at the time, but to be admitted as soon as its population and situation would entitle it to admission....

All we mean to say on this point is, that, as there is no express regulation in the Constitution defining the power which the General Government may exercise over the person or property of a citizen in a Territory thus acquired, the court must necessarily look to the provisions and principles of the Constitution, and its distribution of powers, for the rules and principles by which its decision must be governed.

Taking this rule to guide us, it may be safely assumed that citizens of the United States who migrate to a Territory belonging to the people of the United States, cannot be ruled as mere colonists, dependent upon the will of the General Government, and to be governed by any laws it may think proper to impose.... A power, therefore, in the General Government to obtain and hold colonies and dependent territories, over which they might legislate without restriction, would be inconsistent with its own existence in its present form. Whatever it acquires, it acquires for the benefit of the people of the several States who created it. It is their trustee acting for them, and charged with the duty of promoting the interests of the whole people of the whole Union in the exercise of the powers specifically granted.

At the time when the Territory in question was obtained by cession from France, it contained no population fit to be associated together and admitted as a State; and it therefore was absolutely necessary to hold possession of it, as a Territory belonging to the United States, until it was settled and inhabited by a civilized community capable of self-government, and in a condition to be admitted on equal terms with the other States as a member of the Union. But, as we have before said, it was acquired by the General Government, as the representative and trustee of the people of the United States, and it must therefore be held in that character for their common and equal benefit, for it was the people of the several States, acting through their agent and representative, the Federal Government, who in fact acquired the Territory in question, and the Government holds it for their common use until it shall be associated with the other States as a member of the Union....

But the power of Congress over the person or property of a citizen can never be a mere discretionary power under our Constitution and form of Government.... The Territory being a part of the United States, the Government and the citizen both enter it under the authority of the Constitution, with their respective rights defined and marked out; and the Federal Government can exercise no power over his person or property, beyond what that instrument confers, nor lawfully deny any right which it has reserved....

For example, no one, we presume, will contend that Congress can make any law in a Territory respecting the establishment of religion, or the free exercise thereof, or abridging the freedom of speech or of the press, or the right of the people of the Territory peaceably to assemble, and to petition the Government for the redress of grievances....

These powers, and others, in relation to rights of person, which it is not necessary here to enumerate, are, in express and positive terms, denied to the General Government, and the rights of private property have been guarded with equal care. Thus the rights of property are united with the rights of person, and placed on the same ground by the fifth amendment to the Constitution, which provides that no person shall be deprived of life, liberty, and property, without due process of law. And an act of Congress which deprives a citizen of the United States of his liberty or property, merely because he came himself or brought his property into a particular Territory of the United States, and who had committed no offence against the laws, could hardly be dignified with the name of due process of law....

The powers over person and property of which we speak are not only not granted to Congress, but are in express terms denied, and they are forbidden to exercise them. And this prohibition is not confined to the States, but the words are general, and extend to the whole territory over which the Constitution gives it power to legislate, including those portions of it remaining under Territorial Government, as well as that covered by States. It is a total absence of power everywhere within the dominion of the United States, and places the citizens of a Territory, so far as these rights are concerned, on the same footing with citizens of the States, and guards them as firmly and plainly against any inroads which the General Government might attempt, under the plea of implied or incidental powers. And if Congress itself cannot do this—if it is beyond the powers conferred on the Federal Government—it will be admitted, we presume, that it could not authorise a Territorial Government to exercise them. It could confer no power on any local Government established by its authority, to violate the provisions of the Constitution....

Now, as we have already said in an earlier part of this opinion, upon a different point, the right of property in a slave is distinctly and expressly affirmed in the Constitution. The right to traffic in it, like an ordinary article of merchandise and property, was guaranteed to the citizens of the United States, in every State that might desire it, for twenty years. And the Government in express terms is pledged to protect it in all future time, if the slave escapes from his owner. This is done in plain words—too plain to be misunderstood. And no word can be found in the Constitution which gives Congress a greater power over slave property, or which entitles property of that kind to less protection that property, of any other description. The only power conferred is the power coupled with the duty of guarding and protecting the owner in his rights.

Upon these considerations, it is the opinion of the court that the act of Congress which prohibited a citizen from holding and owning property of this kind in the territory of the United States north of the line therein mentioned, is not warranted by the Constitution, and is therefore void, and that neither Dred Scott himself, nor any of his family, were made free by being carried into this territory; even if they had been carried there by the owner, with the intention of becoming a permanent resident.

We have so far examined the case, as it stands under the Constitution of the United States, and the powers thereby delegated to the Federal Government.

But there is another point in the case which depends on State power and State law. And it is contended, on the part of the plaintiff, that he is made free by being taken to Rock Island, in the State of Illinois, independently of his residence in the territory of the United States, and being so made free, he was not again reduced to a state of slavery by being brought back to Missouri.

Our notice of this part of the case will be very brief, for the principle on which it depends was decided in this court, upon much consideration in the case of *Strader et al. v. Graham*, reported in 10th Howard, 82. In that case, the slaves had been taken from Kentucky to Ohio, with the consent of the owner, and afterwards brought back to Kentucky. And this court held that their *status* or condition, as free or slave, depended upon the laws of Kentucky, when they were brought back into that State, and not of Ohio, and that this court had no jurisdiction to revise the judgment of a State court upon its own laws. This was the point directly before the court, and the decision that this court had not jurisdiction turned upon it, as will be seen by the report of the case.

So in this case. As Scott was a slave when taken into the State of Illinois by his owner, and was there held as such, and brought back in that character, his *status,* as free or slave, depended on the laws of Missouri, and not of Illinois....

Upon the whole, therefore, it is the judgment of this court, that it appears by the record before us that the plaintiff in error is not a citizen of Missouri, in the sense in which that word is used in the Constitution; and that the Circuit Court of the United States, for that reason, had no jurisdiction in the case, and could give no judgment in it. Its judgment for the defendant must, consequently, be reversed, and a mandate issued, directing the suit to be dismissed for want of jurisdiction.

Source:

Roger Taney. "Opinion of the Court," *Scott v. Sandford,* Cornell University Law School, Supreme Court Collection <http://www.law.cornell.edu/supct/html/historics/USSC_CR_0060_0393_ZO.html> [accessed June 20, 2007].

Document 4: Benjamin Curtis's Dissenting Opinion

Supreme Court Justice Benjamin Curtis of Massachusetts won the applause of Northern Republicans for his defiant rebuke of the Court majority in Dred Scott v. Sandford. *Curtis was a conservative Whig, and his opinion revealed displeasure with those who supported Chief Justice Roger B. Taney's apparent readiness to break with both history and past legal rulings. Curtis held that free blacks had in fact been citizens of several states at the start of the republic and that citizenship in the states constituted national citizenship. However, in his dissent he leaves room for states to refuse citizenship to blacks and for states to discriminate among different citizens with regard to specific political and civil rights (for example, voting). His dissent draws on history and the language of the Constitution to support the authority of federal lawmakers to limit slavery. He chides the Court for considering the Missouri Compromise issue after it had concluded that Scott did not hold citizenship in either the state of Missouri or in the United States. As in the case of the Taney selection, this excerpt includes only a small portion of Curtis's final written opinion.*

The Constitution asserts: "the Citizens of each State shall be entitled to all Privileges and Immunities of Citizens in the several States." Yet, Curtis allows individual states to impose specific restrictions on citizens of other states.

Curtis, J., Dissenting Opinion
Supreme Court of the United States

60 U.S. 393
Scott v. Sandford
Argued: — Decided:

Mr. Justice Curtis dissenting.

I dissent from the opinion pronounced by the Chief Justice, and from the judgment which the majority of the court think it proper to render in this case....
the question is whether any person of African descent, whose ancestors were sold as slaves in the United States, can be a citizen of the United States. If any such person can be a citizen, this plaintiff has the right to the judgment of the court that he is so, for no cause is shown by the plea why he is not so, except his descent and the slavery of his ancestors....

Citizens of the United States at the time of the adoption of the Constitution can have been no other than citizens of the United States under the Confederation. By the Articles of Confederation, a Government was organized, the style whereof was "The United States of America." This Government was in existence when the Constitution was framed and proposed for adoption, and was to be superseded by the new Government of the United States of America, organized under the Constitution. When, therefore, the Constitution speaks of citizenship of the United States existing at the time of the adoption of the Constitution, it must necessarily refer to citizenship under the Government which existed prior to and at the time of such adoption....

To determine whether any free persons, descended from Africans held in slavery, were citizens of the United States under the Confederation, and consequently at the time of the adoption of the Constitution of the United States, it is only necessary to know whether any such persons were citizens of either of the States under the Confederation at the time of the adoption of the Constitution.

Of this there can be no doubt. At the time of the ratification of the Articles of Confederation, all free native-born inhabitants of the States of New Hampshire, Massachusetts, New York, New Jersey, and North Carolina, though descended from African slaves, were not only citizens of those States, but such of them as had the other necessary qualifications possessed the franchise of electors, on equal terms with other citizens....

Did the Constitution of the United States deprive them or their descendants of citizenship?

That Constitution was ordained and established by the people of the United States, through the action, in each State, or those persons who were qualified by its laws to act thereon in behalf of themselves and all other citizens of that State. In some of the States, as we have seen, colored persons were among those qualified by law to act on this subject. These colored persons were not only included in the body of "the people of the United States" by whom the Constitution was ordained and established, but, in at least five of the States, they had the power to act, and doubtless did act, by their suffrages, upon the question of its adoption. It would be strange if we were to find in that instrument anything which deprived of their citizenship any part of the people of the United States who were among those by whom it was established.

I can find nothing in the Constitution which, proprio vigore, deprives of their citizenship any class of persons who were citizens of the United States at the time of its adoption, or who should be native-born citizens of any State after its adoption, nor any power enabling Congress to disfranchise persons born on the soil of any State, and entitled to citizenship of such State by its Constitution and laws. And my opinion is that, under the Constitution of the United States, every free person born on the soil of a State, who is a citizen of that State by force of its Constitution or laws, is also a citizen of the United States....

Again, it has been objected that if the Constitution has left to the several States the rightful power to determine who of their inhabitants shall be citizens of the United States, the States may make aliens citizens.

The answer is obvious. The Constitution has left to the States the determination what persons, born within their respective limits, shall acquire by birth citizenship of the United States; it has not left to them any power to prescribe any rule for the removal of the disabilities of alienage. This power is exclusively in Congress.

It has been further objected that, if free colored persons, born within a particular State and made citizens of that State by its Constitution and laws, are thereby made citizens of the United States, then, under the second section of the fourth article of the Constitution, such persons would be entitled to all the privileges and immunities of citizens in the several States, and, if so, then colored persons could vote, and be eligible to not only Federal offices, but offices even in those States whose Constitution and laws disqualify colored persons from voting or being elected to office.

But this position rests upon an assumption which I deem untenable....

One may confine the right of suffrage to white male citizens; another may extend it to colored persons and females; one may allow all persons above a prescribed age to convey property and transact business; another may exclude married women. But whether native-born women, or persons under age, or under guardianship because insane or spendthrifts, be excluded from voting or holding office, or allowed to do so, I apprehend no one will deny that they are citizens of the United States. Besides, this clause of the Constitution does not confer on the citizens of one State, in all other States, specific and enumerated privileges and immunities. They are entitled to such as belong to citizenship, but not to such as belong to particular citizens attended by other qualifications. Privileges and immunities which belong to certain citizens of a State by reason of the operation of causes other than mere citizenship are not conferred. Thus, if the laws of a State require, in addition to citizenship of the State, some qualification for office or the exercise of the elective franchise, citizens of all other States coming thither to reside and not possessing those qualifications cannot enjoy those privileges, not because they are not to be deemed entitled to the privileges of citizens of the State in which they reside, but because they, in common with the native-born citizens of that State, must have the qualifications prescribed by law for the enjoyment of such privileges under its Constitution and laws....

The conclusions at which I have arrived on this part of the case are:

First. That the free native-born citizens of each State are citizens of the United States.

Second. That, as free colored persons born within some of the States are citizens of those States, such persons are also citizens of the United States.

Third. That every such citizen, residing in any State, has the right to sue and is liable to be sued in the Federal courts, as a citizen of that State in which he resides.

Fourth. That, as the plea to the jurisdiction in this case shows no facts, except that the plaintiff was of African descent, and his ancestors were sold as slaves, and as these facts are not inconsistent with his citizenship of the United States and his residence in the State of Missouri, the plea to the jurisdiction was bad, and the judgment of the Circuit Court overruling it was correct.

I dissent, therefore, from that part of the opinion of the majority of the court in which it is held that a person of African descent cannot be a citizen of the United States, and I regret I must go further and dissent both from what I deem their assumption of authority to examine the constitutionality of the act of Congress commonly called the Missouri Compromise Act and the grounds and conclusions announced in their opinion.

Having first decided that they were bound to consider the sufficiency of the plea to the jurisdiction of the Circuit Court, and having decided that this plea showed that the Circuit Court had not jurisdiction, and consequently that this is a case to which the judicial power of the United States does not extend, they have gone on to examine the merits of the case as they appeared on the trial before the court and jury on the issues joined on the pleas in bar, and so have reached the question of the power of Congress to pass the act of 1820. On so grave a subject as this, I feel obliged to say that, in my opinion, such an exertion of judicial power transcends the limits of the authority of the court as described by its repeated decisions, and as I understand, acknowledged in this opinion of the majority of the court....

[Curtis considers the right of Congress to ban slavery in the territories.]

To avoid misapprehension on this important and difficult subject, I will state distinctly the conclusions at which I have arrived. They are:

First. The rules of international law respecting the emancipation of slaves, by the rightful operation of the laws of another State or country upon the status of the slave, while resident in such foreign State or country, are part of the common law of Missouri, and have not been abrogated by any statute law of that State.

Second. The laws of the United States, constitutionally enacted, which operated directly on and changed the status of a slave coming into the Territory of Wisconsin with his master, who went thither to reside for an indefinite length of time, in the performance of his duties as an officer of the United States, had a rightful operation on the status of the slave, and it is in conformity with the rules of international law that this change of status should be recognised everywhere.

Third. The laws of the United States, in operation in the Territory of Wisconsin at the time of the plaintiff's residence there, did act directly on the status of the plaintiff, and change his status to that of a free man.

Fourth. The plaintiff and his wife were capable of contracting, and, with the consent of Dr. Emerson, did contract a marriage in that Territory, valid under its laws, and the validity of this marriage cannot be questioned in Missouri, save by showing that it was in fraud of the laws of that State or of some right derived from them, which cannot be shown in this case, because the master consented to it.

Fifth. That the consent of the master that his slave, residing in a country which does not tolerate slavery, may enter into a lawful contract of marriage, attended with the civil rights and duties which being to that condition, is an effectual act of emancipation. And the law does not enable Dr. Emerson, or anyone claiming under him, to assert a title to the married persons as slaves, and thus destroy the obligation of the contract of marriage and bastardize their issue and reduce them to slavery.

But it is insisted that the Supreme Court of Missouri has settled this case by its decision in Scott v. Emerson, 15 Missouri Reports 576, and that this decision is in conformity with the weight of authority elsewhere, and with sound principles....

To the correctness of such a decision I cannot assent. In my judgment, the opinion of the majority of the court in that case is in conflict with its previous decisions, with a great weight of judicial authority in other slaveholding States, and with fundamental principles of private international law....

I have thus far assumed, merely for the purpose of the argument that the laws of the United States respecting slavery in this Territory were constitutionally enacted by Congress. It remains to inquire whether they are constitutional and binding laws....

[Curtis describes two key constitutional provisions with regard to territories. He holds that the "needful rules" clause of the Constitution give Congress broad powers and applies to territories acquired after the Constitution's ratification.]

It is said this provision has no application to any territory save that then belonging to the United States. I have already shown that, when the Constitution was framed, a confident expectation was entertained, which was speedily realized, that North Carolina and Georgia would cede their claims to that great territory which lay west of those States....

No reason has been suggested why any reluctance should have been felt by the framers of the Constitution to apply this provision to all the territory which might belong to the United States, or why any distinction should have been made, founded on the accidental circumstance of the dates of the cessions ... which I cannot concur.

There is not, in my judgment, anything in the language, the history, or the subject matter of this article which restricts its operation to territory owned by the United States when the Constitution was adopted....

The Constitution declares that Congress shall have power to make "all needful rules and regulations" respecting the territory belonging to the United States.

The assertion is, though the Constitution says "all," it does not mean all—though it says "all" without qualification, it means all except such as allow or prohibit slavery. It cannot be doubted that it is incumbent on those who would thus introduce an exception not found in the language of the instrument to exhibit some solid and satisfactory reason, drawn from the subject matter or the purposes and objects of the clause, the context, or from other provisions of the Constitution, showing that the words employed in this clause are not to be understood according to their clear, plain, and natural signification....

Without going minutely into the details of each case, I will now give reference to two classes of acts, in one of which Congress has extended the Ordinance of 1787, including the article prohibiting slavery, over different Territories, and thus exerted its power to prohibit it; in the other, Congress has erected Governments over Territories acquired from France and Spain, in which slavery already existed, but refused to apply to them that part of the Government under the ordinance which excluded slavery.

Of the first class are the Act of May 7th, 1800, 2 Stat. at Large 58, for the government of the Indiana Territory; the Act of January 11th, 1805, 2 Stat. at Large 309, for the government of Michigan Territory; the Act of May 3d, 1809, 2 Stat. at Large 514, for the government of the Illinois Territory; the Act of April 20th, 1836, 5 Stat. at Large 10, for the government of the Territory of Wisconsin; the Act of June 12th, 1838, for the government of the Territory of Iowa; the Act of August 14th, 1848, for the government of the Territory of Oregon. To these instances should be added the Act of March 6th, 1820, 3 Stat. at Large 548, prohibiting slavery in the territory acquired from France, being northwest of Missouri and north of thirty-six degrees thirty minutes north latitude.

Of the second class, in which Congress refused to interfere with slavery already existing under the municipal law of France or Spain, and established Governments by which slavery was recognised and allowed, are: the Act of March 26th, 1804, 2 Stat. at Large 283, for the government of Louisiana; the Act of March 2d, 1805, 2 Stat. at Large 322, for the government of the Territory of Orleans; the Act of June 4th, 1812, 2 Stat. at Large 743, for the government of the Missouri Territory; the Act of March 30th, 1822, 3 Stat. at Large 654, for the government of the Territory of Florida. Here are eight distinct instances, beginning with the first Congress, and coming down to the year 1848, in which Congress has excluded slavery from the territory of the United States, and six distinct instances in which Congress organized Governments of Territories by which slavery was recognised and continued, beginning also with the first Congress, and coming down to the year 1822. These acts were severally signed by seven Presidents of the United States, beginning with General Washington, and coming regularly down as far as Mr. John Quincy Adams, thus including all who were in public life when the Constitution was adopted.

If the practical construction of the Constitution contemporaneously with its going into effect, by men intimately acquainted with its history from their personal participation in framing and adopting it, and continued by them through a long series of acts of the gravest importance, be entitled to weight in the judicial mind on a question of construction, it would seem to be difficult to resist the force of the acts above adverted to....

If it can be shown by anything in the Constitution itself that, when it confers on Congress the power to make all needful rules and regulations respecting the territory belonging to the United States, the exclusion or the allowance of slavery was excepted, or if anything in the history of this provision tends to show that such an exception was intended by those who framed and adopted the Constitution to be introduced into it, I hold it to be my duty carefully to consider, and to allow just weight to such considerations in interpreting the positive text of the Constitution. But where the Constitution has said all needful rules and regulations, I must find something more than theoretical reasoning to induce me to say it did not mean all....

Looking at the power of Congress over the Territories as of the extent just described, what positive prohibition exists in the Constitution, which restrained Congress from enacting a law in 1820 to prohibit slavery north of thirty-six degrees thirty minutes north latitude?

The only one suggested is that clause in the fifth article of the amendments of the Constitution which declares that no person shall be deprived of his life, liberty, or property, without due process of law. I will now proceed to examine the question whether this clause is entitled to the effect thus attributed to it. It is necessary, first, to have a clear view of the nature and incidents of that particular species of property which is now in question.

Slavery, being contrary to natural right, is created only by municipal law. This is not only plain in itself, and agreed by all writers on the subject, but is inferable from the Constitution and has been explicitly declared by this court. The Constitution refers to slaves as "persons held to service in one State, under the laws thereof." Nothing can more clearly describe a status created by municipal law. In Prigg v. Pennsylvania, 10 Pet. 611, this court said: "The state of slavery is deemed to be a mere municipal regulation, founded on and limited to the range of territorial laws...."

Is it conceivable that the Constitution has conferred the right on every citizen to become a resident on the territory of the United States with his slaves, and there to hold them as such, but has neither made nor provided for any municipal regulations which are essential to the existence of slavery?

Is it not more rational to conclude that they who framed and adopted the constitution were aware that persons held to service under the laws of a State are property only to the extent and under the conditions fixed by those laws that they must cease to be available as property, when their owners voluntarily place them permanently within another jurisdiction, where no municipal laws on the subject of slavery exist, and that, being aware of these principles, and having said nothing to interfere with or displace them, or to compel Congress to legislate in any particular manner on the subject, and having empowered Congress to make all needful rules and regulations respecting the territory of the United States, it was their intention to leave to the discretion of Congress what regulations, if any, should be made concerning slavery therein? Moreover, if the right exists, what are its limits, and what are its conditions? If citizens of the United States have the right to take their slaves to a Territory, and hold them there as slaves, without regard to the laws of the Territory, I suppose this right is not to be restricted to the citizens of slaveholding States. A citizen of a State which does not tolerate slavery can hardly be denied the power of doing the same thing. And what law of slavery does either take with him to the Territory?...

That assumption is that the territory ceded by France was acquired for the equal benefit of all the citizens of the United States. I agree to the position. But it was acquired for their benefit in their collective, not their individual, capacities. It was acquired for their benefit, as an organized political society, subsisting as "the people of the United States," under the Constitution of the United States, to be administered justly and impartially, and as nearly as possible for the equal benefit of every individual citizen, according to the best judgment and discretion of the Congress, to whose power, as the Legislature of the nation which acquired it, the people of the United States have committed its administration....

Nor, in my judgment, will the position that a prohibition to bring slaves into a Territory deprives anyone of his property without due process of law bear examination....

For these reasons, I am of opinion that so much of the several acts of Congress as prohibited slavery and involuntary servitude within that part of the Territory of Wisconsin lying north of thirty-six degrees thirty minutes north latitude and west of the river Mississippi, were constitutional and valid laws.

Source:

Benjamin Curtis. "Dissenting Opinion," *Scott v. Sandford*, Cornell University Law School, Supreme Court Collection <http://www.law.cornell.edu/supct/html/historics/USSC_CR_0060_0393_ZD1.html> [accessed June 21, 2007].

Document 5: Abraham Lincoln's Speech on the Dred Scott Decision

In his June 26, 1857, speech, at Springfield, Illinois, on the Dred Scott decision, Abraham Lincoln offers a vision of the Founders as against slavery and determined to bring the institution to an end. Lincoln believed that since the passing of the Kansas-Nebraska Act in 1854, proslavery forces (including former president Franklin Pierce, current president James Buchanan, Senator Stephen Douglas, and Chief Justice Roger B. Taney) had mounted a conspiracy to make the institution national. For all Republicans, the Dred Scott ruling posed a problem. The newly formed political party was united around the single issue of stopping slavery from expanding to the territories. Here lawyer Lincoln, friend of the Constitution, endeavors to suggest a way around the Taney Court.

Lincoln notes that during the bank war of the 1830s, President Andrew Jackson claimed that the executive and legislative branches, as well as the Supreme Court, had a duty to determine the constitutionality of matters of public policy.

Fellow Citizens:—

And now as to the Dred Scott decision. That decision declares two propositions—first, that a negro cannot sue in the U.S. Courts; and secondly, that Congress cannot prohibit slavery in the Territories. It was made by a divided court—dividing differently on the different points. Judge Douglas does not discuss the merits of the decision; and, in that respect, I shall follow his example, believing I could no more improve on McLean and Curtis, than he could on Taney.

He denounces all who question the correctness of that decision, as offering violent resistance to it. But who resists it? Who has, in spite of the decision, declared Dred Scott free, and resisted the authority of his master over him?

Judicial decisions have two uses—first, to absolutely determine the case decided, and secondly, to indicate to the public how other similar cases will be decided when they arise. For the latter use, they are called "precedents" and "authorities."

We believe, as much as Judge Douglas, (perhaps more) in obedience to, and respect for the judicial department of government. We think its decisions on Constitutional questions, when fully settled, should control, not only the particular cases decided, but the general policy of the country, subject to be disturbed only by amendments of the Constitution as provided in that instrument itself. More than this would be revolution. But we think the Dred Scott decision is erroneous. We know the court that made it, has often over-ruled its own decisions, and we shall do what we can to have it to over-rule this. We offer no resistance to it.

Judicial decisions are of greater or less authority as precedents, according to circumstances. That this should be so, accords both with common sense, and the customary understanding of the legal profession.

If this important decision had been made by the unanimous concurrence of the judges, and without any apparent partisan bias, and in accordance with legal public expectation, and with the steady practice of the departments throughout our history, and had been in no part, based on assumed historical facts which are not really true; or, if wanting in some of these, it had been before the court more than once, and had there been affirmed and re-affirmed through a course of years, it then might be, perhaps would be, factious, nay, even revolutionary, to not acquiesce in it as a precedent.

But when, as it is true we find it wanting in all these claims to the public confidence, it is not resistance, it is not factious, it is not even disrespectful, to treat it as not having yet quite established a settled doctrine for the country—But Judge Douglas considers this view awful. . . .

Why this same Supreme court once decided a national bank to be constitutional; but Gen. Jackson, as President of the United States, disregarded the decision, and vetoed a bill for a re-charter, partly on constitutional ground, declaring that each public functionary must support the Constitution, "as he understands it."

. . . But hear Gen. Jackson further—

"If the opinion of the Supreme court covered the whole ground of this act, it ought not to control the co-ordinate authorities of this Government. The Congress, the executive and the court, must each for itself be guided by its own opinion of the Constitution. Each public officer, who takes an oath to support the Constitution, swears that he will support it as he understands it, and not as it is understood by others."

Again and again have I heard Judge Douglas denounce that bank decision, and applaud Gen. Jackson for disregarding it. It would be interesting for him to look over his recent speech, and see how exactly his fierce philippics against us for resisting Supreme Court decisions, fall upon his own head....

I have said, in substance, that the Dred Scott decision was, in part, based on assumed historical facts which were not really true; and I ought not to leave the subject without giving some reasons for saying this; I therefore give an instance or two, which I think fully sustain me. Chief Justice Taney, in delivering the opinion of the majority of the Court, insists at great length that negroes were no part of the people who made, or for whom was made, the Declaration of Independence, or the Constitution of the United States.

On the contrary, Judge Curtis, in his dissenting opinion, shows that in five of the then thirteen states, to wit, New Hampshire, Massachusetts, New York, New Jersey and North Carolina, free negroes were voters, and, in proportion to their numbers, had the same part in making the Constitution that the white people had....

Again, Chief Justice Taney says: "It is difficult, at this day to realize the state of public opinion in relation to that unfortunate race, which prevailed in the civilized and enlightened portions of the world at the time of the Declaration of Independence, and when the Constitution of the United States was framed and adopted." And again, after quoting from the Declaration, he says: "The general words above quoted would seem to include the whole human family, and if they were used in a similar instrument at this day, would be so understood."

In these the Chief Justice does not directly assert, but plainly assumes, as a fact, that the public estimate of the black man is more favorable now than it was in the days of the Revolution. This assumption is a mistake.... In those days, as I understand, masters could, at their own pleasure, emancipate their slaves; but since then, such legal restraints have been made upon emancipation, as to amount almost to prohibition. In those days, Legislatures held the unquestioned power to abolish slavery, in their respective States; but now it is becoming quite fashionable for State Constitutions to withhold that power from the Legislatures. In those days, by common consent, the spread of the black man's bondage to new countries was prohibited; but now, Congress decides that it will not continue the prohibition, and the Supreme Court decides that it could not if it would. In those days, our Declaration of Independence was held sacred by all, and thought to include all; but now, to aid in making the bondage of the negro universal and eternal, it is assailed, and sneered at, and construed, and hawked at, and torn, till, if its framers could rise from their graves, they could not at all recognize it. All the powers of earth seem rapidly combining against him. Mammon is after him; ambition follows, and philosophy follows, and the Theology of the day is fast joining the cry. They have him in his prison house; they have searched his person, and left no prying instrument with him. One after another they have closed the heavy iron doors upon him, and now they have him, as it were, bolted in with a lock of a hundred keys, which can never be unlocked without the concurrent of every key; the keys in the hands of a hundred different men, and they scattered to a hundred different and distant places; and they stand musing as to what invention, in all the dominions of mind and matter, can be produced to make the impossibility of his escape more complete than it is.

It is grossly incorrect to say or assume, that the public estimate of the negro is more favorable now than it was at the origin of the government...

There is a natural disgust in the minds of nearly all white people, to the idea of an indiscriminate amalgamation of the white and black races; and Judge Douglas evidently is basing his chief hope, upon the chances of being able to appropriate the benefit of this disgust to himself. If he can, by much drumming and repeating, fasten the odium of that idea upon his adversaries, he thinks he can struggle through the storm. He therefore clings to this hope, as a drowning man to the last plank. He makes an occasion for lugging it in from the opposition to the Dred Scott decision. He finds the Republicans insisting that the Declaration of Independence includes ALL men, black as well as white; and forthwith he boldly denies that it includes negroes at all, and proceeds to argue gravely that all who contend it does, do so only because they want to vote, and eat, and sleep, and marry with negroes! He will have it that they cannot be consistent else. Now I protest against that counterfeit logic which concludes that, because I do not want a black woman for a slave I must necessarily want her for a wife. I need not have her for either, I can just leave her alone. In some respects she certainly is not my equal; but in her natural right to eat the bread she earns with her own hands without asking leave of any one else, she is my equal, and the equal of all others.

Chief Justice Taney, in his opinion in the Dred Scott case, admits that the language of the Declaration is broad enough to include the whole human family, but he and Judge Douglas argue that the authors of that instrument did not intend to include negroes, by the fact that they did not at once, actually place them on an equality with the whites. Now this grave argument comes to just nothing at all, by the other fact, that they did not at once, or ever afterwards, actually place all white people on an equality with one or another. And this is the staple argument of both the Chief Justice and the Senator, for doing this obvious violence to the plain unmistakable language of the Declaration. I think the authors of that notable instrument intended to include all men, but they did not intend to declare all men equal in all respects. They did not mean to say all were equal in color, size, intellect, moral developments, or social capacity. They defined with tolerable distinctness, in what respects they did consider all men created equal—equal in "certain inalienable rights, among which are life, liberty, and the pursuit of happiness." This they said, and this meant. They did not mean to assert the obvious untruth, that all were then actually enjoying that equality, nor yet, that they were about to confer it immediately upon them. In fact they had no power to confer such a boon. They meant simply to declare the right, so that the enforcement of it might follow as fast as circumstances should permit. They meant to set up a standard maxim for free society, which should be familiar to all, and revered by all; constantly looked to, constantly labored for, and even though never perfectly attained, constantly approximated, and thereby constantly spreading and deepening its influence, and augmenting the happiness and value of life to all people of all colors everywhere. The assertion that "all men are created equal" was of no practical use in effecting our separation from Great Britain; and it was placed in the Declaration, not for that, but for future use. Its authors meant it to be, thank God, it is now proving itself, a stumbling block to those who in after times might seek to turn a free people back into the hateful paths of despotism. They knew the proneness of prosperity to breed tyrants, and they meant when such should re-appear in this fair land and commence their vocation they should find left for them at least one hard nut to crack....

How differently the respective courses of the Democratic and Republican parties incidentally bear on the question of forming a will—a public sentiment—for colonization, is easy to see. The Republicans inculcate, with whatever of ability—they can, that the negro is a man; that his bondage is cruelly wrong, and that the field of his oppression ought not to be enlarged. The Democrats deny his manhood; deny, or dwarf to insignificance, the wrong of his bondage; so far as possible, crush all sympathy for him, and cultivate and excite hatred and disgust against him; compliment themselves as Union-savers for doing so; and call the indefinite outspreading of his bondage "a sacred right of self-government."

Source:

Abraham Lincoln. June 26, 1857, *Speech at Springfield Illinois, in Collected Works of Abraham Lincoln,* edited by Roy P. Basler, 9 volumes (New Brunswick, N.J.: Rutgers University Press, 1953–1955), volume 2. Ann Arbor: University of Michigan Digital Library Production Services <http://quod.lib.umich.edu/cgi/t/text/text-idx?c=lincoln;cc=lincoln;view=text;idno=lincoln2;rgn=div1;node=lincoln2%3A438>.

Document 6: Abraham Lincoln's Debate with Stephen A. Douglas

During the Lincoln-Douglas debates in 1858, Senator Stephen Douglas accused Abraham Lincoln of thumbing his nose at the rule of law. Lincoln then tried to claim that Douglas had placed himself in a contradictory position by both backing the Supreme Court's Dred Scott decision and insisting on the right of the people of a territory to vote for or against the presence of slavery. In this brief excerpt, Senator Douglas suggests how popular sovereignty and respect for the Court might be reconciled.

Second Debate with Stephen A. Douglas at Freeport, Illinois

August 27, 1858
Mr. Lincoln's Speech.

Q. 2. Can the people of a United States Territory, in any lawful way, against the wish of any citizen of the United States, exclude slavery from its limits prior to the formation of a State Constitution? [Renewed applause.]
Q. 3. If the Supreme Court of the United States shall decide that States cannot exclude slavery from their limits, are you in favor of acquiescing in, adopting and following such decision as a rule of political action? [Loud applause.]

Mr. Douglas's Speech.

The next question propounded to me by Mr. Lincoln is, can the people of a Territory in any lawful way, against the wishes of any citizen of the United States, exclude slavery from their limits prior to the formation of a State

Constitution? I answer emphatically, as Mr. Lincoln has heard me answer a hundred times from every stump in Illinois, that in my opinion the people of a Territory can, by lawful means, exclude slavery from their limits prior to the formation of a State Constitution. Mr. Lincoln knew that I had answered that question over and over again. He heard me argue the Nebraska bill on that principle all over the State in 1854, in 1855, and in 1856, and he has no excuse for pretending to be in doubt as to my position on that question. It matters not what way the Supreme Court may hereafter decide as to the abstract question whether slavery may or may not go into a Territory under the Constitution, the people have the lawful means to introduce it or exclude it as they please, for the reason that slavery cannot exist a day or an hour anywhere, unless it is supported by local police regulations. (Right, right.) Those police regulations can only be established by the local legislature, and if the people are opposed to slavery they will elect representatives to that body who will by unfriendly legislation effectually prevent the introduction of it into their midst. If, on the contrary, they are for it, their legislation will favor its extension. Hence, no matter what the decision of the Supreme Court may be on that abstract question, still the right of the people to make a slave Territory or a free Territory is perfect and complete under the Nebraska bill. I hope Mr. Lincoln deems my answer satisfactory on that point....

The third question which Mr. Lincoln presented is, if the Supreme Court of the United States shall decide that a State of this Union cannot exclude slavery from its own limits, will I submit to it? I am amazed that Lincoln should ask such a question. ["A school boy knows better."] Yes, a school-boy does know better. Mr. Lincoln's object is to cast an imputation upon the Supreme Court. He knows that there never was but one man in America, claiming any degree of intelligence or decency, who ever for a moment pretended such a thing.... He casts an imputation upon the Supreme Court of the United States, by supposing that they would violate the Constitution of the United States. I tell him that such a thing is not possible. (Cheers.) It would be an act of moral treason that no man on the bench could ever descend to. Mr. Lincoln himself would never in his partisan feelings so far forget what was right as to be guilty of such an act. ("Good, good.")

Source:

Lincoln-Douglas Debates, The National Park Service, <http://www.nps.gov/archive/liho/debate2.htm>. Founder's Library: The 19th Century Speeches, Letters and Writings of Abraham Lincoln <http://www.founding.com/library/lbody.cfm?id=321&parent=63>.

BIBLIOGRAPHY

Allen, Austin. *Origins of the Dred Scott Case: Jacksonian Jurisprudence and the Supreme Court, 1837–1857*. Athens: University of Georgia Press, 2006. A revisionist account that concludes that Taney's ruling in *Dred Scott v. Sandford* was "plausible" when set against the larger framework and legal precedents of the period.

Bestor, Arthur. "The American Civil War as a Constitutional Crisis," *American Historical Review*, 69 (January 1964): 327–352. Bestor's article lays out four conflicting interpretations of the Constitution advanced during the 1840s and 1850s as to where legal authority lay to determine slavery's status in the territories.

Ehrlich, Walter. *They Have No Rights: Dred Scott's Struggle for Freedom*. Westport, Conn.: Greenwood Press, 1979. This book is especially useful for those interested in Dred Scott's story and the details surrounding his various legal suits.

Fehrenbacher, Don. *The Dred Scott Case: Its Significance in American Law and Politics*. New York: Oxford University Press, 1978. This study offers a magisterial and authoritative overview of the origins, substance, and consequences of the case. An abridged version of this book is available under the title *Slavery, Law, and Politics: The Dred Scott Case in Historical Perspective*.

———. "Roger B. Taney and the Sectional Conflict," *Journal of Southern History*, 43 (November 1977): 555–566. Fehrenbacher shows how Taney's personal animosity toward antislavery contributed to a partisan decision full of contradictions, inconsistencies, and errors of fact.

Finkelman, Paul. Dred Scott v. Sandford: *A Brief History with Documents*. Boston: Bedford/St. Martin's Press, 1997. This book provides a superior brief introduction to the case. The text also includes selections from the opinions of the nine Supreme Court justices, newspaper reactions from around the nation, and portions of the Lincoln-Douglas debate. Primary materials are prefaced with helpful commentary.

Graber, Marc. *Dred Scott and the Problem of Constitutional Evil*. Cambridge: Cambridge University Press, 2006. A stimulating work of political philosophy deeply informed by history. Graber offers a revisionist critique of Lincoln's view of the Constitution and defends the Taney Court's decision, noting that "no matter how morally wrong and constitutionally egregious," the decision was accepted by enough Americans "to prevent further disruption to an endangered constitutional order."

Hyman, Harold, and Wiecek, William. *Equal Justice under Law: Constitutional Development 1835–1875*. New York: Harper & Row, 1982. Hyman and Wiecek provide a readable survey that connects political and legal developments in the antebellum, Civil War, and Reconstruction eras.

Lincoln, Abraham. "Speech at Springfield, Illinois," June 26, 1857, in *Collected Works of Abraham Lincoln*, edited by Roy P. Basler, 9 volumes. New Brunswick, N.J.: Rutgers University Press, 1953–1955. Ann Arbor: University of Michigan Digital Library Production Services <http://quod.lib.umich.edu/cgi/t/text/text-idx?c=lincoln;cc=lincoln;view=text;idno=lincoln2;rgn=div1;node=lincoln2%3A438> [accessed January 16, 2008].

Lincoln-Douglas Debates, "Second Debate at Freeport Illinois, August, 1858" <http://www.nps.gov/archive/liho/debate2.htm> [accessed July 7, 2007]. In this debate, Lincoln attempts to force Douglas to show how he can reconcile popular sovereignty with his support of the Taney Court's ruling in Dred Scott.

Potter, David. *The Impending Crisis: 1848–1861*. New York: Harper & Row, 1976. Still the best book on the coming of the Civil War, Potter emphasizes the Scott decision as "ruinous" because it "converted the charter of freedom into a safeguard of liberty."

Scott v. Sandford. Supreme Court Collection, Cornell University Law School <http://www.law.cornell.edu/supct/html/historics/USSC_CR_0060_0393_ZO.html> [accessed January 16, 2008]. The Cornell Legal Information Institute has made available on-line the full decisions of all nine justices who ruled on the Dred Scott case.

Simon, James F. *Lincoln and Chief Justice Taney: Slavery, Secession and the President's War Powers*. New York: Simon & Schuster, 2006. Simon writes a popular account of the relationship between Lincoln and Taney that explores the two men's disagreements on slavery and the use of executive power.

Stampp, Kenneth. *America in 1857: A Nation on the Brink*. New York: Oxford University Press, 1990. This narrative frames the Dred Scott decision within the broader context of the year 1857. Stampp contrasts the relatively unified Democratic response to Dred Scott with the deep divisions caused among Democrats by events in Kansas.

Streichler, Stuart. *Justice Curtis in the Civil War Era: At the Crossroads of American Constitutionalism*. Charlottesville: University of Virginia Press, 2005. This useful study details the legal philosophy of the Court's most famous dissenter in the Dred Scott case.

Sunstein, Cass. "*Dred Scott v. Sandford* and Its Legacy," in *Great Cases in Constitutional Law*, edited by Robert P. George. Princeton, N.J.: Princeton University Press, 2000. A brief essay that critiques the legal reasoning of the Court and also suggests that the case "argues against efforts to take the great moral issues out of politics."

Swisher, Carl. *History of the Supreme Court: The Taney Period*, volume 5. New York: Macmillan, 1974. A magisterial treatment of the full body of Supreme Court jurisprudence under Taney's leadership as chief justice, including a substantial discussion of the Dred Scott case.

Wiecek, William. "Slavery and Abolition before the United States Supreme Court, 1820–1860." *Journal of American History*, 65 (June 1978): 34–59. This article provides a succinct summary of relevant court rulings in the period before and after *Dred Scott v. Sandford*. Wiecek holds that the Dred Scott decision "does not appear exceptional or anomalous" in relation to the Taney Court's handling of suits involving slavery.

~ 3 ~

Antebellum Compromises

Slavery continued to be a stumbling block for America as the young nation expounded its destiny as a republic of freedom, democracy, and equality. The Missouri Compromises of 1820 and 1821, the Compromise of 1850, and the Kansas-Nebraska Act of 1854 were all attempts to keep the different sections of the country from destroying the Union of states in the wake of the post-Revolutionary generation.

Several important questions faced the nation at that time: was the United States capable of resolving the incompatibility of slavery and democracy? What role would the federal government, particularly Congress, play in either protecting or restricting slavery in new territories? Was sectional conflict inevitable?

The viability of slavery and its relation to the geographical expansion of the young republic were the underlying issues related to these three "compromises." Each compromise affected the extent to which slavery survived during the development of the United States.

By the time the Missouri Territory sought admission to the Union in February 1819, at least ten thousand slaves resided there. Fearful of a growing "slave power" in American politics in addition to an opposition to slavery, Representative James Tallmadge Jr. of New York offered a remedy representing the views of like-minded Northerners. Tallmadge added to the bill enabling Missouri statehood an amendment that declared freedom to all slaves born after its admission and gradual emancipation for all other slaves (see Document 1). The House, after considerable debate, passed this initial bill with Tallmadge's amendment and sent it to the Senate. The following month, the Senate passed the House's version of the Missouri bill deleting the restrictions on slavery. The House maintained its insistence in keeping the bill with the attached amendment. Without compromise, the Missouri bill died when Congress adjourned its session.

The next session of Congress convened in December 1819 with both houses taking up debate on Missouri statehood. By February 1820 in the Senate, the Missouri bill was attached as an amendment to a bill to admit Maine (then a part of Massachusetts). Senator Jesse Thomas of Illinois attached an additional amendment to exclude slavery, with the exception of Missouri, from territory north of the 36°30′ line of latitude. All territory south of this line would be open to slavery. This "First Missouri Compromise" became law on March 6, 1820, and Maine became the twenty-third state.

Missouri submitted its state constitution, which required its legislature to enact laws barring free persons of color from entering and settling in the state. This caused considerable consternation in Congress during its following session. Several congressmen, including Henry Clay of Kentucky (who had been Speaker of the House in the previous session), believed that this particular clause violated section two of Article IV of the U.S. Constitution, which provided that "citizens of each State shall be entitled to all the privileges and immunities of citizens in the several States."

As things began to reach a crisis point, Clay was given permission to chair a House special committee to meet with a corresponding Senate special committee to resolve the Missouri question. Clay was able to negotiate a conditional resolution that forbade the Missouri legislature from passing any law restricting settlement of

In this illustration by P. F. Rothermel (subsequently engraved by R. Whitechurch), Henry Clay offers the Compromise of 1850 to the U.S. Senate in February 1850 (Library of Congress)

persons of any description who were U.S. citizens or who would become U.S. citizens. By June 1821 the Missouri legislature accepted the conditions for admittance, but stated that the U.S. Congress had no right to bind them with such provisions. Nevertheless, the "Second Missouri Compromise" was approved, and Missouri became the twenty-fourth state in the Union. Very little enforcement of this Second Compromise was undertaken.

Of the three antebellum compromises, the Missouri debates in Congress were the most frank and heated. The Missouri Compromises established definitive areas where slavery could and could not exist, giving both Northerners and Southerners everything they sought in limited areas.

When former president Thomas Jefferson considered the dangers that the Missouri Compromise posed for the future, he wrote, "we have the wolf by the ears, and we can neither hold him, nor safely let him go. Justice is in one scale, and self-preservation in the other" (Risjord, 1994, 192).

The election of Andrew Jackson in 1828 as the seventh U.S. president ushered in the Second American Party System, pitting this "champion of the common man" against Henry Clay and his "American System," which advocated government-sponsored internal improvements and encouraged American industrial growth. By 1834, Clay's political opposition to Jackson and his

Democratic Party was formalized into the Whig Party. During this period, states' rights and threats of secession began to be seriously considered by Southerners.

Viewing Thomas Jefferson's and James Madison's Virginia and Kentucky Resolutions of 1798 to form the basis of his argument, John C. Calhoun reasserted that the United States was a compact among the individual, independent, and sovereign states. When Congress overstepped its legislative powers, he reasoned, states had a right to challenge these acts. In the secretly composed "South Carolina Exposition and Protest" Calhoun argued, with a group of South Carolina politicians, that a single state might suspend a federal law which it regarded as unconstitutional—making it "null and void"—until three-quarters of the states had justified the law through the amendment power. This nullification document was presented as a resolution in the South Carolina House of Representatives in December 1828.

In his 1831 "Fort Hill Address" that circulated as a pamphlet, Calhoun reiterated his belief that the Constitution was a compact of sovereign states, arguing that the tariff issue was indicative of the power of the federal government to infringe on the sovereign power of the states and that such federal power could also threaten other domestic institutions such as slavery. By February 1832, the U.S. Congress passed another tariff that reduced some of its rates from the one passed in 1828, but not to South Carolina's satisfaction. On November 24, 1832, South Carolina passed an ordinance of nullification declaring federal tariffs "null and void and no law." These measures declared that the state did not have to abide by or enforce such laws in the state as of February 1, 1833. In response, President Jackson issued his Nullification Proclamation in December 1832 and urged Congress to pass a "force bill" that would authorize him to use the army and navy to force payment of the appropriate customs duties, particularly in Charleston, South Carolina. This force bill also declared South Carolina's actions as treason. Senator Henry Clay devised a compromise in February 1833 where South Carolina would agree to "nullify" their nullification ordinance in return for a gradual reduction of tariffs over a period of time. South Carolina responded by nullifying Jackson's force bill after Jackson had agreed not to invade the state.

The rise of the abolitionist movement in the North coincided with the growing push for states' rights in the South. In 1833, the American Anti-Slavery Society was formed with state and local affiliates throughout the North. Created to appeal to the moral consciousness of slaveholders, the American Anti-Slavery Society sought to address the general public and lawmakers at every level through the distribution of antislavery literature and petitions. It is estimated that some five hundred thousand petitions were sent to Congress during this decade calling for the abolishment of the domestic slave trade, the end of slavery in the District of Columbia, and the removal of the ³/₅ Clause from the Constitution.

Although Jackson supported the preservation of the Union over states' rights, he was a slaveholder, and in 1835, he called for Northern states to suppress abolitionist and antislavery literature that he considered "incendiary." He also sanctioned Postmaster General Amos Kendall to quietly allow postmasters in the South's major cities to illegally destroy suspected abolitionist material in the mail. From 1836 to 1844, the House of Representatives "tabled" a majority of the petitions sent for consideration by abolitionists.

In December 1845, John O'Sullivan, editor of the *Democratic Review*, wrote that it is "our manifest destiny to overspread and to possess the whole of the continent which Providence has given us for the development of the great experiment of liberty." Manifest Destiny, a concept that had been in practice since the establishment of the American colonies, articulated and perhaps best realized during the 1840s, promised a better future for all who called themselves American with a sense of providential purpose. The annexation of Texas and the subsequent war with Mexico put into question whether this "Manifest Destiny" reflected the views of a majority of Americans or if it was an attempt through patriotic propaganda to unify a fragmented nation over the issue of slavery.

Approximately thirty thousand American nationals resided in East Texas by 1835, outnumbering Mexican residents by a ratio of six to one. And although Mexico outlawed slavery when it achieved independence from Spain in 1821, the American settlers there continued to bring slaves into the province. In 1836, Texans revolted, initially defeated on March 6 by the Mexican Army at the Alamo in present-day San Antonio. Seven months later, the Army of the Republic of Texas defeated Mexican forces and became an independent republic for the next nine years.

President John Tyler of Virginia, who succeeded President William Henry Harrison upon his death in 1841, pushed for the annexation of Texas along with Calhoun, his secretary of state. Calhoun concluded that if Texas was not annexed to the United States, Great Britain could bring it under its sphere of influence, potentially undermining the existence of slavery in the United States and risking another war with the former "mother country." Tyler, who did not run for election in 1844, approved a joint resolution of Congress as one of his last acts in office, annexing Texas as the fifteenth slave state in early 1845.

The presidential campaign of 1844 pitted James K. Polk of Tennessee as the standard-bearer for the Democrats against one of the Whigs' perennial candidates, Henry Clay. Former-slaveholder-turned-antislavery-advocate newspaper editor James G. Birney headed a third-party campaign called the Liberty Party, the first political party designed to weaken the "slave power" by promoting the abolition of slavery.

Polk won the election, becoming the first "dark horse" (or not popularly known) candidate to win the presidency. Hoping to avoid war with Great Britain, President Polk negotiated a treaty that settled the U.S. border at the 49th parallel. Polk wanted the Mexican possessions of California and New Mexico, and he aimed to establish the Texas border with Mexico at the Rio Grande even if meant war. After his offer to pay for the desired territories were spurned by Mexico, Polk ordered U.S. troops under General Zachary Taylor to Texas in late 1845. After the Mexican cavalry crossed into Texas and attacked a small body of American troops, the United States declared war on Mexico on May 13, 1846. The war lasted almost two years and claimed thirteen thousand American lives.

After defeating the Mexican Army, the United States negotiated the Treaty of Guadalupe-Hidalgo, purchasing California and New Mexico, and securing the Texas border at the Rio Grande. The Mexican War and its aftermath was the launching point of renewed debate and conflict over the future of slavery in the newly acquired territories.

Four prevalent "solutions" that dominated the four-year debate dealing with slavery in the territories leading to the Compromise of 1850 were the Wilmot Proviso, "Common Property" Doctrine, the extension of the Missouri Compromise Line, and popular sovereignty. These solutions reflected the political and geographical ideologies involved in this debate.

Representative David Wilmot of Pennsylvania was a first-term Democrat and a supporter of President Polk's war policy, but he voiced concerns over the growing slave power. On August 8, 1846, almost three months after war was declared, Wilmot attached an amendment—soon called the Wilmot Proviso—to a House appropriations bill, which stated that "neither slavery nor involuntary servitude shall ever exist in any part of said territory, except for crime, whereof the party shall first be duly convicted" (see Document 2a). This preemptive measure restricting slavery from potential U.S. territories gained bipartisan support from the northern wings of both the Democratic and Whig Parties. The proviso passed the House but was stricken from the bill when it reached the Senate. Wilmot attached a similar amendment to another appropriations bill the following year with the same result; however, the Wilmot Proviso succeeded in spawning the "Free Soil" Movement among Northerners fearful of the political primacy of the "slave power" and the potential economic competition between white Northerners and slaveholders who were bringing slaves into the territories.

Advocating the constitutional right of slaveholders to carry property into federal territory, Senator Calhoun inaugurated what was called his "Common Property" Doctrine (see Document 3). This doctrine argued that Congress could not promote or exclude slavery from the territories since the holding of slaves as property was guaranteed by the Constitution. Therefore, he reasoned, the Wilmot Proviso and any other congressional mandate on slavery—the Missouri Compromise implied—were unconstitutional. Southerners in both major political parties embraced Calhoun's logic, while many Northerners were repelled by his mode of thinking.

In his final annual message to Congress at the end of 1848, President Polk recommended extending the 36° 30′ parallel of the Missouri Compromise Line to the Pacific Ocean in order to include the majority of the Mexican Cession. While Polk believed that individual states held the exclusive right to determine whether slavery was legal, he acquiesced to this compromise (see Document 4). This posed problems geographically for California, an independent republic that, within two years, sought statehood as a free state.

"Popular sovereignty" gained ground during the presidential election of 1848. Originally attributed to Democratic Party nominee Lewis Cass of Michigan, popular sovereignty advocated giving residents of a territory seeking statehood the power to decide if their future state would support or restrict slavery within its boundaries. For many of its disciples, this concept took away from Congress the decision-making burden regarding slavery that many believed it did not have constitutional authority to legislate. Moreover, popular sovereignty gained broad support, North and South, with the idea that slavery had an equal chance of maintaining a foothold in the territories as it did of being restricted.

These four competing solutions to the escalating debate over slavery in the territories culminated in the Compromise of 1850. This compromise attempted to maintain the peace between the North and the South over both the issue of slavery and the governance of the newly acquired territories by the "old guard" politicians of the Jacksonian era. Henry Clay offered eight resolutions in the Senate in January 1850 (see Document 5) that included the admission of California as a free state, the organization of both Utah and New Mexico Territories under popular sovereignty, the settlement of the boundary issues between Texas and the New Mexico territory, the abolition of the slave trade in the District of Columbia, and the strengthening of the federal fugitive slave law.

In his "Great Compromise" speech on February 5–6, Clay expressed his dismay that Congress had to revisit sectional conflict over slavery that he had helped resolve two decades earlier. He urged the acceptance of his compromise resolutions before the nation realized the fearful consequences of dissolving the Union (see Document 6). Calhoun followed on March 4, arguing that Clay's resolutions benefited Northern antislavery sentiment while at the expense of the South and its desire to protect slavery (see Document 7). Webster's oft-quoted "Seventh of March" speech supported the Compromise Resolutions, but denounced the various antislavery societies in the North that he believed agitated the slavery question. "We all know the fact, and we all know the cause, and everything that this agitating people have done, has been, not to enlarge, but to restrain, not to set free, but to bind faster the slave population of the South," Webster surmised about the abolitionists (see Document 8). Although Webster received great praise for his remarks by supporters of the Compromise Resolutions, many in the North felt betrayed by what they perceived as a son of New England bowing to the pressures of the "Slave Power."

Clay's resolutions faced potential opposition if voted on as a whole package. Senator Stephen A. Douglas of Illinois, a Democrat, reached across party lines and proposed that the legislative package be broken into distinct and separate bills. By doing so, Douglas and others were able to get the needed majorities for all the items to be passed and signed into law by President Millard Fillmore (who succeeded President Zachary Taylor following his death in July) in September 1850.

Capitalizing on his success in skillfully managing the passage of the legislative initiatives included in the Compromise of 1850, Senator Stephen A. Douglas introduced a bill to organize the vast Nebraska Territory in January 1854. The final bill, passed four months later, divided the larger territory into two small sections: Nebraska Territory and Kansas Territory (see Document 9). The residents were authorized to decide whether they would be "slave" or "free" through popular sovereignty, a concept of which Douglas became a champion. The bill gained support from the Southern wings of the two major political parties (Democrats and Whigs) as well as from half of Northern Democrats seeking to avoid sectional conflict. The Kansas-Nebraska Act sought to promote westward expansion at the expense of upsetting the thirty-four-year geographic balance implemented by the Missouri Compromises.

Kansas Territory soon became the testing ground for popular sovereignty as it sat literally on the geographic borderline between slavery and freedom. From 1854 to 1858, violence erupted in Kansas between proslavery and antislavery settlers, bringing about two separate territorial seats of government that was not resolved until late January 1861 when Kansas was admitted to the Union as a free state and six slave states had already left the Union preparing to organize themselves into the Confederate States of America.

The future of slavery and the role of Congress in that decision were influenced by the Supreme Court in *Scott v. Sandford* (1857). Dred Scott, a Missouri slave, sued for his freedom since his owner had taken him into Illinois and later to Wisconsin Territory. The Supreme Court in a 7-2 decision ruled that Dred Scott's status as a slave did not change when he was taken into "free" territory and then returned to Missouri. Chief Justice Roger B. Taney, writing the majority opinion for the Court, stated that as a slave, Scott did not have the rights and privileges accorded to U.S. citizens. Moreover, Taney declared that, since slaves were property protected under the Constitution, Congress had no right to legislate on slavery; therefore, the Missouri Compromise of nearly forty years earlier was unconstitutional (see Document 10).

The three antebellum compromises were temporary measures that delayed definitive action on the institution of slavery for four decades. Once sectional allegiance overcame political party allegiance, national coalitions could not survive. It was abundantly clear by 1857 that the United States could neither live half-slave nor half-free.

James K. Bryant II

CHRONOLOGY

1803

April 30: Final agreement of the Louisiana Purchase treaty is negotiated between the United States and France.

October 21: Louisiana Purchase treaty is ratified by the U.S. Senate and the territory is declared a possession of the United States of America.

October 31: U.S. Congress establishes a territorial government for Louisiana.

1804

March 26: U.S. Congress passes an act that divides Louisiana into two territories: Territory of Orleans (Lower Louisiana below the southern border of Arkansas) and District of Louisiana (encompassing the territory including Arkansas north). The latter "district" is under administrative control of the Indiana Territory.

1805

March 3: U.S. Congress passes an act creating the Territory of Louisiana from the District of Louisiana, separating it from the Indiana Territory, and establishing territorial government.

1812

April 30: Territory of Orleans admitted into the Union as Louisiana the eighteenth state.

June 4: Territory of Louisiana becomes Territory of Missouri.

June 18: The United States declares war on Great Britain, starting the War of 1812.

1814

December 24: American and British representtives sign the Treaty of Ghent, ending the War of 1812.

1815

January 8: General Andrew Jackson's forces, unaware of the Treaty of Ghent, defeat British forces at the Battle of New Orleans.

February 16: The United States ratifies the Treaty of Ghent.

1819

February 13: The U.S. House of Representatives takes up consideration of enabling the people of Missouri Territory to form a state government. Representative James Tallmadge Jr. of New York proposes an amendment restricting new slaves from being brought into Missouri, emancipating slaves currently residing in Missouri by age twenty-five, and declaring free those born in Missouri after it is admitted into the Union. House adjourns without taking any further action.

February 17: Bill to admit Missouri to statehood with slavery restrictions passes the House.

February 27: The U.S. Senate passes the Missouri bill without the slavery restrictions.

March 2: House takes up the Senate's version of the Missouri bill to admit. The House refuses to strike out the slavery restrictions clause. Without concurrence of both Houses of Congress, the bill is dropped.

December 14: Alabama is admitted to the Union as the twenty-second state.

1820

January 3: The U.S. House of Representatives passes a bill admitting Maine (formerly a part of Massachusetts) into the Union.

February 16: The U.S. Senate takes up consideration of admitting Missouri into the Union by attaching it as an amendment to the bill admitting Maine into the Union. Senator Jesse B. Thomas of Illinois proposes a compromise amendment in three parts: 1.) allow Missouri to draft a constitution without slavery restrictions; 2.) admit Maine, that prohibits slavery, as a free state to achieve sectional balance; 3.) prohibit slavery from the area existing north of the 36°30′ line and allow slavery south of the line in the remaining parts of the original Louisiana Purchase Territory.

March 2: Both houses of Congress pass the Maine-Missouri bill.

March 6: The Maine bill with the Missouri admission and slavery amendments are signed into law by President James Monroe, completing the "First Missouri Compromise."

March 15: Maine is admitted as the twenty-third state in the Union.

September 27: Missouri drafts its constitution and includes a clause deeming it a duty of the state legislature "[t]o prevent free negroes and mulattoes from coming to, and settling in, this state, under any pretext whatsoever."

November 14: Proposed Missouri constitution taken up by the U.S. Senate and referred to the appropriate committee.

1821

February 12: A House select committee chaired by Henry Clay of Kentucky offers a resolution to admit Missouri provided that its state legislature does not enact laws barring any description of U.S. citizens or those to become U.S. citizens from residing in the state. This resolution is defeated in the House.

February 23: The House appoints Clay to head another select committee to work with a corresponding Senate committee to resolve the Missouri crisis.

March 2: Both Houses of Congress approve the admission of Missouri.

June: The Missouri state legislature approves of the Congressional measure, but stipulates that Congress does not have the right to bind a state.

August 10: Missouri is admitted as the twenty-fourth state in the Union, completing the "Second Missouri Compromise."

1845

March 1: The United States through a joint resolution of Congress annexes the independent "Lone Star Republic" of Texas.

July 25: General Zachary Taylor lands a force of U.S. troops at Corpus Christi, Texas.

December 29: Texas becomes the twenty-eighth state of the Union and the fifteenth slave state.

1846

May 13: The United States declares war on Mexico.

August 8: Representative David Wilmot of Pennsylvania introduces his amendment to a special appropriation bill outlawing slavery in any territory that might be acquired from Mexico in the war. This becomes commonly known as the "Wilmot Proviso," and the House passes the bill with Wilmot's Amendment.

August 10: The special appropriation bill with the attached Wilmot Proviso dies in the Senate.

1847

February 19: Senator John C. Calhoun of South Carolina submits resolutions guaranteeing constitutional protections for slavery to the Senate.

March 3: Representative David Wilmot of Pennsylvania makes a second attempt to attach the Wilmot Proviso on an appropriation bill that is passed by the House.

1848

February 2: The Treaty of Guadelupe-Hidalgo between the United States and Mexico ends the Mexican War.

December 5: President James K. Polk, in his final Annual Message to Congress, advocates extending the Missouri Compromise Line to the Pacific Ocean to settle growing sectional tensions.

1850

February 5–6: Senator Henry Clay of Kentucky makes his speech in the U.S. Senate in support of his Compromise Resolutions.

March 4: Senator John C. Calhoun of South Carolina makes his last speech (read by Senator James M. Mason of Virginia) against Clay's Compromise Resolutions.

March 7: Senator Daniel Webster of Massachusetts makes his "Seventh of March" Speech in the U.S. Senate in support of Clay's Compromise Resolutions.

March 31: Senator John C. Calhoun of South Carolina dies in Washington, D.C.

July 9: President Zachary Taylor dies in Washington, D.C.

September 9: Clay's Compromise Resolutions admitting California into the Union as a free state; settlement of the Texas-New Mexico boundary issue and organization of New Mexico Territory; and the organization of the Utah Territory passes both houses of Congress.

September 16: Clay's Compromise Resolution on strengthening the federal fugitive slave law (Fugitive Slave Law of 1850) passes both houses of Congress.

September 20: Clay's Compromise Resolution abolishing the slave trade in the District of Columbia passes both houses of Congress.

1852

June 2: Senator Henry Clay of Kentucky dies in Washington, D.C.

October 24: Daniel Webster dies in Marshfield, Massachusetts.

1854

May 20: Congress passes Senator Douglas's Kansas-Nebraska bill.

1857

May 6: Chief Justice Roger B. Taney reads the majority decision in the Supreme Court case *Scott v. Sandford,* declaring that slaves are not recognized as citizens of the United States and that Congress cannot legislate on slavery. The Missouri Compromise is declared unconstitutional.

DOCUMENTS

Document 1: James Tallmadge Jr.'s Proposed Amendment

Inaugurating the forty-year sectional struggle over the future of slavery in the United States, Representative James Tallmadge Jr. of New York (1778–1853) on February 13, 1819, proposed the following amendment to the Missouri statehood enactment bill seeking to halt the extension of slavery in the territories. Tallmadge used this brief clause to influence America's redemption from the "foul stain" of slavery.

Proposed Amendment to a Bill to Authorize the people of Missouri Territory to form a Constitution and State Government, and for the admission of such state into the Union, on an equal footing with the original states by Representative James Tallmadge of New York, February 13, 1819.

And provided also, That the further introduction of slavery or involuntary servitude be prohibited, except for the punishment of crimes, whereof the party shall have been duly convicted; and that all children of slaves, born within the said State [Missouri], after the admission thereof into the Union shall be free, but may be held to service until the age of twenty-five years.

Source:

Annals of Congress, 15th Congress, 2nd session, p. 1170.

Document 2: Failed Amendments Prohibiting Slavery, August 8, 1846, and March 3, 1847

Representative David Wilmot of Pennsylvania, elected as a Democrat in his first Congressional term, supported President James K. Polk's war effort against Mexico. His August 1846 amendment prohibiting slavery in any territory acquired from Mexico stemmed not from a moral repugnance of slavery, but as a protective measure for free white settlers against the growing "Slave Power." Although this amendment passed the House on sectional lines, it died in the Senate. Senator Preston King, a Democrat, offered a similar amendment on a Senate bill in February 1847; this also failed to pass. Wilmot attached a third amendment on March 3, 1847, that met the same fate as the first "proviso."

Amendment to "An Act Making Further Provision for the Expenses Attending the Intercourse between the United States and Foreign Nations" by Representative David Wilmot of Pennsylvania, August 8, 1846

Provided, That, as an express and fundamental condition to the acquisition of any territory from the Republic of Mexico by the United States, by virtue of any treaty which may be negotiated between them, and to the use by the Executive of the moneys herein appropriated, neither slavery nor involuntary servitude shall ever exist in any part of said territory, except for crime, whereof the party shall first be duly convicted.

Source:

Congressional Globe, 29th Congress, 1st Session, p. 1217.

Amendment to "The Three Million Bill" by Representative David Wilmot of Pennsylvania, March 3, 1847

Provided, That there shall be neither slavery nor involuntary servitude in any territory on the continent of America which shall hereafter be acquitted by or annexed to the United states by virtue of this appropriation, or in any other manner whatever, except for crimes, whereof the party shall have been duly convicted. *Provided, always,* That every person escaping into such territory from whom labor or servitude is lawfully claimed in any one of the United States, such fugitive may be lawfully claimed and conveyed out of said territory to the power claiming his or her labor or service.

Source:

Congressional Globe, 29th Congress, 2nd Session, p. 573.

Document 3: John C. Calhoun's Resolutions

John C. Calhoun (1782–1850), former vice president and secretary of state, and a senator from South Carolina when these resolutions were introduced on February 19, 1847, stepped up his agitation for federal policies protecting states' rights and "domestic institutions"—namely, slavery. In response to Representative David Wilmot's "proviso" prohibiting slavery in the territories that might be gained from Mexico and to the growing Northern support for "Free Soil," Calhoun proposed the following resolutions in the Senate. The central element of these resolutions was that Congress did not have constitutional authority to legislate over property (including slaves). These resolutions, better known as the "Common Property Doctrine," strongly influenced the Scott v. Sandford *Supreme Court decision. Although the resolutions did not come up for further debate, they articulated the position of Calhoun and other Southern politicians that soon underlined the basis for an emerging "Solid South."*

Resolutions introduced in the Senate of the United States, by Senator John C. Calhoun of South Carolina, February 19, 1847

Resolved, That the territories of the United States belong to the several States composing the Union, and are held by them as their joint and common property.

Resolved, That Congress as the joint agent and representative of the States of this Union, has no right to make any law, or do any act whatever, that shall directly, or by its effects, make any discrimination between the states of this Union, by which any of them shall be deprived of its full and equal right in any territory of the United States acquired or to be acquired.

Resolved, That the enactment of any law which should directly, or by its effects, deprive the citizens of any of the States of this Union from emigrating, with their property, into any of the territories of the United States, will make such discrimination, and would, therefore, be a violation of the Constitution, and the rights of the States from which such citizens emigrated, and in derogation of that perfect equality which belongs to them as members of this Union, and would tend directly to subvert the Union itself.

Resolved, That it is a fundamental principle in our political creed, that a people, in forming a constitution, have the unconditional right to form and adopt the government which they may think best calculated to secure their liberty, prosperity, and happiness; and that, in conformity thereto, no other condition is imposed by the Federal Constitution on a State, in order to be admitted into this Union, except that its Constitution shall be republican; and that the imposition of any other by Congress would not only be in violation of the Constitution, but in direct conflict with the principle on which our political system rests.

Source:

Congressional Globe, 29th Congress, 2nd Session, p. 455.

Document 4: James K. Polk's Address to Congress

President James K. Polk (1795–1849), in his fourth and final annual address to Congress on December 5, 1848, recommended the extension of the 1820 Missouri Compromise Line to the Pacific Ocean, which would allow the continuation of slavery below the 36°30′ parallel line and restrict it from the territory above it. Although the president was a slaveholder, he believed that the Constitution guaranteed property rights in the territories (including the right to own slaves); Polk believed his suggestion would preserve "the Union, its harmony, and our continued prosperity as a nation." If all else failed, he surmised, the federal courts would ultimately decide the issue; Polk somewhat anticipated the 1857 Scott v. Sandford *decision.*

Excerpts from fourth annual message to Congress President James K. Polk, December 5, 1848

... Whether Congress shall legislate or not, the people of the acquired territories, when assembled in convention to form State constitutions, will possess the sole and exclusive power to determine for themselves whether slavery shall or shall not exist within their limits. If Congress shall abstain from interfering with the question, the people of these territories will be left free to adjust it as they may think proper when they apply for admission as States into the Union. No enactment of Congress could restrain the people of any of the sovereign States of the Union, old or new, North or South, slaveholding or nonslaveholding, from determining the character of their own domestic institutions as they may deem wise and proper.... The people of Georgia might if they choose so alter their constitution as to abolish slavery within its limits, and the people of Vermont might so alter their constitution as to admit slavery within its limits. Both States would possess the right, though, as all know, it is not probable that either would exert it.

It is fortunate for the peace and harmony of the Union that this question is in its nature temporary and can only continue for the brief period which will intervene before California and New Mexico may be admitted as States into the Union. From the tide of population now flowing into them it is highly probable that this will soon occur.

Considering the several States and the citizens of the several States as equals and entitled to equal rights under the Constitution, if this were an original question it might well be insisted on that the principle of noninterference is the true doctrine and that Congress could not, in the absence of any express grant of power, interfere with their relative rights. Upon a great emergency, however, and under menacing dangers to the Union, the Missouri compromise line in respect to slavery was adopted. The same line was extended farther west in the acquisition of Texas. After an acquiescence of nearly thirty years in the principle of compromise recognized and established by these acts, and to avoid the danger to the Union which might follow if it were now disregarded, I have heretofore expressed the opinion that that line of compromise should be extended on the parallel of 36°30′ from the western boundary of Texas, where it now terminates, to the Pacific Ocean. This is the middle ground of compromise, upon which the different sections of the Union may meet, as they have heretofore met. If this be done, it is confidently believed a large majority of the people of every section of the country, however widely their abstract opinions on the subject of slavery may differ, would cheerfully and patriotically acquiesce in it, and peace and harmony would again fill our borders.

The restriction north of the line was only yielded to in the case of Missouri and Texas upon a principle of compromise, made necessary for the sake of preserving the harmony and possibly the existence of the Union.

It was upon these considerations that at the close of your last session I gave my sanction to the principle of the Missouri compromise line by approving and signing the bill to establish "the Territorial government of Oregon." From a sincere desire to preserve the harmony of the Union, and in deference for the acts of my predecessors, I felt constrained to yield my acquiescence to the extent to which they had gone in compromising this delicate and dangerous question. But if Congress shall now reverse the decision by which the Missouri compromise was effected, and shall propose to extend the restriction over the whole territory, south as well as north of the parallel of 36° 30′, it will cease to be a compromise, and must be regarded as an original question.

If Congress, instead of observing the course of noninterference, leaving the adoption of their own domestic institutions to the people who may inhabit these territories, or if, instead of extending the Missouri compromise line to the Pacific, shall prefer to submit the legal and constitutional questions which may arise to the decision of the judicial tribunals, as was proposed in a bill which passed the Senate at your last session, an adjustment may be effected in this mode. If the whole subject be referred to the judiciary, all parts of the Union should cheerfully acquiesce in the final decision of the tribunal created by the Constitution for the settlement of all questions which may arise under the Constitution, treaties, and laws of the United States.

Congress is earnestly invoked, for the sake of the Union, its harmony, and our continued prosperity as a nation, to adjust at its present session this, the only dangerous question which lies in our path, if not in some one of the modes suggested, in some other which may be satisfactory.

SOURCE:

Fred L. Israel, ed. *The State of the Union Messages of the Presidents, 1790–1966*, volume 1 (New York: Chelsea House, 1967), pp. 743–744.

Document 5: FEDERAL FUGITIVE SLAVE LAWS

Senator Henry Clay of Kentucky (1777–1852) offered these resolutions on January 29, 1850, in the midst of the sectional debate over slavery and over the admission of California into the Union as a free state. As a major concession to the Southern states, Clay recommended a stronger federal fugitive slave law. Later in the year, Senator James M. Murray of Virginia (1798–1871) drafted the Fugitive Slave Law of 1850, placing the responsibility of recovering runaway slaves on virtually every American citizen and providing compensation to federal commissioners involved in runaway slave cases.

Resolutions introduced in the Senate of the United States, by Senator Henry Clay of Kentucky, January 29, 1850

It being desirable for the peace, concord, and harmony of the Union of these States, to settle and adjust amicably all existing questions of controversy between them, arising out of the institution of slavery, upon a fair, equitable, and just basis: Therefore,

1st. *Resolved,* That California, with suitable boundaries, ought upon her application to be admitted as one of the States of this Union, without the imposition by Congress of any restriction in respect to the exclusion or introduction of slavery within those boundaries.

2d. *Resolved,* That as slavery does not exist by law, and is not likely to be introduced into any of the territory acquired by the United States from the Republic of Mexico, it is inexpedient for Congress to provide by law either for its introduction into or exclusion from any part of the said territory; and that appropriate Territorial governments ought to be established by Congress in all of the said territory, not assigned as the boundaries of the proposed State of California, without the adoption of any restriction or condition on the subject of slavery.

3d. *Resolved,* That the western boundary of the State of Texas ought to be fixed on the Rio del Norte, commencing one marine league from its mouth, and running up that river to the southern line of New Mexico; thence with that line eastwardly, and so continuing in the same direction to the line as established between the United States and Spain, excluding any portion of New Mexico, whether lying on the east or west of that river.

4th. *Resolved,* That it be proposed to the State of Texas that the United States will provide for the payment of all that portion of the legitimate and *bona fide* public debt of that State contracted prior to its annexation to the United States, and for which the duties on foreign imports were pledged by the said State to its creditors, not exceeding the sum of $——, in consideration of the said duties so pledged having been no longer applicable to that object after the said annexation, but having henceforward become payable to the United States; and upon the condition also that the said State of Texas shall, by some solemn and authentic act of her Legislature, or of a convention, relinquish to the United States any claim which it has to any part of New Mexico.

5th. *Resolved,* That it is inexpedient to abolish slavery in the District of Columbia, whilst that institution continues to exist in the State of Maryland, without the consent of that State, without the consent of the people of the District, and without just compensation to the owners of slaves within the District.

6th. *But Resolved,* That it is expedient to prohibit within the District the slave-trade, in slaves brought into it from States or places beyond the limits of the District, either to be sold therein as merchandise, or to be transported to other markets without the District of Columbia.

7th. *Resolved,* That more effectual provision ought to be made by law, according to the requirement of the Constitution, for the restitution and delivery of persons bound to service or labor in any State, who may escape into any other State or Territory in the Union.

And 8th. *Resolved,* That Congress has no power to prohibit or obstruct the trade in slaves between the slaveholding States; but that the admission or exclusion of slaves brought from one into another of them, depends exclusively upon their own particular laws.

Source:

Congressional Globe, 31st Congress, 1st Session, pp. 246–247.

Document 6: Henry Clay's Last Major Speech on Compromise Resolutions

This is Henry Clay's (1777–1852) last major speech in the U.S. Senate on the compromise resolutions that eventually became the Compromise of 1850. Contrary to arguments made by Southern politicians, Clay argues the case for Congress to play a role in deciding the fate of slavery in the territories. By September 1850, Senator Stephen A. Douglas of Illinois (1813–1861) had modified some of Clay's original resolutions, and he soon guided them as separate pieces of legislation that gained broad support from Whigs and Democrats as well as from Southerners and Northerners in both parties.

Excerpts of speech in the Senate of the United States on the Compromise Resolutions, by Senator Henry Clay of Kentucky, February 5–6, 1850

Mr. President, never on any former occasion, have I risen under feelings of such deep solicitude. I have witnessed many periods of great anxiety, of peril, and of danger even to the country; but I have never before arisen to address any assembly so oppressed, so appalled, so anxious. And, sir, I hope it will not be out of place to do here what again and again I have done in my private chamber—to implore of Him who holds the destinies of nations and individuals in his hands, to bestow upon our country his blessings—to bestow upon our people all his blessings—to calm the violence and rage of party—to still passion—to allow reason once more to resume its empire. And may I not ask of Him, to bestow upon his humble servant, now before Him, the blessing of his smiles, of strength and of ability, to perform the work which now lies before him.

Sir, I have said that I have witnessed other anxious periods in the history of our country; and if I were to mention—to trace to their original source—the cause of all our present dangers and difficulties, I should ascribe them to the violence and intemperance of party spirit. We have had testimony of this in the progress of this session, and Senators, however they may differ in other matters, concur in acknowledging the existence of that cause in originating the unhappy differences which prevail throughout the country upon this subject of the institution of slavery....

When I came to consider this subject, there were two or three general purposes which seemed to me to be most desirable, if possible, to accomplish. The one was to settle all the controverted questions arising out of the subject of slavery; and it seemed to me to be doing very little if we settled one question and left other disturbing questions unadjusted. It seemed to me to be doing but little if we stopped one leak only in the ship of State, and left other leaks capable of producing danger, if not destruction, to the vessel. I therefore turned my attention to every subject connected with the institution of slavery, and out of which controverted questions have sprung, to see if it were possible or practicable to accommodate and adjust the whole of them.

Another principal object which attracted my attention was, to endeavor to frame such a scheme of accommodation that neither of the two classes of States into which our country is unhappily divided should make a sacrifice of any great principle. I believe, sir, the series of resolutions which I have had the honor of presenting to the Senate accomplishes that object.

Another purpose, sir, which I had in view was this: I was aware of the difference of opinion prevailing between these two classes of States. I was aware that, while a portion of the Union was pushing matters, as it seemed to me, to a dangerous extremity, another portion of the Union was pushing them to an opposite, and perhaps to a no less dangerous extremity. It appeared to me, then, that if any arrangement, any satisfactory adjustment could be made of the controverted questions between the two classes of states, that adjustment, that arrangement, could only be successful and effectual by exacting from both parties some concession—not of principle, not of principle at all, but of feeling, of opinion, in relation to the matters in controversy between them. I believe that the resolutions which I have prepared fulfill that object. I believe that you will find upon that careful, rational, and attentive examination of them which I think they deserve, that by them, neither party makes any concession of principle at all, though the concessions of forebearance are ample.

In the next place, in respect to the slaveholding States, there are resolutions making concessions to them by the class of opposite States, without any compensation whatever being rendered by them to the non-slaveholding States.

I think everyone of these characteristics which I have assigned to the measures which I propose is susceptible of clear, satisfactory demonstration, by an attentive perusal and critical examination of the resolutions themselves....

The great principle which was in contest upon the memorable occasion of the introduction of Missouri into the Union was, whether it was competent or was not competent for Congress to impose any restriction which should exist after she became a member of the Union? We, who were in favor of the admission of Missouri, contended that, by the Constitution, no such restriction could be imposed. We contended that, whenever she was once admitted into the Union, she had all the rights and privileges of any preexisting State of the Union; and that of these rights and privileges, one was to decide for herself whether slavery should or should not exist within her limits—that she has as much a right to decide upon the introduction of slavery, or upon its abolition, as New York has a right to decide upon the introduction or abolition of slavery; and that she stood among her peers equal, and invested with all the privileges that any one of the thirteen States, and those subsequently admitted, had a right to enjoy....

The power, Mr. President, in my opinion—and I extend it to the introduction as well as to the prohibition of slavery in the new territories—does exist in Congress; and I think there is this important distinction between slavery outside of the States and slavery inside of the

States; that all outside of the States is debatable, and all inside of the States is not debatable. The Government has no right to attack the institution within the States; but whether she has, and to what extent she has or has not, the right to attack slavery outside of the States, is a debatable question—one upon which men may honorably and fairly differ; and however it may be decided, furnishes, I trust, no just occasion for breaking up this glorious Union of ours. . . .

What do you want?—what do you want?—you who reside in the free States. Do you want that there shall be no slavery introduced into the territories acquired by the war with Mexico? Have you not your desire in California? And in all human probability you will have it in New Mexico also. What more do you want? You have got what is worth more than a thousand Wilmot provisos. You have nature on your side—facts upon your side—and this truth staring you in the face, that there is no slavery in those territories. If you are not infuriated, if you can elevate yourselves from the mud and mire of mere party contentions, to the purer regions of patriotism, what will you not do? Look at the fact as it exists. You will see that this fact was unknown to the great majority of the people; you will see that they acted upon one state of facts, before us; and we will act as patriots—as responsible men, and as lovers of liberty, and lovers, above all, of this Union.

[February 6, 1850]

Now Mr. President, I think that the existing laws for the recovery of fugitive slaves, and the restoration and delivering of them to their owners, being often inadequate and ineffective, it is incumbent upon Congress—(and I hope that hereafter, when a better state of feeling, when more harmony and good-will prevails among the various parts of this Confederacy—I hope it will be regarded by the free States themselves as a part of their duty)—to assist allaying this subject, so irritating and disturbing to the peace of this Union. At all events, whether they do it or not, it is our duty to do it. It is our duty to make laws more effective; and I will go with the farthest Senator from the South in this body to make penal laws, to impose the heaviest sanctions upon the recovery of fugitive slaves, and the restoration of them to their owners. . . .

I have said that I never could vote for it myself, and I repeat that I never can, and never will vote, and no earthly power will ever make me vote to spread slavery over territory where it does not exist. Still, if there be a majority who are for interdicting slavery north of the line, there ought to be a majority, if justice is done to the South, to admit slavery south of the line. And if there be a majority to accomplish both these purposes, although I cannot concur in their action, yet I shall be one of the last to create any disturbance; I shall be one of the first to acquiesce in that legislation, although it is contrary to my own judgment and to my own conscience.

I hope then to keep the whole of these matters untouched by any legislation of Congress upon the subject of slavery, leaving it open and undecided. Non-action by Congress is best for the South, and best for all views which the South have disclosed to us from time to time as corresponding to their wishes. I know it has been said with regard to the territories, and especially has it been said with regard to California, that non-legislation upon the part of Congress implies the same thing as the exclusion of slavery. That we cannot help. That Congress is not responsible for. If nature has pronounced the doom of slavery in these territories—if she has declared, by her immutable laws, that slavery cannot and shall not be introduced there—who can you reproach but nature and nature's God? Congress you cannot. Congress abstains. Congress is passive. Congress is non-acting, south and north of the line; or rather if Congress agrees to the plan which I propose, extending no line, it leaves the entire theatre of the whole cession of these territories untouched by legislative enactments, either to exclude or admit slavery. Well, I ask again, if you will listen to the voice of calm and dispassionate reason—I ask of any man of the South, to rise and tell me if it is not better for that section of the Union, that Congress should remain passive upon both sides of the ideal line, rather than that we should interdict slavery upon the one side of that line and be passive upon the other side of that line?

. . . Sir, do I depict with colors too lively the prosperity which has resulted to us from the operation of the Constitution under which we live? Have I exaggerated in any degree?

Now, let me go a little into detail as to the sway in the councils of the nation, whether of the North or of the South, during the sixty years of unparalleled prosperity that we enjoy. During the first twelve years of the administration of the Government, northern counsels rather prevailed; and out of them sprung the Bank of the United States; the assumption of the State debts; bounties to the fisheries; protection to the domestic manufacturers—I allude to the act of 1789; neutrality in the wars with Europe; Jay's treaty; alien and sedition laws; and a *quasi* war with France. I do not say, sir, that those leading and prominent measures which were adopted during the administration of Washington and the elder Adams were carried exclusively by northern counsels. They could not have been, but were carried mainly by the sway which northern counsels had obtained in the affairs of the country.

So, also, with the latter party, for the last fifty years....

Such is the Union, and such are its glorious fruits. We are told now, and it is rung throughout this entire country, that the Union is threatened with subversion and destruction. Well, the first question which naturally arises is, supposing the Union to be dissolved—having all the causes of grievances which are complained of—how far will a dissolution furnish a remedy for those grievances? If the Union is to be dissolved for any existing causes, it will be dissolved because slavery is interdicted or not allowed to be introduced into the ceded territories; because slavery is threatened to be abolished in the District of Columbia, and because fugitive slaves are not returned, as in my opinion they ought to be, and restored to their masters. These I believe will be the causes, if there be any causes, which can lend to the direful event to which I have referred.

Well, now, let us suppose that the Union has been dissolved. What remedy does it furnish for the grievances complained of in its united condition? Will you be able to push slavery into the ceded territories? How are you to do it, supposing the North—all the States north of the Potomac, and which are opposed to it—in possession of the navy and army of the United States? Can you expect, if there is dissolution of the union, that you can carry slavery into California and New Mexico? You cannot dream of such a purpose....

But, I must take the occasion to say that, in my opinion, there is no right in the part of one or more of the States to secede from the Union. War and the dissolution of the Union are identical and inseparable. There can be no dissolution of the Union, except by consent or by war. No one can expect, in the existing state of things, that that consent would be given, and war is the only alternative by which a dissolution could be accomplished. And, Mr. President, if consent were given—if possibly we were to separate by mutual agreement and by a given line, in less than sixty days after such an agreement had been executed, war would break out between the free and slaveholding portions of this Union—between the two independent portions into which it would be erected in virtue of the act of separation. Yes, sir, sixty days—in *less* time than sixty days, I believe, our slaves from Kentucky would be fleeing over in numbers to the other side of the river, would be pursued by their owners, and the excitable and ardent spirits who would engage in the pursuit would be restrained by no sense of the rights which appertain to the independence of the other side of the river, supposing it, then, to be the line of separation. They would pursue their slaves; they would be repelled, and war would break out. In less than sixty days, war would be blazing forth in every part of this now happy and peaceable land....

I said that I thought that there was no right on the part of one or more of the States to secede from this Union. I think that the Constitution of the thirteen States was made, not merely for the generation which then existed, but for posterity, undefined, unlimited, permanent and perpetual—for their prosperity, and for every subsequent State which might come into the Union, binding themselves by that indissoluble bond. It is to remain for that posterity now and forever. Like another of the great relations of private life, it was a marriage that no human authority can dissolve or divorce the parties from; and, if I may be allowed to refer to this same example in private life, let us say what man and wife say to each other: We have mutual faults; nothing in the form of human beings can be perfect; let us, then, be kind to each other, forbearing, conceding; let us live in happiness and peace.

... Look at history—consult the pages of all history, ancient or modern: look at human nature—look at the character of the contest in which you would be engaged in supposition of a war following the dissolution of the Union, such as I have suggested—and I ask you if it is possible for you to doubt that the final but perhaps distant termination of the whole will be some despot treading down the liberties of the people?—that the final result will be the extinction of this last and glorious light which is leading all mankind, who are gazing upon it, to cherish hope and anxious expectation that the liberty which prevails here will sooner or later be advanced throughout the civilized world? Can you, Mr. President, lightly contemplate the consequences? Can you yield yourself to a torrent of passion, amidst dangers which I have depicted in colors far short of what would be the reality, if the event should ever happen? I conjure gentlemen—whether from the South or the North, by all they hold dear in this world—by all their love of liberty—by all their veneration for their ancestors—by all their regard for posterity—by all their gratitude to Him who has bestowed upon them such unnumbered blessings—by all the duties which they owe to mankind, and all the duties they owe to themselves—by all these considerations I implore them to pause—solemnly to pause—at the edge of the precipice, before the fearful and disastrous leap is taken in the yawning abyss below, which will inevitably lead to certain and irretrievable destruction.

And, finally, Mr. President, I implore, as the best blessing which Heaven can bestow upon me upon earth, that if the direful and sad event of the dissolution of the Union shall happen, I may not survive to behold the sad and heart-rending spectacle.

SOURCE:

Appendix to the Congressional Globe, Senate, 31st Congress, 1st Session, pp. 115–127.

Document 7: CALHOUN DEFENDS THE RIGHTS OF THE SOUTH

When Senator John C. Calhoun of South Carolina (1782–1850) made one of his last appearances in the Senate on March 4, 1850, he was too ill to deliver his remarks; he delegated Senator James M. Mason of Virginia to read them. In his speech, Calhoun defended the rights of the South and called for constitutional amendments to maintain the "equilibrium" between the North and South. He warned that if the compromise resolutions passed, the equilibrium would be destroyed and the Union would be endangered.

Excerpts of speech in the Senate of the United States on the Compromise Resolutions, by Senator John C. Calhoun of South Carolina (Read by Senator James M. Mason of Virginia), March 4, 1850

I have, Senators, believed from the first that the agitation of the subject of slavery would, if not prevented by some timely and effective measure, end in disunion. Entertaining this opinion, I have, on all proper occasions, endeavored to call the attention of each of the two great parties which divided the country to adopt some measure to prevent so great a disaster, but without success. The agitation has been permitted to proceed with almost no attempt to resist it, until it has reached a period when it can no longer be disguised or denied that the Union is in danger. You have thus had forced upon you the greatest and gravest question that can ever come under your consideration: How can the Union be preserved?

To give a satisfactory answer to this mighty question, it is indispensable to have an accurate and thorough knowledge of the nature and the character of the cause by which the Union is endangered. Without such knowledge it is impossible to pronounce with any certainty, by what measure it can be saved; just as it would be impossible for a physician to pronounce, in the case of some dangerous disease, with any certainty, by what remedy the patient could be saved, without familiar knowledge of the nature and character of the cause of the disease. The first question, then, presented for consideration, in the investigation I propose to make in order to obtain such knowledge is: What is it that has endangered the Union?

To this question there can be but one answer: that the immediate cause is the almost universal discontent which pervades all the States composing the southern section of the Union. This widely-extended discontent is not of recent origin. It commenced with the agitation of the slavery question, and has been increasing ever since. The next question, going one step further back, is: What has caused this widely-diffused and almost universal discontent?

It is a great mistake to suppose, as is by some, that it originated with demagogues, who excited the discontent with the intention of aiding their personal advancement, or with the disappointed ambition of certain politicians, who resorted to it as the means of retrieving their fortunes. On the contrary, all the great political influences of the section were arrayed against excitement, and exerted to the utmost to keep the people quiet. The great mass of the people of the South were divided, as in the other section, into Whigs and Democrats. The leaders and the presses of both parties in the South were very solicitous to prevent excitement and to preserve quiet; because it was seen that the effects of the former would necessarily tend to weaken, if not destroy, the political ties which united them with their respective parties in the other section. Those who know the strength of party ties will readily appreciate the immense force which this cause exerted against agitation and in favor of preserving quiet. But, as great as it was, it was not sufficiently so to prevent the wide-spread discontent which now pervades the section. No; some cause, far deeper and more powerful than the one supposed, must exist, to account for discontent so wide and deep. The question, then, recurs: What is the cause of this discontent? It will be found in the belief of the people of the southern States, as prevalent as the discontent itself, that they cannot remain, as things now are, consistently with honor and safety, in the Union. The next question to be considered is: What has caused this belief?

One of the causes is, undoubtedly, to be traced to the long-continued agitation of the slave question on the part of the North, and the many aggressions which they have made on the rights of the South during the time. I will not enumerate them at present, as it will be done hereafter in its proper place.

There is another lying back of it, with which this is intimately connected, that may be regarded as the great and primary cause. That is to be found in the fact that the equilibrium between the two sections in the Government, as it stood when the constitution was ratified and the Government put in action, has been destroyed. At that time there was nearly a perfect equilibrium between the two, which afforded ample means to each to protect itself against the aggression of the other; but, as it now stands, one section has the exclusive power of controlling the Government, which leaves the other without any adequate means of protecting itself against its encroachment and oppression....

The result of the whole is to give the Northern section a predominance in every department of the Government, and thereby concentrate in it the two elements which constitute the Federal Government—a majority of States and a majority of their population, estimated in federal numbers. Whatever section concentrates the two in itself possesses the control of the entire Government.

But we are just at the close of the sixth decade, and the commencement of the seventh. The census is to be taken this year, which must add greatly to the decided preponderance of the North in the House of Representatives and in the electoral college. The prospect is, also, that a great increase will be added to its present preponderance in the Senate during the period of the decade, by the addition of new States. Two Territories, Oregon and Minnesota, are already in progress, and strenuous efforts are making to bring in three additional States from the territory recently conquered from Mexico; which, if successful, will add three other States in a short time to the northern section, making five States, and increasing the present number of its States from fifteen to twenty, and of its Senators from thirty to forty. On the contrary, there is not a single territory in progress in the southern section, and no certainty that any additional State will be added to it during the decade. The prospect then, is, that the two sections in the Senate, should the efforts now made to exclude the South from the newly-acquired territories succeed, will stand, before the end of the decade, twenty northern States to twelve [fourteen] Southern, (considering Delaware as neutral), and forty Northern senators to twenty-four [twenty-eight] southern. This great increase of Senators, added to the great increase of members of the House of Representatives and the electoral college on the part of the North, which must take place under the next decade, will effectually and irretrievably destroy the equilibrium which existed when the Government commenced.

Had this destruction been the operation of time, without the interference of Government, the South would have had no reason to complain; but such was not the fact. It was caused by the legislation of this Government, which was appointed as the common agent of all, and charged with the protection of the interests and security of all. The legislation by which it has been effected may be classed under three heads. The first is, that series of acts by which the South has been excluded from the common territory belonging to all of the States, as members of the Federal Union, and which have had the effect of extending vastly the portion allotted to the Northern section, and restricting within narrow limits the portion left the South; the next consists in adopting a system of revenue and disbursements, by which an undue proportion of the burden of taxation has been imposed upon the South, and an undue proportion of its proceeds appropriated to the North; and the last is a system of political measures by which the original character of the Government has been radically changed. I propose to bestow upon each of these, in the order they stand, a few remarks, with the view of showing that it is owing to the action of this Government that the equilibrium between the two sections has been destroyed, and the whole powers of the system centered in a sectional majority....

I have not included the territory recently acquired by the treaty with Mexico. The North is making the most strenuous efforts to appropriate the whole to herself, by excluding the South from every foot of it. If she should succeed, it will add to that from which the South has already been excluded 526,078 square miles, and would increase the whole which the North has appropriated to herself to 1,764,023, not including the portion that she may succeed in excluding us from in Texas. To sum up the whole, the United States, since they declared their independence, have acquired 2,373,046 square miles of territory, from which the North will have excluded the South, if she should succeed in monopolizing the newly acquired territories, from about three-fourths of the whole, leaving to the South but about one-fourth.

Such is the first and great cause that has destroyed the equilibrium between the two sections in the government.

The next is the system of revenue and disbursements which has been adopted by the Government. It is well known that the Government has derived its revenue mainly from duties on imports. I shall not undertake to show that such duties must necessarily fall mainly on the exporting States, and that the South, as the great exporting portion of the Union, has in reality paid vastly more than her due proportion of the revenue; because I deem it unnecessary, as the subject has on so many occasions been fully discussed. Nor shall I, for the same reason, undertake to show that a far greater portion of the revenue has been disbursed at the North, than its due share, and that the joint effect of these causes has been to transfer a vast amount from South to North, which, under an equal system of revenue and disbursements, would not have been lost to her. If to this be added, that many of the duties were imposed, not for revenue, but for protection; that is, intended to put money, not in the treasury but directly into the pocket of the manufacturers, some conception may be formed of the immense amount which in the long course of sixty years, has been transferred from South to North. There are no data by which it can be estimated with any certainty; but it is safe to say that it amounts to hundreds of millions of dollars. Under the most moderate estimate, it would be sufficient to add greatly to the wealth of the North, and thus greatly increase her population by attracting emigration from all quarters to that section.

This, combined with the great primary cause, amply explains why the North has acquired a preponderance in every department of the Government by its disproportionate increase of population and States. The former, as has been shown, has increased in fifty years, 2,400,000 over that of the South. This increase of population during so long a period, is satisfactorily accounted for by the number of emigrants, and the increase of their descendants, which have been attracted to the Northern section from Europe and the South, in consequence of the advantages derived from the causes assigned. If they had not existed; if the South had retained all the capital which has been extracted from her by the fiscal action of the Government; and, if it had not been excluded by the Ordinance of '87 and the Missouri compromise from the region lying between the Ohio and the Mississippi rivers, and between the Mississippi and the Rocky Mountains north of 36°30′, it scarcely admits of a doubt that it would have divided the emigration with the North, and by retaining her own people, would have at least equalled the North in population under the census of 1840, and probably under that about to be taken. She would also, if she had retained her equal rights in those territories, have maintained an equality in the number of States with the North, and have preserved the equilibrium between the two sections that existed at the commencement of the Government. The loss, then, of the equilibrium is to be attributed to the action of this Government....

But if there was no question of vital importance to the South, in reference to which there was a diversity of views between the two sections, this state of things might be endured without the hazard of destruction to the South. But such is not the fact. There is a question of vital importance to the southern section, in reference to which the views and feelings of the two sections are as opposite and hostile as they can possibly be.

I refer to the relation between the two races in the southern section, which constitutes a vital portion of her social organization. Every portion of the North entertains views and feelings more or less hostile to it. Those most opposed and hostile regard it as a sin, and consider themselves under the most sacred obligation to use every effort to destroy it. Indeed, to the extent that they conceive that they have power, they regard themselves as implicated in the sin, and responsible for not suppressing it by the use of all and every means. Those less opposed and hostile regard it as a crime—an offense against humanity, as they call it; and, although not so fanatical, feel themselves bound to use all efforts to effect the same object; while those who are least opposed and hostile regard it as a blot and a stain on the character of what they call the nation, and feel themselves accordingly bound to give it no countenance or support. On the contrary, the southern section regards the relation as one which cannot be destroyed without subjecting the two races to the greatest calamity, and the section to poverty, desolation, and wretchedness; and accordingly they feel bound by every consideration of interest and safety to defend it....

Unless something decisive is done, I again ask what is to stop this agitation, before the great and final object at which it aims—the abolition of slavery in the States—is consummated? Is it, then, not certain that if something decisive is not done to arrest it, the South will be forced to choose between abolition and secession? Indeed, as events are now moving, it will not require the South to secede in order to dissolve the Union. Agitation will of itself effect it, of which its past history furnishes abundant proof, as I shall next proceed to show.

It is a great mistake to suppose that disunion can be effected by a single blow. The cords which bind these States together in one common Union are far too numerous and powerful for that. Disunion must be the work of time. It is only through a long process, and successively, that the cords can be snapped until the whole fabric falls asunder. Already the agitation of the slavery question has snapped some of the most important, and has greatly weakened all the others. . . .

If the agitation goes on, the same force, acting with increased intensity, as has been shown, will finally snap every cord, when nothing will be left to hold the States together except force. But surely that can, with no propriety of language be called a union, when the only means by which the weaker is held connected with the stronger portion is *force*. It may, indeed, keep them connected; but the connection will partake much more of the character of subjugation on the part of the weaker to the stronger, than the union of free, independent, and sovereign States, in one confederation, as they stood in the early stages of the Government, and which only is worthy of the sacred name of union.

Having now, Senators, explained what it is that endangers the Union, and traced it to its cause, and explained its nature and character, the question again recurs, How can the Union be saved? To this I answer, there is but one way by which it can be, and that is, by adopting such measures as will satisfy the States belonging to the southern section that they can remain in the Union consistently with their honor and their safety. There is, again, only one way by which this can be effected, and that is, by removing the causes by which this belief has been produced. Do *that,* and discontent will cease, harmony and kind feelings between the sections be restored, and every apprehension of danger to the Union removed. The question then is, By what can this be done? . . .

There is but one way by which it can with any certainty; and that is, by a full and final settlement, on the principle of justice, of all the questions at issue between the two sections. The South asks for justice, simple justice, and less she ought not to take. She has no compromise to offer but the Constitution, and no concession or surrender to make. She has already surrendered so much that she has little left to surrender. Such a settlement would go to the root of the evil, and remove all cause of discontent, by satisfying the South that she could remain honorably and safely in the Union, and thereby restore the harmony and fraternal feelings between the sections which existed anterior to the Missouri agitation. Nothing else can, with any certainty, finally and forever settle the question at issue, terminate agitation, and save the Union.

But can this be done? Yes, easily; not by the weaker party, for it can of itself do nothing—not even protect itself—but by the stronger. The North has only to will it to accomplish it—to do justice by conceding to the South an equal right in the acquired territory, and to do her duty by causing the stipulations relative to fugitive slaves to be faithfully fulfilled—to cease the agitation of the slave question, and to provide for the insertion of a provision in the Constitution, by an amendment, which will restore to the South in substance, the power she possessed of protecting herself, before the equilibrium between the sections was destroyed by the action of this Government. There will be no difficulty in devising such a provision—one that will protect the South, and which at the same time will improve and strengthen the Government, instead of impairing and weakening it.

But will the North agree to this? It is for her to answer the question. But, I will say, she cannot refuse, if she has half the love of the Union which she professes to have, or without justly exposing herself to the charge that her love of power and aggrandizement is far greater than her love of the Union. At all events, the responsibility of saving the Union rests on the North, and not on the South. The South cannot save it by any act of hers, and the North may save it without any sacrifice whatever, unless to do justice, and to perform her duties under the Constitution, should be regarded by her as a sacrifice.

It is time, Senators, that there should be an open and manly avowal on all sides, as to what is intended to be done. If the question is not now settled, it is uncertain whether it ever can hereafter be; and we, as the representatives of the States of this Union, regarded as governments, should come to a distinct understanding as to our respective views, in order to ascertain whether the great questions at issue can be settled or not. If you, who represent the stronger portion, cannot agree to settle them on the broad principle of justice and duty, say so; and let the States we both represent agree to separate and part in peace. If you are unwilling we should part in peace, tell us so, and we shall know what to do, when you reduce the question to submission or resistance. If you remain silent, you will compel us to infer by your acts what you intend. In that case, California will become the test question. If you admit her, under all the difficulties that oppose her admission, you compel us to infer that you intend to exclude us from the whole of the acquired territories, with the intention of destroying irretrievably the equilibrium between the two sections. We would be blind not to perceive, in that case, that your real objects are power and aggrandizement, and infatuated not to act accordingly.

I have now, Senators, done my duty in expressing my opinions fully, freely, and candidly on this solemn occasion. In doing so, I have been governed by the motives which have governed me in all the stages of the agitation of the slavery question since its commencement. I have exerted myself, during the whole period, to arrest it, with the intention of saving the Union, if it could be done; and, if it could not, to save the section where it has pleased Providence to cast my lot, and which I sincerely believe has justice and the Constitution on its side. Having faithfully done my duty to the best of my ability, both to the Union and my section, throughout this agitation, I shall have the consolation, let what will come, that I am free from all responsibility.

Source:

Congressional Globe, 31st Congress, 1st Session, pp. 451–456.

Document 8: Speech by Daniel Webster

Prior to his remarks on his compromise resolutions the previous month, Senator Henry Clay (1777–1852) consulted with Senator Daniel Webster of Massachusetts (1782–1852), gaining support from Webster for his resolutions. When Webster gave his last major speech in the Senate on March 7, 1850, the Senate gallery was packed with spectators. The senator who held the floor yielded his time to Webster, remarking that it was evident that the crowd had not come to see him make motions.

Webster called for compromise and criticized Northern abolitionists' agitation of the slavery question. While he gained widespread approval from Southerners and those supporting compromise, many New Englanders in the region he had so long represented felt he had abandoned their principles.

Excerpts of speech in the Senate of the United States on the Compromise Resolutions, by Senator Daniel Webster of Massachusetts, March 7, 1850

Mr. President, I wish to speak to-day, not as a Massachusetts man, nor as a northern man, but as an American, and a member of the Senate of the United States. It is fortunate that there is a Senate of the United States; a body not yet moved from its propriety, not lost to a just sense of its own dignity, and its own high responsibilities, and a body to which the country looks, with confidence, for wise, moderate, patriotic, and healing counsels. It is not to be denied that we live in the midst of strong agitations, and are surrounded by very considerable dangers to our institutions of government. The imprisoned winds are let loose. The East, the West, the North, and the stormy South, all combine to throw the whole ocean into commotion, to toss its billows to the skies, and to disclose its profoundest depths. I do not expect, Mr. President, to hold, or to be fit to hold, the helm in this combat of the political elements; but I have a duty to perform, and I mean to perform it with fidelity—not without a sense of the surrounding dangers, but not without hope. I have a part to act, not for my own security or safety, for I am looking out for no fragment upon which to float away from the wreck, if wreck there must be, but for the good of the whole, and the preservation of the whole; and there is that which will keep me to my duty during this struggle, whether the sun and the stars shall appear, or shall not appear for many days. I speak to-day for the preservation of the Union. "Hear me for my cause." I speak to-day, out of a solicitous and anxious heart, for the restoration to the country of that quiet and that harmony which make the blessings of this Union so rich and so dear to us all. These are the topics that I propose to myself to discuss; these are the motives, and the sole motives, that influence me in the wish to communicate my opinions to the Senate and the country; and if I can do anything, however little, for the promotion of these ends, I shall have accomplished all that I desire....

Now, Sir, upon the general nature, and character, and influence of slavery there exists a wide difference between the northern portion of this country and the southern. It is said, on the one side, that, if not the subject of any injunction or direct prohibition in the New Testament, slavery is a wrong; that it is founded merely in the right of the strongest; and that is an oppression, like all unjust wars—like all those conflicts by which a mighty nation subjects a weaker nation to their will; and that slavery, in its nature, whatever may be said of it in the modifications which have taken place, is not in fact according to the meek spirit of the Gospel. It is not kindly affectioned. It does not "seek another's, and not its own." It does not "let the oppressed go free." These are sentiments that are cherished, and recently with greatly augmented force, among the people of the northern States. It has taken hold of the religious sentiment of that part of the country, as it has, more or less taken hold of the religious feeling of a considerable portion of mankind. The South, upon the other side, having been accustomed to this relation between the two races all their lives, from their birth; having been taught in general to treat the subjects of this bondage with care and kindness—and I believe, in general, feeling for them great care and kindness—have yet not taken this view of the subject which I have mentioned. There are thousands of religious men, with consciences as tender as any of their brethren at the North, who do not see the unlawfulness of slavery; and there are more thousands, perhaps, that, whatsoever they may think of it in its origin, and as a matter depending upon natural right, yet take things as they are, and, finding slavery to be an established relation of the society where they live, can see no way in which—let their opinions on the abstract question be what they may—it is in the power of the present generation to relieve themselves from this relation. And, in this respect, candor obliges me to say, that I believe they are just as conscientious, many of them—and of the religious people, all of them—as they are in the North, in holding different opinions.

Why, sir, the honorable Senator from South Carolina [John C. Calhoun], the other day, alluded to the great separation of that great religious community, the Methodist Episcopal Church. That separation was brought about by differences of opinion upon this particular subject of slavery. I felt great concern, as that dispute went on, about the result; and I was in hopes that the difference of opinion might be adjusted, because I looked upon that religious denomination as one of the great props of religion and morals, throughout the whole country, from Maine to Georgia. The result was against my wishes and against my hopes. I have read all their proceedings, and all their arguments, but I have never yet been able to come to the conclusion, that there was any real ground for that separation; in other words, that no good could be produced by that separation. Sir, when a question of this kind takes hold of the religious sentiments of mankind, and comes to be discussed in religious assemblies of the clergy and laity, there is always to be expected, or always to be feared, a great degree of excitement. It is in the nature of man, manifested in his whole history, that religious disputes are apt to become warm, and men's strength of convictions is proportionate to their views of the magnitude of the questions. In all such disputes, there will sometimes be men found with whom everything is absolute—absolutely wrong, or absolutely right. They see the right clearly; they think others ought to do it, and they are disposed to establish a broad line of distinction between what they think right and what they hold to be wrong. And they are not seldom willing to establish that line upon their own convictions of the truth and the justice of their own opinions, but they are willing to mark and guard that line, by placing along it a series of dogmas, as lines of boundary are marked by posts and stones. There are men, who, with clear perceptions, as they think, of their own duty, do not see how too hot a pursuit of one duty may involve them in the violation of another, or how too warm an embracement of one truth may lead to a disregard of other truths equally important. As I heard it stated strongly, not many days ago, these persons are disposed to mount upon some duty as a war-horse, and to drive furiously on, and upon, and over all other duties, that may stand in the way. There are men, who, in times of that sort, and disputes of that sort, are of opinion, that human duties may be ascertained with the precision of mathematics. They deal with morals as with mathematics, and they think what is right, may be distinguished from what is wrong, with the precision of an algebraic equation. They have, therefore, none too much charity towards others who differ with them. They are apt, too, to think that nothing is good but what is perfect, and that there are no compromises or modifications to be made in submission to difference of opinion, or in deference to other men's judgment. If their perspicacious vision enables them to detect a spot on the face of the sun, they think that a good reason why the sun should be struck down from Heaven. They prefer the chance of running into utter darkness to living in heavenly light, if that heavenly light be not absolutely without any imperfection. There are impatient men—too impatient always to give heed to the admission [admonition] of St. Paul, "that we are not to do evil that good may come"—too impatient to wait for the slow progress of moral causes in the improvement of mankind....

Now, sir, in this state of sentiment, upon the general nature of slavery, lies the cause of a great portion of those unhappy divisions, exasperations, and reproaches, which find vent and support in different parts of the Union. Slavery does exist in the United States. It did exist in the States before the adoption of this Constitution, and at that time.

. . . if we will carry ourselves by historical research back to that day, and ascertain men's opinions by authentic records still existing among us, that there was no great diversity of opinion between the North and South upon the subject of slavery; and it will be found that both parts of the country held it equally an evil—a moral and political evil. . . . They are matters of history on the record. The eminent men, the most eminent men, and nearly all the conspicuous of the South, held the same sentiments, that slavery was an evil, a blight, . . . a mildew, a scourge, and a curse. . . .

But soon a change began at the North and the South, and a severance [difference] of opinion soon showed itself—the North growing much more warm and strong against slavery, and the South growing much more warm and strong in its support. . . . What, then, have been the causes which have created so new a feeling in favor of slavery in the South—which have changed the whole nomenclature of the South on the subject . . . it has now become an institution, a cherished institution there; no evil, no scourge, but a great religious, social, and moral blessing, as I think I have heard it lately [latterly] described? I suppose this, sir, is owing to the sudden uprising and rapid growth of the cotton plantations of the South. So far as any motive of honor, justice, and general judgment could act, it was the cotton interest that gave a new desire to promote slavery, to spread it and to use its labor. I again say that this is produced by the causes, which we must always expect to produce like effects—their whole interests became connected with it. If we look back to the history of the commerce of this country, at the early commencement of this Government, what were our exports? Cotton was hardly, or but to a very limited extent, known. The tables will show that the exports of cotton for the years 1790 and '91, were hardly more than forty or fifty thousand dollars a year. It has gone on increasing rapidly until it may now be, perhaps, in a season of great product and high prices, a hundred millions of dollars. Then there was more of wax, more of indigo, more of rice, more of almost everything of export from the South, than of cotton. . . .

Mr. President, in the excited times in which we live, there is found to exist a state of crimination and recrimination between the North and the South. There are lists of grievances produced by each; and those grievances, real or supposed, alienate the minds of one portion of the country from the other, exasperate the feelings, subdue the sense of fraternal connection, and patriotic love, and mutual regard. I shall bestow a little attention, sir, upon these various grievances produced on the one side and on the other. I begin with complaints of the South: I will not answer, further than I have, the general statements of the honorable Senator from South Carolina [John C. Calhoun], that the North has grown upon the South in consequence of the manner of administering this Government, in the collecting of its revenues, and so forth. These are disputed topics, and I have no inclination to enter into them. But I will state these complaints, especially one complaint of the South, which has in my opinion just foundation; and that is, that there has been found at the North, among individuals and among the Legislatures of the North, a disinclination to perform, fully, their constitutional duties, in regard to the return of persons bound to service, who have escaped into the free States. In that respect it is my judgment that the South is right, and the North is wrong. Every member of every northern Legislature is bound by oath, like every other officer in the country, to support the Constitution of the United States; and the article of the Constitution, which says to these States, that they shall deliver up fugitives from service, is as binding in honor and conscience as any other article. No man fulfills his duty in any Legislature who sets himself to find excuses, evasions, escapes from this constitutional obligation. I have always thought that the Constitution addressed itself to the Legislatures of the States themselves or to the States themselves. It says, that those persons escaping to other States shall be delivered up, and I confess I have always been of the opinion that it was an injunction upon the States themselves. When it is said that a person escaping into another State, and becoming therefore within the jurisdiction of that State, shall be delivered up, it seems to me the import of the passage is, that the State itself, in obedience to the Constitution, shall cause him to be delivered up. That is my judgment. I have always entertained that opinion, and I entertain it now. But when the subject, some years ago, was before the Supreme Court of the United States, the majority of the judges held that the power, to cause fugitives from service to be delivered up, was a power to be exercised under the authority of this Government. I do not know, on the whole, that it may not have been a fortunate decision. My habit is to respect the result of judicial deliberations and the solemnity of judicial decisions. But, as it now stands, the business of seeing that these fugitives are delivered up, resides in the power of Congress, and the national judicature, and my friend at the head of the Judiciary Committee [Senator James M. Mason of Virginia] has a bill on the subject, now before the Senate, with some amendments to it, which I propose to support, with all its provisions, to the fullest extent. And I desire to call the attention of all sober-minded men, of all conscientious men, in the North, of all men who are not carried away by any fanatical idea, or by any false idea whatever, to their constitutional obligations. I put it to all the sober and sound minds at the North, as a question of morals and a question of conscience, What right have they, in all their legislative capacity, or any other, to endeavor to get round this Constitution; to embarrass the free exercise of the rights secured by the Constitution, to the persons whose slaves escape from them? None at all—none at all. Neither in the forum of conscience, nor before the face of the Constitution, are they justified, in my opinion. Of course, it is a matter for their consideration. They probably, in the turmoil of the times, have not stopped to consider of this; they have followed what seemed to be the current of thought and of motives as the occasion arose, and neglected to investigate fully the real question, and to consider their constitutional obligation, as I am sure, if they did consider, they would fulfill them with alacrity. Therefore, I repeat, sir, that here is a ground of complaint against the North, well founded, which ought to be removed—which it is now in the power of the different departments of this Government to remove;—which calls for the enactment of proper laws, authorizing the judicature of this Government, in the several States, to do all that is necessary for the recapture of fugitive slaves, and for the restoration of them to those who claim them. Wherever I go, and whenever I speak on the subject—and when I speak here, I desire to speak to the whole North—I say that the South has been injured in this respect, and has a right to complain; and the North has been too careless of what I think the Constitution peremptorily and emphatically enjoins upon it as a duty....

Then, sir, there are those abolition societies, of which I am unwilling to speak, but in regard to which I have very clear notions and opinions. I do not think them useful. I think their operations for the last twenty years have produced nothing good or valuable. At the same time, I know thousands of them are honest and good men; perfectly well-meaning men. They have excited feelings; they think they must do something for the cause of liberty; and in their sphere of action, they do not see what else they can do, than to contribute to an abolition press, or an abolition society, or to pay an abolition lecturer. I do not mean to impute gross motives even to the leaders of these societies, but I am not blind to the consequences. I cannot but see what mischiefs their interference with the South has produced. And is it not plain to every man? Let any gentleman who doubts of that, recur to the debates in the Virginia House of Delegates in 1832, and he will see with what freedom a proposition made by Mr. [Thomas Jefferson] Randolph for the gradual abolition of slavery, was discussed in that body. Every one spoke of slavery as he thought; very ignominious and disparaging names and epithets were applied to it. The debates in the House of Delegates on that occasion, I believe, were all published. They were read by every colored man who could read, and if there were any who could not read, those debates were read to them by others. At that time Virginia was not unwilling nor afraid to discuss this question, and to let that part of her population know as much of it as they could learn. That was in 1832. As has been said by the honorable member from Carolina [Senator John C. Calhoun], these abolition societies commenced their course of action in 1835. It is said—I do not know how true it may be—that they sent incendiary publications into the slave States; at any event, they attempted to arouse, and did arouse, a very strong feeling; in other words, they created great agitation in the North against southern slavery. Well, what was the result? The bonds of the slaves were bound more firmly than before, their rivets were more strongly fastened. Public opinion, which in Virginia had begun to be exhibited against slavery, and was opening out for the discussion of the question, drew back and shut itself up in its castle. I wish to know whether any body in Virginia can, now, talk as Mr. [Thomas Jefferson] Randolph, Governor [James] McDowell, and others talked there, openly, and sent their remarks to the press, in 1832. We all know the fact, and we all know the cause, and everything that this agitating people have done, has been, not to enlarge, but to restrain, not to set free, but to bind faster the slave population of the South....

There is a more tangible, and irritating cause of grievance, at the North. Free blacks are constantly employed in the vessels of the North, generally as cooks or stewards. When the vessel arrives, these free colored men, are taken on shore, by the police or municipal authority, imprisoned, and kept in prison, till the vessel is again ready to sail. This is not only irritating, but exceedingly inconvenient in practice, and seems altogether unjustifiable, and oppressive. Mr. Hoar's mission, some time ago, to South Carolina, was a well-intended effort to remove this cause of complaint. The North thinks such imprisonment illegal, and unconstitutional; as the cases occur constantly and frequently, they think it a great grievance....

Mr. President, I should much prefer to have heard from every member on this floor, declarations of opinion that this Union should never be dissolved, than the declaration of opinion that in any case, under the pressure of any circumstances, such a dissolution was possible. I hear with pain, and anguish the word secession, especially when it falls from the lips of those who are eminently patriotic, and known to the country, and known all over the world, for their political services. Secession! Peaceable secession! Sir, your eyes and mine are never destined to see that miracle. The dismemberment of this vast country without convulsion! The breaking up of the fountains of the great deep without ruffling the surface! Who is so foolish—I beg every body's pardon—as to expect to see any such thing? Sir, he who sees these States, now revolving in harmony around a common centre, and expects to see them quit their places and fly off without convulsion, may look the next hour to see the heavenly bodies rush from their spheres, and jostle against each other in the realms of space, without producing the crush of the universe. There can be no such thing as a peaceable secession. Peaceable secession is an utter impossibility. Is the great Constitution under which we live here—covering this whole country—is it to be thawed and melted away by secession, as the snows on the mountain melt under the influence of a vernal sun—disappear almost unobserved, and die off? No, Sir! no, Sir! I will not state what might produce the disruption of the States; but, sir, I see it as plainly as I see the sun in heaven—I see that disruption must produce such a war as I will not describe, in its twofold characters.

Peaceable secession! peaceable secession! The concurrent agreement of all the members of this great Republic to separate! A voluntary separation, with alimony on one side and on the other. Why, what would be the result? Where is the line to be drawn? What States are to secede? What is to remain American? What am I to be?—An American no longer? Where is the flag of the Republic to remain? Where is the eagle still to tower? or is he to cower, and shrink, and fall to the ground? Why, sir, our ancestors—our fathers and our grandfathers, those of them that are yet living among us with prolonged lives—would rebuke and reproach us; and our children, and our grandchildren, would cry out, Shame upon us! if we, of this generation, should dishonor these ensigns of the power of the Government and the harmony of the Union, which is every day felt among us with so much joy and gratitude. What is to become of the army? What is to become of the navy? What is to become of the public lands? How is each of the thirty States to defend itself? I know, although the idea has not been stated distinctly, there is to be a southern Confederacy. I do not mean, when I allude to this statement, that any one seriously contemplates such a state of things. I do not mean to say that it is true, but I have heard it suggested elsewhere, that that idea has originated in a design to separate. I am sorry, sir, that it has ever been thought of, talked of, or dreamed of, in the wildest flights of human imagination. But the idea must be of a separation, including the slave States upon one side, and the free States on the other. Sir, there is not—I may express myself too strongly perhaps—but some things, some moral things, are almost impossible as, other natural or physical things; and I hold the idea of a separation of these States—those that are free to form one government, and those that are slaveholding to form another—as a moral impossibility. We could not separate the States by any such line, if we were to draw it. We could not sit down here to-day, and draw a line of separation, that would satisfy any five men in the country. There are natural causes that would keep and tie us together, and there are social and domestic relations which we could not break, if we would, and which we should not if we could. Sir, nobody can look over the face of this country at the present moment—nobody can see where its population is the most dense and growing—without being ready to admit, and compelled to admit, that, ere long, America will be in the valley of the Mississippi.

Well, now, sir, I beg to inquire what the wildest enthusiast has to say, on the possibility of cutting off that river, and leaving free States at its source and on its branches, and slave States down near its mouth? Pray, sir—pray, sir, let me say to the people of this country, that these things are worthy of their pondering and of their consideration. Here, sir, are five millions of freemen in the free States north of the river Ohio: can anybody suppose that this population can be severed by a line that divides them from the territory of a foreign and an alien government, down somewhere, the Lord knows where, upon the lower banks of the Mississippi? What will become of Missouri? Will she join the arrondissement of the slave States? Shall the man from the Yellow Stone and the Platte be connected, in the new Republic with the man who lives on the southern extremity of the

Cape of Florida? Sir, I am ashamed to pursue this line of remark. I dislike it—I have an utter disgust for it. I would rather hear of natural blasts and mildews, war, pestilence, and famine, than to hear gentlemen talk of secession. To break up! to break up this great Government! to dismember this great country! to astonish Europe with an act of folly, such as Europe for two centuries has never beheld in any government! No, Sir! no, Sir! There will be no secession. Gentlemen are not serious when they talk of secession....

And now, Mr. President, I draw these observations to a close. I have spoken freely, and I meant to do so. I have sought to make no display; I have sought to enliven the occasion by no animated discussion; nor have I attempted any train of elaborate argument. I have sought only to speak my sentiments, fully and at large, being desirous, once and for all, to let the Senate know, and to let the country know, the opinions and sentiments which I entertain on all these subjects. These opinions are not likely to be suddenly changed. If there be any future service that I can render to the country, consistently with these sentiments and opinions, I shall cheerfully render it. If there be not, I shall still be glad to have had an opportunity to disburden my conscience from the bottom of my heart, and to make known every political sentiment that therein exists.

And now, Mr. President, instead of speaking of the possibility or utility of secession, instead of dwelling in those caverns of darkness, instead of groping with those ideas so full of all that is horrid and horrible, let us come out into the light of day; let us enjoy the fresh air of Liberty and union; let us cherish those hopes which belong to us; let us devote ourselves to those great objects that are fit for our consideration and action; let us raise our conceptions to the magnitude and the importance of the duties that devolve upon us; let our comprehension be as broad as the country for which we act, our aspirations as high as its certain destiny; let us not be pigmies in a case that calls for men. Never did there devolve, on any generation of men, higher trusts than now devolve upon us for the preservation of this Constitution, and the harmony and peace of all who are destined to live under it. Let us make our generation one of the strongest, and brightest links in that golden chain which is destined, I fully believe, to grapple the people of all the States to this Constitution for ages to come. It is a great, popular Constitutional Government, guarded by legislation, by law, by judicature, and defended by the whole affections of the people. No monarchical throne presses these States together; no iron chain of despotic power encircles them; they live and stand under a Government popular in its form, representative in its character, founded upon principles of equality, and calculated, we hope, to last forever. In all its history, it has been beneficent; it has trodden down no man's liberty; it has crushed no State. Its daily respiration, is liberty and patriotism; its yet youthful veins are full of enterprise, courage, and honorable love of glory and renown. It has received a vast addition of territory. Large before, the country has now, by recent events, become vastly larger. This Republic now extends, with a vast breadth, across the whole continent. The two great seas of the world wash the one and the other shore. We realize, on a mighty scale, the beautiful description of the ornamental edging of the buckler of Achilles....

"Now, the broad shield completed, the artist crowned, With his last hand, and poured the ocean round; In living silver seemed the waves to roll, And beat the bucklers verge, and bound the whole."

SOURCE:

Congressional Globe, 31st Congress, 1st Session, pp. 476–483.

Document 9: KANSAS-NEBRASKA ACT

Senator Stephen A. Douglas of Illinois (1813–1861), influential in getting most of Henry Clay's compromise package enacted into law in 1850, had presidential ambitions. Hoping to make his hometown of Chicago a major railroad hub and to encourage settlement in the remaining areas of the original Louisiana Purchase Territory, Douglas elicited Southern support for his Kansas-Nebraska Act using popular sovereignty—letting the people of a territory decide whether to allow or restrict slavery—effectively repealing the section of the Missouri Compromise of 1820 that had barred slavery in this region. By May 1854, when this act was proposed, Southern Whigs, Southern Democrats, and about half of Northern Democrats voted for it. The influx of settlers in Kansas Territory—of both proslavery and antislavery inclination—led to major acts of violence between 1855 and 1858. This act caused many "Free Soil"

Democrats, disaffected Whigs, and abolitionists to join the infant Republican Party with strongholds in the Northeast and the Midwest.

An Act to organize the Territories of Nebraska and Kansas

Be it enacted by the Senate and House of Representatives of the United States of America in Congress assembled, That all that part of the territory of the United States included ... is hereby, created into a temporary government by the name of the Territory of Nebraska; and when admitted as a State or States, the said Territory, or any portion of the same, shall be received into the Union with or without slavery, as their constitution may prescribe at the time of their admission....

SEC. 10. *And be it further enacted,* That provisions of an act entitled "An act respecting fugitives from justice, and persons escaping from the service of their masters," approved February twelve, seventeen hundred and ninety-three, and the provisions of the act entitles "An act to amend and supplementary to, the aforesaid act," approved September eighteen, eighteen hundred and fifty, be, and the same are hereby, declared to extend to and be in full force within the limits of said Territory of Nebraska....

SEC. 14 ... That the Constitution, and all Laws of the United States which are not locally inapplicable, shall have the same force and effect within the said Territory of Nebraska as elsewhere within the United States, except the eighth section of the act preparatory to the admission of Missouri into the Union, approved March sixth, eighteen hundred and twenty, which, being inconsistent with the principle of non-intervention by Congress with slavery in the States and Territories, as recognized by the legislation of eighteen hundred and fifty, commonly called the Compromise Measures, is hereby declared inoperative and void; it being the true intent and meaning of this act not to legislate slavery into any Territory or State, nor to exclude it therefrom, but to leave the people thereof perfectly free to form and regulate their domestic institutions in their own way, subject only to the Constitution of the United States: *Provided,* That nothing herein contained shall be construed to revive or put in force any law or regulation which may have existed prior to the act of sixth March, eighteen hundred and twenty, either protecting, establishing, prohibiting, or abolishing slavery....

SEC. 19. *And be it further enacted,* That all that part of the Territory of the United States included within the following limits ... is hereby, created into a temporary government by the name of the Territory of Kansas; and when admitted as a State or States, the said Territory, or any portion of the same, shall be received into the Union with or without slavery, as their Constitution may prescribe at the time of their admission....

SEC. 28. *And be it further enacted,* That provisions of the act entitled "An act respecting fugitives from justice, and persons escaping from the service of their masters," approves February twelfth, seventeen hundred and ninety-three, and the provisions of the act entitles "An act to amend, and supplementary to, the aforesaid act," approved September eighteenth, eighteen hundred and fifty, be, and the same are hereby, declared to extend to and be in full force within the limits of said Territory of Kansas....

SEC. 32 ... That the Constitution, and all laws of the United States which are not locally inapplicable, shall have the same force and effect within the said Territory of Kansas as elsewhere within the United States, except the eighth section of the act preparatory to the admission of Missouri into the Union, approved March sixth, eighteen hundred and twenty, which, being inconsistent with the principle of non-intervention by Congress with slavery in the States and Territories, as recognized by the legislation of eighteen hundred and fifty, commonly called the Compromise Measures, is hereby declared inoperative and void; it being the true intent and meaning of this act not to legislate slavery into any Territory or State, nor to exclude it therefrom, but to leave the people thereof perfectly free to form and regulate their domestic institutions in their own way, subject only to the Constitution of the United States: *Provided,* That nothing herein contained shall be construed to revive or put in force any law or regulation which may have existed prior to the act of sixth March, eighteen hundred and twenty, either protecting, establishing, prohibiting, or abolishing slavery....

Approved, May 30, 1854

SOURCE:

George Minot, ed. *The Statutes at Large and Treaties of the United States of America,* Volume 10, *December 1, 1851 to March 3, 1855* (Boston, Mass.: Little, Brown, 1855), pp. 277–290.

BIBLIOGRAPHY

Bartlett, Irving H. *John C. Calhoun: A Biography.* New York: Norton, 1993. An accessible treatment of the Southern statesman whose four-decade political career began when he was an early nationalist and ended when he was a leading advocate for states' rights and for the "positive good" of slavery.

Fehrenbacher, Don E. *Slavery, Law, and Politics: The Dred Scott Case in Historical Perspective*, abridged edition. New York: Oxford University Press, 1981. A readable study of the intersection of slavery and politics in the nineteenth century. The *Dred Scott* case is used as a point of departure in discussing key events in the sectional conflicts of the 1850s.

Forbes, Robert Pierce. *The Missouri Compromise and Its Aftermath: Slavery and the Meaning of America.* Chapel Hill: University of North Carolina Press, 2007. A comprehensive examination of the Missouri Compromise and of the significance of its influence in the early development of the nation. Forbes establishes the Missouri debates of 1819 to 1821 as the only period during which frank and open discussions of slavery were held at the national level; Southern politicians of this period were able to refine the proslavery ideology that sowed the seeds for violent sectional conflict two decades later.

Freheling, William W. *The Road to Disunion*, volume 1, *Secessionists at Bay, 1776–1854*. New York: Oxford University Press, 1990. The Missouri Compromise, the Compromise of 1850, and the Kansas-Nebraska Act are the focus of this examination of the many facets of Southern political thought, in a treatment that opposes the unified and monolithic South assumed by earlier scholars.

———. *The Road to Disunion*, volume 2, *Secessionists Triumphant, 1854–1861*. New York: Oxford University Press, 2007. A continuation of Freheling's examination of Southern political culture in the aftermath of the Kansas-Nebraska Act, including the events leading to the election of 1860.

Morrison, Michael A. *Slavery and the American West: The Eclipse of Manifest Destiny and the Coming of the Civil War*. Chapel Hill: University of North Carolina Press, 1997. An analysis of the growing sectional divide between the North and the South during the 1840s and 1850s. Morrison argues that the intersection of slavery and territorial expansion led both sides to have different understandings of the American Revolution's tenets of liberty and equality.

Nevins, Allan. *Ordeal of the Union*, volume 1, *Fruits of Manifest Destiny, 1847–1852*. New York: Macmillan, 1992 [1947]. A useful political narrative of the United States during its resulting land acquisitions in the aftermath of the U.S.-Mexico War. Nevins argues that the prevalent and consistent issue of slavery in these newly acquired territories led to the unstable Compromise of 1850, divided both major political parties (Democrats and Whigs) internally along sectional lines, and caused a succession of weak presidents between Polk and Lincoln.

———. *Ordeal of the Union*, volume 2, *A House Dividing, 1852–1857*. New York: Macmillan, 1992 [1947]. Nevins continues his narrative of the United States in this volume, tracing history from the political maneuverings of Senator Stephen A. Douglas to the 1854 Kansas-Nebraska Act and its immediate impact on the violent events occurring in Kansas Territory.

Peterson, Merrill D. *The Great Triumvirate: Webster, Clay, and Calhoun*. New York: Oxford University Press, 1987. A useful study of the premier politicians of the Jacksonian era representing three distinct sections of the growing republic: the East (Daniel Webster of Massachusetts); the West (Henry Clay of Kentucky); and the South (John C. Calhoun of South Carolina). Peterson traces their service to the nation and their interaction with each other from their service in the U.S. Congress after the War of 1812 to their final speeches in the U.S. Senate, discussing how each contributed to laying groundwork for the Compromise of 1850.

Potter, David M. *The Impending Crisis, 1848–1861*. New York: Harper, 1977. Potter traces the sectional conflict over slavery in the aftermath of the war with Mexico and suggests that the very success in territorial acquisitions by the United States led to the nation's Civil War.

Remini, Robert V. *Daniel Webster: The Man and His Time*. New York: Norton, 1994. A modern and comprehensive treatment of the multitalented American statesman.

———. *Henry Clay: Statesman for the Union*. New York: Norton, 1991. A modern, comprehensive treatment of Henry Clay of Kentucky by a leading scholar of the Jacksonian era.

~ 4 ~

THE SECESSION CRISIS

Several weeks prior to the presidential election of 1860, Alabama congressman Jabez L. M. Curry addressed a crowd of his constituents in Wetumpka. "As soon as Abe Lincoln takes the Presidential chair," Curry warned, "five hundred thousand wide-awakes, already drilling for the purpose, will rush over the border, lay waste your fields, emancipate your negroes, and amalgamate the poor man's daughter with the rich man's buck [slave]" (Tharin, p. 62). Curry's remarks typified secessionist rhetoric on the election's eve; stories about how the South would be transformed if Abraham Lincoln won the presidential election—invasions by Republican mobs to incite slave revolts, infiltration of Republicans, abolitionists and free blacks into state and local government, and plots to poison drinking wells—circulated prior to the election. As anxieties intensified, the nation stood at an important crossroads in the autumn of 1860—had the slaveholding South feared a Republican administration so much that Lincoln's victory meant imminent secession or would Lincoln's unwillingness to compromise and maintain control of federal property further exacerbate the secession crisis and inaugurate civil war?

Lincoln emerged victorious on November 6, and radical secessionist "fire-eaters" such as South Carolina's Robert Barnwell Rhett—regarded as the father of secession—and Alabama's William Lowndes Yancey—who organized the prosecession League of United Southerners in 1858—called for an immediate break from the Union. Eight days later, Georgia's Alexander Stephens—a seasoned politician and former congressman who became the Confederacy's vice president—remarked, "The election of no man constitutionally chosen to that high office, is sufficient cause for any State to separate from the Union. . . . Let us not anticipate a threatened evil" (Stephens, volume 2, pp. 280–281). As Stephens and other advocates of caution considered when and under what circumstances a state should secede from the Union, they took into consideration what a struggle it would be to convince the South's yeoman farmers, who despised wealthy slave owners, to support an economic system that ultimately would contribute to their financial burdens.

Believing that the South should present a united front against Lincoln, South Carolina governor William H. Gist called Deep South governors to meet one month before the election. North Carolina governor John Ellis and Georgia governor Joseph E. Brown urged restraint. Both men believed that some clear act of aggression against the South had to occur before they severed the bonds of the Union. While Alabama governor Andrew B. Moore and Florida governor Milton Perry seemed to favor secession before Lincoln had the opportunity to perform an aggressive act, they would not secede alone. Mississippi's and Louisiana's chief executives—John Pettus and Thomas Moore respectively—argued that whatever happened, the states should agree to follow the same course. However, the different moods at the meeting made the hope of a united front seem impossible, at which point it became clear to Governor Gist that despite his unwillingness to have South Carolina be the first state to secede, his state—a proponent of secession for more than three decades—would have to take the lead.

On November 10, four days after Lincoln's victory, South Carolina's legislature called for a convention to meet on December 17 to decide on secession. Throughout the month, South Carolinians listened to fire-eaters arguing the merits of disunion; some wondered if secession would lead to war. Rhett so firmly believed there would be no bloodshed that he told a crowd he would eat the bodies of all those who perished in any conflict that resulted from secession. Energized by Rhett's statement, fellow secessionist and senator James Chestnut of South Carolina told Rhett that he would join him and drink the blood of those who died.

As the desire for secession spread throughout South Carolina, other states in the Deep South made preparations for secession and conflict. Governor Perry of Florida bolstered his state militia and Alabama's governor warned a crowd in Montgomery on November 10 that it appeared no other course of action but secession could save the South. Southern senators watching the secession crisis unfold from afar in Washington, D.C., also resigned themselves to the inevitability of secession as the South Carolina convention drew closer. Virginia senator James Mason, who had authored the controversial 1850 Fugitive Slave Law, wrote to his sister-in-law Anne on November 29 that "the dissolution of the Union is a *fixed fact* . . . we have no choice but to accept the 'irrepressible conflict' tendered us by the late election" (Mason, p. 160). A committee of senators from the Deep South gathered four days before the South Carolina convention met. They wrote, "All hope of relief in the Union . . . is extinguished," and concluded, "the sole and primary aim of each slaveholding State ought to be its speedy and absolute separation from an unnatural and hostile Union" (McPherson, p. 37).

Finally, the South Carolina convention met on December 20 and unanimously passed its ordinance of secession. From the delegates' perspective, Lincoln's election was not the cause of secession, but rather, was the culminating event that capped decades of hostility toward slavery. "For seventy-five years this agitation has been steadily increasing," the convention pointed out in its 1860 Declaration of Independence. "A geographical line has been drawn across the Union, and all the states north of that line have united in the election of a man to the high office of President of the United States, whose opinions and purposes are hostile to slavery" (Ford, p. 715).

Despite its bold stand, South Carolina understood that it could not survive alone. Sensing the importance of an alliance of slave states, Rhett proposed that all slave states meet to discuss the formation of a confederacy. While a confederation was certainly necessary, members of the convention knew they first had to convince other

Alexander H. Stephens (National Archives)

states to secede. By December's end, South Carolina's secessionists had chosen commissioners to go to each of the slave states to argue the merits of secession.

By January 11, three states had followed South Carolina's lead—Mississippi, Florida, and Alabama. As the Deep South began to leave the Union all attention focused on Georgia, a state where only approximately 40 percent of its voters owned slaves. The most populous state in the Deep South—with important industries and the vital rail center at Atlanta—Georgia was an essential state for the Confederacy's survival. Those who argued in favor of Georgia's secession had to appeal to both slaveholders and poor farmers who despised slave owners. Although secessionists had little difficulty convincing slaveholders of the necessity of secession, these activists resorted to scare tactics when approaching Georgia's yeomen farmers, suggesting to them that with Lincoln in the White House, slaves would be freed, free blacks and Republicans would infiltrate local governments, and former slaves would compete with poor whites for work and diminish their social status. Secessionists also described the threat of racial amalgamation as a disconcerting possibility.

Union supporters such as Alexander Stephens argued that secession should not occur unless Lincoln violated the Constitution. Yet, despite Stephens's best efforts, Georgia seceded on January 19 by a vote of 208 to 289. While most Georgians, including Stephens, supported Georgia's decision to leave the Union, some worried about the unknown that this crisis would bring with it. The wife of a Methodist minister in Georgia, Rebecca Latimer Felton wrote: "It was an awful crisis to me when we were brought face to face with secession. . . . It gave me almost a nervous chill—because a woman's intuition furnished me the forebodings that we were plunging headlong into the dark unknown" (Felton, p. 25).

As the Union fell apart in the early winter of 1860–1861, President James Buchanan, a lame-duck executive who did not want to inaugurate civil war in his remaining months, offered his opinion on the crisis during his annual message to Congress on December 3, 1860. Buchanan blamed Republicans and Northern abolitionists for the current crisis: "The long-continued and intemperate interference of the Northern people with the question of slavery in the Southern states has at length produced its natural effects," Buchanan stated (Richardson, volume 7, p. 3157). Although Buchanan placed the blame for the current dilemma on Republicans and abolitionists, he also condemned secession as unconstitutional. The framers of the Constitution, Buchanan argued, "never intended to implant in its bosom the seeds of its own destruction, nor were they at its creation guilty of the absurdity of providing for its own dissolution" (Richardson, volume 7, p. 3164).

Secessionists, however, argued that the right of secession was an inferred right in the Constitution; because it was a compact among states, state sovereignty should supersede the power of the federal government. Secessionists also looked to the Declaration of Independence as justification for breaking the bonds between state and federal governments when the latter was usurping or threatening to usurp the rights of its citizens.

Although the question of the constitutionality of secession was especially a question at state levels, the federal government began working to protect the American Republic from being disunited. Sensing the immediacy of the situation, both the House of Representatives and the Senate created committees—the Committee of Thirty-Three and the Committee of Thirteen, respectively—to determine what sort of compromise could be reached to prevent secession and civil war. Several proposals were submitted, and one in particular seemed to have a chance of stemming secession's tide: Kentucky senator John J. Crittenden proposed constitutional amendments that would guarantee the protection of slavery—most significantly, these amendments would guarantee the legality of slavery where it existed, in the South and throughout the extension outlined by the Missouri Compromise to the Pacific coast. While many Congressmen supported the measure, it did not appeal to Republicans who felt that the compromise failed to offer them anything. Among those who did not approve of Crittenden's proposal (or any compromise) was president-elect Abraham Lincoln. "I will suffer death before I will consent or will advise my friends to consent to any concession or compromise which looks like buying the privilege of taking possession of this government to which we have a constitutional right," Lincoln stated in mid January 1861 (Basler, volume 4, pp. 175–176).

With no hope of compromise, delegates from six states in the Deep South—South Carolina, Georgia, Alabama, Mississippi, Florida, and Louisiana—met in Montgomery, Alabama, on February 4 to form the Confederate States of America. By month's end the citizens of Texas had approved a secession resolution, and delegates from the Lone Star state had joined the convention in Montgomery.

Although delegates in Montgomery drafted a constitution and chose provisional leaders—Jefferson Davis as the president and Alexander H. Stephens as the vice president—the greatest problem was figuring out how to convince the remaining eight slave states to join the Confederacy. Including only 20 percent of the U.S. population and around 5 percent of its industry, the Confederacy knew it would need the support of the upper South in order to have any hopes of survival; yet, all attempts to coerce the upper South to secede before Lincoln took office failed.

States that had not yet left the Union believed that the new Republican administration had to perform some act of aggression against the slaveholding South in order to justify secession. A majority of people in the upper South believed that the Union, not secession or an untested Confederacy, was the best way to protect slavery. "A disruption of the union of these states," read an editorial in the *Gazette* of Rockbridge County, Virginia, "reads the doom of African slavery in the South. While the Union exists, there is an influence in the North itself that nearly if not altogether cancels the mad efforts of the abolitionists. . . . Disunion will unsettle the line that divides slavery from free territory" (Morton, p. 116).

Throughout the early phase of the secession crisis Virginia fought for compromise and mediation between the federal government and the seceded states. The Virginia legislature proposed that representatives from all states meet in Washington, D.C., on February 4, 1861, to come up with a peaceable solution to the crisis. Yet, the ensuing Washington Peace Conference, which merely reiterated the points of Senator Crittenden's plan, was doomed because none of the already seceded states sent a delegation. With the attempt at compromise thwarted and the Confederate delegation unable to secure the secession of the upper South, uncertainty colored the political and social climates of the United States as Lincoln's inauguration neared.

During his inaugural address on March 4, Lincoln tried to allay Southerners' fears by iterating that he would not interfere with slavery where it existed, but would only prevent its extension into the territories. Although meant to allay fears, Lincoln's remarks left uncertainty. Upper-South states made it quite clear that they would remain in the Union only if the federal government agreed to protect slavery and not use force against any already seceded state. Lincoln explained that he would not relinquish control of any federal property in the South: "The power confided to me will be used to hold, occupy, and possess the property and places belonging to the Government and to collect the duties and imposts; but beyond what may be necessary for these objects, there will be no invasion, no using of force against or among the people anywhere" (Richardson, volume 6, pp. 7–8). Lincoln's first great challenge as president was to determine to what extent he should go to protect government property.

At the center of this dilemma stood Fort Sumter in South Carolina's Charleston Harbor. Still occupied by a U.S. garrison under command of Major Robert Anderson, Lincoln debated in the late winter and early spring of 1861 whether to send reinforcements and resupply the isolated command with provisions (but not with arms). Many of Lincoln's closest advisors, including General Winfield Scott and Secretary of State William Seward, urged Lincoln to let Fort Sumter alone. They believed that if Lincoln avoided pressing the issue with Fort Sumter the upper South would be likely not to secede, crippling the Confederacy's chances for success. Despite the counsel, Lincoln decided to hold firm to his inaugural promise and to make every effort to secure Fort Sumter. In some parts of the country, this intention was viewed unfavorably, and war began to seem imminent.

When Confederate artillery batteries opened fire against Fort Sumter in the early morning hours of April 12, the secession crisis escalated to military conflict.

Robert Barnwell Rhett (from *Battles and Leaders of the Civil War*, 1956, edited by Ned Bradford; Thomas Cooper Library, University of South Carolina)

Three days after the war's opening shots, Lincoln issued a call for seventy-five thousand volunteers to "maintain the honor, the integrity, and the existence of our National Union and the perpetuity of the popular government and to redress wrongs already long endured" (Richardson, volume 6, p. 13). This measure pushed more states toward secession.

On April 17, Virginia's secession convention held a second vote. This time the convention, which had rejected secession on April 4, now voted for secession by a margin of eighty-eight to fifty-five. Lincoln's attempts to hold onto Fort Sumter and his call for volunteers led Virginia and three other Southern states—North Carolina, Tennessee, and Arkansas—to sever their bonds with the Union. Governor John Ellis of North Carolina regarded Lincoln's proclamation for troops "in violation of the Constitution, and a usurpation of power." Ellis asserted that "he could be no party to the wicked violation of the laws of the country, and to this war upon the liberties of a free people." (Stephens, volume 2, p. 375).

Optimism permeated the new Confederacy in the spring of 1861 following the secession of four upper-South states, and Confederate supporters clamored to support the fight for independence. The excitement they felt in the war's early days, however, soon turned to hopelessness as the war ultimately cost more than 620,000 American lives and ended in the Union's favor in the spring of 1865. Alexander Stephens—the Confederacy's vice president and a voice of moderation in the early days of the secession crisis—correctly prophesied what secession would mean to the South and their institutions. "This step [secession] once taken," Stephens informed the Georgia secession convention in January 1861, "can never be recalled . . . we and our posterity shall see our lovely South desolated by the demon of war" (Bigger, pp. 307–308).

Jonathan Noyalas

CHRONOLOGY

1860

November 6: Abraham Lincoln wins the U.S. presidential election.

December 3: President James Buchanan delivers his fourth annual message to a joint session of Congress. Buchanan condemns secession as unconstitutional, but points out that the federal government does not have the authority to coerce a state back into the Union.

December 18: Kentucky senator John J. Crittenden proposes compromise in an attempt to avoid secession and civil war.

December 20: South Carolina's secession convention unanimously approves ordinance of secession.

1861

January 9: Mississippi's secession convention passes ordinance of secession by a vote of eighty-four to fifteen.

January 10: Florida's secession convention approves secession ordinance by a vote of sixty-two to seven.

January 11: Alabama's secession convention approves secession by a margin of sixty-one to thirty-nine.

January 19: Despite the caution urged by Alexander H. Stephens, Georgia's secession convention agrees to sever its bond with the Union by a vote of 208 to 289.

January 26: Louisiana's secession convention approves secession by a vote of 113 to 17.

February 4: The six seceded states of South Carolina, Mississippi, Louisiana, Alabama, Georgia, and Florida begin meeting in Montgomery, Alabama, to form the Confederate States of America.

February 4: The Washington Peace Conference, urged by Virginia's legislature, meets in Washington, D.C. None of the seceded states attend.

February 9: Jefferson Davis is chosen as the provisional president of the Confederate States of America. Alexander H. Stephens is elected vice president.

February 23: A statewide referendum in Texas favors secession by a vote of 46,153 to 14,747.

March 4: Abraham Lincoln is inaugurated president. During his inaugural address, Lincoln expresses his views about secession's unconstitutionality and remarks that the federal government will maintain control of federal installations in the seceded states.

March 15: Secretary of State William H. Seward urges President Abraham Lincoln not to supply and reinforce Fort Sumter in Charleston Harbor.

April 12: Confederates open fire on Fort Sumter, beginning the Civil War.

April 15: President Abraham Lincoln issues a call for 75,000 volunteers to put down the rebellion.

April 17: Virginia's secession convention approves ordinance of secession by a vote of eighty-eight to fifty-five.

May 6: Tennessee secedes from the Union.

May 7: The secession convention of Arkansas approves secession by a vote of sixty-nine to one.

May 20: North Carolina's secession convention unanimously approves its ordinance of secession, becoming the last state to secede from the Union and join the Confederacy.

DOCUMENTS

Document 1: LETTER FROM JAMES M. MASON

Among the more controversial political figures in the U.S. Senate during the antebellum years was Virginia senator James M. Mason, the author of the Fugitive Slave Law of 1850. Mason viewed secession as inevitable following Abraham Lincoln's election in 1860. In the following excerpt Mason explains in a letter to his sister-in-law Anne why secession has become imminent. Mason contends that all of the slaveholding South will forge an alliance to protect their culture from being threatened by a Republican White House. Mason contends that if military conflict between the North and South results from the secession crisis, that all responsibility should rest with the North since they were responsible for Lincoln's victory.

Selma, November 29, 1860
Dear Sister Anne:

Ida's hand is just now in, from writing for me more than one political letter this evening; and as you seem to want one, you shall be indulged. As the hour is late, however, I can give you little more than my *conclusions*; for the *reasons*, I refer you to the two printed papers enclosed signed 'Henry,' being my latest communications to the Richmond papers.

First, then, the dissolution of the Union is a *fixed fact*. As certain as the sun rises, South Carolina goes out as soon as the *Act of Separation* can be reduced to form, after the 17th of December, when the convention meets—*and she is right*. The incidental meeting of her Legislature on the sixth of this month, to elect Electors, alone gave her the initiative. I have no doubt her example will be followed by State after State as fast as they can assemble in convention, and by Virginia with like speed.

The people at the North really seem to be blind and deaf to the exigency which is upon us, and them. The secession of one State for all purposes of *dissolution,* is as effectual as the secession of a dozen, because it breaks the Union, and involves all the issues incidental to a dissolution.

There are those in the South who think (and I am one of them) that we have no choice but to accept the 'irrepressible conflict' tendered us by the late election. It is a *social war,* declared by the North, a war by one form of society against another distinct form of society. Whether it be conducted in arms, the North, which tenders the issue, will decide. Of one thing be certain: there will be an *undivided South;* in a social war they will realize, and must have, a common destiny.

Most affectionately your *brother,*
J. M. Mason

SOURCE:

Senator James M. Mason to his sister-in-law. November 29, 1860, quoted in *The Public Life and Diplomatic Correspondence of James M. Mason: With Some Personal History,* edited by Virginia Mason (New York: Neale, 1906), pp. 160–161.

Document 2: A MODERATE STANCE ON SECESSION

One of the strongest voices for union in the immediate wake of Abraham Lincoln's election was Georgia's Alexander H. Stephens. A career politician having served in the Georgia senate (1836–1841; 1843–1859) and in the U.S. House of Representatives, Stephens devoted much of his antebellum political career to the protection of slavery and to the preservation of the Union. On November 14, 1860, Stephens addressed his state's legislature on the secession question. While some, such as Georgia's U.S. Senator Robert Toombs—a close friend of Stephens—wanted to dissolve Georgia's ties to the Union, Stephens urged restraint. He informed the legislators that they should not cave in to the threats of what the new Republican administration might do, but rather wait to see what course it pursued and then act accordingly. In Stephens's view, working within the Constitution's framework would provide the best opportunity to preserve slavery and prevent civil war. As with so many in the South who urged moderation, Stephens's unionism was conditional. He stated that if his state decided to secede he would support it.

Fellow Citizens: I appear before you to-night at the request of Members of the Legislature and others, to speak of matters of the deepest interests that can possibly concern us all, of an earthly character. There is nothing, no question or subject connected with this life, that concerns a free people so intimately as that of the Government under which they live. We are now, indeed, surrounded by evils. Never since I entered upon the public stage, has the country been so environed with difficulties and dangers that threatened the mere public peace and the very existence of our Institutions as now....

The first question that presents itself is, shall the people of Georgia secede from the Union in consequence of the election of Mr. Lincoln to the Presidency of the United States? My countrymen, I tell you frankly, candidly and earnestly, that I do not think that they ought. In my judgment, the election of no man, constitutionally chosen to that high office, is sufficient cause to justify any State to separate from the Union. It ought to stand by and aid still in the maintaining the Constitution of the country. To make a point of resistance to the Government, to withdraw from it because any man has been elected, would put us in the wrong. We are pledged to maintain the Constitution. Many of us have sworn to support it. Can we, therefore, for the mere election of any man to the Presidency, and that, too, in accordance with the prescribed forms of the Constitution, make a point of resistance to the Government, without becoming the breakers of that sacred instrument ourselves, by withdrawing ourselves from it? Would we not be in the wrong? Whatever fate is to befall this country, let it never be laid to the charge of the people of the South, and especially to the people of Georgia, that we were untrue to our national engagements. Let the fault and wrong rest upon others. If all our hopes are to be blasted, if the Republic is to go down, let us be found to the last moment standing on the deck with the Constitution of the United States waving over our heads....

But it is said Mr. Lincoln's policy and principles are against the Constitution, and that, if he carries them out, it will be destructive of our rights. Let us not anticipate a threatened evil. If he violates the Constitution, then will come our time to act. Do not let us break it because, forsooth, he may. If he does, that is the time for us to act ... I do not anticipate Mr. Lincoln will do anything, to jeopard[ize] our safety or security, whatever may be his spirit to do it; for he is bound by the Constitutional checks which are thrown around him, which at this time render him powerless to do any great mischief....

Should Georgia determine to go out of the Union, I speak for one, though my views might not agree with them, whatever the result may be, I shall bow to the will of her people. Their cause is my cause, and their destiny; and I trust this will the ultimate course of all. The greatest curse that can befall a free people, is civil war....

I am for exhausting all that patriotism demands, before taking the last step. I would invite, therefore, South Carolina to a conference. I would ask the same of all the other Southern States, so that if the evil has got beyond our control, which God in his mercy grant may not be the case, we may not be divided among ourselves; but if possible, secure the united co-operation of all the Southern States, and then, in the face of the civilized world, we may justify our action, and, with the wrong all on the other side, we can appeal to the God of Battles, if it comes to that, to aid us in our cause. But do nothing, in which any portion of our people, may charge you with rash or hasty action. It is certainly a matter of great importance, to tear this Government asunder.

Source:

Alexander H. Stephens. Union Speech of 1860, November 14, 1860, quoted in Stephens's *A Constitutional View of the Late War Between the States: Its Causes, Character, Conduct and Results*, volume 2 (Philadelphia: National Publishing, 1870), pp. 279–299.

Document 3: President James Buchanan's Opinion of Secession

In the four-month interim between the presidential election of November 1860 and the inauguration of Abraham Lincoln on March 4, 1861, President James Buchanan was pressured by some members of Congress to respond to the secession crisis. Wanting to avoid civil war during his final months in office, Buchanan acted cautiously.

Despite his unwillingness to deal aggressively with secession, Buchanan weighed in on the issue during his annual message to Congress on December 3, 1860. In his address, Buchanan stated that the slaveholding states did not have the right to secede simply because they disagreed with the legitimate winner of a presidential election. Despite his condemnation of secession he also stipulated that the federal government did not possess power to prevent secession.

Washington City, December 3, 1860

Fellow-Citizens of the Senate and House of Representatives:

Throughout the year since our last meeting the country has been eminently prosperous in all its material interests. The general health has been excellent, our harvests have been abundant, and plenty smiles throughout the land. Our commerce and manufactures have been prosecuted with energy and industry, and have yielded fair and ample returns. In short, no nation in the tide of the time has ever presented a spectacle of greater material prosperity than we have done until within a very recent period.

Why is it, then, that discontent now so extensively prevails, and the Union of the States, which is the source of all these blessings, is threatened with destruction?

The long-continued and intemperate interference of the Northern people with the question of slavery in the Southern States has at length produced its natural effects. The different sections of the Union are now arrayed against each other, and the time has arrived, so much dreaded by the Father of his Country, when hostile geographical parties have been formed....

And this brings me to observe that the election of any one of our fellow-citizens to the office of President does not of itself afford just cause for dissolving the Union. This is more especially true if his election has been effected by a mere plurality, and not a majority of the people, and has resulted from transient and temporary causes, which may probably never again occur. In order to justify a resort to revolutionary resistance, the Federal Government must be guilty of a "deliberate, palpable, and dangerous exercise" of powers not granted by the Constitution. The late Presidential election, however, has been held in strict conformity with its express provisions. How, then, can the result justify a revolution to destroy this very Constitution? Reason, justice, a regard for the Constitution, all require that we shall wait for some overt and dangerous act on the part of the President elect before resorting to such a remedy....

After all, he is no more than the chief executive officer of the Government. His province is not to make but to execute laws ... Surely under these circumstances we ought to be restrained from present action by the precept of Him who spake as man never spoke, that "sufficient unto the day is the evil thereof." The day of evil may never come unless we shall rashly bring it upon ourselves....

In order to justify secession as a constitutional remedy, it must be on the principle that the Federal Government is a mere voluntary association of States, to be dissolved at pleasure by any one of the contracting parties. If this be so, the Confederacy is a rope of sand, to be penetrated and dissolved by the first adverse wave of public opinion in any of the States. In this manner our thirty-three States may resolve themselves into as many petty, jarring, and hostile republics, each one retiring from the Union without responsibility whenever any sudden excitement might impel them to such a course. By this process a Union might be entirely broken into fragments in a few weeks which cost our forefathers many years of toil, privation, and blood to establish.

Such a principle is wholly inconsistent with the history as well as the character of the Federal Constitution. After it was framed with the greatest deliberation and care it was submitted to conventions of the people of the several States for ratification. Its provisions were discussed at length in these bodies, composed of the first men of the country. Its opponents contended that it conferred powers upon the Federal Government dangerous to the rights of the States, whilst its advocates maintained that under a fair construction of the instrument there was no foundation for such apprehensions. In that mighty struggle between the first intellects of this or any other country it never occurred to any individual, either among its opponents or advocates, to assert or even to intimate that their efforts were all vain labor, because the moment that any State felt herself aggrieved she might secede from the Union. What a crushing argument would this have proved against those who dreaded that the rights of the States would be endangered by the Constitution....

This Government, therefore, is a great and powerful Government, invested with all the attributes of sovereignty over the special subjects to which its authority extends. Its framers never intended to implant in its bosom the seeds of its own destruction, nor were they at its creation guilty of the absurdity of providing for its own dissolution. It was not intended by its framers to be the baseless fabric of a vision, which at the touch of the enchanter would vanish into thin air, but a substantial and mighty fabric, capable of resisting the slow decay of time and of defying the storms of ages....

Without descending to particulars, it may be safely asserted that the power to make war against a State is at variance with the whole spirit and intent of the Constitution. Suppose such a war should result in the conquest of a State; how are we to govern it afterwards? Shall we hold it as a province and govern it by despotic power? In the nature of things, we would not by physical force control the will of the people and compel them to elect Senators and Representatives to Congress and to perform all the other duties depending upon their own volition and required from the free citizens of a free State as a constituent member of the Confederacy.

But if we possessed this power, would it be wise to exercise it under existing circumstances? The object would doubtless be to preserve the Union. War would not only present the most effectual means of destroying it, but would vanish all hope of its peaceable reconstruction. Besides, in the fraternal conflict a vast amount of blood and treasure would be expended, rendering future reconciliation between the States impossible....

But may I be permitted solemnly to invoke my countrymen to pause and deliberate before they determine to destroy this the grandest temple which has ever been dedicated to human freedom since the world began? It has been consecrated by the blood of our fathers, by the glories of the past, and by the hopes of the future.

SOURCE:

James Buchanan. Fourth Annual Message to Congress, December 3, 1860, quoted in *A Compilation of the Messages and Papers of the Presidents,* volume 7, edited by James D. Richardson (New York: Bureau of National Literature, 1897), pp. 3157–3168.

Document 4: JOHN PARKER HALE OPPOSES SECESSION

Among the Northern politicians who abhorred the secession movement in the South was New Hampshire senator John Parker Hale. A career politician, Hale condemned the threat of secession and lambasted President James Buchanan for taking a weak position on secession. Hale pointed out to his fellow senators in this speech on the Senate floor on on December 5, 1860, that while Buchanan stated there was no constitutional right of secession, there was little the federal government could do to prevent a state from leaving the Union. In the excerpt that follows, Hale condemns Buchanan, and he urges his colleagues in Congress to stand firm against secession and to accept no compromise with the South.

I was in the hopes that the President would have looked in the face the crisis which he says the country is in, and that his message would be either one thing or another. But, sir, I have read it somewhat carefully. I listened to it as it was read at the desk, and if I understand it, and I think I do, it is this: South Carolina has just cause for seceding from the Union; that is the first proposition. The second is that she has no right to secede. The third is that we have no right to prevent her from seceding. That is the President's message, substantially. He goes on to represent this as a great and powerful country, and that no State has a right to secede from it; but the power of the country, if I understand the President, consists in what Dickens made the English constitution to be—a power to do nothing at all.

Now, sir, I think it is incumbent upon the President of the United States to point out definitely and recommend to Congress some rule of action, and to tell us what he recommended us to do. But, in my judgment, he has entirely avoided it. He has failed to look the thing in the face. He has acted like the ostrich, which hides her head and thereby thinks to escape danger.

Sir, the only way to escape danger is to look it in the face. I think the country did expect from the President some exposition of a decided policy, and I confess that, for one, I was rather indifferent as to what that policy was that he recommended, but I hoped that it would be something; that it would be decisive. He has utterly failed in that respect.

I think we may as well look this matter right clearly in the face, and I am not going to be long about doing it. I think that this state of affairs looks to one of two things; it looks to absolute submission, not on the part of our Southern friends and the southern States, but of the North, to the abandonment of their position,—it looks to a surrender of that popular sentiment which has been uttered though the constituted forms of the ballot-box, or it looks to open war.

We need not shut our eyes to the fact. It means war, and it means nothing else; and the State which has put herself in the attitude of secession so looks upon it. She has asked no council, she has considered it as a settled question, and she has armed herself. As I understand the aspect of affairs, it looks to that, and it looks to nothing else except unconditional submission on the part of the majority....

I do not wish, sir, to say a word that shall increase any irritation, that shall add any feeling of bitterness to the state of things which really exists in this country, and I would bear and forbear before I would say anything which would add to this bitterness. But I tell you, sire, the plain, true way is to look this thing in the face—see where we are. And I avow here—I do not know whether or not I shall be sustained by those who usually act with me—if the issue which is presented is that the constitutional will of the public opinion of this country, expressed through the forms of the constitution, will not be submitted to, and war is the alternative, let it come in any form or in any shape.

The Union is dissolved and it cannot be held together as a Union if that is the alternative upon which we go into an election. If it is pre-announced and determined that the voice of the majority, expressed through the regular and constituted forms of the constitution, will not be submitted to, then, sir, this is not a Union of equals; it is a Union of a dictatorial oligarchy on one side and a herd of slaves and cowards on the other. That is it, sir, nothing more, nothing less.... The northern States of the Union are the aggressors in one sense; we have a set of presses and a set of politicians among us traitorous to the public voice and the public interests, ministering to a diseased appetite, that lend their energies to the dissemination of aspersions and slanders upon the people among whom they live and upon whom they feed, and I very much fear that our friends upon the other side have listened too much to their aspersions of their fellow citizens, rather than to their own convictions of what the truth is....

Let me say further, sir, that if there are gentlemen who look to the settlement of this controversy by further concessions from the North, I think they miscalculate and mistake. I believe the difficulty has been that we have conceded too much; we have compromised too much, and we have got to that position of things that whenever any fault is found the ever-recurring remedy to the minds of patriots and statesmen is still further concessions from the North....

Sir, we are trying an experiment. I believe we are in its crisis. I have never been of that number who have been disposed to sympathize with 4th of July orators, who have been in the habit, for the last half or three quarters of a century, of glorifying this country and telling what great things she had done. I have uniformly said, when I have had occasion to address the public on the subject, "We have done nothing; we are but at the beginning of a great experiment."

We talk of our republic! Why, sir, it has not yet outlived the ages of the soldiers who fought its battles and won its victories; but yet we are boasting of our victory. Sir, I think Rome existed as a republic for six hundred years, and they might well boast of something that they had done; but that republic passed away. We have not yet survived the lifetime of men who fought the battles of liberty, or of the patriots and sages who formed our constitution of government. What we have obtained we have obtained by a great effort and a great price. It was not the mere price of the American Revolution; it was not the mere price of the patriot blood that was shed, or of the patriot counsels that formed the constitution; but away back, centuries upon centuries in English history, where power and principle contended against each other with alternate success and defeat—in all those centuries there had been going on the contest which is culminating in our experiment here; and no patriot blood that was poured out on the battle fields in the civil wars of England has been insignificant in relation to this conflict ... we shall present a most humiliating spectacle to the world if at this time, when by the acknowledgement of the President of the United States the blessings of heaven have descended upon this people in all the channels of their efforts and their business to an unexampled degree; when the bounties of heaven have been showered down upon us with no niggard hand; at a time, too, when by the confession of a senator from Georgia, not now in his seat [Mr. Toombs], made last year on the floor of the senate—I cannot quote his very words, but I can his sentiment—this general government was faithfully performing all its functions in relation to the slave States, and in relation to every State, never more faithfully than at the present time; I say, if under such circumstances, with a faithful government, and, I will add, a subservient judiciary, with the blessings of Providence coming down upon us as they are, if at such a time this confederacy should burst, this glorious fraternity of States be dissevered, and we try by the doubtful contingencies of separate State action to carry out the great experiment of human liberty, we shall present a most humiliating spectacle.

Why, sire, the very day, the very hour, that we are coming to such a result and thus developing our experiment, the States of Italy that for centuries have gone through the baptism of fire and blood, groaning beneath the iron heel of despotism, one under this and another under that, are throwing off the yoke and uniting together—I say that at such a time when the classic States of Italy, taught by the bitter experience of centuries by a consolidated constitutional government to come together and unite their energies for liberty, for independence, and for progress, if we, untaught by all the past, reckless of the present blind to the future, should madly dash ourselves upon this dark ocean whose shores no eye of prophecy or of faith can discern, we shall present a sad spectacle to the world....

I know nothing, sir, about the policy of the incoming administration. I have never passed a word by mouth or by letter with the President-elect since he has been nominated for the high office to which the people have elected him. It has been my fortune since I have had a seat upon this floor to find myself uniformly, constantly, and perseveringly in the opposition to the administration. I am far from certain that I have not got to take the same position in regard to the incoming administration—very far. One thing is certain; if that administration shall quail in the performance of its duty, if its head shall hesitate, as Mr. Buchanan has done, to look the thing clearly in the face and mark out a policy consistent with honor and patriotism, he certainly will not find me among the number of his supporters.

SOURCE:

John Parker Hale. "Speech on Secession," December 5, 1860, quoted in *Orations from Homer to William McKinley*, volume 15, edited by Mayo W. Hazeltine (New York: Collier & Son, 1902), pp. 6175–6182.

Document 5: SOUTHERN MANIFESTO

By mid-December 1861 many Southern members of the U.S. House of Representatives and Senate resigned themselves to the fact that no compromise solution could be reached and that the Union's dissolution was inevitable. At the urging of Mississippi representative Reuben Davis, representatives and senators from Alabama, Georgia, Florida, Arkansas, Mississippi, North Carolina, Louisiana, and Texas gathered in Jefferson Davis's Washington, D.C., office on December 13, 1860, and wrote this "Southern Manifesto," which stated that nothing could resolve the sectional crisis. The document, which follows, not only pointed out secession's imminence, but also urged slaveholding states to secede from the Union as that was the only protection a state could erect to defend itself.

Washington, December 13th, 1860

To our Constituents: The argument is exhausted. All hope of relief in the Union through the agency of committees, Congressional legislation, or constitutional amendments, is extinguished, and we trust the South will not be deceived by appearances or the pretence of new guarantees. The Republicans are resolute in the purpose to grant nothing that will or ought to satisfy the South. We are satisfied the honor, safety, and independence of the Southern peoples are to be found only in a Southern Confederacy—a result to be obtained only by separate State secession—and that the sole and primary aim of each slaveholding State ought to be its speedy and absolute separation from an unnatural and hostile Union.

SOURCE:

"Southern Manifesto," December 13, 1860, quoted in *The Political History of the United States of America, during the Great Rebellion*, edited by Edward McPherson (Washington, D.C.: Philp & Solomons, 1865), p. 37.

Document 6: ORDINANCE OF SECESSION

With Abraham Lincoln's election in November 1860, South Carolina fire-eaters, as radical secessionists were known, called for immediate secession. On December 20, 1860, three days after South Carolina's secession convention began, the delegates unanimously voted to leave the Union. They justified their secession on constitutional grounds, arguing that the Constitution was a compact of states wherein state sovereignty superseded the powers of the federal government. For men such as former South Carolina representative and senator Robert Barnwell Rhett—who had clamored for secession for nearly three decades prior to Lincoln's election—this was a momentous occasion. Rhett approached the table to sign the ordinance and, according to one observer, dropped to his knees before the document and lifted his hands in the air in praise.

An ordinance to dissolve the Union between the State of South Carolina and other States united with her under the compact entitled "The Constitution of the United States of America."

We, the People of the State of South Carolina, in Convention assembled, do declare and ordain, and it is hereby declared and ordained, that the Ordinance adopted by us in Convention, on the Twenty-third of May, in the year of our Lord one thousand seven hundred and eighty-eight, whereby the Constitution of the United States was ratified, and also all other Acts and parts of Acts of the General Assembly of the State, ratifying amendments of the said Constitution, are hereby repealed, and the union now subsisting between South Carolina and other States, under the name of the United States of America, is hereby dissolved.

SOURCE:

South Carolina Ordinance of Secession, quoted in *The Federalist: A Commentary on the Constitution of the United States,* edited by Paul Leicester Ford (New York: Holt, 1898), p. 711.

Document 7: SPLIT SENTIMENTS

As in many areas of the upper South, a majority of residents in Virginia's Shenandoah Valley did not favor immediate secession following Abraham Lincoln's election. Valley residents believed that the best way to protect slavery was to remain in the Union. Citizens of the Shenandoah Valley were so adamant about remaining in the Union that fifteen of the nineteen delegates from the Valley who attended the Virginia secession convention in early 1861 were Unionists. During the crisis, Valley newspapers published editorials that largely condemned immediate secession. In the following excerpt from the Gazette, *a newspaper published in Rockbridge County—the home of future Confederate General Thomas J. "Stonewall" Jackson—an editorial published on December 20, 1860, the same date that South Carolina signed its secession ordinance, urges caution and restraint in caving in to the fears of what Lincoln and the Republicans might do to the institution of slavery.*

We do not desire to see this government broken up upon a point of honor more shadowy, more imaginary, more unreal, than any ever alleged by the professional duelist as a ground for demanding satisfaction. There is no dishonor in submitting to Lincoln's administration, because he is legally and constitutionally our president. Secession is a voluntary and complete relinquishment of the rights we hold in virtue of the Union. Peaceable secession is nothing less than a surrender of these rights (to slave property in the territories) to break up the Union upon a mere presumption that the president-elect intends to trample upon the constitution is to drive our Northern friends into union with our enemies. There were more votes against Lincoln in the North than in the entire South. Peaceable secession is really cowardly submission. There is a well-considered policy of a few plotting Catalines to precipitate the cotton states, and ultimately all the slave states, into revolution.

SOURCE:

Editorial condemning secession, December 20, 1860, *Rockbridge Gazette,* quoted in *A History of Rockbridge County, Virginia,* edited by Oren F. Morton (Staunton, Va.: McClure, 1920), p. 117.

Document 8: ANOTHER DECLARATION OF INDEPENDENCE

In concert with South Carolina's secession ordinance the Palmetto State secession convention also issued a declaration of independence on December 24, 1860. This document justified secession on the principle that the United States was a compact of states, which meant that at any time they felt their rights threatened they had the right to leave the Union. The South Carolina convention equated the current crisis with the American Revolution. They argued, as many Southerners soon came to believe, that this conflict was a second revolution for independence. Aside from its constitutional justification for secession, the declaration stated that secession was the only course South Carolina could take if it wanted to protect slavery. The document enumerates the apparent obstacles to maintaining the legality of slavery that Northern states imposed—especially, by their refusal to uphold the Fugitive Slave Law.

The State of South Carolina, having determined to resume her separate and equal place among nations, deems it due to herself, to the remaining United States of America, and to the nations of the world that she should declare the causes which have led to this act.

In the year 1765, that portion of the British empire embracing Great Britain, undertook to make laws for the government of that portion composed of the thirteen American colonies. A struggle for the right of self-government ensued, which resulted, on the 4th of July, 1776, in a declaration by the colonies, "that they are, and of right ought to be, free and independent states, that they have full power to levy war, to conclude peace, contract alliances, establish commerce, and do all other acts and things which independent states may of right do."

They further solemnly declare, that whenever any "form of government becomes destructive of the ends for which it was established, it is the right of that people to alter or abolish it, and to institute a new government." Deeming the government of Great Britain to have become destructive of these ends, they declared that the colonies "are absolved from all allegiance to the British crown, and that all political connection between them and the States of Great Britain is and ought to be totally dissolved."

In pursuance of this declaration of independence, each of the thirteen states proceeded to exercise its separate sovereignty; adopted for itself a constitution, and appointed officers for the administration of government in all its departments—legislative, executive, and judicial. For purpose of defense, they united their arms and their counsels; and, in 1778, they united in a league known as the articles of confederation, whereby they agreed to intrust the administration of their external relations to a common agent, known as the Congress of the United States, expressly declaring in the first article, "that each state retains its sovereignty, freedom, and independence, and every power, jurisdiction, and right which is not, by this confederation, expressly delegated to the United States in Congress assembled."

Under this confederation the war of the Revolution was carried on, and on the 3d of September, 1783, the contest ended, and a definite treaty was signed by Great Britain, in which she acknowledged the independence of the colonies in the following terms:

"Article I. His Britannic Majesty acknowledges the said United States, viz.: New Hampshire, Massachusetts Bay, Rhode Island and Providence Plantation, Connecticut, New York, New Jersey, Pennsylvania, Delaware, Maryland, Virginia, North Carolina, South Carolina, and Georgia, to be free, sovereign, and independent states; that he treats them as such; and for himself, his heirs, and successors, relinquishes all claim to the government, proprietary and territorial rights of the same, and every part thereof."

Thus was established the two great principles asserted by the colonies, namely, the right of a state to govern itself, and the right of a people to abolish a government when it becomes destructive of the ends for which it was instituted. And concurrent with the establishment of these principles was the fact, that each colony became and was recognized by the mother country as a free, sovereign, and independent state.

In 1787, deputies were appointed by the states to revise the articles of Confederation, and on September 17th, 1787, the deputies recommended for the adoption of the states the articles of union known as the Constitution of the United States.

The parties to whom the constitution was submitted were the sovereign states; they were to agree or disagree, and when nine of them agreed, the compact was to take effect among those concurring; and the general government, as the common agent, was then to be vested with their authority.

If only nine of the thirteen stated had concurred, the other four would have remained as they then were—separate, sovereign states, independent of any of the provisions of the constitution. In fact, two of the states did not accede to the constitution until long after it had gone into operation among the other eleven; and during that interval, they exercised the functions of an independent nation.

By this constitution, certain duties were charged on the several states, and the exercise of certain of their powers not delegated to the United States by the constitution, nor prohibited by it to the states, are reserved to the states respectively, or to the people. On the 23d of May, 1788, South Carolina, by a convention of her people, passed an ordinance of assenting to this constitution, and afterwards altering her own constitution to conform herself to the obligation she had undertaken.

Thus was established, by compact between the states, a government with defined objects and powers, limited to the express words of the grant, and to so much more only as was necessary to execute the power granted. The limitations left the whole remaining mass of power subject to the clause reserving it to the state or to the people, and rendered unnecessary the specification of reserved powers.

We hold that the government thus established is subject to the two great principles asserted in the declaration of independence, and we hold further that the mode of its formation subjects it to a third fundamental principle, namely—the law of compact. We maintain that in every compact between two or more parties, the obligation is mutual—that the failure of one of the contracting parties to perform a material part of the agreement entirely releases the obligation of the other, and that, where no arbiter is appointed, each party is remitted to his own judgment to determine the fact of failure with all its consequences.

In the present case that fact is established with certainty. We assert that fifteen of the states have deliberately refused for years past to fulfill their constitutional obligation, and we refer to their own statutes for the proof.

The constitution of the United States, in its fourth article, provides as follows:

"No person held to service or labor in one state, under the laws thereof, escaping into another, shall, in consequence of any law or regulation therein, be discharged from any service of labor, but shall be delivered up, on claim of the party to whom such service or labor may be due."

This stipulation was so material to the compact that without it that compact would not have been made. The greater number of the contracting parties held slaves, and the state of Virginia had previously declared her estimate of its value by making it the condition of cession of the territory which now composes the states north of the Ohio river.

The same article of the Constitution stipulates also for the rendition by the several states of fugitives from justice from the other states.

The general government, as the common agent, passed laws to carry into effect these stipulations of the states. For many years these laws were executed. But an increasing hostility on the part of the northern states to the institution of slavery has led to a disregard of their obligations, and the laws of the general government have ceased to effect the objects of the constitution. The states of Maine, New Hampshire, Vermont, Massachusetts, Connecticut, Rhode Island, New York, Pennsylvania, Illinois, Indiana, Ohio, Michigan, Wisconsin, and Iowa have enacted laws which either nullify the acts of Congress, or render useless any attempt to execute them. In many of these states the fugitive is discharged from the service of labor claimed, and in none of them has the state government complied with the stipulation made in the constitution. The state of New Jersey, at an early day, passed a law for the rendition of fugitive slaves in conformity with her constitutional undertaking; but the current of anti-slavery feeling has led her more recently to enact laws which render inoperative the remedies provided by her own law, and by the laws of Congress. In the state of New York even the right of transit for a slave has been denied by her tribunals, and the states of Ohio and Iowa have refused to surrender to justice fugitives charged with murder and inciting servile insurrection in the state of Virginia. Thus the constitutional compact has been deliberately broken and disregarded by the non-slaveholding states, and the consequence follows that South Carolina is released from its obligation.

The ends for which this constitution was framed are declared by itself to be "to form a more perfect union, establish justice, insure domestic tranquility, provide for the common defense, protect the general welfare and secure the blessings of liberty to ourselves and posterity."

These ends it endeavored to accomplish by a federal government, in which each state was recognized as an equal, and had separate control over its own institutions. The right of property in slaves was recognized by giving to free persons distinct political rights; by giving them the right to represent, and burdening them with direct taxes for three-fifths of their slaves; by authorizing the importation of slaves for twenty years, and by stipulating for the rendition of fugitives from labor.

We affirm that these ends for which this government was instituted have been defeated, and the government itself has been made destructive of them by the action of the non-slaveholding state. These states have assumed the right of deciding upon the propriety of our domestic institutions, and have denied the rights of property established in fifteen of the states and recognized by the constitution; they have denounced as sinful the institution of slavery; they have permitted the open establishment among them of societies whose avowed object is to disturb the peace and claim the property of the citizens of other states. They have encouraged and assisted thousands of our slaves to leave their homes, and those who remain have been incited by emissaries, books, and pictures to servile insurrection.

For seventy-five years this agitation has been steadily increasing, until it has now secure to its aid the power of the common government. Observing the forms of the constitution, a sectional party has found within that article establishing the executive department the means of subverting the constitution itself. A geographical line has been drawn across the United States, whose opinions and purposes are hostile to slavery. He is to be intrusted with the administration of the common government, because he has declared that that "government cannot endure permanently half slave, half free," and that the public mind must rest in the belief that slavery is in the course of ultimate extinction.

This sectional combination for the subversion of the constitution has been aided in some of the states by elevating to citizenship persons, who by the supreme law of the land, are incapable of becoming citizens, and their votes have been used to inaugurate a new policy hostile to the south, and destructive of its peace and safety.

On the 4th of March next, this party will take possession of the government. It has announced that the south shall be excluded from the common territory; that the judicial tribunals shall be made sectional, and that a war must be waged against slavery until it shall cease throughout the United States.

The guarantees of the constitution will then no longer exist; the equal rights of the states will be lost. The slaveholding states will no longer have the power of self-government or self-protection, and the federal government will have become their enemies.

Sectional interest and animosity will deepen the irritation, and all hope of remedy is rendered vain by the fact that public opinion at the north has invested a great political error with the sanctions of a more erroneous religious belief.

We, therefore, the people of South Carolina, by our delegates in convention assembled, appealing to the Supreme Judge of the world for the rectitude of our institutions, have solemnly declared that the union heretofore existing between this state and the other states of North America is dissolved, and that the state of South Carolina has resumed her position among the nations of the world as a free, sovereign, and independent state, with full powers to levy war, conclude peace, and contract alliances, establish commerce, and to do all other acts and things which independent states may, of right, do.

And, for the support of this declaration, with a firm reliance on the protection of Divine Providence, we mutually pledge to each other, our lives, our fortunes, and our sacred honor.

SOURCE:

South Carolina Declaration of Independence, 1860, quoted in *The Federalist: A Commentary on the Constitution of the United States,* edited by Paul Leicester Ford (New York: Holt, 1898), pp. 711–715.

Document 9: CRITTENDEN COMPROMISE

As South Carolina contemplated secession in December 1860, the U.S. Congress made one last attempt to develop a compromise that would prevent secession and civil war. Among those to offer a compromise solution was Senator John J. Crittenden of Kentucky. This proposed joint resolution called for the widespread protection of slavery while allowing slavery to extend to territories south of the old Missouri Compromise line. Appearing less like a compromise and more like giving extra concessions to the South, Crittenden's proposal was defeated.

A joint resolution (S. No. 50) proposing certain amendments to the Constitution of the United States.

Whereas serious and alarming dissensions have arisen between the northern and southern States, concerning the rights and security of the rights of the slaveholding States, and especially their rights in the common territory of the United States; and whereas it is eminently desirable and proper that these dissensions, which now threaten the very existence of the Union, shall be permanently quieted and settled by constitutional provisions, which shall do equal justice to all sections, and thereby restore to the people that peace and good-will which ought to prevail between all the citizens of the United States: Therefore,

Resolved by the Senate and House of Representatives of the United States of America in Congress assembled, (two thirds of both Houses concurring,) That the following articles be, and hereby, proposed and submitted as amendments to the Constitution of the United States, which shall be valid to all intents and purposes, as part of said Constitution, when ratified by conventions of three fourths of the several States:

Article 1. In all the territory of the United States now held, or hereafter acquired, situate north of latitude 36° 30′, slavery or involuntary servitude, except as punishment for a crime, is prohibited while such territory shall remain under territorial government. In all the territory south of said line of latitude, slavery of the African race is hereby recognized as existing, and shall not be interfered with by Congress, but shall be protected as property by all the departments of territorial government during its continuance. And when any Territory, north or south of said line, within such boundaries as Congress may prescribe, shall contain the population requisite for a member of Congress according to the then Federal ratio of representation of the people of the United States, it shall, if its form of government be republican, be admitted to the Union, on an equal footing with the original States, with or without slavery, as the continuation of such new State may provide.

Article 2. Congress shall have no power to abolish slavery in places under its exclusive jurisdiction, and situate within the limits of States that permit the holding of slaves.

Article 3. Congress shall have no power to abolish slavery within the District of Columbia, so long as it exists in the adjoining States of Virginia and Maryland, or either, nor without the consent of the inhabitants, nor without just compensation first made to such owners of slaves as do not consent to abolishment. Nor shall Congress at any time prohibit officers of the Federal Government, or members of Congress, whose duties require them to be in said District, from bringing with them their slaves, and holding them as such during the time their duties may require them to remain there, and afterwards taking them from the District.

Article 4. Congress shall have no power to prohibit or hinder the transportation of slaves from one State to another, or to a Territory in which slaves are by law permitted to be held, whether that transportation be by land, navigable rivers, or by sea.

Article 5. That in addition to the provisions of the third paragraph of the second section of the fourth article of the Constitution of the United States, Congress shall have power to provide by law, and it shall be its duty so to provide, that the United States shall pay to the owner who shall apply for it, the full value of his fugitive slave in all cases when the marshal or other officer whose duty it was to arrest said fugitive was prevented from so doing by violence or intimidation, or when, after arrest, said fugitive was rescued by force, and the owner thereby prevented and obstructed in the pursuit of his remedy for the recovery of his fugitive slave under the said clause of the Constitution and the law made in pursuance thereof. And in all such cases, when the United States shall pay for such fugitive, they shall have the right, in their own name, to sue the county in which said violence, intimidation, or rescue was committed, and to recover from it, with interest and damages, the amount paid by them for said fugitive slave. And the said county, after it has paid said amount to the United States, may, for its indemnity, sue and recover from the wrong-doers or rescuers by whom the owner was prevented from the recovery of his fugitive slave, in like manner as the owner himself might have sued and recovered.

Article 6. No future amendment of the Constitution shall affect the five preceding articles; nor the third paragraph of the second section of the first article of the Constitution; nor the third paragraph of the second section of the fourth article of said Constitution; and no amendment shall be made to the Constitution which shall authorize or give to Congress any power to abolish or interfere with slavery in any of the States by whose laws it is, or may be, allowed or permitted.

And whereas, also, besides those causes of dissension embraced in the foregoing amendments proposed to the Constitution of the United States, there are others which come within the jurisdiction of Congress, and may be remedied by its legislative power; and whereas it is the desire of Congress, as far as its power will extend, to remove all just cause for the popular discontent and agitation which now disturb the peace of the country, and threaten the stability of its institutions: Therefore:

1. Resolved by the Senate and House of Representatives of the United States of America in Congress assembled, That the laws now in force for the recovery of fugitive slaves are in strict pursuance of the plain and mandatory provisions of the Constitution, and have been sanctioned as valid and constitutional by the judgment of the Supreme Court of the United States; that the slaveholding States are entitled to the faithful observance and execution of those laws, and that they ought not to be repealed, or so modified or changed as to impair the efficiency; and that laws ought to be made for the punishment of those who attempt by rescue of the slave, or other illegal means, to hinder or defeat the due execution of said laws.

2. That all State laws which conflict with the fugitive slave acts of Congress, or any other constitutional acts of Congress, or which, in their operation, impeded, hinder, or delay the free course and due execution of any of said acts, are null and void by the plain provisions of the Constitution of the United States; yet those States laws, void as they are, have given color to practices, and led to consequences, which have obstructed the due administration and execution of acts of Congress, and especially the acts for the delivery of fugitive slaves, and have thereby contributed much to the discord and commotion now prevailing. Congress, therefore, respectfully and earnestly to recommend the repeal of those laws to the several States which have enacted them as may prevent their being used or perverted to such mischievous purposes.

3. That the act of the 18th of September, 1850, commonly called the fugitive slave law, ought to be so amended as to make the fee of the commissioner, mentioned in the eighth section of the act, equal in amount in the cases decided by him, whether his decision be in favor of or against the claimant. And to avoid misconstruction, the last clause of the fifth section of said act, which authorizes the person holding a warrant for the arrest or detention of a fugitive slave, to summon to his aid the *posse comitatus*, and which declares it to be so amended as expressly limit the authority and duty to cases in which there shall be resistance or danger of resistance and rescue.

4. That the laws of suppression for the African slave trade, and especially those prohibiting the importation of slaves in the United States, ought to be made effectual, and ought to be thoroughly executed; and all further enactments necessary to those ends ought to be promptly made.

Source:

"Crittenden Compromise," quoted in William MacDonald, ed., *Select Documents Illustrative of the History of the United States, 1776–1861* (New York: Macmillan, 1898), pp. 438.

Document 10: Alexander H. Stephens's Speech at the Secession Convention

As the most populous state in the Deep South, Georgia's participation was crucial to the success of any slaveholding confederation. While Georgians decided their fate at their secession convention in mid-January 1861, cautious voices stood up in favor of union. Alexander H. Stephens, the future Confederate vice president, was among those who favored remaining loyal to the Union. On January 17, Stephens addressed the convention and informed his colleagues that the election of one man would not threaten their institutions. In the excerpt that follows from Stephens's convention speech he points out that the North has made every effort to appease the South regarding slavery and that the majority of the government has been and continues to be dominated by the South. Stephens warned fellow members of the convention that secession would forever change the South and bring about a speedy end to slavery.

This step [secession] once taken, can never be recalled, and all the baleful and withering consequence that must follow (as you will see), will rest upon this convention for all coming time. When we and our posterity shall see our lovely South desolated by the demon of war, which this act of yours will inevitably provoke, when our green fields and waving harvest shall be trodden down by a murderous soldiery, and the fiery car of war sweeps over our land, our temples of justice laid in ashes, and every horror and desolation upon us, who but this convention will be held responsible for it, and who but him who shall give his vote for this unwise and ill-timed measure shall be held to a strict account for this suicidal act by the present generation, and be cursed and execrated by posterity in all coming time?. . . Pause, I entreat you, and consider for a moment what reasons you can give that will satisfy yourselves in calmer moments. What right has the North assailed? What interest in the South has been invaded? What justice has been denied? Can any of you name today one governmental act of wrong deliberately, and purposely done by the government at Washington, of which the South has a right to complain? I challenge and answer. On the other hand, let me show the facts of which I wish you to judge, and I will only state facts which are clear and undeniable, and which now stand in the authentic record of the history of our county. When we of the South demanded the slave trade, did they not yield the right for twenty years? When we asked a three-fifths representation in Congress for our section, was it not granted? When we demanded the return of any fugitive from justice, or the recovery of those persons owing labor or allegiance, was it not incorporated in the Constitution, and again ratified and strengthened in the Fugitive Slave Law of 1850? Do you reply that in many instances they have violated this compact? As individuals and local communities they may have done so, but not by the sanction of the government, for that has always been true to Southern interests. When we asked that more territory should be added, that we might spread the institution of slavery, did they not yield to our demands in giving us Louisiana, Florida, and Texas, out of which four States have been carved, and ample territory left for four more to be added in due time, if you by this unwise and impolitic act do not destroy this hope, and perhaps by it lost all, and have your last slave wrenched from you by stern military rule, or by the vindictive decree of universal emancipation, which may reasonably be expected to follow? We have always had control of the government and can yet have it, if we remain in it, and are united as we have been. We have had a majority of the presidents chosen from the South, as well as the control and management of those chosen from the North. We had had sixty years of Southern presidents to their twenty-four, thus controlling the executive department. So of the judges of the Supreme Court. We have had eighteen from the South but eleven from the North. Although nearly four-fifths of the judicial business has arisen in the free States, yet a majority of the court has always been from the South. This we have required so as to guard against any interpretation unfavorable to us. . . . In choosing the presiding officer, *pro tem,* of the Senate, we have had twenty-four and they eleven. Speakers of the House we have had twenty-three, they twelve. While the majority of the representatives, from their greater population, have always been from the North, yet we have generally secured the speaker, because he, to a great extent, shapes and controls the legislation of the country. Nor have we had less control in every other department of the general government. Attorney-generals, we have had fourteen, while the North has had but five. Foreign ministers we have had eighty-six, and they but fifty-four. While three-fourths of the business which demands diplomatic agents abroad is clearly from the free States, because of their greater commercial interests, we have, nevertheless, had the principal embassies, so as to secure the world markets for our cotton, tobacco, and sugar on the best possible terms. We have had a vast majority of the higher officers of both army and navy, while a larger proportion of the soldiers and sailors were drawn from the North. Equally so of clerks, auditors, and comptrollers filling the Executive Department. The records show for the last fifty years that of the three thousand thus employed, we have had more than two-thirds, while we have only one-third of the white population of the Republic.

SOURCE:

Alexander H. Stephens. Speech delivered at Georgia Secession Convention, January 17, 1861, quoted in *Ohio's Silver-Tongued Orator: Life and Speeches of General William H. Gibson,* edited by David Dwight Bigger (Dayton, Ohio: United Brethren, 1901), pp. 307–310.

Document 11: THE FATE OF FORT SUMTER

In the aftermath of Abraham Lincoln's inauguration on March 4, 1861, the upper-South states watched intently to see what methods Lincoln would employ to hold on to federal installations in seceded territory—especially Fort Sumter in Charleston Harbor, which had a garrison of approximately one hundred, with supplies running dangerously low. Fully understanding that if Fort Sumter were resupplied and reinforced the upper South would secede, Lincoln sought the advice of top cabinet and military officials as to what should be done with Fort Sumter. Among those who weighed in on the matter was Secretary of State William H. Seward. An ardent Republican who vehemently disagreed with secession and slavery, Seward urged Lincoln to let Fort Sumter go because holding on to it would not end the secession crisis, but rather, would exacerbate it and prompt the secession of the upper South and potentially start a civil war. Following is Seward's "Cabinet Paper" on Fort Sumter.

Department of State
Washington, March 15, 1861

The President submits to me the following question: "Assuming it to be possible to now provision Fort Sumter, under all the circumstances, is it wise to attempt it?"

If it were possible to peacefully provision Fort Sumter, of course I should answer that it would be both unwise and inhuman not to attempt it. But the facts of the case are known to be that the attempt must be made with the employment of a military and marine force which would provoke combat and probably initiate a civil war, which the Government of the United States would be committed to maintain through all changes to some definitive conclusion.

History must record that a sectional party, practically constituting a majority of the people of the fifteen slave states, excited to a high state of jealous apprehension for the safety of life and property by impassioned though groundless appeals, went into the late election with a predetermined purpose, if unsuccessful at the polls, to raise the standard of secession immediately afterwards, and to separate the slave states, or so many of them as could be detached from the Union, and to organize them in a new, distinct, and independent confederacy. That party was unsuccessful at the polls.

In the frenzy which followed the announcement of their defeat, they put the machinery of the state legislatures and conventions into motion, and within the period of three months they have succeeded in obtaining ordinances of secession by which seven of the slave states have seceded and organized a new confederacy under the name of the "Confederate States of America."

These states, finding a large number of the mints, custom houses, forts, and arsenals of the United States situated within their limits, unoccupied, undefended, and virtually abandoned by the late administration, have seized and appropriated them to their own use, and under the same circumstances have seized and appropriated to their own use large amounts of money and other public property of the United States found within their limits. The people of the other slave states, divided and balancing between sympathy with the seceding slave states and loyalty to the Union, have been intensely excited, but at the present moment indicate a disposition to adhere to the Union if nothing extraordinary shall occur to renew excitement and produce popular exasperation. This is the stage in this premeditated revolution at which we now stand.

The opening of this painful controversy at once raised the question, whether it would be for the interest of the country to admit the projected dismemberment with its consequent evils, or whether patriotism and humanity require that it shall be prevented.

As a citizen, my own decision on this subject was promptly made, namely, that the Union is inestimable and even indispensable to the welfare and happiness of the whole country and to the best interests of mankind. As a statesman in the public service, I have not hesitated to assume that the Federal government is committed to maintain, preserve, and defend the Union, peacefully if it can, forcibly if it must, to every extremity.

Next to disunion itself, I regard civil war as the most disastrous and deplorable of national calamities, and as the most uncertain and fearful of all remedies for political disorders. I have, therefore, made it the study and labor of the hour how to save the Union from dismemberment by peaceful policy and without civil war.

Influenced by these sentiments, I have felt that it is exceedingly fortunate that, to a great extent, the Federal government occupies thus far not an aggressive attitude, but practically a defensive one, while the necessity for action, if civil war is to be initiated, falls on those who seek to dismember and to subvert the Union.

It has seemed to me equally fortunate that the disunionists are absolutely without any justifications for the rash and desperate designs. The administration of the government had been for a long time virtually in their own hands, and controlled and directed by themselves, when they began the work of the revolution.

They had, therefore, no other excuse than apprehension of oppression from the new and adverse administration which was about to come into power.

It seemed to me, farther, to be a matter of good fortune that the new adverse administration must come in with both Houses of Congress containing majorities opposed to its policy, so that, even if it would, it could commit no wrong or injustice against the states which were being madly goaded into revolution. Under these circumstances, disunion could have no better basis to stand upon than a blind, unreasoning, popular excitement, arising out of a simple and harmless disappointment in a Presidential election; that excitement, if it should find no new material, must soon subside and leave disunion without any real support. On the other hand, I have believed firmly that everywhere, even in South Carolina, devotion to the Union is a profound and permanent national sentiment, which, although it may be suppressed and silenced by terror for a time, could, if encouraged, be ultimately relied upon to rally the people of the seceding states to reverse, upon due deliberation, all the popular acts of legislature and conventions by which they were hastily and violently committed to disunion.

The policy of the time, therefore, has seemed to me to consist in conciliation, which should deny to disunionists any new provocation or apparent offence, while it would enable the Unionists in the slave states to maintain with truth and with effect that the alarms and apprehensions put forth by the disunionists are groundless and false.

I have not been ignorant of the objections that the administration was elected through the activity of the republican party; that it must continue to deserve and retain the confidence of that party; while conciliation towards the slave states tends to demoralize the republican party itself, on which party the main responsibility of maintaining the Union must rest.

But it has seemed to me a sufficient answer first, that the administration could not demoralize the republican party without making some sacrifice of its essential principles, while no such sacrifice is necessary, or is anywhere authoritatively proposed; and secondly, if it be indeed true that pacification is necessary to prevent dismemberment of the Union and civil war, or either of them, no patriot and lover of humanity could hesitate to surrender party for the higher interests of country and humanity.

Partly by design, partly by chance, this policy has been hitherto pursued by the late administration of the Federal government, and by the republican party in its corporate action. It is by this policy, thus pursued, I think, that the progress of dismemberment has been arrested after the seven Gulf States had seceded, and the border states yet remain, although they do so uneasily, in the Union.

It is to a perseverance of this policy for a short time longer that I look as the only peaceful means of assuring the continuance of Virginia, Maryland, North Carolina, Kentucky, Tennessee, Missouri, and Arkansas, or most of those states in the Union. It is through their good and patriotic offices that I look to see the Union sentiment revived and brought once more into activity in the seceding states, and through this agency those states themselves returning into the Union.

I am not unaware that I am conceding more than can reasonably be demanded by the people of the border states. They could, speaking justly, demand nothing. They are bound by the Federal obligation to adhere to the Union without concession or conciliation, just as much as the people of the free states are. But in administration we must deal with men, facts, and circumstances, not as they ought to be, but as they are.

The fact then is that while the people of the border states desire to be loyal, they are at the same time sadly, though temporarily, demoralized by a sympathy for the slave states, which makes them forget their loyalty whenever there are any grounds for apprehending that the Federal government will resort to military coercion against the seceding states, even though such coercion should be necessary to maintain the authority, or even the integrity, of the Union. This sympathy is unreasonable, unwise, and dangerous, and therefore cannot, if left undisturbed, be permanent. It can be banished, however, only in one way, and that is by giving time to wear out, and for reason to resume its sway. Time will do this, if it be not hindered by new alarms and provocations.

South Carolina opened the revolution. Apprehending the chastisement by the military arm of the United States, she seized all the forts of the United States in the harbor of Charleston, except Fort Sumter, which, garrisoned by less than one hundred men, stands practically in a state of siege, but at the same time defying South Carolina, and, as the seceding states imagine, menacing her with conquest.

Every one knows first, that even if Sumter were adequately reinforced, it would still be practically useless to the government, because the administration in no case could attempt to subjugate Charleston, or the State of South Carolina.

It is held now because it is the property of the United States, and is a monument of their authority and sovereignty. I would so continue to hold it so long as it can be done without involving some danger or evil greater than the advantage of continued possession. The highest military authority tells us that without supplies the garrison must yield in a few days to starvation—that its numbers are so small that it must yield in a few days to attack by the assailants now lying around it,—and that the case in this respect would remain the same even if it were supplied, but not reinforced. All the military and naval authorities tell us that any attempt at supplies would be unavailing without the employment of armed military and naval force. If we employ armed force for the purpose of supplying the fort, we give all the provocation that could be offered by combining reinforcement with supply.

The question submitted to us then practically is: Supposing it to be possible to reinforce and supply Fort Sumter, is it wise now to attempt it, instead of withdrawing the garrison?

The most that could be done by any means now in our hands would be to throw two hundred and fifty to four hundred men into the garrison with provisions for supplying it five or six months. In this active and enlightened country, in this season of excitement, with a daily press, daily mails, and an incessantly operating telegraph, the design to reinforce and supply the garrison must become known to the opposite party at Charleston as soon at least as preparation for it should begin. The garrison would then almost certainly fall by assault before the expedition could reach the harbor of Charleston. But supposing the secret kept, the expedition must engage in conflict on entering the harbor of Charleston; suppose it to be overpowered and destroyed, is that new outrage to be avenged, or are we then to return our attitude of immobility? Should we be allowed to do so? Moreover, in that event, what becomes of the garrison?

I suppose the expedition successful. We have then a garrison at Fort Sumter that can defy assault for six months. What is it to do then? Is it to make war by opening its batteries and attempting to demolish the defences of the Carolinians? Can it demolish them if it tries? If it cannot, what is the advantage we shall have gained? If it can, how will it serve to check or prevent disunion?

In either case it seems to me that we will have inaugurated a civil war by our own act, without an adequate object, after which reunion will be hopeless, at least under this administration which unnecessarily commenced it. Fraternity is the element of union—war is the very element of disunion. Fraternity if practiced by this administration, will rescue the Union from all its dangers. If this administration, on the other hand, take up the sword, then an opposite party will offer the olive branch, and will, as it ought, profit by the restoration of peace and union.

I may be asked whether I would in no case, and at no time, advise force—whether I purpose to give up everything. I reply—No, I would not initiate war to regain a useless unnecessary position on the soil of the seceding states. I would not provoke war in any way *now*. I would resort to force to protect the collection of the revenue, because that is a necessary as well as a legitimate public object. Even then it should be only a naval force that I would employ for that necessary purpose, which I would defer military action on land until a case should arise where we would hold the defensive. In that case we should have the spirit of the country and the approval of mankind on our side. In the other, we should peril peace and union, because we had not the courage to practice prudence and moderation at the cost of temporary misapprehension.

SOURCE:

William H. Seward. "Reinforcement of Fort Sumter: A Cabinet Paper," March 15, 1861, quoted in *The Diplomatic History of the War for the Union, Being the Fifth Volume of the Works of William H. Seward*, edited by George E. Baker (Boston: Houghton, Mifflin, 1890), pp. 606–609.

Document 12: LINCOLN'S INAUGURAL ADDRESS

During his inaugural address on March 4, 1861, President Abraham Lincoln tried to allay Southerners' fears, saying that he would not do anything to abolish slavery in states where it already existed. Despite Lincoln's conciliatory rhetoric regarding slavery, he did make it clear that he regarded secession as unconstitutional and that it was the president's responsibility to do everything necessary to prevent it. Lincoln stated that he would use whatever means necessary to hold on to federal installations in already seceded states.

I hold that in contemplation of universal law and of the Constitution the Union of these States is perpetual. Perpetuity is implied, if not expressed, in the fundamental law of all national governments. It is safe to assert that no government proper ever had a provision in its organic law for its own extermination. . . .

If the United States be not a government proper, but an association of States in the nature of contract merely, can it, as a contract, be peaceably unmade by less than all the parties who made it? One party to a contract may violate it—break it, so to speak—but does it not require all to lawfully rescind it?

Descending from these general principles, we find the proposition that in legal contemplation the Union is perpetually confirmed by the history of the Union itself. The Union is much older than the Constitution. It was formed, in fact, by the Articles of Association in 1774. It was matured and continued by the Declaration of Independence in 1776. It was further matured, and the faith of all the then thirteen States expressly plighted and engaged that it should be perpetual, by the Articles of Confederation in 1778. And finally, in 1787, one of the declared objects for ordaining and establishing the Constitution was "to form a more perfect Union."

But if destruction of the Union by one or by a party only of the States be lawfully possible, the Union is *less* perfect than before the Constitution, having lost the vital element of perpetuity.

It follows from these views that no State upon its own mere motion can lawfully get out of the Union; that *resolves* and *ordinances* to that effect are legally void, and that acts of violence within any State or States against the authority of the United States are insurrectionary, according to circumstances.

I therefore consider that in view of the Constitution and the laws the Union is unbroken, and to the extent of my ability I shall take care, as the Constitution itself expressly enjoins upon me, that the laws of the Union be faithfully executed in all the States. Doing this I deem to be only a simple duty on my part, and I shall perform it so far as practicable unless my rightful masters, the American people, shall withhold the requisite means or in some authoritative manner direct the contrary. I trust this will not be regarded as a menace, but only as the declared purpose of the Union that it *will* constitutionally defend and maintain itself.

In doing this there needs to be no bloodshed or violence, and there shall be none unless it be forced upon the national authority. The power confided to me will be used to hold, occupy, and possess the property and places belonging to the Government and to collect the duties and imposts; but beyond what may be necessary for these objects, there will be no invasion, no using of force against or among the people anywhere. Where hostility to the United States in any interior locality shall be so great and universal as to prevent competent resident citizens from holding the Federal offices, there will be no attempt to force obnoxious strangers among the people for that object.

Source:

Abraham Lincoln. First Inaugural Address, March 4, 1861, quoted in *A Compilation of the Messages and Papers of the Presidents, 1789–1902*, edited by James D. Richardson (New York.: Bureau of National Literature and Art, 1907), pp. 7–8.

BIBLIOGRAPHY

Abrahamson, James L. *The Men of Secession and Civil War: 1859–1861.* Wilmington, Del.: Scholarly Resources, 2000. Provides a sweeping overview of the secession crisis and an examination of the major figures involved in the crisis.

Barney, William L. *The Secessionist Impulse: Alabama and Mississippi in 1860.* Princeton, N.J.: Princeton University Press, 1974. Examines both the secession crisis in Alabama and Mississippi and the challenges that confronted secessionists. Especially significant is the author's explanation of how secessionists used fear as a great weapon to promote secession.

Basler, Roy P., ed. *The Collected Works of Abraham Lincoln,* 8 volumes. New Brunswick, N.J.: Rutgers University Press, 1953. The most comprehensive assemblage of primary documents related to Abraham Lincoln. Volume four is especially significant as it contains a number of primary documents dealing with Lincoln's views on the secession crisis.

Carey, Anthony Gene. *Parties, Slavery, and the Union in Antebellum Georgia.* Athens: University of Georgia Press, 1997. Examines how secession sentiment evolved in Georgia during the three decades prior to the Civil War.

Channing, Steven A. *Crisis of Fear: Secession in South Carolina.* New York: Simon & Schuster, 1970. Examines the role that paranoia and anxiety played in South Carolina's secession. The book portrays South Carolina as a state that feared, more than anything else, the threat of insurrection and emancipated slaves.

Crofts, Daniel W. *Reluctant Confederates: Upper South Unionists in the Secession Crisis.* Chapel Hill: University of North Carolina Press, 1989. Provides an excellent study of the circumstances that led to the secession of Virginia, North Carolina, and Tennessee.

Davis, William C. *"A Government of Our Own": The Making of the Confederacy.* Baton Rouge: Louisiana State University Press, 1994. While largely a study of the issues that confronted the Confederate delegation in Montgomery, Alabama, in early 1861, Davis's book also provides an assessment of the secession of the Deep South and examines the measures that the newly formed Confederate government undertook to promote secession in the Upper South.

————. *Rhett: The Turbulent Life and Times of a Fire-Eater.* Columbia: University of South Carolina Press, 2001. A highly detailed and readable study of Robert Barnwell Rhett, the father of secession.

———— and James I. Robertson Jr., eds. *Virginia at War: 1861.* Lexington: University Press of Kentucky, 2005. Offers insightful essays on various topics related to the first year of the war. Of particular importance to the secession crisis is James I. Roberston Jr.'s "The Virginia State Convention of 1861," which offers a clear and succinct account of Virginia's decision to secede.

Freehling, William W. *The Road to Disunion: Secessionists Triumphant, 1854–1861,* volume 2. Oxford: Oxford University Press, 1990. A lengthy academic study and the sequel to Freehling's earlier work, *The Road to Disunion: Secessionists at Bay, 1776–1854,* this book presents a very detailed account of the myriad factors that led to secession and how the minority of radical fire-eaters helped fuel the secession crisis.

———— and Craig M. Simpson, eds. *Secession Debated: Georgia's Showdown in 1860.* New York: Oxford University Press, 1992. Provides an excellent introduction to the secession crisis in Georgia and a series of seven primary documents addressing the pros and cons of secession.

Gunderson, Robert Gray. *Old Gentlemen's Convention: The Washington Peace Conference of 1861.* Madison: University of Wisconsin Press, 1961. Provides a detailed analysis of the failed Washington Peace Conference inaugurated by Virginia as a means to avoid secession and military conflict.

Johnson, Michael P. *Toward a Patriarchal Republic: The Secession of Georgia.* Baton Rouge: Louisiana State University Press, 1977. Examines slavery's role in Georgia's secession and how the state's upper-class slaveholders overcame obstacles to promote secession. In the author's view, secession in Georgia was not only motivated by preventing the influence of Republican rule, but it was also a way for the state's slaveholders—a minority in Georgia—to assert themselves politically.

Knoles, George Harmon, ed. *The Crisis of the Union 1860–1861.* Baton Rouge: Louisiana State University Press, 1965. A compilation of four papers originally presented at an academic conference at Stanford University in March 1963 addressing the rise of the Republican Party to power, the split of the Democratic Party, explanations for understanding why secession occurred, and a discussion of reasons why Republicans did not favor compromise.

Link, William A. *Roots of Secession: Slavery and Politics in Antebellum Virginia.* Chapel Hill: University of North Carolina Press, 2003. Examines slavery's role and opposition to the federal government in Virginia during the antebellum years.

Potter, David M. *The Impending Crisis: 1848–1861.* New York: Harper & Row, 1976. A classic study of the years leading up to the Civil War. Potter's work addresses the issues that divided the nation during the thirteen years prior to the Civil War. Especially significant to a study of the secession crisis are chapters 16 through 20.

Reynolds, Donald E. *Editors Make War: Southern Newspapers in the Secession Crisis.* Nashville: Vanderbilt University Press, 1970. Offers examinations of the role of newspapers in promoting secession.

Stampp, Kenneth M. *And the War Came: The North and the Secession Crisis, 1860–1861.* Baton Rouge: Louisiana State University Press, 1950. A classic study on the secession crisis. Stampp's book examines the secession crisis from a northern perspective and offers explanations as to why compromise was not a viable solution to prevent secession and civil war.

Stephens, Alexander H. *A Constitutional View of the Late War Between the States; Its Causes, Character, Conduct and Results,* 2 volumes. Philadelphia: National Publishing, 1870. This two-volume study offers Stephens's analysis of why secession and civil war occurred. Of particular importance to a study of secession are Stephens's speeches against secession which appear primarily in volume 2.

Walther, Eric H. *William Lowndes Yancey and the Coming of Civil War.* Chapel Hill: University of North Carolina Press, 2006. A full biographical treatment of William Lowndes Yancey—one of the most ardent secessionists. The work addresses the issues that occurred throughout Yancey's life that compelled him to favor disunion.

~ 5 ~

ARMED CONFLICT: LOGISTICS, STRATEGY, AND THE EXPERIENCE OF BATTLE

The Civil War (1861–1865) is one of the most passionately argued subjects in American history. It was a monumental struggle that resulted in more than 618,000 soldiers dead and another 471,000 wounded—more casualties than all the other conflicts in U.S. history combined. What made this conflict so bloody? How did the North win? Why did the South lose? In an attempt to answer these questions, one is best served by examining the logistical concerns of both sides, the strategies employed, and the experience of battle.

On the surface, it appears that the North was capable of defeating the South quickly. A survey of key economic resources in 1861 reveals that the Union held a decided advantage over the Confederacy in ten areas: bank deposits, 4.4 to 1; value of manufactured goods, 11 to 1; railroad mileage, 2.4 to 1; shipping tonnage, 16 to 1; value of textiles produced, 18 to 1; pig iron production, 26 to 1; coal production, 21 to 1; corn and wheat production, 2.2 to 1; draft animals, 2 to 1; and value of firearms produced, 31 to 1. A closer look at this last ratio provides a striking illustration of Northern might. In 1860 the Federal government could produce twenty-two thousand rifled muskets a year; within two years it had increased production to five thousand per day. At its height, the South could only manufacture three hundred rifled muskets a day.

The Union, with its twenty-three states (including the Border States of Maryland, Delaware, Kentucky, and Missouri), had a total population of 23.3 million. Its white male population of military age (18 to 45 years) amounted to 4.6 million, which outnumbered the South's 1.1 million by 4.2 to 1. The significance of this reservoir of manpower was evident by 1864 when only 44 percent of Northern males were fighting, while the South had already tapped into 90 percent of its male population (see Document 1).

Yet, for all its advantages, the Union suffered from significant disadvantages. It may have had the larger navy, but it was nearly impossible for it to blockade some 3,600 miles of Southern coastline and 190 harbors and navigable river mouths effectively. Federal forces had to fight along "exterior lines," meaning that they had to penetrate into territory occupied by troops who could easily and quickly respond to incoming threats. Anywhere from 20 percent to 25 percent of Northern troops were foreign born and subsequently did not have the patriotic zeal of their native-born comrades. More important, Union leadership was less than stellar. Between 1861 and 1863 the Army of the Potomac, the main Union army throughout the course of the war, had six different commanders. Irvin McDowell was replaced after the disastrous First Battle of Bull Run in 1861. George B. McClellan won the Battle of Antietam in 1862 but was removed because of his slow response in following up that victory (see Document 2). That same year, John Pope lost at the Second Battle of Bull Run, and his replacement Ambrose Burnside fared no better at Fredericksburg. At Chancellorsville in 1863 Joseph Hooker nearly lost his entire command. Not until

Ulysses S. Grant (Illinois State Military Museum)

George Meade took over the Army of the Potomac did it have a general on par with Southern leadership.

The Confederacy consisted of eleven states; of its total population of 9.1 million, one-third was enslaved. As already illustrated, its industrial capacity was extremely limited, and it had to depend on foreign aid for arms, textiles, and manufactured goods. It was self-sufficient in agricultural output only (see Document 3). Many supplies had to be brought in from Europe on blockade runners (small, fast vessels) (see Document 4).

Nevertheless, the South had some important assets. First, it was fighting a defensive war, and its troops were familiar with the terrain and could make good use of interior lines of communication and supply. Second, man for man, the Southerner made for a better soldier, as he was raised in a rural society and more familiar with firearms and living off the land. Third, cotton, the one area where the South outproduced the North (124 to 1), represented a trump card for the Confederacy. Southern exports were the primary source of raw cotton for the mills in England and France, and possible European intervention in the American domestic squabble could forestall Southern industrial collapse. As for leadership, the Army of Northern Virginia had the best commander of the entire war, Robert E. Lee. Last but not least, a strong sense of honor pervaded Confederate ranks and instilled the average soldier with determination (see Document 5).

Overall, both sides sought a hard, fast victory. No one truly anticipated the duration and intensity of the fighting (see Document 6). For the Confederacy, it just needed to survive and ride out the Federal government's efforts to subdue it. An inherent danger existed in a war of attrition for the South, because Northern capabilities would eventually come to bear.

One cause for this conflict being so bloody was the improvements made in technology and weaponry over the preceding few decades. During the course of the war, railroads transported troops; hot-air balloons provided a means to observe enemy formations and movements; ironclad vessels engaged in combat (see Document 7); and the first successful submarine attack in history occurred. The average soldier fought with a rifled musket, either the Springfield Model 1861 or the Enfield Model 1853. A muzzle-loading weapon relying upon a percussion cap for ignition, the rifled musket had an effective range of five hundred to six hundred yards, a marked improvement over its predecessor, the smoothbore flintlock musket, which had an effective range of only one hundred yards. Artillery pieces also improved and became more powerful. The breech-loading rifled cannons used at the war's end could shoot up to three miles.

By its nature, any military organization is a conservative organ of government, and it is usually reluctant to change. Tried-and-true methods of combat exist long after their effectiveness has worn away, because any army or navy is only as good as its last victory. During the Civil War, it became evident early on that the technology of the day surpassed the standard tactics. Both sides' armies relied upon the previous century's linear tactics (long lines of infantrymen firing at close ranges to maximize the effectiveness of their inaccurate weapons). The result was horrendous casualties. For example, at the Battle of Shiloh in 1862, more than 1,700 were killed and 8,000 wounded on each side (see Document 8). Later that same year at Antietam, total losses for both armies amounted to 23,000 killed and wounded, making that day the single bloodiest one in American history (see Document 9). Consequently, by 1865 trench warfare became the norm on many battlefields, as the contending forces could not achieve victory by simple frontal assaults.

Given the limited medical knowledge of the time, many of those wounded had to endure operations, including amputations, without the benefit of anesthesia (see Document 10). In addition, the simple fact that this conflict was a civil war, pitting father against father and brother against brother, added to the vehemence of the fighting. A case in point can be seen with the guerrillas who operated in Kansas and Missouri (see Document 11). Indeed, as Confederate cavalryman Nathan Bedford Forrest observed, "war means fighting. And fighting means killing."

During the course of the war, military operations occurred in two theaters: the East and the West. Although the first Union strategic plan was sound, the Northern press quickly derided it as the "Anaconda Plan" because of its resemblance to how the large snake constricts its prey. Sketched out by War of 1812 veteran (and octogenarian) Winfield Scott, commander in chief of all Union armies to October 1861, the strategy was a slow process and called for the raising, equipping, and training of large forces. Meanwhile, a tight blockade of the Southern coastline would be implemented and the inland borders sealed off. At that stage Federal armies would drive down the major rivers of the Confederacy (such as the Mississippi), dividing the regions and establishing fortified posts. President Abraham Lincoln, who liked a hands-on approach when it came to military strategy, and his cabinet deemed this plan too ponderous and soon replaced Scott. Nevertheless, even though Scott's vision was initially ignored, it oddly enough turned out to be the strategy needed to defeat the South, a lesson the North did not learn until the last stages of the conflict.

Lee became commander of the Army of Northern Virginia in 1862, after General Joseph E. Johnston was wounded at Seven Pines, and he quickly proved himself to be a shrewd adversary. According to historian Russell F. Weigley, Lee employed a Napoleonic strategy. Named after the famed French emperor and general Napoleon Bonaparte, this approach to war relied upon grand maneuvers that forced opposing enemy forces into disadvantageous positions so they could be defeated in climactic battle. The Confederate general advocated an offensive-defensive approach; in other words, he would

General Robert E. Lee; photograph taken by Julian Vannerson in 1863 (Virginia Historical Society)

stay on the defensive until presented with the chance to attack Union forces. In 1862, he invaded the North for the first time but was halted in Maryland, at Antietam. The following year, he conducted his second invasion (see Document 12) but lost the decisive battle of Gettysburg in Pennsylvania (see Document 13). Thereafter, the Confederacy conducted a strictly defensive war.

By this point, the conflict had taken on a moral tone, as Lincoln had turned the war into one of not only preserving the Union but also of freeing African Americans by virtue of issuing the Emancipation Proclamation, which went into effect on January 1, 1863. In addition, Lincoln appointed Ulysses S. Grant as general in chief of all Union forces in 1864. A reliable and steady commander who had served up until this time in the Western theater, he had proven his worth, having captured the strategic river fortress of Vicksburg in July 1863.

George N. Barnard took this photograph of Columbia, South Carolina, from the state capitol, after the city was burned in 1865 (National Archives).

Grant favored a war of annihilation (see Document 14) against his opponent and believed the conflict could not be won without heavy loss of life. He attacked on all fronts, never letting up the pressure against the South. Grant accompanied the Army of the Potomac under Meade and relentlessly attacked Lee at the Wilderness, Spotsylvania Courthouse, and Cold Harbor. Meanwhile, in order to tie down as many enemy forces as possible and to undermine the resolve of the civilian population, Grant sent General William T. Sherman on a mission to march from Tennessee into Georgia and up through the Carolinas. Sherman's army of some sixty-two thousand men conducted a total war, cutting a swath of destruction sixty miles wide throughout the heartland of the South, destroying railroads, supply depots, and farmsteads (see Document 15). The level of devastation was so exact that even anvils were destroyed so that they could not be used to shoe horses, whether for civilian or military use. Sherman took the cities of Atlanta, Savannah, and Columbia (see Document 16) before proceeding into North Carolina.

Meanwhile, Grant tied down the Army of Northern Virginia at the siege of Petersburg. Eventually breaching the lines, Grant pursued Lee away from the Richmond area. Cornered at Appomattox Courthouse in Virginia, Lee surrendered the Army of Northern Virginia on April 9, 1865, having been "compelled to yield to overwhelming numbers and resources" (see Document 17).

If the American Revolution made America, the Civil War certainly remade it. The nation was finally united and stretched from sea to sea. Nevertheless, the deep wounds of the Civil War took long to heal, and Southern despair and defiance became readily apparent in the Reconstruction era.

Anthony J. Scotti Jr.

CHRONOLOGY

1860

November 6: Abraham Lincoln is elected President.

December 20: South Carolina secedes from the Union. Within two months Mississippi, Florida, Alabama, Georgia, Louisiana, and Texas also secede.

1861

March 4: Abraham Lincoln is sworn in as the sixteenth president of the United States.

April 12–13: Confederate forces lay siege upon Fort Sumter in Charleston, South Carolina.

April 17: Virginia secedes from the Union, followed by Arkansas, North Carolina, and Tennessee.

April 19: Lincoln issues a blockade against Southern ports. Although its legality and effectiveness were in question for a variety of reasons, the blockade reduced the ability of the South to trade and obtain resources.

April 20: Robert E. Lee resigns his commission in the U.S. Army and accepts command of the forces of his home state of Virginia.

July 21: Battle of Bull Run/Manassas. Expectations of a limited conflict are shattered by the military defeat of General Irvin McDowell's Union forces twenty-five miles south of Washington, D.C.

July 27: Lincoln replaces McDowell by appointing George D. McClellan as Commander of the Department of the Potomac. Three months later McClellan is named commander of all Union forces, replacing the aging Winfield Scott.

September 11: Lincoln revokes the proclamation of General John C. Fremont authorizing emancipation as a matter of military necessity in Missouri.

November 8: U.S. Navy seizes Confederate envoys James Mason and John Slidell, creating an international diplomatic crisis between Britain and the United States.

1862

February 16: Fort Donelson falls to Ulysses S. Grant, marking the first major victory for the Union.

March–July: Peninsula Campaign. McClellan attempts to flank Confederate forces around Richmond by making an amphibious assault up the Virginia Peninsula. The attack quickly loses momentum, and Union forces retreat after the Seven Days Battles.

March 8–9: After sinking two Union ships, the Confederate ironclad *Merrimac* battles the Union's ironclad *Monitor* to a draw, effectively ending the utility of wooden ships in battle.

April 6–7: Battle of Shiloh. Confederates surprise Grant's unprepared forces, resulting in twenty-three thousand fatalities, more than the total in all previous American wars combined.

April 25: Naval forces under David Farragut capture New Orleans for the Union.

June 25–July 1: Seven Days Battles. Lee launches a series of counterattacks against McClellan's larger army, pushing the conservative Union general to a withdrawal and ending the Peninsula Campaign.

August 29–30: Second Battle of Bull Run. Stonewall Jackson and James Longstreet defeat the Union Army of Virginia, forcing its commander John Pope to retreat to Washington, D.C.

September 5: Hoping to capitalize on his momentum, Lee launches an offensive campaign through Maryland in hopes of forcing the Union to surrender.

September 17: Battle of Antietam: McClellan fails to exploit his tactical advantage to destroy Lee's army, but his forces are able to halt Lee's offensive and end the threat of Confederate invasion. The conflict's twenty-three thousand casualties make September 17 the bloodiest day in American history.

September 22: Preliminary Emancipation Proclamation. Although the Battle of Antietam was tactically inconclusive, Lee's withdrawal from Maryland provided the "victory" that Lincoln required to publicly announce that all slaves in rebel territory would be considered free by the federal government beginning January 1, 1863.

November 5: Citing his repeated failure to exploit his tactical advantages, Lincoln replaces McClellan with Ambrose Burnside in hopes of a more aggressive command strategy.

December 13: Lee defeats the larger Union force under Burnside at Fredericksburg, Virginia. The battle causes another Union offensive to end in retreat and leads to Burnside's removal a month later.

1863

January 26: Burnside is replaced as Commander of the Army of the Potomac by Joseph "Fighting Joe" Hooker.

May 2: Stonewall Jackson is mortally wounded during the Confederate victory over Hooker's forces in the Battle of Chancellorsville. Lee is able to defeat the much larger Union force by dividing his army and attacking Hooker at several points. Lee once again seeks to seize his momentum by invading the North. Hooker moves to intercept Lee in Pennsylvania but is replaced by George Meade on June 28.

July 1-3: Union victory at Gettysburg, Pennsylvania. Lee's army is forced to retreat from his invasion of the North after three days of intense fighting that result in 50,000 casualties. The final day of fighting culminates in a massive charge of 12,500 Confederate soldiers under George Pickett. The attack is repulsed by Union soldiers and artillery, forcing Lee to withdraw his depleted forces back to Virginia.

July 4: Union forces under Ulysses S. Grant capture Vicksburg, Mississippi, the last Confederate garrison on the Mississippi River. This victory gives the Union control of the river and strengthens Grant's reputation as an effective general.

July 13-16: Draft riots throughout New York City reveal the latent racism of many Northerners as they attack African Americans. The draft riots also reveal frustration with provisions allowing middle- and upper-class draftees to hire a substitute, thus avoiding service.

October 19-20: The most significant defeat of Union forces in the West occurs in the Battle of Chickamauga, along the Tennessee-Georgia border. Although the Union advance was halted, the "victory" proved costly to the Confederacy, as they suffered more casualties than Union forces.

November 23-25: A Confederate siege on the Union-controlled city of Chattanooga is repulsed by Union forces under Grant. The victory effectively ends Confederate control in Tennessee and allows the Union the opportunity to invade the Deep South.

1864

March 12: Grant becomes general in chief of the Union army.

May 6-20: Both sides suffer heavy casualties during the Wilderness Campaign and Battle of Spotsylvania, but Grant continues to advance toward Richmond. Grant orders William T. Sherman to command forces in the West, beginning the Atlanta Campaign.

June 3: Grant orders a futile assault against fortified Confederate forces at Cold Harbor.

June 15: Following the bloody battles in May, Grant and Robert E. Lee's forces begin what will become a nine-month battle of attrition around the city of Petersburg, Virginia.

September 1: Federal forces under Sherman occupy the city of Atlanta after a series of battles.

November 8: Lincoln is reelected as President, largely owing to the recent military success of Union forces.

November 15: After burning most of the city of Atlanta, Sherman begins his notorious March to the Sea. Within five weeks Sherman's forces waged total warfare on the Southern countryside, burning fields and destroying livestock before capturing the seaport city of Savannah, Georgia.

1865

January 31: Congress submits the Thirteenth Amendment to the states for ratification.

April 2-4: After Union forces under Phillip Sheridan defeat George Pickett's forces at Five Forks, Grant's forces are able to break through Confederate lines and take the city of Richmond without a fight.

April 9: Lee surrenders the Army of Northern Virginia at Appomattox Court House in Virginia. Although other Confederate armies continue the war in the West for another month, the Civil War is effectively over.

April 14: Confederate sympathizer John Wilkes Booth assassinates Abraham Lincoln at Ford's Theater.

DOCUMENTS

Document 1: CALL FOR TROOPS

In 1861 both Union and Confederate forces were woefully unprepared for the struggle. The federal government at the time had a regular army of only 16,000 men, and, with secession, many of the Southerners left to join the armed forces of their respective states. As a result, in this proclamation of April 15, 1861, President Abraham Lincoln called up some 75,000 militiamen from the Northern states and territories to serve three-month enlistments. The initial response soon proved to be less than adequate, and within a few months the Lincoln administration had raised another 500,000 troops. Ultimately, an estimated 2.8 million men passed through Union ranks, while as many as 1.5 million served in the Confederate Army.

Whereas the laws of the United States have been for some time past and now are opposed and the execution thereof obstructed in the States of South Carolina, Georgia, Alabama, Florida, Mississippi, Louisiana, and Texas by combinations too powerful to be suppressed by the ordinary course of judicial proceedings or by the powers vested in the marshals by law:

Now, therefore, I, Abraham Lincoln, President of the United States, in virtue of the power in me vested by the Constitution and the laws, have thought fit to call forth, and hereby do call forth, the militia of the several states of the Union to the aggregate number of 75,000, in order to suppress said combinations and to cause the laws to be duly executed.

The details for this object will be immediately communicated to the State authorities through the War Department.

I appeal to all loyal citizens to favor, facilitate, and aid this effort to maintain the honor, the integrity, and the existence of our National Union and the perpetuity of popular government and to redress wrongs already long enough endured.

I deem it proper to say that the first service assigned to the forces hereby called forth will probably be to re-possess the forts, places, and property which have been seized from the Union; and in every event the utmost care will be observed, consistently with the objects aforesaid, to avoid any devastation, any destruction of or interference with property, or any disturbance of peaceful citizens in any part of the country.

And I hereby command the persons composing the combinations aforesaid to disperse and retire peaceably to their respective abodes within twenty days from this date....

SOURCE:

Leslie E. Decker, and Robert Seager II, eds. *America's Major Wars: Crusaders, Critics, and Scholars, Volume 1 (1775–1865)* (Reading, Mass.: Addison-Wesley, 1973), pp. 299–300.

Document 2: MCCLELLAN V. LINCOLN

George B. McClellan is regarded by some military historians as one of the ten worst generals in American history. Appointed to command the Army of the Potomac in 1861, McClellan initially showed his administrative aptitude by thoroughly organizing and training his men. Called the "Young Napoleon" by some, he instilled good morale in the troops, and they loved him in return. However, once put to the test of battle, he demonstrated an inordinate amount of caution. President Abraham Lincoln, impatient for a decisive victory, could not tolerate his subordinate's timidity and frequently goaded him to take more assertive action. Meanwhile, the egotistical McClellan thought of Lincoln as nothing more than a nosy buffoon. The letter of October 13, 1862, reproduced below, demonstrates the president's exasperation at the general's delay in annihilating the Army of Northern Virginia following the victory at Antietam in September 1862. Soon after this missive was written Lincoln fired McClellan.

To General G. B. McClellan.
Executive Mansion, Washington, October 13, 1862

My Dear Sir:

You remember my speaking to you of what I called your over-cautiousness. Are you not over cautious when you assume that you cannot do what the enemy is constantly doing? Should you not claim to be at least his equal in prowess, and act upon the claim?

As I understand, you telegraphed General Halleck that you cannot subsist your army at Winchester unless the rail road from Harper's Ferry to that point be put in working order. But the enemy does now subsist his army at Winchester, at a distance nearly twice as great from railroad transportation as you would have to do, without the railroad last named. He now wagons from Culpepper Court-House, which is just about twice as far as you would have to do from Harper's Ferry. He is certainly not more than half as well provided with wagons as you are. I certainly should be pleased for you to have the advantage of the railroad from Harper's Ferry to Winchester; but it wastes all the remainder of autumn to give it to you, and in fact, ignores the question of *time*, which cannot and must not be ignored.

Again, one of the standard maxims of war, as you know, is "to operate upon the enemy's communications as much as possible, without exposing your own." You seem to act as if this applies *against* you, but cannot apply in your *favor*. Change positions with the enemy, and think you not he would break your communication with Richmond within the next twenty-four hours? You dread his going into Pennsylvania. But if he does so in full force, he gives up his communications to you absolutely, and you have nothing to do but to follow and ruin him, if he does so with less than full force, fall upon and beat what is left behind all the easier.

Exclusive of the water line, you are now nearer to Richmond than the enemy is, by the route that you *can* and he *must* take. Why can you not reach there before him, unless you admit that he is more than your equal on a march? His route is the arc of a circle, while yours is the chord. The roads are as good on yours as on his.

You know I desired, but did not order, you to cross the Potomac below instead of above the Shenandoah and the Blue Ridge. My idea was, that this would at once menace the enemy's communications, which I would seize if he would permit. If he should move northward, I would follow him closely, holding his communications. If he should prevent our seizing his communications, and move toward Richmond, I would press closely to him, fight him if a favorable opportunity should present, and at least try to beat him to Richmond on the inside track. I say "try;" if we never try, we shall never succeed. If he makes a stand at Winchester, moving neither north or south, I would fight him there, on the idea that if we cannot beat him when he bears the wastage of coming to us, we never can when we bear the wastage of going to him. This proportion is a simple truth, and is too important to be lost sight of for a moment. In coming to us he tenders us an advantage which we should not waive. We should not so operate as to merely drive him away. As we must beat him somewhere or fail finally, we can do it, if at all, easier near to us than far away. If we cannot beat the enemy where he now is, we never can, he again being within the intrenchments of Richmond....

It is all easy if our troops march as well as the enemy, and it is unmanly to say they cannot do it. This letter is in no sense an order.

Yours truly,
A. Lincoln

Source:

Henry Steele Commager, ed. *The Civil War Archive: The History of the Civil War in Documents,* revised by Erik Bruun (New York: Tess, 2000), pp. 192–193.

Document 3: A Vengeful President

President Abraham Lincoln's war message of April 15, 1861, in which he called up seventy-five thousand troops to crush the rebellion, evoked strong responses from Southern newspapers. The following article appeared in the Charlottesville (Va.) Review, *and it accuses Lincoln of waging a war of revenge. Note that the reference to the year 1832 concerns Southern opposition to the existing high protective tariff of that time. Unlike many observers, the editors of the* Review *accurately predicted a long and bloody conflict in the making.*

When War—and Civil War—has come, it is neither politic nor in good taste to recur to the past. Political foes will soon stand side by side in the shock of battle. We accept War as a fact. From wickedness, or from some strange hallucination, the President has summoned the country to arms—to fight among themselves. Whoever is to blame about Fort Sumter, why the affair was not dropped there, or confined to Fort Pickens, we are at a loss to conjecture. What object but *revenge*, can have stimulated the immense military preparations in progress, or a purpose to "re-capture" other forts, we cannot discover. We have desired to weigh fairly both sides of this question. We know there is one sentiment at the North, and one sentiment at the South. The Northern journals rest the coercive measures which are being initiated on the necessity of maintaining the Union, and vindicating the Government. We admit very freely that in any ordinary case of resistance to the constituted authorities, force, even war, ought to be resorted to. In 1832 the Government would in our opinion have been fully justified in putting into execution the Force bill. The object of Government is to perpetuate itself, and to uphold its authority.

In the present case a section of country comprising some eight hundred thousand square miles, and eleven millions of people is about to be arrayed in hostility to the government. A sectional line has been drawn, the people on one side of which under the name of "the Government," are marshalling to compel to their ways of thinking the people on the other side. In 1861, it is proposed to carry conviction to fourteen American States by the sword. The Government so far from establishing and perpetuating its authority, is driving from itself new States, and laying the foundation of permanent separation and undying enmity. It is not a case of insubordination. It is the protest of one half of a confederation against the other half.

After ten years—or a generation—have passed—and every green field has been stained with blood—and many a gallant soldier has bit the dust—and bereavement or impoverishment has entered every home in the South, will the South be prepared to go back to the old ways? Shall the free spontaneous outgoings of the American spirit draw its impulses from the instructive promptings of improved artillery and rifled muskets? Will Virginia and Alabama be chastised into the peaceable election of members to the Federal Congress? Will blows with the edge or the flat-side of cavalry sabres teach them to cast electoral votes for a Northern president?

In case of success, the most that the "United States Government" can hope for, is the permanent military occupation of the Southern States. We through this journal have battled for the cause of the American Union, until we exposed ourselves at the hands of some of the best men in the community to the charge of being wanting in patriotism and sectional pride. We have reprobated the dismemberment of this Union in terms of the bitterest and most unmeasured condemnation. Upon an humble theatre, and with humble abilities, we have contended for the Union as a man contends for his life. We have encountered pecuniary injury, and the estrangement of valued friends, in the path of what we believed to be a duty to the welfare of the State, the interests of the American nation, and the cause of human liberty. And now while President Lincoln holds in suspense the uplifted gauge of battle, we warn him in the name of the former Union party in Virginia, that there are no divisions here now that the curtain has begun to rise. If he sends war upon the people of the South, he will meet a united and continued resistance until he will retreat as Pyrrhus did from Italy, or the legions of France retired from Moscow. Peradventure he will retrace his steps as the Persians fled from Marathon, or the English from Bannockburn. The history of Scotland may afford him an instructive lesson. After centuries of war—after the fields of Falkirk and Flodden—Scotland was still unconquered. After four hundred years that Union was effected peaceably which could never be established by force.

We find it difficult to believe that Abraham Lincoln, speaking the same language, professing the same religion, belonging to the same advanced race—born even upon Southern soil—really contemplates serious war. We can hardly realise that any man of fair ability and fair morality in the United States would in earnest inaugurate civil war between Americans. If he were to let loose the devils in hell, he could not get up such a tragedy. We still hope in conformity with his reply to the Virginia Commissioners that his design is at present limited to "the border of the country." That would be trifling in its results to a collision of large armies in the interior. It is the policy of both parties to settle this contest at sea, and at the frontier forts. Mr. Lincoln may try the experiment of coercion to this extent. It will probably only drive all the border States to secession, and succeed in establishing the permanent division of the Union by the slave line. When he should be weary, he would have the satisfaction of having added six or eight States to those already seceded.

This method of conducting the war, *may* be his policy. The danger is that, even if he has the inclination, he may not be able to restrain the storm which he has roused. The conflict will, we fear, gradually extend, and a long and bloody continental war be the result.

Judging by the temper of the people of this community, this last result will be rather invited than avoided. The public heart is stirred to its lowest depths. The War feeling is swelling and surging like the waves of the sea. Who can resist a whole people, thoroughly aroused, brave to rashness, fighting for their existence?

SOURCE:

Charlottesville (Va.) *Review*, April 19, 1861.

Document 4: Lee's Resignation

Robert E. Lee is one of the most beloved figures in Southern history. The son of famed Revolutionary War Lieutenant Colonel Henry "Light-Horse Harry" Lee, Robert E. Lee was a man of deep, abiding principles. He opposed secession and freed his slaves before the fighting commenced. Although offered the command of the Union army, he turned down that tempting position and remained loyal to his home state of Virginia. Below is his letter of resignation as a commissioned officer in the U.S. Army. It is addressed to Winfield Scott, general in chief of federal forces.

Arlington, Va., April 20, 1861.

General:

Since my interview with you on the 18th inst. I have felt that I ought not longer to retain my commission in the army. I therefore tender my resignation, which I request you will recommend for acceptance. It would have been presented at once, but for the struggle it has cost me to separate myself from a service to which I have devoted the best years of my life and all the ability I possessed. During the whole of that time—more than a quarter of a century—I have experienced nothing but kindness from my superiors and a most cordial friendship from my comrades. To no one, general, have I been as much indebted as to yourself for uniform kindness and consideration, and it has always been my ardent desire to merit your approbation. I shall carry to the grave the most grateful recollections of your kind consideration, and your name and fame will always be dear to me.

Save in the defence of my native State, I never desire again to draw my sword. Be pleased to accept my most earnest wishes for the continuance of your happiness and prosperity, and believe me most truly yours,

R. E. Lee.

Source:

A. L. Long, ed. *Memoirs of Robert E. Lee; His Military and Personal History, Embracing a Large Amount of Information Hitherto Unpublished* (New York & Philadelphia: J. M. Stoddart, 1886), p. 94.

Document 5: Campaign Life

The following account was written by Confederate Captain Randolph A. Shotwell, who served in the ranks until his capture in 1864 and was a journalist in North Carolina afterward. His vivid description of the harsh conditions of campaign life is more than the mere grumbling of a typical soldier found in any era and in any conflict: it reveals how utterly bankrupt the Southern economic system had become by the last year of the conflict. Soldiers and civilians suffered alike, as the residents of Richmond, Virginia, could attest. There families were paying ten times more for food than they did in 1860. Northern economic preponderance had truly come to bear.

Our Quarter Master's department . . . really did a great deal more to break down the army than to keep it up. I mean that their shortcomings, their negligence, improvidence, and lack of energy counterbalanced their services. It is a well-known fact, and a most disgraceful one, that when General Lee crossed the Potomac fully *ten thousand* of his men were *barefooted, blanketless,* and *hatless!* The roads were lined with stragglers limping on swollen and blistered feet, shivering all night, (for despite the heat of the day the nights were chilly), for want of blankets; and utterly devoid of underclothes—if indeed they possessed so much as one shirt!

And the lack of proper equipment gradually made itself felt on the *morale* of the men. In the earlier stages of the war when our men were well dressed and cleanly every company having its wagon for extra baggage enabling the private soldiers to have a change of clothing and necessary toilet articles—the men retained much of their individuality as citizen-soldiers, volunteering to undergo for a time, the privations and perils of army life, but never forgetting that they were *citizens* and *gentlemen*, with a good name and reputation for gentlemanliness to maintain. Hence, when in battle array, these gallant fellows, *each had a pride in bearing himself bravely;* and when the hour of conflict arrived they rushed upon the foe with an impetuosity and fearlessness that amazed the old army officers; and caused foreign military men to declare them the best fighters in the world. After a while the spirit of the men became broken. Constant marching and fighting were sufficient of themselves to gradually wear out the army; but it was more undermined by the continual neglect and ill-provision to which the men were subjected.

Months on months they were without a change of underclothing, or a chance to wash that they had worn so long, hence it became actually coated with grease and dust, moistened with daily perspiration under the broiling sun.

Pestiferous vermin swarmed in every camp, and on the march—an indescribable annoyance to every well-raised man yet seemingly uneradicable. Nothing would destroy the little pests but *hours of steady boiling,* and of course, we had neither kettles, nor the time to boil them, if we had been provided with ample means.

As to purchasing clothes, the private soldiers did not have an opportunity of so doing once in six months, as their miserable pittance of $12 per month was generally withheld that length of time, or longer—(I only drew pay *three* times in *four* years, and after the first year, I could not have bought a *couple of shirts* with a *whole month's pay.*) Naturally fastidious in tastes, and habituated to the strictest personal cleanliness and neatness, I chafed from morning till night at the insuperable obstacles to decency by which I was surrounded, and as a consequence there was not one time in the whole four years of the war that I could not have blushed with mortification at meeting with any of my old friends.

It is impossible for such a taste of things to continue for years without breaking down one's self-respect, wounding his *amour propre,* stirring his deepest discontent, and very materially impairing his efficiency as a soldier.

Starvation, rags, dirt, and vermin may be borne *for a time* by the neatest of gentlemen; but when he has become habituated to them, he is no longer a gentleman. The personal pride which made many a man act the *hero* during the first year of the war was gradually worn out and undermined by the open, palpable neglect, stupidity, and indifference of the authorities until during the last year of the war, the hero became a "shirker," and finally a "deserter."

Source:

J. G. de Roulhac Hamilton, ed. *The Papers of Randolph Abbott Shotwell,* volume 1 (Raleigh: North Carolina Historical Commission, 1929), pp. 314–316.

Document 6: Shiloh

The initial engagements fought in the Eastern theater of operations went badly for the North. Mean- *while, in the West, federal forces did much better, and by the spring of 1862, they controlled most of Tennessee, Kentucky, and Missouri, and portions of Arkansas. Confederate General Albert Sidney Johnston, recognizing the need to stop the enemy advance, launched a surprise attack on the Union encampment near Shiloh Church at Pittsburg Landing along the Cumberland River in southwestern Tennessee. Shiloh (the Hebrew word for "place of peace") was the bloodiest battle ever fought in North America up to that point. This two-day engagement on March 6 and 7, 1862, resulted in some twenty-four thousand casualties for both sides. General Ulysses S. Grant's account from* Century Magazine, *February 1865, reproduced below, illustrates the sheer ferocity of the fighting found on many Civil War battlefields. This costly Northern victory resulted in Union control of western Tennessee and northern Mississippi.*

The Battle of Shiloh, or Pittsburg Landing, fought on Sunday and Monday, the 6th and 7th of April, 1862, has been perhaps less understood, or, to state the case more accurately, more persistently misunderstood, than any other engagement between National and Confederate troops during the entire rebellion. Correct reports of the battle have been published, notably by Sherman, Badeau, and, in a speech before a meeting of veterans, by General Prentiss; but all of these appeared long subsequent to the close of the rebellion, and after public opinion had been most erroneously formed.

Events had occurred before the battle, and others subsequent to it, which determined me to make no report to my then chief, General Halleck, further than was contained in a letter, written immediately after the battle, informing him that an engagement had been fought, and announcing the result. The occurrences alluded to are these: After the capture of Fort Donelson, with over fifteen thousand effective men and all their munitions of war, I believed much more could be accomplished without further sacrifice of life.

Clarksville, a town between Donelson and Nashville, in the State of Tennessee, and on the east bank of the Cumberland, was garrisoned by the enemy. Nashville was also garrisoned, and was probably the best-provisioned depot at the time in the Confederacy. Albert Sidney Johnston occupied Bowling Green, Ky., with a large force. I believed, and my information justified the belief, that these places would fall into our hands without a battle, if threatened promptly. I determined not to miss this chance. But being only a district commander, and under the immediate orders of the department commander, General Halleck, whose headquarters were at St. Louis, it was my duty to communicate to him all I proposed to do, and to get his approval, if possible. I did so communicate, and, receiving no reply, acted upon my own judgment. The result proved that my information was correct, and sustained my judgment. What, then, was my surprise, after so much had been accomplished by the troops under my immediate command between the time of leaving Cairo, early in February, and the 4th of March, to receive from my chief a dispatch of the latter date, saying: "You will place Major-General C. F. Smith in command of expedition, and remain yourself at Fort Henry. Why do you not obey my orders to report strength and positions of your command?" I was left virtually in arrest on board a steamer, without even a guard, for about a week, when I was released and ordered to resume my command.

Again: Shortly after the battle of Shiloh had been fought, General Halleck moved his headquarters to Pittsburg Landing, and assumed command of the troops in the field. Although next to him in rank, and nominally in command of my old district and army, I was ignored as much as if I had been at the most distant point of territory within my jurisdiction; and although I was in command of all the troops engaged at Shiloh, I was not permitted to see one of the reports of General Buell or his subordinates in that battle, until they were published by the War Department, long after the event. In consequence, I never myself made a full report of this engagement.

When I was restored to my command, on the 13th of March, I found it on the Tennessee River, part at Savannah and part at Pittsburg Landing, nine miles above, and on the opposite or western bank. I generally spent the day at Pittsburg, and returned by boat to Savannah in the evening. I was intending to remove my headquarters to Pittsburg, where I had sent all the troops immediately upon my reassuming command, but Buell, with the Army of the Ohio, had been ordered to reinforce me from Columbia, Tenn. He was expected daily, and would come in at Savannah. I remained, therefore, a few days longer than I otherwise should have done, for the purpose of meeting him on his arrival.

General Lew Wallace, with a division, had been placed by General Smith at Crump's Landing, about five miles farther down the river than Pittsburg, and also on the west bank. His position I regarded as so well chosen that he was not moved from it until the Confederate attack in force at Shiloh.

The skirmishing in our front had been so continuous from about the 3d of April up to the determined attack, that I remained on the field each night until an hour when I felt there would be no further danger before morning. In fact, on Friday, the 4th, I was very much injured by my horse falling with me and on me while I was trying to get to the front, where firing had been heard. The night was one of impenetrable darkness, with rain pouring down in torrents; nothing was visible to the eye except as revealed by the frequent flashes of lightning. Under these circumstances I had to trust to the horse, without guidance, to keep the road. I had not gone far, however, when I met General W. H. L. Wallace and General (then Colonel) McPherson coming from the direction of the front. They said all was quiet so far as the enemy was concerned. On the way back to the boat my horse's feet slipped from under him, and he fell with my leg under his body. The extreme softness of the ground, from the excessive rains of the few preceding days, no doubt saved me from a severe injury and protracted lameness. As it was, my ankle was very much injured; so much so, that my boot had to be cut off. During the battle, and for two or three days after, I was unable to walk except with crutches.

On the 5th General Nelson, with a division of Buell's army, arrived at Savannah, and I ordered him to move up the east bank of the river, to be in a position where he could be ferried over to Crump's Landing or Pittsburg Landing, as occasion required. I had learned that General Buell himself would be at Savannah the next day, and desired to meet me on his arrival. Affairs at Pittsburg Landing had been such for several days that I did not want to be away during the day. I determined, therefore, to take a very early breakfast and ride out to meet Buell, and thus save time. He had arrived on the evening of the 5th, but had not advised me of the fact, and I was not aware of it until some time after. While I was at breakfast, however, heavy firing was heard in the direction of Pittsburg Landing, and I hastened there, sending a hurried note to Buell, informing him of the reason why I could not meet him at Savannah. On the way up the river I directed the dispatch boat to run in close to Crump's Landing, so that I could communicate with General Lew Wallace. I found him waiting on a boat, apparently expecting to see me, and I directed him to get his troops in line ready to execute any orders he might receive. He replied that his troops were already under arms and prepared to move.

Up to that time I had felt by no means certain that Crump's Landing might not be the point of attack. On reaching the front, however, about 8 A.M., I found that the attack on Shiloh was unmistakable, and that nothing more than a small guard, to protect our transports and stores, was needed at Crump's. Captain A. S. Baxter, a quartermaster on my staff, was accordingly directed to go back and order General Wallace to march immediately to Pittsburg, by the road nearest the river. Captain Baxter made a memorandum of his order. About 1 P.M., not hearing from Wallace, and being much in need of reënforcements, I sent two more of my staff, Colonel James B. McPherson and Captain W. R. Rowley, to bring him up with his division....

Shiloh was a log meeting-house, some two or three miles from Pittsburg Landing, and on the ridge which divides the waters of Snake and Lick creeks, the former entering into the Tennessee just north of Pittsburg Landing, and the latter south. Shiloh was the key to our position, and was held by Sherman. His division was at that time wholly raw, no part of it ever having been in an engagement, but I thought this deficiency was more than made up by the superiority of the commander. McClernand was on Sherman's left, with troops that had been engaged at Fort Donelson, and were therefore veterans so far as Western troops had become such at that stage of the war. Next to McClernand came Prentiss, with a raw division, and on the extreme left, Stuart, with one brigade of Sherman's division. Hurlbut was in rear of Prentiss, massed, and in reserve at the time of the onset. The division of General C. F. Smith was on the right, also in reserve. General Smith was sick in bed at Savannah, some nine miles below, but in hearing of our guns. His services on those two eventful days would no doubt have been of inestimable value had his health permitted his presence. The command of his division devolved upon Brigadier-General W. H. L. Wallace, a most estimable and able officer—a veteran, too, for he had served a year in the Mexican war, and had been with his command at Henry and Donelson. Wallace was mortally wounded in the first day's engagement, and with the change of commanders thus necessarily effected in the heat of battle, the efficiency of his division was much weakened.

The position of our troops made a continuous line from Lick Creek, on the left, to Owl Creek, a branch of Snake Creek, on the right, facing nearly south, and possibly a little west. The water in all these streams was very high at the time, and contributed to protect our flanks. The enemy was compelled, therefore, to attack directly in front. This he did with great vigor, inflicting heavy losses on the National side, but suffering much heavier on his own.

The Confederate assaults were made with such disregard of losses on their own side, that our line of tents soon fell into their hands. The ground on which the battle was fought was undulating, heavily timbered, with scattered clearings, the woods giving some protection to the troops on both sides. There was also considerable underbrush. A number of attempts were made by the enemy to turn our right flank, where Sherman was posted, but every effort was repulsed with heavy loss. But the front attack was kept up so vigorously that, to prevent the success of these attempts to get on our flanks, the National troops were compelled several times to take positions to the rear, nearer Pittsburg Landing. When the firing ceased at night, the National line was all of a mile in rear of the position it had occupied in the morning.

In one of the backward moves, on the 6th, the division commanded by General Prentiss did not fall back with the others. This left his flanks exposed, and enabled the enemy to capture him, with about 2,200 of his officers and men. General Badeau gives 4 o'clock of the 6th as about the time this capture took place. He may be right as to the time, but my recollection is that the hour was later. General Prentiss himself gave the hour as half-past five. I was with him, as I was with each of the division commanders that day, several times, and my recollection is that the last time I was with him was about half-past four, when his division was standing up firmly, and the general was as cool as if expecting victory. But no matter whether it was four or later, the story that he and his command were surprised and captured in their camps is without any foundation whatever. If it had been true, as currently reported at the time, and yet believed by thousands of people, that Prentiss and his division had been captured in their beds, there would not have been an all-day struggle with the loss of thousands killed and wounded on the Confederate side.

With the single exception of a few minutes after the capture of Prentiss, a continuous and unbroken line was maintained all day from Snake Creek or its tributaries on the right to Lick Creek or the Tennessee on the left, above Pittsburg. There was no hour during the day when there was not heavy firing and generally hard fighting at some point on the line, but seldom at all points at the same time. It was a case of Southern dash against Northern pluck and endurance.

Three of the five divisions engaged on Sunday were entirely raw, and many of the men had only received their arms on the way from their States to the field. Many of them had arrived but a day or two before, and were hardly able to load their muskets according to the manual. Their officers were equally ignorant of their duties. Under these circumstances, it is not astonishing that many of the regiments broke at the first fire. In two cases, as I now remember, colonels led their regiments from the field on first hearing the whistle of the enemy's bullets. In these cases the colonels were constitutional cowards, unfit for any military position. But not so the officers and men led out of danger by them. Better troops never went upon a battle-field than many of these officers and men afterward proved themselves to be who fled panic-stricken at the first whistle of bullets and shell at Shiloh.

During the whole of Sunday I was continuously engaged in passing from one part of the field to another, giving directions to division commanders. In thus moving along the line, however, I never deemed it important to stay long with Sherman. Although his troops were then under fire for the first time, their commander, by his constant presence with them, inspired a confidence in officers and men that enabled them to render services on that bloody battle-field worthy of the best of veterans. McClernand was next to Sherman, and the hardest fighting was in front of these two divisions. McClernand told me on that day, the 6th, that he profited much by having so able a commander supporting him. A casualty to Sherman that would have taken him from the field that day would have been a sad one for the troops engaged at Shiloh. And how near we came to this! On the 6th Sherman was shot twice, once in the hand, once in the shoulder, the ball cutting his coat and making a slight wound, and a third ball passed through his hat. In addition to this he had several horses shot during the day.

The nature of this battle was such that cavalry could not be used in front; I therefore formed ours into line, in rear, to stop stragglers, of whom there were many. When there would be enough of them to make a show, and after they had recovered from their fright, they would be sent to reënforce some part of the line which needed support, without regard to their companies, regiments, or brigades....

The situation at the close of Sunday was as follows: Along the top of the bluff just south of the log-house which stood at Pittsburg Landing, Colonel J. D. Webster, of my staff, had arranged twenty or more pieces of artillery facing south, or up the river. This line of artillery was on the crest of a hill overlooking a deep ravine opening into the Tennessee. Hurlbut, with his division intact, was on the right of this artillery, extending west and possibly a little north. McClernand came next in the general line, looking more to the west. His division was complete in its organization and ready for any duty. Sherman came next, his right extending to Snake Creek. His command, like the other two, was complete in its organization and ready, like its chief, for any service it might be called upon to render. All three divisions were, as a matter of course, more or less shattered and depleted in numbers from the terrible battle of the day. The division of W. H. L. Wallace, as much from the disorder arising from changes of division and brigade commanders, under heavy fire, as from any other cause, had lost its organization, and did not occupy a place in the line as a division; Prentiss's command was gone as a division, many of its members having been killed, wounded, or captured. But it had rendered valiant service before its final dispersal, and had contributed a good share to the defense of Shiloh.

There was, I have said, a deep ravine in front of our left. The Tennessee River was very high, and there was water to a considerable depth in the ravine. Here the enemy made a last desperate effort to turn our flank, but was repelled. The gun-boats *Tyler* and *Lexington,* Gwin and Shirk commanding, with the artillery under Webster, aided the army and effectually checked their further progress. Before any of Buell's troops had reached the west bank of the Tennessee, firing had almost entirely ceased; anything like an attempt on the part of the enemy to advance had absolutely ceased. There was some artillery firing from an unseen enemy, some of his shells passing beyond us; but I do not remember that there was the whistle of a single musket-ball heard. As his troops arrived in the dusk, General Buell marched several of his regiments part way down the face of the hill, where they fired briskly for some minutes, but I do not think a single man engaged in this firing received an injury; the attack had spent its force.

General Lew Wallace, with 5,000 effective men, arrived after firing had ceased for the day, and was placed on the right. Thus night came, Wallace came, and the advance of Nelson's division came, but none—unless night—in time to be of material service to the gallant men who saved Shiloh on that first day, against large odds. Buell's loss on the 6th of April was two men killed, and one wounded, all members of the 36th Indiana Infantry. The Army of the Tennessee lost on that day at least 7,000 men. The presence of two or three regiments of his army on the west bank before firing ceased had not the slightest effect in preventing the capture of Pittsburg Landing.

So confident was I before firing had ceased on the 6th that the next day would bring victory to our arms if we could only take the initiative, that I visited each division commander in person before any reënforcements had reached the field. I directed them to throw out heavy lines of skirmishers in the morning as soon as they could see, and push them forward until they found the enemy, following with their entire division in supporting distance, and to engage the enemy as soon as found. To Sherman I told the story of the assault at Fort Donelson, and said that the same tactics would win at Shiloh. Victory was assured when Wallace arrived even if there had been no other support. The enemy received no reënforcements. He had suffered heavy losses in killed, wounded, and straggling, and his commander, General Albert Sidney Johnston, was dead. I was glad, however, to see the reënforcements of Buell and credit them with doing all there was for them to do. During the night of the 6th the remainder of Nelson's division, Buell's army, crossed the river, and were ready to advance in the morning, forming the left wing. Two other divisions, Crittenden's and McCook's, came up the river from Savannah in the transports, and were on the west bank early on the 7th. Buell commanded them in person. My command was thus nearly doubled in numbers and efficiency.

During the night rain fell in torrents, and our troops were exposed to the storm without shelter. I made my headquarters under a tree a few hundred yards back from the river-bank. My ankle was so much swollen from the fall of my horse the Friday night preceding, and the bruise was so painful, that I could get no rest. The drenching rain would have precluded the possibility of sleep, without this additional cause. Some time after midnight, growing restive under the storm and the continuous pain, I moved back to the loghouse on the bank. This had been taken as a hospital, and all night wounded men were being brought in, their wounds dressed, a leg or an arm amputated, as the case might require, and everything being done to save life or alleviate suffering. The sight was more unendurable than encountering the enemy's fire, and I returned to my tree in the rain.

The advance on the morning of the 7th developed the enemy in the camps occupied by our troops before the battle began, more than a mile back from the most advanced position of the Confederates on the day before. It is known now that they had not yet learned of the arrival of Buell's command. Possibly they fell back so far to get the shelter of our tents during the rain, and also to get away from the shells that were dropped upon them by the gun-boats every fifteen minutes during the night.

The position of the Union troops on the morning of the 7th was as follows: General Lew Wallace on the right, Sherman on his left; then McClernand, and then Hurlbut. Nelson, of Buell's army, was on our extreme left, next to the river; Crittenden was next in line after Nelson, and on his right; McCook followed, and formed the extreme right of Buell's command. My old command thus formed the right wing, while the troops directly under Buell constituted the left wing of the army. These relative positions were retained during the entire day, or until the enemy was driven from the field.

In a very short time the battle became general all along the line. This day everything was favorable to the Federal side. We had now become the attacking party. The enemy was driven back all day, as we had been the day before, until finally he beat a precipitate retreat. The last point held by him was near the road leading from the landing to Corinth, on the left of Sherman and right of McClernand. About 3 o'clock, being near that point and seeing that the enemy was giving way everywhere else, I gathered up a couple of regiments, or parts of regiments, from troops near by, formed them in line of battle and marched them forward, going in front myself to prevent premature or long-range firing. At this point there was a clearing between us and the enemy favorable for charging, although exposed. I knew the enemy were ready to break, and only wanted a little encouragement from us to go quickly and join their friends who had started earlier. After marching to within musket-range, I stopped and let the troops pass. The command, *Charge*, was given, and was executed with loud cheers, and with a run, when the last of the enemy broke....

After the rain of the night before and the frequent and heavy rains for some days previous, the roads were almost impassable. The enemy, carrying his artillery and supply trains over them in his retreat, made them still worse for troops following. I wanted to pursue, but had not the heart to order the men who had fought desperately for two days, lying in the mud and rain whenever not fighting, and I did not feel disposed positively to order Buell, or any part of his command, to pursue. Although the senior in rank at the time, I had been so only a few weeks. Buell was, and had been for some time past, a department commander, while I commanded only a district. I did not meet Buell in person until too late to get troops ready and pursue with effect; but, had I seen him at the moment of the last charge, I should have at least requested him to follow....

Shiloh was the severest battle fought at the West during the war, and but few in the East equaled it for hard, determined fighting. I saw an open field, in our possession on the second day, over which the Confederates had made repeated charges the day before, so covered with dead that it would have been possible to walk across the clearing, in any direction, stepping on dead bodies, without a foot touching the ground. On our side National and Confederate were mingled together in about equal proportions; but on the remainder of the field nearly all were Confederates. On one part, which had evidently not been plowed for several years, probably because the land was poor, bushes had grown up, some to the height of eight or ten feet. There was not one of these left standing unpierced by bullets. The smaller ones were all cut down.

Contrary to all my experience up to that time, and to the experience of the army I was then commanding, we were on the defensive. We were without intrenchments or defensive advantages of any sort, and more than half the army engaged the first day was without experience or even drill as soldiers. The officers with them, except the division commanders, and possibly two or three of the brigade commanders, were equally inexperienced in war. The result was a Union victory that gave the men who achieved it great confidence in themselves even after.

The enemy fought bravely, but they had started out to defeat and destroy an army and capture a position. They failed in both, with very heavy loss in killed and wounded, and must have gone back discouraged and convinced that the "Yankee" was not an enemy to be despised.

After the battle I gave verbal instructions to division commanders to let the regiments send out parties to bury their own dead, and to detail parties, under commissioned officers from each division, to bury the Confederate dead in their respective fronts, and to report the numbers so buried. The latter part of these instructions was not carried out by all; but they were by those sent from Sherman's division, and by some of the parties sent out by McClernand. The heaviest loss sustained by the enemy was in front of these two divisions.

The criticism has often been made that the Union troops should have been intrenched at Shiloh; but up to that time the pick and spade had been but little resorted to at the West. I had, however, taken this subject under consideration soon after reassuming command in the field. McPherson, my only military engineer, had been directed to lay out a line to intrench. He did so, but reported that it would have to be made in rear of the line of encampment as it then ran. The new line, while it would be nearer the river, was yet too far away from the Tennessee, or even from the creeks, to be easily supplied with water from them; and in case of attack, these creeks would be in the hands of the enemy. Besides this, the troops with me, officers and men, needed discipline and drill more than they did experience with the pick, shovel, and axe. Reënforcements were arriving almost daily, composed of troops that had been hastily thrown together into companies and regiments—fragments of incomplete organizations, the men and officers strangers to each other. Under all these circumstances I concluded that drill and discipline were worth more to our men than fortifications....

General Albert Sidney Johnston, who commanded the Confederate forces at the beginning of the battle, was disabled by a wound in the afternoon of the first day. His wound, as I understood afterward, was not necessarily fatal, or even dangerous. But he was a man who would not abandon what he deemed an important trust in the face of danger, and consequently continued in the saddle, commanding, until so exhausted by the loss of blood that he had to be taken from his horse, and soon after died. The news was not long in reaching our side, and, I suppose, was quite an encouragement to the National soldiers. I had known Johnston slightly in the Mexican war, and later as an officer in the regular army. He was a man of high character and ability. His contemporaries at West Point, and officers generally who came to know him personally later, and who remained on our side, expected him to prove the most formidable man to meet that the Confederacy would produce. Nothing occurred in his brief command of an army to prove or disprove the high estimate that had been placed upon his military ability.

General Beauregard was next in rank to Johnston, and succeeded to the command, which he retained to the close of the battle and during the subsequent retreat on Corinth, as well as in the siege of that place. His tactics have been severely criticised by Confederate writers, but I do not believe his fallen chief could have done any better under the circumstances. Some of these critics claim that Shiloh was won when Johnston fell, and that if he had not fallen the army under me would have been annihilated or captured. *Ifs* defeated the Confederates at Shiloh. There is little doubt that we would have been disgracefully beaten *if* all the shells and bullets fired by us had passed harmlessly over the enemy, and *if* all of theirs had taken effect. Commanding generals are liable to be killed during engagements; and the fact that when he was shot Johnston was leading a brigade to induce it to make a charge which had been repeatedly ordered, is evidence that there was neither the universal demoralization on our side nor the unbounded confidence on theirs which has been claimed. There was, in fact, no hour during the day when I doubted the eventual defeat of the enemy, although I was disappointed that reënforcements so near at hand did not arrive at an earlier hour.

The Confederates fought with courage at Shiloh, but the particular skill claimed I could not, and still cannot, see; though there is nothing to criticise except the claims put forward for it since. But the Confederate claimants for superiority in strategy, superiority in generalship, and superiority in dash and prowess are not so unjust to the Union troops engaged at Shiloh as are many Northern writers. The troops on both sides were American, and united they need not fear any foreign foe. It is possible that the Southern man started in with a little more dash than his Northern brother; but he was correspondingly less enduring.

The endeavor of the enemy on the first day was simply to hurl their men against ours—first at one point, then at another, sometimes at several points at once. This they did with daring and energy, until at night the rebel troops were worn out. Our effort during the same time was to be prepared to resist assaults whenever made. The object of the Confederates on the second day was to get away with as much of their army and material as possible. Ours then was to drive them from our front, and to capture or destroy as great a part as possible of their men and material. We were successful in driving them back, but not so successful in captures as if further pursuit could have been made. As it was, we captured or recaptured on the second day about as much artillery as we lost on the first; and, leaving out on the one great capture of Prentiss, we took more prisoners on Monday than the enemy gained from us on Sunday. On the 6th Sherman lost 7 pieces of artillery, McClernand 6, Prentiss 8, and Hurlbut 2 batteries. On the 7th Sherman captured 7 guns, McClernand 3, and the Army of the Ohio 20.

At Shiloh the effective strength of the Union force on the morning of the 6th was 33,000. Lew Wallace brought five thousand more after nightfall. Beauregard reported the enemy's strength at 40,955. According to the custom of enumeration in the South, this number probably excluded every man enlisted as musician, or detailed as guard or nurse, and all commissioned officers—everybody who did not carry a musket or serve a cannon. With us everybody in the field receiving pay from the Government is counted. Excluding the troops who fled, panic-stricken, before they had fired a shot, there was not a time during the 6th when we had more than 25,000 men in line. On the 7th Buell brought twenty thousand more. Of his remaining two divisions, Thomas's did not reach the field during the engagement; Wood's arrived before firing had ceased, but not in time to be of much service.

Our loss in the two-days fight was 1,754 killed, 8,408 wounded, and 2,885 missing. Of these 2,103 were in the Army of the Ohio. Beauregard reported a total loss of 10,699, of whom 1,728 were killed, 8,012 wounded, and 959 missing. This estimate must be incorrect. We buried, by actual account, more of the enemy's dead in front of the divisions of McClernand and Sherman alone than here reported, and four thousand was the estimate of the burial parties for the whole field. Beauregard reports the Confederate force on the 6th at over 40,000, and their total loss during the two days at 10,699; and at the same time declares that he could put only 20,000 men in battle on the morning of the 7th.

The navy gave hearty support to the army at Shiloh, as indeed it always did, both before and subsequently, when I was in command. The nature of the ground was such, however, that on this occasion it could do nothing in aid of the troops until sundown on the first day. The country was broken and heavily timbered, cutting off all view of the battle from the river, so that friends would be as much in danger from fire from the gun-boats as the foe. But about sundown, when the National troops were back in their last position, the right of the enemy was near the river and exposed to the fire of the two gun-boats, which was delivered with vigor and effect. After nightfall, when firing had entirely ceased on land, the commander of the fleet informed himself, proximately, of the position of our troops, and suggested the idea of dropping a shell within the lines of the enemy every fifteen minutes during the night. This was done with effect, as is proved by the Confederate reports.

Up to the battle of Shiloh, I, as well as thousands of other citizens, believed that the rebellion against the Government would collapse suddenly and soon if a decisive victory could be gained over any of its armies. Henry and Donelson were such victories. An army of more than 21,000 men was captured or destroyed. Bowling Green, Columbus, and Hickman, Ky., fell in consequence, and Clarksville and Nashville, Tenn., the last two with an immense amount of stores, also fell into our hands. The

Tennessee and Cumberland rivers, from their mouths to the head of navigation, were secured. But when Confederate armies were collected which not only attempted to hold a line farther south, from Memphis to Chattanooga, Knoxville and on to the Atlantic, but assumed the offensive, and made such a gallant effort to regain what had been lost, then, indeed, I gave up all idea of saving the Union except by complete conquest. Up to that time it had been the policy of our army, certainly of that portion commanded by me, to protect the property of the citizens whose territory was invaded, without regard to their sentiments, whether Union or Secession. After this, however, I regarded it as humane to both sides to protect the persons of those found at their homes but to consume everything that could be used to support or supply armies. Protection was still continued over such supplies as were within lines held by us, and which we expected to continue to hold. But such supplies within the reach of Confederate armies I regarded as contraband as much as arms or ordnance stores. Their destruction was accomplished without bloodshed, and tended to the same result as the destruction of armies. I continued this policy to the close of the war. Promiscuous pillaging, however, was discouraged and punished. Instructions were always given to take provisions and forage under the direction of commissioned officers, who should give receipts to owners, if at home, and turn the property over to officers of the quartermaster or commissary departments, to be issued as if furnished from our Northern depots. But much was destroyed without receipts to owners when it could not be brought within our lines, and would otherwise have gone to the support of secession and rebellion. This policy, I believe, exercised a material influence in hastening the end.

Source:

Ned Bradford, ed. *Battles and Leaders of the Civil War* (New York: Fairfax, 1979), pp. 83–94.

Document 7: CLASH OF THE IRONCLADS

The first use of ironclad vessels did not occur in the U.S. Civil War but in the Crimean War of 1853–1856. Such heavily armored ships revolutionized naval warfare in the nineteenth century. The most famous duel between ironclads occurred on March 8, 1862, near Hampton Roads, Virginia, and pitted the CSS Virginia *against the USS* Monitor. *The* Virginia *had originally been the Union frigate* Merrimac, *which had been scuttled by federal forces when they evacuated Norfolk. The Confederate Navy then raised the hulk and fitted the wooden framework with a series of four-inch metal plates. Meanwhile, the* Monitor *was more of a true ironclad and was designed by the Swedish-born engineer John Ericsson. The following account of the fateful encounter between the two ships was written by U.S. Navy Lieutenant S. Dana Greene.*

U.S. Steamer *Monitor*, Hampton Roads, Va.—At 4 P.M. [March 8, 1862] we passed Cape Henry and heard heavy firing in the direction of Fortress Monroe. As we approached, it increased, and we immediately cleared ship for action. When about halfway between Fortress Monroe and Cape Henry we spoke the pilot boat. He told us the *Cumberland* was sunk and the *Congress* was on fire and had surrendered to the *Merrimac*. We could not credit it at first, but as we approached Hampton Roads, we could see the fine old *Congress* burning brightly; and we knew it must be true. Sad indeed did we feel to think those two fine old vessels had gone to their last homes with so many of their brave crews. Our hearts were very full, and we vowed vengeance on the *Merrimac* if it should be our lot to fall in with her. At 9 P.M. we anchored near the frigate *Roanoke*, the flagship, Captain Marston. Captain Worden immediately went on board and received orders to proceed to Newport News and protect the *Minnesota* (then aground) from the *Merrimac*.

We got under way and arrived at the *Minnesota* at 11 P.M. I went on board in our cutter and asked the captain what his prospects were of getting off. He said he should try to get afloat at 2 A.M., when it was high water. I asked him if we could render him any assistance, to which he replied, "No!" I then told him we should do all in our power to protect him from the *Merrimac*. He thanked me kindly and wished us success. Just as I arrived back to the *Monitor* the *Congress* blew up, and certainly a grander sight was never seen; but it went straight to the marrow of our bones. Not a word was said, but deeply did each man think and wish we were by the side of the *Merrimac*. At 1 A.M. we anchored near the *Minnesota*. The captain and myself remained on deck, waiting for the appearance of the *Merrimac*. At 3 A.M. we thought the *Minnesota* was afloat and coming down on us; so we got under way as soon as possible and stood out of the channel. After backing and filling about for an hour, we found we were mistaken and anchored again. At daylight we discovered the *Merrimac* at anchor with several vessels under Sewall's Point. We immediately made every preparation for battle. At 8 A.M. on Sunday the *Merrimac* got under way accompanied by several steamers, and started direct for the *Minnesota*. When a mile distant she fired two guns at her. By this time our anchor was up, the men at quarters, the guns loaded, and everything ready for action. As the *Merrimac* came close, the captain passed the word to commence firing. I triced up the port, ran out the gun, and fired the *first* gun, and thus commenced the great battle between the *Monitor* and the *Merrimac*.

Now mark the condition our men and officers were in. Since Friday morning, forty-eight hours, they had had no rest and very little food, as we could not conveniently cook. They had been hard at work all night, and nothing to eat for breakfast except hard bread, and were thoroughly worn out. As for myself, I had not slept a wink for fifty-one hours and had been on my feet almost constantly.

But after the first gun was fired we forgot all fatigues, hard work, and everything else and fought as hard as men ever fought. We loaded and fired as fast as we could. I pointed and fired the guns myself. Every shot I would ask the captain the effect, and the majority of them were encouraging. The captain was in the pilothouse, directing the movements of the vessel; Acting Master Stodder was stationed at the wheel which turns the tower but, as he could not manage it, was relieved by Steiners. The speaking trumpet from the tower to the pilothouse was broken; so we passed the word from the captain to myself on the berth deck by Paymaster Keeler and Captain's Clerk Toffey.

Five times during the engagement we touched each other, and each time I fired a gun at her, and I will vouch the hundred and sixty-eight pounds penetrated her sides. Once she tried to run us down with her iron prow but did no damage whatever. After fighting for two hours we hauled off for half an hour to hoist shot in the tower. At it we went again as hard as we could, the shot, shell, grape, canister, musket, and rifle balls flying in every direction but doing no damage. Our tower was struck several times, and though the noise was pretty loud it did not affect us any. Stodder and one of the men were carelessly leaning against the tower when a shot struck it exactly opposite them and disabled them for an hour or two.

At about 11:30 A.M. the captain sent for me. I went forward, and there stood as noble a man as lives, at the foot of the ladder to the pilothouse, his face perfectly black with powder and iron, and apparently perfectly blind. I asked him what was the matter. He said a shot had struck the pilot-house exactly opposite his eyes and blinded him, and he thought the pilothouse was damaged. He told me to take charge of the ship and use my own discretion. I led him to his room, laid him on the sofa, and then took his position. On examining the pilothouse I found the iron hatch on top, on the forward side, was completely cracked through.

We still continued firing, the tower being under the direction of Steiners. We were between two fires, the *Minnesota* on one side and the *Merrimac* on the other. The latter was retreating to Sewall's Point, and the *Minnesota* had struck us twice on the tower. I knew if another shot should strike our pilothouse in the same place, our steering apparatus would be disabled, and we should be at the mercy of the batteries on Sewall's Point. We had *strict* orders to act on the defensive and protect the *Minnesota*. We had evidently finished the *Merrimac* as far as the *Minnesota* was concerned. Our pilothouse was damaged, and we had orders *not* to follow the *Merrimac* up; therefore, after the *Merrimac* had retreated. I went to the *Minnesota* and remained by her until she was afloat. General Wool and Secretary Fox both commended me for acting as I did and said it was the strict military plan to follow. This is the reason we did not sink the *Merrimac*, and every one here capable of judging says we acted perfectly right.

Source:

Lydia Minturn Post, ed. *Soldiers' Letters from Camp, Battlefield and Prison* (New York: Bunce & Huntington, 1865), pp. 109–113.

Document 8: Upcoming Battle

The first Confederate invasion of federal territory in the Eastern Theater resulted in a bloody battle near Sharpsburg, Maryland, at Antietam Creek on September 17, 1862. Robert E. Lee had several reasons for taking the war to Maryland. Aside from desiring to draw this slave state into the Confederacy, he wanted to threaten Washington, D.C. In addition, his aggressiveness would hopefully sway the peace candidates in the upcoming Northern elections as well as convince European powers to officially recognize the Confederacy. The resulting engagement proved more violent than Shiloh. In some spots the bodies piled up two or three deep, and the sunken road in the middle of the battlefield became known as "Bloody Lane." The account reproduced below is that of Private David L. Thompson, Company G, Ninth New York Volunteers, and describes a ranker's view of the approach to the upcoming battle. His regiment consisted of Zouaves, Union troops who wore French-style uniforms with red caps, baggy trousers, and white leggings.

On the 5th of September, 1862, Hawkins's Zouaves, as a part of Burnside's corps, from Fredericksburg, landed at Washington to assist in the defense of the capital, then threatened by Lee's first invasion of Maryland, and, as events proved, to join in the pursuit of the invaders. Here, in pursuance of a measure for shortening the baggage train which had lately been decided on, we were deprived of our Sibley tents—those cumbersome, conical caravansaries, in which eighteen men lie upon the ground with their feet toward the center.

Shelter tents came soon to replace the "Sibleys," and with them came marching orders—the army was moving west. At dusk we set up our new houses. A shelter or dog tent is like a bargain—it takes two to make it. Each man is provided with an oblong piece of thick, unbleached muslin about the length of a man—say six feet—and two-thirds as wide, bordered all round with buttons and button-holes alternately matching respectively button-holes and buttons of the comrade's piece. To set it up, cut two crotched stakes, each about four feet long, point them at the uncrotched end, and drive them into the ground about six feet apart; cut a slender pole to lie horizontally from one crotch to the other, button the two pieces of muslin together and throw the resulting piece over the pole, drawing out the corners tight and pinning them down to the ground by means of little loops fastened in them. You will thus get a wedge-shaped structure—simply the two slopes of an ordinary roof—about three and a half feet high at its highest point, and open at both ends. This will accommodate two men, and in warm, pleasant weather is all that is needed. In rainy weather a third man is admitted. A piece of rope about four feet long is then tied to the top of one of the stakes and then stretched out in the line of direction of the ridge pole, the free end being brought down to the ground and pinned there. The third man then buttons his piece of muslin to one slope of the roof, carries the other edge of the piece out and around the tightened rope and brings it back to the edge of the other slope, to which it is buttoned. This third piece is shifted from one end of the tent to the other, according to the direction of the wind or storm. You thus get an extension to your tent in which knapsacks can be stored, leaving the rest of the space clear for sleeping purposes. This is large enough to accommodate three men lying side by side.

But will such a structure keep out rain? Certainly, just as your umbrella does—unless you touch it on the inside when it is soaked. If you do, the rain will come in, drop by drop, just where you have touched it. To keep the water from flowing in along the surface of the ground, dig a small trench about three inches deep all around the tent, close up, so that the rain shed from the roof will fall into it. Such a house is always with you potentially, for you carry the materials on your back and can snap your fingers at the baggage wagon. For three-fourths of the year it is all the shelter needed, as it keeps out rain, snow, and wind perfectly, being penetrable only by the cold.

We marched at last, and the 12th of September entered Frederick, wondering all the way what the enemy meant. We of the ranks little suspected what sheaves he was gathering in at Harper's Ferry, behind the curtain of his main body. We guessed, however, as usual, and toward evening began to get our answer. He was right ahead, his rear-guard skirmishing with our advance. We came up at the close of the fight at Frederick, and, forming line of battle, went at double-quick through cornfields, potato patches, gardens, and backyards—the German washer-women of the 103d New York regiment going in with us on the run. It was only a measure of precaution, however, the cavalry having done what little there was to do in the way of driving out of the city a Confederate rear-guard not much inclined to stay. We pitched tents at once in the outskirts, and after a hearty supper went to explore the city.

The next morning the feeling of distrust which the night before had seemed to rule the place had disappeared, and a general holiday feeling took its place. The city was abloom with flags, houses were open everywhere, trays of food were set on the window-sills of nearly all the better class of houses, and the streets were filled with women dressed in their best, walking bareheaded, singing, and testifying in every way the general joy. September 13th in Frederick City was a bright one in memory for many a month after—a pleasant topic to discuss over many a camp-fire.

The next day our regiment went on a reconnoissance to a speck of a village, rather overweighted by its name—

Jefferson—about eight miles from Frederick and on our left. Far up the mountainside ahead of us we could see, in the fields confronting the edge of the woods that crowned the ridge, the scattered line of Rush's Lancers, their bright red pennons fluttering gayly from their spear heads.

We reached camp again about 10 o'clock at night, and found awaiting us marching orders for 2 o'clock the following morning. Late as it was, one of my tent-mates—an enterprising young fellow—started out on a foraging expedition, in pursuance of a vow made several days before to find something with which to vary his monotonous regimen of "hard-tack" and "salt horse." He "ran the guard"—an easy thing to do in the darkness and hubbub—and returned shortly after, struggling with a weight of miscellaneous plunder; a crock of butter, a quantity of apple-butter, some lard, a three-legged skillet weighing several pounds, and a live hen. It was a marvel how he managed to carry so much; but he was a rare gleaner always, with a comprehensive method that covered the ground. That night we had several immense flapjacks, the whole size of the pan; then, tethering the hen to one of the tent pegs, we went to sleep, to be roused an hour or so later by hearing our two-legged prize cackling and fluttering off in the darkness.

Up to the 10th the army had not marched so much as it had drifted, but from this point on our purpose seemed to grow more definite and the interest deepened steadily. There had been sporadic fighting through the day (the 13th), but it was over the hills to the west, and we heard nothing of it beyond those airy echoes that take the shape of rumor. Now, however, the ferment at the front, borne back by galloping orderlies, was swiftly leaving the mass. Occasionally, on our march we would pass a broken gun wheel or the bloated body of a slaughtered horse, and in various ways we knew that we were close upon the enemy, and that we could not now be long delayed. This would have been told us by the burden of our daily orders, always the same, to hold ourselves "in readiness to march at a moment's notice," with the stereotyped addendum, "three days' cooked rations and forty rounds." Every one lay down to sleep that night with a feeling of impending battle.

By daylight next morning we were in motion again—the whole army. The gathering of such a multitude is a swarm, its march a vast migration. It fills up every road leading in the same direction over a breadth of many miles, with long ammunition and supply trains disposed for safety along the inner roads, infantry and artillery next in order outwardly, feelers of cavalry all along its front and far out on its flanks; while behind, trailing along every road for miles (ravelings from the great square blanket which the enemy's cavalry, if active, snip off with ease), are the rabble of stragglers—laggards through sickness or exhaustion, squads of recruits, convalescents from the hospital, special duty men going up to rejoin their regiments. Each body has its route laid down for it each day, its time of starting set by watch, its place of bivouac or camp appointed, together with the hour reaching it. If two roads come together, the corps that reaches the junction first moves on, while the other flies out into the fields, stacks arms, builds fires, and boils its coffee. Stand, now, by the roadside while a corps is filing past. They march "route step," as it is called—that is, not keeping time—and four abreast, as a country road seldom permits a greater breadth, allowing for the aides and orderlies that gallop in either direction continually along the column. If the march has just begun, you hear the sound of voices everywhere, with roars of laughter in spots, marking the place of the company wag—generally some Irishman, the action of whose tongue bears out his calling. Later on, when the weight of knapsack and musket begins to tell, these sounds die out; a sense of weariness and labor rises from the toiling masses streaming by, voiced only by the shuffle of a multitude of feet, the rubbing and straining of innumerable straps, and the flop of full canteens. So uniformly does the mass move on that it suggests a great machine, requiring only its directing mind. Yet such a mass, without experience in battle, would go to pieces before a moderately effective fire. Catch up a handful of snow and throw it, it flies to fluff; pack it, it strikes like stone. Here is the secret of organization—the aim and crown of drill, to make the units one, that when the crisis comes, the missile may be thoroughly compacted. Too much, however, has been claimed for theoretic discipline—not enough for intelligent individual action. No remark was oftener on the lips of officers during the war than this: "Obey orders! *I* do your thinking for you." But that soldier is the best whose good sense tells him when to be merely a part of a machine and when not.

The premonitions of the night were not fulfilled next day. That day—the 14th of September—we crossed the Catoctin range of mountains, reaching the summit about noon, and descended its western slope into the beautiful valley of Middletown. Half-way up the valley's western side we halted for a rest, and turned to look back on the moving host. It was a scene to linger in the memory. The valley in which Middletown lies is four or five miles wide, as I remember it, and runs almost due north and south between the parallel ranges of Catoctin and South Mountains. From where we stood the landscape lay below us, the eye commanding the opposite slope of the valley almost at point-blank. An hour before, from the same spot, it had been merely a scene of quiet pastoral beauty. All at once, along its eastern edge the heads of the columns began to appear, and grew and grew, pouring over the ridge and descending by every road, filling them completely and scarring the surface of the gentle landscape with the angry welts of war. By the farthest northern road—the farthest we could see—moved the baggage wagons, the line stretching from the bottom of the valley back to the top of the ridge, and beyond, only the canvas covers of the wagons revealing their character. We knew that each dot was a heavily loaded army wagon, drawn by six mules and occupying forty feet of road at least. Now they looked like white beads on a string. So far away were they that no motion was perceptible. The constant swelling of the end of the line down in the valley, where the teams turned into the fields to park, gave evidence that, in this way, it was being slowly reeled along the way. The troops were marching by two roads farther south. The Confederates fighting on the western summit must have seen them plainly. Half a mile beyond us the column broke abruptly, filing off into line of battle, right and left, across the fields. From that point backward and downward, across the valley and up the farther slope, it stretched with scarcely a gap, every curve and zigzag of the way defined more sharply by its somber presence. Here, too, on all the distant portions of the line, motion was imperceptible, but could be inferred from the casual glint of sunlight on a musket barrel miles away. It was 3 o'clock when we resumed our march, turning our backs upon the beautiful, impressive picture—each column a monstrous, crawling, blue-black snake, miles long, quilled with the silver slant of muskets at a "shoulder," its sluggish tail writhing slowly up over the distant eastern ridge, its bruised head weltering in the roar and smoke upon the crest above, where was being fought the battle of South Mountain.

We were now getting nearer to the danger line, the rattle of musketry going on incessantly in the edges of the woods and behind the low stone fences that seamed the mountain-side. Then we came upon the fringes of the of the contest—slightly wounded men scattered along the winding road on their way to the hospital, and now and then a squad of prisoners, wounded and unwounded together, going under guard to the rear.

The brigade was ordered to the left of the road to support a regular battery posted at the top of a steep slope, with a cornfield on the left, and twenty yards or so in front, a thin wood. We formed behind the battery and a little down the slope—the 89th on the left, and the 9th next, then the 103d. We had been in position but a few minutes when a stir in front advised us of something unusual afoot, and the next moment the Confederates burst out of the woods and made a dash at the battery. We had just obeyed a hastily given order to lie down, when the bullets whistled over our heads, and fell far down the slope behind us. Then the guns opened at short range, full-shotted with grape and canister. The force of the charge was easily broken, for though it was vigorously made it was not sustained—perhaps was not intended to be, as the whole day's battle had been merely an effort of the enemy to check our advance till he could concentrate for a general engagement. As the Confederates came out of the woods their line touched ours on the extreme left only, and there at an acute angle, their men nearly treading on those of the 89th, who were on their faces in the cornfield, before they discovered them. At that instant the situation just there was ideally, cruelly advantageous to us. The Confederates stood before us not twenty feet away, the full intention of destruction on their faces—but helpless, with empty muskets. The 89th simply rose up and shot them down.

It was in this charge that I first heard the "rebel yell"; not the deep-breasted Northern cheer, given in unison and after a struggle, to signify an advantage gained, but a high shrill yelp, uttered without concert, and kept up continually when the fighting was approaching a climax, as an incentive to further effort. This charge ended the contest for the day on that part of the line. Pickets were set well forward in the woods, and we remained some time in position, waiting. How a trivial thing will often thrust itself upon the attention in a supreme moment was well exemplified here. All about us grew pennyroyal, bruised by the tramping of a hundred feet, and the smell of it has always been associated in my memory with that battle.

Before the sunlight faded, I walked over the narrow field. All around lay the Confederate dead—undersized men mostly, from the coast district of North Carolina, with sallow, hatchet faces, and clad in "butternut"—a color running all the way from a deep, coffee brown up to the whitish brown of ordinary dust. As I looked down on the poor, pinched faces, worn with marching and scant fare, all enmity died out. There was no "secession" in those rigid forms, nor in those fixed eyes staring blankly at the sky. Clearly it was not "their war." Some of our men primed their muskets afresh with the finer powder from the cartridge-boxes of the dead. With this exception, each remained untouched as he had fallen. Darkness came on rapidly, and it grew very chilly. As little could be done at that hour in the way of burial, we unrolled the blankets of the dead, spread them over the bodies, and then sat down in line, munching a little on our cooked rations in lieu of supper, and listening to the firing, which was kept up on the right, persistently. By 9 o'clock this ceased entirely. Drawing our blankets over us, we went to sleep, lying upon our arms in line as we had stood, living Yankee and dead Confederate side by side, and indistinguishable.—This was Sunday, the 14th of September.

The next morning, receiving no orders to march, we set to work collecting the arms and equipments scattered about the field, and burying the dead. The weather being fine, bowers were built in the woods—generally in fence corners—for such of the wounded as could not be moved with safety; others, after stimulants had been given, were helped down the mountain to the rude hospitals. Before we left the spot, some of the country people living thereabout, who had been scared away by the firing, ventured back, making big eyes at all they saw, and asking most ridiculous questions. One was, whether we were from Mexico! Those belated echoes, it seemed, were still sounding in the woods of Maryland.

Source:

Ned Bradford, ed. *Battles and Leaders of the Civil War* (New York: Fairfax, 1979), pp. 233–239.

Document 9: Moving North

In mid-1863, Confederate general Robert E. Lee decided again to go on the offensive. Aside from needing to procure provisions for his troops in the farmlands north of the Potomac, he wanted to influence the growing peace movement in the federal government, especially among the Copperheads, an extreme wing of the Democrats (named because they were considered as deadly as the snake). In addition, as was the case with the first invasion in 1862, Lee hoped that a successful campaign would finally induce either England or France to enter the conflict on behalf of the Confederacy. In this missive, Lee succinctly explains his decision to Confederate Secretary of War James A. Seddon.

(Confidential.) hdqrs. Army of Northern Virginia
June 8, 1863
Hon. James A. Seddon
Secretary of War, Richmond, Va.:

Sir:

. . . As far as I can judge, there is nothing to be gained by this army remaining quietly on the defensive, which it must do unless it can be reinforced. I am aware that there is difficulty and hazard in taking the aggressive with so large an army in front, intrenched behind a river, where it cannot be advantageously attacked. Unless it can be drawn out in a position to be assailed, it will take its own time to prepare and strengthen itself to renew its advance upon Richmond, and force this army back within the intrenchments of that city. This may be the result in any event; still, I think it is worth a trial to prevent such a catastrophe. Still, if the Department thinks it better to remain on the defensive, and guard as far as possible all the avenues of approach, and await the time of the enemy, I am ready to adopt this course. You have, therefore, only to inform me.
R. E. Lee,
General.

Source:

Henry Steele Commager, ed. *The Civil War Archive: The History of the Civil War in Documents.* Revised by Erik Bruun (New York: Tess, 2000), p. 432.

Document 10: Gettysburg

Between July 1 and 3, 1863, the Army of Northern Virginia assaulted the positions of the Army of the Potomac near Gettysburg, Pennsylvania. This engagement proved not to be Robert E. Lee's best battle. Ill at the time with dysentery and piles, he attempted to turn one flank of the Union positions, then the other, and finally attacked in the center. Lee's trusted subordinate Lieutenant General James Longstreet thought the battle to be fruitless and disagreed with his commander's plan of action. The climactic charge conducted by three divisions under Major General George Pickett is related below by

Brigadier General E. Porter Alexander. Pickett's Charge, made by 13,500 troops on a one-mile front, lasted forty minutes and resulted in a bloodbath. The divisions involved failed in the attempt and lost 50 percent of their strength. Gettysburg represented the greatest Union victory of the war. Meanwhile, the South suffered another major defeat with the fall of Vicksburg, Mississippi, on July 4. The year 1863 was the turning point of the war.

We marched quite steadily, with a good road and a bright moon, until about 7 A.M. on the 2d, when we halted in a grassy open grove about a mile west of Seminary Ridge, and fed and watered. Here, soon afterward, I was sent for by General Longstreet, and, riding forward, found him with General Lee on Seminary Ridge. Opposite, about a mile away, on Cemetery Ridge, overlooking the town, lay the enemy, their batteries making considerable display, but their infantry, behind stone walls and ridges, scarcely visible. In between us were only gentle rolling slopes of pasture and wheat-fields, with a considerable body of woods to the right and front. The two Round Tops looked over everything, and a signal-flag was visible on the highest. Instinctively the idea arose, "If we could only take position here and have them attack us through this open ground!" But I soon learned that we were in no such luck—the boot, in fact, being upon the other foot.

It was explained to me that our corps was to assault the enemy's left flank, and I was directed to reconnoiter it and then to take charge of all the artillery of the corps and direct it in the attack, leaving my own battalion to the command of Major Huger. I was particularly cautioned, in moving the artillery, to keep it out of sight of the signal-station upon Round Top. . . .

We waited quite a time for the infantry, and I think it was about 4 o'clock when at last the word was given for Hood's division to move out and endeavor to turn the enemy's left, while McLaws awaited the development of Hood's attack, ready to assault the Peach Orchard. Henry's battalion moved out with Hood and was speedily and heavily engaged; Cabell was ready to support him, and at once went into action near Snyder's house, about seven hundred yards from the Peach Orchard.

The Federal artillery was ready for us and in their usual full force and good practice. The ground at Cabell's position gave little protection, and he suffered rapidly in both men and horses. To help him I ran up Huger with 18 guns of my own 26, to Warfield's house, within 500 yards of the Peach Orchard, and opened upon it. This made fifty-four guns in action, and I hoped they would crush that part of the enemy's line in a very short time, but the fight was longer and hotter than I expected. So accurate was the enemy's fire, that two of my guns were fairly dismounted, and the loss of men was so great that I had to ask General Barksdale, whose brigade was lying down close behind in the wood, for help to handle the heavy 24-pounder howitzers of Moody's battery. He gave me permission to call for volunteers, and in a minute I had eight good fellows, of whom, alas! we buried two that night, and sent to the hospital three others mortally or severely wounded. At last I sent for my other two batteries, but before they arrived McLaws's division charged past our guns, and the enemy deserted their line in confusion. Then I believed that Providence was indeed "taking the proper view," and that the war was very nearly over. Every battery was limbered to the front, and the two batteries from the rear coming up, all six charged in line across the plain and went into action again at the position the enemy had deserted. I can recall no more splendid sight, on a small scale—and certainly no more inspiring moment during the war—than that of the charge of these six batteries. An artillerist's heaven is to follow the routed enemy, after a tough resistance, and throw shells and canister into his disorganized and fleeing masses. Then the explosions of the guns sound louder and more powerful, and the very shouts of the gunners, ordering "Fire!" in rapid succession, thrill one's very soul. There is no excitement on earth like it. It is far prettier shooting than at a compact, narrow line of battle, or at another battery. Now we saw our heaven just in front, and were already breathing the very air of victory. Now we would have our revenge, and make them sorry they had staid so long. Everything was in a rush. The ground was generally good, and pieces and caissons went at a gallop, some cannoneers mounted, and some running by the sides—not in regular line, but a general race and scramble to get there first.

But we only had a moderately good time with Sickles's retreating corps after all. They fell back upon fresh troops in what seemed a strong position extending along the ridge north of Round Top. Hood's troops under Law gained the slope of Little Round Top, but were driven back to its base. Our infantry lines had become disjoined in the advance, and the fighting became a number of isolated combats between brigades. The artillery took part whenever it could, firing at everything in sight, and a sort of pell-mell fighting lasted until darkness covered the field and the fuses of the flying shells looked like little meteors in the air. But then both musketry and artillery slackened off, and by 9 o'clock the field was silent....

Early in the morning General Lee came around, and I was then told that we were to assault Cemetery Hill, which lay rather to our left. This necessitated a good many changes of our positions, which the enemy did not altogether approve of, and they took occasional shots at us, though we shifted about, as inoffensively as possible, and carefully avoided getting into bunches. But we stood it all meekly, and by 10 o'clock, Dearing having come up, we had seventy-five guns in what was virtually one battery, so disposed as to fire on Cemetery Hill and the batteries south of it, which would have a fire on our advancing infantry. Pickett's division had arrived, and his men were resting and eating. Along Seminary Ridge, a short distance to our left, were sixty-three guns of A. P. Hill's corps, under Colonel R. L. Walker. As their distance was a little too great for effective howitzer fire, General Pendleton offered me the use of nine howitzers belonging to that corps. I accepted them, intending to take them into the charge with Pickett; so I put them in a hollow behind a bit of wood, with no orders but to wait there until I sent for them. About 11, some of Hill's skirmishers and the enemy's began fighting over a barn between the lines, and gradually his artillery and the enemy's took part, until over a hundred guns were engaged, and a tremendous roar was kept up for quite a time. But it gradually died out, and the whole field became as silent as a churchyard until 1 o'clock. The enemy, aware of the strength of his position, simply sat still and waited for us. It had been arranged that when the infantry column was ready, General Longstreet should order two guns fired by the Washington Artillery. On that signal all our guns were to open on Cemetery Hill and the ridge extending toward Round Top, which was covered with batteries. I was to observe the fire and give Pickett the order to charge. I accordingly took position, about 12, at the most favorable point, just on the left of the line of guns and with one of Pickett's couriers with me. Soon after I received the following note from Longstreet:

COLONEL: If the artillery fire does not have the effect to drive off the enemy or greatly demoralize him, so as to make our efforts pretty certain, I would prefer that you should not advise General Pickett to make the charge. I shall rely a great deal on your good judgment to determine the matter, and shall expect you to let General Pickett know when the moment offers.

This note rather startled me. If that assault was to be made on General Lee's judgment it was all right, but I did not want it made on mine. I wrote back to General Longstreet to the following effect:

GENERAL: I will only be able to judge of the effect of our fire on the enemy by his return fire, for his infantry is but little exposed to view and the smoke will obscure the whole field. If, as I infer from your note, there is any alternative to this attack, it should be carefully considered before opening our fire, for it will take all the artillery ammunition we have left to test this one thoroughly, and, if the result if unfavorable, we will have none left for another effort. And even if this is entirely successful, it can only be so at a very bloody cost.

To this presently came the following reply:

COLONEL: The intention is to advance the infantry if the artillery has the desired effects of driving the enemy's off, or having other effect such as to warrant us in making the attack. When the moment arrives advise General Pickett, and of course advance such artillery as you can use in aiding the attack.

I hardly knew whether this left me discretion or not, but at any rate it seemed decided that the artillery must open. I felt that if we went that far we could not draw back, but the infantry must go too. General A. R. Wright, of Hill's corps, was with me looking at the position when these notes were received, and we discussed them together. Wright said, "It is not so hard to *go* there as it looks: I was nearly there with my brigade yesterday. The trouble is to *stay* there. The whole Yankee army is there in a bunch."

I was influenced by this, and somewhat by a sort of camp rumor which I had heard that morning, that General Lee had said that he was going to send every man he had upon that hill. At any rate, I assumed that the question of supports had been well considered, and that whatever was possible would be done. But before replying I rode to see Pickett, who was with his division a short distance in the rear. I did not tell him my object, but only tried to guess how he felt about the charge. He seemed very sanguine, and thought himself in luck to have the chance. Then I felt that I could not make any delay or let the attack suffer by any indecision on my part. And that General Longstreet might know my intention, I wrote him only this: "GENERAL: When our artillery fire is at its best, I shall order Pickett to charge."

Then, getting a little more anxious, I decided to send for the nine howitzers and take them ahead of Pickett up nearly to musket range, instead of following close behind him as at first intended: so I sent a courier to bring them up in front of the infantry, but under cover of the wood. The courier could not find them. He was sent again, and only returned after our fire was opened, saying they were gone. I afterward learned that General Pendleton had sent for a part of them, and the others had moved to a neighboring hollow to get out of the line of the enemy's fire at one of Hill's batteries during the artillery duel they had had an hour before.

At exactly 1 o'clock by my watch the two signal-guns were heard in quick succession. In another minute every gun was at work. The enemy were not slow in coming back at us, and the grand roar of nearly the whole artillery of both armies burst in on the silence, almost as suddenly as the full notes of an organ would fill a church.

The artillery of Ewell's corps, however, took only a small part, I believe, in this, as they were too far away on the other side of the town. Some of them might have done good service from positions between Hill and Ewell, enfilading the batteries fighting us. The opportunity to do that was the single advantage in our having the exterior line, to compensate for all its disadvantages. But our line was so extended that all of it was not well studied, and the officers of the different corps had no opportunity to examine each other's ground for chances to coöperate.

The enemy's position seemed to have broken out with guns everywhere, and from Round Top to Cemetery Hill was blazing like a volcano. The air seemed full of missiles from every direction....

Before the cannondale opened I had made up my mind to give Pickett the order to advance within fifteen or twenty minutes after it began. But when I looked at the full development of the enemy's batteries, and knew that his infantry was generally protected from our fire by stone walls and swells of the ground, I could not bring myself to give the word. It seemed madness to launch infantry into that fire, with nearly three-quarters of a mile to go at midday under a July sun. I let the 15 minutes pass, and 20, and 25, hoping vainly for something to turn up. Then I wrote to Pickett: "If you are coming at all you must come at once, or I cannot give you proper support; but the enemy's fire has not slackened at all; at least eighteen guns are still firing from the cemetery itself." Five minutes after sending that message, the enemy's fire suddenly began to slacken, and the guns in the cemetery limbered up and vacated the position.

We Confederates often did such things as that to save our ammunition for use against infantry, but I had never before seen the Federals withdraw their guns simply to save them up for the infantry fight. So I said, "If he does not run fresh batteries in there in five minutes, this is our fight." I looked anxiously with my glass, and the five minutes passed without a sign of life on the deserted position, still swept by our fire, and littered with dead men and horses and fragments of disabled carriages. Then I wrote Pickett, urgently: "For God's sake, come quick. The eighteen guns are gone; come quick, or my ammunition won't let me support you properly."

I afterward heard from others what I took place with my first note to Pickett.

Pickett took it to Longstreet, Longstreet read it, and said nothing. Pickett said, "General, shall I advance?" Longstreet, knowing it had to be, but unwilling to give the word, turned his face away. Pickett saluted and said, "I am going to move forward, sir," galloped off to his division and immediately put it in motion.

Longstreet, leaving his staff, came out alone to where I was. It was then about 1:40 P.M. I explained the situation, feeling then more hopeful, but afraid our artillery ammunition might not hold out for all we would want. Longstreet said, "Stop Pickett immediately and replenish your ammunition." I explained that it would take too long, and the enemy would recover from the effect our fire was then having, and we had, moreover, very little to replenish with. Longstreet said, "I don't want to make this attack. I would stop it now but that General Lee ordered it and expects it to go on. I don't see how it can succeed."

I listened, but did not dare offer a word. The battle was lost if we stopped. Ammunition was far too low to try anything else, for we had been fighting three days. There was a chance, and it was not my part to interfere. While Longstreet was still speaking, Pickett's division swept out of the wood and showed the full length of its gray ranks and shining bayonets, as grand a sight as ever a man looked on. Joining it on the left, Pettigrew stretched farther than I could see. General Dick Garnett, just out of the sick ambulance, and buttoned up in an old blue overcoat, riding at the head of his brigade passed us and saluted Longstreet. Garnett was a warm personal friend, and we had not met before for months. We had served on the plains together before the war. I rode with him a short distance, and then we wished each other luck and a good-bye, which was our last.

Then I rode down the line of guns, selecting such as had enough ammunition to follow Pickett's advance, and starting them after him as fast as possible. I got, I think, fifteen or eighteen in all, in a little while, and went with them. Meanwhile, the infantry had no sooner debouched on the plain than all the enemy's line, which had been nearly silent, broke out again with all its batteries. The eighteen guns were back in the cemetery, and a storm of shell began bursting over and among our infantry. All of our guns—silent as the infantry passed between them—reopened over their heads when the lines had got a couple hundred yards away, but the enemy's artillery let us alone and fired only at the infantry. No one could have looked at that advance without feeling proud of it.

But, as our supporting guns advanced, we passed many poor, mangled victims left in its trampled wake. A terrific infantry fire was now opened upon Pickett, and a considerable force of the enemy moved out to attack the right flank of his line. We halted, unlimbered, and opened fire upon it. Pickett's men never halted, but opened fire at close range, swarmed over the fences and among the enemy's guns—were swallowed up in smoke, and that was the last of them. The conflict hardly seemed to last five minutes before they were melted away, and only disorganized stragglers pursued by a moderate fire were coming back. Just then, Wilcox's brigade passed by us, moving to Pickett's support. There was no longer anything to support, and with the keenest pity at the useless waste of life, I saw them advance. The men, as they passed us, looked bewildered, as if they wondered what they were expected to do, or why they were there. However, they were soon halted and moved back. They suffered some losses, and we had a few casualties from canister sent at them at rather long range.

From the position of our guns the sight of this conflict was grand and thrilling, and we watched it as men with a life-and-death interest in the result. If it should be favorable to us, the war was nearly over; if against us, we each had the risks of many battles yet to go through. And the event culminated with fearful rapidity. Listening to the rolling crashes of musketry, it was hard to realize that they were made up of single reports, and that each musket-shot represented nearly a minute of a man's life in that storm of lead and iron. It seemed as if 100,000 men were engaged, and that human life was being poured out like water. As soon as it appeared that the assault had failed, we ceased firing in order to save ammunition in case the enemy should advance. But we held our ground as boldly as possible, though we were entirely without support, and very low in ammunition. The enemy gave us an occasional shot for a while and then, to our great relief, let us rest. About that time General Lee, entirely alone, rode up and remained with me for a long time. He then probably first appreciated the full extent of the disaster as the disorganized stragglers made their way back past us. The Comte de Paris, in his excellent account of this battle, remarks that Lee, as a soldier, must at this moment have foreseen Appomattox—that he must have realized that he could never again muster so powerful an army, and that for the future he could only delay, but not avert, the failure of his cause. However this may be, it was certainly a momentous thing to him to see that superb attack end in such a bloody repulse. But, whatever his emotions, there was no trace of them in his calm and self-possessed bearing. I thought at the time his coming there very imprudent, and the absence of all his staff-officers and couriers strange. It could only have happened by his express intention. I have since thought it possible that he came, thinking the enemy might follow in pursuit of Pickett, personally to rally stragglers about our guns and make a desperate defense. He had the instincts of a soldier within him as strongly as any man. Looking at Burnside's dense columns swarming through the fire of our guns toward Marye's Hill at Fredericksburg, he had said: "It is well war is so terrible or we would grow too fond of it." No soldier could have looked on at Pickett's charge and not burned to be in it. To have a personal part in a close and desperate fight at that moment would, I believe, have been at heart a great pleasure to General Lee, and possibly he was looking for one. We were here joined by Colonel Fremantle of Her Majesty's Coldstream Guards, who was visiting our army. He afterward published an excellent account of the battle in "Blackwood," and described many little incidents that took place here, such as General Lee's encouraging the retreating stragglers to rally as soon as they got back to cover, and saying that the failure was his fault, not theirs. Colonel Fremantle especially noticed that General Lee reproved an officer for spurring a foolish horse, and advised him to use only gentle measures. The officer was Lieutenant F. M. Colston of my staff, whom General Lee had requested to ride off to the right and try to discover the cause of a great cheering we heard in the enemy's lines. We thought it might mean an advance upon us, but it proved to be only a greeting to some general officer riding along the line.

That was the end of the battle. . . . Night came very slowly, but came at last; and about 10 the last gun was withdrawn to Wiloughby Run, whence we had moved to the attack the afternoon before.

Of Pickett's three brigadiers, Garnett and Armistead were killed and Kemper dangerously wounded. Fry, who commanded Pettigrew's brigade, which adjoined Garnett on the left, and in the charge was the brigade of direction for the whole force, was also left on the field desperately wounded. Of all Pickett's field-officers in the three brigades only one major came out unhurt. The men who made the attack were good enough: the only trouble was, there were not enough of them.

SOURCE:

Ned Bradford, ed. *Battles and Leaders of the Civil War* (New York: Fairfax, 1979), pp. 391–398.

Document 11: QUANTRILL'S RAIDERS

One of the uglier aspects of the Civil War was the contest between guerrilla forces in the border region of Kansas and Missouri. The person most associated with such activity was the enigmatic William C. Quantrill. A former schoolteacher, the Ohio-born Quantrill moved to Kansas in 1857. With the outbreak of hostilities, he formed a band of irregular Confederate fighters who soon terrorized the region. The most infamous deed perpetrated by Quantrill's raiders occurred when they rode into Lawrence, Kansas, in August 1863 and killed some 150 men, women, and children before burning the town. Although Federal authorities declared him an outlaw, Quantrill managed to escape capture. He met his end in Kentucky in the last year of the war. Gurdon Grovenor survived the Lawrence massacre and left this detailed account of that horrible day.

The raid occurred on the morning of Aug. 21st, 1863. It was a clear, warm, still morning, in the midst of one of the hot, dry, dusty spells of weather common in Kansas in the month of August. The guerrillas reached Lawrence just be fore sunrise after an all night's ride from the border of Missouri. Myself and family were yet in bed and asleep. They passed directly by our house, and we were awakened by their yelling and shouting.

I thought at first that the noise came from a company of colored recruits who were camped just west of our house; thought that they had got to quarrelling among themselves. I got up and went to the window to see what was the matter, and as I drew aside the curtain the sight that met my eyes was one of terror—one that I shall never forget. The bushwhackers were just passing by my house. There were 350 of them, all mounted and heavily armed; they were grim and dirty from their night's ride over the dusty roads and were a reckless and bloodthirsty set of men. It was a sight we had somewhat anticipated, felt that it might come, and one that we had dreaded ever since the commencement of the war. I turned to my wife and said: "The bushwhackers are here."

They first made for the main street, passing up as far as the Eldridge House to see if they were going to meet with any opposition, and when they found none they scattered out all over town, killing, stealing and burning. We hastily dressed ourselves and closed up the house tightly as possible and began to talk over what was best to do. My first thought was to get away to some hiding place, but on looking out there seemed no possibility of that as the enemy were everywhere, and I had a feeling that I ought not to leave my family, a young wife and two children, one a babe of three months old, and so we sat down and awaited developments. We saw men shot down and fires shooting up in all directions.

Just on the north of our house, a half a block away and in full view was a camp of recruits twenty-two in all, not yet mustered into service and unarmed. They were awakened by the noise, got up and started to run but were all shot down but five. I saw this wholesale shooting from my window, and it was sight to strike terror to a stouter heart than mine. But we had not long to wait before our time came. Three of the guerillas came to the house, stepped up on the front porch, and with the butt of a musket smashed in one of the front windows; my wife opened the door and let them in. They ransacked the house, talked and swore and threatened a great deal, but offered no violence. They set the house on fire above and below, took such things as they fancied, and left. After they had gone I put the fire out be low, but above it had gotten too strong a hold, and I could not put it out.

Not long after a single man rode up the front gate, he was a villainous looking fellow, and was doubly villainous from too much whiskey. He saw me standing back in the hall of the house, and with a terrible oath he ordered me to come out. I stepped out on the plaza, and he leveled his pistol at me and said: "Are you union or secesh?"

It was my time of trial; my wife with her little one in her arms, and our little boy clinging to her side, was standing just a little ways from me. My life seemingly hung on my answer, my position may be imagined but it cannot be described. The thought ran through me like an electric shock, that I could not say that I was a secessionist, and deny my loyalty to my country; that I would rather die than to live and face that disgrace; and so I answered that I was a union man. He snapped his pistol but it failed to fire. I stepped back into the house and he rode around to the north door and met me there, and snapped his pistol at me again, and this time it failed. Was there a providence in this?

Just then a party of a half dozen of the raiders came riding towards the house from the north, and seeing my enemy, hallooed to him "Don't shoot that man." They rode up to the gate and told me to come there; I did so and my would be murderer came up to me and placed the muzzle of his revolver in my ear. It was not a pleasant place to be in, but the leader of the new crowd told him not to shoot, but to let me alone until he could inquire about me, so he asked me if I had ever been down in Missouri stealing niggers or horses; I told him "No that I never had been in Missouri, except to cross the state going and coming from the east." This seemed to be satisfactory so he told my old enemy to let me alone and not kill me. This seemed to make him very angry, and he cursed me terribly, but I ventured to put my hand up and push away his revolver. The leader of the party then told me if I did not expect to get killed, I must get out of sight, that they were all getting drunk, and would kill everybody they saw; I told him that that was what I had wanted to do all morning, but I could not; "Well," he says, "you must hide or get killed." And they all rode away.

After they had gone I told my wife that I would go into the cellar, and stay until the fire reached me, and if any more of the raiders inquired for me to tell them that I had been taken a prisoner and carried off. Some years ago I read an article in the *Sunday School Times*, saying that a lie under any circumstances was a sin. I thought then that I should like to see that writer try my experiences at the time of the raid and see what he would think then; I did not feel my lie a sin then and never have since.

The cellar of my house was under the ell and the fire was in the front and in the upper story. There was an outside bulk-head door, where I knew I could get out after the fire had reached the floor above me. I had not been in the cellar long before my wife came and said they had just killed my neighbor across the street.

Soon after the notorious Bill Anderson, passing by the house, saw my wife standing in the yard, stopped and commenced talking with her; told her how many men he had killed that morning, and inquiring where her husband was; she told him that he had been taken prisoner and carried away—was it my wife's duty to tell him the truth, tell him where I was and let him come and shoot me as he would a dog, which he would have done? Awhile after wife came and said she thought the raiders had all gone, and so I came out of my prison just as the fire was eating through the floor over my head, thankful that I had passed through that dreadful ordeal and was safe.

Such was my experience during those four or five terrible hours. Our home and its contents was in ashes, but so thankful were we that my life was spared that we thought but little of our pecuniary loss. After the raiders had left and the people could get out on the street, a most desolate and sickening sight met their view. The whole business part of the town, except two stores, was in ashes. The bodies of dead men, some of them partly burned away, were laying in all directions. A large number of dwellings were burned to the ground, and the moaning of the grief stricken people was heard from all sides. Gen. Lane, who was in the city at the time, told me that he had been over the battle-ground of Gettysburg a few days before but the sight was not so sickening as the one which the burned and sacked city of Lawrence presented. The exact number killed was never known, but it was about 150, many of them of the best citizens.

SOURCE:

William E. Connelley. *Quantrill and the Border Wars* (Cedar Rapids, Iowa: Torch, 1910), pp. 362–365.

Document 12: GRISLY SIGHTS

The surgeons on both sides of the Civil War did as well as they could given the limited medical knowledge of the day. Armies of the time were more geared toward fighting than succoring the wounded. Many soldiers viewed the sights and sounds of the improvised hospitals as more grim than the actual field of battle. Captain Augustus C. Brown of the Fourth New York Heavy Artillery vividly relates the reality of being wounded in the Civil War.

Tuesday, May 10th [1864]. Heavy cannonading from 8 A.M. to 1 P.M. The Pontoon train has been sent back to Fredericksburg, apparently to get it out of the way, and the army horses are put on half-rations, that is, five pounds of food. Ambulances and army wagons with two tiers of flooring, loaded with wounded and drawn by four and six mule teams, pass along the plank, or rather, corduroy road to Fredericksburg, the teamsters lashing their teams to keep up with the train, and the wounded screaming with pain as the wagons go jolting over the corduroy. Many of the wounds are full of maggots. I saw one man with an arm off at the shoulder, with maggots half an inch long crawling in the sloughing flesh, and several poor fellows were holding stumps of legs straight up in the air so as to ease the pain the rough road and the heartless drivers subjected them to. These men had been suffering in temporary field hospitals, as no opportunity had been afforded to send them to the rear until we got within reach of the road running to Fredericksburg.

And this reminds me of a scene I witnessed a day or two since which seemed to me to cap the climax of the horrors of war. Passing along a little in the rear of the lines when a battle was raging in which my battalion was not engaged, I came upon a field-hospital to which the stretcher-bearers were bringing the men wounded in the conflict. Under three large "tent flies," the center one the largest of all, stood three heavy wooden tables, around which were grouped a number of surgeons and their assistants, the former bareheaded and clad in long linen dusters reaching nearly to the ground, which were covered with blood from top to bottom and had the arms cut off or rolled to the shoulders. The stretcher-bearers deposited their ghastly freight side by side in a winrow on the ground in front of the table under the first tent fly. Here a number of assistants took charge of the poor fellows, and as some of them lifted a man on to the first table others moved up the winrow so that no time nor space should be lost. Then some of the surgeons administered as anaesthetic to the groaning and writhing patient, exposed his wound and passed him to the center table. There the surgeons who were operating made a hasty examination and determined what was to be done and did it, and more often than not, in a very few moments an arm or a leg or some other portion of the subject's anatomy was flung out upon a pile of similar fragments behind the hospital, which was then more than six feet wide and three feet high, and what remained of the man was passed on to the third table, where other surgeons finished the bandaging, resuscitated him and posted him off with others in an ambulance. Heaven forbid that I should ever again witness such a sight!

SOURCE:

Augustus C. Brown. *The Diary of a Line Officer* (New York: Privately printed, 1906), pp. 43–44.

Document 13: BLOCKADE RUNNERS

Because of the Union naval blockade, the Confederacy had to rely upon special ships to bring in badly needed supplies during the Civil War. Initially, these blockade runners were operated by private individuals who were not above making money off civilian desires for luxury items such as perfumes and silks. Starting in 1863, however, the government started purchasing the ships and banned all nonessential items. A typical blockade runner was fast and sleek, painted in drab colors, and burned nearly smokeless anthracite coal in its steam engines. On a dark moonless night, such a ship was practically invisible as it darted in and out of inlets. In 1861, 90 percent of all blockade runners were successful; by 1865, only 50 percent. Nevertheless, these ships brought in an impressive haul, including 600,000 firearms, 624,000 pairs of shoes, and millions of pounds of ammunition. The account below from Harper's New Monthly, *August 1865, concerns what blockade running meant to the port of Charleston, South Carolina, late in the war.*

During those long wearisome days and weeks when the city was under fire almost the only event of joy which would occur would be the arrival of some one of these blockade runners. The business was finally reduced to a science. Even in the darkest night the cunning craft would work their way in or out through the tortuous channels of the harbor. When outward-bound the captain generally went down to Sullivan's Island upon the evening of sailing to learn the disposition of the Union fleet and plan the course of his exit. Lights also were always prearranged along the shores of the island, or suspended from boats in the harbor in order to indicate the channel.

The most dangerous point, and that which demanded the exercise of the greatest skill to avoid, was a narrow tongue of land which ran out from Sullivan's Island just opposite Sumter, and which was known as the Breakwater Jetty. Here the channel is not only very narrow but takes a sudden turn, and it was in making this turn that the vessel was in danger of getting aground. The Union artillerists after a while learned many of the cunning arts of the blockade-runner, and when ever they saw a light from the opposite shore of Morris Island, which they supposed was intended for the guidance of a vessel, they would immediately open fire. They had a way too of sending out picketboats which would quietly allow the vessel to pass till it had rounded the jetty and return became impossible, and then by means of rockets would signalize the fleet outside.

The chase of a blockade-runner was the most exciting thing imaginable. Like a hunted deer it would speed through the water, its fierce avenger after it, every beam from stem to stern quivering through the violent pulsations of its great iron heart, and the dash of the paddles as in their lightning like revolutions they would strike the water. Sometimes not only was one half of the cargo thrown overboard, but every combustible thing that could be laid hold of crowded into the furnaces to increase the steam. Some of these blockade runners were very successful. I knew of one which had run the gauntlet no less than nineteen times, and had consequently proved a mine of wealth to its owners. When a vessel had once run the blockade it was considered to have paid for itself, and every subsequent trip was consequently clear gain. The captain generally cleared on each round trip ten thousand dollars in gold, and the pilot and mate in proportion.

To be at all connected with or interested in a blockade runner was in those days esteemed in Charleston a signal piece of good fortune. It insured at least a partial supply of the comforts and luxuries of life; for the ladies an occasional new silk dress, the envy and admiration of the streets; for the gentlemen a good supply of Bourbon—a box or two of cigars, or a larder filled with Stilton cheese or West India fruits. By-and-by came an edict from Richmond forbidding the importation of luxuries of this kind, and restricting the cargo of a vessel entirely to those articles which the country needed in its military operations, or which contributed to a supply of the actual necessities of the people. One half of the cargo of the vessel going out was also required to be devoted to government account, and one half of the cargo of the vessel coming in. This, of course, greatly curtailed the profits of the owners, but still immense fortunes continued to be made on both sides of the water.

SOURCE:

W. F. G. Peck. "Four Years Under Fire at Charleston," *Harper's New Monthly Magazine*, 31 (August 1865): 364.

Document 14: ATTACK ON ALL FRONTS

On March 9, 1864, Ulysses S. Grant, victor of the siege of Vicksburg, received the rank of lieutenant general, the first officer to hold that commission in the U.S. Army since George Washington. The Lincoln administration placed much confidence in this man. Grant became commander of all Union field armies and quickly developed a strategy to defeat the Confederacy: he would attack on all fronts. Northern armies advanced toward Atlanta and Mobile, up the Peninsula in eastern Virginia, and down the Shenandoah Valley. Meanwhile, Grant accompanied the Army of the Potomac under Major General George Meade and concentrated on the main prize: Robert E. Lee's Army of Northern Virginia. Between May and June the two main armies fought three big battles in Virginia as related below in this account by Confederate Major General E. M. Law. The Wilderness (May 5–6), Spotsylvania Courthouse (May 8–19), and Cold Harbor (June 1–3) were some of the bloodiest engagements of the entire war, and Lee's army suffered more losses than it could sustain, especially among the officer ranks. In one month alone, Lee lost twenty-two generals out of a total of fifty-eight. The Union finally had a general who knew the secret of defeating the South: a relentless war of attrition.

On the 2d of May, 1864, a group of officers stood at the Confederate signal station on Clark's Mountain, Virginia, south of the Rapidan, and examined closely through their field-glasses the position of the Federal army then lying north of the river in Culpeper county. The central figure of the group was the commander of the Army of Northern Virginia, who had requested his corps and division commanders to meet him there. Though some demonstrations had been made in the direction of the upper fords, General Lee expressed the opinion that the Federal army would cross the river at Germanna or Ely's. Thirty-six hours later General Meade's army, General Grant, now commander-in-chief, being with it, commenced its march to the crossings indicated by General Lee.

The Army of the Potomac, which had now commenced its march toward Richmond, was more powerful in numbers than at any previous period of the war. It consisted of three corps: the Second (Hancock's), the Fifth (Warren's), and the Sixth (Sedgwick's); but the Ninth (Burnside's) acted with Meade throughout the campaign. Meade's army was thoroughly equipped, and provided with every appliance of modern warfare. On the other hand, the Army of Northern Virginia had gained little in numbers during the winter just passed and had never been so scantily supplied with food and clothing. The equipment as to arms was well enough for men who knew how to use them, but commissary and quartermasters' supplies were lamentably deficient. A new pair of shoes or an overcoat was a luxury, and full rations would have astonished the stomachs of Lee's ragged Confederates. But they took their privations cheerfully, and complaints were seldom heard. I recall an instance of one hardy fellow whose trousers were literally "worn to a frazzle" and would no longer adhere to his legs even by dint of the most persistent patching. Unable to buy, beg, or borrow another pair, he wore instead a pair of thin cotton drawers. By nursing these carefully he managed to get through the winter. Before the campaign opened in the spring a small lot of clothing was received, and he was the first man of his regiment to be supplied.

I have often heard expressions of surprise that these ragged, barefooted, half-starved men would fight at all. But the very fact that they remained with their colors through such privations was sufficient to prove that they would be dangerous foes to encounter upon the line of battle. The *morale* of the army at this time was excellent, and it moved forward confidently to the grim death-grapple in the wilderness of Spotsylvania with its old enemy, the Army of the Potomac.

General Lee's headquarters were two miles northeast of Orange Court House; of his three corps, Longstreet's was at Gordonville, Ewell's was on and near the Rapidan, above Mine Run, and Hill's on his left, higher up the stream. When the Federal army was known to be in motion, General Lee prepared to move upon its flank with his whole force as soon as his opponent should clear the river and begin the march southward. The route selected by General Grant led entirely around the right of Lee's position on the river above. Grant's passage of the Rapidan was unopposed, and he struck boldly out on the direct road to Richmond. Two roads lead from Orange Court House down the Rapidan toward Fredericksburg. They follow the general direction of the river, and are almost parallel to each other, the "Old turnpike" nearest the river, and the "Plank road" a short distance south of it. The route of the Federal army lay directly across these two roads, along the western borders of the famous Wilderness.

About noon on the 4th of May, Ewell's corps was put into motion on and toward the Orange turnpike, while A. P. Hill, with two divisions, moved parallel with him on the Orange Plank road. The two divisions of Longstreet's corps encamped near Gordonsville were ordered to move rapidly across the country and follow Hill on the Plank road. Ewell's corps was the first to find itself in the presence of the enemy. As it advanced along the turnpike on the morning of the 5th, the Federal column was seen crossing it from the direction of Germanna Ford. Ewell promptly formed line of battle across the turnpike, and communicated his position to General Lee, who was on the Plank road with Hill. Ewell was instructed to regulate his movements by the head of Hill's column, whose progress he could tell by the firing in its front, and not to bring on a general engagement until Longstreet should come up. The position of Ewell's troops, so near the flank of the Federal line of march, was anything but favorable to a preservation of the peace, and a collision soon occurred which opened the campaign in earnest.

General Warren, whose corps was passing when Ewell came up, halted, and turning to the right made a vigorous attack upon Edward Johnson's division, posted across the turnpike. J. M. Jones's brigade, which held the road, was driven back in confusion. Steuart's brigade was pushed forward to take its place. Rodes's division was thrown in on Johnson's right, south of the road, and the line, thus reëstablished, moved forward, reversed the tide of battle, and rolled back the Federal attack. The fighting was severe and bloody while it lasted. At some points the lines were in such close proximity in the thick woods which covered the battle-field that when the Federal troops gave way several hundred of them, unable to retreat without exposure to almost certain death, surrendered themselves as prisoners.

Ewell's entire corps was now up—Johnson's division holding the turnpike, Rodes's division on the right of it, and Early's in reserve. So far Ewell had been engaged only with Warren's corps, but Sedgwick's soon came up from the river and joined Warren on his right. Early's division was sent to meet it. The battle extended in that direction, with steady and determined attacks upon Early's front, until nightfall. The Confederates still clung to their hold on the Federal flank against every effort to dislodge them.

When Warren's corps encountered the head of Ewell's column on the 5th of May, General Meade is reported to have said: "They left a division to fool us here, while they concentrate and prepare a division on the North Anna." If the stubborn resistance to Warren's attack did not at once convince him of his mistake, the firing that announced the approach of Hill's corps along the Plank road, very soon afterward, must have opened his eyes to the bold strategy of the Confederate commander. General Lee had deliberately chosen this as his battle-ground. He knew this tangled wilderness well, and appreciated fully the advantages such a field afforded for concealing his great inferiority of force and for neutralizing the superior strength of his antagonist. General Grant's bold movement across the lower fords into the Wilderness, in the execution of his plan to swing past the Confederate army and place himself between it and Richmond, offered the expected opportunity of striking a blow upon his flank while his troops were stretched out on the line of march. The wish for such an opportunity was doubtless in a measure "father to the thought" expressed by General Lee three days before, at the signal station on Clark's Mountain.

Soon after Ewell became engaged on the Old turnpike, A. P. Hill's advance struck the Federal outposts on the Plank road at Parker's store, on the outskirts of the Wilderness. These were driven in and followed up to their line of battle, which was so posted as to cover the junction of the Plank road with the Stevensburg and Brock roads, on which the Federal army was moving toward Spotsylvania. The fight began between Getty's division of the Sixth Corps and Heth's division, which was leading A. P. Hill's column. Hancock's corps, which was already on the march for Spotsylvania by way of Chancellorsville, was at once recalled, and at 4 o'clock in the afternoon was ordered to drive Hill "out of the Wilderness." Cadmus Wilcox's division went to Heth's support, and Poague's battalion of artillery took position in a little clearing on the north side of the Plank road, in rear of the Confederate infantry. But there was little use for artillery on such a field. After the battle was fairly joined in thickets in front, its fire might do as much damage to friend as to foe; so it was silent. It was a desperate struggle between the infantry of the two armies, on a field whose physical aspects were as grim and forbidding as the struggle itself. It was a battle of brigades and regiments rather than of corps and divisions. Officers could not see the whole length of their commands, and could tell whether their troops on their right and left were driving or being driven only by the sound of the firing. It was a fight at close quarters too, for as night came on, in those tangled thickets of stunted pine, sweet-gum, scrub-oak, and cedar, the approach of the opposing lines could be discerned only by the noise of their passage through the underbrush or the flashing of their guns. The usually silent Wilderness had suddenly become alive with the angry flashing and heavy roar of musketry, mingled with the yells of the combatants as they swayed to and fro in the gloomy thickets....

When the battle closed at 8 o'clock, General Lee sent an order to Longstreet to make a night march, so as to arrive upon the field at daylight the next morning. The latter moved at 1 A.M. of the 6th, but it was already daylight when he reached the Plank road at Parker's store, three miles in rear of Hill's battle-field. During the night the movements of troops and preparations for battle could be heard on the Federal line, in front of Heth's and Wilcox's divisions, which had so far sustained themselves against every attack by six divisions under General Hancock. But Heth's and Wilcox's men were thoroughly worn out. Their lines were ragged and irregular, with wide intervals, and in some places fronting in different directions. In the expectation that they would be relieved during the night, no effort was made to rearrange and strengthen them to meet the storm that was brewing.

As soon as it was light enough to see what little could be seen in that dark forest, Hancock's troops swept forward to the attack. The blow fell with greatest force upon Wilcox's troops south of the Orange Plank road. They made what front they could and renewed the fight, until, the attacking column overlapping the right wing, it gave way, and the whole line "rolled up" from the right and retired in disorder along the Plank road as far as the position of Poague's artillery, which now opened up upon the attacking force. The Federals pressed their advantage and were soon abreast of the artillery on the opposite side, their bullets flying across the road among the guns where General Lee himself stood. For a while matters looked very serious for the Confederates. General Lee, after sending a messenger to hasten the march of Longstreet's troops and another to prepare the trains for movement to the rear, was assisting in rallying the disordered troops and directing the fire of the artillery, when the head of Longstreet's corps appeared in double column, swinging down the Orange Plank road at a trot. In perfect order, ranks well closed, and no stragglers, those splendid troops came on, regardless of the confusion on every side, pushing their steady way onward like a "river in the sea" of confused and troubled human waves around them. Kershaw's division took the right of the road, and, coming into line under a heavy fire, moved obliquely to the right (south) to meet the Federal left, which had "swung round" in that direction. The Federals were checked in their sweeping advance and thrown back upon their front line of breastworks, where they made a stubborn stand. But Kershaw, urged on by Longstreet, charged with his whole command, swept his front, and captured the works.

Nearly at the same moment Field's division took the left of the road, with Gregg's brigade in front, Benning's behind it, Law's next, and Jenkins's following. As the Texans in the front line swept past the batteries where General Lee was standing, they gave a rousing cheer for "Marse Robert," who spurred his horse forward and followed them in the charge. When the men became aware that he was "going in" with them, they called loudly to him to go back. "We won't go unless you go back," was the general cry. One of the men dropped to the rear, and taking the bridle turned the general's horse around, while General Gregg came up and urged him to do as the men wished. At that moment a member of his staff (Colonel Venable) directed his attention to General Longstreet, whom he had been looking for, and who was sitting on his horse near the Orange Plank road. With evident disappointment General Lee turned off and joined General Longstreet.

The ground over which Field's troops were advancing was open for a short distance, and fringed on its farther edge with scattered pines, beyond which began the Wilderness. The Federals were advancing through the pines with apparently resistless force, when Gregg's eight hundred Texans, regardless of numbers, flanks, or supports, dashed directly upon them. There was a terrific crash, mingled with wild yells, which settled down into a steady roar of musketry. In less than ten minutes one-half of that devoted eight hundred were lying upon the field dead or wounded; but they had delivered a staggering blow and broken the force of the Federal advance. Benning's and Law's brigades came promptly to their support, and the whole swept forward together. The tide was flowing the other way. It ebbed and flowed many times that day, strewing the Wilderness with human wrecks....

About 10 o'clock it was ascertained that the Federal left flank rested only a short distance south of the Orange Plank road, which offered a favorable opportunity for a turning movement in that quarter. General Longstreet at once moved Mahone's, Wofford's, Anderson's, and Davis's brigades, the whole under General Mahone, around this end of the Federal line. Forming at right angles to it, they attacked in flank and rear, while a general advance was made in front. So far the fight had been one of anvil and hammer. But this first display of tactics at once changed the face of the field. The Federal left wing was rolled up in confusion toward the Plank road and then back upon the Brock road.

This partial victory had been a comparatively easy one. The signs of demoralization and even panic among the troops of Hancock's left wing, who had been hurled back by Mahone's flank attack, were too plain to be mistaken by the Confederates, who believed that Chancellorsville was about to be repeated. General Longstreet rode forward and prepared to press his advantage. Jenkins's fresh brigade was moved forward on the Plank road to renew the attack, supported by Kershaw's division, while the flanking column was to come into position on its right. The latter were now in line south of the road and almost parallel to it. Longstreet and Kershaw rode with General Jenkins at the head of his brigade as it pressed forward, when suddenly the quiet that had reigned for some moments was broken by a few scattering shots on the north of the road, which were answered by a volley from Mahone's line on the south side. The firing in their front, and the appearance of troops on the road whom they failed to recognize as friends through the intervening timber, had drawn a single volley, which lost to them all the fruits of the splendid work they had just done. General Jenkins was killed and Longstreet seriously wounded by our own men. The troops who were following them faced quickly toward the firing and were about to return it; but General Kershaw called out, "They are friends!" every musket was lowered, and the men dropped upon the ground to avoid the fire.

The head of the attack had fallen, and for a time the movements of the Confederates were paralyzed. Lee came forward and directed the dispositions for a new attack, but the change of commanders after the fall of Longstreet, and the resumption of the thread of operations, occasioned a delay of several hours, and then the tide had turned, and we received only hard knocks instead of victory. When at 4 o'clock an attack was made upon the Federal line along the Brock road, it was found strongly fortified and stubbornly defended. The log breastworks had taken fire during the battle, and at one point separated the combatants by a wall of fire and smoke which neither could pass. Part of Field's division captured the works in their front, but were forced to relinquish them for want of support. Meanwhile Burnside's corps, which had reënforced Hancock during the day, made a vigorous attack on the north of the Orange Plank road. Law's (Alabama) and Perry's (Florida) brigades were being forced back, when, Heth's division coming to their assistance, they assumed the offensive, driving Burnside's troops beyond the extensive line of breastworks constructed previous to their advance.

The battles fought by Ewell on the Old turnpike and by A. P. Hill on the Plank road, on the 5th of May, were entirely distinct, no connected line existing between them. Connection was established with Ewell's right by Wilcox's division, after it had been relieved by Longstreet's troops on the morning of the 6th. While the battle was in progress on the Orange Plank road, on the 6th, an unsuccessful attempt was made to turn Ewell's left next the river, and heavy assaults were made upon the line of Early's division. So persistent were these attacks on the front of Pegram's brigade, that other troops were brought up to its support, but the men rejected the offer of assistance.

Late in the day General Ewell ordered a movement against the Federal right wing, similar to that by which Longstreet had "doubled up" Hancock's left in the morning. Two brigades, under General John B. Gordon, moved out of their works at sunset, and lapping the right of Sedgwick's corps made a sudden and determined attack upon it. Taken by surprise, the Federals were driven from a large portion of their works with the loss of six hundred prisoners—among them Generals Seymour and Shaler. Night closed the contest, and with it the battle of the Wilderness.

When Lee's army appeared on the flank of the Federal line of march on the 5th of May, General Grant had at once faced his adversary and endeavored to push him out of the way. Grant's strongest efforts had been directed to forcing back the Confederate advance on the Orange Plank road, which, if successful, would have enabled him to complete his plan of "swinging past" that army and placing himself between it and Richmond. On the other hand, Lee's principal effort had been to strike the head of Grant's column a crushing blow where it crossed the Plank road, in order to force it from its route and throw it in confusion back to the Wilderness. Both attempts had failed. What advantages had been gained by the two days' fighting remained with the Confederates. They held a position nearer the Federal line of march than when the battle began, and had inflicted losses incomparably heavier than they had themselves sustained. Both sides were now strongly intrenched, and neither could well afford to attack. And so the 7th of May was spent in skirmishing, each waiting to see what the other would do. That night the race for Spotsylvania began. General Lee had been informed by "Jeb" Stuart of the movement of the Federal trains southward during the afternoon. After dark the noise of moving columns along the Brock road could be heard, and it was at once responded to by a similar movement on the part of Lee. The armies moved in parallel columns separated only by a short interval. Longstreet's corps (now commanded by R. H. Anderson) marched all night and arrived at Spotsylvania at 8 o'clock on the morning of the 8th, where the ball was already in motion. Stuart had thrown his cavalry across the Brock road to check the Federal advance, and as the Federal cavalry had failed to dislodge him, Warren's corps had been pushed forward to clear the way. Kershaw's, Humphrey's and Law's brigades were at once sent to Stuart's assistance. The head of Warren's column was forced back and immediately commenced intrenching. Spotsylvania Court House was found occupied by Federal cavalry and artillery, which retired without a fight. The Confederates had won the race.

The troops on both sides were now rapidly arriving. Sedgwick's corps joined Warren's, and in the afternoon was thrown heavily against Anderson's right wing, which, assisted by the timely arrival of Ewell's corps, repulsed the attack with great slaughter. Hill's corps (now under command of General Early) did not arrive until the next morning, May 9th. General Lee's line now covered Spotsylvania Court House, with its left (Longstreet's corps) resting on the Po river, a small stream which flows on the south-west; Ewell's corps in the center, north of the Court House, and Hill's on the right, crossing the Fredericksburg road. These positions were generally maintained during the battles that followed, though brigades and divisions were often detached from their proper commands and sent to other parts of the field to meet pressing emergencies.

No engagement of importance took place on the 9th, which was spent in intrenching the lines and preparing places of refuge from the impending storm. But the 10th was "a field-day." Early in the morning it was found that Hancock's corps had crossed the Po above the point where the Confederate left rested, had reached the Shady Grove road, and was threatening our rear, as well as the trains which were in that direction on the Old Court House road leading to Louisa Court House. General Early was ordered from the right with Mahone's and Heth's divisions, and, moving rapidly to the threatened quarter, attacked Hancock's rear division as it was about to recross the Po—driving it, with severe loss, through the burning woods in its rear, back across the river.

Meanwhile General Grant was not idle elsewhere. He had commenced his efforts to break through the lines confronting him. The first assault was made upon Field's division of Longstreet's corps and met with a complete and bloody repulse. Again at 3 o'clock in the afternoon, the blue columns pressed forward to attack, and were sent back torn and bleeding, leaving the ground covered with their dead and wounded. Anticipating a renewal of the assaults, many of our men went out in front of their breastworks, and, gathering up the muskets and cartridge-boxes of the dead and wounded, brought them in and distributed them along the line. If they did not have repeating-rifles, they had a very good substitute—several loaded ones to each man. They had no reserves, and knew that if they could not sufficiently reduce the number of their assailants to equalize matters somewhat before they reached the works, these might become untenable against such heavy and determined attacks.

A lull of several hours succeeded the failure of the second attack, but it was only a breathing spell preparatory to the culminating effort of the day. Near sunset our skirmishers were driven in and the heavy, dark lines of attack came into view, one after another, first in quick time, then in a trot, and then with a rush toward the works. The front lines dissolved before the pitiless storm that met them, but those in the rear pressed forward, and over their dead and dying comrades reached that portion of the works held by the Texas brigade. These gallant fellows, now reduced to a mere handful by their losses in the Wilderness, stood manfully to their work. Their line was bent backward by the pressure, but they continued the fight in rear of the works with bayonets and clubbed muskets. Fortunately for them, Anderson's brigade had cleared its own front, and a portion of it turned upon the flank of their assailants, who were driven out, leaving many dead and wounded inside the works.

While this attack was in progress on Field's line, another, quite as determined, was made farther to the right, in front of Rodes's division of Ewell's corps. Doles's brigade was broken and swept out of its works with the loss of three hundred prisoners. But as the attacking force poured through the gap thus made, Daniel's brigade on one side and Steuart's on the other drew back from their lines and fell upon its flanks, while Battle's and Johnston's brigades were hurried up from the left and thrown across its front. Assailed on three sides at once, the Federals were forced back to the works, and over them, whereupon they broke in disorderly retreat to their own lines.

The next day was rainy and disagreeable, and no serious fighting took place. There were movements, however, along the Federal lines during the day that indicated a withdrawal from the front of Longstreet's corps. Late in the afternoon, under the impression that General Grant had actually begun another flanking movement, General Lee ordered that all artillery on the left and center that was "difficult of access" should be withdrawn from the lines, and that everything should be in readiness to move during the night if necessary. Under this order, General Long, Ewell's chief of artillery, removed all but two batteries from the line of General Edward Johnson's division, for the reason given, that they were "difficult of access." Johnson's division held an elevated point somewhat advanced from the general line, and known as "the salient" [or "Bloody Angle"], the breastworks there making a considerable angle, with its point toward the enemy. This point had been held because it was a good position for artillery, and if occupied by the enemy would command portions of our line. Such projections on a defensive line are always dangerous if held by infantry alone, as an attack upon the point of the angle can only be met by a diverging fire; or if attacked on either face, the troops holding the other face, unless protracted by traverses or by works in rear (as were some of the Confederates), are more exposed than those on the side attacked. But with sufficient artillery, so posted as to sweep the sides of the angle, such a position may be very strong. To provide against contingencies, a second line had been laid off and partly constructed a short distance in the rear, so as to cut off this salient.

After the artillery had been withdrawn on the night of the 11th, General Johnson discovered that the enemy was concentrating in his front, and, convinced that he would be attacked in the morning, requested the immediate return of the artillery that had been taken away. The men in the trenches were kept on alert all night and were ready for the attack, when at dawn on the morning of the 12th a dense column emerged from the pines half a mile in the front of the salient and rushed to the attack. They came on, to use General Johnson's words, "in great disorder, with a narrow front, but extending back as far as I could see." Page's battalion of artillery, which had been ordered back to the trenches at 4 o'clock in the morning, was just arriving and was not in position to fire upon the attacking column, which offered so fair a mark for artillery. The guns came only in time to be captured. The infantry in the salient fought as long as fighting was of any use; but deprived of the assistance of the artillery, which constituted the chief strength of the position, they could do little to check the onward rush of the Federal column, which soon overran the salient, capturing General Johnson himself, 20 pieces of artillery, and 2,800 men—almost his entire division. The whole thing happened so quickly that the extent of the disaster could not be realized at once. Hancock's troops, who had made the assault, had recovered their formation, and, extending their lines across the works on both sides of the salient, had resumed their advance, when Lane's brigade of Hill's corps, which was immediately on the right of the captured works, rapidly drew back to the unfinished line in rear, and poured a galling fire upon Hancock's left wing, which checked its advance and threw it back with severe loss. General Gordon, whose division (Early's) was in reserve and under orders to support any part of the line about the salient, hastened to throw it in front of the advancing Federal column. As the division was about to charge, General Lee rode up and joined General Gordon, evidently intending to go forward with him. Gordon remonstrated, and the men, seeing his intention, cried out, "General Lee to the rear!" which was taken up all along the line. One of the men respectfully but firmly took hold of the general's bridle and led his horse to the rear, and the charge went on. The two moving lines met in the rear of the captured works, and after a fierce struggle in the woods the Federals were forced back to the base of the salient. But Gordon's division did not cover their whole front. On the left of the salient, where Rodes's division had connected with Johnson's, the attack was still pressed with great determination. General Rodes drew out Ramseur's brigade from the left of his line, and sent it to relieve pressure on his right and restore the line between himself and Gordon. Ramseur swept the trenches the whole length of his brigade, but did not fill the gap, and his right was exposed to a terrible fire from the works still held by the enemy. Three brigades from Hill's corps were ordered up. Perrin's, which was the first to arrive, rushed forward through a fearful fire and recovered a part of the line on Gordon's left. General Perrin fell dead from his horse just as he reached the works. General Daniel had been killed, and Ramseur painfully wounded, though remaining in the trenches with his men. Rodes's right being still hard pressed, Harris's (Mississippi) and McGowan's (South Carolina) brigades were ordered forward and rushed through the blinding storm into the works on Ramseur's right. The Federals still held the greater part of the salient, and though the Confederates were unable to drive them out, the Federals could get no farther. Hancock's corps, which had made the attack, had been reënforced by Russell's and Wheaton's divisions of the Sixth Corps and one-half of Warren's corps, as the battle progressed. Artillery had been brought up on both sides, the Confederates using every piece that could be made available upon the salient. Before 10 o'clock General Lee had put in every man that could be spared for the restoration of his broken center. It then became a matter of endurance with the men themselves. All day long and until far into the night the battle raged with unceasing fury, in the space covered by the salient and the adjacent works. Every attempt to advance on either side was met and repelled from the other. The hostile battle-flags waved over different portions of the same works, while the men fought like fiends for their possession.

During the day diversions were made on both sides, to relieve the pressure in the center. An attack upon Anderson's (Longstreet's) corps by Wright's Sixth Corps (Sedgwick having been killed on the 9th) was severely repulsed, while, on the other side of the salient, General Early, who was moving with a part of Hill's corps to strike the flank of the Federal force engaged there, met and defeated Burnside's corps, which was advancing at the same time to attack Early's works.

While the battle was raging at the salient, a portion of Gordon's division was busily engaged in constructing in the rear of the old line intrenchments a new and shorter one, to which Ewell's corps retired before daylight on the 13th. Never was respite more welcome than the five days of comparative rest that followed the terrible battle of the 12th to our wearied men, who had been marching and fighting almost without intermission since the 4th of May. Their comfort was materially enhanced, too, by the supply of coffee, sugar, and other luxuries to which they had long been strangers, obtained from the haversacks of the Federal dead. It was astonishing into what close places a hungry Confederate would go to get something to eat. Men would sometimes go out under a severe fire, in the hope of finding a full haversack. It may seem a small matter to the readers of war history, but to the *makers* of it who were in the trenches, or on the march, or engaged in battle night and day for weeks without intermission, the supply of the one article of coffee, furnished by the

Army of the Potomac to the Army of Northern Virginia, was *not* a small matter, but did as much as any other material agency to sustain the spirits and bodily energies of the men, in a campaign that taxed both to their utmost limit. Old haversacks gave place to better ones, and tin cups now dangled from the accouterments of the Confederates, who at every rest on the march or interval of quiet on the lines could be seen gathered around small fires, preparing the coveted beverage.

In the interval from the 12th to the 18th our army was gradually moving east to meet corresponding movements on the other side. Longstreet's corps was shifted from the left to the extreme right, beyond the Fredericksburg road. Ewell's corps still held the works in the rear of the famous salient, when on the morning of the 18th a last effort was made to force the lines of Spotsylvania at the only point where previous efforts had met with even partial success. This was destined to a more signal failure than any of the others. Under the fire of thirty pieces of artillery, which swept all the approaches to Ewell's line, the attacking force was broken and driven back in disorder before it became well within reach of the muskets of the infantry. After the failure of this attack, the "sidling" movement, as the men expressed it, again began, and on the afternoon of the 19th Ewell's corps was thrown around the Federal left wing to ascertain the extent of this movement. After a severe engagement, which lasted until night, Ewell withdrew, having lost about nine hundred men in the action. This seemed a heavy price to pay for information that might have been otherwise obtained, but the enemy had suffered more severely, and General Grant was delayed in his turning movement for twenty-four hours. He however got the start in the race for the North Anna; Hancock's corps, leading off on the night of the 20th, was followed rapidly by the remainder of his army.

On the morning of the 21st Ewell's corps moved from the left to the right of our line, and later on the same day it was pushed southward on the Telegraph road, closely followed by Longstreet's corps. A. P. Hill brought up the rear that night, after a sharp "brush" with the Sixth Corps, which was in the act of retiring from its lines. Lee had the inside track this time, as the Telegraph road on which he moved was the direct route, while Grant had to swing round on the arc of a circle of which this was the chord. About noon on the 22nd the head of our column reached the North Anna, and that night Lee's army lay on the south side of the river. We had won the second heat and secured a good night's rest besides, when the Federal army appeared on the other side in the forenoon of the 23d.

Warren's corps crossed the river that afternoon without opposition at Jericho Ford, four miles above the Chesterfield bridge on Telegraph road; but as it moved out from the river it met Cadmus Wilcox's division of Hill's corps, and a severe but indecisive engagement ensued, the confronting lines intrenching as usual. Meanwhile a small earth-work, that had been built the year before, covering the approaches to the bridge on the Telegraph road and now held by a small detachment from Kershaw's division, was attacked and now held by a small detachment from Kershaw's division, was attacked and carried by troops of Hancock's corps, the Confederates retiring across the river with the loss of a few prisoners.

It did not seem to be General Lee's purpose to offer any serious resistance to Grant's passage of the river at the points selected. His lines had been retired from it at both these points, but touched it at Ox Ford, a point intermediate between them. Hancock's corps, having secured the Chesterfield bridge, crossed over on the morning of the 24th, and, extending down the river, moved out until it came upon Longstreet's and Ewell's corps in position and ready for battle. The Sixth Corps (General Wright) crossed at Jericho Mill and joined Warren. The two wings of Grant's army were safely across the river, but there was no connection between them. Lee had only thrown back his flanks and let them in on either side, while he held the river between; and when General Grant attempted to throw his center, under Burnside, across between the ford and the bridge, it was very severely handled and failed to get a foothold on the south side. A detachment from Warren's corps was sent down on the south side to help Burnside across, but was attacked by Mahone's division, and driven back with heavy loss, narrowly escaping capture. General Grant found himself in what may be called a military dilemma. He had cut his army in two by running it upon the point of a wedge. He could not break the point, which rested upon the river, and the attempt to force it out of place by striking on its sides must of necessity be made without much concert of action between the two wings of his army, neither of which could reënforce the other without crossing the river twice; while his opponent could readily transfer his troops, as needed, from one wing to the other across the narrow space between them.

The next two days were consumed by General Grant in fruitless attempts to find a vulnerable point in our lines. The skirmishers were very active, often forcing their way close up to our works. The line of my brigade crossed the Richmond and Fredericksburg railroad. It was an exposed point and the men stationed there, after building their log breastwork, leant their muskets against it and moved out on one side, to avoid the constant fire that was directed upon it....

On the morning of May 27th General Grant's army had disappeared from our front. During the night it had, "folded its tents like the Arab and as quietly stolen away," on its fourth turning movement since the opening of the campaign. The Army of the Potomac was already on its march for the Pamunkey River at Hanovertown, where the leading corps crossed on the morning of the 27th. Lee moved at once to head off his adversary, whose advance column was now eight miles nearer Richmond than he was. In the afternoon of the 28th, after one of the severest cavalry engagements of the war, in which Hampton and Fitz Lee opposed the advance of Sheridan at Hawe's Shop, the infantry of both armies came up and again confronted each other along the Totopotomoy. Here the Confederate position was found too strong to be attacked in front with any prospect of success, and again the "sidling" movements began—this time toward Cold Harbor.

Sheridan's cavalry had taken possession of Cold Harbor on the 31st, and had been promptly followed up by two corps of infantry. Longstreet's and a part of Hill's corps, with Hoke's and Breckenridge's divisions, were thrown across their front. The fighting began on the Cold Harbor line, late in the afternoon of the 1st of June, by a heavy attack upon the divisions of Hoke and Kershaw. Clingman's brigade on Hoke's left gave way, and Wofford's on Kershaw's right, being turned, was also forced back; but the further progress of the attack was checked and the line partly restored before night. By the morning of the 2d of June the opposing lines had settled down close to each other, and everything promised a repetition of the scenes at Spotsylvania.

Three corps of Grant's army (General W. F. Smith's Eighteenth Corps having arrived from Drewry's bluff) now confronted the Confederate right wing at Cold Harbor, while the other two looked after Early's (Ewell's) corps near Bethesda Church. In the afternoon of June 2d, General Early, perceiving a moment that indicated a withdrawal of the Federal force in his front, attacked Burnside's corps while it was in motion, striking also the flank of Warren's corps, and capturing several hundred prisoners. This was accomplished with small loss, and had the effect of preventing the coöperation of these two corps in the attack at Cold Harbor the next day.

Early in the morning of the 2d I was ordered to move with my own and Anderson's brigades, of Field's division, "to reënforce the line on the right," exercising my own discretion as to the point where assistance was most needed. After putting the troops in motion I rode along the line, making a personal inspection as I went. Pickett's division, the first on our right, held a strong position along the skirt of the wood, with open fields in front, and needed no strengthening. The left of Kershaw's division, which was the next in order, was equally strong; but on calling at General Kershaw's quarters I was informed of the particulars of the attack upon his own and Hoke's divisions the evening before, and requested by him to place my troops as a support to his right wing, which had been thrown back by the attack. On examining the line I found it bent sharply back at almost a right angle, the point of which rested upon a body of heavy woods. The works were in open ground and were ill-adapted to resist an attack. The right face of the angle ran along a slope, with a small marshy stream behind and higher ground in front. The works had evidently been built just where the troops found themselves at the close of the fight the previous evening.

Convinced that under such assaults as we had sustained at Spotsylvania our line would be broken at that point, I proposed to cut off the angle by building a new line across its base, which would throw the marshy ground in our front and give us a clear sweep across it with our fire from the slope on the other side. This would not only strengthen but shorten the line considerably and I proposed to General Kershaw to build and occupy it with my two brigades that night.

Meanwhile the enemy was evidently concentrating in the woods in front, and every indication pointed to an early attack. Nothing could be done upon the contemplated line during the day, and we waited anxiously the coming of night. The day passed without an attack. I was as well satisfied that it would come at dawn the next morning as if I had seen General Meade's order directing it. That no mistake should be made in the location of the works, I procured a hatchet, and accompanied by two members of my staff, each with an armful of stakes, went out after dark, located the line, and drove every stake upon it. The troops were formed on it at once, and before morning the works were finished. Artillery was placed at both ends of the new line, abreast of the infantry. General Kershaw then withdrew that portion of his division which occupied the salient, the men having leveled the works as far as possible before leaving them.

Our troops were under arms and waiting, when with the misty light of early morning the scattering fire of our pickets, who now occupied the abandoned works in the angle, announced the beginning of the attack. As the assaulting column swept over the old works a loud cheer was given, and it rushed on into the marshy ground in the angle. Its front covered little more than the line of my own brigade of less than a thousand men; but line followed line until the space inclosed by the old salient became a mass of writhing humanity, upon which our artillery and musketry played with cruel effect. I had taken position on the slope in the rear of the line and was carefully noting the firing of the men, which soon became so heavy that I feared they would exhaust the cartridges in the boxes before the attack ceased. Sending an order for a supply of ammunition to be brought into the lines, I went down to the trenches to regulate the firing. On my way I met a man, belonging to the 15th Alabama regiment of my brigade, running to the rear through the storm of bullets that swept the hill. He had left his hat behind in his retreat, was crying like a big baby, and was the bloodiest man I ever saw. "Oh General," he blubbered out, "I am dead! I am killed! Look at this!" showing his wound. He was a broad, fat-faced fellow, and a minieball had passed through his cheek and the fleshy part of his neck, letting a large amount of blood. Finding it was only a flesh wound, I told him to go on; he was not hurt. He looked at me doubtfully for a second as if questioning my veracity or my surgical knowledge, I didn't know which; then, as if satisfied with my diagnosis, he broke into a broad laugh, and, the tears still running down his cheeks, trotted off, the happiest man I saw that day.

On reaching the trenches, I found the men in fine spirits, laughing and talking as they fired. There, too, I could see more plainly the terrible havoc made in the ranks of the assaulting column. I had seen the dreadful carnage in front of Marye's Hill at Fredericksburg, and on the "old railroad cut" which Jackson's men held at the Second Manassas; but I had seen nothing to exceed this. It was not war; it was murder. When the fight ended, more than a thousand men lay in front of our works either killed or too badly wounded to leave the field. Among them were some who were not hurt, but remained among the dead and wounded rather than take the chances of going back under that merciless fire. Most of these came in and surrendered during the day, but were fired on in some instances by their own men (who still held a position close to our front) to prevent them from doing so. The loss in my command was fifteen or twenty, most of them wounded about the head and shoulders, myself among the number. Our artillery was handled superbly during the action. Major Hamilton, chief of artillery of Kershaw's division, not only coöperated with energy in strengthening our line on the night of June 2d, but directed the fire of his guns with great skill during the attack on the 3d, reaching not only the front of the attacking force, but its flanks also, as well as those of the supporting troops.

While we were busy with the Eighteenth Corps on the center of the general line, the sounds of the battle could be heard both on the right and left, and we knew from long use what that meant. It was a general advance of Grant's whole army. Early's corps below Bethesda Church was attacked without success. On our right, where the line extended toward the Chickahominy, it was broken at one point, but at once restored by Finegan's (Florida) brigade, with heavy loss to Hancock's troops who were attacking there. The result of the action in the center, which has been described, presents a fair picture of the results along the entire line—a grand advance, a desperate struggle, a bloody and crushing repulse. Before 8 o'clock A.M. on the 3d of June the battle of Cold Harbor was over, and with it Grant's "overland campaign" against Richmond....

The results of the "overland campaign" against Richmond, in 1864, cannot be gauged simply by the fact that Grant's army found itself within a few miles of the Confederate capital when it ended. It might have gotten there in a much shorter time and without any fighting at all. Indeed, one Federal army under General Butler was already there, threatening Richmond, which was considered by the Confederates much more secure after the arrival of the armies of Lee and Grant than it had been before. Nor can these results be measured only by the losses of the opposing armies on the battle-field, except as they affected the *morale* of armies themselves; for their losses were about proportional to their relative strength. So as far as the Confederates were concerned, it would be idle to deny that they (as well as General Lee himself) were disappointed at the result of their efforts in the Wilderness on the 5th and 6th of May, and that General Grant's constant "hammering" with his largely superior force had, to a certain extent, a depressing effect upon both officers and men. "It's no use killing these fellows; a half-dozen take the place of every one we kill," was a common remark in the army. We knew that our resources of men were exhausted, and that the vastly greater forces of the Federal Government, if brought fully to bear, even in this costly kind of warfare, must wear us out in the end. The question with us (and one often asked at the time) was, "How long will the people of the North, and the army itself, stand it?" We heard much about the demoralization of Grant's army, and of the mutterings of discontent at home with the conduct of the campaign, and we verily believed that their patience would soon come to an end.

SOURCE:

Ned Bradford, ed. *Battles and Leaders of the Civil War* (New York: Fairfax, 1979), pp. 473–489.

Document 15: WAR IS HELL

While Ulysses S. Grant pushed through northern Virginia in 1864, another Northern army launched its own offensive. Major General William T. Sherman led a force of sixty-two thousand men over the mountains in Tennessee and penetrated into western Georgia. A proponent of total war (that is, undermining the will of the enemy to resist by targeting his economic infrastructure and civilian morale), Sherman believed that "war is hell." He certainly brought that belief to reality, and today he is one of the most reviled figures in Southern history, the devil incarnate to many. Captain Daniel Oakey of the Second Massachusetts Volunteers describes how the "flying column" rendered Georgia and the Carolinas into "a howling waste" and left a path of destruction never seen before (or since) on the North American continent.

To us of the Twelfth Corps who had gone West with the Eleventh Corps from the Army of the Potomac, the distant thunder of "the battle of the clouds" was the first sound of conflict in the new field. Some of our "Potomac airs," which had earned us the name of "Kid gloves and paper collars," began to wear away as we better understood the important work to be done by the great army organizing around us, and of which we were to form a considerable part. A most interesting feature of these preparations was the reënlistment of the old three-years regiments. The two Potomac corps were consolidated, and we of the Twelfth who wore "the bloody star" were apprehensive lest different insignia should be adopted; but the star became the badge of the new (Twentieth) corps, the crescent men amiably dropping their Turkish emblem....

We observed in the Western troops an air of independence hardly consistent with the nicest discipline; but this quality appeared to some purpose at the battle of Resaca, where we saw our Western companions deliberately leave the line, retire out of range, clean their guns, pick up ammunition from the wounded, and return again to the fight. This cool self-reliance excited our admiration. On we went in a campaign of continual skirmishes and battles that ended in the capture of Atlanta. The morale of the troops had been visibly improved by this successful campaign.

On my way to army headquarters at Atlanta to call upon a staff friend, I met General Sherman, who acknowledged my salute with a familiar "How do you do, Captain." Scrutinizing the insignia on my cap, he continued, "Second Massachusetts? Ah, yes, I know your regiment; you have very fine parades over there in the park."

Sherman could be easily approached by any of his soldiers, but no one could venture to be familiar. His uniform coat, usually wide open at the throat, displayed a not very military black cravat and linen collar, and he generally wore low shoes and one spur. On the march he rode with each column in turn, and often with no larger escort than a single staff-officer and an orderly. In passing us on the march he acknowledged our salutations as if he knew us all, but hadn't time to stop. On "the march to the sea" a soldier called out to Sherman, "Uncle Billy, I guess Grant's waiting for us at Richmond." Sherman's acquaintance among his officers was remarkable, and of great advantage, for he learned the character of every command, even of regiments, and could assign officers to special duties, with knowledge of those who were to fill the vacancies so made. The army appreciated these personal relations, and every man felt that in a certain sense that Sherman had his eye on him.

Before the middle of November, 1864, the inhabitants of Atlanta, by Sherman's orders, had left the place. Serious preparations were making for the march to the sea. Nothing was to be left for the use or advantage of the enemy. The sick were sent back to Chattanooga and Nashville, along with every pound of baggage that could be dispensed with. The army was reduced, one might say, to its fighting weight, no man being retained who was not capable of a long march. Our communications were then abandoned by destroying the railroad and telegraph. There was something intensely exciting in this perfect isolation.

The engineers had peremptory orders to avoid any injury to dwellings, but to apply gunpowder and the torch to public buildings, machine-shops, depots, and arsenals. Sixty thousand of us witnessed the destruction of Atlanta, while our post band and that of the 33d Massachusetts played martial airs and operatic selections. It was a night never to be forgotten. Our regular routine was a mere form, and there could be no "taps" amid the brilliant glare and excitement.

The throwing away of superfluous conveniences began at day break. The old campaigner knows what to carry and what to throw away. Each group of messmates decided which hatchet, stew-pan, or coffee-pot should be taken. The single wagon allowed to a battalion carried scarcely more than a grip-sack and a blanket, and a bit of shelter tent about the size of a large towel, for each officer, and only such other material as was necessary for regimental business. Transportation was reduced to a minimum, and fast marching was to be the order of the day. Wagons to carry the necessary ammunition in the contingency of battle, and a few days' rations in case of absolute need, composed the train of each army corps, and with one wagon and one ambulance for each regiment made very respectable "impedimenta," averaging about eight hundred wagons to a corps.

At last came the familiar "Fall in"; the great "flying column" was on the march, and the last regiment in Atlanta turned its back upon the smoking ruins. Our left wing (the Fourteenth and Twentieth corps under Slocum) seemed to threaten Macon, while the right wing (the Fifteenth and Seventeenth corps under Howard) bent its course as if for Augusta. Skirmishers were in advance, flankers were out, and foraging parties were ahead gathering supplies from the rich plantations. We were all old campaigners, so that a brush with the militia now and then or with Hardee's troops made no unusual delay; and Wheeler's cavalry was soon disposed of. We were expected to make fifteen miles a day; to corduroy the roads where necessary; to destroy such property as was designated by our corps commander, and to consume everything eatable by man or beast.

Milledgeville proved to be Sherman's first objective, and both wings came within less than supporting distance in and around the capital of the State. Our colored friends, who flocked to us in embarrassing numbers, told many stories about the fear and flight of the inhabitants at the approach of Sherman.

Cock-fighting became one of the pastimes of the "flying column." Many fine birds were brought in by our foragers. Those found deficient in courage and skill quickly went to the stew-pan in company with the modest barnyard fowl, but those of redoubtable valor won an honored place and name, and were to be seen riding proudly on the front seat of an artillery caisson, or carried tenderly under the arm of an infantry soldier.

Our next objective was Savannah. Hazen's capture of Fort McAllister opened the gates of that beautiful city, while Hardee managed to escape with his little army; and Sherman, in a rather facetious dispatch, presented the city to Mr. Lincoln as a Christmas gift. Flushed with the success of our march, we settled down for a rest. Our uniforms were the worse for wear, but the army was in fine condition and fully prepared for the serious work ahead.

In the middle of December in the neighborhood of Savannah, after Hardee's troops had nearly exhausted the country, which was now mainly under water, there was little opportunity for the foragers to exercise their talents, and some of them returned to the ranks. The troops bivouacked here and there in comparatively dry spots, while picket duty had to be performed at many points in the water. In going from Sister's Ferry to Robertsville, where my regiment was in bivouac, I waded for a mile and a half in water knee-deep. At Purysburg the pickets were all afloat in boats and scows and on rafts, and the crestfallen foragers brought in nothing but rice, which became unpalatable when served three times a day for successive weeks. At length, when we left Savannah and launched cheerily into the untrodden land of South Carolina, the foragers began to assume their wonted spirit. We were proud of our foragers. They constituted a picked force from each regiment, under an officer selected for command, and were remarkable for intelligence, spirit, and daring. Before daylight, mounted on horses captured on the plantations, they were in the saddle and away, covering the country sometimes seven miles in advance. Although I have said "in the saddle," many a forager had nothing better than a bit of carpet and rope halter; yet this simplicity of equipment did not abate his power of carrying off hams and sweet-potatoes in the face of the enemy. The foragers were also important as a sort of advance guard, for they formed virtually a curtain of mounted infantry screening us from the inquisitive eyes of parties of Wheeler's cavalry, with whom they did not hesitate to engage when it was a question of a rich plantation.

When compelled to retire, they resorted to all the tricks of infantry skirmishers, and summoned reënforcements of foragers from other regiments to help drive the "Johnnies" out. When success crowned their efforts, the plantation was promptly stripped of live stock and eatables. The natives were accustomed to bury provisions, for they feared their own soldiers quite as much as they feared ours. These subterranean stores were readily discovered by the practiced "Yankee" eye. The appearance of the ground and a little probing with a ramrod or bayonet soon decided whether to dig. Teams were improvised; carts and vehicles of all sorts were pressed into the service and loaded with provisions. If any antiquated militia uniforms were discovered, they were promptly donned, and a comical procession escorted the valuable train of booty to the point where the brigade was expected to bivouac for the night. The regimentals of the past, even to those of revolutionary times, were often conspicuous.

On an occasion when our brigade had the advance, several parties of foragers, consolidating themselves, captured a town from the enemy's cavalry, and occupied the neighboring plantations. Before the arrival of the main column hostilities had ceased; order had been restored, and mock arrangements were made to receive the army. Our regiment in the advance was confronted by a picket dressed in a continental uniform, who waved his plumed hat in response to the gibes of the men, and galloped away on his bareback mule to apprise his comrades of our approach. We marched into the town and rested on each side of the main street. Presently a forager, in ancient militia uniform indicating high rank, debouched from a side street to do the honors of the occasion. He was mounted on a raw-boned horse with a bit of carpet for a saddle. His old plumed chapeau in hand, he rode with gracious dignity through the street, as if reviewing the brigade. After him came a family carriage laden with hams, sweet-potatoes, and other provisions, and drawn by two horses, a mule, and a cow, the two latter ridden by postilions....

The march through Georgia has been called a grand military promenade, all novelty and excitement. But its moral effect on friend and foe was immense. It proved our ability to lay open the heart of the Confederacy, and left the question of what we might do next a matter of doubt and terror. It served also as a preliminary training for the arduous campaign to come. Our work was incomplete while the Carolinas, except at a few points on the sea-coast, had not felt the rough contact of war. But their swamps and rivers, swollen and spread into lakes by winter floods, presented obstructions almost impracticable to an invading army, if opposed by even a very inferior force.

The task before us was indeed formidable. It involved exposure and indefatigable exertion. To succeed, our forward movement had to be continuous, for even the most productive regions would soon be exhausted by our 60,000 men and more, and 13,000 animals.

Although we were fully prepared, with our great trains of ammunition, to fight a pitched battle, our mission was not to fight, but to consume and destroy. Our inability to care properly for the wounded, who must necessarily be carried along painfully in jolting ambulances to die on the way from exhaustion and exposure, was an additional and very serious reason for avoiding collision with the enemy. But where he could not be evaded, his very presence across our path increased the velocity of our flying column. We repelled him by a decisive blow and without losing our momentum.

The beginning of our march in South Carolina was pleasant, the weather favorable, and the country productive. Sometimes at the midday halt a stray pig that had cunningly evaded the foragers would venture forth in the belief of having escaped "the cruel war," and would find his error, alas! too late, by encountering our column. Instantly an armed mob would set upon him, and his piercing shrieks would melt away in the scramble for fresh pork. But the midday support of the main column and the happy life of the forager were sadly interrupted. The sun grew dim, and the rain came and continued. A few of our excellent foragers were reported captured by Wheeler's cavalry, while we sank deeper and deeper in the mud as we approached the Salkehatchie Swamp, which lay between us and the Charleston and Augusta railroad. As the heads of column came up, each command knew what it had to do. Generals Mower and G. A. Smith got their divisions across by swimming, wading, and floating, and effected lodgments in spite of the enemy's fire. An overwhelming mass of drenched and muddy veterans swept away the enemy, while the rest of our force got the trains and artillery over by corduroying, pontooning, and bridging. It seemed a grand day's work to have accomplished, as we sank down that night in our miry bivouac....

We destroyed about forty miles of the Charleston and Augusta railroad, and, by threatening points beyond the route we intended to take, we deluded the enemy into concentrating at Augusta and other places, while we marched rapidly away, leaving him well behind, and nothing but Wade Hampton's cavalry, and the more formidable obstacle of the Saluda River and its swamps, between us and Columbia, our next objective. As the route of our column lay west of Columbia, I saw nothing of the oft-described and much-discussed burning of that city.

During the hasty removal of the Union prisoners from Columbia two Massachusetts officers managed to make their escape. Exhausted and almost naked, they found their way to my command. My mess begged for the privilege of caring for one of them. We gave him a mule to ride with a comfortable saddle, and scraped together an outfit for them, although our clothes were in the last stages. Our guest found the mess luxurious, as he sat down with us at the edge of a rubber blanket spread upon the ground for a table-cloth, and set with tin cups and platters. Stewed fighting-cock and bits of fried turkey were followed by fried corn-meal and sorghum. Then came our coffee and pipes, and we lay down by a roaring fire of pine-knots, to hear our guest's story of life in a rebel prison. Before daybreak the tramp of horses reminded us that our foragers were sallying forth. The red light from the countless camp-fires melted away as the dawn stole over the horizon, casting its wonderful gradations of light and color over the masses of sleeping soldiers, while the smoke from burning pine-knots befogged the chilly morning air. Then the bugles broke the impressive stillness, and the roll of drums was heard on all sides. Soon the scene was alive with blue coats and the hubbub of roll-calling, cooking, and running for water to the nearest spring or stream. The surgeons looked to the sick and footsore, and weeded from the ambulances those who no longer needed to ride.

It was not uncommon to hear shots at the head of the column. The foragers would come tumbling back, and ride alongside the regiment, adding to the noisy talk their account of what they had seen, and dividing among their comrades such things as they had managed to bring away in their narrow escape from capture. A staff-officer would gallop down the roadside like a man who had forgotten something which must be recovered in a hurry. At the sound of the colonel's ringing voice, silence was instant and absolute. Sabers flashed from their scabbards, the men brought their guns to the "carry," and the battalion swung into line at the roadside; cats, fighting-cocks, and frying-pans passed to the rear rank; officers and sergeants buzzed round their companies to see that the guns were loaded and the men ready for action. The color-sergeant loosened the water-proof cover of the battle flag, a battery of artillery flew past on its way to the front, following the returning staff-officer, and we soon heard the familiar bang of shells. Perhaps it did not amount to much after all, and we were soon swinging into "route step" again.

At times when suffering from thirst it was hard to resist the temptation of crystal swamp water, as it rippled along the side of a causeway, a tempting sight for the weary and unwary. In spite of oft-repeated cautions, some contrived to drink it, but these were on their backs with malarial disease at the end of the campaign, if not sooner....

We marched into Cheraw with music and with colors flying. Stacking arms the main street, we proceeded to supper, while the engineers laid the pontoons across the Pedee River. The railing of the town pump, and the remains of a buggy, said to belong to Mr. Lincoln's brother-in-law, Dr. Todd, were quickly reduced to kindling-wood to boil the coffee. The necessary destruction of property was quickly accomplished, and on we went. A mile from the Lumber River the country, already flooded ankle-deep, was rendered still more inhospitable by a steady down-pour of rain. The bridges had been partly destroyed by the enemy, and partly swept away by the flood. An attempt to carry heavy army wagons and artillery across this dreary lake might have seemed rather foolhardy, but we went to work without loss of time. The engineers were promptly floated out to the river, to direct the rebuilding of bridges, and the woods all along the line of each column soon rang with the noise of axes. Trees quickly became logs, and were brought to the submerged roadway. No matter if logs disappeared in the floating mud; thousands more were coming from all sides. So, layer upon layer, the work went bravely on. Soon the artillery and wagons were jolting over our wooden causeway.

As my regiment was the rear-guard for the day, we had various offices to perform for the train, and it was midnight before we saw the last wagon over the bridge by the light of our pine torches. It seemed as if that last wagon was never to be got over. It came bouncing and bumping along, its six mules smoking and blowing in the black, misty air. The teamster, mounted on one of the wheelers, guided his team with a single rein and addressed each mule by name, reminding the animal of his faults, and accusing him of having, among other peculiarities, "a black military heart." Every sentence of his oath-adorned rhetoric was punctuated with a dexterous whip-lash. At last, drenched to the skin and covered with mud, I took my position on the bridge, seated in a chair which one of my men had presented to me, and waited for the command to "close up."...

As we advanced into the wild pine regions of North Carolina the natives seemed wonderfully impressed at seeing every road filled with marching troops, artillery, and wagon trains. They looked destitute enough as they stood in blank amazement gazing upon the "Yanks" marching by. The scene before us was very striking; the resin pits were on fire, and great columns of black smoke rose high into the air, spreading and mingling together in gray clouds, and suggesting the roof and pillars of a vast temple. All traces of habitation were left behind, as we marched into that grand forest with its beautiful carpet of pine-needles. The straight trunks of the pine-tree shot up to a great height, and then spread out into a green roof, which kept us in perpetual shade. As night came on, we found that the resinous sap in the cavities cut in the trees to receive it, had been lighted by "bummers" in our advance. The effect of these peculiar watch-fires on every side, several feet above the ground, with flames licking their way up the tall trunks, was particularly striking and beautiful. But it was sad to see this wanton destruction of property, which, like the firing of the resin pits, was the work of "bummers," who were marauding through the country committing every sort of outrage. There was no restraint except with the column or the regular foraging parties. We had no communications, and could have no safeguards. The country was necessarily left to take care of itself, and became a "howling waste." The "coffee-coolers" of the Army of the Potomac were archangels compared to our "bummers," who often fell to the tender mercies of Wheeler's cavalry, and were never heard of again, earning a fate richly deserved.

On arriving within easy distance of the Cape Fear River, where we expected to communicate with the navy, detachments were sent in rapid advance to secure Fayetteville. Our division, after a hard day of corduroying in various spots over a distance of twelve miles, went into camp for supper, and then, taking the plank-road for Fayetteville, made a moonlight march of nine miles in three hours, but our friends from the right wing arrived there before us.

Hardee retired to a good position at Averysboro', where Kilpatrick found him intrenched and too strong for the cavalry to handle unassisted. It was the turn of our brigade to do special duty, so at about 8 o'clock in the evening we were ordered to join the cavalry. We were not quite sure it rained, but everything was dripping. The men furnished themselves with pine-knots, and our weapons glistened in the torch-light, a cloud of black smoke from the torches floating back over our heads. The regimental wits were as ready as ever, and amid a flow of lively badinage we toiled on through the mud....

The clear wintry dawn disclosed a long line of bluecoats spread over the ground in motionless groups. This was the roaring torch-light brigade of the night before. The orders "Fall in!" "Forward!" in gruff tones broke upon the chilly air, and brought us shivering to our feet. We moved to the edge of the woods with the cavalry. The skirmish-line, under Captain J. I. Grafton, had already disappeared into the opposite belt of woods, and evidently were losing no time in developing the enemy and ascertaining his force. They were drawing his fire from all points, indicating a force more than double that of our brigade. Dismounted cavalry were now sent forward to prolong the skirmish-line. Captain Grafton was reportedly badly wounded in the leg, but still commanding with his usual coolness. Suddenly he appeared staggering out of the wood into the open space in our front, bareheaded, his face buried in his hands, his saber hanging by the sword-knot from his wrist, one leg bound up with a handkerchief, his uniform covered with blood; in a moment he fell toward the colors. Officers clustered about him in silence, and a gloom spread through the brigade as word passed that Grafton was dead.

The main column was now arriving, and as troops filed off to the right and left of the road, and the field-guns galloped into battery, we moved forward to the attack. The enemy gave us a hot reception, which we returned with a storm of lead. It was a wretched place for a fight. At some points we had to support our wounded until they could be carried off, to prevent their falling into the swamp water, in which we stood ankle-deep. Here and there a clump of thick growth in the black mud broke the line as we advanced. No ordinary troops were in our front. They would not give way until a division of Davis's corps was thrown upon their right, while we pressed them closely. As we passed over their dead and wounded, I came upon the body of a very young officer, whose handsome, refined face attracted my attention. While the battle swept past me I knelt at his side for a moment. His buttons bore the arms of South Carolina. Evidently we were fighting the Charleston chivalry. Sunset found us in bivouac on the Goldsboro' road, and Hardee in retreat.

As we trudged on toward Bentonville, distant sounds told plainly that the head of the column was engaged. We hurried to the front and went into action, connecting with Davis's corps. Little opposition having been expected, the distance between our wing and the right wing had been allowed to increase beyond supporting distance in the endeavor to find easier roads for marching as well as for transporting the wounded. The scope of this paper precludes a description of the battle of Bentonville, which was a combination of mistakes, miscarriages, and hard fighting on both sides. It ended in Johnston's retreat, leaving open the road to Goldsboro', where we arrived ragged and almost barefoot. While we were receiving letters from home, getting new clothes, and taking our regular doses of quinine, Lee and Johnson surrendered, and the great conflict came to an end.

Source:

Ned Bradford, ed. *Battles and Leaders of the Civil War* (New York: Fairfax, 1979), pp. 591–599.

***Document 16:* COLUMBIA IS BURNING**

The army of Major General William T. Sherman reached Columbia, South Carolina, on February 17, 1865, and what exactly happened later that night has been hotly debated since. Most of the city was destroyed by a massive fire; while some assert that the Federal troops went on a rampage of pillaging and burning, others maintain that retreating Confederates had fired some cotton bales, and with a strong wind that night, these fires quickly got out of control. The truth is that both sides bear responsibility for the conflagration. Brevet Major George Ward Nichols, an aide-de-camp to General Sherman, left this account.

A Scene of Shameful Confusion

Columbia, February 17th [1865]—It is with a feeling of proud exultation that I write the date of Columbia. We have conquered and occupy the capital of the haughty state that instigated and forced forward the treason which has brought on this desolating war. The city which was to have been the capital of the Confederacy if Lee and Rebel hosts had been driven from Richmond is now overrun by Northern soldiers. The beautiful capital building bears the marks of Yankee shot and shell, and the old flag which the Rebels insulted at Sumter now floats freely in the air from the house tops of the central city in South Carolina....

General Sherman and General Howard were the first to cross the bridge, and entered the city, followed by their staffs. A scene of shameful confusion met their eyes. On every side were evidences of disorder; bales of cotton scattered here and there; articles of household furniture and merchandise of every description cast pell-mell 'in every direction by the frightened inhabitants, who had escaped from a city which they supposed was doomed to destruction....

The three or four days' notice of our approach enabled the government officials to remove most of the material belonging to the branch of the Treasury Department which was located at this point; yet large quantities of paper for printing Confederate notes and bonds, with type, printing-presses, etc., has fallen into our hands. This loss is irreparable to the Rebel government.

The arsenal was found well stocked with shot, shell, fixed ammunition, powder, Enfield rifles, carbines, and other material of war. A full battery of four rifled English Blakely guns, which were in a battery commanding the bridge, was also taken, with caissons and other material. Connected with the arsenal are shops full of costly machinery for the manufacture of arms and ammunition, with foundries for all sorts of castings. A little way down the river there is a large powder-mill. All of this will be thoroughly destroyed....

The store-houses are filled with all sorts of supplies—flour, meal, bacon, corn, harness, hardware, etc.—while cotton is found in every direction. As there is no treasury agent of our government to appropriate this costly material for somebody's benefit, I doubt if a very correct record of the quantity will be made before it is burned....

I began to-day's record early in the evening, and while writing I noticed an unusual glare in the sky, and heard a sound of running to and fro in the streets, with the loud talk of servants that the horses must be removed to a safer place. Running out, I found, to my surprise and real sorrow, that the central part of the city, including the main business street, was in flames, while the wind, which had been blowing a hurricane all day, was driving the sparks and cinders in heavy masses over the eastern portion of the city, where the finest residences are situated. These buildings, all wooden, were instantly ignited by the flying sparks. In half an hour the conflagration was raging in every direction, and but for a providential change of the wind to the south and west, the whole city would in a few hours have been laid in ashes.

As it is, several hundred buildings, including the old State House, one or two churches, most of the carved work stored in the sheds round about the new capitol, and a large number of public store-houses, have been destroyed. In some of the public buildings the Rebels had stored shot, shell, and other ammunition, and when the flames reached these magazines we had the Atlanta experience all over again—the smothered boom, the huge columns of fire shooting heavenward, the red-hot iron flying here and there. But there was one feature, pitiable indeed, which we did not find at Atlanta. Groups of men, women, and children were gathered in the streets and squares, huddled together over a trunk, a mattress, or a bundle of clothes. Our soldiers were at work with a will, removing household goods from the dwellings which were in the track of the flames, and here and there extinguishing a fire when there was hope of saving a building. General Sherman and his officers worked with their hands until long after midnight, trying to save life and property. The house taken for headquarters is now filled with old men, women, and children who have been driven from their homes by a more pitiless enemy than the detested "Yankees."

Various causes are assigned to explain the origin of the fire. I am quite sure that it originated in sparks flying from the hundreds of bales of cotton which the Rebels had placed along the middle of the main street, and fired as they left the city. Fire from a tightly-compressed bale of cotton is unlike that of a more open material, which burns itself out. The fire lies smouldering in a bale of cotton long after it appears extinguished; and in this instance, when our soldiers supposed they had extinguished the fire, it suddenly broke out again with the most dangerous effect.

There were fires, however, which must have been started independent of the above-named cause. The source of these is ascribed to the desire for revenge from some two hundred of our prisoners, who had escaped from the cars as they were being conveyed from this city to Charlotte, and, with the memories of long sufferings in the miserable pens I visited yesterday on the other side of the river, sought this means of retaliation. Again, it is said that the soldiers who first entered the town, intoxicated with success and a liberal supply of bad liquor, which was freely distributed among them by designing citizens, in an insanity of exhilaration set fire to unoccupied houses.

Whatever may have been the cause of the disaster, the direful result is deprecated by General Sherman most emphatically; for however heinous the crimes of this people against our common country, we do not war against women and children and helpless persons.

SOURCE:

George Ward Nichols. *The Story of the Great March, from the Diary of a Staff Officer* (New York: Harper, 1865), pp. 160–166.

Document 17: APPOMATTOX

On the afternoon of Sunday, April 9, 1865, a somber Robert E. Lee surrendered the Army of Northern Virginia at Appomattox Courthouse, Virginia. Outnumbered five to one and surrounded, his troops lacked ammunition and food. The formalities occurred in the parlor of the home of Wilmer McLean. Lee, wearing his best dress uniform and accompanied by his military secretary Colonel Charles Marshall, sat in marked contrast to Lieutenant General Ulysses S. Grant with his mud-splattered boots and rumpled officers. The following day, Lee issued his last address to his troops, General Order No. 9.

Headquarters, Army of Northern Virginia,
April 10th, 1865.

After four years of arduous service, marked by unsurpassed courage and fortitude, the Army of Northern Virginia has been compelled to yield to overwhelming numbers and resources. I need not tell the survivors of so many hard-fought battles, who have remained steadfast to the last, that I have consented to this result from no distrust of them, but, feeling that valor and devotion could accomplish nothing that could compensate for the loss that would have attended the continuation of the contest, I have determined to avoid the useless sacrifice of those whose past services have endeared them to their countrymen.

By the terms of the agreement, officers and men can return to their homes, and remain there until exchanged. You will take with you the satisfaction that proceeds from the consciousness of duty faithfully performed; and I earnestly pray that a merciful God will extend to you his blessing and protection.

With an increasing admiration for your constancy and devotion to your country, and a grateful remembrance of your kind and generous consideration of myself, I bid you an affectionate farewell.

R. E. Lee, General.

SOURCE:

Ned Bradford, ed. *Battles and Leaders of the Civil War* (New York: Fairfax, 1979), p. 620.

BIBLIOGRAPHY

Burton, William L. *Melting Pot Soldiers: The Union's Ethnic Regiments.* Ames: Iowa State University Press, 1988. Examines how ethnic politicians and entrepreneurs impacted the organization of these units.

Carter, Samuel, III. *The Final Fortress: The Campaign for Vicksburg, 1862–1863.* New York: St. Martin's Press, 1980. Analysis of Ulysses S. Grant's successful siege of the strategic post on the Mississippi River.

Catton, Bruce. *Grant Takes Command.* Boston: Little, Brown, 1969. The Union general is portrayed as the most innovative strategist of the conflict.

Catton. *A Stillness at Appomattox.* Garden City, N.Y.: Doubleday, 1953. The third book in the author's trilogy on the Army of the Potomac, following *Mr. Lincoln's Army* (1951) and *Glory Road: The Bloody Route from Fredericksburg to Gettysburg* (1952). Winner of the Pulitzer Prize and the National Book Award, *A Stillness at Appomattox* examines the last year of the conflict.

Donald, David, ed. *Why the North Won the Civil War.* Baton Rouge: Louisiana State University Press, 1960. Collection of essays by notable historians on military, economic, and social issues.

Escott, Paul D. *After Secession: Jefferson Davis and the Failure of Confederate Nationalism.* Baton Rouge: Louisiana State University Press, 1978. Maintains that the Confederacy lost because it lacked a viable nationalism that could inspire its population.

Fellman, Michael. *Inside War: The Guerrilla Conflict in Missouri During the American Civil War.* New York: Oxford University Press, 1989. Firsthand accounts of the bitter struggle. This state experienced the most widespread and destructive guerrilla activity in the entire war.

Foote, Shelby. *The Civil War: A Narrative.* 3 volumes. New York: Random House, 1958–1974. A popular and eloquent history of the conflict from the Southern point of view.

Fowler, William M., Jr. *Under Two Flags: The American Navy in the Civil War.* New York: Norton, 1990. A popular account of Union and Confederate naval operations.

Freeman, Douglas Southall. *Lee's Lieutenants: A Study in Command.* 3 volumes. New York: Scribners, 1942–1944. Biographies of some 150 officers of the Army of Northern Virginia.

———. *R. E. Lee: A Biography.* 4 volumes. New York: Scribners, 1934–1935. The single best biography on the famed Confederate general.

Geary, James W. *We Need Men: The Union Draft in the Civil War.* De Kalb: Northern Illinois University Press, 1991. Examination of an important homefront issue in the North.

Glatthaar, Joseph T. *Forged in Battle: The Civil War Alliance of Black Soldiers and White Officers.* New York: Free Press, 1990. Examines the bond created by shared adversity and the racial tension in the Federal Army as revealed in personal letters and official documents.

Griffith, Paddy. *Battle Tactics of the Civil War.* New Haven, Conn.: Yale University Press, 1989. Explains how the rifled musket's effectiveness depended on battlefield conditions.

Nevis, Allan. *The War for the Union.* 4 volumes. New York: Scribners, 1959–1971. A classic multivolume study.

Oates, Stephen B. *With Malice Toward None: The Life of Abraham Lincoln.* New York: Harper & Row, 1977. Lincoln is seen as a shrewd politician, devoted husband, and determined wartime leader.

Persico, Joseph E. *My Enemy, My Brother: Men and Days of Gettysburg.* New York: Viking, 1977. A study of the pivotal battle from the participants' point of view.

Ramsdell, Charles W. *Behind the Lines in the Southern Confederacy.* Baton Rouge: Louisiana State University Press, 1944. Asserts that deficiencies on the homefront were fundamental to the collapse of the Confederacy.

Royster, Charles. *The Destructive War: William Tecumseh Sherman, Stonewall Jackson, and the Americans.* New York: Knopf, 1991. Argues that these two "fire and sword" generals were not unusual and that from 1862 onward many on both sides of the struggle saw terror as a useful weapon.

Sears, Stephen W. *Landscape Turned Red: The Battle of Antietam.* New Haven, Conn.: Ticknor & Fields, 1983. A vivid description of the battle that portrays Union General George B. McClellan in a negative light.

Wise, Stephen R. *Lifeline of the Confederacy: Blockade Running During the War.* Columbia: University of South Carolina Press, 1988. A good study, although it downplays the fragility of this supply line.

~ 6 ~

African Americans in the Military: Contrabands, Freemen, and Women

The question of whether African Americans should participate in the military during the Civil War was a contentious issue. Politically, the service of African Americans, most of whom were slaves, meant the demise of slavery and thus threatened the Union's coalition with slaveholding border states. Socially, black and white soldiers fighting side by side implied equality, the political and social implications of which alarmed many Americans and galvanized others. Americans who opposed African American participation in the military cited the potential increase in political and social equality for blacks, while abolitionists supported African American involvement because of the same possible outcome. The politics of black enlistment and emancipation were inseparable, and deeply rooted ideologies of white supremacy clashed with measures that promoted racial equality.

The contradictions between the democratic and republican ideals associated with American independence and the realities of institutionalized slavery yielded a pervasive ideology of racism in nineteenth-century America. In this context, Americans struggled with central questions of debate including: whether the institution of slavery should be eliminated; whether former slaves should continue to live in the United States; and whether African Americans had the same mental and emotional capacities as European Americans. With the outbreak of the Civil War, the question of arming black soldiers became a hotly debated issue. When hundreds of thousands of slaves liberated themselves and entered Union lines, the debate became an urgent one.

At the start of the Civil War it was illegal for free black men and slaves to serve in the military. Although black Americans had fought in every American engagement from the colonial period through the American Revolution and the War of 1812, Congress had officially prohibited African Americans from enlisting in militias or in the U.S. Army in 1792 and again in 1820. Federal policy from 1793 and 1850 legislating that fugitive slaves must be returned to their owners meant that, legally, escaped slaves could not serve in the military in any capacity.

During the first years of the Civil War, combat status for African Americans was intensely debated by politicians, military commanders, abolitionists, and the general public. President Abraham Lincoln's concern for maintaining the loyalty of slaveholding border states and his sensitivity to Northern racism initially prevented him from initiating policy to permit black men to serve in the Union army. Lincoln's primary aim for the war was not to end slavery but to preserve the Union.

Days after the Confederate attack on Fort Sumter, free blacks in the North began offering their services to the Union. Within weeks fugitive slaves reached Union camps and volunteered for the war effort. By the end of 1862, between five hundred thousand and seven hundred thousand fugitive slaves had entered Federal lines. For two years, politicians and the public debated how to handle the issue of black enlistment while individual

Christian A. Fleetwood, who earned a Congressional Medal of Honor for his service at the Battle of New Market Heights on September 29, 1864 (Library of Congress)

Union generals had to make practical decisions about how to handle the huge influx of African American volunteers.

Ultimately, the actions of the hundreds of thousand of slaves who freed themselves and fled to Union lines made black military service and emancipation inevitable. Motivated by military exigency, Lincoln issued an Emancipation Proclamation in 1863, officially liberating slaves in Confederate states and permitting their armed service. The controversial proclamation initiated the first large-scale use of African American men as combat soldiers in American history. However, Lincoln's policy did not address whether African Americans who served the Union would receive the same treatment as their white counterparts, and as black men and women risked their lives to support the Federals, deeply rooted racial prejudice among white Americans often meant that the work of these black men and women went largely unrecognized and uncompensated.

Lincoln initially attempted to avoid the fractious issues of emancipation and racial equality by avoiding the enlistment of blacks, free or slave. However, the flood of escaped slaves into Federal lines at the onset of the war forced Union officers to consider their military use despite legal restrictions. In several cases, Union generals engaged slaves and pursued the recruitment of black men without congressional authority. When African Americans arrived at Fort Monroe in May 1861, General Benjamin Butler declared the fugitive slaves "contraband of war" and refused their return despite the Fugitive Slave Act still in effect in Federal territory. Butler reasoned that since many of the fugitive slaves in his camp had escaped from working on Confederate fortifications, their return would aid the enemy. Butler instead put the men to work, with compensation, in his quartermaster department, and Lincoln permitted Butler's policy to stand.

Four months later, in August 1861, Congress passed the First Confiscation Act, which nullified the claims of slave owners to slaves who had aided the Confederate war effort. Both Union commanders and slaves quickly took advantage of the legislation. Over the course of the war, an estimated two hundred thousand contrabands worked for the Union army in noncombat capacities such as teamsters, cattle drivers, stevedores, laborers, and camp aides. At the end of August of 1861, the head of the Department of the West, General John C. Frémont, invoked martial law and issued an edict freeing the slaves of disloyal Missouri rebels. This time a Union general's unauthorized proclamation was overruled by the president, who feared that such a policy would alienate slaveholders in the border states. When Frémont refused to modify the edict, Lincoln ordered him to do so. Still, enslaved men and women continued to free themselves by entering Federal lines.

When Secretary of War Simon Cameron issued his annual report in December 1861, he had, at Lincoln's prompting, removed passages advocating emancipation and the engagement of former slaves in the Union army. In March 1862, Congress enacted an additional article of war that further undermined the fugitive-slave laws by prohibiting military and naval personnel from "returning fugitives from service or labor, who may have escaped from any persons to whom such service or labor is claimed to be due." President Lincoln began to urge the border states to enact gradual, compensated abolition, and he advocated the colonization of former slaves outside of the United States.

A step ahead of federal policy, Union general David Hunter, commander of the Department of the South, began arming slaves at Port Royal, South Carolina, in April 1862 and declared free all slaves in South Carolina, Alabama, and Florida in the following month. Lincoln issued a proclamation to nullify Hunter's edict, and the War Department initially refused to pay or equip his black soldiers. Nevertheless, Hunter's First South Carolina Volunteers was the first unit of former slaves to unofficially join the Union army. They served in combat under Colonel Thomas Wentworth Higginson and were ultimately designated the Thirty-third Regiment of U.S. Colored Troops in February 1864. In the summer of 1862, a few months after Hunter began to arm former slaves in South Carolina, Kansas senator James H. Lane began to recruit former slaves from Missouri and Arkansas to form the First Kansas Colored Volunteer Infantry, later known as the Seventy-ninth Infantry Regiment.

As federal policy began to take a turn, in July 1862 Congress passed two measures that directly linked African American enlistment to emancipation. The Second Confiscation Act freed slaves of rebel owners and permitted the seizure of the latter's property; it also prohibited military personnel from surrendering fugitives or deciding on the validity of an escaped slave's claim to freedom. Finally, the act authorized the president to employ "persons of African descent" in any capacity to suppress the rebellion. The Militia Act, also passed in July, provided for the employment of African Americans in "any military or naval service for which they may be found competent," and also granted freedom to slaves so employed and to their families if their owners were rebels. On September 22, 1862, Lincoln issued the preliminary Emancipation Proclamation that would go into effect at the start of the following year.

A small detachment from the First Kansas Colored Volunteer Infantry fought in an engagement at Island Mound, Missouri, in October 1862, initiating the use of black troops in active combat. A month earlier in Louisiana, General Butler had officially mustered the first three all-black units in the Union army, known as the First, Second, and Third Louisiana Native Guards or the Corps D'Afrique, initially led by African American commanders. In December 1862, in protest of the use of black soldiers, Jefferson Davis issued a Confederate proclamation that former slaves serving as Union soldiers would not be treated as prisoners of war and that their white officers would be executed.

Lincoln's final Emancipation Proclamation of January 1, 1863, authorized that emancipated slaves "will be received into the armed service of the United States to garrison forts, positions, stations, and other places, and to man vessels of all sorts in said service." While the proclamation only liberated slaves in Confederate territory not under Union control, and left slavery in the border states intact, it established emancipation as an official objective of the war. Lincoln's 1863 proclamation also instigated an active recruitment policy for African American soldiers, paving the way for the first large-scale use of black combat soldiers in U.S. history. In May 1863 the federal government established the Bureau for Colored Troops to systematize African American recruitment and enlistment.

Approximately 180,000 African American soldiers fought in the Union army, constituting 10 percent of all Union combat troops. More than half of these enlisted black soldiers were from Confederate states, the vast majority of whom were former slaves, as were most of the African American soldiers from border states who comprised almost a quarter of the troops. About 50,000 of the Union's black soldiers, roughly 20 percent, were from Northern states and were free from birth, manumission, or escape.

Reluctant to commission black officers, the Union army commissioned between 80 and 100 African American officers during the Civil War. Eight black men served as Federal army surgeons, including Lieutenant Colonel Alexander T. Augusta, the highest-ranking black soldier in the Civil War. Fourteen African Americans served as army chaplains. The Union's black soldiers were organized into 133 infantry regiments, 4 independent companies, 12 regiments of heavy artillery, 10 batteries of light artillery, and 7 cavalry regiments. The United States Colored Troops (USCT) fought in approximately 450 engagements, including 40 major battles.

The engagement of the Louisiana Native Guard units at Port Hudson, Louisiana, in March 1863 was the first major assault by black troops. Many of the members of the Louisiana Native Guards were free men of color who had previously cast their lot with the Confederacy but had never been put into service; others were former slaves. While the assault failed, the valor of the black soldiers impressed observers. Two months later the First Mississippi Volunteers of African Descent, composed of former Mississippi and Louisiana slaves, repelled a Confederate attack at Milliken's Bend, Louisiana. Their efforts, described by Ulysses S. Grant as "gallant," smoothed the

Company E, the Fourth U.S. Colored Infantry, at Fort Lincoln, Washington (Library of Congress)

way for the systematic recruitment and utilization of USCT regiments for the remainder of the war.

In July 1863, the Fifty-fourth Massachusetts Volunteer Infantry, the first black regiment raised in a free state, spearheaded an assault on Fort Wagner, South Carolina, that was a military failure but a political victory. Greatly outnumbered, Union forces were not able to take the fort and sustained heavy casualties. The Fifty-fourth Massachusetts lost two-thirds of their officers, including their commander, Robert Gould Shaw, and half of their troops. For his heroism during the Fort Wagner assault, Sergeant William H. Carney became the first African American to receive the Congressional Medal of Honor in August 1863. The skill and sacrifice of the soldiers of the Fifty-fourth garnered national attention and widely signaled the success of black military recruitment.

Confederate troops were often particularly cruel to black Union soldiers, and debates continue over whether particular events constituted outright massacres. At Fort Pillow, Tennessee, in April 1864, Confederate troops killed 64 percent of the Union's African American soldiers, double the death toll for the equivalent number of white Union troops there. Congressional inquiries found that many of the killings took place after black soldiers had surrendered. Days later in Poison Spring, Arkansas, Confederates killed troops from the First Kansas Colored Infantry who had surrendered. While black troops contributed to the success of the Siege of Petersburg, Virginia, cutting off supplies to the Confederate capital of Richmond, the vast majority of those who fought in Petersburg's Battle of the Crater on July 30, 1864, were killed by Confederate troops. African American soldiers at the Crater sustained the heaviest single-day casualties of the entire war.

The greatest number of USCT served in the Virginia theater as part of General Grant's Petersburg-Richmond campaigns that helped bring the Civil War to an end. African American units fought in all of the significant Virginia campaigns and were especially active in the fighting around Petersburg during the summer of 1864. In September, two months after the Battle of the Crater, black troops experienced victory but also heavy casualties at the Battle of New Market Heights near Richmond. Fourteen black soldiers received the Medal of Honor for their bravery and leadership during this battle.

The U.S. Colored Cavalry (USCC) was primarily put into service on scouting and reconnaissance missions. However, in December 1864 and January 1865 the Third USCC joined white cavalry troops in a 450-mile raid in Mississippi, liberating some one thousand slaves. In April 1865 the Fifth Massachusetts Cavalry, composed of African American horsemen, was among the first of the Federal troops to enter Richmond upon its capture. Black troops were among the Union forces at the Appomattox Court House when General Robert E. Lee surrendered. African American troops from the Sixty-second U.S. Colored Infantry Regiment fought in the war's final battle at Palmito Ranch, Texas, in May 1865.

The Union army discriminated against black soldiers, providing them substandard supplies, equipment, rations, training, medical care, and pay—and black troops and their white commanders strongly protested salary discrepancies. The Fifty-fourth Massachusetts Regiment served a year without pay rather than accept substandard wages. In 1864 the War Department sanctioned equal wages for black soldiers. Most Northern states provided local and state aid for the dependents of white soldiers but not for their black counterparts. In July 1864 the federal government began to give assistance to the families of African Americans killed in service; yet, enslaved family members were not eligible.

The Confederacy ultimately recognized the necessity of recruiting black soldiers, but not until the war was at its close. Confederates had long debated the use of African Americans in the military, generally limiting their service to noncombat roles such as laboring on fortifications. On March 13, 1865, Confederacy president Jefferson Davis signed a bill authorizing the enlistment of slaves and their emancipation beginning on April 3. Six days later, on April 9, 1865, General Lee surrendered at the Appomattox Court House.

While black troops did not appear on the battlefield in large numbers until after the Emancipation Proclamation, black sailors fought from the onset of the war. African American men had long served on American naval vessels in substantial numbers, and black sailors faced much less official discrimination than African American soldiers during the Civil War. Unlike their counterparts in the army, black sailors served in integrated crews and received the same pay, benefits, promotion opportunities, legal recourse, and living standards as white sailors. Approximately twenty thousand black men served as sailors during the Civil War. Recent estimates suggest that as many as one in every six Union sailors was black.

At the war's outbreak, escaped slaves sought refuge on navy vessels, and many provided intelligence on Confederate movements and fortifications. By July 1861, Secretary of the Navy Gideon Welles had established a policy to recruit black sailors. Within months, thousands of men of African descent, including fugitive slaves and freemen, many of whom had been born outside the United States, enlisted as sailors, serving in every major naval battle and campaign and transforming the composition of the Union navy. (After the Civil War, the Navy began to restrict black enlistment.)

Several of the men who served in the Union navy had survived daring escapes from slavery. On May 23, 1862, Robert Smalls, an enslaved man in Charleston, South Carolina, employed by Confederates to pilot the *Planter*, masqueraded as the ship's white captain and delivered the war ship along with his family and twelve other slaves to Union lines. After meeting with President Lincoln, who authorized an award of federal monies for the delivery of Confederate supplies, Smalls served the Union as the first African American captain of a U.S. Navy vessel for the remainder of the war. Smalls went on to serve in the U.S. Congress in 1875 and 1876.

African American women served the Union effort as nurses, spies, scouts, camp aides, and laborers. Mary Ann Shadd Cary was appointed by the Union army as a recruiting officer. Maria Lewis served with the Eighth New York Cavalry, while Mary Dyson, a former slave, fought in several battles disguised as a man. Harriet Tubman served the Union for three years as a spy, nurse, and scout. Her intelligence facilitated several successful raids by the Second South Carolina Volunteers, a black regiment, on Confederate strongholds. Tubman was reported to have led one of these raids, which liberated close to eight hundred slaves. Upon her death in 1913, Tubman received a full military funeral.

Susie King Taylor, a former slave, joined the First South Carolina Volunteers initially as a laundress and teacher. Taylor ultimately served on several expeditions as a camp aide cleaning and loading firearms and, primarily, as an army nurse. Many Southern black women provided Union soldiers with intelligence and supplies. Ellen Bower, a free woman, went undercover as a slave named Ellen Bond in Jefferson Davis's Richmond home, where, pretending to be illiterate and mentally impaired, she collected information for Union soldiers. When she came under suspicion, Bower escaped to Union lines after attempting to burn the Confederate White House in January 1864.

Days after the Confederate attack on Fort Sumter initiated the Civil War, free blacks in the North offered their services to the Union, and within weeks the first of the roughly half a million fugitive slaves who escaped to Federal lines volunteered for the war effort. During 1861 and 1862 politicians and the public debated how to handle the issues surrounding black military service, while individual Union generals made on-the-ground decisions about how to handle the vast influx of black volunteers. In 1863 President Lincoln recognized African American enlistment as a necessity and initiated federal policy to systematize black recruitment. Between 1863 and 1865 more than two hundred thousand African Americans served in the Federal army and navy. These enlisted black soldiers and sailors, as well as countless black men and women who served the Union forces in unofficial capacities, played varied and vital roles in the Union's military victory. The treatment and use of black combatants remained controversial throughout the war. The Union's black supporters faced discrimination and hostility not only from Confederate ranks but from Union forces as well.

Although Lincoln was initially opposed to arming African Americans, he ultimately acknowledged that the emancipation and arming of slaves were crucial to the Union's victory. In addition to the African American units that were officially mustered, numerous black men and women aided Union forces in unofficial capacities, supplying labor, resources, and information. Between forty thousand and sixty thousand enlisted African Americans lost their lives in the Civil War. Twenty-three African American soldiers and sailors received the Medal of Honor for their Civil War service. After the war, several black regiments assisted the Army of Occupation and Reconstruction efforts until 1867. The Spanish American War in 1898 brought many of these conflicts to surface once again. While African American soldiers played a crucial role in the success of U.S. forces in Cuba, these soldiers faced discrimination and violence at home.

Christina Proenza-Coles

CHRONOLOGY

1861

April 12: Confederates attack Fort Sumter, inaugurating the Civil War.

May 24: General Benjamin Butler declares fugitive slaves at Fort Monroe, Virginia, "contraband" and puts them to work for the Union with pay.

August 6: The First Confiscation Act nullifies slave owners' claims to fugitive slaves who have previously been put to use in the Confederate war effort.

August 30: General John C. Frémont declares all slaves of rebel slave owners in Missouri free; Lincoln will order Frémont to rescind his proclamation the following month.

September 21: Navy secretary Gideon Wells authorizes recruiters to enlist former slaves in the Union navy.

1862

April 3: General David Hunter begins to recruit black soldiers in South Carolina on his own authority after his request for permission has gone unanswered.

May 9: General Hunter declares all slaves in South Carolina, Georgia, and Florida free.

May 19: President Abraham Lincoln nullifies General Hunter's emancipation edict and urges border states to embrace gradual, compensated emancipation and colonization.

June–August: Senator James H. Lane begins to recruit the First Kansas Colored Volunteer Infantry, making Kansas the first state to officially recruit and train military units comprised of black soldiers.

July 17: Congress passes the Second Confiscation Act and the Militia Act.

August 22: General Butler incorporates several Louisiana Native Guard units of free black soldiers into Union forces and musters the first official all-black forces in the Union army.

August 25: After having withheld permission, the War Department authorizes Hunter's recruitment of black soldiers in the South Carolina Sea Islands.

September 22: Lincoln issues the preliminary Emancipation Proclamation, announcing that all slaves in areas still in rebellion as of January 1, 1863, will be declared free.

October 28: In the first use of black troops in combat during the Civil War, the First Kansas Colored Volunteer Infantry fight at Island Mound, Missouri.

December 23: Protesting the use of black soldiers, Jefferson Davis issues a proclamation ordering that black Union soldiers captured by Confederate troops are not to be treated as prisoners of war but remanded to Confederate state authorities and that their white officers will be executed.

1863

January 1: Lincoln issues the Emancipation Proclamation, liberating slaves in Confederate states and announcing the Union's intention to enlist black soldiers and sailors.

March 26: Adjutant General of the Army, Lorenzo Thomas, begins a large-scale effort to raise and administer black troops in the Mississippi Valley.

May 22: The Bureau of Colored Troops is established.

May 27: The Louisiana Native Guards play a vital role in the assault on Port Hudson, Louisiana.

June 7: The First Mississippi Volunteers of African Descent soldiers repel a Confederate attack at Milliken's Bend, Louisiana.

July 13–16: In what becomes known as the New York City Draft Riots, predominantly Irish mobs, angered by congressional laws initiating a draft, attack African Americans in New York City and burn down an orphanage for black children.

July 18: The Fifty-fourth Massachusetts spearheads an assault on Fort Wagner, South Carolina.

July 30: Lincoln's Order of Retaliation states that Union soldiers, black or white, are entitled to equal protection if captured by the enemy. The order threatens retaliation for Confederates who enslave or kill black prisoners of war.

October 3: The War Department orders full-scale recruitment of black soldiers in Maryland, Missouri, and Tennessee, with compensation to loyal owners.

1864

April 12: Confederate troops massacre black soldiers at Fort Pillow, Tennessee.

June 15: Congress equalizes the pay of black and white soldiers.

June 15: United States Colored Troops (USCT) Eighteenth Corps help to capture and secure regions around Petersburg, the supplier of the Confederate capital, Richmond, initiating the longest siege in American history.

July 30: USCT Ninth Corps fight at the Battle of the Crater in Petersburg.

September 29: Black soldiers are crucial to the success of the Battle of New Market Heights near Richmond. Fourteen black soldiers later receive the Medal of Honor for this battle.

December 15: USCT regiments help to achieve victory at the Battle of Nashville, Tennessee.

1865

March 23: The Confederate War Department issues an order to recruit enslaved men as soldiers starting in April and to emancipate them upon completion of loyal service.

April 9: Black Union troops are present for Lee's surrender at Appomattox.

May 12: The Sixty-second U.S. Colored Infantry fight in the final battle of the Civil War at Palmito Ranch, Texas.

DOCUMENTS

Document 1: Our Historic Development—Shall It Be Superceded by a War of Races?

This anonymous writer in the New York Herald *on September 19, 1860, demonstrates the primacy of white supremacy in the psyche and culture of many white Americans, both in the North and in the South, during this period. For many white Americans, white supremacy was fundamental to their national as well as their individual identity; therefore, for these individuals, the idea of African American equality threatened to degrade the nation as well as white people personally.*

Party divisions among us have hitherto been based on questions of policy in government, but without departing from the great principles of the rightful preponderance of the white race. Thus, in the first division of parties after the establishment of the constitution, the lines of the federal and republican organization were drawn on the great questions of a stronger or weaker form of federal government, involving the right of controlling personal liberty, the freedom of the press, and other questions of similar character which marked our legislation and political agitation during the closing years of the last century. This was succeeded by party divisions on the question of a second war with England in defense of our rights on the ocean, and the patriotic sacrifices the war party then led the country to make in the face of the bitter opposition of "the Massachusetts school" were the foundations of our present commercial glory. After this came the great division under Jackson, on the questions of bank, tariff and internal improvements by the general government. All of these questions were discussed with partisan bitterness, but in them the doubt of the right of the white man to rule never entered.

The only party division that exists to-day, aside from the bickering of the selfish and unscrupulous leaders, who each endeavoring, with their petty cockle boats, to gather the fragments upon the tide of party revolution, involves a far deeper and older question than any that has previously been discussed among us during our national career. The issue that is presented by the black republican party involves the whole question of our social and national existence. Black republicanism, founded on and animated by the anti-slavery idea, and pursuing an exaggerated notion of individual rights, involves not only an attempt to equalize dissimilar and discordant races in their social and immunities, but also the most destructive theories in regard to the organization of society....

This anti-slavery idea aims to establish a new social policy in this country—the policy of an equalization of the white and black races—which had never produced anything but bloodshed in other parts of the world, and which can only result in the subjugation or destruction of the numerically weaker race. There is no possibility of the black and the white existing harmoniously together in social and political equality....

[T]he Southern States, where four millions of blacks are now held in a position of social subjection, which contributes to their own moral and material welfare, and to that the whole community in which they exist. The triumph of antislavery sentiment, through the election of Lincoln to the Presidency, will initiate a social revolution among us will require generations, and perhaps centuries, for its consummation, if we exist through it so long. Such a war of races will absorb all the power of our society, diverting them from the prosecution of domestic industry and foreign trade. Above all, it will produce division and conflict among ourselves, as it has divided the whites everywhere that it has prevailed, while the blacks, without other policy or impulses, will be united by the bond of color....

The real question, therefore, now presented to the people of the United States is the question of our social development for generations yet to come, and involving our very existence as a nation. If we once begin the war of races, which will inevitably follow from the triumph of the abolition idea and its control of our government, it cannot cease until the black race has been exterminated or driven from among us. Such a war will involve the cessation of the prosecution of many of the industrial pursuits that now constitute our prosperity and national greatness. It will consume all the elements that now contribute to our intellectual and material development. With such certainty before us, involving our posterity for centuries in conflict and ruin, it becomes every man to take heart and do his utmost to defeat the fanatical and revolutionary black republicans, who, blinded by their own zeal, following a fallacy that elsewhere has conducted only to destruction, and obstinately refusing to learn wisdom from the experience and disasters from other lands and nations, are bent on establishing here the most destructive conflict of races that the world has ever witnessed.

Source:

Published by an anonymous author in the *New York Herald*, September 19, 1860, reprinted in *The Civil War: Primary Documents on Events from 1860 to 1865*, edited by Ford Risely (Westport, Conn.: Greenwood Press, 2004), pp. 19–21.

Document 2: The Late Election

After the election of President Abraham Lincoln, one of the nation's most prominent abolitionists, Frederick Douglass, published the following essay in his publication Douglass' Monthly *in December 1860. Because the issues surrounding abolition, racial equality, and the arming of black soldiers became inextricable with the start of the Civil War, it is useful to examine Lincoln's stance on slavery prior to the start of the conflict. While Douglass did not feel confident that Lincoln would further the cause of abolition, a charge he believed was issued by Lincoln's opponents, Douglass argued that Lincoln's election was significant because it signaled a challenge to the South's long-standing domination of national politics. Douglass ultimately served as a recruiter for the U.S. Army during the war, and two of his sons served in the Fifty-fourth Massachusetts.*

The clamor now raised by the slaveholders about "Northern aggression," "sectional warfare," as a pretext of dissolving the Union, has this basis only: The Northern people have elected, against the opposition of the slaveholding South, a man for President who declared his opposition to the further extension of slavery over the soil belonging to the United States. Such is the head and front, and the full extent of the offense, for which "minute men" are forming, drums are beating, flags are flying, people are arming, "banks are closing," "stocks are falling," and the South generally taking on dreadfully.

By referring to another part of our present monthly, our respected readers will find a few samples of the spirit of the Southern press on this subject. They are full of intrigue, smell of brimstone, and betoken a terrific explosion. Unquestionably, "secession," "disunion," "Southern Confederacy," and the like phrases are the most popular political watch words of the cotton-growing States of the Union. Nor is this sentiment to be entirely despised. If Mr. Lincoln were really an Abolition President, which he is not; if he were a friend to the Abolition movement, instead of being, as he is, its most powerful enemy, the dissolution of the Union might be the only effective mode of perpetuating slavery in the Southern States—since if it could succeed, it would place slavery beyond the power of the President and his Government. But the South has now no such cause for disunion. The present alarm and perturbation will cease; the Southern fire-eaters will be appeased and will retrace their steps.—There is no sufficient cause for the dissolution of the Union. Whoever lives through the next four years will see Mr. Lincoln and his Administration attacked more bitterly for their pro-slavery truckling, than for doing any anti-slavery work. He and his party will become the best protectors of slavery where it now is, and just such protectors as slaveholders will most need. In order to defeat him, the slaveholders took advantage of the ignorance and stupidity of the masses, and assured them that Lincoln is an Abolitionist. This, Mr. Lincoln and his party will lose no time in scattering to the winds as false and groundless. With the single exception of the question of slavery extension, Mr. Lincoln proposes no measure which can bring him into antagonistic collision with the traffickers in human flesh, either in the States or in the District of Columbia....

With an Abolition President we should consider a successful separation of slave from the free states a calamity, greatly damaging to the prospects of our long enslaved, bruised and mutilated people; but under what may be expected of the Republican party, with its pledges to put down the slaves should they attempt to rise, and to hunt them should they run away, a dissolution of the Union would be highly beneficial to the cause of liberty....

What, then, has been gained to the anti-slavery cause by the election of Mr. Lincoln? Not much in itself considered, but very much when viewed in the light of its relations and bearings. For fifty years the country has taken its law from the lips of an exacting, haughty and imperious slave oligarchy. The masters of slave have been masters of the Republic.... Lincoln's election has vitiated their authority, and broken their power. It has taught the North its strength, and shown the South its weakness. More important still, it has demonstrated the possibility of electing, if not an Abolitionist, at least an *anti-slavery reputation* to the Presidency of the United States.

... Notwithstanding the many cowardly disclaimers, and miserable concessions to popular prejudice against the colored people, which Republican orators have felt themselves required, by an intense and greedy desire of success, to make, they have been compelled also to recur to first principles of human liberty, expose the baseless claim of property in man, exhibit the hideous features of slavery, and to unveil, for popular execration, the brutal manners and morals of the guilty slave-masters.

SOURCE:

Frederick Douglass. *Douglass' Monthly, December 1860*, reprinted in *Lincoln on Black and White: A Documentary History*, edited by Arthur Zilversmit (Malabar, Fla.: Krieger, 2000), pp. 70–73.

Document 3: LINCOLN'S REPLY TO HENRY RAYMOND

This letter is president-elect Abraham Lincoln's reply to Henry Raymond, who had sent the president a letter from a member of the Mississippi legislature, William Smedes. The reply speaks to the profound anxiety of many white Americans regarding the idea of African American equality.

Springfield, Illinois
Dec. 18, 1860
Confidential
Hon. H. J. Raymond

My dear Sir

Yours of the 14th. is received. What a very mad-man your correspondent, Smedes is. Mr. Lincoln is not pledged to the ultimate extinctinction [sic] of slavery; does not hold the black man to the equal of the white, unqualifiedly as Mr. S. states it; and never did stigmatize their white people as immoral & unchristian; and Mr. S. can not prove one of his assertions true.

    ... Yours truly
    A. Lincoln

SOURCE:

There is a photocopy of this letter in the collections of the Abraham Lincoln Association, Springfield, Illinois. It has been reprinted in *The Collected Works of Abraham Lincoln*, volume 4, edited by Roy Basler (New Brunswick, N.J.: Rutgers University Press, 1990 [1953]), p. 156.

Document 4: LETTER FROM JACOB DODSON

This letter from Jacob Dodson to Secretary of War Simon Cameron indicates the desire on the part of many free black men to serve in the Union army in April 1861. Dodson was a free black man from Missouri who had accompanied John C. Frémont on expeditions to Utah and California in the 1840s. Abraham Lincoln refused the service of the three hundred men Dodson recruited.

Washington, April 23, 1861
Hon. Simon Cameron,
Secretary of War:

Sir:

I desire to inform you that I know some 300 reliable colored free citizens of this city who desire to enter the service for the defense of the city.

    I have been three times across the Rocky Mountains in the service of the country with Frémont and others.

    I can be found about the Senate Chamber, as I have been employed about the premises for some years.

    Yours, respectfully,
    Jacob Dodson (Colored).

SOURCE:

From *The War of Rebellion: A Compilation of the Official Records of the Union and Confederate Armies* compiled by Robert N. Scott (Washington: Government Printing Office, 1880).

Document 5: LINCOLN'S LETTER TO ORVILLE H. BROWNING

This is a letter Abraham Lincoln wrote on September 22, 1861, to his friend Orville H. Browning, a Repub-

lican senator from Illinois. In it, Lincoln expresses his concern that arming African Americans would turn the border states against the Union, and he writes the now famous line that "to lose Kentucky is nearly the same as to lose the whole game."

Executive Mansion, Washington
September 22, 1861
Private & confidential
Hon. O. H. Browning

My dear Sir

Yours of the 17th is just received; and coming from you, I confess it astonishes me. That you should object to my adhering of a law, which you had assisted in making, and presenting to me, less than a month before, is odd enough. But this is a very small part. Genl. Freemont's proclamation, as to confiscation of property, and the liberation of slaves, is *purely political,* and not within the range of *military* law, or necessity. If a commanding General finds a necessity to seize the farm of a private owner, for a pasture, an encampment, or a fortification, he has the right to do so, and to so hold it, as long as the necessity lasts; and this is within military law, because within military necessity. But to say the farm shall no longer belong to the owner, or his heirs forever; and this as well when the farm is not needed for military purposes as when it is, is purely political, without the savor of military law about it. And the same is true of slaves. If the General needs them, he can seize them, and use them; but when the need is past, it is not for him to fix their permanent future condition. That must be settled according to laws to make by law-makers, and not by military proclamations. The proclamation in the point in question, is simply "dictatorship." It assumes that the general may do *anything* he pleases—confiscate the lands and free the slaves of *loyal* people, as well as of disloyal ones. And going the whole figure I have no doubt would be more popular with some thoughtless people, than that which has been done! But I cannot assume this reckless position; nor allow others to assume it on my responsibility. You speak of it as being the only means of *saving* the government. On the contrary it is itself the surrender of the government. Can it be pretended that it is any longer the government of the U.S.—any government of Constitution and laws,—wherein a General, or a President, may make permanent rule of property by declaration?

I do not say that Congress might not with propriety pass a law, on the point, just such as General Freemont proclaimed. I do not say I might not, as a member of Congress, vote for it. What I object to, is, that I as President, shall expressly or impliedly seize and exercise the permanent legislative functions of the government.

So much as to principle. Now as to policy. Now doubt the thing was popular in some quarters, and would have been more so had it been a general declaration of emancipation. The Kentucky Legislature would not budge till that proclamation was modified; and Gen. Anderson telegraphed me that on the new of Gen. Freemont having actually issued deeds of manumission, a whole company of our Volunteers threw down their arms and disbanded. I was so assured, as to think it probable, that the very arms we had furnished Kentucky would be turned against us. I think to lose Kentucky is nearly the same as to lose the whole game. Kentucky gone, we can not hold Missouri, nor, as I think, Maryland. These all against us, and the job on our hands is too large for us. We would as well consent to separation at once, including the surrender of this capitol. On the contrary, if you will give up your restlessness for new positions, and back me manfully on the grounds upon which you and other kind friends gave me the election, and have approved in my public documents, we shall go through triumphantly.

. . . Your friend as ever
A. Lincoln

Source:

This letter is in the Illinois State Historical Library, Springfield, Illinois. It has been reprinted in *The Collected Works of Abraham Lincoln,* volume 4, edited by Roy Basler (New Brunswick, N.J.: Rutgers University Press, 1990 [1953]), pp. 531–533.

Document 6: Letter from William Scott

Ohio Democrat William Scott published this letter in the Marietta Register *on November 22, 1861. Scott correctly predicted that hundreds of thousands of slaves would liberate themselves during the conflict of the war. A supporter of the war, Scott worried about how to manage former slaves, whom he viewed neither as his equals nor as American citizens.*

Whatever may be the result of the civil war in our Country, many thousands, yes hundreds of thousands, of negroes will escape from their masters. When the way, along the borders of the Slave States, becomes opened by the Federal troops, there will doubtless be a continual stampede of slaves. The Union men will suffer in this way as will the rebels. We can see no way to avoid it. In the face of all this, what is to be done for the helpless blacks, to preserve them from starvation and ruin, as well as to protect ourselves from such a horde of semibarbarians let loose upon the public?

Shall the Government arm them—as some have suggested, and employ them against their masters? We think a Christian people could never think of such a thing. If our course is of such a nature, as to be necessary to resort to such means to forward it, it is high time for us to consider whether we ought not to abandon it at once. Shall the Government employ them in its fortifications until the close of the war and then have them disposed of, paying the loyal men for their services? 3,000,000 or 4,000,000 will not be easily taken care of for that length of time.

Shall they be colonized in South Carolina—as the [Marietta] Intelligencer has suggested, making the whites *their* slaves—thus making an independent nation of them? Or shall they be permitted to run at large, flooding the entire North with a worthless set of paupers? This would be a fatal step, both for their own interests as well as ours. They, when thus situated, would be a greater barrier to the prosecution of the war, than they would be were they at the disposal of the rebels.... Surely, this is a very inopportune time to have such a care, when our entire country is in a state ill prepared to supply the wants of our own poor citizens.

This will undoubtedly be a question for our State Legislature, the coming winter. Some of the Western States have already legislated against their coming within their borders. It is very likely—the rest will be compelled to do the same thing.

Source:

From the *Marietta Register*, November 22, 1861, written by William Scott; reprinted in *Ohio's War: The Civil War in Documents*, edited by Christine Dee (Athens: Ohio University Press, 2006), pp. 66–67.

Document 7: John Boston's Letter

John Boston was a fugitive slave from Maryland who served in a Brooklyn regiment. In this letter to his wife he expresses his gratitude for his successful escape to freedom as well as the pain caused by his separation from his family.

Upton Hill [Va.]
January the 12 1862

My Dear Wife

it is with grate joy I take this time to let you know Whare I am i am now in Safety in the 14th Regiment of Brooklyn this Day i can Adress you thank god as a free man I had a little truble in giting away But as the lord led the Children of Isrel to the land of Canon So he led me to a land Whare fredom Will rain in spite Of earth and hell Dear you must make your Self content i am free from al the Slavers Lash and as you have chose the Wise plan Of Serving the lord i hope you Will pray Much and i Will try by the help of god To Serv him With all my hart I am With a very nice man and have All that hart Can Wish But My Dear I Cant express my grate desire that i Have to See you i trust the time Will Come When We Shal meet again And if We dont met on earth We Will Meet in heven Whare Jesas ranes Dear Elizabeth tell Mrs Own[ees] That i trust that She Will Continue Her kindness to you and that god Will Bless her on earth and Save her In grate eternity My Acomplements To Mrs Owens and her Children may They Prosper through life I never Shall forgit her kindness to me Dear Wife i must Close rest yourself Contented i am free i Want you to rite To me Soon as you Can Without Delay Direct your letter to the 14th Reigment New york State malitia Uptons Hill Virginea In Care of Mr Cranford Comary Write my Dear Soon As you C Your Affectionate Husband Kiss Daniel For me
   John Boston
   Give my love to Father and Mother

John Boston to Mrs. Elizabeth Boston, 12 Jan. 1862, enclosed in Maj. Genl. Geo. B. McClellan to Hon. Edwin Stanton, 21 Jan. 1862, A-587 1862, Letters Received, ser. 12, Adjutant General's Office, Record Group 94, National Archives. The envelope is addressed, in a different handwriting, to "Mrs. Elizabeth Boston Care Mrs. Prescia Owen Owensville Post Office Maryland."

Source:

Ira Berlin, Barbara J. Fields, Steven F. Miller, Joseph P. Reidy, and Leslie S. Rowland, eds. *Free at Last: A Documentary History of Slavery, Freedom, and the Civil War* (New York: New Press, 2007); <http://www.history.umd.edu/Freedmen/boston.htm> (accessed February 6, 2008).

Document 8: Sambo's Right to Be Kilt

The Civil War song "Sambo's Right to Be Kilt" was first published in the New York Herald *in 1862. Writing under the pen name Private Miles O'Reilly, the author of the verse was Charles C. Halpine, a staff officer who served under the command of General David Hunter. In April of that year Hunter had issued a proclamation, initially overturned by Lincoln, freeing the slaves of South Carolina, Georgia, and Florida as well as enlisted black soldiers. Even when federal policy began to support Hunter's practices, many Northern whites were highly critical. Halpine's verse was an effort to defend Hunter's decision; it countered the unease of many whites who believed that serving alongside black soldiers would demean them.*

Some tell me 'tis a burnin' shame
To make the naygers fight,
And that the trade of bein' kilt
Belongs but to the white.
But as for me, upon my soul!
So lib'ral are we here,
I'll let Sambo be shot instead of myself
On ev'ry day in the year.

Chorus:
On ev'ry day in the year, boys,
And in ev'ry hour in the day,
The right to be kilt I'll divide wid him,
And devil a word I'll say.

In battle's wild commotion,
I shouldn't at all object,
If Sambo's body should stop a ball
That's coming for me direct;
And the prod of a Southern bagnet
So ginerous are we here,
I'll resign and let Sambo take it
On every day in the year.

Chorus:
On ev'ry day in the year, boys,
And wid none 'iv your nasty pride,
All my right in a Southern bagnet prod
Wid Sambo I'll divide.

The men who object to Sambo
Should take his place and fight;
And it's better to have a nayger's hue
Than a liver that's wake and white.
Though Sambo's black as the ace of spades,
His fingers a trigger can pull,
And his eye runs straight on the barrel sight,
From under his thatch of wool.

Chorus:
On ev'ry day in the year, boys,
Don't think that I'm tippin' you chaff,
The right to be kilt we'll divide with him, boys,
And give him the largest half.

[bagnet=bayonet]

Source:

Thanks to Benjamin Tubb of *The Music of the American Civil War (1861–1865)* <http://www.civilwarpoetry.org/union/songs/sambo.html>.

Document 9: The Diary of Salmon P. Chase

The following is a series of excerpts from the diary of Salmon P. Chase from July 1862. At the time, Chase was secretary of the treasury. Chase's entries shed light on the federal government's shifting attitudes toward arming African Americans.

Monday, July 21, 1862

. . . I received a notice to attend a Cabinet meeting, at 10 o'clock. It has been so long since any consultation has been held that it struck me as a novelty.

I went at the appointed hour, and found that the President had been profoundly concerned at the present aspect of affairs, and had determined to take some definitive steps in respect to military action and slavery. He had prepared several Orders, the first of which contemplated authority to Commanders to subsist their troups in the hostile territory—the second, authority to employ negroes as laborers—the third requiring that both in the case of property taken and of negroes employed, accounts should be kept with such degrees of certainty as would enable compensation to made in proper cases—another provided for the colonization of negroes in some tropical country.

A good deal of discussion took place on these points. The first Order was universally approved. The second was approved entirely; and the third, by all except myself. I doubted the expedience of attempting to keep accounts for the benefit of the inhabitants of rebel States. The Colonization project was not much discussed.

Tuesday, July 22, 1862

Went to Cabinet at the appointed hour. It was unanimously agreed that the Order in respect to Colonization should be dropped; and the other were adopted unanimously, except that I wished North Carolina included among the States named in the first order.

The question of arming slaves was then brought up and I advocated it warmly. The President was unwilling to adopt this measure, but proposed to issue a proclamation, on the basis of the Confiscation Bill, calling upon the States to return their allegiance—warning the rebels the provisions of the Act would have full force at the expiration of sixty days—adding, on his own part, a declaration of his intention to renew, at the next session of Congress, his recommendation of compensation to States adopting the gradual abolishment of slavery—and proclaiming the emancipation of all slaves within States remaining in insurrection on the first of January, 1863.

I said that I should give to such a measure my cordial support; but I should prefer that no new expression on the subject of compensation should be made, and I thought that the measure of Emancipation could be much better and more quietly accomplished by allowing Generals to organize and arm the slaves (thus avoiding depredation and massacre on the one hand, and support to the insurrection on the other) and by directing the Commanders of Departments to proclaim emancipation within their Districts as soon as practicable; but I regarded this as so much better than inaction on the subject, that I should give it my entire support.

The President determined to publish the first three Orders forthwith, and to leave the other for some further consideration. The impression left upon my mind by the whole discussion was, that while the President thought that the organization, equipment and arming of negroes, like other soldiers, would be productive of more evil than good, he was not willing that Commanders should, at their discretion, arm, for purely defensive purposes, slaves coming within their line.

Sunday, August 3

. . . I received a summons to a Cabinet meeting.

There was a good deal of conversation on the connection of the Slavery question with the rebellion. I expressed my conviction for the tenth or twentieth time, that the time for the suppression of the rebellion without interference with slavery had passed; that it was possible, probably, at the outset, by striking the insurrectionists wherever found, strongly and decisively; but we had elected to act on the principles of a civil war, in the which the whole population of every seceding state was engaged against the Federal Government, instead of treating the active secessionists as insurgents and exerting our utmost energies for their arrest and punishment;—that the bitterness of the conflict had now substantially united the white population of the rebel states against us;—that the loyal whites remaining, if they would not prefer the Union without Slavery, certainly would not prefer Slavery to the Union; that the blacks were really only the loyal population worth counting; and that, in the Gulf States at least, their right to Freedom ought to be at once recognized, while, in the Border States, the President's plan of emancipation might be made the basis of the necessary measures for their enfranchisement;—that the practical mode of effecting this seemed to me quite simple;—that the President had already spoken of the importance of making of the freed blacks on the Mississippi, below Tennessee, a safeguard to the navigation of the river;—that Mitchell, with a few thousand soldiers, could take Vicksburgh;—assure the blacks freedom on condition of loyalty; organize the best of them in companies, regiments etc. and provide, as far as practicable for the cultivation of the plantations by the rest;—that Butler should signify to the slaveholders of Louisiana that they must recognize the freedom of their workpeople by paying them wages;—and that Hunter should do the same thing in South-Carolina.

Mr. Seward expressed himself as in favor of any measures likely to accomplish the results I contemplated, which could be carried into effect without Proclamations; and the President said he was pretty well cured of objections to any measure except want of adaptedness to put down the rebellion; but did not seem satisfied that the time had come for the adoption of such a plan as I had proposed.

SOURCE:

From "Diary and Correspondence of Salmon P. Chase," *American Historical Association, Annual Report for the Year 1902*, 2 volumes (Washington, D.C.: Government Printing Office, 1903); reprinted in *Lincoln on Black and White: A Documentary History*, edited by Arthur Zilversmit (Malabar, Fla.: Krieger, 2000 [1971]), pp. 91–94.

Document 10: NEGRO SOLDIERS ON DUTY

The following article from the New-York Tribune *on February 11, 1863, praises the courage of a black South Carolina regiment after a successful raiding expedition into St. Mary's, Georgia. This letter, written by a white author, attempted to counter public concerns over the efficacy of black combatants.*

The bravery and good conduct of the regiment more than equaled the high anticipation of its commander. The men were repeatedly under fire, were opposed by infantry, cavalry, and artillery, fought on board of a steamer exposed to heavy musketry from the back of a narrow river—were tried in all ways, and came off invariably with honor and success. They brought away property to a large amount, capturing also a cannon and a flag, which the Colonel asks leave to keep for the regiment, and which he and they have fairly won.

It will not need many such reports as this—and there have been several before it—to shake our inveterate Saxon prejudice against the capacity and courage of negro troops.... No officer who has commanded black troops had yet reported against them. They are tried in the most unfavorable and difficult circumstances, but never fail. When shall we learn to use the full strength of our formidable ally who is only waiting for a summons to rally under the flag of the Union?

Col. Higginson says: "No officer in this regiment now doubts that the key to the successful prosecution of this war lies in the unlimited employment of black troops." The remark is true in a military sense, and it has a still deeper political significance. When Hunter has scattered 50,000 muskets among the negroes of the Carolinas, and Butler has organized the 100,000 or 200,000 blacks for whom he may perhaps shortly carry arms to New Orleans, the possibility of restoring the Union as it was, with Slavery again its dominant power, will be seen to have finally passed away. The negro is indeed the key to our success.

SOURCE:

Published by an anonymous author in the *New-York Tribune*, February 11, 1863; republished in *The Civil War: Primary Documents on Events from 1860 to 1865*, edited by Ford Risely (Westport, Conn.: Greenwood Press, 2004), pp. 203–204.

Document 11: C. B. WILDER'S TESTIMONY

Captain C. B. Wilder, the superintendent of contraband at Fort Monroe, testified regarding the actions of fugitive slaves, officially deemed "contrabands," before the American Freedmen's Inquiry Commission on May 9, 1863. Over the course of the Civil War, hundreds of thousands of slaves liberated themselves and fled to Union lines. Slaves had liberated themselves in large numbers during earlier conflicts as well; while some former slaves served alongside other Americans during the Revolutionary War and the War of 1812, others took the opportunity afforded by the uprisings to permanently flee slavery and resettle in the Caribbean and Canada.

May 9, 1863.

Question: How many of the people called contrabands, have come under your observation?

Answer: Some 10,000 have come under our control, to be fed in part, and clothed in part, but I cannot speak accurately in regard to the number. This is the rendezvous. They come here from all about, from Richmond and 200 miles off in North Carolina. There was one gang that started from Richmond 23 strong and only 3 got through.

Q: In your opinion, is there any communication between the refugees and the black men still in slavery?

A: Yes Sir, we have had men here who have gone back 200 miles.

Q: In your opinion would a change in our policy which would cause them to be treated with fairness, their wages punctually paid and employment furnished them in the army, become known and would it have any effect upon others in slavery?

A: Yes—Thousands upon Thousands. I went to Suffolk a short time ago to enquire into the state of things there— for I found I could not get any foot hold to make things work there, through the Commanding General, and I went to the Provost Marshall and all hands—and the colored people actually sent a deputation to me one morning before I was up to know if we put black men in irons and sent them off to Cuba to be sold or set them at work and put balls on their legs and whipped them, just as in slavery; because that was the story up there, and they were frightened and didn't know what to do. When I got at the feelings of these people I found they were not afraid of the slaveholders. They said there was nobody on the plantations but women and they were not afraid of them One woman came through 200 miles in Men's clothes. The most valuable information we received in regard to the Merrimack and the operations of the rebels came from the colored people and they got no credit for it. I found hundreds who had left their wives and families behind. I asked them "Why did you come away and leave them there?" and I found they had heard these stories, and wanted to come and see how it was. "I am going back again after my wife" some of them have said "When I have earned a little money" "What as far as that?" "Yes" and I have had them come to me to borrow money, or to get their pay, if they had earned a months wages, and to get passes. "I am going for my family" they say. "Are you not afraid to risk it?" "No I know the Way" Colored men will help colored men and they will work along the by paths and get through. In that way I have known quite a number who have gone up from time to time in the neighborhood of Richmond and several have brought back their families; some I have never heard from. As I was saying they do not feel afraid now. The white people have nearly all gone, the blood hounds are not there now to hunt them and they are not afraid, before they were afraid to stir. There are hundreds of negroes at Williamsburgh with their families working for nothing. They would not get pay here and they had rather stay where they are. "We are not afraid of being carried back" a great many have told us and "if we are, we can get away again." Now that they are getting their eyes open they are coming in. Fifty came this morning from Yorktown who followed Stoneman's Cavalry when they returned from their raid. The officers reported to their Quartermaster that they had so many horses and fifty or sixty negroes. "What did you bring them for" "Why they followed us and we could not stop them." I asked one of the men about it and he said they would leave their work in the field as soon as they found the Soldiers were Union men and follow them sometimes without hat or coat. They would take best horse they could get and every where they rode they would take fresh horses, leave the old ones and follow on and so they came in. I have questioned a great many of them and they do not feel much afraid; and there are a great many courageous fellows who have come from long distances in rebeldom. Some men who came here from North Carolina, knew all about the [Emancipation] Proclammation and they started on the belief in it; but they had heard these stories and they wanted to know how it was. Well, I gave them the evidence and I have no doubt their friends will hear of it. Within the last two or three months the rebel guards have been doubled on the line and the officers and privates of the 99th New York between Norfolk and Suffolk have caught hundreds of fugitives and got pay for them.

Q: Do I understand you to say that a great many who have escaped have been sent back?

A: Yes Sir, The masters will come in to Suffolk in the day time and with the help of some of the 99th carry off their fugitives and by and by smuggle them across the lines and the soldier will get his $20. or $50.

Source:

Published in *Freedom: Volume 1, Series 1: The Destruction of Slavery: A Documentary History of Emancipation, 1861–1867,* edited by Ira Berlin and others (Cambridge University Press, 1986), pp. 88–90; *The Freedmen and Southern Society Project,* University of Maryland <http://www.history.umd.edu/Freedmen/wilder.htm> (accessed January 12, 2008).

Document 12: Letter from Elias Strunke

In his letter to a recruiter of African American troops in Louisiana, a white Union officer, Elias Strunke, describes the valor of black soldiers, many of whom were former slaves, at Port Hudson, Louisiana. Strunke's letter challenged the common charge by whites that black soldiers would not fight.

Baton Rouge [La.]
May 29th/63.

General.

feeling deeply interested in the cause which you have espoused, I take the liberty to transmit the following concerning the colored Troops engaged in the recent battles at Port Hudson.

I have arrived here the evening of the 26th Inst, was mustered and reported to Maj. Tucker for duty—

During the night I heard heavy connonadeing at Port Hudson. Early next morning I obtained permission and went to the front. But so much was detained, I did not reach our lines until the fighting for the day had nearly ceased—There being no renewal of the engagement the following day—I engaged in removing and administering to the wounded, gathering meantime as much information as possible concerning the battle and the conduct of our Troops. My anxiety was to learn all I could concerning the Bravery of the Colored Reg. engaged, for their good conduct and bravery would add to your undertakings and make more popular the movement. Not that I am afraid to meet unpopular doctrines, for I am not. But that we may show our full strength. the cause should be one of general sanction.

I have ever believed, from my idea of those traits of character which I deemed necessary to make a good soldier, together with their history, that in them we should find those characteristics necessary, for an effective army. And I rejoice to learn, in the late engagements the fact is established beyond a doubt.

The following is (in substance) a statement personally made to me, by 1st Lt. Co. F. 1st R[egiment]. La. Native Guard who was wounded during the engagement.

"We went into action about 6. A.M. and was under fire most of the time until sunset.

The very first thing after forming line of battle we were ordered to charge—My Co. was apparently brave. Yet they are mostly contrabands, and I must say I entertained some fears as to their pluck. But I have now none—The moment the order was given, they entered upon its execution. Valiantly did the heroic decendants of Africa move forward cool as if Marshaled for dress parade, under a most murderous fire from the enemies guns, until we reached the main ditch which surrounds the Fort. finding it impassible we retreated under orders to the woods and deployed as skirmishes—In the charge we lost our Capt. and Colored sergeant, the latter fell wraped in the flag he had so gallantly borne—Alone we held our position until 12. o'clock when we were relieved—

At two o'clock P.M. we were again ordered to the front where we made two separate charges each in the face of a heavy fire from the enemies Battery of seven guns—whose destructive fire would have confuse and almost disorganized the bravest troops. But these men did not swerve, or cowardice. I have been in several engagements, and I never before beheld such coolness and daring—

Their gallantry entitles them to a special praise. And I already observe, the sneers of others are being tempered to eulogy—

It is pleasant to learn these things, and it must be indeed gratifying to the General to know that his army will be composed of men of almost unequaled coolness & bravery—

The men of our Reg. are very ready in learning the drills, and the officers have every confidence in their becoming excellent soldiers.

Assuring you that I will always, both as an officer of the U.S. Army and as a man, endeavor to faithfully & fully discharge the duties of my office, I am happy to Subscribe Myself, Very Respectfully, Your Most Obt. Servt,

ALS

Elias D. Strunke

SOURCE:

Ira Berlin, et al., eds., *Freedom's Soldiers: A Documentary History* (Cambridge: Cambridge University Press, 1993), pp. 94–96.

Document 13: HARRIET TUBMAN

This July 10, 1863, Boston Commonwealth article describes a successful raid led by Harriet Tubman in June 1863. In addition to her work during the Civil War as a Union nurse, spy, courier, and scout, Tubman became the first American woman to command an armed military raid when she guided Colonel James Montgomery and the Second South Carolina Volunteers up the Combahee River.

Col. Montgomery and his gallant band of 300 black soldiers, under the guidance of a black woman, dashed into the enemy's country, struck a bold and effective blow, destroying millions of dollars worth of commissary stores, cotton and lordly dwellings, and striking terror into the heart of rebeldom, brought off near 800 slaves and thousands of dollars worth of property, without losing a man or receiving a scratch. It was a glorious consummation.

After they were all fairly well disposed of in the Beaufort charge, they were addressed in strains of thrilling eloquence by their gallant deliverer, to which they responded in a song. "There is a white robe for thee," a song so appropriate and so heartfelt and cordial as to bring unbidden tears.

The Colonel was followed by a speech from the black woman, who led the raid and under whose inspiration it was originated and conducted. For sound sense and real native eloquence, her address would do honor to any man, and it created a great sensation....

Since the rebellion she had devoted herself to her great work of delivering the bondman, with an energy and sagacity that cannot be exceeded. Many and many times she has penetrated the enemy's lines and discovered their situation and condition, and escaped without injury, but not without extreme hazard.

SOURCE:

Boston Commonwealth, number 45, July 10, 1863.

Document 14: LINCOLN'S LETTER TO HIS CRITICS

President Abraham Lincoln's letter addressing critics in Illinois regarding his policy of arming black troops was published in the Richmond Daily Dispatch *on September 7, 1863. His description of the policy's resounding success illustrates a dramatic change in his attitude toward arming African Americans.*

September 7, 1863
Richmond Dispatch
Latest from the North
Letter from Lincoln—how and when peace is to be obtained—the Enlistment of negro troops.

Executive Mansion, Washington, August 26.
Hon. James E. Conkling:

My Dear Sir

—Your letter inviting me to attend a mass meeting of unconditional Union men, to be held at the Capitol of Illinois on the 3d day of September, has been received. It would be very agreeable to me to thus meet my old friends at my own home, but I cannot just now be absent from this city so long as a visit there would require.

The meeting is to be of all those who maintain unconditional devotion to the Union, and I am sure my old political friends will thank me for tendering, as I do, the nation's gratitude to those other noble men whom no partisan malice or partisan hope can make false to the nation's life. They are those who are dissatisfied with me. To such I would say: You desire peace, and you blame me that we do not have it. But how can we obtain it? There are but three conceivable ways. First, to suppress the rebellion by force of arms. This I am trying to do. Are you for it? If you are, so far we are agreed. If you are not for it, we are not agreed.

A second way is to give up the Union. I am against this. If you are, you should say so plainly. If you are not for force, nor yet for dissolution, there only remains some imaginary compromises. I do not believe that any compromises embracing the maintenance of the Union is now possible. All that I learn leads to directly the opposite belief. The strength of the rebellion is its military—its army. That army dominates all the country and all the people within its range. Any offer of terms made by any man or men within that range, in opposition to that army is simply nothing, for the present, because such man or men have no power whatever to enforce their side of the compromise, if one were made with them.

To illustrate: Suppose a refugee from the South and the peace men of the North get together and frame and proclaim a compromise embracing the restoration of the Union, in what way can that compromise be used to keep Gen. Lee's army out of Pennsylvania? Gen. Meade's army can keep Lee's army out of Pennsylvania, and I think can ultimately drive it out of existence, but no paper compromise to which the controllers of Gen. Lee's army are not agreed can at all affect that army. In an effort at such compromise we would waste time which the enemy would improve to our disadvantage, and that would be all.

A compromise, to be effective, must be made either with those who control the army or with the people first liberated from the domination of that army by the success of our army. Now, allow me to assure you that no word or intimation from the rebel army, or from any of the men controlling it, in relation to any peace compromise has ever come to my knowledge or belief. All charges or intimations to the contrary are deceptive and groundless, and I promise you that if any such proposition shall hereafter come it shall not be rejected and kept secret from you.

I freely acknowledge myself to be the servant of the people according to the bond of service—the United States Constitution—and that as such I am responsible to them. But, to be plain, you are dissatisfied with me about the negro. Quite likely there is a difference of opinion between you and myself upon that subject. I certainly wish that all men could be free, while you, I suppose, do not. Yet, I have neither adopted nor proposed any measure which is not consistent with even your views, provided you are for the Union. I suggested compensated emancipation, to which you replied that you wished not to be taxed to buy negroes. But I had not asked you to be taxed to buy negroes, except in such a way as to save you from greater taxation, to save the Union exclusively by other means. You dislike the emancipation proclamation, and, perhaps, you want to have it retracted. You say it is unconstitutional. I think differently. I think that the Constitution invests its Commander-in-Chief with the law of war in time of war. The most that can be said—if so much — is that slaves are property. Is there, has there ever been, any question that by the law of war the property both of enemies and friends may be taken when needed? And is it not needed whenever taken it helps us or hurts the enemy? Armies, the world over, destroy the enemy's property when they cannot use it, and even destroy their own to keep it from the enemy. Civilized belligerents do all in their power to help themselves or hurt the enemy, except a few things recorded as barbarous or cruel. Among the exceptions are the massacre of vanquished foes and non-combatants, male and female.

But the proclamation as a law is valid or is not valid. If it is not valid it needs no retraction. If it is valid it cannot be retracted any more than the dead can be brought to life. Some of you profess to think that its retraction would operate favorably for the Union. Why better after the retraction than before the issue? There was more than a year and a half for trial to suppress the rebellion before the proclamation was issued, the last one hundred days of which passed under explicit notice it was coming unless averted by those in revolt returning to their allegiance.

The war has certainly progressed as favorably for us since the issue of the proclamation as before. I know, as fully as one can know the opinions of others, that some of the commanders of our armies in the field who have given us our most important victories, believe that the emancipation policy and the aid of the colored troops constitutes the heaviest blows yet dealt to the rebellion; and that at least one of those important successes could not have been achieved when it was, but for the aid of the black soldiers.

Among the commanders holding these views are some who have never had any affinity with what is called Abolitionism, or with Republican party polities, but who hold them purely as military opinions. I submit their opinions as being entitled to some weight against the objections often urged that emancipation and the arming of the blacks are unwise as military measures, and were not adopted as such in good faith.

You say that you will not fight to free negroes. Some of them seem to be willing to fight for you; but no matter, fight you, then, exclusively to save the Union. I issued the proclamation on purpose to aid you in saving the Union. Whenever you shall have conquered all resistance to the Union, if I shall urge you to continue fighting, it will be an apt time then for you to declare that you will not fight to free negroes.

I thought that in your struggle for the Union, to whatever extent the negro should cease helping the enemy, to that extent it weakens the enemy in his resistance to you. Do you think differently? I thought that whatever negroes can be got to do as soldiers, leaves just so much less for white soldiers to do in saving the Union.

Does it appear otherwise to you? But negroes, like other people, act upon motives. Why should they do anything for us if we will do nothing for them? If they stake their lives for us they must be prompted by the strongest motive, even the promise of freedom; and the promise being made must be kept.

The signs look better. The Father of Waters again goes unvexed to the sea; thanks to the great Northwest for it; nor yet wholly to them. Three hundred miles up they met New England, the Empire, Keystone, and New Jersey showing their way right and left. The Sunny South, too, in more colors than ours, also lent a hand on the spot. Their part of history was jotted down in black and white. The poet was a great national one, and let none be banned who bore an honest part in it; while those who have cleared the great river may well be proud.

Even that is not all. It is hard to say that anything has been more bravely and better done than at Antietam, Murfreesboro', Gettysburg, and on many fields of less note.

Nor must Uncle Sam's noble fleet be forgotten. At all the water's margins they have been present. Not only on the deep sea, the broad bay, the rapid river, but also up the narrow, muddy bayon, and wherever the ground was a little damp, they have been and made their tracks.

Thanks to all, for the great Republic, for the principles by which it lives and keeps alive for man's vast future! Thanks to all!

Peace does not appear so distant as it did. I hope it will come soon, come to stay, and so come as to be worth the keeping in all future time. It will then have been proved that among freemen there can be no successful appeal from the ballot to the bullet, and that they who take such an appeal are sure to lose their case and pay the cost; and then there will be some black men who can remember that, with silent tongues, and clenched teeth, and steady eye, and well poised bayonet, they have helped mankind on to this great consummation, while I fear that there will be some white men unable to forget that with malignant heart and deceitful speech they have to hinder it.—Still, let us not be over sangume of a speedy and final triumph. Let us be quite sober, let us diligently apply the means, never doubting that a just God, in his own good time, will give us the rightful result.

Yours, very truly,
A. Lincoln.

Source:

Abraham Lincoln. *The Daily Dispatch,* September 7, 1863; *The Richmond Daily Dispatch,* University of Richmond Libraries <http://dlxs.richmond.edu/cgi/t/text/text-idx?c=ddr;cc=ddr;view=text;idno=ddr0882.0025.058;rgn=div4;node=ddr0882.0025.058%3A3.2.1.1> (accessed December 12, 2007).

Document 15: LETTER FROM JAMES HENRY GOODING

African American Corporal James Henry Gooding wrote this letter on September 28, 1863, to the president on behalf of the Massachusetts Fifty-fourth to protest racial disparity in soldiers' pay. His is but one of several such letters of protest. The soldiers also protested the injustice by refusing to accept the substandard wages. Note the distinction Gooding makes here between black freemen and former slaves and his invocation of Lincoln's Order of Retaliation to support his case.

Morris Island [S.C.].
Sept 28th 1863.

Your Excelency will pardon the presumtion of an humble individual like myself, in addressing you. but the earnest Solicitation of my Comrades in Arms, besides the genuine interest felt by myself in the matter is my excuse, for placing before the Executive head of the Nation our Common Grievance: On the 6th of the last Month, the Paymaster of the department, informed us, that if we would decide to recieve the sum of $10 (ten dollars) per month, he would come and pay us that sum, but, that, on the sitting of Congress, the Regt would, in his opinion, be allowed the other 3 (three.) He did not give us any guarantee that this would be, as he hoped, certainly he had no authority for making any such guarantee, and we can not supose him acting in any way interested. Now the main question is. Are we Soldiers, or are we LABOURERS. We are fully armed, and equipped, have done all the various Duties, pertaining to a Soldiers life, have conducted ourselves, to the complete satisfaction of General Officers, who, were if any, prejudiced against us, but who now accord us all the encouragement, and honour due us: have shared the perils, and Labour, of Reducing the first stronghold, that flaunted a Traitor Flag: and more, Mr President. Today, the Anglo Saxon Mother, Wife, or Sister, are not alone, in tears for departed Sons, Husbands, and Brothers. The patient Trusting Decendants of Africs Clime, have dyed the ground with blood, in defense of the Union, and Democracy. Men too your Excellency, who know in a measure, the cruelties of the Iron heel of oppression, which in years gone by, the very Power, their blood is now being spilled to maintain, ever ground them to the dust. But When the war trumpet sounded o'er the land, when men knew not the Friend from the Traitor, the Black man laid his life at the Altar of the Nation,—and he was refused. When the arms of the Union, were beaten, in the first year of the War, And the Executive called more food. for its ravaging maw, again the black man begged, the privelege of Aiding his Country in her need, to be again refused, And now, he is in the War: and how has he conducted himself? Let their dusky forms, rise up, out the mires of James Island, and give the answer. Let the rich mould around Wagners parapets be upturned, and there will be found an Eloquent answer. Obedient and patient, and Solid as a wall are they. all we lack, is a paler hue, and a better acquaintance with the Alphabet. Now Your Excellency, We have done a Soldiers Duty. Why cant we have a Soldiers pay? You caution the Rebel Chieftain, that the United States, knows, no distinction, in her Soldiers: She insists on having all her Soldiers, of whatever, creed or Color, to be treated, according to the usages of War. Now if the United States exacts uniformity of treatment of her Soldiers, from the Insurgents, would it not be well, and consistent, to set the example herself, by paying all her Soldiers alike? We of this Regt. were not enlisted under any "contraband" act. But we do not wish to be understood, as rating our Service, of more Value to the Government, than the service of the exslave, Their Service is undoubtedly worth much to the Nation, but Congress made express, provision touching their case, as slaves freed by military necessity, and assuming the Government, to be their temporary Gaurdian:— Not so with us—Freemen by birth, and consequently, having the advantage of thinking, and acting for ourselves, so far as the Laws would allow us. We do not consider ourselves fit subjects for the Contraband act. We appeal to You, Sir: as the Executive of the Nation, to have us Justly Dealt with. The Regt, do pray, that they be assured their service will be fairly appreciated, by paying them as american SOLDIERS, not as menial hierlings. Black men You may well know, are poor, three dollars per month, for a year, will suply their needy Wives, and little ones, with fuel. If you, as chief Magistrate of the Nation, will assure us, of our whole pay. We are content, our Patriotism, our enthusiasm will have a new impetus, to exert our energy more and more to aid Our Country. Not that our hearts ever flagged, in Devotion, spite the evident apathy displayed in our behalf, but We feel as though, our Country spurned us, now we are sworn to serve her.

Please give this a moments attention
James Henry Gooding

Source:

Ira Berlin, et al., eds. *Freedom's Soldiers: The Black Military Experience in the Civil War* (Cambridge University Press, 1998), pp. 114–116; *The Freedmen and Southern Society Project*, University of Maryland <http://www.history.umd.edu/Freedmen/gooding.htm> (accessed January 12, 2008).

Document 16: The Ovation for the Black Regiment

This New York Times *article from March 7, 1864, makes a stark comparison between the assault on African Americans during the New York City Draft Riots in July 1863 and the city's reception of black troops eight months later, in March 1864. During the Draft Riots, numerous white residents of New York City, many of whom were of Irish descent, grew violent in response to Lincoln's issuing the Enrollment Act of Conscription (which permitted exemptions for wealthier Americans), and many made African Americans their target. The author here contrasts the violence that African Americans met with during the riots with the exaltation of black soldiers months later. In some respects the author is correct to recognize the arming of black soldiers as a "revolution" signaling the beginning of African American social equality and citizenship; however, in light of the persistence of racial discrimination after the Civil War, the claims may seem overly optimistic in retrospect.*

There has been no more striking manifestation of the marvelous times that are upon us than the scene in our streets at the departure of the first of our colored regiments. Had any man predicted it last year he would been thought a fool, even by the wisest and most discerning. History abounds with strange contrasts. It always has been an ever-shifting melo-drama. But never, in this land at least, has it presented a transition so extreme and yet so speedy as what our eyes have just beheld.

Eight months ago the African race in this City were literally hunted down like wild beasts. They fled for their lives. When caught, they were shot down in cold blood, or stoned to death, or hung to the trees or the lamp-posts. Their houses were pillaged; the asylum which Christian charity had provided for their orphaned children was burned; and there was no limit to the persecution but in the physical impossibility of finding further material on which the mob could wreak its ruthless hate. Nor was it solely the raging horde in the streets that visited upon the black man the nefarious wrong. Thousands and tens of thousands of men of higher social grade, of better education, cherished precisely the same spirit. It found expression in the contumelious speech rather than in the violent act, but it was persecution none the less for that. In fact the mob would never have entered upon that career of outrage but for the fact that it was fired and maddened by the prejudice which had been generated by the ruling influences, civil and social, here in New York, till it had enveloped the City like some infernal atmosphere. The physical outrages which were inflicted on the black race in those terrible days were but the outburst of malignant agencies which had been transfusing the whole community from top to bottom, year after year.

How astonishingly has all this been changed! The same men who could not have shown themselves in the most obscure street in the City without peril or instant death, even though in the most suppliant attitude, now march in solid platoons, with shouldered muskets, slung knapsacks, and buckled cartridge-boxes down through our gayest avenues and our busiest thoroughfares to the pealing strains of martial music, and are everywhere saluted with waving handkerchiefs, with descending flowers, and with the acclimations and plaudits of countless beholders. They are halted at our most beautiful square, and, amid an admiring crowd, in the presence of many of our prominent citizens, are addressed in an eloquent and most complementary speech by the President of our chief literary institution, and are presented with a gorgeous stand of colors in the name of a large number of the first ladies of the City, who attest on parchment, signed by their own fair hands, that they "will anxiously watch your career, glorying in your heroism, ministering to you when wounded and ill, and honoring your martyrdom with benedictions and tears."

It is only by such occasions that we can at all realize the prodigious revolution which the public mind everywhere is experiencing. Such developments are infallible tokens of a new epoch.

SOURCE:

New York Times, March 7, 1864.

Document 17: LETTER FROM COLONEL C. T. TROWBRIDGE

Under the command of General David Hunter, Charles Taylor Trowbridge served as the white captain of the First South Carolina Volunteer Infantry. His response here on April 7, 1902, to the manuscript of Susie King Taylor confirms her account and acknowledges her service as an army nurse despite the failure of official recognition, pay, or pension. Taylor, a slave during her childhood, had attended secret schools in Savannah, Georgia, in an era when it was illegal for a slave to do so. Her education made her a valuable asset to the Union army.

St. Paul, Minn.,
April 7, 1902.
Mrs. Susan King Taylor:

Dear Madam,

—The manuscript of the story of your army life reached me to-day. I have read it with much care and interest, and I most willingly and cordially indorse it as a truthful account of your unselfish devotion and service through more than three long years of war in which the 33d Regiment bore a conspicuous part in the great conflict for human liberty and the restoration of the Union. I most sincerely regret that through a technicality you are debarred from having your name placed on the roll of pensioners, as an Army Nurse; for among all the number of heroic women whom the government is now rewarding, I know of no one more deserving than yourself.

Yours in F. C.&L.,
C. T. Trowbridge,
Late Lt.-Col. 33d U. S. C. T.

SOURCE:

From *Reminiscences of My Life in Camp with the 33D United States Colored Troops Late 1st S.C. Volunteers,* written by Susie King Taylor (Boston: Published by the author, 1902); Documenting the American South, University of North Carolina at Chapel Hill <http://docsouth.unc.edu/neh/taylorsu/taylorsu.html> (accessed January 12, 2008).

BIBLIOGRAPHY

Berlin, Ira, Joseph Reidy, and Leslie S. Rowland. *Freedom's Soldiers: The Black Military Experience in the Civil War.* Cambridge: Cambridge University Press, 1998—The editors use letters, affidavits, and memorials (reprinted from the National Archives) to describe the complexity of the experiences and impact of black soldiers and sailors during the Civil War. Their analysis highlights how the actions and persistence of African Americans forced both their service in Union forces and the end of the institution of slavery despite formidable political and social obstacles.

Burkhardt, George S. *Confederate Rage, Yankee Wrath: No Quarter in the Civil War.* Carbondale: Southern Illinois University Press, 2007—Contemporary newspaper accounts and soldiers' letters are used to explore the reactions of white soldiers to the U.S. Colored Troops during the Civil War. Burkhardt's study examines the Confederate practice of executing the Union's African American soldiers rather than treating them as prisoners of war.

Cornish, Dudley Taylor. *The Sable Arm: Negro Troops in the Union Army, 1861–1865.* New York: Longmans, Green, 1956—Among the earliest works to chronicle the experiences of the Civil War's African American soldiers, this pioneering and detailed military history is now considered a classic.

Forbes, Ella. *African American Women during the Civil War.* New York: Garland, 1998—An examination of the experiences and contributions of black women as nurses, spies, recruiters, laundresses, cooks, camp aides, educators, and combatants during the Civil War.

Glatthaar, Joseph T. *Forged in Battle: The Civil War Alliance of Black Soldiers and White Officers.* Baton Rouge: Louisiana State University, 1990—An in-depth and well-researched study of the relationships between white officers and black soldiers that brings to the fore the entrenched racism and prejudice faced by black soldiers as well as their triumphs.

Higginson, Thomas Wentworth. *Army Life in a Black Regiment.* Boston: Houghton, Mifflin, 1910—A memoir of a white colonel and abolitionist who commanded the First South Carolina Volunteers, the first regiment of former slaves raised during the Civil War.

McPherson, James M. *The Negro's Civil War: How American Negroes Felt and Acted during the War for the Union.* New York: Ballentine, 1991—An analysis of the experiences of African Americans during the Civil War based on and interwoven with relevant documents from the period.

Ramold, Steven J. *Slaves, Sailors, Citizens: African Americans in the Union Navy.* De Kalb: Northern Illinois University Press, 2002—An engaging and well-documented analysis of the conditions and battles faced by black Union sailors during the Civil War. Ramold's study suggests that black sailors faced far less discrimination than their counterparts in the army.

Risley, Ford. *The Civil War: Primary Documents on Events from 1860–1865.* Westport, Conn.: Greenwood Press, 2004—This book is a collection of newspaper articles published during the Civil War. The chapters "Lincoln Elected President," "Black Soldiers," and "Arming the Slaves" are particularly useful for illuminating the issues that surrounded the question of arming African American men in the minds of several Americans at the time.

Shaffer, Donald R. *After the Glory: The Struggles of Black Civil War Veterans.* Lawrence: University Press of Kansas, 2004—Examines the lives of African American soldiers during and after the Civil War. Shaffer's study illuminates the difficulties black veterans faced in a white supremacist society and their achievements as community leaders.

Smith, John David, ed. *Black Soldiers in Blue: African American Troops in the Civil War Era.* Chapel Hill: University of North Carolina Press, 2002—This collection of fourteen essays examines different aspects of the experiences of African American soldiers during the Civil War with a shared focus on their performance under fire. The essays effectively illuminate the controversies that surrounded African American military service.

Taylor, Susie King. *A Black Woman's Civil War Memoirs: Reminiscences of My Life in Camp with the 33rd U.S. Colored Troops, Late 1st South Carolina Volunteers.* New York: Markus Weiner, 1988 [1902]—An account of the war through the eyes of a formerly enslaved woman who served as an army nurse and camp aide.

Zilversmit, Arthur. *Lincoln on Black and White: A Documentary History.* Malabar, Fla.: Krieger, 1971. This volume is a collection of documents, primarily letters and speeches, that illuminate Lincoln's views on race and slavery. Several of the documents, particularly those written during the years of the Civil War, speak directly to the issues surrounding the arming of African American soldiers.

~ 7 ~

Violent Abolitionism: John Brown and the Raid on Harpers Ferry

At midnight on October 16, 1859, John Brown gave the order: "Men, get on your arms; we will proceed to the Ferry." With his band of five black men and sixteen whites, Brown—a white abolitionist, tanner, farmer, and failed businessman—launched an attack against the institution of slavery. He captured the town of Harpers Ferry, Virginia, intending for slaves to use weapons from the federal arsenal to rise up and claim their freedom. Federal forces led by Colonel Robert E. Lee overwhelmed the band after thirty-six hours, and Brown was taken to a Virginia jail cell. He was later indicted on counts of assault, murder, conspiracy, and treason. On November 2 he made his final address to the court and heard his sentence: he was to be hanged in Charles Town on December 2, 1859.

The Harpers Ferry raid appeared to mark a point of no return in the growing conflict over slavery.

Both in 1859 and in the years that followed, Brown symbolized the controversial notion of principled violence. His violent methods seemed at odds with abolitionist calls for democratic brotherhood. His actions were treasonous; yet, he declared them to be patriotic. He seemed lawless, yet idealistic. He condemned the violence of slavery while taking violent action himself. What did the public responses of his fellow abolitionists to the conflicts outlined above suggest about their tactics of resisting and ending slavery? Did commentators seek to diffuse the conflict and make Brown's violence more palatable—was it possible to do so?

Some abolitionists used Brown's raid and his prison letters to prepare the North for a supposed holy war that would bring divine retribution upon the South for the crime of slavery. Although Brown's raid had failed, Northern sympathizers turned him into a martyr, inflaming passions in the South. About 40 percent of the Southern population was black, and the ratio of blacks to whites on larger plantations exceeded ten to one; consequently, fears of a large-scale slave revolt were acute. Southern leaders argued that the South's interests were not adequately represented in federal law. The debate became bitter as Southern politicians charged that their voices were not being heard in Congress. In 1860, when Northern and Southern Democrats had splintered into three parties, Republican Abraham Lincoln was elected president.

Brown's raid set off a chain of events that widened the chasm between proslavery causes and abolitionists. But, if Brown's raid was a turning point in the growing conflict over slavery, it also marked the beginning of a series of political and philosophical conflicts within the abolitionist movement. As David W. Blight said in 2000 of Brown's raid and execution, it "provokes us to think about the meaning and uses of martyrdom. His story is a template for our understanding of revolutionary violence in any age . . . he represents some of our deepest political ambivalences, standing as he does for high ideals and ruthless deeds" (45).

Brown's tipping point with regard to slavery had come in 1850, with the passage of the Fugitive Slave Law, which ordered that any person who helped a fugitive slave to avoid recapture was subject to a fine and imprisonment. In 1851 Brown organized the United States League of Gileadites, a

This daguerreotype from 1846 or 1847 by August Washington is the earliest known image of John Brown (National Portrait Gallery, Smithsonian Institution).

black self-defense unit named after the biblical army tested by God before battle. He wrote a document titled "Words of Advice," which included descriptions of guerilla tactics; he suggested, for example, in capturing slave catchers, "A lasso might possibly be applied...."

Brown's eldest son, John Jr., and several of Brown's other sons moved to Kansas in 1854, after the Kansas-Nebraska Bill placed the issue of slavery into the hands of settlers who were given the power to decide by popular vote whether the state would be free or slave. Proslavery "Border Ruffians" and antislavery Free-Staters were pouring into Kansas, contending over the future of slavery in the state. In May 1855, John Jr. asked his father for help in procuring weapons for the fight against slavery.

Having decided to join his sons in Kansas, Brown headed west, stopping on the way to give a speech in Syracuse on June 26, 1855, the first day of the inaugural convention of the Radical Political Abolitionists. Brown hoped to garner support for his plan of armed resistance and raise money for arms. He quoted from Hebrews, chapter 9, insisting that "without the shedding of blood there is no remission of sin"; when he recommended to the other delegates that they help arm all the free-state settlers in Kansas, there was some argument over whether the group wanted to encourage violence. Eventually, only one delegate dissented (Stauffer, 13), and the convention agreed that Brown's way was the only way forward. By the end of the meeting the group had agreed they were God's disciples, had declared slavery a state of war, and had passed a resolution to resist any attempted return of fugitive slaves. The following year, at their National Nominating Convention in Syracuse on May 28, 1856, one Radical Political Abolitionist characterized conditions in Kansas as a state of revolution. In response to the situation, Frederick Douglass suggested that "Slaveholders must be met at the point of the bayonet"—and added that liberty "must either cut the throat of slavery or slavery . . . cut the throat of liberty" (Stauffer, 21).

Unbeknownst to Douglass, Brown and his men had already begun to turn Douglass's rhetoric into action. Participating in the era of conflict (later called "Bleeding Kansas") between factions who were fighting over the status of slavery in Kansas, Brown and seven others (including four of his sons and his son-in-law Henry Thompson) had entered the proslavery settlement at Pottawatomie Creek on the night of May 24 and hacked to death five unarmed settlers.

Even after the pillaging of Lawrence, Kansas, by proslavery settlers (called the "sacking of Lawrence"), the violence committed by Brown and his cohorts was considered barbarous by proslavery advocates—even, at best, difficult for Brown's admirers to understand: the men who had been murdered—mutilated, apparently—had neither owned slaves nor participated in the violence in Lawrence. Seemingly undeterred, Brown told his friend Franklin Sanborn a few months after the murders, in January 1857, that violent death was better than a continuation of the slave system: "I have always been delighted with the doctrine that all men are created equal; and to my mind it is like the Saviour's command, 'Thou shalt love thy neighbor as thyself,' for how can we do that unless our neighbor is equal to ourself? That is the doctrine, sir; and rather than have that fail in the world, or in these States, 't would be better for a whole generation to die a violent death" (Sanborn 1885, 620). In his attempt to push America closer to a finalizing conflict, Brown meant the killings to terrify proslavery forces, to build a wall of protection around free-state settlers, and to focus the attention of the country on the issue of slavery.

Brown remained focused on ending slavery through violent insurrection. At Douglass's home in Rochester, the following January, he wrote his "provisional constitution," which declared that "whole generation" was *already* at war. Echoing the Radical Political Abolitionists' definition of slavery in his constitution's "preamble," he argued that it was "none other than a most barbarous, unprovoked, and unjustifiable *war* of one portion of its citizens upon another portion." He justified armed resistance to end the war and preserve peace. In April 1858 he went to Ontario and convened a provisional constitutional convention in order to ratify his constitution. There, he outlined his plans to attack western Virginia, arm his men, and march south. After arming liberated slaves with stolen weapons, Brown intended to establish a slave-free state under the constitution adopted at the convention. Freed blacks would be organized, and a new state would be founded in the southern Appalachian Mountains.

In July 1859 Brown began to put his war plans in motion. He rented a farm five miles from Harpers Ferry, where slaves could be outfitted from the armory—close to the mountains, where he could hide. Men gathered as weapons arrived. Brown and his men raided Harpers Ferry on October 16, and of the twenty-one men who fought beside him, ten died in the battle, six escaped, and five were later hung. As dawn broke on the morning of his execution, Brown handed his last prison letter to a guard. Just two sentences, it read: "I John Brown am now quite certain that the crimes of this guilty land will never be purged away; but with Blood. I had as I now think; vainly flattered myself that without very much bloodshed; it might be done."

Commentators sought to downplay Brown's violence and introduced a new angle: gentleness and compassion. A story sprang up that Brown had stopped on his way to the gallows to kiss the child of a slave woman. John Greenleaf Whittier wrote the poem "Brown of Osawatomie," which features the kiss at its center, and the scene was painted by Louis Ransom in 1860, Thomas Satterwhite Noble in 1867, and Thomas Hovenden in 1884. Ransom's painting, *John Brown Meeting the Slave Mother and Her Child*, drew a favorable review from *Harper's Weekly*: "It is one of the incidents that history will always fondly record and art delineate," wrote a reviewer on June 13, 1863. "The fierce and bitter judgment of the moment upon the old man is already tempered. Despised and forsaken in his own day, the heart of another generation may treat him as he treated the little outcast child."

With similar results, some tempered the horror of the event by comparing Brown's violence to images of natural force. The Reverend Fales Henry Newhall called Brown "a volcanic blaze that rises as if to 'lick the stars,'" and the Reverend Moncure Conway concurred, explaining that Brown's actions were therefore impossible to judge: "We may as well question the moral propriety of a streak of lightning or an earthquake as of [Brown's] deed," he insisted (Redpath, 195, 355).

A series of other cultural representations addressed Brown's violence by making him a representative American, part of the country's revolutionary heritage. A Quaker woman, identifying herself only as E.B. and writing to Brown on October 27, 1859, had first made the connection: "If the American people honor Washington for resisting with bloodshed for seven years an unjust tax, how much more ought thou be honored for seeking to free the poor slaves?" (Sanborn, 1885, 582). Parallels followed after Brown's death: "But was he not a rebel, guilty of sedition and treason?" asked the Reverend Newhall; "Yes, all this. But we are to remember that the words 'rebel' and 'treason' have been made holy in the American language" (Redpath, 204). Sanborn added in 1885 that "so much was [Brown] in accord with what is best in the American character, that he will stand in history as one type of our people, as Franklin and Lincoln do" (185).

Sanborn also invoked the Puritans: "[Brown] embodied the distinctive qualities of the Puritan, but with a strong tincture of the humane sentiments of later times" (1885, 185). Others identified the same tradition: William Lloyd Garrison declared Brown was of old Puritan stock, and Ralph Waldo Emerson was intrigued by Brown's direct descent from Peter Brown, a Plymouth colonist of the Mayflower. The abolitionist Wendell Phillips even wondered if Brown's "Puritan" identity explained his militancy—again seeking a palatable explanation for the violence: "You cannot expect to put a real Puritan Presbyterian, as John Brown is—a regular Cromwellian dug up for two centuries—in the midst of our New England civilization, that dares not say its soul is its own. . . . Put a Christian in the presence of a sin, and he will spring at its throat, if he is a true Christian" (Redpath, 55).

In the years that followed, abolitionists and observers continued to grapple with the conflict between Brown's violence and his professed patriotism. As they tried to explain the meaning of his violence, they called him Socrates, Ironsides, Spartacus, Martin Luther, John Milton, William Tell, George Washington, Giuseppe Garibaldi, Marquis de Lafayette, Henry Wadsworth Longfellow, King Arthur, Joan of Arc, Moses, David, and Saint Paul. They described him as an archetypal tragic character. Distanced from the bloodshed by a move to make him mythological, Brown was simplified, and his violence was made palatable.

Engraving of The Storming of the Engine-House by the United States Marines, *illustration by Porte Crayon (pseudonym of David H. Strother), featured in* Harper's Weekly (Library of Congress)

Yet, Brown's infamous strategy of violent resistance was no mythic anomaly. His actions, which terrified Southern slaveholders and seemed extreme to some moderate abolitionists, were part of a violent strand in American abolitionism. By the time of the Civil War, more than 250 small-scale slave revolts had occurred in the South. The most significant of these was Nat Turner's revolt of 1831 in Virginia. Turner led seventy other slaves in a rebellion in Southampton County, Virginia, and the rampage left dead sixty whites and one hundred blacks. Aboard slave ships, slaves had revolted at least fifty-five times between 1699 and 1845. Such forcible resistance made the antislavery crusade a precursor of the violence of the Civil War.

Abolitionists, indeed, had long advocated violent resistance to slavery. In his pamphlet *Appeal to the Coloured Citizens of the World* (1829), David Walker had instructed blacks to kill anyone who tried to enslave them. "Do not trifle, for they will not trifle with you," he instructed. Addressing all blacks who might rebel, he continued: "they want us for their slaves, and think nothing of murdering us in order to subject us to that wretched condition—therefore, if there is an *attempt* made by us, kill or be killed" (28). The pamphlet prophesied millennial violence if slavery were not abolished, and called blacks to action, to "go to work and prepare the way of the Lord" (31). In 1848 Brown helped republish Walker's pamphlet (alongside an oration by the militant black abolitionist Henry Highland Garnet).

Two years after this republication, the Fugitive Slave Law passed. Black abolitionists advocated responses to the law ranging from nonviolent civil disobedience to violent resistance. One, Joshua B. Smith, circulated weapons at an abolitionist meeting, and another, William P. Newman, wrote to Frederick Douglass in a letter published in *The North Star* on October 24, 1850: "I am frank to declare that it is my fixed and changeless purpose to kill any so-called man who attempts to enslave me or mine, if possible.... To do this ... would be an act of the highest virtue." At a meeting in Philadelphia, on October 14, 1850, several hundred free blacks passed a resolution that they would resist to the death any attempt to enforce the Fugitive Slave Law, and the following year, when fugitives fought slave catchers trying to reenslave them in Pennsylvania, the black radical James McCune Smith proclaimed: "Our white brethren cannot understand us unless we speak to them in their own language; they recognize only force."

John Brown's infamous strategies of violent resistance had a bloodline, traceable through the history of black abolitionism. And sure enough, numerous defenses of Brown in the wake of his raid came from African Americans. On November 29, 1859, before Brown's execution, the black congregation at the Wylie Street A.M.E. Church in Pittsburgh met and resolved that: "John Brown, in taking up arms to liberate the slaves, only acted upon the maxim that 'resistance to tyrants is obedience to God.'" For his part, Douglass explained Brown's actions as an attempt to meet "persecution with persecution, war with war, strategy with strategy, assassination and house-burning with signal and terrible retaliation, till even the blood-thirsty propagandists of slavery were compelled to cry for quarter." While the incident, and the "horrors wrought by [Brown's] iron hand," could not be "contemplated without a shudder," as Douglass acknowledged, this was "the shudder which one feels at the execution of a murderer" (1881, 744).

By the time the Civil War began, black abolitionists' defense of Brown perhaps seemed justified as his violent actions seemed suddenly to have foreshadowed the greater conflict and to make him a prophet. While Union soldiers marched to the song "John Brown's Body," the *Illinois Weekly Mirror* noted: the "apotheosis of old John Brown is fast taking place.... All over the country, the John Brown song may be heard at all times of the night or day in the streets of Chicago and all other cities." For years commentators would insist that he began the war that ended slavery: "not Carolina, but Virginia, not Fort Sumter, but Harpers Ferry and the arsenal, not Col. Anderson, but John Brown, began the war that ended American slavery and made this a free Republic," observed Douglass in 1881 (1999, 648). The shots fired at Harpers Ferry had arguably been the first of the Civil War.

Zoe Trodd

CHRONOLOGY

1800
In Philadelphia, free blacks petition Congress to repeal the 1793 Fugitive Slave Act.
May 9: John Brown is born in Torrington, Connecticut. His father, a strict Calvinist, believes slavery to be a sin against God.
August 30: Gabriel Prosser's plan to lead Virginia slaves in rebellion is revealed.

1805
June: The Brown family joins the westward migration of New Englanders and moves to Hudson, Ohio, a town eventually known for its strong abolitionist views.

1816
The American Colonization Society is founded to resettle free blacks in Africa.

1817
James Forten leads 3,000 blacks in a Philadelphia protest meeting against colonization.

1820
The Missouri Compromise admits Missouri and Maine as slave and free states respectively.
June 21: Brown marries Dianthe Lusk in Hudson, Ohio.

1821
The Republic of Liberia in West Africa is established as a refuge for freed American slaves. In 1847 this becomes the independent nation of Liberia.
July 25: Brown's first child and namesake, John Brown Jr., is born in Hudson, Ohio.

1822
Denmark Vesey, a free black, is convicted and hanged along with thirty-five others in Charleston, S.C., when his plans to lead a slave uprising are uncovered.

1825
A fugitive slave and his wife appear at Brown's house. Brown feeds and hides the pair.

1826
Brown and family move to Randolph, Pennsylvania, where Brown establishes a tannery.

Secretary of State Henry Clay asks Canada to return escaped slaves and Canada refuses.

1827

The first black newspaper, *Freedom's Journal,* is published in New York.

1829

August 10: White mobs attack black freedmen in Cincinnati, Ohio, and one thousand blacks leave for Canada.

1831

January 1: William Lloyd Garrison begins publishing *The Liberator,* the first newspaper in the country to demand an immediate end to slavery.

August 22: Nat Turner leads a slave uprising in Southampton County, Virginia.

1832

The New England Anti-Slavery Society is founded.

August 10: Dianthe Brown dies of heart failure in New Richmond.

1833

Britain adopts an emancipation and apprenticeship plan that prepares eight hundred thousand slaves for freedom.

July 11: John Brown marries seventeen-year-old Mary Day.

December: Garrison and sixty delegates found the American Anti-Slavery Society.

1835

October 21: A mob pursues Garrison through Boston and nearly lynches him.

1836

January: During a period of extreme land speculation, Brown moves his family to Franklin Mills, Ohio, and borrows money to buy land.

1837

Brown is almost ruined financially by the Panic of 1837.

November 7: Upon hearing that abolitionist newspaperman Elijah Lovejoy has been shot and killed in Illinois by a proslavery mob, Brown commits himself to working for the destruction of slavery.

1839

The Spanish slave ship *Amistad,* carrying fifty-three slaves, is taken over in a mutiny by their leader, Cinque, who orders the two surviving whites to sail the ship to Africa. The ship is seized off the coast of Long Island, and the Africans are jailed.

1841

November 7: Slaves aboard the *Creole* en route from Virginia to New Orleans revolt and sail the ship to a British port in the Bahamas, where they are freed.

1846

Gerritt Smith sells land to Brown in North Elba, New York, where Brown will live on and off, among a small community of freed slaves, until his death.

1850

January: Henry Clay introduces the Compromise of 1850, which admits California as a free state and Texas as a slave state.

September 18: The new Fugitive Slave Act is passed. This allows slaveholders to retrieve slaves in Northern states and free territories without due process of law, prohibits anyone from helping fugitives, and requires government officials to assist in the retrieval of escaped slaves. Captured blacks are denied any legal power to prove their freedom. At Thanksgiving, Brown speaks on the Fugitive Slave Act to the congregation at his church.

1851

Brown establishes the United States League of Gileadites, a black self-defense organization. Senator Charles Sumner meets with Brown and the Gileadites.

1852

Harriet Beecher Stowe's novel *Uncle Tom's Cabin* sells one million copies within the year.

1853

Brown, now living with his family in Akron, Ohio, becomes involved with the Underground Railroad.

1854

May 30: The Kansas-Nebraska Act is passed, sweeping aside the Missouri Compromise, which restricted the expansion of slavery. Those settling the new territories will decide, by popular vote, whether to be "free" or "slave." The violence of "Bleeding Kansas" begins, as hundreds of proslavery and antislavery advocates move into the area.

June 2: Fifty thousand people in Boston watch Anthony Burns, a fugitive slave, taken in shackles to a ship.

October: Brown's unmarried sons, Owen, Frederick, and Salmon, leave for Kansas territory in the wake of the Kansas-Nebraska Bill.

1855

June: Brown decides to follow his sons to Kansas and leaves Mary and their children behind at North Elba.

December 7: Brown and four of his sons help defend Lawrence, Kansas, during the Wakarusa War.

1856

May 22: Senator Charles Sumner of Massachusetts is almost caned to death on the floor of the Senate in Washington, D.C., by Congressman Preston Brooks of South Carolina, after delivering an antislavery speech titled "The Crime against Kansas."

May 24: Brown directs his men in the murder of five proslavery settlers at Pottawatomie Creek.

June 2: At the Battle of Black Jack in southeastern Douglas County, Brown defeats Henry Clay Pate.

August 30: Brown fights at the Battle of Osawatomie, where his second son, Frederick, is killed.

1857

March: The Dred Scott Decision rules that Scott, a Missouri slave who was suing for freedom on grounds that he had become a free man when his master took him into territory made free by the Missouri Compromise, is not a citizen and so is not eligible to sue. With a Southern majority, it also ruled that no black person, free or slave, is a U.S. citizen; that slaveholders have the right to take slaves into free territory; and that Congress has no power to prevent slavery in the territories.

March 12: Brown tells a Concord audience that he hates violence but accepts it as God's will.

1858

February 22: Brown meets with Gerrit Smith and Franklin Sanborn in Peterboro, New York, and outlines a plan to raid Harpers Ferry.

May 8: Brown's Constitutional Convention of the Oppressed People of the United States is held in Chatham, Ontario, Canada. Brown produces and presents his Provisional Constitution for government in a slave-free nation, and plans his Harpers Ferry raid.

June 16: At Springfield, Illinois, senatorial candidate Abraham Lincoln gives his "House Divided" speech at the close of the Republican state convention.

August–October: The Lincoln/Douglas Debates, an exchange between Republican Abraham Lincoln and Democrat Stephen Douglas, bring Lincoln into the national spotlight, influencing his nomination for president in 1860.

December 20–21: Brown leads a raid on two proslavery homesteads in Missouri, confiscates property, and liberates eleven slaves. He then travels for eighty-two days, covering more than one thousand miles, to escort the slaves along the Underground Railroad to Canada.

1859

January: In response to Brown's Missouri raid, President Buchanan offers a $250 reward for his capture.

Mid March: Brown reaches Detroit and moves the slaves into Canada.

July 3: Brown arrives at Harpers Ferry and rents a farm five miles away. His men slowly gather.

October 16: Brown and his men capture the armory at Harpers Ferry. They take as hostages some local militia leaders, including Colonel Lewis W. Washington, a grandnephew of George Washington.

October 17: At 7:00 A.M. the local railroad conductor at Harpers Ferry alerts railroad officials to the situation. Officials telegraph President Buchanan and local militia move on Harpers Ferry. Several of Brown's men are killed, and at nightfall Brown ignores demands for his surrender. Lieutenant Colonel Robert E. Lee and Lieutenant J. E. B. Stuart arrive.

October 18: At dawn, Lee's marines break into the engine house. Lieutenant Israel Green attacks Brown with the dress sword he brought by mistake, then hits Brown over the head with the sword's handle and knocks him unconscious.

October 25–November 2: Brown goes on trial at Charlestown.

December 2: Brown is hanged for murder, treason, and conspiracy to incite a slave insurrection and is buried at North Elba.

1861

April 12: Confederate batteries open fire on Fort Sumter.

1863

January 1: President Lincoln signs the Emancipation Proclamation.

1865

December 6: The Thirteenth Amendment to the United States Constitution is ratified, abolishing slavery as a legal institution.

DOCUMENTS

Document 1: LETTER FROM JOHN BROWN TO HIS BROTHER

John Brown's November 21, 1834, letter to his brother Frederick was his first written reference to any strategy for helping slaves. Nothing came of the ideas he outlines (he took no African Americans into his family and received no help from "first-rate abolitionist families"), and the letter hints at Brown's sense that his interest in abolitionism might not be compatible with his business commitments and family life. At this moment in 1834 he is also struggling with what it means to "effect" change, returning to the word repeatedly as he tries to balance concepts of human action and divine will.

By 1839 his business was failing. Creditors foreclosed and took him to court. In 1841 he was arrested when he tried to prevent the eviction of his family and barricaded himself in a cabin with three of his sons. He lost almost everything he owned in various settlements, and in 1842 he applied for bankruptcy. But the Panic of 1837 and eviction apparently transformed his outlook, and he moved closer to the spiritual realm, seeking an escape from the material world.

Randolph, Nov. 21, 1834.

Dear Brother,

—As I have had only one letter from Hudson since you left here, and that some weeks since, I begin to get uneasy and apprehensive that all is not well. I had satisfied my mind about it for some time, in expectation of seeing father here, but I begin to give that up for the present. Since you left me I have been trying to devise some means whereby I might do something in a practical way for my poor fellow-men who are in bondage, and having fully consulted the feelings of my wife and my three boys, we have agreed to get at least one negro boy or youth, and bring him up as we do our own,-viz., give him a good English education, learn him what we can about the history of the world, about business, about general subjects, and, above all, try to teach him the fear of God. We think of three ways to obtain one: First, to try to get some Christian slave-holder to release one to us. Second, to get a free one if no one will let us have one that is a slave. Third, if that does not succeed, we have all agreed to submit to considerable privation in order to buy one. This we are now using means in order to effect, in the confident expectation that God is about to bring them all out of the house of bondage.

I will just mention that when this subject was first introduced, Jason had gone to bed; but no sooner did he hear the thing hinted, than his warm heart kindled, and he turned out to have a part in the discussion of a subject of such exceeding interest. I have for years been trying to devise some way to get a school a-going here for blacks, and I think that on many accounts it would be a most favorable location. Children here would have no intercourse with vicious people of their own kind, nor with openly vicious persons of any kind. There would be no powerful opposition influence against such a thing; and should there be any, I believe the settlement might be so effected in future as to have almost the whole influence of the place in favor of such a school. Write me how you would like to join me, and try to get on from Hudson and thereabouts some first-rate abolitionist families with you. I do honestly believe that our united exertions alone might soon, with the good hand of our God upon us, effect it all.

This has been with me a favorite theme of reflection for years. I think that a place which might be in some measure settled with a view to such an object would be much more favorable to such an undertaking than would any such place as Hudson, with all its conflicting interests and feelings; and I do think such advantages ought to be afforded the young blacks, whether they are all to be immediately set free or not. Perhaps we might, under God, in that way do more towards breaking their yoke effectually than in any other. If the young blacks of our country could once become enlightened, it would most assuredly operate on slavery like firing powder confined in rock, and all slaveholders know it well. Witness their heaven-daring laws against teaching blacks. If once the Christians in the Free States would set to work in earnest in teaching the blacks, the people of the slaveholding States would find themselves constitutionally driven to set about the work of emancipation immediately. The laws of this State are now such that the inhabitants of any township may raise by a tax in aid of the State school-fund any amount of money they may choose by a vote, for the purpose of common schools, which any child may have access to by application. If you will join me in this undertaking, I will make with you any arrangement of our temporal concerns that shall be fair. Our health is good, and our prospects about business rather brightening.

Affectionately yours,
John Brown

SOURCE:

Franklin B. Sanborn. *The Life and Letters of John Brown, Liberator of Kansas and Martyr of Virginia* (Boston: Roberts, 1885), pp. 40–41.

Document 2: WORDS OF ADVICE

John Brown did not begin to practice guerrilla warfare in earnest until 1854, but his militant approach to abolitionism was visibly on the horizon in January 1851, when he founded the League of Gileadites and launched its first (and only) branch in Springfield, Massachusetts. The Fugitive Slave Law, passed on September 18, 1850, demanded that law-enforcement officials everywhere arrest anyone suspected of being a runaway slave. In addition, any person aiding a runaway slave was subject to six months' imprisonment and a $1,000 fine. The passage of the law prompted action from Brown and the formation of the league.

In June 1854, a few days after federal and state forces arrived in Boston to return Anthony Burns to slavery, the black abolitionist William Wells Brown visited Springfield and commented that the league members were more than ready to carry out Brown's "Words of Advice." When slave catchers came calling, "the authorities, foreseeing a serious outbreak, advised them to leave, and feeling alarmed for their personal safety, these disturbers of the peace had left on the evening train for New York," he remembered in an article for The Independent *on March 10, 1870. "No fugitive slave was ever afterwards disturbed at Springfield."*

Branch of the United States League of Gileadites. Adopted January 15, 1851, as written and recommended by John Brown.

"Union is Strength"

Nothing so charms the American people as personal bravery. Witness the case of Cinques, of everlasting memory, on board the "Amistad." The trial for life of one bold and to some extent successful man, for defending his rights in good earnest, would arouse more sympathy throughout the nation than the accumulated wrongs and sufferings of more than three millions of our submissive colored population. We need not mention the Greeks struggling against the oppressive Turks, the Poles against Russia, nor the Hungarians against Austria and Russia combined, to prove this. *No jury can be found in the Northern States that would convict a man for defending his rights to the last extremity. This is well understood by Southern Congressmen, who insisted that the right of trial by jury should not be granted to the fugitive.* Colored people have more fast friends amongst the whites than they suppose, and would have ten times the number they now have were they but half as much in earnest to secure their dearest rights as they are to ape the follies and extravagances of their white neighbors, and to indulge in idle show, in ease, and in luxury. Just think of the money expended by individuals in your behalf in the past twenty years. Think of the number who have been mobbed and imprisoned on your account. Have any of you seen the Branded Hand? Do you remember the names of Lovejoy and Torrey?

Should one of your number be arrested, you must collect together as quickly as possible, so as to outnumber your adversaries who are taking an active part against you. Let no able-bodied man appear on the ground unequipped, or with his weapons exposed to view; let that be understood beforehand. Your plans must be known only to yourself, and with the understanding that all traitors must die, wherever caught and proven to be guilty. 'Whosoever is fearful or afraid, let him return and depart early from Mount Gilead.' (Judges, vii. chap., 3 verse; Deut., xx chap., 8 verse.) Give all cowards an opportunity to show it on condition of holding their peace. *Do not delay one moment after you are ready you will lose all your resolution if you do. Let the first blow be the signal for all to engage, and when engaged do not do your work by halves; but make clean work with your enemies, and be sure you meddle not with any others.* By going about your business quietly, you will get the job disposed of before the number that an uproar would bring together can collect;

and you will have the advantage of those who come out against you, for they will be wholly unprepared with either equipments or matured plans; all with them will be confusion and terror. Your enemies will be slow to attack you after you have once done up the work nicely; and if they should, they will have to encounter your white friends as well as you, for you may safely calculate on a division of the whites, and may by that means get to an honorable parley.

Be firm, determined, and cool; but let it be understood that you are not to be driven to desperation without making it an awful job to others as well as to you. Give them to know distinctly that those who live in wooden houses should not throw fire, and that you are just as able to suffer as your white neighbors. *After effecting a rescue, if you are assailed, go into the houses of your most prominent and influential white friends with your wives, and that will effectually fasten upon them the suspicion of being connected with you, and will compel them to make a common cause with you, whether they would otherwise live up to their profession or not. This would leave them no choice in the matter.* Some would, doubtless, prove themselves true of their own choice; others would flinch. That would be taking them at their own words. You may make a tumult in the court-room where a trial is going on by burning gunpowder freely in paper packages, if you cannot think of any better way to create a momentary alarm, and might possibly give one or more of your enemies a hoist. But in such case the prisoner will need to take the hint at once and bestir himself and so should his friends improve the opportunity for a general rush.

A lasso might possibly be applied to a slave-catcher for once with good effect. Hold on to your weapons, and never be persuaded to leave them, part with them, or have them far away from you. *Stand by one another, and by your friends, while a drop of blood remains; and be hanged, if you must, but tell no tales out of school. Make no confession.*

Union is strength. Without some well-digested arrangements nothing to any good purpose is likely to be done, let the demand be never so great. Witness the case of Hamlet and Long in New York, when there was no well-defined plan of operations or suitable preparation beforehand.

The desired end may be effectually secured by the means proposed; namely, the enjoyment of our inalienable rights.

Source:

Franklin B. Sanborn. *The Life and Letters of John Brown, Liberator of Kansas and Martyr of Virginia* (Boston: Roberts, 1885), pp. 124–126.

***Document 3:* Eyewitness Testimony**

On May 24, 1856, John Brown and seven others entered the proslavery settlement at Pottawatomie Creek, Kansas, and hacked five men to death. The victims included James P. Doyle and his two sons, who were proslavery but not slave owning, and Allen Wilkinson, who was a member of the proslavery legislature. Mrs. Doyle and Mrs. Wilkinson provided eyewitness testimonies. The fifth man killed was William Sherman, a border ruffian and horse thief. He was taken from the house of James Harris, who also provided a testimony. All three accounts were given in the William Howard Committee Report to Congress of 1860. There is still some mystery surrounding the murders, caused in part by Brown's refusal to confess formally. Brown may not have slain anyone himself: most accounts concur that the younger Brown boys and Henry Thompson killed the five men, and Brown only fired a shot after the murders were over, possibly as a signal to those in his band who were waiting at a distance.

Testimony of Mrs. Doyle:

I am the widow of the late James P. Doyle. We moved into the Territory—that is, my husband, myself, and children—moved into the Territory of Kansas some time in November, A.D. 1855, and settled upon Musketo creek, about one mile from its mouth, and where it empties into Pottawatomie creek, in Franklin county. On Saturday, the 24th of May, A.D. 1855, about eleven o'clock at night, after we had all retired, my husband, James P. Doyle, myself, and six children, five boys and one girl—the eldest is about twenty-two years of age; his name is William. The next is about twenty years of age; his name is Drury. The next is about seventeen years of age; his name is John. The next is about thirteen years of age; her name is Polly Ann. The next is about eight years of age; his name is James. The next is about five years of age; his name is Henry. We were all in bed, when we heard some persons come into the yard, and rap at the door, and call for Mr. Doyle, my husband. This was about eleven o'clock on Saturday night, of the 24th of May last. My husband got up and went to the door. Those outside inquired for Mr. Wilkinson, and where he lived. My husband said he would tell them. Mr. Doyle, my husband, and several came into the house, and said they were from the army. My husband was a pro-slavery man. They told my husband that he and the boys must surrender; they were then prisoners. The men were armed with pistols and large knives. They first took my husband out of the house; then took two of my sons—William and Drury—out, and then took my husband and these two boys (William and Drury) away. My son John was spared, because I asked them, in tears, to spare him.

In a short time afterwards I heard the report of pistols; I heard two reports. After which I heard moaning as if a person was dying. Then I heard a wild whoop. They had asked before they went away for our horses. We told them that our horses were out on the prairie. My husband and two boys, my sons, did not come back any more. I went out next morning in search of them, and found my husband and William, my son, lying dead in the road, near together, about two hundred yards from the house. They were buried the next day. On the day of the burying, I saw the dead body of Drury. Fear of myself and the remaining children, induced me to leave the home where we had been living. We had improved our claim a little. I left and went to the State of Missouri.

―――~―――

Testimony of Mrs. Wilkinson:

I was sick with measles, and woke up Mr. Wilkinson, and asked if he heard the noise and what it meant? He said it was only someone passed about, and soon after was again asleep. It was not long before the dog raged and barked furiously, awakening me once more; pretty soon I heard footsteps as of men approaching; saw one pass by the window, and some one knocked at the door. I asked, who is that? No one answered. I awoke my husband who asked, who is that? Someone replied, "I want you to tell me the way to Dutch Henry's." He commenced to tell them, and they said to him, "Come out and show us." He wanted to go, but I would not let him; he then told them it was difficult to find his clothes, and could tell them as well without going out of doors. The men out of doors, after that, stepped back, and I thought I could hear them whispering; but they immediately returned, and, as they approached, one of them asked my husband, "Are you a northern armist?" He said "I am!" I understood the answer to mean that my husband was opposed to the northern or freesoil party. I cannot say that I understood the question. My husband was a pro-slavery man, and was a member of the territorial legislature held at Shawnee Mission. When my husband said "I am," one of them said "you are a prisoner. Do you surrender?" He said, "Gentlemen, I do." They said, "open the door." Mr. Wilkinson told them to wait till he made a light; and they replied, "if you don't open it, we will open it for you." He opened the door against my wishes, and four men came in, and my husband was told to put on his clothes, and they asked him if there were not more men about; they searched for arms, and took a gun and powder flask, all the weapon that was about the house. I begged them to let Mr. Wilkinson stay with me, saying that I was sick and helpless, and could not stay by myself. My husband also asked them to let him stay with me, until he could get some one to wait on me; told them that he would not run off, but he would be there the next day, or whenever called for; the old man who seemed to be in command looked at me, and then around at the children, and replied, "you have neighbors." I said, "so I have, but they are not here, and I cannot go for them." The old man replied, "it matters not," and told him to get ready. My husband wanted to put on his boots, and get ready, so as to be protected from the damp and night air, but they would not let him. They then took my husband away. After they were gone I thought I heard my husband's voice in complaint, but do not know; went to the door and all was still. Next morning Mr. Wilkinson's body was found about one hundred and fifty yards from the house, in some dead brush. A lady who saw my husband's body said that there was a gash in his head and side. Others said he was cut in the throat twice.

―――~―――

Testimony of James Harris:

On Sunday morning, May 25, 1856, about two A.M., while my wife and child and myself were in bed in the house where we lived, near Henry Sherman's, we were aroused by a company of men who said they belonged to the Northern army, and who were each armed with a sabre and two revolvers, two of whom I recognized; namely, a Mr. Brown, whose given name I do not remember (commonly known by the appellation of "old man Brown"), and his son Owen Brown. They came into the house and approached the bedside where we were lying and ordered us, together with three other men who were in the same house with me, to surrender; that the Northern army was upon us, and it would be no use for us to resist. The names of these other men who were in the house with me were William Sherman and John S. Whiteman; the other man I did not know.

They were stopping with me that night. They had bought a cow from Henry Sherman, and intended to go home the next morning. When they came up to the bed, some had drawn sabers in their hands, and some revolvers. They then took into their possession two rifles and a bowie-knife, which I had there in the room (there was but one room in my house), and afterwards ransacked the whole establishment in search of ammunition. They then took one of these three men, who were staying in my house, out. (This was the man whose name I did not know.) He came back. They then took me out, and asked me if there were any more men about the place. I told them there were not. They searched the place, but found no others but us four. They asked me where Henry Sherman was. (Henry was a brother to William Sherman.) I told them he was out on the plains in search of some cattle which he had lost. They asked me if I had ever taken any hand in aiding proslavery men in coming to the Territory of Kansas, or had ever taken any hand in the last troubles at Lawrence; they asked me whether I had ever done the Free-State party any harm, or ever intended to do that party any harm; they asked me what made me live at such a place. I then answered that I could get higher wages there than anywhere else. They asked me if there were any bridles or saddles about the premises. I told them there was one saddle, which they took: and they also took possession of Henry Sherman's horse, which I had at my place, and made me saddle him. They then said if I would answer no to all the questions which they had asked me, they would let me loose. Old Mr. Brown and his son then went into the house with me. The other three men—Mr. William Sherman, Mr. Whiteman, and the stranger—were in the house all this time. After old man Brown and his son went into the house with me, old man Brown asked Mr. Sherman to go out with him; and Mr. Sherman then went out with old Mr. Brown, and another man came into the house in Brown's place. I heard nothing more for about fifteen minutes. Two of the Northern army, as they styled themselves, stayed in with us until we heard a cap burst, and then these two men left. That morning, about ten o'clock, I found William Sherman dead in the creek near my house. I was looking for him; as he had not come back, I thought he had been murdered. I took Mr. William Sherman out of the creek and examined him. Mr. Whiteman was with me. Sherman's skull was split open in two places, and some of his brains were washed out by the water. A large hole was cut in his breast, and his left hand was cut off except a little piece of skin on one side. We buried him.

Source:

Kansas Affairs, Special Committee Appointed to Investigate the Troubles in the Territory of Kansas, 34th Congress, 1st session, Washington, 1856, H. Rept. 200, serial 869, pp. 1193–1199.

Document 4: **Provisional Constitution and Ordinances for the People of the United States**

In April 1858, John Brown went to Chatham, Ontario. There, a project he had contemplated for years took form. He had drafted a "constitution" for a provisional government in a slave-free nation during a recent two-week stay at Frederick Douglass's home in Rochester, and now completed it, also organizing a convention for the following month. The area had a large free-black community, several of whom attended the convention. Douglass did not attend, although he kept a copy of the constitution until the end of his life. The "provisional constitutional convention" convened on May 8 and ran for two days. By the end of the first day the convention had ratified the "provisional constitution and ordinances" and had elected Brown as commander in chief of the whole paper government. On May 10, Brown appointed a committee to fill all the executive, legislative, judicial, and military offices named in the constitution.

Preamble:

Whereas slavery, throughout its entire existence in the United States, is none other than a most barbarous, unprovoked, and unjustifiable war of one portion of its citizens upon another portion—the only conditions of which are perpetual imprisonment and hopeless servitude or absolute extermination—in utter disregard and violation of those eternal and self-evident truths set forth in our Declaration of Independence: Therefore we, citizens of the United States, and the oppressed people who, by a recent decision of the Supreme Court, are declared to have no rights which the white man is bound to respect, together with all other people degraded by the laws thereof, do, for the time being, ordain and establish for ourselves the following Provisional Constitution and

Ordinances, the better to protect our persons, property, lives, and liberties, and to govern our actions:

Article I. Qualifications for Membership

All persons of mature age, whether proscribed, oppressed, and enslaved citizens, or of the proscribed and oppressed races of the United States, who shall agree to sustain and enforce the Provisional Constitution and Ordinances of this organization, together with all minor children of such persons, shall be held to be fully entitled to protection under the same.

Article II. Branches of Government

The provisional government of this organization shall consist of three branches, viz.: legislative, executive, and judicial.

Article III. Legislative

The legislative branch shall be a Congress or House of Representatives, composed of not less than five nor more than ten members, who shall be elected by all citizens of mature age and of sound mind connected with this organization, and who shall remain in office for three years, unless sooner removed for misconduct, inability, or by death. A majority of such members shall constitute a quorum.

Article IV. Executive

The executive branch of this organization shall consist of a President and Vice-President, who shall be chosen by the citizens or members of this organization, and each of whom shall hold his office for three years, unless sooner removed by death or for inability or misconduct.

Article V. Judicial

The judicial branch of this organization shall consist of one Chief Justice of the Supreme Court and of four associate judges of said court, each constituting a circuit court. They shall each be chosen in the same manner as the President, and shall continue in office until their places have been filled in the same manner by election of the citizens. Said court shall have jurisdiction in all civil or criminal causes arising under this constitution, except breaches of the rules of war.

Article VI. Validity of Enactments

All enactments of the legislative branch shall, to become valid during the first three years, have the approbation of the President and the Commander-in-chief of the army.

Article VII. Commander-in-Chief

A Commander-in-chief of the army shall be chosen by the President, Vice-President, a majority of the Provisional Congress, and of the Supreme Court, and he shall receive his commission from the President, signed by the Vice-President, the Chief Justice of the Supreme Court, and the Secretary of War, and he shall hold his office for three years, unless removed by death or on proof of incapacity of misbehavior. He shall, unless under arrest, (and until his place is actually filled as provided for by this constitution), direct all movements of the army and advise with any allies. He shall, however, be tried, removed, or punished, on complaint of the President, by at least three general officers, or a majority of the House of Representatives, or of the Supreme Court; which House of Representatives, (the President presiding), the Vice-President, and the members of the Supreme Court, shall constitute a court-martial for this trial; with power to remove or punish, as the case may require, and to fill his place, as above provided.

Article VIII. Officers

A Treasurer, Secretary of State, Secretary of War, and Secretary of the Treasury, shall each be chosen for the first three years, in the same way and manner as the Commander-in-Chief; subject to trial or removal on complaint of the President, Vice-President, or Commander-in-Chief, to the Chief Justice of the Supreme Court; or on complaint of the majority of the members of said court, or the Provisional Congress. The Supreme Court shall have power to try or punish either of those officers; and their places shall be filled as before.

Article IX. Secretary of War

The Secretary of War shall be under the immediate direction of the Commander-in-Chief; who may temporarily fill his place, in case of arrest, or of any inability to serve.

Article X. Congress or House of Representatives

The House of Representatives shall make ordinances for the appointment (by the President or otherwise) of all civil officers excepting those already named; and shall have power to make all laws and ordinances for the general good, not inconsistent with this Constitution and these ordinances.

Article XI. Appropriation of Money, etc

The Provisional Congress shall have power to appropriate money or other property actually in the hands of the Treasurer, to any object calculated to promote the general good, so far as may be consistent with the provisions of this Constitution; and may in certain cases, appropriate, for a moderate compensation of agents, or persons not members of this organization, for important service they are known to have rendered.

Article XII. Special Duties

It shall be the duty of Congress to provide for the instant removal of any civil officer or policeman, who becomes habitually intoxicated, or who is addicted to other immoral conduct, or to any neglect or unfaithfulness in the discharge of his official duties. Congress shall also be a standing committee of safety, for the purpose of obtaining important information; and shall be in constant communication with the Commander-in-Chief; the members of which shall each, as also the President, Vice-President, members of the Supreme Court, and Secretary of State, have full power to issue warrants returnable as Congress shall ordain (naming witnesses, etc.) upon their own information, without the formality of a complaint. Complaint shall be made immediately after arrest, and before trial; the party arrested to be served with a copy at once.

Article XIII. Trial of President and Other Officers

The President and Vice-President may either of them be tried, removed, or punished, on complaint made to the Chief-Justice of the Supreme Court, by a majority of the House of Representatives, which House, together with the Associate Judges of the Supreme Court, the whole to be presided over by the Chief-Justice in cases of the trial of the Vice-President, shall have full power to try such officers, to remove, or punish as the case may require, and to fill any vacancy so occurring, the same as in the case of the Commander-in-Chief.

Article XIV. Trial of Members of Congress

The members of the House of Representatives may any and all of them be tried, and on conviction, removed or punished on complaint before the Chief-Justice of the Supreme Court, made by any number or members of said House, exceeding one-third, which House, with the Vice-President and Associate Judges of the Supreme Court, shall constitute the proper tribunal, with power to fill such vacancies.

Article XV. Impeachment of Judges

Any member of the Supreme Court, tried, convicted, or punished by removal or otherwise, on complaint to the President, who shall, in such case, preside; the Vice-President, House of Representatives, and other members of the Supreme Court, constituting the proper tribunal (with power to fill vacancies); on complaint of a majority of said House of Representatives, or of the Supreme Court; a majority of the whole having power to decide.

Article XVI. Duties of President and Secretary of State

The President, with the Secretary of State, shall immediately upon entering on the duties of their office, give special attention to secure, from amongst their own people, men of integrity, intelligence, and good business habits and capacity; and above all, of first-rate moral and religious character and influence, to act as civil officers of every description and grade, as well as teachers, chaplains, physicians, surgeons, mechanics, agents of every description, clerks, and messengers. They shall make special efforts to induce at the earliest possible period, persons and families of that description, to locate themselves within the limits secured by this organization; and shall, moreover, from time to time, supply the names and residence of such persons to the Congress, for their special notice and information, as among the most important of their duties, and the President is hereby authorized and empowered to afford special aid to such individuals, from such moderate appropriations as the Congress shall be able and may deem it advisable to make for that object. The President and Secretary of State, and in cases of disagreement, the Vice-President shall appoint all civil officers, but shall not have power to remove any officer. All removals shall be the result of a fair trial, whether civil or military.

Article XVII. Further Duties

It shall be the duty of the President and Secretary of State, to find out (as soon as possible) the real friends, as well as the enemies of this organization in every part of the country; to secure among them, innkeepers, private postmasters, private mail-contractors, messengers, and agents : through whom may be obtained correct and regular information, constantly; recruits for the service, places of deposit and sale; together with all needed supplies: and it shall be a matter of special regard to secure such facilities through the Northern States.

Article XVIII. Duties of the President

It shall be the duty of the President, as well as the House of Representatives, at all times, to inform the Commander-in-Chief of any matter that may require his attention, or that may affect the public safety.

Article XIX. Duty of President—Continued

It shall be the duty of the President to see the provisional ordinances of this organization, and those made by Congress, are promptly and faithfully executed; and he may in cases of great urgency call on the Commander-in-Chief of the army, or other officers for aid; it being, however, intended that a sufficient civil police shall always be in readiness to secure implicit obedience to law.

Article XX. The Vice President

The Vice-President shall be the presiding officer of the Provisional Congress; and in cases of tie shall give the casting vote.

Article XXI. Vacancies

In case of death, removal, or inability of the President, the Vice-President, and next to him the Chief-Justice of the Supreme Court, shall be the President during the remainder of the term: and the place of Chief-Justice thus made vacant shall be filled by Congress from some of the members of said court; and places of the Vice-President and Associate Justice thus made vacant, filled by an election by the united action of the Provisional Congress and members of the Supreme Court. All other vacancies, not heretofore specially provided for, shall, during the first three years, be filled by the united action of the President, Vice-President, Supreme Court, and Commander-in-Chief of the Army.

Article XXII. Punishments of Crimes

The punishment of crimes not capital, except in case of insubordinate convicts or other prisoners, shall be (so far as may be) by hard labor on the public works, roads, etc.

Article XXIII. Army Appointments

It shall be the duty of all commissioned officers of the army to name candidates of merit for office or elevation to the Commander-in-Chief, who, with the Secretary of War, and, in cases of disagreement, the President, shall be the appointing power of the army: and all commissions of military officers shall bear the signatures of the Commander-in-Chief and the Secretary of War. And it shall be the special duty of the Secretary of War to keep for constant reference of the Commander-in-Chief a full list of names of persons nominated for office, or elevation, by the officers of the army, with the name and rank of the officer nominating, stating distinctly but briefly the grounds for such notice or nomination. The Commander-in-Chief shall not have power to remove or punish any officer or soldier; but he may order their arrest and trial at any time, by court-martial.

Article XXIV. Courts-Martial

Courts-martial for Companies, Regiments, Brigades, etc., shall be called by the chief officer of each command, on complaint to him by any officer, or any five privates, in such command, and shall consist of not less than five nor more than nine officers, non-commissioned officers, and privates, one-half of whom shall not be lower in rank than the person on trial, to be chosen by the three highest officers in the command, which officers shall not be a part of such court. The chief officer of any command shall, of course, be tried by a court-martial of the command above his own. All decisions affecting the lives of persons, or office of persons holding commission, must, before taking full effect, have the signature of the Commander-in-Chief, who may also, on the recommendation of, at least, one-third of the members of the court-martial finding any sentence, grant a reprieve or communication of the same.

Article XXV. Salaries

No person connected with this organization shall be entitled to any salary, pay, or emolument, other than a competent support of himself and family, unless it be from an equal dividend, made of public property, on the establishment of peace, or of special provisions by treaty; which provision shall be made for all persons who may have been in any active civil or military service at any time previous to any hostile action for Liberty and Equality.

Article XXVI. Treaties of Peace

Before any treaty of peace shall take full effect, it shall be signed by the President and Vice-President, the Commander-in-Chief, a majority of the House of Representatives, a majority of the Supreme Court, and majority of all general officers of the army.

Article XXVII. Duty of the Military

It shall be the duty of the Commander-in-Chief, and all officers and soldiers of the army, to afford special protection when needed, to Congress, or any member thereof; to the Supreme Court, or any member thereof; to the President, Vice-President, Treasurer, Secretary of State,

Secretary of Treasury, and Secretary of War; and to afford general protection to all civil officers, other persons having right to the same.

Article XXVIII. Property

All captured or confiscated property, and all property the product of the labor of those belonging to this organization and of their families, shall be held as the property of the whole, equally, without distinction; and may be used for the common benefit, or disposed of for the same object; and any person, officer or otherwise, who shall improperly retain, secret, use or needlessly destroy such property, or property found, captured, or confiscated, belonging to the enemy, or shall willfully neglect to render a full and fair statement of such property by him so taken or held, shall be deemed guilty of a misdemeanor and, on conviction, shall be punished accordingly.

Article XXIX. Safety or Intelligence Fund

All money, plate, watches, or jewelry, captured by honorable warfare, found, taken, or confiscated, belonging to the enemy, shall be held sacred, to constitute a liberal safety or intelligence fund; and any person who shall improperly retain, dispose of, hide, use, or destroy such money or other article above named, contrary to the provisions and spirit of this article, shall be deemed guilty of theft, and, on conviction, thereof, shall be punished accordingly. The Treasurer shall furnish the Commander-in-Chief at all times with a full statement of the condition of such fund and its nature.

Article XXX. The Commander-in-Chief and the Treasury

The Commander-in-Chief shall have power to draw from the Treasury the money and other property of the fund provided for in ARTICLE twenty-ninth, but his orders shall be signed also by the Secretary of War, who shall keep strict account of the same; subject to examination by any member of Congress, or general officer.

Article XXXI. Surplus of the Safety or Intelligence Fund

It shall be the duty of the Commander-in-Chief to advise the President of any surplus of the Safety or Intelligence Fund; who shall have power to draw such surplus (his order being also signed by the Secretary of State) to enable him to carry out the provisions of Article Seventeenth.

Article XXXII. Prisoners

No person, having surrendered himself or herself a prisoner, and who shall properly demean himself or herself as such, to any officer or private connected with this organization, shall afterward be put to death, or be subject to any corporal punishment, without first having had the benefit of a fair and impartial trial: nor shall any prisoner be treated with any kind of cruelty, disrespect, insult, or needless severity: but it shall be the duty of all persons, male and female, connected herewith, at all times and under all circumstances, to treat all such prisoners with every degree of respect and kindness the nature of the circumstances will admit of; and to insist on a like course of conduct from all others, as in the fear of Almighty God, to whose care and keeping we commit our cause.

Article XXXIII. Voluntaries

All persons who may come forward and shall voluntarily deliver up their slaves, and have their names registered on the Books of the organization, shall, so long as they continue at peace, be entitled to the fullest protection of person and property, though not connected with this organization, and shall be treated as friends, and not merely as persons neutral.

Article XXXIV. Neutrals

The persons and property of all non-slaveholders who shall remain absolute neutral, shall be respected so far as the circumstances can allow it; but they shall not be entitled to any active protection.

Article XXXV. No Needless Waste

The needless waste or destruction of any useful property or article, by fire, throwing open of fences, fields, buildings, or needless killing of animals, or injury of either, shall not be tolerated at any time or place, but shall be promptly and properly finished.

Article XXXVI. Property Confiscated

The entire and real property of all persons known to be acting either directly or indirectly with or for the enemy, or found in arms with them, or found willfully holding slaves, shall be confiscated and taken, whenever and wherever it may be found, in either free or slave States.

Article XXXVII. Desertion

Persons convicted, in impartial trial, of desertion to the enemy after becoming members, acting as spies, or of treacherous surrender of property, arms, ammunition, provisions, or supplies of any kind, roads, bridges, persons, or fortifications, shall be put to death and their entire property confiscated.

Article XXXVIII. Violation of Parole of Honor

Persons proven to be guilty of taking up arms after having been set at liberty on parole of honor, or, after the same, to have taken any active part with or for the enemy, direct or indirect, shall be put to death and their entire property confiscated.

Article XXXIX. All Must Labor

All persons connected in any way with this organization, and who may be entitled to full protection under it: shall be held as under obligation to labor in some way for the general good; and persons refusing, or neglecting so to do, shall on conviction receive a suitable and appropriate punishment.

Article XL. Irregularities

Profane swearing, filthy conversation, indecent behavior, or indecent exposure of the person, or intoxication, or quarrelling, shall not be allowed or tolerated; neither unlawful intercourse of the sexes.

Article XLI. Crimes

Persons convicted of the forcible violation of any female prisoner shall be put to death.

Article XLII. The Marriage Relation— Schools—the Sabbath

The marriage relation shall be at all times respected; and families kept together as far as possible; and broken families encouraged to re-unite, and intelligence offices established for that purpose, schools and churches established, as soon as may be, for the purpose of religious and other instructions and the first day of the week regarded as a day of rest and appropriated to moral and religious instruction and improvement; relief to the suffering, instruction of the young and ignorant, and the encouragement of personal cleanliness nor shall any persons required on that day to perform ordinary manual labor, unless in extremely urgent cases.

Article XLIII. Carry Arms Openly

All persons known to be of good character, and of sound mind and suitable age, who are connected with this organization, whether male or female, shall be encouraged to carry arms openly.

Article XLIV. No Person to Carry Concealed Weapons

No person within the limits of the conquered territory, except regularly appointed policemen, express officers of the army, mail carriers, or other fully accredited messengers of the Congress, President, Vice-President, members of the Supreme Court, or commissioned officer of the army—and those only under peculiar circumstances—shall be allowed, at any time, to carry concealed weapons and any person not specifically authorized so to do, who shall be found so doing, shall be deemed a suspicious person, and may at once be arrested by any officer, soldier, or citizen, without the formality of a complaint or warrant, and may at once be subjected to thorough search, and shall have his or her case thoroughly investigated; and be dealt with as circumstances, on proof, shall require.

Article XLV. Persons to Be Seized

Persons within the limits of the territory holden by this organization, not connected with this organization, having arms at all, concealed or otherwise, shall be seized at once; or be taken in charge of some vigilant officer; and their case thoroughly investigated : and it shall be the duty of all citizens and soldiers, as well as officers, to arrest such parties as are named in this and the preceding Section or Article, without the formality of complaint or warrant: and they shall be placed in charge of some proper officer for examination, or for safe keeping.

Article XLVI. These Articles Not for the Overthrow of Gov'm't

The foregoing Articles shall not be construed so as in any way to encourage the overthrow of any State Government of the United States: and look to no dissolution of the Union, but simply to Amendment and Repeal. And our flag shall be the same that our Fathers fought under in the Revolution.

Article XLVII. No Plurality of Offices

No two of the offices specially provided for, by this Instrument, shall be filled by the same person, at the same time.

Article XLVIII. Oath

Every officer, civil or military, connected with this organization, shall, before entering upon the duties of his office, make solemn oath or affirmation, to abide by and support this Provisional Constitution and these Ordinances. Also, every Citizen and Soldier, before being fully recognized as such, shall do the same.

SOURCE:

James Redpath. *The Public Life of Capt. John Brown* (Boston: Thayer & Eldridge, 1860), pp. 234–236.

Document 5: JOHN BROWN'S TESTIMONY

Just after midnight on October 16, 1859, John Brown and his band of allies took the armory and the arsenal at Harpers Ferry, Virginia, intending that slaves rise up and claim their freedom. Early in the morning on October 18 they were overpowered by marines, led by Lieutenant Colonel Robert E. Lee and Lieutenant J. E. B. Stuart. Brown was carried from the engine house and taken to the armory. On October 19, Lee, Governor Henry Wise, Andrew Hunter, Senator James Murray Mason, Representatives Charles James Faulkner, Clement L. Vallandigham, and others arrived to interview Brown, as reported here. The only question he would not answer concerned the identities of his co-conspirators. After the interview, Brown was taken eight miles down the road to the prison at Charles Town, and later indicted on counts of assault, murder, conspiracy, and treason.

Mason: Can you tell us who furnished money for your expedition?

Brown: I furnished most of it myself: I cannot implicate others. It is by my own folly that I have been taken. I could easily have saved myself from it, had I exercised my own better judgment rather than yielded to my feelings.

Mason: You mean if you had escaped immediately?

Brown: No. I had the means to make myself secure without any escape; but I allowed myself to be surrounded by a force by being too tardy. I should have gone away; but I had thirty odd prisoners, whose wives and daughters were in tears for their safety, and I felt for them. Besides, I wanted to allay the fears of those who believed we came here to burn and kill. For this reason I allowed the train to cross the bridge, and gave them full liberty to pass on. I did it only to spare the feelings of those passengers and their families, and to allay the apprehensions that you had got here in your vicinity a band of men who had no regard for life and property, nor any feelings of humanity.

Mason: But you killed some people passing along the streets quietly.

Brown: Well, sir, if there was anything of that kind done, it was without my knowledge. Your own citizens who were my prisoners will tell you that every possible means was taken to prevent it. I did not allow my men to fire when there was danger of killing those we regarded as innocent persons, if I could help it. They will tell you that we allowed ourselves to be fired at repeatedly, and did not return it.

A Bystander: That is not so. You killed an unarmed man at the corner of the house over there at the water-tank, and another besides.

Brown: See here, my friend; it is useless to dispute or contradict the report of your own neighbors who were my prisoners.

Mason: If you would tell us who sent you here,—who provided the means,—that would be information of some value.

Brown: I will answer freely and faithfully about what concerns myself,—I will answer anything I can with honor,—but not about others.

Mr. Vallandigham (who had just entered): Mr. Brown, who sent you here?

Brown: No man sent me here; it was my own prompting and that of my Maker, or that of the Devil,— whichever you please to ascribe it to. I acknowledge no master in human form.

Vallandigham: Did you get up the expedition yourself?

Brown: I did.

Vallandigham: Did you get up this document that is called a Constitution?

Brown: I did. They are a constitution and ordinances of my own contriving and getting up.

Vallandigham: How long have you been engaged in this business?

Brown: From the breaking out of the difficulties in Kansas. Four of my sons had gone there to settle, but because of the difficulties.

Mason: How many are there engaged with you in this movement?

Brown: Any questions that I can honorably answer I will,—not otherwise. So far as I am myself concerned, I have told everything truthfully. I value my word, sir.

Mason: What was your object in coming?

Brown: We came to free the slaves, and only that.

A Volunteer. How many men, in all, had you?

Brown: I came to Virginia with eighteen men only, besides myself.

Volunteer: What in the world did you suppose you could do here in Virginia with that amount of men?

Brown: Young man, I do not wish to discuss that question here.

Volunteer: You could not do anything.

Brown: Well, perhaps your ideas and mine on military subjects would differ materially.

Mason: How do you justify your acts?

Brown: I think, my friend, you are guilty of a great wrong against God and humanity,—I say it without wishing to be offensive,—and it would be perfectly right for any one to interfere with you so far as to free those you willfully and wickedly hold in bondage. I do not say this insultingly.

Mason: I understand that.

Brown: I think I did right, and that others will do right who interfere with you at any time and at all times. I hold that the Golden Rule, "Do unto others as ye would that others should do unto you," applies to all who would help others to gain their liberty.

Lieutenant Stuart: But don't you believe in the Bible?

Brown: Certainly I do.

Mason: Did you consider this a military organization in this Constitution? I have not yet read it.

Brown: I did, in some sense. I wish you would give that paper close attention.

Mason: You consider yourself the commander-in-chief of these "provisional" military forces?

Brown: I was chosen, agreeably to the ordinance of a certain document, commander-in-chief of that force.

Mason: What wages did you offer?

Brown: None.

Stuart: "The wages of sin is death."

Brown: I would not have made such a remark to you if you had been a prisoner, and wounded, in my hands.

A Bystander: Did you not promise a Negro in Gettysburg twenty dollars a month?

Brown: I did not.

Mason: Does this talking annoy you?

Brown: Not in the least.

Vallandigham: Have you lived long in Ohio?

Brown: I went there in 1805. I lived in Summit County, which was then Portage County. My native place is Connecticut; my father lived there till 1805.

Vallandigham: Have you been in Portage County lately?

Brown: I was there in June last.

Vallandigham: When in Cleveland, did you attend the Fugitive Slave Law Convention there?

Brown: No. I was there about the time of the sitting of the court to try the Oberlin rescuers. I spoke there publicly on that subject; on the Fugitive Slave Law and my own rescue. Of course, so far as I had any influence at all, I was supposed to justify the Oberlin people for rescuing a slave, because I have myself forcibly taken slaves from bondage. I was concerned in taking eleven slaves from Missouri to Canada last winter. I think I spoke in Cleveland before the Convention. I do not know that I had conversation with any of the Oberlin rescuers. I was sick part of the time I was in Ohio with the ague, in Ashtuba County.

Vallandigham: Did you see anything of Joshua R. Giddings there?

Brown: I did meet him.

Vallandigham: Did you converse with him?

Brown: I did. I would not tell you, of course, anything that would implicate Mr. Giddings; but I certainly met with him and had conversations with him.

Vallandigham: About that rescue case?

Brown: Yes; I heard him express his opinions upon it very freely and frankly.

Vallandigham: Justifying it?

Brown: Yes, sir; I do not compromise him, certainly, in saying that.

Vallandigham: Will you answer this; Did you talk with Giddings about your expedition here?

Brown: No, I won't answer that; because a denial of it I would not make, and to make any affirmation of it I should be a great dunce.

Vallandigham: Have you had correspondence with parties at the North on the subject of this movement?

Brown: I have had correspondence.

A Bystander: Do you consider this a religious movement?

Brown: It is, in my opinion, the greatest service man can render to God.

Bystander: Do you consider yourself an instrument in the hands of Providence?

Brown: I do.

Bystander: Upon what principle do you justify your acts?

Brown: Upon the Golden Rule. I pity the poor in bondage that have none to help them: that is why I am here; not to gratify any personal animosity, revenge, or vindictive spirit. It is my sympathy with the oppressed and the wronged, that are as good as you and as precious in the sight of God.

Bystander: Certainly. But why take the slaves against their will?

Brown: I never did.

Bystander: You did in one instance, at least.

[Stephens, the other wounded prisoner, here said, "You are right. In one case I know the negro wanted to go back."]

Bystander: Where did you come from?

Stephens: I lived in Ashtabula County, Ohio.

Vallandigham: How recently did you leave Ashtabula County?

Stephens: Some months ago. I never resided there any length of time; have been through there.

Vallandigham: How far did you live from Jefferson?

Brown: Be cautious, Stephens, about any answers that would commit any friend. I would not answer that.

[Stephens turned partially over with a groan of pain, and was silent.]

Vallandigham: Who are your advisors in this movement?

Brown: I cannot answer that. I have numerous sympathizers throughout the entire North.

Vallandigham: In northern Ohio?

Brown: No more than anywhere else; in all the free states.

Vallandigham: But you are not personally acquainted in southern Ohio?

Brown: Not very much.

A Bystander: Did you ever live in Washington City?

Brown: I did not. I want you to understand, gentlemen, and [to the reporter of the "Herald"] you may report that,—I want you to understand that I respect the rights of the poorest and weakest of colored people, oppressed by the slave system, just as much as I do those of the most wealthy and powerful. This is the idea that has moved me, and that alone. We expected no reward except the satisfaction of endeavoring to do for those in distress and greatly oppressed as we would be done by. The cry of distress of the oppressed is my reason, and the only thing that prompted me to come here.

Bystander: Why did you do it secretly?

Brown: Because I thought that necessary to success; no other reason.

Bystander: Have you read Gerrit Smith's last letter?

Brown: What letter do you mean?

Bystander: The "New York Herald" of yesterday, in speaking of this affair, mentions a letter in this way:— "Apropos of this exciting news, we recollect a very significant passage in one of Gerrit Smith's letters, published a month or two ago, in which he speaks of the folly of attempting to strike the shackles off the slaves by the force of moral suasion or legal agitation, and predicts that the next movement made in the direction of negro emancipation would be an insurrection in the South."

Brown: I have not seen the "New York Herald" for some days past; but I presume, from your remark about the gist of the letter, that I should concur with it. I agree with Mr. Smith that moral suasion is hopeless. I don't think the people of the slave States will ever consider the subject of slavery in its true light till some other argument is resorted to than moral suasion.

Vallandigham: Did you expect a general rising of the slaves in case of your success?

Brown: No, sir; nor did I wish it. I expected to gather them up from time to time and set them free.

Vallandigham: Did you expect to hold possession here till then?

Brown: Well, probably I had quite a different idea. I do not know that I ought to reveal my plans. I am here a prisoner and wounded, because I foolishly allowed myself to be so. You overrate your strength in supposing I could have been taken if I had not allowed it. I was too tardy after commencing the open attack,—in delaying my movements through Monday night, and up to the time I was attacked by the government troops. It was all occasioned by my desire to spare the feelings of my prisoners and their families and the community at large. I had no knowledge of the shooting of the negro Heywood.

Vallandigham: What time did you commence your organization in Canada?

Brown: That occurred about two years ago; in 1858.

Vallandigham: Who was the secretary?

Brown: That I would not tell if I recollected; but I do not recollect. I think the officers were elected in May, 1858. I may answer incorrectly, but not intentionally. My head is a little confused by wounds, and my memory obscure on dates, etc.

Dr. Biggs: Were you in the party at Dr. Kennedy's house?

Brown: I was the head of that party. I occupied the house to mature my plan. I have not been in Baltimore to purchase caps.

Dr. Biggs: What was the number of men at Kennedy's?

Brown: I decline to answer that.

Dr. Biggs: Who lanced that woman's neck on the hill?

Brown: I did. I have sometimes practiced in surgery when I thought it a matter of humanity and necessity, and there was no one else to do it; but I have not studied surgery.

Dr. Biggs: It was done very well and scientifically. They have been very clever to the neighbors, I have been told, and we had no reason to suspect them, except that we could not understand their movements. They were represented as eight or nine persons; on Friday there were thirteen.

Brown: There were more than that.

Reporter: I do not wish to annoy you; but if you have anything further you would like to say, I will report it.

Brown: I have nothing to say, only that I claim to be here in carrying out a measure I believe perfectly justifiable, and not to act the part of an incendiary or ruffian, but to aid those suffering great wrong. I wish to say, furthermore, that you had better—all you people at the South—prepare yourselves for a settlement of this question, that must come up for settlement sooner than you are prepared for it. The sooner you are prepared the better. You may dispose of me very easily,—I am nearly disposed of now; but this question is still to be settled,—this negro question I mean; the end of that is not yet. These wounds were inflicted upon me—both sabre cuts on my head and bayonet stabs in different parts of my body—some minutes after I had ceased fighting and had consented to surrender, for the benefit of others, not for my own. I believe the Major would not have been alive; I could have killed him just as easy as a mosquito when he came in, but I supposed he only came in to receive our surrender. There had been loud and long calls of "surrender" from us,—as loud as men could yell: but in the confusion and excitement I suppose we were not heard. I do not think the Major, or any one, meant to butcher us after we had surrendered.

An Officer: Why did you not surrender before the attack?

Brown: I did not think it was my duty or my interest to do so. We assured the prisoners that we did not wish to harm them, and they should be set at liberty. I exercised my best judgment, not believing the people would wantonly sacrifice their own fellow-citizens, when we offered to let them go on condition of being allowed to change our position about a quarter of a mile. The prisoners agreed by a vote among themselves to pass across the bridge with us. We wanted them only as a sort of guarantee of our safety,—that we should not be fired into. We took them, in the first place, as hostages and to keep them from doing any harm. We did kill some men in defending ourselves, but I saw no one fire except directly in self-defense. Our orders were strict not to harm any one not in arms against us.

An Officer: Brown, suppose you had every nigger in the United States, what would you do with them?

Brown: Set them free.

A Bystander: Your intention was to carry them off and free them?

Brown: Not at all.

A Bystander: To set them free would sacrifice the life of every man in this community.

Brown: I do not think so.

Bystander: I know it. I think you are fanatical.

Brown: And I think you are fanatical. "Whom the gods would destroy they first make mad," and you are mad.

A Bystander: Was it your only object to free the negroes?

Brown: Absolutely our only object.

A Bystander: But you demanded and took Colonel Washington's silver and watch?

Brown: Yes; we intended freely to appropriate the property of the slaveholders to carry out our object. It was for that, and only that, and with no design to enrich ourselves with any plunder whatever.

Bystander: Did you know Sherrod in Kansas? I understand you killed him.

Brown: I killed no man except in fair fight. I fought at Black Jack Point and at Osawatomie; and if I killed anybody, it was at one of these places.

Source:

James Redpath. *The Public Life of Capt. John Brown* (Boston: Thayer & Eldridge, 1860), pp. 276–285.

Document 6: Last Address of John Brown to the Virginia Court

John Brown went on trial before Judge Richard Parker in the courthouse at Charles Town on October 25, 1859, just seven days after his capture at Harpers Ferry. Sensing the magnitude of what was unfolding in Virginia, reporters flocked to Charles Town. Newspaper artists sketched Brown, lying wounded on his cot in the courtroom. On November 2, 1859, Brown made this, his final address to the court, mocking the accusations made against him and commenting on the frailty of his allies. Judge Thomas Russell wrote in the Boston Traveler *on November 5 that Brown had "delivered [a] remarkable speech, speaking with perfect calmness of voice and mildness of manner, winning the respect of all for his courage and firmness." And the* New York Tribune *observed on November 3 that Brown's "soft and gentle tones, yet calm and manly . . . touched the hearts of many who had come only to rejoice at the heaviest blow their victim was to suffer." After making his final address, Brown heard his sentence read. He was hanged on December 2.*

I have, may it please the Court, a few words to say.

In the first place, I deny everything but what I have all along admitted,—the design on my part to free slaves. I intended certainly to have made a clean thing of that matter, as I did last winter, when I went into Missouri and there took slaves without the snapping of a gun on either side, moved them through the country, and finally left them in Canada. I designed to do the same thing again, on a larger scale. That was all I intended. I never did intend murder, or treason, or the destruction of property, or to excite or incite slaves to rebellion, or to make insurrection.

I have another objection; and that is, it is unjust that I should suffer such a penalty. Had I interfered in the manner which I admit, and which I admit has been fairly proved (for I admire the truthfulness and candor of the greater portion of the witnesses who have testified in this case),—had I so interfered in behalf of the rich, the powerful, the intelligent, the so-called great, or in behalf of any of their friends,—either father, mother, sister, wife, or children, or any of that class,—and suffered and sacrificed what I have in this interference, it would have been all right; and every man in this court would have deemed it an act worthy of reward rather than punishment.

The court acknowledges, as I suppose, the validity of the law of God. I see a book kissed here which I suppose to be the Bible, or at least the New Testament. That teaches me that all things whatsoever I would that men should do to me, I should do even so to them. It teaches me further to "remember them that are in bonds, as bound with them." I endeavored to act up to that instruction. I say, I am too young to understand that God is any respecter of persons. I believe that to have interfered as I have done—as I have always freely admitted I have done—in behalf of His despised poor, was not wrong, but right.

Now if it is deemed necessary that I should forfeit my life for the furtherance of the ends of justice, and mingle my blood further with the blood of my children and with the blood of millions in this slave country whose rights are disregarded by wicked, cruel, and unjust enactments,—I submit; so let it be done!

Let me say one word further.

I feel entirely satisfied with the treatment I have received on my trial. Considering all the circumstances, it has been more generous than I expected. I feel no consciousness of my guilt. I have stated from the first what was my intention, and what was not. I never have had any design against the life of any person, nor any disposition to commit treason, or excite slaves to rebel, or make any general insurrection. I never encouraged any man to do so, but always discouraged any idea of that kind.

Let me say also, a word in regard to the statements made by some to those connected with me. I hear it has been said by some of them that I have induced them to join me. But the contrary is true. I do not say this to injure them, but as regretting their weakness. There is not one of them but joined me of his own accord, and the greater part of them at their own expense. A number of them I never saw, and never had a word of conversation with, till the day they came to me; and that was for the purpose I have stated.

Now I have done.

SOURCE:

Franklin B. Sanborn. *The Life and Letters of John Brown, Liberator of Kansas and Martyr of Virginia* (Boston: Roberts, 1885), pp. 584–585.

Document 7: CAPTAIN JOHN BROWN NOT INSANE

Frederick Douglass first met John Brown in 1847, and later remarked that Brown was the only entirely non-racist white man he had ever met. Brown was just as impressed by Douglass, becoming an early advocate of his newspaper, The North Star *(titled* Frederick Douglass' Paper *after 1851). Brown desperately wanted to recruit Douglass for the raid on Harpers Ferry. During a meeting in August 1859, in a disused quarry pit in Chambersburg, Pennsylvania, Brown outlined his plans and urged Douglass to join his group of men. Douglass refused, warning Brown that it was a "perfect steel-trap" (1881, 759). He did, however, come to Brown's defense in November of that year, denying accusations that Brown was insane. During Brown's trial, affidavits claiming insanity in Brown's family were presented by his counsel. They came from Brown's well-meaning neighbors, who hoped to help mitigate his crimes, and were sent by telegram from Asahel H. Lewis, an abolitionist newspaper editor in Ohio. Brown rejected the claims vehemently, however, as did his wife, Mary, when interviewed by reporters.*

One of the most painful incidents connected with the name of this old hero, is the attempt to prove him insane. Many journals have contributed to this effort from a friendly desire to shield the prisoner from Virginia's cowardly vengeance. This is a mistaken friendship, which seeks to rob him of his true character and dim the glory of his deeds, in order to save his life. Was there the faintest hope of securing his release by this means, we would choke down our indignation and be silent. But a Virginia court would hang a crazy man without a moment's hesitation, if his insanity took the form of hatred of oppression; and this plea only blasts the reputation of this glorious martyr of liberty, without the faintest hope of improving his chance of escape.

It is an appalling fact in the history of the American people, that they have so far forgotten their own heroic age, as readily to accept the charge of insanity against a man who has imitated the heroes of Lexington, Concord, and Bunker Hill.

It is an effeminate and cowardly age, which calls a man a lunatic because he rises to such self-forgetful heroism, as to count his own life as worth nothing in comparison with the freedom of millions of his fellows. Such an age would have sent Gideon to a mad-house, and put Leonidas in a straight-jacket. Such a people would have treated the defenders of Thermopylae as demented, and shut up Caius Marcus in bedlam. Such a marrowless population as ours has become under the debaucheries of Slavery, would have struck the patriot's crown from the brow of Wallace, and recommended blisters and bleeding to the heroic Tell. Wallace was often and again desperately forgetful of his own life in defence of Scotland's freedom, as was Brown in striking for the American slave; and Tell's defiance of the Austrian tyrant, was as far above the appreciation of cowardly selfishness as was Brown's defiance of the Virginia pirates. Was Arnold Winkelried insane when he rushed to his death upon an army of spears, crying "make way for Liberty!" Are heroism and insanity synonyms in our American dictionary? Heaven help us! When our loftiest types of patriotism, our sublimest historical ideals of philanthropy, come to be treated as evidence of moonstruck madness. Posterity will owe everlasting thanks to John Brown for lifting up once more to the gaze of a nation grown fat and flabby on the garbage of lust and oppression, a true standard of heroic philanthropy, and each coming generation will pay its instalment of the debt. No wonder that the aiders and abettors of the huge, overshadowing and many-armed tyranny, which he grappled with in its own infernal den, should call him a mad man; but for those who profess a regard for him, and for human freedom, to join in the cruel slander, "is the unkindest cut of all."

Nor is it necessary to attribute Brown's deeds to the spirit of vengeance, invoked by the murder of his brave boys. That the barbarous cruelty from which he has suffered had its effect on intensifying his hatred of slavery, is doubtless true. But his own statement, that he had been contemplating a bold strike for the freedom of the slaves for ten years, proves that he had resolved upon his present course long before he, or his sons, ever set foot in Kansas. His entire procedure in this matter disproves the charge that he was prompted by an impulse of mad revenge, and shows that he was moved by the highest principles of philanthropy. His carefulness of the lives of unarmed persons—his humane and courteous treatment of his prisoners—his cool self-possession all through his trial—and especially his calm, dignified speech on receiving his sentence, all conspire to show that he was neither insane or actuated by vengeful passion; and we hope that the country has heard the last of John Brown's madness. The explanation of his conduct is perfectly natural and simple on its face. He believes the Declaration of Independence to be true, and the Bible to be a guide to human conduct, and acting upon the doctrines of both, he threw himself against the serried ranks of American oppression, and translated into heroic deeds the love of liberty and hatred of tyrants, with which he was inspired by both these forces acting upon his philanthropic and heroic soul. This age is too gross and sensual to appreciate his deeds, and so calls him mad; but the future will write his epitaph upon the hearts of a people freed from slavery, because he struck the first effectual blow.

Not only is it true that Brown's whole movement proves him perfectly sane and free from merely revengeful passion, but he has struck the bottom line of the philosophy which underlies the abolition movement. He has attacked slavery with the weapons precisely adapted to bring it to the death. Moral considerations have long since been exhausted upon slaveholders. It is in vain to reason with them. One may as well hunt bears with ethics and political economy for weapons, as to seek to "pluck the spoiled out of the hand of the oppressor" by the mere force of moral law. Slavery is a system of brute force. It shields itself behind *might,* rather than right. It must be met with its own weapons. Capt. Brown has initiated a new mode of carrying out the crusade of freedom, and his blow has sent dread and terror throughout the entire ranks of the piratical army of slavery. His daring deeds may cost him his life, but priceless as is the value of that life, the blow he has struck, will, in the end, prove to be worth its mighty cost. Like Samson, he has laid his hands upon the pillars of this great national temple of cruelty and blood, and when he falls, that temple will speedily crumble to its final doom, burying its denizens in its ruins.

SOURCE:

Frederick Douglass' Paper (November 1859), in *Frederick Douglass: Selected Speeches and Writings,* edited by Philip S. Foner and Yuval Taylor (Chicago: Lawrence Hill Books, 1999), pp. 374–375.

Document 8: LETTERS FROM PRISON

In the time before his sentencing and execution, John Brown converted many to his point of view in letters to family and friends that were swiftly published in dozens of newspapers across the land. In the prison letters below, he sets his violence alongside the realities of family life, biblical themes, and his wider political philosophies. The letters position his life and actions in the Judeo-Christian tradition. He compares himself to St. Peter on November 1, 1859, to Samson on November 15, to St. Paul on November 23, and to Moses on November 25. Brown claims divine authority for his raid on Harpers Ferry. He saw the potential value of his execution to the abolitionist cause, writing on November 30: "in no other possible way could I be used to so much advance the cause of God."

Charlestown, Jefferson Co., Va.,
31st. Oct. 1859

My dear Wife, and Children every one

I suppose you have learned before this by the newspapers that two weeks ago today we were fighting for our lives at Harpers Ferry: that during the fight Watson was mortally wounded; Oliver killed, Wm Thompson killed, & Dauphin slightly wounded. That on the following day I was taken prisoner immediately after which I received several Sabre cuts in my head; & Bayonet stabs in my body. As nearly as I can learn Watson died of his wound on Wednesday the 2d or on Thursday the 3d day after I was taken. Dauphin was killed when I was taken; & Anderson I suppose also. I have since been tried, & found guilty of treason, &c; and of murder in the first degree. I have not yet received my sentence. No others of the company with whom you were acquainted were so far as *I can learn* either killed or taken. Under all these terrible calamities; I feel quite cheerful in the assurance that God reigns; & will overrule all for his glory; & the best possible good. I feel *no* consciousness of *guilt* in the matter: nor even mortification on account of my imprisonment; & irons; & I feel perfectly assured that very soon no member of my family will feel any possible disposition to "blush on my account." Already dear friends at a distance with kindest sympathy are cheering me with the assurance that *posterity* at least: will do me justice. I shall commend you all together with my beloved; but bereaved daughters in law to their sympathies which I have no doubt will soon reach you. I also commend you all to him "whose mercy endureth forever": to the God of my *fathers* "whose I am; & whom I serve." "He will never leave you or forsake you" unless you forsake him. Finally my dearly beloved be of good comfort. Be as it has been consistent with the holy religion of Jesus Christ in which I remain a most firm, & humble believer. Never forget the poor nor think any thing you bestow on them to be lost, to you even though they may be as *black* as Ebedmelch, the Ethiopian eunuch one to whom Phillip preached Christ. Be sure to entertain strangers for thereby some have—"Remember them that are in bonds as bound with them." I am in charge of a jailor *like* the one who took charge of "Paul & Silas;" & you may rest assured that both *kind hearts* and *kind faces* are more or less about me: whilst thousands are thirsting for my blood. "These *light* afflictions which are but *for a moment* shall work out for us a far *more exceeding &* eternal weight of glory." I hope to be able to write you again. My wounds are doing well. Copy this & send it to your sorrow stricken brothers, *Ruth*; to comfort them. Write me a few words in regard to the welfare of all. God Almighty bless you all: & make you "joyful in the midst of all your tribulations." Write to John Brown, Charlestown, Jefferson Co, Va, care of Capt John Avis

Your Affectionate Husband, & Father. John Brown Nov. 3d 1859

P.S. Yesterday Nov 2d I was sentenced to be hanged on 2 Decem next. Do not grieve on my account. I am still quite cheerful.

Charlestown, Jefferson County, Va.,
Nov. 1, 1859.

My Dear Friend E.B. of R.I.,

Your most cheering letter of the 27th of October is received; and may the Lord reward you a thousandfold for the kind feeling you express toward me; but more especially for your fidelity to the "poor that cry, and those that have no help." For this I am a prisoner in bonds. It is solely my own fault, in a military point of view, that we met with our disaster. I mean that I mingled with our prisoners and so far sympathized with them and their families that I neglected my duty in other respects. But God's will, not mine, be done.

You know that Christ once armed Peter. So also in my case I think he put a sword into my hand, and there continued it so long as he saw best, and then kindly took it from me. I mean when I first went to Kansas. I wish you could know with what cheerfulness I am now wielding the "sword of the Spirit" on the right hand and on the left. I bless God that it proves "mighty to the pulling down of strongholds." I always loved my Quaker friends, and I commend to their kind regard my poor bereaved widowed wife and my daughters and daughters-in-law, whose husbands fell at my side. One is a mother and the other likely to become so soon. They, as well as my own sorrow-stricken daughters, are left very poor, and have much greater need of sympathy than I, who, through Infinite Grace and the kindness of strangers, am "joyful in all my tribulations."

Dear Sister, write them at North Elba, Essex County, N.Y., to comfort their sad hearts. Direct to Mary A. Brown, wife of John Brown. There is also another—a widow, wife of Thompson, who fell with my poor boys in the affair at Harper's Ferry—at the same place.

I do not feel conscious of guilt in taking up arms; and had it been in behalf of the rich and powerful, the intelligent, the great (as men count greatness), or those who form enactments to suit themselves and corrupt others, or some of their friends, that I interfered, suffered, sacrificed, and fell, it would have been doing very well. But enough of this. These light afflictions, which endure for a moment, shall but work for me "a far more exceeding and eternal weight of glory." I would be very grateful for another letter from you. My wounds are healing. Farewell. God will surely attend to his own cause in the best possible way and time, and he will not forget the work of his own hands.

Your friend, John Brown.

Charlestown, Jefferson County, Va.,
Nov. 8, 1859.

Dear Wife and Children, Every One,

I will begin by saying that I have in some degree recovered from my wounds, but that I am quite weak in my back and sore about my left kidney. My appetite has been quite good for most of the time since I was hurt. I am supplied with almost everything I could desire to make me comfortable, and the little I do lack (some articles of clothing which I lost) I may perhaps soon get again. I am, besides, quite cheerful, having (as I trust) "the peace of God, which passeth all understanding," to "rule in my heart," and the testimony (in some degree) of a good conscience that I have not lived altogether in vain. I can trust God with both the time and the manner of my death, believing, as I now do, that for me at this time to seal my testimony for God and humanity with my blood will do vastly more toward advancing the cause I have earnestly endeavored to promote, than all I have done in my life before. I beg of you all meekly and quietly to submit to this, not feeling yourselves in the least *degraded* on the account. Remember, dear wife and children all, that Jesus of Nazareth suffered a most excruciating death on the cross as a felon, under the most aggravating circumstances. Think also of the prophets and apostles and Christians of former days, who went through greater tribulations than you or I, and try to be reconciled. May God Almighty comfort all your hearts, and soon wipe away all tears from your eyes! To him be endless praise! Think, too, of the crushed millions who "have no comforter." I charge you all never in your trials to forget the griefs "of the poor that cry, and of those that have none to help them." I wrote most earnestly to my dear and afflicted wife not to come on for the present, at any rate. I will now give her reasons for doing so. First, it would use up all the scanty means she has, or is at all likely to have, to make herself and children comfortable hereafter. For let me tell you that the sympathy that is now aroused in your behalf may not always follow you. There is but little more of the romantic about helping poor widows and their children than there is about trying to relieve poor "niggers." Again, the little comfort it might afford us to meet again would be dearly bought by the pains of a final separation. We must part; and I feel assured for us to meet under such dreadful circumstances would only add to our distress. If she comes on here, she must be only a gazing-stock throughout the whole journey, to be remarked upon in every look, word, and action, and by all sorts of creatures, and by all sorts of papers, throughout the whole country. Again, it is my most decided judgment that in quietly and submissively staying at home vastly more of generous sympathy will reach her, without such dreadful sacrifice of feeling as she must put up with if she comes on. The visits of one or two female friends that have come on her have produced great excitement, which is very annoying; and they cannot possibly do me any good. Oh, Mary! do not come, but patiently wait for the meeting of those who love God and their fellow-men, where no separation must follow. "They shall go no more out forever." I greatly long to hear from some one of you, and to learn anything that in any way affects your welfare. I sent you ten dollars the other day; did you get it? I have also endeavored to stir up Christian friends to visit and write to you in your deep affliction. I have no doubt that some of them, at least, will heed the call. Write to me, care of Captain John Avis, Charlestown, Jefferson County, Virginia.

"Finally, my beloved, be of good comfort." May all your names be "written in the Lamb's book of life!"—may you all have the purifying and sustaining influence of the Christian religion!—is the earnest prayer of

Your affectionate husband and father, John Brown

P.S.—I cannot remember a night so dark as to have hindered the coming day, nor a storm so furious and dreadful as to prevent the return of warm sunshine and a cloudless sky. But, beloved ones, do remember that this is not your rest,—that in this world you have no abiding place or continuing city. To God and his infinite mercy I always commend you.

—∽—

Charlestown, Jefferson County, Va.,
Nov. 12, 1859.

Dear Brother Jeremiah,

Your kind letter of the 9th inst. is received, and also one from Mr. Tilden; for both of which I am greatly obliged.

You inquire, "Can I do anything for you or your family?" I would answer that my sons, as well as my wife and daughters, are all very poor; and that anything that may hereafter be due me from my father's estate I wish paid to them, as I will endeavor hereafter to describe, without legal formalities to consume it all. One of my boys has been so entirely used up as very likely to be in want of comfortable clothing for winter. I have, through the kindness of friends, fifteen dollars to send him, which I will remit shortly. If you know where to reach him, please send him that amount at once, as I shall remit the same to you by a safe conveyance. If I had a plain statement from Mr. Thompson of the state of my accounts with the estate of my father, I should then better know what to say about that matter. As it is, I have not the least memorandum left me to refer to. If Mr. Thompson will make me a statement, and charge my dividend fully for his trouble, I would be greatly obliged to him. In that case you can send me any remarks of your own. I am gaining in health slowly, and am quite cheerful in view of my approaching end,—being fully persuaded that I am worth inconceivably more to hang than for any other purpose. God Almighty bless and save you all!

Your affectionate brother, John Brown.

November 13.

P.S. Say to my poor boys never to grieve for one moment on my account; and should many of you live to see the time when you will not blush to own your relation to Old John Brown, it will not be more strange than many things that have happened. I feel a thousand times more on account of my sorrowing friends than on my own account. So far as I am concerned, I "count it all joy." "I have fought the good fight," and have, as I trust, "finished my course." Please show this to any of my family that you may see. My love to all; and may God, in his infinite mercy, for Christ's sake, bless and save you all!

—∽—

Charlestown, Jefferson Co. Va,
15th. Nov. 1859.
Rev. H L Vaill

My Dear Steadfast Friend

Your most *kind & most welcome* letter of the 8th inst reached me in due time. *I am very grateful* for all the good feeling you express & also for the kind counsels you give together—with your prayers in my behalf. Allow me here to say notwithstanding "my soul is amongst lions," still I believe that "God in very deed is with me." You will not therefore feel surprised when I tell you that I am "joyful in all my tribulations": that I do not feel condemned of Him whose judgment is just; nor of my own conscience. Nor do I feel degraded by my imprisonment, my chains or prospect of the Gallows. I have not only been *(though utterly unworthy)* permitted to suffer affliction with God's people," but have also had *a great many rare* opportunities for "preaching *righteousness* in the great congregation." I trust it will not all be lost. *The jailor* (in whose charge I am) *& his family; & assistants* have all been most kind: & notwithstanding he was one of the bravest of all who *fought me:* he is *now* being abused for humanity. So far as my observation goes; *none but brave* men: are likely to be *humane;* to a fallen foe. "Cowards *prove* their *courage* by their *ferocity.*" It may be done in that way with but little risk. I wish I could write you about a few only of the interesting times, I here experience with different classes of men; *clergymen* among others. Christ the great Captain of *liberty;* as well as of salvation; & who began his mission, as foretold of him; by proclaiming it, *saw fit* to take from me a sword of steel after I had carried it for a time but he has put another in my hand ("The sword of the Spirit;") & I pray God to make me a faithful soldier wherever he may send me, not less on the scaffold, than when surrounded by the warmest sympathizers. My dear old friend I do assure you I have not forgotten our last meeting nor our retrospective look over the route by which God had then led us; & I bless his name that he has again enabled me to hear your words of cheering; & comfort, at a time when I at least am on the "brink of Jordan." See Bunyan's Pilgrim. God in Infinite mercy grant us *soon* another meeting on the opposite shore. I have often passed under the rod of him whom I *call my* Father; & certainly no son ever needed it oftener; & yet I have enjoyed much of life, as I was enabled to discover the secret of this; somewhat early. It has been in making the prosperity, & the happiness of others *my own:* so that really I have had a great deal of prosperity. I am very prosperous still; & looking forward to a time when "peace on Earth & good will to *men* shall every where prevail." I have no murmuring thoughts of *envious* feelings to fret my mind. "I'll praise my *maker* with my *breath.*" I am *an unworthy* nephew of Deacon John; & I loved him much; & in view of the many choice friends *I have had* here I am led the more earnestly to pray; "gather *not* my soul with the *unrighteous.*" Your assurance of the earnest sympathy of the friends in my native land is very grateful to my feelings; & allow me to say a word of comfort to them. As I believe most firmly that God reigns; I cannot believe that any thing I have *done suffered or may yet suffer will be lost;* to the *cause of God or of humanity:* & before I began my work at Harpers Ferry; I felt assured that in the *worst event;* it would certainly PAY. I often expressed that belief; & I can now see no possible cause to alter my mind. I am not as yet in the *main* at all disappointed. I have been *a good deal* disappointed as it regards *myself* in not keeping up to *my own plans;* but I now feel entirely reconciled to that even: for Gods plan, was Infinitely better; *no doubt:* or I should have kept to my own. Had Samson kept to his *determination* of not telling Delilah wherein his great strength lay; he would probably have never overturned the house. I did not tell Delilah; but I was induced to act very *contrary* to my *better judgment:* & I have lost my two noble boys; & *other friends, if not my two eyes.*

But "Gods will not *mine* be done." I feel a comfortable hope that like the *erring servant* of whom I have just been writing *even I* may (through Infinite mercy in Christ Jesus) yet "die in faith." As to both the time, & manner of my death: I have but very little trouble on that score; *& am able* to be (as you exhort) "of good cheer." I send through you my best wishes to Mrs. Woodruff & her son George; & to all dear friends. May the God of the *poor* and *oppressed;* be the God & Savior of you all.

Farewell till we "*meet again.*"

Your friend in truth, John Brown

Charlestown, Jefferson Co. Va.
17th Nov. 1859
J B Musgrave Esqr

My Dear Young Friend

I have just received your most kind; & welcome letter of the 15th inst but did not get any other from you. I am under many obligations *to you & to your Father* for all the kindness you have shown me, especially since my disaster. *May God* & your own consciousness ever be your rewarders. Tell your Father that I am quite cheerful that I do not feel myself in the least degraded by my imprisonment, my chain, or the *near prospect* of the Gallows. *Men* cannot *imprison,* or *chain;* or *hang* the *soul.* I go joyfully in behalf of millions that "have no rights" that this "great, & glorious"; "this Christian Republic," "is bound to respect." Strange *change in morals political;* as well as *Christian;* since 1776. I look forward to *other changes* to take place *in "Gods good time;"* fully believing that "the fashion of this world passeth away." (I am unable *now* to tell you where my friend is; that you inquire after. Perhaps my Wife who I suppose is still with Mrs. Spring, may have some information of him. I think it quite uncertain however.) Farewell; may God abundantly bless you all.

    Your Friend, John Brown

Jail, Charlestown, Wednesday,
Nov. 23, 1859
Rev. McFarland,

Dear Friend:

Although you write to me as a stranger, the spirit you show towards me and the cause for which I am in bonds, makes me feel towards you as a dear friend. I would be glad to have you, or any of my liberty-loving ministerial friends here, to talk and pray with me. I am not a stranger to the way of salvation by Christ. From my youth I have studied much on that subject, and at one time hoped to be a minister myself; but God had another work for me to do. To me it is given in behalf of Christ, not only to believe on him, but also to *suffer* for his sake. But while I trust that I have some experimental and saving knowledge of religion, it would be a great pleasure to me to have some one better qualified than myself to lead my mind in prayer and meditation, now that my time is so near a close. You may wonder, are there no ministers of the gospel here? I answer, No. There are no ministers of *Christ* here. These ministers who profess to be Christian, and hold slaves or advocate slavery, I cannot abide them. My knees will not bend in prayer with them while their hands are stained with the blood of souls. The subject you mention as having been preaching on, the day before you wrote to me, is one which I have often thought of since my imprisonment. I think I feel as happy as Paul did when he lay in prison. He knew if they killed him it would greatly advance the cause of Christ; that was the reason he rejoiced so. On that same ground "I do rejoice, yea, and will rejoice." Let them hang me; I forgive them, and may God forgive them, for they know not what they do. I have no regret for the transaction for which I am condemned. I went against the laws of men, it is true; but "whether it be right to obey *God* or *men,* judge ye." Christ told me to remember them that are in bonds, as *bound with them,* to do towards them as I would wish them to do towards me in similar circumstances. My conscience bade me do that. I tried to do it, but failed. Therefore I have no regret on that score. I have no sorrow either as to the result, only for my poor wife and children. They have suffered much, and it is hard to leave them uncared for. But God will be a husband to the widow, and a father to the fatherless.

I have frequently been in Wooster; and if any of my old friends from Akron are there, you can show them this letter. I have but a few more days, and I feel anxious to be away, "where the wicked cease from troubling, and the weary are at rest." Farewell.

    Your friend, and the friend of all friends of liberty, John Brown.

Charlestown, Prison, Jefferson Co. Va.
30th Nov. 1859.

My Dearly beloved Wife, Sons: & Daughters, *every one*

As I now begin what is probably the last letter I shall ever write to any of you; I conclude to write you all at the same time. I will mention some little matters particularly applicable to little property concerns in another place. I yesterday received a letter from my wife from near Philadelphia: dated Nov 27th, by which it would seem that she has about given up the idea of seeing me again. I had written her to come on; if *she* felt equal to the undertaking; but I do not know as she will get my letter in time. It was on her *own account chiefly* that I asked her to stay *back* at first. I had a most strong desire to see her again; but there appeared to be very serious objections; & should we never meet in *this life;* I trust she will in the end be satisfied it was *for the best at least;* if not most for her comfort. I enclosed in my last letter to her a Draft of $50, Fifty Dollars from John Jay made payable to her order. I have now another to send her from my excellent old friend Edward Harris of Woonsocket Rhode Island for $100, One Hundred Dollars; which I shall *also make payable to her* order. I am writing the hour of my public *murder* with great composure of mind, & cheerfulness; feeling the strongest assurance that in no other possible way could I be used to so much advance the cause of God; & of humanity; & that nothing that either I or all my family have sacrificed or suffered: *will be lost.* The reflection that a *wise, & merciful, as well as Just, & holy God:* rules not only the affairs of *this world;* but of all worlds; is a rock to set our feet upon; under all circumstances; *even* those more severely *trying ones:* into which our own follies; & [w]rongs have placed us. I have now no doubt but that our seeming *disaster:* will ultimately result in the most *glorious success.* So my dear *shattered; & broken* family; be of good cheer; & believe & trust in God; "with all your heart; & with all your soul;" for *he* doeth *All things well."* Do not feel ashamed on my account; nor *for one moment* despair of the cause; or grow *weary* of *well doing.* I bless God; I never felt stronger confidence in the certain & near approach of a *bright Morning; & glorious day;* than I have felt; & do now feel; since my confinement here. I am endeavoring to "return" like a "poor Prodigal" *as I am;* to my Father: against whom I have *always* sinned: *in the hope;* that he may kindly, & forgivingly "meet me: though; *a verry great way off."* Oh my dear Wife & Children would "to God" you could know how I have been "traveling in birth for you" all; that no one of you "may fail of the grace of God, through Jesus Christ:" that no one of you may be blind to the truth: & glorious "light of *his* word;" in which Life; & Immortality; are brought to light." I beseech you *every one* to make the bible your *daily & nightly study;* with a *childlike honest, candid, teachable spirit:* out of love and respect for your Husband; & Father: & I beseech *the God* of *my Fathers;* to open all your eyes to a discovery of *the truth.* You *cannot imagine* how much *you* may *soon need* the consolations of the Christian religion.

Circumstances like my own; for more than a month past; convince me beyond *all doubt* of our great need: of something more to rest our hopes on; than merely our own vague theories framed up, while our *prejudices* are excited; *or* our *Vanity* worked up to its highest pitch. Or do not trust your eternal all upon the boisterous Ocean, without *even a Helm;* or *Compass* to *aid* you in steering. I do *not ask any* of you; to throw *away your reason:* I only *ask* you, to make a candid, & sober *use of your reason:* My dear younger children will you listen to this last poor admonition of one who can *only* love you? Oh be determined at once to give your whole hearts to God; & let *nothing shake; or alter;* that resolution. You need have no fear *of* REGRETTING *it.* Do not be in vain; and thoughtless: but *sober minded.* And let me entreat you all to love *the whole remnant* or our once great family: "with a pure *heart fervently."* Try to *build again:* your broken walls: & to make *the utmost* of every *stone* that is left. Nothing can so tend to make life a blessing as the consciousness that you *love: & are beloved:* & "love ye the stranger" *still.* It is a ground of the utmost comfort to *my mind:* to know that so many of you as have had *the opportunity;* have given full proof of your fidelity to the great family of man. *Be faithful* until *death.* From the exercise of habitual love to man: *it cannot* be very *hard:* to *learn to love* his *maker.* I must *yet* insert a reason for my firm belief in the Divine inspiration of the Bible: notwithstanding I am (perhaps naturally) skeptical. (certainly not, *credulous.*) I wish you all to consider *it most thoroughly;* when you read that blessed book; & see whether you *can not* discover such evidence yourselves. It is the purity of *heart, feeling, or motive:* as well as *word, & action* which is every where insisted on; that distinguish it from *all other teachings;* that *commends it*

to *my conscience:* whether *my heart* be "willing, & obedient" *or not.* The inducements that it holds out; are another reason *of my conviction* or its *truth: & genuineness;* that I cannot here *omit;* in this my *last argument,* for the Bible *Eternal life:* is that my soul *is "panting after"* this moment. I mention this; as reason for endeavoring to leave a valuable copy of the Bible to be carefully *preserved* in remembrance of *me:* to so many of my posterity; *instead* of some *other* thing: of equal *cost.* I beseech you all to live in habitual contentment with verry *moderate* circumstances: & gains, of *worldly store:* & most earnestly to teach this: to your *children; & children's children;* after you: by *example: as well;* as precept. Be determined to know by experience *as soon as may be:* whether Bible instruction is of *Divine origin* or not; which says; "Owe no man anything but to love one another." John Rogers wrote to his children, "Abhor that arrant whore of Rome." John Brown writes to his children to abhor with *undying hatred,* also: that "sum of all vilanies;" Slavery. *Remember* that "he that is *slow* to *anger* is *better* than the mighty: and he that ruleth his *spirit;* than he that taketh a city." Remember also: *that* "they that be *wise* shall *shine:* and they that *turn* many to *righteousness:* as the stars forever; & ever." And now dearly beloved *Farewell* To God & the word of his grace I commend you all.

Your Affectionate Husband & Father, John Brown

Charlestown, Va,
2d, December, 1859.

I John Brown am now quite certain that the crimes of this guilty land: will never be purged away but with Blood. I had as I now think; vainly flattered myself that without *very much* bloodshed; it might be done.

Source:

Franklin B. Sanborn. *The Life and Letters of John Brown, Liberator of Kansas and Martyr of Virginia* (Boston: Roberts, 1891), pp. 579–580, 582–583, 585–591, 593, 598–599, 613–615, 620.

Document 9: Brown of Osawatomie

Soon after John Brown's execution on December 2, 1859, a story circulated that he had stopped on his way to the gallows to kiss the child of a slave woman. Though untrue, the story was reported by the New York Tribune *on December 6, 1859, and then depicted by poets, commentators, and painters in the years that followed. Wendell Phillips spoke in admiring tones of the kiss in his eulogy at Brown's funeral, Lydia Maria Child composed the poem "John Brown and the Colored Child," and Frederick Douglass remembered the incident in a speech of 1881. The poet John Greenleaf Whittier, a pacifist Quaker and a gradualist abolitionist, was horrified by Brown's violent raid on Harpers Ferry, but impressed by the kiss. His poem "Brown of Osawatomie," reported here, cemented the story that was fast becoming a national myth.*

John Brown of Osawatomie spake on his dying day:
"I will not have to shrive my soul a priest in Slavery's pay;
But let some poor slave-mother whom I have striven to free,
With her children, from the gallows-stair put up a prayer for me!"

John Brown of Osawatomie, they led him out to die;
And lo! a poor slave-mother with her little child pressed nigh;
Then the bold, blue eye grew tender, and the old harsh face grew mild,
As he stooped between the jeering ranks and kissed the negro's child!

The shadows of his stormy life that moment fell apart,
And they who blamed the bloody hand forgave the loving heart;
That kiss from all its guilty means redeemed the good intent,
And round the grisly fighter's hair the martyr's aureole bent!

Perish with him the folly that seeks through evil good!
Long live the generous purpose unstained with human blood!
Not the raid of midnight terror, but the thought which underlies;
Not the borderer's pride of daring, but the Christian's sacrifice.

Nevermore may yon Blue Ridges the Northern rifle hear,
Nor see the light of blazing homes flash on the negro's spear;
But let the free-winged angel Truth their guarded passes scale,
To teach that right is more than might, and justice more than mail!

So vainly shall Virginia set her battle in array;
In vain her trampling squadrons knead the winter snow with clay!
She may strike the pouncing eagle, but she dares not harm the dove;
And every gate she bars to Hate shall open wide to Love!

SOURCE:

James Redpath. *Echoes of Harpers Ferry* (Boston: Thayer & Eldridge), 1860, pp. 303–304.

Document 10: Nat Turner's Rebellion

In 1831, Nat Turner led seventy other slaves in a rebellion in Southampton County, Virginia. The rampage left dead sixty whites and a hundred blacks. After John Brown's raid in 1859, comparisons between the two men became popular: the abolitionist Wendell Phillips compared Turner and Brown on November 1, 1859, explaining that if Virginia was made anxious by Turner, it would be even more scared by Brown. Frederick Douglass noted in October 1859 that the South saw Brown's raid as a repetition of the Turner insurrection. In December 1859 an anonymous article, possibly written by the black intellectual James McCune Smith, appeared in Anglo-African Magazine. *This article places Brown's raid against a backdrop of more extreme violence. If the country did not respond to Brown's methods, Turner's would take over, it declared. The article was printed alongside Turner's public confession so that readers could compare the two men. In fact, Brown admired Turner as much as he admired George Washington, and both rebels were at the forefront of his mind as he planned his own violent insurrection.*

There are two reasons why we present our readers with the "Confessions of Nat Turner." First, to place upon record this most remarkable episode in the history of human slavery, which proves to the philosophic observer that in the midst of this most perfectly contrived and apparently secure system of slavery, humanity will out, and engender from its bosom forces that will contend against oppression, however unsuccessfully; and secondly, that the two methods of Nat Turner and of John Brown may be compared. The one is the mode in which the slave seeks freedom for his fellows, and the other mode in which the white man seeks to set the slave free. There are many points of similarity between these two men; they were both idealists; both governed by their views of the teachings of the Bible; both had harbored for years the purpose to which they gave up their lives; both felt themselves swayed as by some divine, or at least, spiritual impulse; the one seeking in the air, the earth, and the heavens for signs which came at last; and the other, obeying impulses which he believes to have been foreordained from the eternal past; both cool, calm, and heroic in prison and in the prospect of inevitable death; both confess with childlike frankness and simplicity the object they had in view the pure and simple emancipation of their fellow men; both win from the judges who sentenced them, expressions of deep sympathy—and here the parallel ceases. Nat Turner's terrible logic could only see the enfranchisement of one race compassed by the extirpation of the other; and he followed his gory syllogism with rude exactitude. John Brown, believing that the freedom of the enthralled could only be effected by placing them on an equality with the enslavers, and unable in the very effort at emancipation to tyrannize himself, is moved with compassion for tyrants, as well as slaves, and seeks to extirpate this formidable cancer, without spilling one drop of Christian blood.

These two narratives present a fearful choice to the slaveholders, nay, to this great nation—which of the two modes of emancipation shall take place? The method of Nat Turner, or the method of John Brown?

Emancipation must take place, and soon. There can be no long delay in the choice of methods. If John Brown's be not soon adopted by the free North, then Nat Turner's will be by the enslaved South.

Had the order of events been reversed—had Nat Turner been in John Brown's place at the head of these twenty-one men, governed by his inexorable logic and cool daring, the soil of Virginia and Maryland and the far South would by this time be drenched in the blood and the wild and sanguinary course of these men, no earthly power could stay.

The course which the South is now frantically pursuing will engender in its bosom and nurse into maturity a hundred Nat Turners, whom Virginia is infinitely less able to resist in 1860, than she was in 1831.

So, people of the South, people of the North! Men and brethren, choose ye which method of emancipation you prefer—Nat Turner's or John Brown's?

SOURCE:

Anglo-African Magazine (December 31, 1859): 225.

BIBLIOGRAPHY

Abels, Jules. *Man on Fire: John Brown and the Cause of Liberty*. New York: Macmillan, 1971. Part historical scholarship, part popular biography, Abels's book includes otherwise neglected information on Brown's family after 1859.

Anderson, Osborne P. *A Voice from Harpers Ferry*. Boston: Printed for the author, 1861. As the only man left alive who was at Harpers Ferry throughout the whole raid, Anderson recounts the events of October 1859.

Benet, Stephen Vincent. *John Brown's Body*. New York: Farrar & Rinehart, 1928. This long narrative poem identifies Brown's raid on Harpers Ferry as the cause of the Civil War.

Blight, David W. "John Brown: Triumphant Failure," *American Prospect*, vol. 11 (March 13, 2000): 44–45. In a review of *John Brown's Holy War*, a documentary directed by Robert Kenner and written by Ken Chowder that aired on the public television series *The American Experience* on February 28, 2002, Blight examines the meaning of Brown's martyrdom.

Boyer, Richard. *The Legend of John Brown*. New York: Knopf, 1973. Boyer considers Brown's early life and positions him as a man of his times, rather than as an isolated fanatic.

Carton, Evan. *Patriotic Treason: John Brown and the Soul of America*. New York: Free Press, 2006—Carton argues that Brown's cross-racial empathy partially explains his violent actions.

DeCaro, Louis A. *Fire from the Midst of You: A Religious Life of John Brown*. New York: New York University Press, 2002. DeCaro argues for Brown's religious integrity and sets him in an evangelical tradition that decried pacifism, as well as in a tradition of Puritan abolitionism.

Douglass, Frederick. "John Brown, Speech Delivered at Storer College, Harper's Ferry, West Virginia, May 30, 1881," in *Frederick Douglass: Selected Speeches and Writings*, edited by Philip S. Foner and Yuval Taylor. Chicago: Lawrence Hill Books, 1999, pp. 633–649. Douglass pays tribute to Brown as a martyr whose actions marked the beginning of the end of slavery.

———. *The Life and Times of Frederick Douglass*, in *Douglass Autobiographies*. New York: Library of America, 1996 [1881]—Douglass's third autobiography recounts his associations, activism, and travels during the antebellum era, the Civil War, Reconstruction and the Gilded Age.

Furnas, J. C. *The Road to Harpers Ferry.* New York: Sloane, 1959. Furnas argues that Brown was a deviant and that he was mentally disturbed.

Keller, Allan. *Thunder at Harpers Ferry.* Englewood Cliffs, N.J.: Prentice-Hall, 1958. Keller provides a compelling account of the Harpers Ferry raid hour-by-hour.

Malin, James C. *John Brown and the Legend of Fifty-Six.* Philadelphia: American Philosophical Society, 1942. Portraying Brown unsympathetically, Malin focuses entirely on Brown's activities in Kansas in 1856, including the Pottawatomie murders.

Nudelman, Franny. *John Brown's Body: Slavery, Violence, and the Culture of War.* Chapel Hill: University of North Carolina Press, 2004. Comparing martyred soldiers with brutalized slaves, Nudelman argues that responses to wartime death need to be understood in the context of violence against slaves during the antebellum era and that Brown's death helped create a self-sacrificial nationalism during the Civil War.

Oates, Stephen B. *To Purge This Land with Blood: A Biography of John Brown.* New York: Harper & Row, 1970. Oates focuses on Brown's activities in Kansas and the Harpers Ferry raid, setting his actions in their cultural context.

Quarles, Benjamin. *Allies for Freedom: Blacks and John Brown.* New York: Oxford University Press, 1974. Quarles traces Brown's life as an abolitionist and examines black attitudes toward Brown from the 1850s into the 1960s.

Redpath, James, ed. *Echoes of Harpers Ferry.* New York: Arno, 1969 [1860]. A collection of antislavery papers, speeches, and poems commemorative of Brown, which also contains reprints of letters addressed to Brown while he was in prison at Charlestown.

Reynolds, David S. *John Brown, Abolitionist: The Man Who Killed Slavery, Sparked the Civil War, and Seeded Civil Rights.* New York: Knopf, 2005. Reynolds argues that if Brown was a terrorist, he was right to terrorize a slave system that showed no signs of responding to peaceful tactics, and that far from insane, Brown was a deeply religious, if overconfident, reformer.

Rossbach, Jeffrey S. *Ambivalent Conspirators: John Brown, the Secret Six, and a Theory of Slave Violence.* Philadelphia: University of Pennsylvania Press, 1982. The author focuses on the six abolitionists who conspired with Brown and furnished him arms and money for the purpose of destroying slavery by violent means.

Sanborn, Franklin B. *Recollections of Seventy Years.* Boston: R. G. Badger, 1909. Reminiscences of Sanborn's life in Concord and of the national politics that permeated the town.

———, ed. *The Life and Letters of John Brown, Liberator of Kansas, and Martyr of Virginia.* Boston: Roberts, 1885. Brown's friend and supporter offers an eyewitness view of Brown's life, and describes the process by which Brown was made into a mythical figure.

Stauffer, John. *The Black Hearts of Men: Radical Abolitionists and the Transformation of Race.* Cambridge, Mass.: Harvard University Press, 2002. Stauffer braids together Brown's life with the stories of white philanthropist Gerrit Smith, former slave Frederick Douglass, and black intellectual James McCune Smith.

Stavis, Barrie. *John Brown: The Sword and the Word.* South Brunswick, N.J.: A. S. Barnes, 1970. Defending Brown's character and actions, Stavis argues that he acted rationally, if autocratically.

Villard, Oswald Garrison. *John Brown, 1800–1859: A Biography Fifty Years After.* Boston: Houghton Mifflin, 1910. The most comprehensive study of Brown's career and the spectrum of his political attitudes, including interviews with eyewitnesses.

Walker, David. *Appeal to the Coloured Citizens of the World,* edited by Peter P. Hinks. University Park: Pennsylvania State University Press, 2000 [1829]. One of America's most provocative political documents, Walker's *Appeal* challenges slaves to cast off their chains.

Warren, Robert Penn. *John Brown: The Making of a Martyr.* New York: Payson & Clarke, 1929. Warren tries to debunk the myths surrounding Brown, terming him a self-glorifying fanatic.

Wilson, Hill Peebles. *John Brown, Soldier of Fortune: A Critique.* Lawrence, Kans.: Wilson, 1913. Wilson decries the image of Brown as a martyr or saint, calling him a mere pirate.

~ 8 ~

Temperance: Religion, Politics, and Ethnic Groups

America had a drinking problem in the decades leading up to the Civil War—at least, in 1833 that was the message that reformers began to send out through churches and media. At its root, the Temperance campaign was designed to enforce moderation, to ensure that Americans would "temper" their consumption of alcohol.

The Temperance Movement reflected a trend taking place with other social issues as well. The abolition movement, utopian experiments with communal living, and investigations into treatment of the imprisoned and insane all raised the question: Which behaviors remained subject to personal choice, and when was it appropriate for the government to regulate behavior? From the formation of the first temperance society to the repeal of Prohibition, the pivotal issues for temperance reformers were, on one hand, how to get individuals to curb alcohol consumption, and, on the other hand, whether it was appropriate for government to regulate personal consumption of alcoholic beverages.

The Temperance Movement at times led to strange alliances and occasionally resulted in bitter contests. Religious denominations disagreed over the core problem of alcohol; Nativists and ethnic groups clashed over alcohol-related cultural practices; Northerners and Southerners bitterly disagreed about how much power government should have to legislate individual behavior; and members of different socio-economic classes saw the "proper" use of alcohol as an indicator of social stature. These conflicts were complicated by the question of whether women should be allowed to participate in the political process, especially by voting.

Before Americans even began discussing how to moderate alcohol consumption, reformers examined public views on alcohol intake. At the end of the American Revolution, Dr. Benjamin Rush started urging Americans to see their habits of alcohol consumption as excessive. His perspective gained a following after the Whiskey Rebellion, when the new nation had to put down the first internal uprising against the federal government. In this conflict, the new federal government attempted to collect excise taxes on whiskey, which was largely a product of the western part of the United States. The tax struck at a core product of Americans on the frontier, who imbibed at almost every social or political event, used whiskey as currency on the frontier, and relied on selling whiskey because it cost less to ship than wagons full of grain. As frontiersmen rebelled against the excise tax by tormenting tax collectors and rising up in armed mobs, President George Washington sent troops to western Pennsylvania to put down the rebellion. The event caused Americans to recognize the integral role that hard drink played in daily life, and it caused a shift toward the realization that alcohol dependence was a problem facing the young country.

On an individual level, in the early part of the nineteenth century, Americans changed their attitude about alcohol abuse from regarding it as a sin to seeing it as a personal vice and a social problem. Protestant church leaders were the first to advocate "tempering" the consumption of alcohol. By 1826 the Temperance Movement began to take shape with the founding of the American Temperance Society, which produced the American Temperance Union. These two groups worked with Protestant evangelicals to persuade the groups' members to make a personal commitment to temperance by taking a pledge, or making a public promise to stay "dry."

During the late antebellum period, relationships between the organizations and religious leaders became strained, because the organizations wanted churches to do more to enforce temperance principles among church members. Religious leaders felt concern over being allied with organizations that had begun to adopt political activity. Religious leaders did not all support Prohibition legislation, in part because of disagreement over whether wine should be banned, especially in light of its role in the liturgy of some Christian sects. Some religious leaders also felt that concentrating on the vice of intemperance would detract from a balanced rebuke against all sin. While moral support for temperance and admonitions against "demon rum" remained a source of strength for the Temperance Movement throughout its existence, temperance organizations eventually began to seek a political answer to the alcohol problem in America.

The debate over a national political Temperance Movement revealed class division and religious transformations in the nineteenth century. Early temperance was supported by elites in American society, politically represented by Federalists and religiously represented by Congregationalists and Presbyterians, part of the New England church establishment. During the Second Great Awakening, revivalism swept through the country and the Baptist and Methodist sects grew. These and other new evangelical religions, generally connected with people in the lower classes or on the frontier, took up the temperance crusade. The evangelical churches supported government control through legislative measures, while the earlier religious support for temperance by elites had advocated individual responsibility through education and personal reform. Older denominations remained more hesitant than the evangelical churches to enforce temperance through political action.

Though the American Temperance Union used the religious rhetoric of "moral suasion" to persuade Americans of the evils of alcoholic beverages, many Americans did not respond to moralistic arguments. Two new organizations that were founded in the 1840s, The Washingtonians and the Sons of Temperance, appealed to working-class men who were looking for socialization, self-improvement, and self-advancement by participating and networking in temperance societies. The Sons of Temperance, organized in September 1842, added two features to the temperance support group: peer pressure to remain dry and space where men could gather for recreation without alcohol. Eventually, the Sons of Temperance adopted political activity as well, endorsing prohibition legislation by the end of the 1840s.

During the 1850s temperance overlapped with the abolition reform movement, with many reformers supporting both causes. Many of the same people who advocated improved treatment of enslaved African Americans were also willing to advocate better treatment for dependent women and children as victims of the alcoholism that impoverished and endangered families. This connection between the two causes hampered temperance expansion, however, since many Southerners dismissed temperance as another attempt by Northern reformers to impose public will on personal choices—something Southerners defiantly rejected.

Temperance organizations began trying to distance themselves from abolition organizations because temperance leaders did not want to risk losing support for their cause over the controversy of slavery. In some temperance meetings, speakers would even have their speeches cut short or cancelled if they tried to raise the issue of abolition in connection with temperance, as happened at the World Temperance Convention in 1846, when William Lloyd Garrison was silenced.

The connection between temperance and abolition also caused an Irish temperance activist, Father Theobald Mathew, some embarrassment as he toured the United States from 1849 to 1851. Father Mathew had achieved remarkable success in Ireland in persuading followers to take the temperance pledge, and he was hailed as a kind of miracle worker when he arrived in the United States. Abolitionists invited him to attend a celebration in New England of abolition in the West Indies, which he declined because of his plans to visit slaveholding states. This stirred up controversy in abolitionist circles, since at one point Father Mathew had signed a letter of support for abolition.

When he arrived in Washington, D.C., Father Mathew was entertained by President Zachary Taylor, and he was invited to hold an honorary seat in the House of Representatives. Senator Isaac P. Walker of Wisconsin then proposed that Father

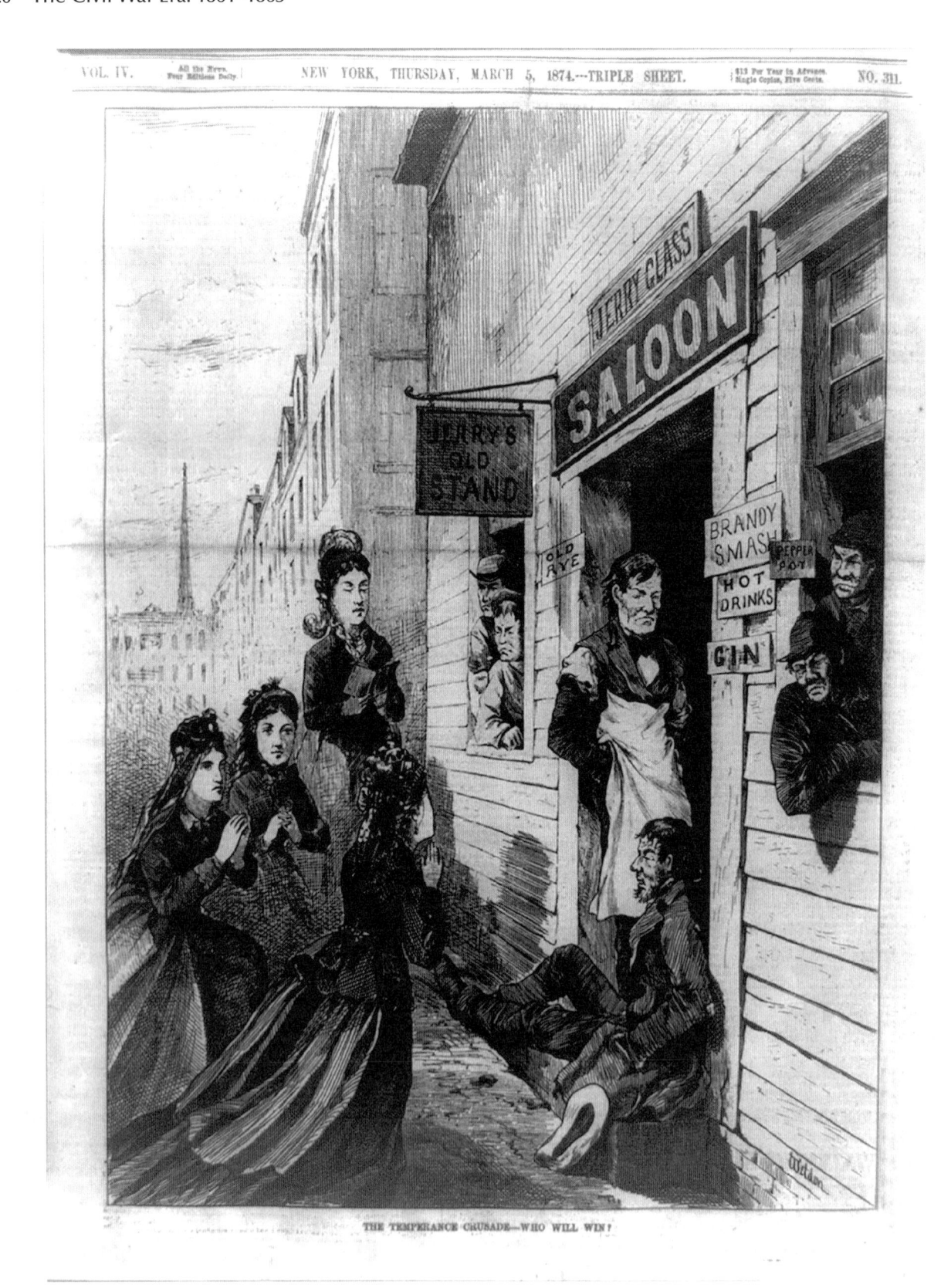

"The Temperance Crusade—Who Will Win?" in The Daily Graphic, *March 5, 1874* (Library of Congress)

Mathew be invited to visit the Senate, but the invitation was opposed by Southern senators. Eventually, the Senate passed a vote to invite Father Mathew to visit the Senate, although it was opposed by eighteen Southern senators. The controversy about his affiliation with abolitionists hung over Father Mathew's head through the rest of his tour of the South.

Although many Southerners resented temperance as another attempt by Northerners to infringe on state and personal rights, some organizations found ways to draw in Southern members. Because the Sons of Temperance were not affiliated with evangelicals or the abolition movement, they made headway in gaining members in Southern states. The nature of membership in the club, with secret handshakes, rituals, and oaths, also protected the identity of members of the Sons, which meant that Southern members could participate in the organization without fear of reprisal from neighbors who objected to affiliation with Northern reform movements. More importantly, the Sons focused on the honor of secret society and personal pledge, and both of these emphases supported Southern pride and complemented Southern insistence on limited government.

Despite Southern objections to Prohibition initiatives, beginning in 1850 the Free Soil Party sought to gain popular appeal by supporting Prohibition legislation, which was proposed at the state and local level. State Prohibition laws, called "Maine Laws" after the first state to pass such a law (in 1851), connected temperance societies politically and introduced means of working with politicians to accomplish temperance goals.

The Maine Law serves as an example of the power of strong individuals in the Temperance Movement, and points to the problems and advantages such individuals could present. Neal Dow, called the "Napoleon of Temperance," was the mayor of Portland, Maine, and he vigorously fought for prohibition legislation. He used his political acumen and his personal charisma to persuade the legislature to pass a law that restricted the manufacture and sale of alcoholic beverages in the state of Maine. In order to ensure enforcement of the prohibition, the Maine Law provided that citizens could conduct their own search and seizure of an establishment if they believed that illegal trade in alcohol was taking place. At least one vigilante group, the Carson League in Massachusetts, credited itself with ensuring multiple convictions under Massachusetts's version of the Maine Law. Members of the League sought out places where alcohol was served or stored in violation of the Maine Law, and the vigilantes destroyed alcohol and brought the people responsible to the legal authorities. Some of the Maine Laws were overturned because of the search-and-seizure clause, which was ruled in violation of the Constitution's protections against unlawful search and seizure.

Political activism by temperance societies reflected a decade of social change in the 1850s that troubled Americans and pitted them against each other. Growing industrialization in the North, along with the wealth generated by cotton in the South, caused Americans to enjoy a period of prosperity that was unprecedented. At the same time that Americans faced social change because of increasing national wealth and changes in the standard of living, the country was also experiencing a redefinition of freedom. The South defended a strong, individualistic freedom. Northerners intensified their demand that the South end the corrupting influence of slavery on free society, and the coercion of the Fugitive Slave Act seemed evidence to them that slavery undermined the principle of liberty throughout the entire republic. Although Northerners rebelled against the Fugitive Slave Act, many of them accepted restrictions on their behavior that were imposed by Prohibition laws because they perceived alcohol, pushed by liquor dealers, to be equally as enslaving as the institutional slave system of the South. These Northerners saw Prohibition laws as *liberating* them from the domineering designs of alcohol dealers, rather than as oppressive measures of government. Slavery as an institution was geographically removed from many Northerners, but the "enslaving" influences of alcohol abuse were visible all around.

Emotional arguments were presented by temperance societies, especially in stories that heavily stressed moral decay and family decline that accompanied alcoholism. Popular plays and novels of the 1850s such as *The Drunkard*, which was performed at P. T. Barnum's American Museum, and *Ten Nights in a Barroom*, a novel later performed as a gas-lantern slide show and then as a play, worked on emotional and moral sentiments of the public. Alcohol was dramatically associated with mental illness, domestic abuse, physical waste, and spiritual damnation, all of which hampered the progress of individuals and the nation. This portrayal made the case for government regulation of alcohol, because alcohol abusers were simplified as weaklings or villains chained to the "master" of alcohol, and producers of alcohol were seen as heartless monsters who would tie down a family to alcoholism for the sake of a profit.

In the economic domain, the decade of the 1850s showed a tendency toward standardization in the workforce and an increasing pragmatism in American outlook on life. As the economy grew stronger, class division be-

'THE DRUNKARD, or, The Fallen Saved.'

Conceded to be one of the most powerful auxiliaries that the Temperance Cause has ever received in this country, and to which was awarded the approbation and countenance of the great body of clergymen, the religious community at large, and of all the first families in this city.

'The Drunkard' is one of the most perfect and real Pictures of Life ever placed before the public. In the first act we behold

THE MODERATE DRINKER

In the second act, we have his progress, step by step, to ruin; his increased appetite for strong drink; the distress of his relations; the embarrassment of himself and family. In the third act, we have his

DRUNKEN ORGIES

in Broadway, his bar-room debauchery, the degradation of himself and vileness of his associates, loss of time, &c. In the fourth act we have

DESPAIR AND ATTEMPTED SUICIDE

and in the fifth act, his restitution to sobriety and society, by the aid of a Temperance Philanthropist. It is a most thrilling and affecting performance.

The whole drama is relieved with lively sparks of wit and humor, and the comic characters, funny scenes, country dances, songs, choruses, &c. serve to render the piece as amusing as it is instructive.

As always, the entertainments that take place in this Saloon every day consist in part of highly moral and instructive Domestic Dramas, written expressly for this establishment and so constructed as to please and edify while they possess a powerful reformatory tendency.

NO BAR OR INTOXICATING DRINKS
allowed upon the premises.

Poster advertising W. H. Smith's Temperance play at the reopening of P. T. Barnum's American Museum on July 8, 1850 (The Temperance Archive at the Lost Museum)

came deeper, and alcohol became a marker and even a weapon of class division. Industrialists, whose success depended on steady labor to improve its efficiency and to make a greater profit, saw in alcohol consumption the waste of energy and the dissipation of skill. Growing national prosperity fed into the belief that the American economy offered the opportunity for wealth to all who would work hard, and the waste of financial and human capital through drunkenness violated this principle. Temperance illustrated class conflict, because the owners of capital wanted to limit alcohol consumption by laborers, believing that a sober workforce was more efficient and productive.

The mass immigration of Germans and Irish before and during the Civil War led to a conflict between ethnic groups that affected the temperance debate through the end of the Reconstruction period. Nativists, who wanted to curb German and Irish cultural expression (and therefore prevent the influence by their ethnic cultures on American culture), attacked the drinking practices of immigrants; for example, Nativists did not support the practice of drinking for leisure or during family time on Sunday afternoons. The enforcement of prior bans on Sunday drinking or Sunday saloon-closing laws targeted German social habits.

The very drink of choice of Germans, malt liquor or beer, introduced complexity into the temperance debate, because the alcohol content was lower than that of whiskey, the traditional problem drink. By 1865 the per capita consumption of beer was twice that of the level of 1850, in part because of the growing number of immigrants who preferred beer to distilled liquor. Some immigrants viewed beer as a healthy beverage, especially compared to water available in cities, and breweries expanded in number and increased the quantity of their product in the 1850s.

The conflict over immigrant drinking practices with beer and Sunday beer-hall activities erupted in Chicago's first episode of civil disturbance on April 21, 1855, in an event now known as the "Lager Beer Riot." A temperance faction had swept the elections the month before, and once in power they raised the liquor-license fees, in a targeted attempt to shut down German beer halls. Germans raised funds to finance the new liquor-license fees, but the mayor's decision to close beer halls on Sundays led to a trial as a test case on April 21. The courtroom was packed with supporters of the defendants, and when the mayor ordered police to clear the courthouse area, violence erupted, resulting in one death and sixty arrests. The Germans organized themselves and in the next election, they forced the temperance officials out of office and restored former license fees and regulations of beer halls. The lasting effect of this episode was a polarization in city politics, which centered on ethnic division.

During the Civil War, temperance dropped into the background of American politics. Before the Emancipation Proclamation, Maine Laws represented some of the greatest successes in antebellum reform movements; by the end of the war, many of the Maine Laws had been repealed. Robert Wiebe, renowned historian, argues that Americans felt disappointed by the minimal "progressive gains" of temperance, so they turned to abolition as a cause that could yield greater advancement for the nation. In fact, the 1862 Internal Revenue Act, designed to generate additional funds for the government's war effort, took advantage of increased consumption of alcohol during the war. This act required that retailers who sold alcoholic beverages should hold liquor licenses, and it directly taxed distilled and malt liquor. Temperance advocates decried this legislation, objecting that it drew the government into an immoral connection with alcohol interests. Senator Harry Wilson stated that "the Federal Government ought not to derive a revenue from the sale of intoxicating drinks" (Pegram 45), which summarized the temperance objection to the revenue measure. The Revenue Act actually strengthened alcohol interests, because in 1862 the United States Brewers' Association formed as a lobbying group to address tax rates on alcohol. This positioned alcohol producers to be ready to fight future Prohibition legislation, because the brewers would be organized and have connections with legislative bodies.

In the larger social sphere, temperance was suspended during the Civil War because alcohol was a part of coping with a war for which there was little anesthetic available. Americans self-medicated with alcohol for a variety of war-related ailments, and soldiers on both sides of the conflict were issued alcohol as part of their rations.

Once the war ended, though, temperance societies experienced a resurgence in membership. At that time, the conflict over temperance changed from *how* to curb alcohol abuse to *who* would play a part in controlling "demon rum." In an attempt to get the national political parties to resume Prohibition legislation, a third political party was created, a party of outsiders who had little influence on national politics. After the war, women engaged in the Temperance Movement and used it as a platform to lobby for the right to vote. Americans also used membership in temperance societies as a test of limits of integration, especially in the South. Each of these conflicts focused on empowerment of marginal political players, especially women and newly emancipated African Americans.

After the Civil War, reformers continued to see control of the behavior of other people through legislation as necessary to rid society of problems associated with alcohol.

The National Temperance Society influenced national attitudes about the evils of alcohol by a constant production of articles, broadsheets, and tracts related to temperance. Yet, while the priority in politics after the war had become equilibrium, the swing between the rejection and support of prohibition measures remained the focus of the Temperance Movement and threatened the stability of political parties of the period. Although the Republican Party was perceived as the party of reform, it avoided prohibition measures, largely because it found itself consumed with problems of legislating Reconstruction. Republicans simply could not afford to lose support for the Reconstruction agenda by taking up the controversial issue of prohibition, which did not find neat alliances with other political initiatives.

The Third Party System arose in reaction to the mainstream party's rejection of reform efforts. The Prohibition Party was created at its first national convention in 1869 by members of the Grand Lodge of the Good Templars, who suggested that a third political party would be necessary if any legislation were to pass for prohibition, since Democrats and Republicans were avoiding the issue. A key leader of this party, James Black, eventually ran for president in 1872 as the Prohibition candidate. The party never became strong enough to accomplish more than forcing Prohibition as an agenda item for Democrats and Republicans, though.

During the period of Reconstruction, the antebellum alliance of reformers for abolition, temperance, and women's suffrage broke up when abolitionists accomplished their goal of suffrage for black males. This left women working with the Temperance Movement as allies in the drive for greater women's rights. In 1873, women acted out in frustration about being the most common victims of alcohol abuse, with no voting power to implement change. They embarked upon a Woman's Crusade, for which "Mother" Eliza Daniel Stewart was an important leader. In December, an itinerant preacher named Dio Lewis in Western New York called for women to march against saloons and pray and protest until the owners ceased selling liquor. Women responded in large numbers, eventually taking action in most areas of the country except in the Deep South. The movement was short-lived, lasting only until the spring of 1874, but it demonstrated enough zeal that women who had been active in the Independent Order of Good Templars formed a new temperance organization exclusively for women, The Women's Christian Temperance Union (WCTU), upon the suggestion of Martha McClellan Brown. The Woman's Crusade demonstrated to women that they needed an organization in which they represented their own interests, because of the treatment they received from men during the Crusade, which ranged from mocking and abusive language to having excrement dumped on their heads as they marched in front of saloons.

The WCTU provided a socially acceptable forum for women to become politically active at a time when, in some areas, women had barely gained the right to speak in public. During the period of Reconstruction, under the leadership of the reformer Annie Wittenmyer, the WCTU emphasized moral suasion as the key to promoting temperance. The organization became divided about whether or not to continue the traditional role of women of arguing and asking for change from male legislators and male voters, to women demanding political power for themselves through female suffrage. In 1874 Frances Willard was named the corresponding secretary for the WCTU, and her strong personality and sense of vision quickly dominated the organization, leading the WCTU to pursue greater political rights for women. Under her leadership, members adopted the maxim "Do Everything" and the WCTU became committed to the goal of legislative prohibition, which they hoped to accomplish by first achieving women's suffrage. This equal drive for prohibition and women's suffrage turned some would-be temperance supporters away, because during Reconstruction, temperance and even prohibition were more socially acceptable than women's suffrage.

In the South, temperance carried American conflict into the most socially difficult question of the age when reform groups tried to recruit African American members into their ranks. The National Sons of Temperance allowed for each division (or state organization) to create its own plan for promoting temperance among blacks in 1866, but by 1871 it had banned separate chapters of the organization based on the race of the chapter members. During the Civil War the Templars accepted a dual-lodge system, tolerating racial segregation among members. However, some members protested by breaking off and forming the Right Worthy Grand Lodge of the World, which would not tolerate segregation.

Southerners reacted to Northern temperance societies by forming temperance groups of their own, including the United Friends of Temperance and the Temple of Templars, both all-white societies. Not only did these groups reject integration, but they also tended to reject prohibition, preferring the principle of the individual pledge of temperance over legislative coercion.

The end of Reconstruction left the North and the South with the idea that the temperate life was a moral ideal. Yet, the unpopular nature of women's suffrage, racial integration, and even conflicts among temperance organizations over priorities and practices meant that little in the way of legislative accomplishments occurred during Reconstruction. The reorganization of temperance societies during this period, though, prepared them for success in passing prohibition laws during the upcoming Gilded Age.

Laura A. Cruse

CHRONOLOGY

1850
The Independent Order of Good Templars, a temperance organization that includes elements of secrecy such as a handshake and ritual, is founded.

1851
June 2: The first of a series of state prohibition laws called "Maine Laws" is passed, thanks to the efforts of the mayor of Portland, Neal Dow.

1852
George Schneider begins a brewery in St. Louis, Missouri, that will later become the Anheuser-Busch Brewing Company.

Vermont, Massachusetts, and Rhode Island adopt versions of the Maine Law. Minnesota Territory passes a short-lived prohibition law.

The New York State Women's Temperance Society is formed after The Sons of Temperance refuse a request by Susan B. Anthony to address the Sons.

1853
Michigan passes "Maine Law" prohibition.

1854
Elizabeth Cady Stanton asks the New York legislature to support prohibition and to pass divorce laws that will allow women to separate from intemperate husbands.

The Carson League, a citizens-action group in Maine, is formed to seek out evidence of violations of the Maine Prohibition law, under the liberal "search-and-seizure" clause of the law. In their records of October 1854 the organization boasts having contributed to twenty-five convictions for violations of the Maine Law as a result of evidence they obtained during raids.

Connecticut passes "Maine Law" prohibition.

The Republican Party is founded, due to the dissolution of the Whig Party and the weakening of other third parties.

The Massachusetts Supreme Court rules the search-and-seizure provisions of its Maine Law to be unconstitutional.

1855
Prohibition laws, modeled after Maine Law, are passed in New York, Indiana, Delaware, Iowa, Nebraska, and New Hampshire.

April 21: The Lager Beer Riot in Chicago results in one death and sixty arrests as a result of the German and Irish reaction to the mayor's Nativist-motivated decision to close saloons on Sundays.

June 2: The Portland Rum Riot occurs when citizens gather at city hall in Portland, Maine, upon hearing rumors that a stash of alcohol is being stored there. Neal Dow, mayor of Portland, calls in the militia, which fires into the crowd, killing one man and injuring another seven.

1856
The New York Supreme Court strikes down the search-and-seizure clause of its prohibition law.

1862
The *1862 Internal Revenue Act* taxes distilled and malt liquors and requires that retail distributors of alcoholic beverages purchase a federal liquor license. This measure is designed to generate revenue for the federal government to offset the costs of the Civil War. The measure is opposed by temperance reformers as a compromise of principle.

Thirty-seven breweries from New York form an association that in 1864 will become the United States' Brewers Association as a response to the new federal tax on distilled and malt liquor.

1863
Rhode Island repeals prohibition.

1865

The National Temperance Society and Publication House is formed in Saratoga, New York.

Massachusetts creates a state constabulary to enforce the Prohibition Law of 1855.

1867

Maine creates a state police force to enforce prohibition. Pennsylvania's legislature bans sale of liquor on Sunday. Germans in Pittsburgh gather to weaken liquor-license restrictions. Germans in Kansas organize to oppose temperance advances. Iowans form the political group "People's Party" to successfully fight prohibition.

1869

A new prohibition law is passed in Massachusetts. The Prohibition Party is formed.

1872

Prohibition Party candidate James Black polls 5,608 votes in the presidential election. Southerners leave the Sons of Temperance to found the United Friends of Temperance, a whites-only temperance society.

1873

The Women's Crusade takes place from December to spring 1874 in response to an exhortation by Dio Lewis, an itinerant temperance speaker, for women to march on saloons and urge liquor sellers to destroy their stock.

1874

November: The Women's Christian Temperance Union is founded by women who leave the Templars to create a women-only organization, following the demonstration of female influence for temperance enforcement during the Women's Crusade.

1875

Massachusetts Prohibition law of 1869 is repealed.

DOCUMENTS

Document 1: CATHOLIC TEMPERANCE ASSOCIATION

What did members of temperance societies promise regarding alcohol, when they took "the pledge"? How did the rhetoric of the pledge empower the person making the promise to resist the urge to imbibe? Especially during the period after the Civil War, when prohibition legislation was too risky for passage, the pledge was the means by which temperance advocates recruited supporters, and held those followers accountable to the promise to abstain from intoxicating drink. Because many of the larger temperance organizations had ties to evangelical Protestant sects, some Catholic priests encouraged male parishioners to take the Catholic Temperance Pledge. This pledge, printed in the shape of a cross and signed on March 28, 1844, was typical.

New York Catholic Temperance Association

Neil James Sweeney was admitted on the 28 of March 1844 by the Very Rev. Felix Varela, and made the following pledge:

I do solemnly promise to avoid intemperance, and should it be necessary in order to attain this object to abstain *totally* from all intoxicating liquors, I do hereby pledge myself to abstain from every one of them. I also promise by my advice and example to induce others to do the same.

Temperance: Religion, Politics, and Ethnic Groups 227

SOURCE:

"Temperance pledge filled in by Neil James Sweeney, 28 of March, 1844." *An American Time Capsule: Three Centuries of Broadsides and Other Printed Ephemera.* Library of Congress American Memory Collection. <http://memory.loc.gov/cgi-bin/ampage?collId=rbpe&fileName=rbpe11/rbpe119/11902600/rbpe11902600.db&recNum=0&itemLink=D?rbpebib:3:./temp/~ammem_Lvlf::@@@mdb=ftvbib,rbpebib,calbkbib,cic,curt,dag,fsaall,cmns,flwpabib,afcreed,cowellbib,toddbib,afcnyebib,lomaxbib,ngp,afcwwgbib,raelbib,wpa,ncpm,afcwip,omhbib,pan,afcpearl,wpapos,lhbprbib,qlt,ncr,papr,afc911bib,afcesnbib,mesnbib,denn,fpnas,lhbtnbib&linkText=0> [accessed January 13, 2008].

Document 2: CELEBRATING TEMPERANCE

How did temperance leaders link patriotic sentiment to support for curbing consumption of alcoholic beverages? In the decade preceding the Civil War, prohibition was a controversial subject in the South. Prohibition reformers were often associated with abolitionists, although they tried to distance themselves from that movement, and that tended to make prohibition a less popular movement in the South than in the North. In the diary entry below, for July 4, 1849, North Carolina temperance advocate Thomas M. Garrett writes about a Fourth of July celebration sponsored by the Sons of Temperance. Temperance rallies were often held in conjunction with Independence Day celebrations, because temperance leaders wanted to emphasize their cause as "independence" from addiction.

The diary entry is introduced by a short biography of Garrett.

Thomas Miles Garrett (1830–1864) of Hertford County, NC, entered the University in 1848, was a member of the Philanthropic Society, and graduated in 1851. He became a lawyer and during the Civil War served as a colonel in the Confederate army. He was killed at Spotsylvania.

SOURCE:

Documenting the American South. The University Library at the University of North Carolina at Chapel Hill, 2005 <http://docsouth.unc.edu/global/getBio.html?type=bio&id=pn0000565&name=Garrett, Thomas Miles> [accessed January 13, 2008].

From the Diary of Thomas M. Garrett

July 4th

Surely there can not be a prouder feeling than that the of love of country. No day can come more joyous than that of which a nation's boast is to her and all mankind the gift of freedom. It is true that this alone is enough to fill the bigest measure a nation's pride but the coming of this day brings to rembrance brighter feelings and brighter joys. All that is great and good is bound up in the remembrance of our great sires. The sweetest joy is to pay them the listless praise of example, and only let the heart move the acsent. "Sleep on Great Farthers a nation's pride is thy memory. We will never disturb nor let be disturbed they peaceful sleep." The unexampled prosperity our country is truly a subject of congratulation. The freedom which we have enjoyed is beyond all conception, and the proudest words upon earth are "I am an American citizen," words of in which the most haughty being would rejoice, if he would know. To know that I have am a sovreighn of the greatest of nations, and can claim the protection of the freest government upon amongst mankind raises even my little self to feel as big as a king, who can claim no more. What have we of which we may boast? All do and should join in the celebration of this great day, and raise a song of triump and praise to God to our farthers and to freedom—I met with serious disappointment to day. A great celebration was to come off at Hillboro', under the direction principly by of the Sons of Temperance, and I was verry much in hope of being able to join in it, because I am a member of that order. I failed however to get a conveyance and it was impossible to get there It seemed that the whole village of C. Hill poured out, and every horse cart waggon, buggy, carriage, and whatever else that was ever made to ride in were filled, besides not a few "rode their mother's colts" We had however a celebration here.

SOURCE:

"Excerpts from the Diary of Thomas M. Garrett, July 4 and August 31, 1849." *Documenting the American South.* The University Library at the University of North Carolina, Chapel Hill, 2005 <http://docsouth.unc.edu/true/mss04-23/mss04-23.html> [accessed January 13, 2008].

Document 3: The Prohibitory Liquor Law of Maine

How could alcohol consumption be controlled in a more regular manner than by personal commitment alone? The following text includes key passages from the "Maine Law," enacted in 1851, the first of a series of prohibition laws passed by states before the Civil War. The Maine Law passed in 1851 served as the model for other states that wanted to prevent the sale and public consumption of alcoholic beverages. Maine was the first state to prohibit the manufacture or sale of alcohol, except for medicinal or mechanical purposes.

An Act for the Suppression of Drinking Houses and Tippling Shops

Be it enacted by the Senate and House of Representatives in Legislature assembled, as follows:

Section 1. Manufacture and Sale Prohibited

The manufacturing, sale, keeping, or depositing for sale of intoxicating liquors, is prohibited except as is hereinafter provided. The term intoxicating liquor used in the Act, means and includes every liquid preparation that will produce intoxication. No such liquor shall be sold except for medicinal and mechanical uses, by agents duly appointed for that purpose, as in this Act is provided. Such agents may sell to the Selectmen of towns, the Mayor and Aldermen of cities, and to the assessors of plantations, for the supply of agencies as established by this Act, in their respective cities, towns, and plantations. No other person shall sell such liquors for any purpose. Agents may be appointed under this Act by the Mayor and Aldermen of cities, and the Selectmen of towns, and assessors of plantations, as soon after the annual March meeting in each year as may conveniently be done. He shall hold his office one year, and until another is appointed in his place, unless sooner removed. The appointing board have the power of removal. Vacancies by removal or otherwise shall be filled as soon as may be. His compensation shall be such as the board shall prescribe. He shall conform to such rules and regulations in the sales of liquors as this Act provides, and as the board shall in writing prescribe, not inconsistent with this Act; which rules and regulations, and his appointment, shall be in writing, and shall within seven days after the appointment be recorded in the records of such city or town. He shall sell only for cash, and shall keep an accurate account of all purchases made for him by the Selectmen, assessors, or Mayor and Aldermen of his city, town, or plantation, with the date, the quantity and price of each purchase or parcel; also, of every sale by him made, with the name of the purchaser, the purchase for which purchased, the quantity, price, and date of the sale, which account shall always be open to the inspection of the appointing board. He shall annually, on the first day of December, make a report, by him signed and sworn to, to the board appointing him, of the quantity of each kind of liquor sold by him under this Act for the year ending that day, and of the amount of money received for the same, and the said board shall, before the 20th day of said December, transmit a certified copy of the same to the Secretary of State, to be by him laid before the legislature. He shall sell to no one unless he knows him to be an inhabitant of his city, town, or plantation. He shall not sell to any minor, servant, or apprentice, without the written order of his parent, guardian, or master, nor to any intemperate person, nor to any Indian. He shall not sell to any person by reason of having himself prescribed the medical use of the liquors sold. He shall have no interest in the liquor sold, nor in the profits of the agency. He shall be a person of sober life, and not addicted to the use of intoxicating liquors. No one who has been convicted of selling liquor contrary to the law shall be appointed such agent. No innholder, tavern-keeper, or trader shall be appointed such agent. He shall, whenever requested by any Justice of the Peace of his County, exhibit to him his said appointment, and the said accounts of the purchases and sales, and permit him to take minutes or copies of the same. If the Justice find that he has violated any of the provisions of this Act, he may require the appointing board to inquire into the charge, and to remove him if sufficient cause appear, and to put his bond in suit. If such agent knowingly violate any of the provisions or restrictions of this section, he shall be liable to be indicted and punished as a common seller. Before entering upon the duties of his office, he shall give a bond to the city, town, or plantation, with two good and sufficient sureties, in a sum not less than six hundred dollars, which bond shall be in substance as follows:

Know all men, that we, _____ as principal, and _____ and as sureties, are holden and stand firmly bound to the inhabitants of the town of _____ (or city, as the case may be), in the sum of _____ hundred dollars, to be paid by them, to which payment we bind ourselves, our heirs, executors, and administrators, firmly by these presents. Sealed with our seals, and dated this _____ day of _____, A.D. _____.

The condition of this obligation is such, that whereas the above bounden _____ has been duly appointed an agent of the town (or city) of _____, to sell within, and on account of said town (or city), intoxicating liquors for medicinal and mechanical purposes, and no other, until the _____ of _____ A.D. _____, unless sooner removed from said agency.

Now if the said _____ shall in all respects conform to the provisions of the law relating to the business for which he is appointed, and to such rules and regulations as now are or shall be from time to time established by the board making the appointment, then this obligation to be void; otherwise to remain in full force. The Mayor and Aldermen of any city, and the Selectmen of any town, and assessors of any plantation, whenever complaint shall be made to them that a breach of the conditions of the bond given by any person appointed under this Act, has been committed, shall notify the person complained of, and if upon the hearing of the parties it shall appear that any breach has been committed, they shall revoke and make void his appointment. And whenever any breach of any bond given to the inhabitants of any city or town in pursuance of any of the provisions of this Act shall be made known to the Mayor and Aldermen, or Selectmen, or shall in any manner come to their knowledge, they or some one of them shall, at the expense and for the use of said city or town, cause the bond to be put in suit in any court proper to try the same.

Section 2. Fines And Imprisonment For Sale

If any person shall, by himself, clerk, servant, or agent, at any time sell any intoxicating liquors in violation of the provisions of this Act, he shall, for the first conviction, pay a fine of twenty dollars and costs, and be imprisoned thirty days; for the second conviction, he shall pay a fine of twenty dollars and costs, and be imprisoned sixty days; and for the third conviction, he shall pay a fine of twenty dollars and costs, and be imprisoned ninety days; for the fourth and every subsequent conviction, he shall be deemed a common seller, and he shall pay a fine of two hundred dollars and costs, and be imprisoned six months in the common jail or house of correction; and in default of the payment of fines and costs prescribed by this section, for the first and second and third conviction, the convict shall not be entitled to the benefit of chapter one hundred and seventy-five of the Revised Statutes, until he shall have been imprisoned two months; and in default of payment of fines and costs provided for in the fourth and every subsequent conviction, he shall not be entitled to the benefit of said chapter one hundred and seventy-five of the Revised Statutes, until he shall have been imprisoned four months after the said six months. And if any clerk, servant, agent, or other person in the employment or in the premises of another, shall violate any of the provisions of this section, he shall be held equally guilty with the principal, and on conviction shall suffer the same penalty.

Section 3. Fines and Imprisonment for Manufacturing

No person shall be allowed to be a manufacturer of any intoxicating liquor, on pain of forfeiting on the first conviction the sum of two hundred dollars and costs of prosecution, and six months' imprisonment in the common jail or house of correction; and on the second conviction, the person so convicted shall pay the sum of four hundred dollars and costs of prosecution, and shall be imprisoned nine months in the common jail or house of correction; and on the third and every subsequent conviction, shall pay the sum of one thousand dollars and costs, and shall be imprisoned one year in the State Prison; said penalties to be recovered by indictment in any court of competent jurisdiction.

Section 4. Regulations Regarding Apothecaries

No apothecary or druggist shall keep or use any such liquors for any other purpose than the preparation of medicines ordered by a physician of sober life and not addicted to the use of intoxicating liquors, whose name shall be subscribed to the prescription to be put up or prepared by such druggist or apothecary, in his own shop; and he shall not suffer any such liquor to be drank on his premises, or to be carried away to be drank or used elsewhere. No druggist, apothecary, artist, or manufacturer shall keep or use such liquors for any other purposes than the common uses made thereof in his art or manufactory, and he shall not suffer any such liquors to be drank on his premises or to be carried away therefrom. If any apothecary or druggist, artist or manufacturer, shall violate any of the provisions of this section, he shall, on conviction for the first offense, be punished by a fine of one hundred dollars and costs, and three months' imprisonment in the common jail or house of correction, and for the second, and every subsequent conviction, by a fine of two hundred dollars and costs, and imprisonment in the common jail or house of correction, six months.

Section 5. Regulations Regarding Travelers

No person shall travel from place to place in this State, conveying with him personally or in any carriage or vehicle, any intoxicating liquors, including every kind of beer, cordials, and liquid preparations, purporting to be medicinal, a part of which is composed of intoxicating liquors, with the intention to sell or use the same, in any manner forbidden by this Act, under the penalty for the first conviction of a fine twenty dollars and costs, and thirty days' imprisonment; for the second conviction, twenty dollars and costs, and sixty days' imprisonment; for the third conviction, a fine of twenty dollars and costs, and ninety days' imprisonment, and for the fourth and every subsequent conviction, he shall be deemed a common seller, and punished by a fine of two hundred dollars and costs, and six months' imprisonment in the common jail or house of correction. Any person offending against the provisions of this section shall be liable to be arrested on a warrant on the complaint or oath of any citizen of the State, on which warrant his person, carriage, or vehicle may be searched, and such liquors, if found thereon, seized. Such complaint and warrant, and the subsequent proceedings thereon, shall be substantially the same in form and substance as in this Act is provided in cases of arrest, search, and seizure of liquors kept and deposited in the manner forbidden by this Act.

Section 6. Liquors Conveyed Through this State

All such liquors brought into this State for the purpose of being conveyed through the State to places beyond its borders, shall not be kept or deposited in any city or town in this State for the space of more than twenty-four hours (the hours of Sunday excepted), except in the case of inevitable accident, and if so kept, shall be liable to be seized and forfeited, under the provisions of this Act, as being kept and deposited for unlawful sale; and if such liquors shall be seized on a warrant, and proceeded with as this Act required and directs, and the respondent shall allege in defense against such process, that such liquors were in transitu, and not intended for sale in the State, it shall be sufficient to show on the other side that such liquors were kept or deposited in any city or town in the State for the space of more than twenty-four hours. Whenever any such liquors shall be seized, and on trial the owner or keeper shall claim that they were in transitu, and therefore exempt from seizure, he shall set forth in the claim the name of the place to which they were about to be carried, and if on trial it shall appear that the liquors are of such description, as to the quantities of the casks or packages in which they are contained, or in other respects as are by the revenue or other laws of the Province or State to which they were so to be carried, prohibited to be introduced therein, that fact shall be sufficient evidence that they were kept and deposited for unlawful sale within this State.

Section 7. Regulations Regarding Express-Men, Carriers, etc.

No stage driver, express-man, common-carrier, teamster, or other agent, shall carry from place to place within this State any such liquors, except for agencies provided for in this Act, under a penalty of a fine of twenty dollars and costs for the first conviction, twenty dollars fine and costs and thirty days' imprisonment for the second conviction, two hundred dollars fine and costs and three months' imprisonment for the third conviction, and four hundred dollars fine and six months' imprisonment for the fourth and every other subsequent offense. Such carrying shall be prima facie evidence of intention to violate the provisions of this section, subject however to such evidence as may be adduced on the part of the defendant to show that he had no such intention.

Section 8. Search and Seizure

If three persons who are competent to be witnesses in civil suits, resident in the county within which the complaint shall be made, shall make complaint upon oath or affirmation before any judge of a municipal or police court or justice of the peace, that they have reason to believe, and do believe, that intoxicating liquors are kept or deposited in any building or place, other than a dwelling-house, no part of which is used as a shop, or for purposes of traffic, by a person or persons named in said complaint, or by a person or persons unknown, not authorized by law to sell the same, within the city, town, or plantation where they are alleged to be so kept or deposited, and that said liquors are intended for sale within this State in violation of the law, such magistrate shall issue his warrant, directed to any sheriff, deputy sheriff, marshal, deputy marshal, constable, or police officer, having power to serve such process, commanding such officer to search the premises described in such complaint, which premises shall also be described in said warrant; also to search any yard or building (other than such dwelling-house), adjoining the premises described in said warrant, if occupied by the same person occupying the premises described in said warrant; and if any such intoxicating liquors are there found, to seize the same, with the vessels in which they might be contained, and to convey them to some proper place of security to be there kept until final action upon such complaint. And the officer having such warrant shall be authorized by virtue thereof to make the search directed by such warrant to be made, and to seize and dispose of any such liquors as in this Act is provided. And such officer shall, in his return on such warrant, designate and describe the liquors by him so seized, and the vessels in which they are contained, with reasonable certainty. And if the name of the person or persons by whom such liquors are alleged to be so kept or deposited shall be stated in said complaint, the officer shall be commanded in and by said warrant, if he find such liquors, to arrest such person or persons, and have them forthwith before the judge or justice by whom such warrant was issued, to answer to said complaint, and show cause why said liquors should not be forfeited. Any such person so arrested and brought before such judge or justice may not plead guilty to such complaint and may show in defense thereto that said liquors were not so kept and deposited intended for sale contrary to law, or that they were imported under the laws of the United States, and in accordance therewith; that they are contained in the original packages in which they were imported, and in quantities not less than the laws of the United States prescribe. And such defense being established, the judge or justice may order such liquors to be restored to the defendant, if satisfied that he is the lawful owner or keeper thereof. But custom-house certificates of importation, and proofs of marks on the casks and packages corresponding thereto, shall not be received as evidence that the identical liquors contained in said packages and casks were actually imported therein. And if upon the trial neither of the said grounds of defense shall be established, and if in the opinion of the court, upon the evidence produced, said liquors were kept or deposited by such person or persons for the purposes of sale contrary to law, such person or persons being found guilty shall each be punished by a fine of twenty dollars and costs and thirty days' imprisonment, and also shall be imprisoned thirty days' in default of payment of the fine and costs. And the liquors so seized, with the vessels in which they are contained, shall be declared forfeited, and such adjudication shall be a bar to any claim for the recovery of the same, or the value thereof, and they shall on written order of said judge or justice be destroyed. And the officer to whom such order is directed, shall make return thereon of his doings in the premises. If, however, upon trial the judge or justice shall find the person or persons so charged in the complaint, not guilty, or if it shall appear that he is not the lawful owner or keeper thereof, he shall, if satisfied that the liquors so seized were so as aforesaid kept and deposited for unlawful sale by some person or persons not named in the complaint, decline to order them to be restored, and shall proceed therewith as in hereinafter provided.

❖   ❖   ❖

Section 11. Search of Private Dwellings only on Oath

No warrant shall issue for the search of any dwelling-house in which a family resides, or in which or part of which a shop is not kept, or other place is not kept for the sale of such liquors, unless it shall be first shown to the Magistrate, before a warrant is issued for such search, by the testimony of witnesses upon oath, that there is reasonable ground for believing that such liquors are kept or deposited in such dwelling-house or its appurtenances, intended for unlawful sale in such dwelling-house or elsewhere, which testimony the Magistrate shall reduce to writing and cause to be signed and verified by oath or affirmation of such witnesses, and upon such testimony so produced and verified, he may, upon complaint of three persons competent to be witnesses in civil suits, resident in the county, issue his warrant in like manner and form as is provided in the 8th section of this Act, commanding the Officer to search such dwelling-house and its appurtenances, and if any such liquors are found therein, to seize the same, together with the vessels in which they are contained, and also to arrest the owner or keeper thereof if named in said complaint, and the subsequent proceedings shall be conformable to the 8th, 9th, and 10th sections of this Act, as the case may be. No dwelling-house, inn, tavern, or other building in which or part of which a shop is kept for traffic, or office, bar, or other place is kept for the sale of liquors shall be entitled to the protection from search provided in this section, but shall be liable to be searched in the manner provided in the 8th section of this Act. And any of the said witnesses who shall be convicted of giving false testimony knowingly and willfully in the statements so subscribed and verified shall be punished therefor by imprisonment in the State Prison for the term of two years. The finding of such liquors upon search in a dwelling-house shall not of itself be evidence that they are kept or deposited therein intended for unlawful sale.

Section 12. Arrest When Seizure is Prevented

If any Officer, having a warrant issued under this Act committed to him directing him to seize any such liquors and to arrest the owner or keeper thereof, shall be prevented from seizing the liquors by their being poured out or otherwise destroyed, he shall arrest the owner or keeper and bring him before the Magistrate, and he shall make return upon the warrant that he was prevented from seizing the liquors by their being poured out or otherwise destroyed, as the case may be, and in his return he shall state the quantity so poured out or destroyed, and that the liquors so poured out or destroyed were such as were described in the warrant, and that they were so kept or deposited intended for unlawful sale; and if the person so arrested shall be found to be the owner or keeper thereof, he shall be fined and sentenced in the same manner as he would be if the liquors described in the warrant and in the return had been seized on the warrant and brought before the Magistrate by the Officer.

Section 13. Sale of Liquor at Public Places

It shall be the duty of any Mayor, Alderman, Selectman or Assessor, City Marshal or Deputy, or Constable, or Police Officer of any place, if he shall have information that any intoxicating liquors are kept for sale or sold in any tent, shanty, hut, or place of any kind for selling refreshments in any public place, or near the ground of any camp-meeting, cattle show, agricultural exhibition, military muster, or public occasion of any kind, and shall believe said information to be true, forthwith to enter a complaint before some Judge of a Municipal or a Police Court or Justice of the Peace, against the keeper or keepers of such place, alleging in said complaint that he has reason to believe, and does believe, that such liquors are so kept in such place (describing the same) by such keeper or keepers contrary to law. And upon such complaint the said Judge or Justice shall issue his warrant, commanding the Officer who may serve the same to search the place described in said complaint, and which shall be described in said warrant. And if he shall find upon said premises any such liquor, to seize the same with the vessels in which they may be contained, and to arrest the keeper or keepers thereof, and have said keeper or keepers, with the liquors and vessels so seized, as soon as may be, before said Judge or Justice, to be dealt with according to law. And the Officer to whom said warrant may be committed shall forthwith execute the same, and said keeper or keepers when arrested shall be tried thereon in due course of law, and upon proof that said liquors are intoxicating, that they were found in possession of the accused in a tent, shanty, hut, or other place as aforesaid, he or they shall be found guilty, and sentenced to be punished by imprisonment in the County jail for thirty days, and to pay all costs of such proceedings, and the liquors and vessels so seized shall be destroyed by order of the Court in the manner before provided in this Act. Any Mayor or Alderman, Selectman, Assessor, City Marshal or his deputy, Constable, Police Officer, or Watchman in his City or Town, or Plantation, may take into his custody any such liquors, and the vessels in which they are contained, which he shall find at any place, by day or night, if he have reason to believe they are kept or deposited and intended for unlawful sale in this State, and detain the same until a warrant can be procured under which proceedings shall be had against such liquors and the owner or keeper, in like manner as is provided in case of such liquors taken in a shanty, hut, or other place. If any person arrested, tried, and sentenced, as set forth in this section, shall appeal from such sentence, the Judge or Justice shall grant the appeal, and order him to recognize in the sum of one hundred dollars, with sufficient sureties for his appearance, and for prosecuting his appeal, and he shall stand committed till the order is complied with; and the Judge or Justice whose judgment is appealed from shall furnish full copies of all the proceedings in the case at the expense of the appellant. And if judgment is rendered against the appellant in the Appellate Court he shall be punished, and the liqours seized and vessels dealt with as is above provided in this section; and if said appellant shall fail to appear and prosecute his appeal, or to abide and perform the judgment of the Appellate Court, the recognizance shall be forfeited, and the liquors and vessels shall be disposed of as aforesaid by Order of the Court.

◆   ◆   ◆

Section 16. Delivery an Evidence of Sale

Whenever, an unlawful sale is alleged, and a delivery proved, it shall not be necessary to prove a payment, but such a delivery shall be a sufficient evidence of sale.

Section 18. Persons Found Intoxicated

Any person hereafter found intoxicated in any of the streets or highways, or being intoxicated in his own house, or in any other building or place, and who, in such house, building, or place, shall become quarrelsome, or in any way disturb the public peace, or that of his own or any other family, so as to render it necessary for the police or peace officers to interfere, may be taken into custody by any sheriff, deputy sheriff, constable, marshal, deputy marshal, police officer, or watchman, and committed to the watch-house or restrained in some other suitable place, till a complaint can be made and warrant issued in due form, upon which he may be arrested and tried, and if found guilty of being intoxicated in the streets or highways, or of being intoxicated in his own house, or any other building or place, and becoming quarrelsome and disturbing the public peace, or that of his own or any other family, he shall be punished by imprisonment in the common jail for thirty days; but said Judge or Justice may remit any portion of said punishment, and order the prisoner to be discharged, whenever the person so arrested shall make such disclosures or furnish such evidence as will authorize a warrant to be issued for an offense against some of the provisions of this Act, against the person of whom he procured or received the liquors whereby he became intoxicated.

SOURCE:

Henry S. Clubb. *The Maine Liquor Law: Its Origins, History, and Results, Including a Life of Hon. Neal Dow* (New York: For the Maine Law Statistical Society by Fowler and Wells, 1856), pp. 331–342.

Document 4: LETTER FROM THE NEW JERSEY SONS OF TEMPERANCE

How did temperance reformers react to the government's tolerance of alcohol during the Civil War, as intoxicating beverages were distributed as part of rations, and as public distribution of alcohol was used as a source of tax revenue to fund the war? Notice in the following letter to President Abraham Lincoln in 1863 that temperance activists appealed to the moral high ground of temperance, and even suggested that delays in the military success of Union forces were a consequence of intemperance.

From Trenton New Jersey Sons of Temperance to Abraham Lincoln, February 23, 1863

Trenton Feb'y 23rd 1863

Honored Sir:

The undersigned, Officers of the Grand Division, Sons of Temperance of New Jersey, respectfully represent that they were appointed at the last session of that body to memorialise the President of the United States "that the Executive influence may be interposed for the exclusion of intoxicating liquors from the Army, and for the immediate removal of all intemperate persons, incumbents of office, from the civil and military service of the Union."

Deeply impressed by the condition of our beloved country, and recognizing our solemn responsibility as citizens, and members of a great reformatory organization, we earnestly appeal to you in behalf of action that shall present a spectacle of patriotism, honor and morality, which cannot fail to secure the blessing of the God of Nations on your Administration in this trying and solemn crisis in our National affairs.

When we remember that "Righteousness exalteth a Nation," that "Sin is a reproach to any people," and that among the sins emphatically denounced in the Bible is that of drunkenness, we look upon the state of our country with undissembled sorrow, in view of the striking facts every day exhibited in high places of degrading habits of intemperance. It is a prevailing impression among the people that such habits pervade the army, especially, and that, to their pernicious influence many of the reverses that have attended military movements, are justly attributable.

It is therefore, not alone as representatives of a society banded together to promote good morals in the community, but as patriots, lovers of our country, that we appeal to you in behalf of the object of this memorial, and earnestly pray that you will avert such danger and disgrace to the National cause, by the exercise of your high prerogative as the chief Executive, and appointing power, and dismiss from the service of the government every officer addicted to the debasing habit of intemperance, or who, by his example or influence, countenances or encourages the use of intoxicating drinks. By thus setting the seal of your stern condemnation on an immoral and dangerous practice, you will remove a blighting and demoralizing example from the army, and commend yourself as a wise, patriotic and religious Magistrate of a free, christian people, whose petitions before the throne of the heavenly favor, will secure for you and the Nation, the blessing of the Lord God of Battle,—the God of Purity, Truth and Righteousness.

And as in duty bound, we will ever pray, &c.

In behalf of the Grand Division:
—P. G. W. P.
Hoxley Rheem — G. W. P.
Benjamin D [Donennty?] — G. W. A.
x Henry B. Howell — G. Scribe
Frank [Devereny?] — G. Treas.
Jno D Lee — G. Cond.
Robt Travis Jr — G. Chaplain
Jno. Riley — G. Lieut.
S L. Condit, M D
Past Most Worthy Patriarch
Natl Divn. S. of. T of N. America

Source:

"Trenton New Jersey Sons of Temperance to Abraham Lincoln, Monday, February 23, 1863 (Request that Lincoln exclude intoxicating drink from the army)." Abraham Lincoln Papers at the Library of Congress. Transcribed and Annotated by the Lincoln Studies Center, Knox College. Galesburg, Illinois <http://memory.loc.gov/cgi-bin/query/r?ammem/mal:@field(DOCID+@lit(d2192500))> [accessed February 6, 2008].

Document 5: Minutes of the Proceedings of the Ten Islands Baptist Association

How did churches, which originally advocated temperance, react to the movement as it became social and political? During the Civil War, prohibition was virtually suspended in both the North and the South. In fact, both armies provided soldiers with rations of alcoholic beverages, and in the North a revenue measure was passed that taxed alcoholic beverages as a means of financing the war. The minutes for the September 26–28, 1863, meeting of the Ten Islands Baptist Association of Alabama, which follow, show the continuing concern, though, for abuse of intoxicating beverages. The minutes also show the leadership role that evangelical churches provided in the temperance campaign. At a time when temperance had faded in importance as a social evil, Baptist leaders were still expressing concern about it.

The Association on motion proceeded to the election of Moderator and Clerk, by ballot. Elder T P Gwin was chosen Moderator, & John M Crook, Clerk. After a few feeling remarks by the Moderator, accepting the position, he called for petitionary letters—none were offered.

The Moderator then called for correspondence, when the following named brethren presented themselves:

From Coosa River—Elder E T Smyth. From Tallassehatchee—brethren Chandler and Allen. From Cherokee—Elder A B Smith with a letter of correspondence, all of whom were duly received and invited to seats with the body.

The following committees were on motion appointed. On the arrangement of Business—John M Crook, Silas Woodruff, James C Wood, Theodore Turk, and Smith Lipscomb. On Finance—M Dickinson and Elias Read, On Documents—Green Griffin and Silas Woodruff. John M Crook was appointed Treasurer.

Committee to arrange preaching—brethren M Dickinson, Matthew Allen, John Brewton, J C Wood, and John Vise.

On motion, agreed to meet in the church house in special prayer meeting for the success of our armies, the independence of our country, and for the success of the Gospel, in building up the Churches of Christ, at half after nine o'clock to-morrow morning.

On motion, it was resolved that at the close of the morning services to-morrow, we will take up a collection for the purpose of sending a Missionary to the army. Adjourned to eight o'clock Monday morning—prayer by Elder James D Read.

Monday Morning the Association met agreeably to adjournment—prayer by the Moderator, The roll was called, and the body proceeded to business.

The Rules of Decorum were read by the Clerk. The report of the committee to prepare business for the action of the Association was read and received.

Appointments

To preach the Introductory Sermon at our next session, Elder Woodruff, Elder E T Read, Alternate. To preach the Missionary Sermon, Elder Gwin, Elder E T Read, Alternate.

Received the report of committee on documents, and committee discharged.

Committees were then appointed on the following subjects:

On Temperance, brethren Crook, Turk and Bowls. On the Religious instruction of Servants, brethren Ragan, Ingram and Vise. On Domestic Missions, brethren J D Read, Hodges and Alford. On Sabbath Schools and Bible Classes, brethren Woodruff, M Dickinson and Griffin.

The next session of this Association to be held with the Church at Mount Zion, Calhoun county Ala on Saturday before the fourth Sabbath in September, 1864.

The Treasurer is authorised to settle with the former Treasurer.

Resolved,

That we do recommend to our membership, daily prayer to Almighty God, for the preservation of our gallant army in the field of battle, and for the independence and prosperity of our beloved country, the Confederate States of America.

Resolved,

That the clerk have published in the Minutes a general letter for all of our correspondents.

Resolved,

That any member of this body who shall think proper, is hereby authorised and requested to act as a messenger from us to any one or more of the bodies with whom we correspond.

Resolved,

That the Associational funds be divided with corresponding messengers by the Treasurer, according to the time thus spent.

Resolved,

That the clerk is hereby appointed agent for the distribution of the minutes among the churches, and if the funds be sufficient that he have eight hundred copies printed, and that he receive ten dollars for superintending the same.

Resolved,

That we return our thanks to our heavenly Father for his care over us, and to our brethren at Post Oak Spring, for their kindness and attention to us during our session.

After singing an appropriate hymn and extending the parting hand, prayer was offered by Elder Silas Woodruff, when the Moderator after a few feeling and appropriate remarks, declared the body adjourned sine die.

Resolved,

That during this unholy war, our churches be requested to hold prayer meetings, specially to ask the interposition of Almighty God in behalf of our country and our institutions, and to crown us with independence and lasting peace.

Whereas, a collection was taken up on Sabbath morning, amounting to $—for the purpose of army missions, by order of this body, therefore Resolved, That Elders Silas Woodruff, T P Gwin, E T Read and John M Crook be and are hereby appointed a committee to give said funds a proper direction.

T. P. Gwin, Moderator.

John M. Crook, Clerk.

The Clerk failed to find in the correspondence any appointment of Union meetings in the first second and fourth districts.

3rd District—Mount Gilead, on Friday before the first Sabbath in August next; Elder Silas Woodruff to preach the Introductory sermon, Elder E T Read, Alternate. To preach on the duties of churches to their pastors, Elder E T Read, and Elder T P Gwin alternate.

Corresponding Letter

Post Oak Spring, Calhoun Co. Ala.

The Ten Islands Association sendeth Christian Salutation:

Dear Brethren:

At the close of one of the most pleasant and agreeable sessions that we recollect ever to have witnessed, we feel happy to again confer with you by letter and messengers. We are at all times rejoiced to receive your correspondence; and would respectfully enquire why this pleasant duty of intercommunication between christian bodies is so often neglected. True the present surroundings are seriously felt in all our deliberations; therefore we feel that we should more earnestly supplicate a throne of grace for that great blessing which we all so much desire, the independence of our beloved South, with its accompanying blessings. With this we send you a token of our love, with assurances of our christian affection. Our minutes will show who we have appointed as Messengers to your body.

Respectfully,

John M. Crook, Sec'y.

T. P. Gwin, Mod.

Report on Domestic Missions

We your committee beg leave to report, that we have had the subject of Home Missions under consideration; and do feel to lament that a subject of such vast importance is so much neglected. And as we believe that Home Missions are so well understood that they need no explanation, and that the field of labor has opened so large and wide in our midst, and the Macedonian cry is heard from so many directions, that we as an Association are called upon to come up to the help of the Lord against the mighty. The Savior's admonition is appropriate to us;

"Lift up your eyes and look upon the fields, for they are white already to harvest." Say not brethren, four months and we will attend to this but let us come to the work at once. We would suggest and recommend, that as the Lord of the harvest has crowned our fields with plenty, and filled our pockets with money, that this Association employ missionaries one to preach to our fathers, husbands, brothers and sons in the army; the other to our mothers, wives, sisters and children at home especially in the destitute bounds of our churches, unsupplied by a regular pastor. Dear brethren, to think of the poor soldier dying without hope in Jesus, who has sacrificed all the pleasures of association with father, mother, brother; sisters, wives and children, all the loved ones at home and all that interests man on earth, and take his life in his hand as it were to stand, fight and defend; not only home and firesides, but our religious altars and principles, handed down to us by the great Head of the Churches, through our forefathers. The heart is enlisted in this great struggle for moral and religious liberty. All of which is submitted.

Report on Temperance

The different societies in our common country, when united, constitute one great family, mutually interested and morally bound for each other's protection; and are under an imperious obligation to feed and clothe such as are physically or mentally disqualified for supplying their own wants. Hence, every man ought to feel it to be his duty, not only to abstain from every indulgence that will have a demoralising tendency upon his own mind, but also to exert himself to the extent of the ability with which God has endowed him, in the suppression of whatever impairs the intellect, produces debility, or blunts the sensibilities of others. Inasmuch therefore, as the habitual use of intoxicating liquors legitimately tends to drunkenness, produces physical debility, mental imbecility, and spreads blight and mildew in the social circle, is a public nuisance; and by beggaring its votaries; thrusts them as paupers upon the State. It follows inevitably that the habitual use of intoxicating spirits ought to be frowned upon, as being in direct antagonism to that principle which is the chief corner stone of social happiness, and to which the Saviour referred when he said to his disciples;

"All things whatsoever ye would that men should do unto you, do ye even so unto them; for this is the law and the prophets."

While all men as good citizens ought to enlist in the cause of temperance, the churches are in a higher and peculiar sense, most solemnly and imperatively bound to enter unitedly and singly upon the duty of suppressing, by every laudable means, the use of ardent spirits as a beverage. Then let our churches assume the high and uncompromising position on this question, which the interests of our holy christianity demand, and then as the leader in the crusade against intemperance, will they occupy the high potion as the light of the world, which will be well pleasing to the great Lawgiver of Zion. When freed from the shackles of intemperance, they will present a galaxy in the temperance cause that will strike with terror and dismay the sordid retailers of the hellish poison, and snatch them from a drunkard's grave; and should unitedly pray to God to save them from the consequences of that death that never dies. In conclusion; we offer the following resolutions:

1st Resolved,

That it is the sense of this Association, that the habitual use of intoxicating liquors is productive of physical debility; is injurious to the mind, and has a demoralizing effect upon those who thus use them.

2nd Resolved,

That all christians ought to abstain from the use of ardent spirits as a beverage, themselves, and as far as practicable influence offers to follow their example.

Report on Religious Instruction of Colored People

We your committee upon instruction to colored people, beg leave to report, that while we have had the subject to some extent under consideration, and from the best information that we have been able to arrive at, while some churches and some masters seem alive to the subject, too many seem to neglect to a great extent the religious instruction of this class of our population. We would suggest that our churches adopt some plan for the stated instruction of our blacks, either by stated preaching for their benefit, or by separate apartments, (as many of our churches have) for their occupation; which plan we prefer; at least for our country churches, where this class of our population is small, as calling for less labor at the hands of the ministry. And further, we would earnestly present the subject to our brethren who are masters (believing that while God sanctions the institution of slavery, he requires you to regard the spiritual welfare of your slaves,) and beg you to see that your servants are regular and orderly in their attendance at our churches on the Sabbath, instead of desecrating as is too often the case, God's holy day by labor or, traffic, or idle roving about; which is demoralising. These things are deemed worthy of our consideration, even in view of our present good, knowing that the religious servant is always the obedient. Respectfully submitted.

REPORT ON DOCUMENTS

The committee reported no matter worthy of the attention of the body had been presented during the session.
ORDINATIONS.—During this associational year, our estimable brother E. T. Read was, by a Presbytery called for that purpose, duly examined and ordained to the great work of the Gospel ministry.
REVIVAL MEETING.—After the adjournment of the Association at Post Oak Spring, the church continued the meeting until the ensuing Sabbath, during which they received by baptism 18 & by letter 5 additional members.

 Report of Committee on Finance.

 The committee on finance report; that they received on Sabbath,

 for army missions, ...$353.00
 For Printing the Minutes, ... 73.20
 Associational purposes, ... 39.75
 All of which is submitted and paid
  over to the Treasurer. $465.95
 M. Dickinson, Chairman.

SOURCE:

"Minutes of the Proceedings of the Ten Islands Baptist Association. Held with the Church at Post Oak Spring, Calhoun County, Alabama, on the 26th, 27th and 28th Days of September, 1863." The University Library at the University of North Carolina at Chapel Hill, 2001 < http://docsouth.unc.edu/imls/tenislands/tenislands.xml> [accessed January 13, 2008].

Document 6: THE TEMPLE OF HONOR

How did temperance organizations persuade people to put aside the social act of drinking in company? This broadsheet dated January 1, 1870, from the Temple of Honor in Rhode Island reflects the type of communication that was popular in temperance clubs as members supported each other in the resolve to stay dry. The message to remain dry was absolute, expressed in the phrase, "Touch Not! Taste Not!" Stories were a popular way to highlight the dangers inherent in even the smallest slip in the commitment to abstain from alcohol.

Address to Temperance Societies everywhere.

(*Written for the Temple of Honor.*)

You have banded together in a glorious cause,—
To fight against evil, and inhuman laws.
As your numbers increase may it strengthen your power,
While each, at his post, stands firm as a tower.
The sad fruits of drinking are everywhere met,
While the rumseller's snare for his victims is set;—
Wives' hearts throb with anguish as the dim lamp doth burn,
And breathless they listen for the lost one's return;
They watch over their children and blush for the stain
Transmitted to them, to sully their name.
Fond memory rolls back, like a summer day tide
To the hour when each mother stood a beautiful bride;—
Confiding in him who a traitor has proved.
While he turns from his home and the wife he once loved.
O, ye who are pledged by your oaths before heaven,
As in mercy you hope that you may be forgiven:
Sit not down an idler, but heed the sad call;
Be true to your mission, —there's work for you all.
Feed the hungry, clothe the naked, take the drunkard by the hand;
With kind words invite him to join with your band;
Let him feel you're his friend and will help him all you can
And ere another New Year shall dawn on the earth,
May each harbor for liquor to temperance give birth;
While the carols of angels join in the glad strain,—
"King Alcohol's dead! with all his dark train.
Let the children of earth hold a grand jubilee.
The fathers have conquered, posterity's free!"
 A.E.H.
 Pawtucket, Jan. 1, 1870.

Touch Not! Taste Not!

Friends of freedom! swell the song;
    Young and old, the strain prolong;
Make the temperance army strong,
    And on to victory!
Lift up your banners, let them wave—
Onward march, a world to save:
Who would fill a drunkard's grave
    And bear his infamy?

Shrink not when the foe appears;
Spurn the coward's guilty fears;
Hear the shrieks, behold the tears,
    Of ruined families!
Raise the cry in every spot,
"Touch not, taste not, handle not!"
Who would be a drunken sot,
    The worst of miseries?

Give the aching bosom rest;
Carry joy to every breast;
Make the wretched drunkard blest,
    By living soberly.
Raise the glorious watchword high,
"Touch not, taste not till you die!"
Let the echo reach the sky.
    And earth keep jubilee.

God of mercy, hear us plead:
For thy help we intercede:
See how many bosoms bleed,
    And heal them speedily.
When beneath its gentle ray,
TEMPERANCE all the world shall sway,
    And reign triumphantly.

Select Tales

Resisting Temptation

A young man, or rather boy, for he was seventeen years of age, was a clerk in one of the great mercantile establishments of New York. An orphan and poor, he must rise, if he rose at all, by his own exertions. His handsome, honest face, and free, cordial manner, won him the friendship of all his fellow-laborers, and many were the invitations he received to join them in the club-room, in the theatre, and even the bar-room. But Alfred Harris had the pure teachings of a Christian mother to withhold him from rushing headlong into dissipation and vice, and all the persuasions of his comrades could not induce him to join them in scenes like this. He feared the consequences.

One evening, one of his fellow clerks, George Warren, the most high-toned and moral one among them, invited Alfred to go home with him to supper and make the acquaintance of his family. The boy gladly assented, for he spent many lonely evenings, with only his books and his thoughts for company.

He found his friend's family very social and entertaining. Mrs. Warren, the mother, was a pleasant, winning, I might almost say, fascinating woman; one of the kind whose every little speech seems of consequence, and whose every act, praiseworthy. Mr. Warren was a cheery, social gentleman, fond of telling stories and amusing young people. And George's sister, Jessie—how shall I describe her? A girl about Alfred's own age, a half-bashful, half-saucy, dimpled-faced, rosy-cheeked maiden, sparkling with wit and pleasantry, and pretty enough for any young man to fall in love with at first sight.

This was Mr. Warren's family, and it was no wonder that Alfred was charmed with them. They were not very wealthy people, but were in easy circumstances, and on a promising road to fortune. Alfred very soon felt as well acquainted with them as if he had known them for years. The supper was delicious, especially to a boy whose small salary could afford him only the plainest living.

After supper, wine was brought in. Mrs. Warren poured it out herself, and with a winning smile passed a glass of the sparkling liquid to their guest. Alfred took it with some hesitation, but did not raise it to his lips. Each of the family held a glass, waiting to pledge their visitor. But Alfred feared to drink. He set the goblet on the table, while a burning flush overspread his face.

"What! do you not drink wine?" asked Mrs. Warren in her pleasant tones.

"I have been taught not to drink it," said Alfred.

"You have had good teaching, I doubt not," said the lady, "and I honor you for respecting it, but I think it makes a difference where and in what company you take it. I should not be willing for George to go into a barroom in company with dissipated young men and call for wine, but at home, in the family circle, it is different. A moderate use of wine never hurts any one. It is only when carried to excess that it is injurious. You had better drink yours. So little as that will never hurt you."

Jessie was sitting by Alfred. She took up the glass he had set on the table and gave it to him with a charming smile.

"Drink it for my sake," she said.

Again he took the goblet in his hand. The glowing wine was tempting, but the faces around him were more tempting still. He raised it toward his lips. But at that moment there rose up before him a pale, sweet face, with pleading eyes—the face of his mother in heaven. The boy laid down the glass with a firm hand, and with firm tones he said:

"I cannot drink it. It was my mother's dying request that I should never taste of wine, and if I disregard it now, I fear greater temptations will follow. You must pardon my seeming discourtesy, but I cannot drink it."

A silence fell upon the little circle. None spoke for several minutes.

Then Mrs. Warren said in a voice choked with emotion:

"Forgive me, my boy, for tempting you to violate your conscience. Would that all young men would show as high a sense of duty."

Every one of the family put down their wine untasted.

"The boy is right," said Mr. Warren. "Drinking wine leads to deeper potations. We have done wrong in setting such an example before our children. Here, Ellen," he called to the servant, "take away this decanter."

And as the table was cleared of the wine and glasses, Mr. Warren said, solemnly:

"Now here, in the presence of you all, I make a solemn vow never to have any more wine on my table, or drink it myself as a beverage; and may my influence and precepts be as binding on my children as the request of this boy's mother to him."

And Mrs. Warren softly responded:

"Amen!"

Mr. Warren turned to Alfred.

"We are not drunkards or wine bibbers, here, my boy. I have always preached temperance to my children, but I have never realized before how an occasional glass of wine, if partaken of in good society, could injure. I see it now. If a person can drink one glass, he can drink another, and yet another, and it is hard to know just where to draw the line. I thank you for this lesson. I will show that I have as much manliness as a mere boy. My children, will you follow my example and pledge to abstain totally from wine as a beverage?"

"We will, father," was the response.

This pledge was never broken by any of the family, and never did Alfred Harris have cause to regret that he resisted the temptation to drink one cup of wine.

Years afterward, when he was a prosperous and worthy merchant, and sweet Jessie Warren was his wife, they often spoke of the consequences which might have followed, had he yielded to that one temptation; and Jessie tries to impress as firm principles upon the minds of her children as her husband's mother instilled into the heart of her boy.

Temperance Notes

A Terrible Enemy.—The rumseller is a terrible enemy to the happiness of every family circle. He sits in the lurking places of the villages, like a beast of prey. He fastens his eyes upon the youth and sets forth the most tempting bait to draw them into his net. If some huge serpent lurking near, should now and then glide along the street and wind his fatal folds around somebody's son and crush him, who could remain indifferent and inactive? Every parent, every citizen would rise up, and that serpent would be dragged forth and destroyed, though his den were a rocky fortress. That serpent could kill but the body. The rumseller kills the body and soul together. And yet persons who know all this, and who would sooner follow a son to the grave in life's fair morning, than see him live to become a victim to the rumseller, will all sit still with folded hands and see the work of ruin go on busily around him. Once a fierce wolf, went prowling over the hills and valleys, thinning the flocks of the farmers. The men rose up, pursued the enemy to his lair, the bravest of them went in and confronted and destroyed him. The wolf preyed only upon the flocks, the rumsellers prey upon the precious youth. Had that wolf been endowed with perpetual life, and had he devoured the sons instead of the lambs, he would not have been at all so terrible an enemy to the homes of the country as are the rumsellers, who are fattening by the ruin of souls.

When I Was a Boy.—Boys, I want to tell you a story of an accident that happened when I was a boy.

Thirty-eight years ago—some seven boys or more, were at a boarding school on the North river. Near the school lived a widow who was very kind to all of us, and gave us many a handful of fruit, and also kind words.

One day she sent us all an invitation to attend a children's party at her house. We were all there in the evening, and had a very pleasant time with looking at pictures, playing, and listening to the welcome stories she told us. About nine o'clock, she invited us to another room to eat the good things she had provided. After we had finished all the cake, oranges, nuts, &c., she brought out a decanter of wine, and pouring it out into a number of wine glasses, invited us to drink it. We remember well how we felt. We did not like to decline, and still we could not take it. By-and-by our turn came. We blushed as red in the face as a boy could, and stammered out our thanks, but declined; three other boys followed our example. One of these boys died a thorough temperance man three years since, and the others are living, all staunch temperance men. One of the boys who took that wine died before he was seventeen years old, a drunkard. Another at eighteen years of age and another at twenty five—all drunkards. The youngest of the number who drank that night, we could show you today in a city not far off, who is also a drunkard.

Boys, it requires *courage* to resist the wine cup, especially under the circumstances in which we were placed. A boy on a canal boat, some years ago (on the Erie canal) was importuned all day by a company of travellers to drink liquor. He declined time after time. At last one of the men said, "Come, boy, why won't you drink?" Said he, "The word of God says, 'My son, if sinners entice thee, consent thou not.'" The men had nothing to say, and the noble boy was not troubled any more. Will *you* stand up for the right?

Source:

"The Temple of Honor: Devoted to the Cause of Temperance." Olive Branch Temple of Honor Publishers. Jan. 1, 1870. Alcohol, Temperance, & Prohibition: A Brown University Digital Collection <http://dl.lib.brown.edu/jpegs/1092325886662125.jpg> [accessed January 24, 2008].

Document 7: "O, Come and Sign the Pledge"

How were the arts and popular entertainment used to spread the message of the ills of alcohol, and that it was possible to have fun without alcoholic drinks? Many working-class men who joined temperance societies did so out of a desire to replace the camaraderie of the bar with other forms of fellowship. Temperance songs, such as this one published in 1876, reflect the socialization that was an important part of men's temperance societies and clubs.

To My Friend J.K. Osgood

Song and Chorus.
Written and composed by E.W. Locke.

Ho, ye who love the winecup, and quaff the flowing bowl,
Too long you've been in bondage, come free yourself today;
Your comrades are deserting, their names are on our roll;
Salvation is so easy—just dash the cup away:
This is the golden moment, come now within the fold
Tho' long amidst the desert, like sheep you've been astray;
Tho' covered o'er with bruises and hungry, wet, and cold,
There's all you need in waiting, you may be saved today.

O, dash away the poison, it has a fearful spell,
It binds you ere you know it, and gives you no release;
It fills the soul with anguish no mortal tongue can tell;
O, come and join our numbers, and find a life of peace:—
Hear ye the wail of thousands, who're writhing in their chains?
Hear ye their plea for pity, their cry to come and save?
Your hearts are not so stony, you do not heed their pains,
Then come with us to seek them, and rescue from the grave.

O, ye who're undecided, who feel your flesh is weak,
Who feel you are not able, to keep the better way;
There's no time like the present, the little word to speak;
And if you lack the courage, just look above and pray:
Behold the converts coming, they crowd on every side,
They're ready for enrollment, and will you longer wait?
Just now it is so easy to join the swelling tide,
O, wait not till tomorrow, it then may be too late.

We have no party quarrels, we've no discordant creeds,
We do not want an office, are slaves to no one's will;
Our mission's with the drunkard, to meet his many needs;
For tho' he's like a leper, he is a brother still;

Come, stand in line among us, and dash the cup away,
One manly resolution, the battle's nearly fought;
Assert in pride your manhood, but don't forget to pray,
For one there is who helpeth, when all our strength is naught.

CHORUS (harmonized)
O, come and sign the pledge, O, come and sign the pledge;
Just break away, and firmly say, "O, yes I'll sign the pledge."
O, come and sign the pledge, O, come and sign the pledge;
You'll bless the day you threw away Your strong drink for the pledge.

SOURCE:

E. W. Locke. "O, Come and Sign the Pledge," sheet music (Boston: G. D. Russell, 1876) <http://memory.loc.gov/cgi-bin/ampage> [accessed January 13, 2008].

Document 8: A Man of Unique Methods

Was temperance just about personal improvement, or did it cultivate a sense of sociality and "belonging" among its followers? Did temperance presentations even double as entertainment? During the period of Reconstruction, because political parties were reluctant to take on the divisive issue of prohibition, temperance gatherings took on a decidedly social air. Note that the following article from the April 22, 1878, New York Times *reports as much on the "delivery," or entertainment value, of Francis Murphy's temperance address as it does on the surprisingly large response to his appeal for the audience to take the temperance pledge.*

The Blue Ribbon Orator.

Francis Murphy's Debut in New-York—
A Vehement Temperance Exhortation, in Which the Speaker's Feet Play an Important Part—Hundreds of Pledges and Yards of Ribbon Given Away.

The announcement that Francis Murphy would deliver his first public address in this City, before the American Temperance Union, yesterday afternoon, brought together a throng of people that filled the great hall of the Cooper Union to repletion. Shortly after 3 o'clock the President, Mr. Mundy, the Chaplain, and a third gentleman entered amid subdued applause, and took their seats. The third gentleman was Francis Murphy, and, seating himself, he began to twirl his thumbs in Quaker fashion and to glance around upon the sea of faces with a pleasant smile. His costume was rather out of the ordinary style. He wore a very long frock coat, black trousers, a piccadilly collar, and boots that shone with a mirror-like polish. In the snow-white bosom of his shirt shone a gem, the brilliant glitter of which at once attracted the attention of the audience.

After the singing of a hymn, Mr. Mundy, in a brief speech, introduced Mr. Murphy, who was greeted with prolonged applause. Mr. Murphy said he was about to speak on Gospel temperance, and he hoped all his auditors would pray for him in order that what he said might be blessed. His motto in the work was, "With malice toward none, with charity for all." He had no quarrel with those who drank or those who sold liquor. Men had a perfect right to do both. He knew that if men did not drink men would not sell. Osman Pasha had to surrender Plevna because he had no supplies. As soon as the liquor-seller found he had no supply he would cease his traffic. The plain fact was that men must come to a knowledge of the truth that they have all a personal responsibility in the cause of total abstinence, and then the traffic would stop and liquor-drinking would stop. "My theme will be from real life this afternoon," he said, after breaking off abruptly to greet a friend, "and when I speak of myself and my experiences, I hope none will take offense." He then went on to describe some of the "true old Irish hospitality," and in his description assume a rich brogue, and, at times, gesticulated with the index fingers of both hands in a manner that much resembled the rather amusing peculiarity of the natives of Japan. After describing in a touching manner his parting from his mother, his departure for America, his sea voyage, he narrated his landing. He was met by three or four young acquaintances from the "old country," and together they repaired to a saloon. Here they received the warmest of warm greetings, the smiling bar-tender greeting them, strangers though they were, as heartily as if he had known them all his life. Then everybody treated, they "set them up," and "put them down" again and again, and kept it up until it was impossible to tell who set them up or who put them down, and everything became frightfully confused. "Can any one wonder," the speaker exclaimed, "why those bar-keepers should keep friends with our young men when churches cannot attract them? The reason is there is too much religion done up in broadcloth and kid gloves." And, amid general laughter, the speaker gave an imitation of the freezing dignity with which the ushers of some churches receive a stranger who happens to enter a sacred edifice. The speaker next described his downfall, his incarceration in the County Jail at Portland, and spoke of the kindness shown him at that time by Capt. Cyrus Sturtevant, to whose compassionate interest in his reformation was due, he said, any good he might have since done. In the peroration the speaker's painfully excessive vehemence produced an anticlimax that was almost ludicrous. He had undertaken to picture of a vision of the liquor curse just previous to its destruction. He described a tree, the branches of which were covered with hideous black serpents that were hissing at human beings beneath the branches. He screamed vehemently that he would crush the monsters to death, and began to stamp wildly about the platform, pounding so vigorously as to raise small clouds of dust. "Oh, how I hate, hate, hate you!" he yelled, as he annihilated imaginary reptiles. "I will kill you! kill you! kill you! I thank God that I am an Irishman and that I can handle a spade and dig your graves." This sentiment he followed with more resounding stamps with both feet, and then stopping abruptly said in an ordinary tone of voice, "Good afternoon, God bless you," and stepped back to his seat. He arose quickly, however, and exclaimed rapidly and loudly, "Where are those pledges?" A great pile of large cards issued by the National Temperance Union and bearing Mr. Murphy's portrait above the motto: "With malice toward none, with charity for all," were brought out, together with countless strips of blue ribbon, and placed on a table. Stepping to the edge of the platform, Murphy said, "All those wishing to sign the pledge will have an opportunity to do so." He then cried out aloud very many times, "Come all men! Come all men!" A very unusual spectacle was then witnessed. Hundreds crowded around the platform to shake hands with the speaker and to receive the pledges and bands of blue ribbon. Cards were flung in the midst of the audience by many ready hands, and yards and yards of ribbon were distributed. This continued, the assemblage in the meantime singing "Hold the Fort" for some time, during which, probably, more pledges were issued than were ever before given away in any public assemblage in New York City.

SOURCE:

"A Man of Unique Methods." The New York Times. April 22, 1878 <http://query.nytimes.com/gst/abstract.html?res=9801E3DB113AE63BBC4A51DFB2668383669FDE> [accessed January 7, 2008].

***

Document 9: **Two Methods of Reform**

In an era before broadcast speeches, how could temperance organizers ensure that the messages delivered by individual orators would be powerful and uniform? By the end of the Reconstruction era, the National Temperance Society and Publication House was producing thousands of pamphlets designed to motivate public opinion against intoxicating drink. This particular address was published in an 1881 book of arguments and speeches that could be used by a local temperance society to persuade members of a community to take the pledge, or to support prohibition legislative measures, or both.

The temperance reform, broad as it is, divides itself naturally into two branches; it is a reform of two methods. It is a reform, you know, in the first place, of the individual; it is a struggle against inward temptation; and then, as applied to society, it is a struggle against the outward incitement. So that, again, it divides itself into moral and legal suasion. We need moral suasion, of course, as the foundation of everything; we need correct public sentiment as the foundation of all correct action, and nobody can overvalue this. It is always to be present in our efforts, and nobody should think, if we make but little mention of it in our conventions, that we therefore ignore it. It is because we do not wish perpetually to go laying against the foundations. The foundations have all been laid. We all believe in it; we all know it; we were all brought up to appreciate the value of it, and we do not wish to be repeatedly naming to wearisomeness the platitudes that have been repeated so often in regard to this cause. We know it all by heart; we value and cling to it, and we expect to as long as we are engaged in this temperance warfare. But out of this grows the necessity for legal suasion. I have a very short method with those who advocate moral suasion alone. I say, "Practice it upon yourself first. Persuade yourselves first to be total-abstinence men; for nine-tenths of the men who talk about this are not total-abstinence men themselves. Persuade yourselves, then try it upon your neighbor; then go hand-in-hand with those noble organizations that are lifting up the weak. Do the work of moral suasion; lift men up from the gutter; and then, depend upon it, there will be no man more earnest and pronounced than you in an effort to make the streets safe for the men you have rescued from the gutter." No man who has a Christian heart, who has wept and prayed over the victim of intemperance, and has succeeded in elevating him into the image of God, with a clean heart and a pure soul—no man trembles more than that man when he sends him forth to his daily work, to run the gauntlet of the legalized grogshops that lie in his path; and no matter what that man's theory may have been when he started, he comes back from the work of benevolence indignant at the civilization that allows the weak to be tempted back to destruction again by this public incitement to vice and iniquity. So that let every man follow moral suasion to the end, not with mouth and word only, but with the heart and hand, and I will risk his feeling upon this subject of moral suasion.

Hon. R. C. Pitman

SOURCE:

R. C. Pitman. "Two Methods of Reform," in *The National Temperance Orator,* edited by Miss L. Penney (New York: National Temperance Society and Publication House, 1881), pp. 13–15.

Document 10: FRANCES WILLARD

What particular strategies did women use to build support for political action, before they were allowed to vote and before they had much access to media outlets? The following excerpt from Caroline Merrick's 1901 memoir reveals one of Frances Willard's strategies in building support for the Women's Christian Temperance Union (WCTU). Willard was president of the WCTU from 1879 to 1898, and she built it into the largest organization of women in the nineteenth century. Willard's personal charm played an important role in her recruiting, but more important, she was able to identify community leaders quickly and enlist them as leaders in the temperance cause. Note that when Caroline Merrick was reluctant to become a WCTU leader, Willard got Mr. Merrick to persuade his wife to accept the role. Caroline Merrick was an active suffragist and president of the Louisiana WCTU.

Chapter XIII Frances Willard

In June, 1881, I spoke by invitation before the Alumnae Association of Whitworth College, at Brookhaven, Mississippi,—a venerable institution under the care of the Methodist Episcopal Church South. I did not give those young women strong doctrine, but I set before them the duty to

"Learn the mystery of progression truly:—Nor dare to blame God's gifts for incompleteness."

Bishop Keener, the well-known opponent of women's public work, sat beside me on the platform. When the addresses were concluded, he pronounced them "very good." "For women?" I asked. "No," he returned, "for *anybody!*" I treated the gentlemen to some of the extemporaneous "sugar plums" which for a half century they have been accustomed to shower from the rostrum upon women—"just to let them see how it sounded." Though it was against the rules, they applauded as if they were delighted.

I said, "Lest they should feel overlooked and slighted, I will say a word to the men—God bless them. Our hearts warm toward the manly angels—our rulers, guides, and protectors, to whom we confide all our troubles and on whom we lay all our burdens. Oh! what a noble being is an honest, upright, fearless, generous, manly man! How such men endear our firesides, and adorn and bless our homes. How sweet is their encouragement of our timid efforts in every good word and work, and how grateful we are to be loved by these noble comforters, and how utterly wretched and sad this world would be, deprived of their honored and gracious presence. Again, I say God bless the men."

This occasion was of moment to me, because it led to one of the chief events of my life—my friendship and work with Frances E. Willard. She had seen in the New Orleans *Times* the address I made at Brookhaven, and was moved to ask me if I could get her an audience in my city, which she had already visited without results. I had been invited to join the little band enlisted by Mrs. Annie Wittenmeyer, the first president of the National Woman's Christian Temperance Union; but I had declined, saying that this temperance work was the most unpopular and hardest reform ever attempted. However, I looked up the remnant of the first society, and went with their good president, Mrs. Frances A. Lyons, to call on every minister in town, requesting each to announce the date of Miss Willard's address, and to urge upon their congregations that they should hear her speak. We were uncommonly successful, even that princely Christian, Rev. B. F. Palmer D. D., departing from the usual Presbyterian conservatism. The result was a large audience in Carondelet Methodist Church, of which Rev. Felix R. Hill was the brave pastor;—for it required no little moral courage at that time to introduce a woman to speak, and to do it in a church, and on a subject upon which the public conscience was not only asleep, but which affronted even many Christians' sense of personal liberty.

I remember that I remonstrated when Miss Willard removed her bonnet and stood with uncovered head. But I could find no fault with the noble expression of serene sadness on her clear-cut features and with the gentle humility and sweetness which emanated from her entire personality. Heavenly sentiments dropped in fitly chosen sentences with perfect utterance, as she argued for the necessity of a clear brain and pure habits in order to establish the Master's kingdom on earth. The hearts of the people went out to her in spontaneous sympathy and admiration; and the brethren were ready to bid her Godspeed, for they felt that this public appearance was due to an impelling conviction that would not let her be silent. Thus the New Orleans Methodist Church, that indomitable pioneer of reform, proclaimed "All hail! to Frances Willard and the glorious cause."

Some effort had been made to attain this success. With Miss Willard's telegram in hand, I had despatched a message to my son, Edwin T. Derrick, jr., and to the W. C. T. U., but the train arriving ahead of time, a carriage brought the expected guest and her companion, Miss Anna Gordon, to my door, where I alone received and welcomed them. After weary travels over thousands of miles and stoppages in as many towns, they were glad to rest a week in my home. I had sent out hundreds of cards for a reception. My house was thronged. Distinguished members of the bench, the bar, the pulpit, the press and the literary world were present, and a large number of young women and men. Frances Willard came to most of these as a revelation—this unassuming, delicate, progressive woman, with her sweet, intellectual face, her ready gaiety and her extraordinarily enlarged sympathies, which seemed to put her spirit at once in touch with every one who spoke to her. She wore, I remember, a black brocaded silk and point lace fichu. She ever had the right word in the right place as she greeted each one who was presented.

She particularly desired to see Geo. W. Cable, who was present with his wife. "This is our literary lion tonight," I said. "Oh, no!" he replied, "I come nearer being your house cat!" at which sally Miss Willard laughed. This visit was in March, 1882.

I did not attend all of Miss Willard's meetings, and was greatly surprised when on returning from one of them she informed me that I was the president of the W. C. T. U. of New Orleans. I protested, and let her know I did not even have a membership in that body of women, she herself being for me the only object of interest in it. Finding that the source of power in my family resided ultimately in the head of the house, she wisely directed her persuasions in his direction. It was not long before I was advised by Mr. Merrick to come to terms and do whatever Miss Willard requested. This was the beginning of my work in the Woman's Christian Temperance Union and of a friendship which lasted until God called this lovely and gifted being to come up into a larger life.

SOURCE:

Caroline E. Merrick. *Old Times in Dixie Land: A Southern Matron's Memories* (New York: Grafton Press, 1901) <http://docsouth.unc.edu/fpn/merrick/merrick.html> [accessed January 13, 2008].

BIBLIOGRAPHY

Blocker, Jack S. *American Temperance Movements: Cycles of Reform.* Boston: Twayne, 1989. In this work, Blocker looks at areas of temperance reform and searches for patterns in approaches to temperance. The work includes photographs.

Burns, Eric. *The Spirits of America: A Social History of Alcohol.* Philadelphia: Temple University Press, 2004. A journalist, Burns tells the stories of the Temperance Movement and prohibition efforts in a highly readable style. Notes are included at the end of the book.

Gusfield, Joseph R. *Symbolic Crusade.* Urbana: University of Illinois Press, 1963. Gusfield examines the Temperance Movement from a sociological perspective.

Key, V. O., Jr. *Politics, Parties, and Pressure Groups,* fifth edition. New York: Crowell, 1964. Key examines special-interest groups in American politics and suggests how they influence political parties and political action. The text provides a short but useful discussion of how temperance groups affected prohibition laws.

Krout, John Allen. *The Origins of Prohibition.* New York: Russell & Russell, 1925. Krout provides a detailed explanation of the Temperance Movement up to the beginning of the Civil War.

Lipset, Seymour M. "Religion and Politics in the American Past and Present," in *Religion and Social Conflict,* edited by Robert Lee and Martin E. Marty. New York: Oxford University Press, 1964. This article discusses the role of religion in the Temperance Movement, with a focus on how the approaches of established American denominations differed from those of evangelicals.

Pegram, Thomas R. *Battling Demon Rum: The Struggle for a Dry America, 1800–1933.* Chicago: Ivan R. Dee, 1998. Pegram's work provides a chronological overview of the Temperance Movement with many anecdotes and details.

Rorabaugh, W. J. *The Alcoholic Republic: An American Tradition.* New York: Oxford University Press, 1979. Rorabaugh's work is considered a classic analysis of the social and political concerns that led to changes in the Temperance Movement and that ultimately gave reformers the power to pass prohibition.

Rumbarger, John J. *Profits, Power, and Prohibition: Alcohol Reform and the Industrializing of America, 1800–1930.* Albany: State University of New York Press, 1989. Rumbarger looks at the Temperance Movement from an economic perspective, especially considering men of wealth who influenced the formation of temperance societies and the passage of legislation.

Stokes, Anson Phelps, and Leo Pfeffer. *Church and State in the United States,* revised edition. New York: Harper, 1950. This one-volume edition contains a concise discussion of the role of religious leaders in the Temperance and Prohibition Movements.

Szymanski, Ann-Marie E. *Pathways to Prohibition: Radicals, Moderates, and Social Movement Outcomes.* Durham, N.C.: Duke University Press, 2003. Szymanski examines the Temperance Movement in detail, including regional information and data as she explains the national movement for temperance and prohibition.

Wiebe, Robert H. *The Opening of American Society, from the Adoption of the Constitution to the Eve of Disunion.* New York: Knopf, 1984. Wiebe surveys the development of American political and social culture up to the Civil War.

~ 9 ~

Religion in the Age of Slavery

On March 4, 1865, President Abraham Lincoln gave his second inaugural address as the Civil War was coming to a close. In his speech, Lincoln sought to explain the hundreds of thousands of deaths. Asserting that slavery was "somehow the cause of the war," Lincoln noted that in many ways, the Civil War was a religious conflict. He commented that both sides "read the same Bible and pray to the same God"; his implication was, perhaps, that the prayers of both sides could not be answered (Lincoln, 1905, 46–47).

Slaves, abolitionists, and defenders of slavery all wrestled with the definition of slavery and freedom. Abolitionists drew upon the Christian doctrine of the equality of all humans in the eyes of God to support their denouncement of slavery as a grievous sin. Southern supporters of slavery defended a literal interpretation of the Bible that seemed to prove that slavery was divinely ordained, and they envisioned slavery as a Christian institution that both cared for and converted slaves who adopted Christianity to affirm their worth as human beings. Slaves constructed an alternate vision of Christianity as a religion that guaranteed freedom in this world as well as in the next. How is it possible for sincere Christians to use religion, especially the Bible, for such divergent purposes?

The number of Christian churches multiplied during the antebellum era, and although many Christians viewed the early national era (1790–1810) as a low point for American churches—with low attendance and widespread skepticism toward religion—Protestant evangelical denominations, especially the Baptists and the Methodists, grew by leaps and bounds beginning with the Second Great Awakening. The Methodists increased from 50 congregations in 1780 to 20,000 in 1860, while the Baptists increased over the same period from 400 churches to 12,150. A major reason for this explosive growth was the popularity of revivals, in which thousands gathered together to hear direct emotional preaching calling sinners to repentance. Evangelicals espoused a popular faith that emphasized an immediate, personal conversion experience. Many evangelicals believed that God had chosen the United States as a "providential nation" to perfect Christian civilization and to spread it throughout the world. To achieve this goal, evangelical Protestants created organizations dedicated to reforming American society; these private groups sought to improve prisons, help the poor, and send missionaries abroad. These societies flourished in both the North and the South—and with the emergence of the most radical of these movements, abolitionism, the sections came into conflict.

Until the 1830s, most critics of slavery advocated the improvement of the condition of slaves or a gradual emancipation spread over decades or longer. With the formation of the American Anti-Slavery Society (AAS) in New York in 1833, a new radicalism entered the antislavery movement. Although a majority of Northern churches continued to resist the immediate emancipation of slaves, the AAS influenced abolitionist insistence upon both immediate emancipation and the inclusion of freed blacks into American society as citizens.

While abolitionists certainly drew upon secular concepts of freedom in the Declaration of Independence, Christianity was the most powerful source of their attacks on slavery. Abolitionists like William Lloyd Garrison and Frederick Douglass condemned slavery as a sin against God and humanity. Abolitionists called upon masters to repent and free their slaves. Abolitionists employed "moral suasion," or moral pressure, in their attempts to convert masters. In 1835 the AAS flooded Southern post offices with thousands of tracts and pamphlets denouncing slavery as unchristian and predicting that the nation—particularly the South—would face God's wrath unless they reformed. In reaction, mobs of white Southerners burned the offending pamphlets and passed laws making it a capital offense to possess abolitionist literature.

Conservative ministers denounced abolitionists as fanatics who endangered the Union and placed abolition above the salvation of souls. In response, abolitionists attacked many Northern churches as being proslavery, denouncing them as "bulwarks of slavery." Antislavery advocates agitated within the major Protestant denominations, sending petitions to the periodic annual conventions. In 1837 the Presbyterian Church split into so-called New School and Old School denominations after bitter debates over the morality of slavery, although other issues also played a role. In 1844 the Methodists and the Baptists divided internally over slavery. When Georgia bishop James O. Andrew inherited a slave through marriage, he was attacked by antislavery Methodists. Southerners defended slavery as a Christian institution and seceded to form the Methodist Episcopal Church, South. Disputes over whether missionaries could own slaves led to the division within Baptist sects. Despite such splits, not all Northern churches fully embraced antislavery.

Under attack from abolitionists, Southern whites developed a sophisticated defense of slavery as a Christian institution. Proslavery writers pointed out that the patriarchs of the Old Testament, Abraham, Isaac, Jacob, and Job all owned slaves. Abraham was blessed by God as the founder of his chosen people. Also, slavery was expressly recognized and regulated in the laws God gave the Hebrew nation. Both the fourth and the tenth commandments mention "man-servants" and "maid-servants."

Lev. 25:44–46 were probably the most quoted verses defending slavery. "Both thy bondsmen, and thy bondsmaids, which thou shalt have, shall be of the heathen that are around you; of them shall ye buy bondsmen and bondsmaids." The verses continue: "And ye shall take them as an inheritance for your children after you, to inherit them for a possession." Proslavery advocates engaged abolitionists in an endless battle over whether the Bible was referring to slaves or hired servants. Slave

THE

RELIGIOUS INSTRUCTION

OF THE

NEGROES,

IN THE UNITED STATES

BY CHARLES C. JONES.

SAVANNAH:
PUBLISHED BY THOMAS PURSE.
1842.

Title page for the volume by the South's leading advocate of reforming slavery to "Bible Standards" (New York Public Library)

owners pointed out that under the Law of Moses, if a slave was killed during punishment, the master suffered no penalty except the loss of the slave, because the slave was his "own money."

In the New Testament, defenders of slavery argued that Christ and his Apostles never condemned slavery, although a majority of people in the Roman Empire were slaves. Proslavery writers constantly cited verses explicitly recognizing slavery. In the Book of Philemon, Paul returned the slave Onesimus back to his master after he had run away. One writer summed up the biblical argument: "If Christian ministers held slaves during the apostolic age; if one of them was addressed by the great apostle [St. Paul] himself as a beloved brother in the Lord Jesus; his faith and life commended, and his runaway slave restored to him... and their reciprocal duties made a part of the volume of inspiration..." how could slavery be sinful? (*Southern Christian Advocate,* November 29, 1844). Proslavery Christians condemned abolitionists as "infidels" who placed their own individual conscience above the "plain meaning" of the Word of God.

Southern ministers focused on Col. 4:1, which advised, "Masters, give unto your servants that which is just and equal, knowing that ye also have a Master in heaven." For Southern whites, slavery was a benevolent institution in which masters cared not only for the physical but also for the religious welfare of their slaves. White Christians believed that God ordained slavery to bring the gospel to heathen Africans. It was the "providential mission" of the Southern churches to convert the slaves. Virginia Baptist Thornton Stringfellow wrote that slavery "has brought within the range of gospel influence, millions of Ham's descendants among ourselves, who but for this institution, would have sunk down to eternal ruin; knowing not God, and strangers to the Gospel" (Stringfellow, 1860, p. 491).

Until the late 1820s only scattered efforts were made to preach to the slaves. Methodist William Capers organized the first formal "domestic mission" to the slaves in South Carolina in 1829. The most prominent Southern missionary to the slaves was Presbyterian minister Charles Colcock Jones of Georgia. Widely known as "the Apostle to the Blacks," Jones preached to thousands of slaves.

Southern white preachers gave black slaves a mixed message. In the face of fierce white racism, they insisted that all the races were created in the image of God and that African American souls were equally valuable in God's eyes. Many whites believed that teaching blacks these doctrines would subvert slavery. However, white preachers also accommodated the demands of a slave society. In return for a chance to convert slaves, they agreed to give only oral instruction. All slave states by the 1830s had passed laws against teaching slaves to read, fearing that literacy would spark discontent and rebellions. These laws violated a central doctrine in Protestantism: that all believers should read the Bible for themselves.

Despite these limitations, the domestic missions brought thousands of slaves into the white churches. Within the churches, slaves and free blacks were definitely not equal; they were relegated to segregated seating, often in balconies or the back of churches. In most churches they could not vote on issues as full members, or become ministers. There were a few semi-independent black churches with black ministers, usually in urban areas; however, legally, they needed white sponsors who usually owned the church property.

Although white ministers valued black converts, they seemed to believe that religion was something given by benevolent whites to ignorant blacks. Even the most sympathetic whites viewed slave religion without white guidance as deeply flawed. As one Presbyterian minister asserted, black religion consisted of "bodily exercise, under repetitious and noisy songs and exhortations and producing a Christian experience which consisted of little more than a tissue of dreams, visions, travels" (Stiles, 1850, p. 33). To white eyes, African American religion was excessively emotional, immoral, and "heathenish."

White ministers preached obedience to masters, citing Bible verses that warned against running away, stealing, and laziness. Slaves remembered being told by white preachers not to steal chickens, fake illnesses, or talk back to their masters—all without hearing any mention of their souls. White clergymen often told slave owners that Christian slaves would be harder-working and more content. Charles C. Jones learned, however, that slaves had their own ideas on religion. Jones tells of quoting the Book of Philemon to a black congregation on the Georgia seacoast: "When I insisted on fidelity and obedience as Christian virtues in servants and upon the authority of Paul, condemned the practice of *running away,* one half of my audience deliberately rose up and walked off with themselves." Those who remained looked dissatisfied. After the service, many declared "that there was no such epistle in the Bible" and others "objected against me as a preacher, because I was a *master*" (Jones, 1845, pp. 24–25). Southern whites made a firm distinction between the spiritual freedom of Christianity and freedom within this world. Christianity could free a sinner from damnation, but it did not free him from slavery.

Historians agree that instead of being indoctrinated by white Christians into obedience, slaves constructed their own Christianity. Blending elements of African religious life with Christianity, slaves used their own religion to stave off the dehumanizing effects of slavery, to construct communities, and to actively resist their enslavement. Historians have long debated how much of African religious life survived into American slavery. A consensus has emerged that although much was lost, many basic religious beliefs and practices survived and fused with white Christianity.

Many African beliefs were similar to Christian ones, including faith in one supreme Deity and the prevalence of an ecstatic spiritual possession that paralleled the conversion experience. More specifically, spirituals and practices such as the ring shout contained African elements. One of the carryovers from African religion was a refusal to separate the worldly from the spiritual.

Slaves songs and chants were used to send coded messages of freedom and resistance. Frederick Douglass remembered that when plotting with fellow slaves to escape, "A keen observer might have detected in our repeated singing of 'O Canaan, sweet Canaan / I am bound for the land of Canaan,' something more than a hope of reaching heaven. We meant to reach the *North,* and the North was our Canaan" (Douglass, 1855, pp. 159–160).

Slaves demonstrated their commitment to freedom in their use of biblical imagery. Whites in the North and South often portrayed themselves as the "New Israel" chosen by God. In their songs and preaching, slaves saw themselves as the children of Israel enslaved in Egypt, confident that God would send a Moses to free them.

Although hundreds of thousands of Southern blacks worshiped in biracial churches, they also conducted their own hidden services and listened to their own preachers. Labeled by one historian the "invisible institution" of the antebellum South, independent worship allowed slaves the freedom to express their sorrow over slavery and their desire for freedom. Slaves snuck away at night after laboring long hours in the fields to "hush arbors," where they could practice their religion away from white eyes. The slave preacher was one of the most influential members of the plantation community. He gained his prominence through his unique gifts to preach the gospel and to minister to the needs of the slave community.

Throughout the 1850s the tensions between North and South and between slave and free were increasingly expressed in terms of religion. A sense of impending crisis filled the air, whether it was the hope of a new millennium or the fear of doom. A radical who rejected the possibilities behind moral suasion, John Brown saw himself as an Old Testament prophet sent by God to scourge a sinful people. In October 1859 he led a raid on the federal armory in Harpers Ferry, Virginia, hoping to spark a slave rebellion, although his plan quickly failed as forces killed many of his followers and captured him. Tried for treason by the state of Virginia and condemned to be hanged, Brown turned his trial into a morality play by presenting himself as a Christian martyr. Brown inspired thousands of Northerners with his sacrifice. Abolitionists praised him as a Christlike figure suffering death for a sinning nation. The famous essayist Ralph Waldo Emerson pronounced that Brown now made the gallows as holy as the cross. White Southerners were outraged that Northerners could celebrate a man they saw as a murderer and a fanatic. Brown became the symbol for all antislavery advocates and a precursor to further bloodshed—while the religious conflict entered into a new, more violent phase.

When Republican Abraham Lincoln was elected, and war broke out, the conflicting sides interpreted the war through their own religious perspectives. For white Confederates, the new nation was fulfilling God's will by preserving the Christian institution of slavery from the "infidelity" of antislavery. The Southern churches rallied to the new nation and were among the strongest supporters of the war effort. Charles Colcock Jones was one of many ministers who saw the war as a divinely appointed opportunity to reform slavery. Before the war, many white ministers called for the securing of the rights of slaves to literacy, religious instruction, and the sanctity of their marriages and families (under Southern law, slave marriages had no legal recognition). Jones, in the inaugural address to the Confederate Presbyterian Church, contended that the mission of the new nation was to complete the Christianization of the slaves, now that it was free of abolitionist interference. Throughout the war, Southern ministers called upon the states to reform their slave laws, but to no avail. As defeat followed defeat, ministers preached that the South's suffering was God's punishment for not living up to their Christian duty to the slaves.

Abolitionists saw the war as both God's judgment on the nation for the sin of slavery, and as a God-given opportunity to end slavery. Abolitionists like Frederick Douglass interpreted early Union defeats as God's punishment for not making freedom a war aim. When Abraham Lincoln issued the Emancipation Proclamation in September 1862, abolitionists rejoiced.

For the slaves, the war was the fulfillment of God's will in ending slavery. Slaves drew upon the Book of Exodus, seeing themselves as the children of Israel freed from slavery in Egypt. As Union armies advanced, slaves greeted them as liberators sent by God and praised Lincoln as a new Moses. Many slaves did not wait to be freed, but used the chaos of war to escape and join the Northern armies. Those who stayed behind used the collapse of white supervision to openly preach a gospel of freedom and to conduct their own services. Slaves celebrated emancipation as the "Year of Jubilo."

Henry McNeal Turner, organizer of the African Methodist Episcopal Church in Georgia and, in 1863, of the First Regiment of U.S. Colored Troops (Thomas Cooper Library, University of South Carolina)

After the defeat of the Confederacy, the South lay in ruins. In the next couple of years, the religious landscape also profoundly changed. Biracial churches split as newly freed blacks created their own independent congregations. White and black Northerners came South to organize churches. The African Methodist Episcopal Church, in particular, drew thousands of blacks away from the Southern white churches. Led by ministers such as Henry McNeal Turner, blacks sought the freedom to worship as equals in their own churches, free from white oversight. They selected their own ministers, organized their own reform societies, and made their churches the centers of the black community. The newly independent black churches became centers of political organization. Black ministers were at the forefront of agitating for black civil rights, including the right to vote. Many black ministers, including Turner and Hiram Revels, were elected to office. Black preachers, as in times of slavery, were leaders of their communities.

For many Southern whites, the defeat of the Confederacy brought on a profound religious crisis. These individuals constructed a "Lost Cause" argument that defended the Confederacy as a righteous nation overwhelmed by superior resources. They proclaimed that God punished those he loved best, and that Southern principles would ultimately prevail. Overwhelmingly opposed to Radical Reconstruction, which gave the former slaves legal equality, these Southern whites took control of their states and systematically reduced blacks to second-class citizens through violence and fraud—something they celebrated as the so-called Redemption of the South. They consciously used religious language to proclaim the restoration of the white supremacy as divinely ordained. Southern white churches overwhelmingly rejected black equality and lost most of their black members.

With the end of Reconstruction, the religious conflicts of the era changed. In the South, racism and segregation made it difficult for former slaves to find acceptance within the church; black and white Christians were increasingly separate and alienated. Most white Southern Christians abandoned their efforts to convert blacks and began to defend the oppression of African Americans as second-class citizens. Northern abolitionists, with few exceptions, believed their mission was accomplished and moved on to new causes. Northern whites looked back on the war and on emancipation as proof that God favored America above all other nations, and they increasingly turned their attention to spreading Christianity throughout the world. African Americans, despite an environment of harsh racism, were able to construct their own religious life in independent churches that later played a central role in the Civil Rights Movement of the twentieth century.

Christopher Luse

CHRONOLOGY

1816

The African Methodist Episcopal (AME) Church is founded in Philadelphia. It is the first independent African American denomination in America.

December 21: The American Colonization Society is founded in Washington, D.C. Supported by leading clergymen, the society's mission is to send freed blacks back to Africa.

1822

June 22: Citing Old Testament verses calling for God's vengeance against slave owners, Denmark Vesey attempts a slave revolt in Charleston, South Carolina. When the plot is uncovered, more than thirty-five blacks are executed, many of them members of the Charleston AME Church. Whites institute a wave of repression against independent black religious life; the AME church is outlawed.

1829

Methodist William Capers organizes the first formal domestic mission to the slaves in the South Carolina low country.

1831

January 1: William Lloyd Garrison publishes *The Liberator* in Boston.

August 22: A rebellion led by slave preacher Nat Turner erupts in Southampton County, Virginia.

1832

Charles Colcock Jones organizes the Association for the Religious Instruction of the Negroes of Liberty County, Georgia.

1833

December 4: The American Anti-Slavery Society (AAS) is founded in Philadelphia, dedicated to the immediate abolition of slavery.

1835

The AAS begins mailing antislavery literature throughout the South, employing "moral suasion" to call upon slave owners to repent of the sin of slavery.

1837

The Presbyterian Church splits into the "Old School" and the "New School." The "Old School" faction denounces the increasing antislavery orientation of many Northern "New School" churches.

1844

April: The Baptist Church splits over slavery, with controversy centering on whether slave owners can be appointed missionaries. Southerners form the Southern Baptist Convention in April 1845, in Augusta, Georgia.

May: The Methodist Church splits over slavery. In the General Conference, Northern antislavery delegates protest Georgia bishop James O. Andrew's inheritance of a slave through marriage, asserting that Northern Methodists will not accept a slave-owning bishop.

1845

May: Frederick Douglass publishes his *Narrative of the Life of Frederick Douglass, An American Slave.*

Southern delegates secede and form the Methodist Episcopal Church, South, in Louisville, Kentucky.

1847

December: Douglass founds the *North Star* in Rochester, New York. The paper is dedicated to immediate abolitionism and black rights based on the inherent equality of all children of God.

1852

March: Harriet Beecher Stowe publishes *Uncle Tom's Cabin.* Stowe's novel becomes a literary phenomenon, selling three hundred thousand copies in less than a year. Stowe creates the character of Uncle Tom as a Christlike martyr, the perfect pious Christian destroyed by the evil of slavery.

1856

May 25: John Brown and his followers massacre five proslavery settlers in Kansas as revenge for the sacking of Lawrence by proslavery forces.

1859

October 16: Brown launches his raid against the Harpers Ferry federal arsenal with a force that includes escaped slaves. They are quickly defeated and Brown is captured.

December 2: Brown is hanged after being convicted of treason against the state of Virginia.

1860

December 20: South Carolina secedes from the Union, setting in motion a series of state secessions leading to the formation of the Confederate States of America.

1861

November: The Christian Commission, an organization of Northern evangelicals dedicated to supplying soldiers with chaplains, religious tracts, food, and medical supplies, is founded by the Young Men's Christian Association as an alternative to the Unitarian-dominated Sanitary Commission, which has been performing the same functions in support of the war effort.

December 10: Charles Colcock Jones delivers the inaugural address at the first meeting of the Presbyterian Church in the Confederate States of America, in Augusta, Georgia. The Old School Presbyterians split when Northern members force a resolution pledging support for the Union war effort and denouncing secession.

1862

February: "The Battle Hymn of the Republic" is published. Written by abolitionist Julia Ward Howe after hearing soldiers sing "John Brown's Body," the song is an excellent example of the use of millennial religious symbols dedicating the nation to the cause of freedom.

1863

January 1: The Emancipation Proclamation goes into effect.

1865

March 4: President Abraham Lincoln delivers his Second Inaugural Address.

April 14: President Lincoln is shot, and he dies on Good Friday. Many Northerners interpret this as the last sacrifice for the sacred cause of freedom and the Union. Lincoln is compared to Christ in numerous sermons and speeches as the nation mourns.

1865–1877

Throughout Reconstruction, the Southern churches undergo a profound change. Hundreds of thousands of African Americans leave white churches to form their own congregations. Missionaries, both African American and Caucasian, come from the North to assist in the reorganization of the South.

1868

Henry McNeal Turner, along with every other black representative, is expelled from the Georgia legislature.

1877

President Rutherford B. Hayes agrees to withdraw federal support from the last Republican-controlled states, effectively ending Reconstruction. White, Southern Democrats take complete control of the former Confederate States, calling it the Redemption of the South from the "tyranny" of Negro Rule.

DOCUMENTS

Document 1: THE MARTYR

This section from Harriet Beecher Stowe's novel Uncle Tom's Cabin *(1852) portrays Uncle Tom's martyrdom as he is whipped to death for refusing to reveal the hiding place of escaped slaves. Historians argue that the popularity of the novel can be attributed to Stowe's effective combination of the conventions of the domestic novel with the horrors of slavery. Stowe's novel heavily concentrated on the home and religious life of the slaves, demonstrating that even the most benevolent owners could not prevent the separations of families and the abuse of the slaves' religious faith. Uncle Tom is presented as a pious Christian who is eventually "sold down the river" to his doom. Stowe, instead of making arguments concerning the equality of all races or citing the Declaration of Independence, showed how slavery destroyed the personal lives of African Americans.*

Chapter XL

Deem not the just by Heaven forgot!
Though life its common gifts deny,—

> Though, with a crushed and bleeding heart,
> And spurned of man, he goes to die!
> For God hath marked each sorrowing day,
> And numbered every bitter tear;
> And Heaven's long years of bliss shall pay
> For all his children suffer here.
>
> Bryant

The longest way must have its close,—the gloomiest night will wear on to a morning. An eternal, inexorable lapse of moments is ever hurrying the day of the evil to an eternal night, and the night of the just to an eternal day. We have walked with our humble friend thus far in the valley of slavery; first through flowery fields of ease and indulgence, then through heart-breaking separations from all that man holds dear. Again, we have waited with him in a sunny island, where generous hands concealed his chains with flowers; and, lastly, we have followed him when the last ray of earthly hope went out in night, and seen how, in the blackness of earthly darkness, the firmament of the unseen has blazed with stars of new and significant lustre.

The morning-star now stands over the tops of mountains, and gales and breezes, not of earth, show that the gates of day are unclosing.

The escape of Cassy and Emmeline irritated the before surly temper of Legree to the last degree; and his fury, as was expected, fell upon the defenceless head of Tom. When he hurriedly announced the tidings among his hands, there was a sudden light in Tom's eye, a sudden upraising of his hands, that did not escape him. He saw that he did not join the muster of pursuers. He thought of forcing him to do it; but, having had, of old, experience of his inflexibility when commanded to take part in any deed of inhumanity, he would not, in his hurry, stop to enter into any conflict with him.

Tom, therefore, remained behind, with a few who had learned of him to pray, and offered up prayers for the escape of the fugitives.

When Legree returned, baffled and disappointed, all the long-working hatred of his soul towards his slave began to gather in a deadly and desperate form. Had not this man braved him,—steadily, powerfully, resistlessly,—ever since he bought him? Was there not a spirit in him which, silent as it was, burned on him like the fires of perdition?

"I *hate* him!" said Legree, that night, as he sat up in his bed; "I *hate* him! And isn't he MINE? Can't I do what I like with him? Who's to hinder, I wonder?" And Legree clenched his fist, and shook it, as if he had something in his hands that he could rend in pieces.

But, then, Tom was a faithful, valuable servant; and, although Legree hated him the more for that, yet the consideration was still somewhat of a restraint to him.

The next morning, he determined to say nothing, as yet; to assemble a party, from some neighboring plantations, with dogs and guns; to surround the swamp, and go about the hunt systematically. If it succeeded, well and good; if not, he would summon Tom before him, and—his teeth clenched and his blood boiled—*then* he would break that fellow down, or—there was a dire inward whisper, to which his soul assented.

Ye say that the *interest* of the master is a sufficient safeguard for the slave. In the fury of man's mad will, he will wittingly, and with an open eye, sell his own soul to the devil to gain his ends; and will he be more careful of his neighbor's body?

"Well," said Cassy, the next day, from the garret, as she reconnoitred through the knot-hole, "the hunt's going to begin again, to-day!"

Three or four mounted horsemen were curvetting about, on the space front of the house; and one or two leashes of strange dogs were struggling with the negroes who held them, baying and barking at each other.

The men are, two of them, overseers of plantations in the vicinity; and others were some of Legree's associates at the tavern-bar of a neighboring city, who had come for the interest of the sport. A more hard-favored set, perhaps, could not be imagined. Legree was serving brandy, profusely, round among them, as also among the negroes, who had been detailed from the various plantations for this service; for it was an object to make every service of this kind, among the negroes, as much of a holiday as possible.

Cassy placed her ear at the knot-hole; and, as the morning air blew directly towards the house, she could overhear a good deal of conversation. A grave sneer overcast the dark, severe gravity of her face, as she listened, and heard them divide out the ground, discuss the rival merits of the dogs, give orders about firing, and the treatment of each, in case of capture.

Cassy drew back; and, clasping her hands, looked upward, and said, "O, great Almighty God! we are *all* sinners; but what have *we* done, more so than the rest of the world, that we should be treated so?"

There was a terrible earnestness in her face and voice, as she spoke.

"If it wasn't for *you*, child," she said, looking at Emmeline, " I'd *go* out to them; and I'd thank any one of them that *would* shoot me down; for what use will freedom be to me? Can it give me back my children, or make me what I used to be?"

Emmeline, in her child-like simplicity, was half afraid of the dark moods of Cassy. She looked perplexed, but made no answer. She only took her hand, with a gentle, caressing movement.

"Don't!" said Cassy, trying to draw it away; "you'll get me to loving you; and I never mean to love anything, again!"

"Poor Cassy!" said Emmeline, "don't feel so! If the Lord gives us liberty, perhaps he'll give back your daughter; at any rate, I'll be a daughter to you. I know I'll never see my poor old mother again! I shall love you, Cassy, whether you love me or not!"

The gentle, child-like spirit conquered. Cassy sat down by her, put her arm around her neck, stroked her soft, brown hair; and Emmeline then wondered at the beauty of her magnificent eyes, now with soft tears.

"O, Em!" said Cassy, "I've hungered for my children, and thirsted for them, and my eyes fail with longing for them! Here! here!" she said, striking her breast, "it's all desolate, all empty! If God would give me back my children, then I could pray."

"You must trust him, Cassy," said Emmeline; "he is our Father!"

"His wrath is upon us," said Cassy; "he has turned away in anger."

"No, Cassy! He will be good to us! Let us hope in Him," said Emmeline,—"I always have had hope."

❖   ❖   ❖

The hunt was long, animated, and thorough, but unsuccessful; and, with grave, ironic exultation, Cassy looked down on Legree, as, weary and dispirited, he alighted from his horse.

"Now, Quimbo," said Legree, as he stretched himself down in the sitting-room, "you jest go and walk that Tom up here, right away! The old cuss is at the bottom of this yer whole matter; and I'll have it out of his old black hide, or I'll know the reason why!"

Sambo and Quimbo, both, though hating each other, were joined in one mind by a no less cordial hatred of Tom. Legree had told them, at first, that he had bought for him a general overseer, in his absence; and this had begun an ill will, on their part, which had increased, in their debased and servile natures, as they saw him becoming obnoxious to their master's displeasure. Quimbo, therefore, departed, with a will, to execute his orders.

Tom heard the message with a forewarning heart; for he knew all the plan of the fugitives' escape, and the place of their present concealment;—he knew the deadly character of the man he had to deal with, and his despotic power. But he felt strong in God to meet death, rather than betray the helpless.

He sat his basket down by the row, and, looking up, said, "Into thy hands I commend my spirit! Thou hast redeemed me, oh Lord God of truth!" and then quietly yielded himself to the rough, brutal grasp with which Quimbo seized him.

"Ay, ay!" said the giant, as he dragged him along; "ye'll cotch it, now! I'll boun' Mas'r's back's up *high*! No sneaking out, now! Tell ye, ye'll get it, and no mistake! See how ye'll look, now, helpin' Mas'r's niggers to run away! See what ye'll get!"

The savage words none of them reached that ear!—a higher voice there was saying, "Fear not them that kill the body, and, after that, have no more that they can do." Nerve and bone of that poor man's body vibrated to those words, as if touched by the finger of God; and he felt the strength of a thousand souls in one. As he passed along, the trees and bushes, the huts of his servitude, the whole scene of degradation, seemed to whirl by him as the landscape by the rushing car. His soul throbbed,—his home was in sight,—and the hour of release seemed at hand.

"Well, Tom!" said Legree, walking up and seizing him grimly by the collar of his coat, and speaking through his teeth, in a paroxysm of determined rage, "do you know I've made up my mind to KILL you?"

"It's very likely, Mas'r," said Tom, calmly.

"I *have*," said Legree, with grim, terrible calmness, "*done—just—that—thing*, Tom, unless you'll tell me what you know about these yer gals!"

Tom stood silent.

"D'ye hear?" said Legree, stamping, with a roar like that of an incensed lion. "Speak!"

"*I han't got nothing to tell, Mas'r*," said Tom, with a slow, firm, deliberate utterance.

"Do you dare to tell me, ye old black Christian, ye don't *know*?" said Legree.

Tom was silent.

"Speak!" thundered Legree, striking him furiously. "Do you know anything?"

"I know, Mas'r; but I can't tell anything. *I can die!*"

Legree drew in a long breath; and, suppressing his rage, took Tom by the arm, and, approaching his face almost to his, said, in a terrible voice, "Hark'e, Tom!—ye think, 'cause I've let you off before, I don't mean what I say; but this time, I've *made up my mind,* and counted the cost. You've always stood it out agin' me: now, I'll *conquer ye, or kill ye!*—one or t'other. I'll count every drop of blood there is in you, and take 'em, one by one, till ye give up!"

Tom looked up to his master, and answered, "Mas'r, if you was sick, or in trouble, or dying, and I could save ye, I'd *give* ye my heart's blood; and, if taking every drop of blood in this poor old body would save your precious soul, I'd give 'em freely, as the Lord gave his for me. O, Mas'r! don't bring this great sin on your soul! It will hurt you more than 't will me! Do the worst you can, my troubles 'll be over soon; but, if ye don't repent, yours won't *never* end!"

Like a strange snatch of heavenly music, heard in the lull of a tempest, this burst of feeling made a moment's blank pause. Legree stood aghast, and looked at Tom; and there was such a silence, that the tick of the old clock could be heard, measuring, with silent touch, the last moments of mercy and probation to that hardened heart.

It was but a moment. There was one hesitating pause,—one irresolute, relenting thrill,—and the spirit of evil came back, with seven-fold vehemence; and Legree, foaming with rage, smote his victim to the ground.

◆ ◆ ◆

Scenes of blood and cruelty are shocking to our ear and heart. What man has nerve to do, man has not nerve to hear. What brother-man and brother-Christian must suffer, cannot be told us, even in our secret chamber, it so harrows up the soul! And yet, oh my country! these things are done under the shadow of thy laws! O, Christ! thy church sees them, almost in silence!

But, of old, there was One whose suffering changed an instrument of torture, degradation and shame, into a symbol of glory, honor, and immortal life; and where His spirit is, neither degrading stripes, nor blood, nor insults, can make the Christian's last struggle less than glorious.

Was he alone, that long night, whose brave, loving spirit was bearing up, in that old shed, against buffeting and brutal stripes?

Nay! There stood by him One,—seen by him alone,—"like unto the Son of God."

The tempter stood by him, too,—blinded by furious, despotic will,—every moment pressing him to shun that agony by the betrayal of the innocent. But the brave, true heart was firm on the Eternal Rock. Like his Master, he knew that, if he saved others, himself he could not save; nor could utmost extremity wring from him words, save of prayer and holy trust.

"He's most gone, Mas'r," said Sambo, touched, in spite of himself, by the patience of his victim.

"Pay away, till he gives up! Give it to him!—give it to him!" shouted Legree. "I'll take every drop of blood that he has, unless he confesses!"

Tom opened his eyes, and looked upon his master. "Ye poor miserable critter!" he said, "there an't no more ye can do! I forgive ye, with all my soul!" and he fainted entirely away.

"I b'lieve, my soul, he's done for, finally," said Legree, stepping forward, to look at him. "Yes, he is! Well, his mouth's shut up, at last,—that's one comfort!"

Yes, Legree; but who shall shut up that voice in thy soul? that soul, past repentance, past prayer, past hope, in whom the fire that never shall be quenched is already burning!

Yet Tom was not quite gone. His wondrous words and pious prayers had struck upon the hearts of the imbruted blacks, who had been the instruments of cruelty upon him; and, the instant Legree withdrew, they took him down, and, in their ignorance, sought to call him back to life,—as if *that* were any favor to him.

"Sartin, we's been doin' a dreful wicked thing!" said Sambo; "hopes Mas'r 'll have to 'count for it, and not we."

They washed his wounds,—they provided a rude bed, of some refuse cotton, for him to lie down on; and one of them, stealing up to the house, begged a drink of brandy of Legree, pretending that he was tired, and wanted it for himself. He brought it back, and poured it down Tom's throat.

"O, Tom!" said Quimbo, "we's been awful wicked to ye!"

"I forgive ye, with all my heart!" said Tom, faintly.

"O, Tom! do tell us who is *Jesus,* anyhow?" said Sambo; "Jesus, that's been a standin' by you so, all this night!—Who is he?"

The word roused the failing, fainting spirit. He poured forth a few energetic sentences of that wondrous One,—his life, his death, his everlasting presence, and power to save.

They wept,—both the two savage men.

"Why didn't I never hear this before?" said Sambo; "but I do believe!—I can't help it! Lord Jesus, have mercy on us!"

"Poor critters!" said Tom, "I'd be willing to bar' all I have, if it'll only bring ye to Christ! O, Lord! give me these two more souls, I pray!"

That prayer was answered!

SOURCE:

Harriet Beecher Stowe. *Uncle Tom's Cabin; or, Life among the Lowly,* volume 2 (Boston: Jewett; Cleveland, Ohio: Jewett, Proctor & Worthington, 1852), pp. 267–275.

Document 2: SKETCHES OF SLAVE LIFE

The narratives of escaped slaves were among the most powerful literature presented by abolitionists. Historians are somewhat wary when using this material, because they cannot be absolutely certain how much of the narrative is from the former slave and how much ghostwritten by abolitionists. However, many of them give detailed accounts of the religious life of slaves, which can be confirmed by other sources. Peter Randolph was born a slave on a Virginia plantation on the James River and was later freed in his master's will in 1844. He went north soon afterward, forced out by a state law making it illegal for freed slaves to remain in Virginia. In his narrative, Randolph describes how he became a slave preacher. In his early teens he experienced a "call" from God to preach and set out to teach himself to read the Bible, which he had to do in secret, owing to white hostility to slave literacy.

Slave preachers were generally selected by the slave community, instead of chosen by whites. Slave preachers were among the most influential members of the slave community, which looked to them to provide community support. This section of Randolph's 1855 account describes the major features of slave religious life. Note especially how he contrasts white church services and the slaves' own worship practices. Randolph gives a good account of the hidden "hush arbors" used by slaves for hidden meetings.

Illustrations of the "Peculiar Institution."

by Rev. Peter Randolph, an Emancipated Slave.

RELIGIOUS INSTRUCTION

Many say the negroes receive religious education—that Sabbath worship is instituted for them as for others, and were it not for slavery, they would die in their sins—that really, the institution of slavery is a benevolent missionary enterprise. Yes, they are preached to, and I will give my readers some faint glimpses of these preachers, and their doctrines and practices.

In Prince George County, there were two meeting-houses intended for public worship. Both were occupied by the Baptist denomination. These houses were built by William and George Harrison, brothers. Mr. G. Harrison's was built on the line of his brother's farm, that their slaves might go there on the Sabbath and receive instruction, such as slaveholding ministers would give. The prominent preaching to the slaves was, "'Servants, obey your masters.'" Do not *steal* or *lie,* for this is very wrong. Such conduct is sinning against the Holy Ghost, *"and is base ingratitude to your kind masters, who feed, clothe, and protect you."* All Gospel, my readers! It was great policy to build a church for the *"dear slave,"* and allow him the wondrous privilege of such holy instruction! Edloe's slaves sometimes obtained the consent of Harrison to listen to the Sabbath teachings so generously dealt out to his servants. Shame! shame! to take upon yourselves the name of Christ, with all that blackness of heart. I should think, when making such statements, the slaveholders would feel the rebuke of the Apostle, and fall down and be carried out from the face of day, as were Ananias and Sapphira, when they betrayed the trust committed to them, or refused to bear true testimony in regard to that trust.

There was another church, about fourteen miles from the one just mentioned. It was called "Brandon's church," and there the white Baptists worshipped. Edloe's slaves sometimes went there. The colored people had a very small place allotted them to sit in, so they used to get as near the window as they could to hear the preacher talk to his congregation. But sometimes, while the preacher was exhorting to obedience, some of those outside would be selling refreshments, cake, candy, and rum, and others would be horse-racing. This was the way, my readers, the Word of God was delivered and received in Prince George County. The Gospel was so mixed with Slavery, that the people could see no beauty in it, and feel no reverence for it.

There was one Brother Shell, who used to preach. One Sabbath, while exhorting the poor, impenitent, hard-hearted, ungrateful slaves, so much beloved by their masters, to repentance and prayerfulness, while entreating them to lead good lives, that they might escape the wrath (of the lash) to come, some of his crocodile tears overflowed his cheek, which so affected his hearers, that they shouted and gave thanks to God, that brother

Shell had at length felt the spirit of the Lord in his heart; and many went away rejoicing that a heart of stone had become softened. But, my readers, Monday morning, brother Shell was afflicted with his old malady, hardness of heart, so that he was obliged to catch one of the sisters by the throat, and give her a terrible flogging.

The like of this is the preaching, and these are the men that spread the Gospel among the slaves. Ah! such a Gospel had better be buried in oblivion, for it makes more heathens than Christians. Such preachers ought to be forbidden by the laws of the land ever to mock again at the blessed religion of Jesus, which was sent as a light to the world.

Another Sunday, when Shell was expounding, (very much engaged was he in his own attempts to enlighten his hearers), there was one Jem Fulcrum became so enlightened that he fell from his seat, quite a distance, to the floor. Brother Shell thought he had preached unusually well so to affect Jem; so he stopped in the midst of his sermon, and asked, "Is that poor Jemmy? poor fellow!" But, my readers, he did not know the secret,—*brother Jem had fallen asleep.* Poor Shell did not do so much good as he thought he had, so Monday morning he gave Jem enough of his raw hide spirit to last him all the week; at least, till the next Sabbath, when he could have an opportunity to preach to him.

I could only think, when Shell took so much glory to himself for the effect of his preaching upon the slaves, of the man who owned colored Pompey. This slaveholder was a great fighter, (as most of them are), and had prepared himself for the contest with great care, and wished to know how he looked; so he said, "Pompey, how do I look?" "O, massa, *mighty*." "What do you mean by 'mighty,' Pompey?" "Why, massa, you look noble." "What do you mean by 'noble?'" "Why, sar, you look just like one *lion*." "Why, Pompey, where have you ever seen a lion?" "I see one down in yonder field the other day, massa." "Pompey, you foolish fellow, that was a *jackass*." "Was it, massa? Well, you look just like him."

This may seem very simple to my readers, but surely, nothing more noble than a jackass, without his simplicity and innocence, can that man be, who will rise up as an advocate of this system of wrong. He who trains his dogs to hunt foxes, and enjoys the hunt or the horse-race on the Sabbath, who teaches his blood-hounds to follow upon the track of the freedom-loving negro, is not more guilty or immoral than he who stands in a Northern pulpit, and hunts down the flying fugitive, or urges his hearers to bind the yoke again upon the neck of the escaped bondman. He who will lisp one word in favor of a system which will send blood-hounds through the forests of Virginia, the Carolinas, Georgia, Kentucky, and all the South, chasing human beings, (who are seeking the inalienable rights of all men, "life, liberty, and the pursuit of happiness,") possesses no heart; and that minister of religion who will do it is unworthy his trust, knows not what the Gospel teaches, and had better turn to the heathen for a religion to guide him nearer the right; for the heathen in their blindness have some regard for the rights of others, and seldom will they invade the honor and virtue of their neighbors, or cause them to be torn in pieces by infuriated beasts.

Mr. James L. Goltney was a Baptist preacher, and was employed by Mr. M. B. Harrison to give religious instruction to his slaves. He often used the common text: "Servants, obey your masters." He would try to make it appear that he knew what the slaves were thinking of,—telling them they thought they had a right to be free, but he could tell them better,—referring them to some passages of Scripture. "It is the devil," he would say, "who tells you to try and be free." And again he bid them be patient at work, warning them that it would be his duty to whip them, if they appeared dissatisfied,—all which would be pleasing to God! "If you run away, you will be turned out of God's church, until you repent, return, and ask God and your master's pardon." In this way he would continue to preach his slaveholding gospel.

This same Goltney used to administer the Lord's Supper to the slaves. After such preaching, let no one say that the slaves have the Gospel of Jesus preached to them.

One of the Baptist ministers was named B. Harrison. He owned slaves, and was very cruel to them. He came to an untimely end. While he was riding out one afternoon, the report of a gun was heard, and he was found dead,—his brains being blown out. It could never be found who killed him, and so he went to judgment, with all his sins on his head.

Mr. L. Hanner was a Christian preacher, selecting texts like the following: "The Spirit of the Lord is upon me, because he hath anointed me to preach deliverance to the captives, he hath sent me to bind up the brokenhearted." But Hanner was soon mobbed out of Prince George's County, and had to flee for his life, and all for preaching a true Gospel to colored people.

I did not know of any other denomination where I lived in Virginia, than the Baptists and Presbyterians. Most of the colored people, and many of the poorer class of whites, were Baptists.

Sabbath and Religious Meetings

On the Sabbath, after doing their morning work, and breakfast over, (such as it is), that portion of the slaves who belong to the church ask of the overseer permission to attend meeting. If he is in the mood to grant their request, he writes them a pass, as follows:—

"Permit the bearer to pass and repass to ——, this evening, unmolested."

Should a pass not be granted, the slave lies down, and sleeps for the day—the only way to drown his sorrow and disappointment....

Not being allowed to hold meetings on the plantation, the slaves assemble in the swamps, out of reach of the patrols. They have an understanding among themselves as to the time and place of getting together. This is often done by the first one arriving breaking boughs from the trees, and bending them in the direction of the selected spot. Arrangements are then made for conducting the exercises. They first ask each other how they feel, the state of their minds, &c. The male members then select a certain space, in separate groups, for their division of the meeting. Preaching in order, by the brethren; then praying and singing all round, until they generally feel quite happy. The speaker usually commences by calling himself unworthy, and talks very slowly, until, feeling the spirit, he grows excited, and in a short time, there fall to the ground twenty or thirty men and women under its influence. Enlightened people call it excitement; but I wish the same was felt by everybody, so far as they are sincere.

The slave forgets all his sufferings, except to remind others of the trials during the past week, exclaiming: "Thank God, I shall not live here always!" Then they pass from one to another, shaking hands, and bidding each other farewell, promising, should they meet no more on earth, to strive and meet in heaven, where all is joy, happiness and liberty. As they separate, they sing a parting hymn of praise.

Sometimes the slaves meet in an old log-cabin, when they find it necessary to keep a watch. If discovered, they escape, if possible; but those who are caught often get whipped. Some are willing to be punished thus for Jesus' sake. Most of the songs used in worship are composed by the slaves themselves, and describe their own sufferings. Thus:

"O, that I had a bosom friend,
To tell my secrets to,
One always to depend upon
In every thing I do!"

"How I do wander, up and down!
I seem a stranger, quite undone;
None to lend an ear to my complaint,
No one to cheer me, though I faint."

Some of the slaves sing—

"No more rain, no more snow,
No more cowskin on my back;"

then they change it by singing—

"Glory be to God that rules on high."

In some places, if the slaves are caught praying to God, they are whipped more than if they had committed a great crime. The slaveholders will allow the slaves to dance, but do not want them to pray to God. Sometimes, when a slave, on being whipped, calls upon God, he is forbidden to do so, under threat of having his throat cut, or brains blown out. O, reader! this seems very hard,—that slaves cannot call on their Maker, when the case most needs it. Sometimes the poor slave takes courage to ask his master to let him pray, and is driven away with the answer, that if discovered praying, his back will pay the bill.

Source:

Peter Randolph. *Sketches of Slave Life: or, Illustrations of the "Peculiar Institution"* (Boston: Published for the author, 1855).

Document 3: "The 'Infidelity' of Abolitionism"

William Lloyd Garrison (1805–1879), the most famous (and most reviled) antebellum abolitionist, was best known for founding and editing the radical paper The Liberator. *Early in his career he supported the American Colonization Society (ACS) and advocated a program of gradual emancipation. However, after extensive contact with free blacks who bitterly denounced the ACS as a proslavery organization, Garrison became an uncompromising abolitionist. In the first issue of* The Liberator *in 1831, he denounced moderation: "I will be as harsh as the truth, and as uncompromising as justice . . .*

I will not equivocate—I will not excuse—I will not retreat a single inch—AND I WILL BE HEARD." Garrison was one of the founders and leaders of the American Anti-Slavery Society. He was bitterly attacked by both slave owners and Northern conservatives. Despite his vehement rhetoric, he consistently advocated "moral suasion" and a peaceful means to end slavery.

This article, originally published in The Liberator *on December 25, 1855, discusses many of the major religious arguments against slavery. In particular, abolitionists frequently cited the "Golden Rule" in which Christ commanded his followers to "do unto others as you would have them do unto you." Abolitionists consistently appealed to the "spirit" of the New Testament that condemned all forms of injustice. The "infidelity" mentioned in the article refers to Southern accusations that abolitionists abandoned the literal truth of the Bible because it supported slavery.*

Every great reformatory movement, in every age, has been subjected alike to popular violence and to religious opprobium. The history of one is essentially that of every other. Its origin is ever in obscurity; its earliest supporters are destitute of resources, uninfluential in position, without reputation; it is denounced as fanatical, insane, destructive, treasonable, infidel. The tactics resorted to for its suppression are ever the same, whether it be inaugurated by the prophets, by Jesus and his apostles, by Wickliffe, Luther, Calvin, Fox, or any of their successors. Its opponents have scornfully asked, as touching its pedigree, "Is not this the carpenter's son?" They have patriotically pronounced it a seditious attempt to play into the hands of the Romans, to the subversion of the State and nation. They have piously exclaimed against it as open blasphemy. They have branded it as incomparably more to be feared and abhorred than robbery and murder.

No other result has been possible, under the circumstances. The wrong assailed has grown to a colossal size: its existence not only implies, but demonstrates, universal corruption. It has become organic—a part of the habits and customs of the times. It is incorporated into the State; it is nourished by the Church. Its support is the test of loyalty, patriotism, piety. It holds the reins of government with absolute mastery—rewarding the venal, stimulating the ambitious, terrifying the weak, inflaming the brutal, satisfying the pharisaical, ostracising the incorruptible. It has its temple, its ritual, its priesthood, its divine paternity, in the prevailing religion, no matter what may be the title or pretension thereof.

Now, to attack such a wrong, without fear or compromise,—to strip off the mask, and exhibit it in all its naked deformity,—to demand its immediate suppression, at whatever cost to reputation or worldly interest,—must, of necessity, put the reformer seemingly in antagonism to public quietude and good order, and make the whole social, political and religious structure tremble to its foundations. He cannot be a good citizen; for he refuses to be law-abiding, and treads public opinion, legislative enactment, and governmental edict, alike under his feet. He cannot be sane; for he arraigns, tries and condemns, as the greatest sinners and worst criminals, the most reputable, elevated, revered and powerful members of the body politic. He cannot love his country; for he declares it to be "laden with iniquity," and liable to the retributive judgments of Heaven. He cannot possess humility; for he pays no regard to usage, precedent, authority, or public sentiment, but defies them all. He cannot be disinterested; for it is not supposable that he is actuated by any higher motive than the love of notoriety, a disposition to be facetious, or the consummation of some ulterior design. He cannot be virtuous; for he is seen in the company of publicans and sinners, and is shunned by the chief priests, scribes and pharisees. He cannot be religiously sound in the faith; for he impeaches whatever is popularly accounted piety as but an empty observance, a lifeless tradition, a sanctified villany, or a miserable delusion. He ought not to live; for "it is better that one man should die, than that a whole nation should perish."

Every nation has its "peculiar institution," its vested interest, its organized despotism, its overmastering sin, distinct from every other nation. The conflict of reform is ever geographical as an issue, because the evil assailed is never world-wide: it may be universal in its tendencies, but it is local in its immediate results. It is easy to denounce Monarchy in America, Slavery in Europe, Protestantism in Italy, Democracy in Russia, Judaism in Turkey; because it is to take the popular side, in every such case. An iniquitous system, which, if vigorously assailed in one country, may excite a bloody persecution, and cause the whole land to tremble with consternation and fury, in another country may be denounced not only with impunity, but to general acceptance; for the special abomination thus opposed not existing therein, it is seen in its true character. Hence, what may serve to reveal the exact moral condition of one people, may not be applicable in any other case. Kossuth found that pleading for "material aid" in America was quite a different thing from contending with Austrian despotism in Hungary.

The one great, distinctive, all-conquering sin in America is its system of chattel slavery—co-existent with the settlement of the country—for a considerable time universally diffused—at first, tolerated as a necessary evil—subsequently, deplored as a calamity—now, defended in every slave State as a most beneficent institution, upheld by natural and revealed religion—in its feebleness, able to dictate terms in the formation of the Constitution—in its strength, controlling parties and sects, courts and legislative assemblies, the army and navy, Congress, the national Executive, the Supreme Court—and having at its disposal all the offices, honors and revenues of the government, wherewith to defy all opposition, and to extend its dominion indefinitely. Gradually abolished in six of the thirteen States which formed the union, it has concentrated itself in the southern and south-western portion of the Republic, covering more than one half of the national territory, and aiming at universal empire.

The victims of this terrible system being of African extraction, it has engendered and established a complexional caste, unknown to European civilization; pervading all parts of the United States like a malaria-tainted atmosphere; in its development more malignant at the North than at the South; poisoning the life-blood of the most refined and the most depraved alike; and making the remotest connection with the colored race a leprous taint. Its spirit is as brutal as it is unnatural; as mean as it is wicked; as relentless as it is monstrous. It is capable of committing any outrage upon the person, mind or estate of the negro, whether bond or free. It carries with it the venom of the rattlesnake, the rapacity of the wolf, the fury of the tiger. It is "set on fire of hell," and the flame is never quenched. No religious creed, no form of worship, no evangelical discipline, no heretical liberality, either mitigates or restrains it. Christian and Infidel, Calvinist and Universalist, Trinitarian and Unitarian, Episcopalian and Methodist, Baptist and Swedenborgian, Old School and New School Presbyterian, Orthodox and Hicksite Quaker, all are infected by it, and equally ready to make an innocent natural distinction the badge of eternal infamy, and a warrant for the most cruel proscription. As a nation sows, so shall it also reap. The retributive justice of God was never more strikingly manifested than in this all-prevailing color-phobia, the dreadful consequence of chattel slavery.

The vitality, the strength, the invulnerability of slavery, are found in the prevailing religious sentiment and teaching of the people. While it has been pronounced an evil, a calamity, wrong in the abstract, as a system to be deplored, and gradually to be exterminated,—the act of individual and general slaveholding, the right to have property in man, has been universally recognized as compatible with Christian faith and fellowship, and sanctioned by the Holy Scriptures. More than half a million slaves at the South are owned by ministers, office-bearers, and church members, who buy, sell, bequeath, inherit, mortgage, divide, and barter slave property as they do any other portion of their personal or real estate. At the North, every sect, desirous of nation extension, can secure it only by acknowledging slaveholders and brethren in Christ. All the great, controlling ecclesiastical and religious denominations in the land,—constituting the American, comprehensively speaking,—are one in sentiment on the subject. All the leading Bishops, Doctors of Divinity, Theological Professors, ministers, and religious journalists, find ample justification for slaveholding at the South. Professor Stuart, of Andover, found it in the Decalogue—Bishop Hedding, in the Golden Rule! Rev. Dr. Lord, President of Dartmouth College, finds it in natural and revealed religion—Rev. Nehemiah Adams, in the beneficent workings of slavery, suppressing pauperism, preventing mobocratic violence, upholding law and order, nourishing affection, cultivating the religious sentiment, and extending the kingdom of God on earth! Rev. Dr. Spring avows that if, by offering up a single prayer, he could emancipate every slave in America, he would deem it a rash and censurable act!

Such, then, was the system,—so buttressed and defended,—to be assailed and conquered by the Abolitionists. And who were they? In point of numbers, as drops to the ocean; without station or influence; equally obscure and destitute of resources. Originally, they were generally members of the various religious bodies, tenacious of their theological views, full of veneration for the organized church and ministry, but ignorant of the position in which these stood to "the sum of all villanies." What would ultimately be required of them by a faithful adherence to the cause of the slave, in their church relations, in their political connections, their social affinities, their worldly interest and reputation, they knew not. Instead of seeking a controversy with the pulpit and the church, they confidently looked to both for efficient aid to their cause. Instead of suddenly withdrawing from the pro-slavery religious organizations with which they were connected, they lingered long and labored hard to bring them to repentance. They were earnest, but well-balanced; intrepid, but circumspect; importunate, but long-suffering. Their controversy was neither personal nor sectional; their object, neither to arraign any sect nor to assail any party, primarily. They sought to liberate the slave by every righteous instrumentality—nothing more. But, to their grief and amazement, they were gradually led to perceive, by the terrible revelations of the hour, that the religious forces on which they had relied were all arrayed on the side of the oppressor; that the North was as hostile to emancipation as the South; that the spirit of slavery was omnipresent, invading every sanctuary, infecting every pulpit, controlling every press, corrupting every household, and blinding every vision; that no other alternative was presented to them, except to wage war with "principalities, and powers, and spiritual wickedness in high places," and to separate themselves from every slaveholding alliance, or else to daub with untempered mortar, substitute compromise for principle, and thus betray the rights and liberties of the millions in thraldom, at a fearful cost to their own souls.

Religion is, in every land, precisely and only what is popularly recognized as such. To pronounce it corrupt, oppressive, and especially to demonstrate it to be so, is ever a proof of "infidelity"—whether among Pagans or Mohammedans, Jews or Christians, Catholics or Protestants. In the United States it is the bulwark of slavery—the untiring enemy of abolitionism. How, then, has it been possible for the abolitionists to establish a religious character, while in necessary and direct conflict with such a religion? To say that they ought not to have assailed it, is to denounce them for refusing to go with the multitude to do evil, for being governed by the standard of eternal justice, for adhering to the Golden Rule.

To what, or to whom, have they been infidel? If to the cause of the enslaved, let it be shown. But this is not pretended; and yet this is the only test by which they are to be tried. They have not but one bond of agreement—the inherent sinfulness of slavery, and, consequently, the duty of immediate emancipation. As *individuals*, they are all of theological and political opinions; having an undeniable right to advocate those opinions, and to make as many converts to them as possible. As an *organization*, they meet for a common object in which they are agreed, and endorse nothing but the right of the slave to himself as paramount to every other claim, and to apply no other principle as a rule whereby to measure sects, parties, institutions and men. No sectarian, no party exaction can be made, without destroying unity of spirit and general co-operation. The Episcopalian, the Presbyterian, the Baptist, the Methodist, the "Infidel," surrender not one jot or tittle of their right to be such, by uniting together for the abolition of slavery. No sectarian or party object can be sought, without a breach of good faith, and the perversion of the object ostensibly aimed at. No member can justly complain of any other member, or seek to weaken his testimony against slavery and its abettors, on account of any opinions held or promulgated by him on his individual responsibility.

Whence, then, this outcry of "infidelity"? It has never proceeded from a manly spirit; it has never been raised by any one truly remembering the slave as bound with him; useless, indeed, it be true, that the Anti-Slavery organization has perfidiously turned aside from its original object, to accomplish some ulterior purpose, still assuming to be unchanged and deviating. But it is not true:—though the charge has been repeated ten thousand times, at home and abroad, it is ten thousand times a calumny, uttered either through ignorance, sectarian enmity, personal jealousy, or pro-slavery malice. Abolitionism has never arraigned or criticized any religious body, on account of its peculiar creed; it has never taken any action on theological matters; it has never discussed, never attempted to settle the question, whether the Bible is plenarily inspired, or whether the first day of the week is the Sabbath, or any other question foreign to its avowed purpose. Of the Sabbath it has declared, as Jesus did, that it is as lawful and obligatory to heal the sick, release the bound, and plead for the oppressed, on that day, as it is to succor cattle in distress. Of the Bible, as an anti-slavery instrumentality, it has made a constant and most powerful use against the pro-slavery interpretations of a time-serving clergy; though not deriving the rights of man from any book, but from its own nature. Of the true Church it has ever spoken with veneration, and vindicated it as animated and controlled by the spirit of impartial liberty, to the exclusion of all tyrants. Of the Gospel it has proclaimed, that in all its doctrines, teachings and examples, it is utterly at war with slavery, and for universal freedom. Of Jesus it has affirmed, that he is ever with the down-trodden and oppressed, whose case he has literally made his own, and that he has gloriously vindicated the brotherhood of the human race, to the confusion of all who desecrate the image of God. Its appeals have been unceasingly to the conscience and the heart; it has called to repentance a guilty nation, as the only condition of salvation; it has refused to compromise with sin.

If, therefore, abolitionism be an infidel movement, it is only so in the sense in which Jesus was a blasphemer, and the Apostles were "pestilent and seditious fellows, seeking to turn the world upside down." It is infidel to Satan, the enslaver; it is loyal to Christ, the redeemer. It is infidel to a Gospel which makes man the property of man; it is bound up with the Gospel which requires us to love our neighbors as ourselves, and to call no man master. It is infidel to a Church which receives to its communion the "traffickers in slaves and the souls of men"; it is loyal to the Church which is not stained in blood, nor polluted by oppression. It is infidel to the Bible as a pro-slavery interpreted volume; it is faithful to it as constructed on the side of justice and humanity. It is infidel to a Sabbath, on which it is hypocritically pronounced unlawful to extricate the millions who lie bound and bleeding in the pit of slavery; it is true to the Sabbath, on which it is well-pleasing to God to bind up the broken hearted, and to let the oppressed go free. It is infidel to all blood-stained compromises, sinful concessions, unholy compacts, respecting the system of slavery; it is devotedly attached to whatever is honest, straight-forward, invincible for the right. No reformatory struggle has ever erected a higher moral standard, or more disinterestedly pursued its object, or more unfalteringly walked by faith, or more confidingly trusted in the living God for succor in every extremity, and for a glorious victory at last. At the jubilee, its vindication shall be triumphant and universal.

Source:
William Lloyd Garrison. "The 'Infidelity' of Abolitionism," *The Liberator* (December 21, 1855).

Document 4: "The Bible Argument"

Thornton Stringfellow (1788–1869) was born in Fauquier County, Virginia, to a wealthy slave-owning family. Stringfellow became a Baptist minister and was accepted as pastor of Stevenburg Baptist Church in Culpeper County, Virginia. Stringfellow gained prominence as one of the more able and popular defenders of slavery as a "biblical institution." Like Charles Colcock Jones (see Document 5), Stringfellow was active in the mission movement to convert slaves. In 1846 he was elected vice president of the Southern Baptist Convention's Domestic Mission Board. Stringfellow frequently preached to large slave audiences. Slaves composed more than half of his congregation. Stringfellow was also active in other reform societies such as the Sunday-school movement and religious tract societies. Stringfellow wrote Christian defenses of slavery, including A Brief Examination of Scripture Testimony on the Institution of Slavery *(1850) and* Scriptural and Statistical Views in Favor of Slavery *(1856). This essay was published in 1860.*

Slavery in the Light of Divine Revelation

CIRCUMSTANCES exist among the inhabitants of these United States, which make it proper that the Scriptures should be carefully examined by Christians in reference to the institution of slavery, which exists in several of the States, with the approbation of those who profess unlimited subjection to God's revealed will.

It is branded by one portion of people, who take their rule of moral rectitude from the Scriptures, as a great sin; nay, the greatest of sins that exist in the nation. And they hold the obligation to exterminate it, to be paramount to all others.

If slavery be thus sinful, it behooves all Christians who are involved in the sin, to repent in dust and ashes, and wash their hands of it, without consulting with flesh and blood. Sin in the sight of God is something which God in his word makes known to be wrong, either by preceptive prohibition, by principles of moral fitness, or examples of inspired men, contained in the sacred volume. When these furnish no law to condemn human conduct, there is no transgression. Christians should produce a "thus saith the Lord," both for what they condemn as sinful, and for what they approve as lawful, in the sight of heaven.

It is to be hoped, that on a question of such vital importance as this to the peace and safety of our common country, as well as to the welfare of the church, we shall be seen cleaving to the Bible, and taking all our decisions about this matter, from its inspired pages. With men from the North, I have observed for many years a palpable ignorance of the Divine will, in reference to the institution of slavery. I have seen but a few who made the Bible their study, that had obtained a knowledge of what it did reveal on this subject. Of late their denunciation of slavery as a sin, is loud and long....

I hope the importance of the subject to Christians as well as to statesmen will be my apology. I have written it, not for victory over an adversary, or to support error or falsehood, but to gather up God's will in reference to holding men and women in *bondage, in the patriarchal age*. And it is clear, in the first place, that God decreed this state before it existed. Second. It is clear that the highest manifestations of good-will which he ever gave to mortal man, was given to Abraham, in that covenant in which he required him to circumcise all his *male servants, which he had bought with his money,* and that were *born of them* in his house. Third. It is certain that he gave *these servants* as *property* to Isaac. Fourth. It is certain that, as the owner of *these slaves,* Isaac received similar tokens of God's favor. Fifth. It is certain that Jacob, who inherited from Isaac his father, received like tokens of divine favor. Sixth. It is certain, from a fair construction of language, that Job, who is held up by God himself as a model of human perfection, was a great slaveholder. Seventh. It is certain, when God showed honor, and came down to bless Jacob's posterity, in taking them by the hand to lead them out of Egypt, *they were the owners of slaves that were bought with money, and treated as property; which slaves* were allowed of God to unite in celebrating the divine goodness to their *masters,* while *hired servants* were excluded. Eighth. It is certain that God interposed to give Joseph the power in Egypt, which he used, to create a state, or condition, among the Egyptians, which *substantially agrees* with *patriarchal* and *modern slavery*. Ninth. It is certain, that in references to this institution in Abraham's family, and the surrounding nations, for five hundred years, it is never censured in any communication made from God to men. Tenth. It is certain, when God put a *period* to *that dispensation,* he *recognized slaves as property on Mount Sinai*. If, therefore, it has become sinful since, it cannot be from the *nature of the thing,* but from the *sovereign pleasure of God in its prohibition*....

The Apostle Paul decides in reference to the relative duties of men, that whether written out in preceptive form in the law or not, they are all comprehended in this saying, viz: "thou shalt love thy neighbor as thyself." With these views to guide us, as to the acknowledged design of the law, viz: that of revealing the eternal principles of moral rectitude, by which human conduct is to be measured, so that sin may abound, or be made apparent, and righteousness be ascertained or known, we may safely conclude, that the institution of slavery, which legalizes the holding one person in bondage as property forever by another, if it be morally wrong, or at war with the principle which requires us to love God supremely, and our neighbor as ourself, will, if noticed at all in the law, be noticed, for the purpose of being condemned as sinful. And if the modern views of abilitionists be correct, we may expect to find the institution marked with such tokens of divine displeasure, as will throw all other sins into the shade, as comparatively small, when laid by the side of this monster. What, then, is true? Has God ingrafted hereditary slavery upon the constitution of government he condescended to give to his chosen people—that people, among whom he promised to dwell, and that he required to be holy? I answer, he has. It is clear and explicit. He enacts, first, that his chosen people may take their money, go into the slave markets of the surrounding nations, (the seven devoted nations excepted,) and purchase men-servants and women-servants, and give them, and their increase, to their children and their children's children, forever; and worse still for the refined humanity of our age—he guarantees to the foreign slaveholder perfect protection, while he comes in among the Israelites, for the purpose of dwelling, the raising and selling slaves, who should be acclimated and accustomed to the habits and institutions of the country. And worse still for the sublimated humanity of the present age, God passes with the right to buy and possess, the right to govern, by a severity which knows no bounds but the master's discretion. And if worse can be, for the morbid humanity we censure, he enacts that his own people may sell themselves and their families for limited periods, with the privilege of extending the time at the end of the sixth year to the fiftieth year or jubilee, if they prefer bondage to freedom. Such is the precise character of two institutions, found in the constitution of the Jewish commonwealth, emanating directly from Almighty God. For the fifteen hundred years, during which these laws were in force, God raised up a succession of prophets to reprove that people for the various sins into which they fell; yet there is not a reproof uttered against the institution of *involuntary slavery,* for any species of abuse that ever grew out of it. A severe judgment is pronounced by Jeremiah, (chapter xxxiv: see from the 8th to the 22d verse,) for an abuse or violation of the law, concerning the *voluntary* servitude of Hebrews; but the prophet pens it with caution, as if to show that it had no reference to any abuse that had taken place under the system of *involuntary slavery,* which existed by law among that people; the sin consisted in making hereditary bond-men and bond-women of Hebrews, which was positively forbidden by the law, and not for buying and holding one of another nation in hereditary bondage, which was as positively allowed by the law....

I will now proceed to make them good to the letter, see Levit. xxv: 44, 45, 46; "Thy bond-men and thy bond-maids which thou shalt have, shall be of the heathen that are round about you; of them shall ye buy bond-men and bond-maids. Moreover, of the children of the strangers that do sojourn among you, of them shall ye buy, and of their families that are with you, which they begat in your land. And they shall be your possession. And ye shall take them as an inheritance for your children after you, to inherit them for a possession they shall be your bond-men forever." I ask any candid man, if the words of this institution could be more explicit? It is from God himself; it authorizes that people, to whom he had become *king and lawgiver*, to purchase men and women as property; to hold them and their posterity in bondage; and to will them to their children as a possession forever; and more, it allows *foreign slaveholders* to *settle* and *live among them*; to *breed slaves* and *sell them*....

It will be evident to all, that here are *two states* of servitude; in reference to *one* of which, *rigid* or *compulsory* authority, is *prohibited,* and that its *exercise is authorized in the other.*

...In the criminal code, that conduct is punished with death, when done to a *freeman*, which is not punishable at all, when done *by a master to a slave*, for the express reason, that the slave is the *master's money*. "He that smiteth a man so that he die, shall surely be put to death."—Exod. xxi: 20, 21. "If a man smite his servant or his maid, with a rod, and he die under his hand, he shall be surely punished; notwithstanding, if he continue a day or two, he shall not be punished, for he is his money."—Exod. xxi: 20. Here is precisely the same crime: smiting a man so that he die; if it be a freeman, he shall surely be put to death, whether the man die under his hand, or live a day or two after; but if it be a servant, and the master continued the rod until the servant died under his hand, then it must be evident that such a chastisement could not be necessary for any purpose of wholesome or reasonable authority, and therefore he may be punished, but not with death. But if the death did not take place for a day or two, then it is to be *presumed,* that the master only aimed to use the rod, so far as was necessary to produce subordination, and for this, the law which allowed him to lay out his money in the slave, would protect him against all punishment. This is the common-sense principle which has been adopted substantially in civilized countries, where involuntary slavery has been instituted, from that day until this. Now, here are laws that authorize the holding of men and women in bondage, and chastising them with the rod, with a severity that terminates in death. And he who believes the Bible to be of divine authority, believes these laws were given by the Holy Ghost to Moses. I understand modern abolition sentiments to be sentiments of marked hatred against such laws; to be sentiments which would hold God himself in abhorrence, if he were to give such laws his sanction; but he has given them his sanction; therefore, they must be in harmony with his moral character. Again, the divine Lawgiver, in guarding the property right in slaves among his chosen people, sanctions principles which may work the separation of man and wife, father and children. Surely, my reader will conclude, if I make this good, I shall force a part of the saints of the present day to blaspheme the God of Israel. All I can say is, truth is mighty, and I hope it will bring us all to say, let God be true, in settling the true principles of humanity, and every man a liar who says slavery was inconsistent with it, in the days of the Mosaic law. Now for the proof: "If thou buy a Hebrew servant, six years shall he serve thee, and in the seventh he shall go out free for nothing; if he came in by himself, he shall go out by himself; if he were married, then his wife shall go out with him; if his master have given him a wife (one of his bond-maids) and she have borne him sons and daughters, the wife and her children shall be her master's and he shall go out by himself."—Exod. xxi: 2, 3, 4....

Under every view we are allowed to take of the subject, the conviction is forced upon the mind, that from Abraham's day, until the coming of Christ, (a period of two thousand years,) this institution found favor with God. No marks of his displeasure are found resting upon it. It must, therefore, in its moral nature, be in harmony with those moral principles which he requires to be exercised by the law of Moses, and which are the principles that secure harmony and happiness to the universe, viz: supreme love to God, and the love of our neighbor as ourself.—Deut. vi: 5.—Levit. xix: 18. To suppose that God has laid down these fundamental principles of moral rectitude in his law, as the soul that must inhabit every preceptive requirement of that law, and yet to suppose he created relations among the Israelites, and prescribed relative duties growing out of these relations, that are hostile to the spirit of the law, is to suppose what will never bring great honor or glory to our Maker. But if I understand that spirit which is now warring against slavery, this is the position which the spirit of God forces it to occupy, viz: that God has ordained slavery, and yet slavery is the greatest of sins. Such was the state of the case when Jesus Christ made his appearance. We propose . . . [t]o show that Jesus Christ recognized this institution as one that was lawful among men, and regulated its relative duties. . . .

And first, I may take it for granted, without proof, that he has not abolished it by commandment, for none pretend to this. This, by the way, is a singular circumstance, that Jesus Christ should put a system of measures into operation, which have for their object the subjugation of all men to him as a law-giver—kings, legislators, and private citizens in all nations; at a time, too, when hereditary slavery existed in all; and after it had been incorporated for fifteen hundred years into the Jewish constitution, immediately given by God himself. I say, it is passing strange, that under such circumstances, Jesus should fail to prohibit its further existence, if it was his intention to abolish it. Such an omission or oversight cannot be charged upon any other legislator the world has ever seen. But, says the abolitionist, he has introduced new moral principles, which will extinguish it as an unavoidable consequence, without a direct prohibitory command. What are they? "Do to others as you would they should do to you." Taking these words of Christ to be a body, inclosing a moral soul in them, what soul, I ask, is it?

The same embodied in these words of Moses, Levit. xix: 18; "thou shalt love thy neighbor as thyself;" or is it another? It cannot be another, but it must be the very same, because Jesus says, there are but two principles in being in God's moral government, *one* including all that is *due to God*, the *other* all that is *due to men*.

If, therefore, doing to others as we would they should do to us, means precisely what loving our neighbor as ourself means, then Jesus has added no new moral principle above those in the law of Moses, to prohibit slavery, for in his law is found this principle, and slavery also.

The very God that said to them, they should love him supremely, and their neighbors as themselves, said to them also, "of the heathen that are round about you, thou shalt buy bond-men and bond-women, and they shall be your possession, and ye shall take them as an inheritance for your children after you, to inherit them as a possession; they shall be your bond-men forever." Now, to suppose that Jesus Christ left his disciples to find out, without a revelation, that slavery must be abolished, as a natural consequence from the fact, that when God established the relation of master and servant under the law, he said to the master and servant, each of you must love the other as yourself, is, to say the least, making Jesus to presume largely upon the intensity of their intellect, that they would be able to spy out a discrepancy in the law of Moses, which God himself never saw. Again: if "do unto others as ye would they should do to you," is to abolish slavery, it will for the same reason, level all inequalities to human condition. It is not to be admitted, then, that Jesus Christ introduced any new moral principle that must, of necessity, abolish slavery. The principle relied on to prove it, stands boldly out to view in the code of Moses, as the *soul*, that must *regulate*, and *control*, the *relation* of *master and servant*, and therefore cannot abolish it.

Why a master cannot do to a servant, or a servant to a master, as he would have them do to him, as soon as a wife to a husband or a husband to a wife, I am utterly at a loss to know. The wife is "subject to her husband in all things" by divine precept. He is her "head," and God "suffers her not to usurp authority over him." Now, why in such a relation as this, we can do to others *as we* would they should do to us, any sooner than in a relation, securing to us what is just and equal as servants, and due respect and faithful service rendered with good will to us as masters, I am at a loss to conceive. I affirm then, first, (and no man denies,) that Jesus Christ has not abolished slavery by a prohibitory command: and second, I affirm, he has introduced no new moral principle which can work its destruction, under the gospel dispensation. . . .

The relative duties of each state are pointed out; those between the servant and master in these words: "Servants be obedient to them who are your masters, according to the flesh, with fear and trembling, in singleness of your heart as unto Christ; not with eye service as men pleasers, but as the servants of Christ, doing the will of God from the heart, with good-will, doing service, as to the Lord, and not to men, knowing that whatesoever good thing any man doeth, the same shall he receive of the Lord, whether he be bond or free. And ye masters do the same things to them, forbearing threatening, knowing that your master is also in heaven, neither is there respect of persons with him." Here, by the Roman law, the servant was property, and the control of the master unlimited, as we shall presently prove.

. . . Paul in his letter to them, recognizes the three relations of wives and husbands, parents and children, servants and masters, as relations existing among the members; (here the Roman law was the same;) and to the servants and masters he thus writes: "Servants obey in all things your masters, according to the flesh: not with eye service, as men pleasers, but in singleness of heart, fearing God: and whatsoever you do, do it heartily, as to the Lord and not unto men; knowing that of the Lord ye shall receive the reward of the inheritance, for ye serve the Lord Christ.

But he that doeth wrong shall receive for the wrong he has done; and there is no respect of persons with God. Masters give unto your servants that which is just and equal, knowing that you also have a master in heaven."

The same Apostle writes a letter to the church at Corinth. Under the direction of the Holy Ghost, he instructs the church, that, on this particular subject, *one general principle* was ordained of God, applicable alike in all countries and at all stages of the church's future history, and that it was this: *"as the Lord has called every one, so let him walk."* "Let every man wherein he is called, therein abide with God." . . . "Art thou called, being a servant? Care not for it, but if thou mayest be made free, use it rather;" vii: 18, 21. Here, by the Roman law, slaves were property,—yet Paul ordains, in this, and all other churches, that Christianity gave them no title to freedom, but on the contrary, required them not to care for being slaves, or in other words, to be contented with their *state,* or *relation,* unless they could be *made free,* in a lawful way.

Again, we have a letter by Peter, . . . addressed especially to the Jews, who were scattered through various provinces of the Roman empire; comprising those provinces especially, which were the theater of their dispersion, under the Assyrians and Babylonians. . . . Those revolutionary scenes of violence left one half the human race (within the range of their influence,) in abject bondage to the other half. This was the state of things in these provinces addressed by Peter, when he wrote. The chances of war, we may reasonably conclude, had assigned a full share of bondage to this people, who were despised of all nations. In view of their enslaved condition to the Gentiles; knowing, as Peter did, their seditious character; forseeing, from the prediction of the Saviour, the destined bondage of those who were then free in Israel, which was soon to take place, as it did, in the fall of Jerusalem, when all the males of seventeen, were sent to work in the mines of Egypt, as slaves to the State, and all the males under, amounting to upwards of ninety-seven thousand, were sold into domestic bondage;—I say, in view of these things, Peter was moved by the Holy Ghost to write to them, and his solicitude for such of them as were in slavery, is very conspicuous in his letter; (read carefully from 1 Peter, 2d chapter, from the 13th verse to the end;) but it is not the solicitude of an abolitionist. He thus addresses them: "Dearly beloved, I beseech you." He thus instructs them: "Submit yourselves to every ordinance of man for the Lord's sake." "For so is the will of God." "Servants, be subject to your masters with all fear, not only to the good and gentle, but also to the froward."—1 Peter ii: 11, 13, 15, 18. What an important document is this! enjoining political subjection to *governments of every form,* and Christian subjection on the part of servants to their masters, whether good or bad; for the purpose of showing forth to advantage, the *glory of the gospel,* and putting to silence the ignorance of foolish men, who might think it seditious. . . .

When such enslaved persons came into the church of Christ let them (says Peter) "be subject to their masters with all fear," whether such masters be good or bad. It is worthy of remark, that he says much to secure civil subordination to the State, and hearty and cheerful obedience to the masters, on the part of servants; yet he says nothing to masters in the whole letter. It would seem from this, that danger to the cause of Christ was on the side of *insubordination among the servants,* and a *want of humility with inferiors,* rather than *haughtiness among superiors* in the church. . . .

Now, I ask, can any man in his proper senses, from these premises, bring himself to conclude that slavery is *abolished by Jesus Christ,* or that obligations are imposed by him upon his disciples that are subversive of the institution? Knowing as we do from contemporary historians, that the institution of slavery existed at the time and to the extent stated by Gibbon—what sort of a soul a man must have, who, with these facts before him, will conceal the truth on this subject, and hold Jesus Christ responsible for a scheme of treason that would, if carried out, have brought the life of every human being on earth at the time, into the most imminent peril, and that must have worked the destruction of half the human race? . . .

Abolition sentiments had not dared to show themselves so near the imperial sword. To warn the church against their treasonable tendency, was therefore unnecessary. Instead, therefore, of special precepts upon the subject of relative duties between master and servant, [Paul] lays down a system of practical morality, in the 12th chapter of his letter, which must commend itself equally to the king on his throne, and the slave in his hovel; for while its practical operation leaves the subject of earthly government to the discretion of man, it secures the exercise of sentiments and feelings that must exterminate every thing inconsistent with doing to others as we would they should do unto us: a system of principles that will give moral strength to governments; peace, security, and good-will to individuals; and glory to God in the highest. . . .

But we are furnished with additional light, and if we are not greatly mistaken, with light which arose out of circumstances analogous to those which are threatening at the present moment to overthrow the peace of society, and deluge this nation with blood....

In an age filled with literary men, who are employed in transmitting historically, to future generations, the structure of society in the Roman Empire; that would put it in our power at this distant day, to know the state or condition of a slave in the Roman Empire, as well as if we had lived at the time, and to know beyond question, that his condition was precisely that one, which is now denounced as sinful: in such an age, and in such circumstances, Jesus Christ causes his will to be published to the world; and it is this, that if a Christian slave have an unbelieving master, who acknowledges no allegiance to Christ, this believing slave must count his master worthy of all honor, according to what the Apostle teaches the Romans, "Render, therefore, to all their dues, tribute to whom tribute is due, custom to whom custom is due, fear to whom fear, honor to whom honor."—Rom. xiii: 7. Now, honor is enjoined of God in the Scriptures, from children to parents—from husbands to wives—from subjects to magistrates and rulers, and here by Jesus Christ, from Christian slaves to unbelieving masters, who held them as property by law, with power over their very lives. And the command is remarkable. While we are commanded to honor father and mother, without adding to the precept "all honor," here a Christian servant is bound to render to his unbelieving master "all honor." Why is this? Because in the one case nature moves in the direction of the command; but in the other, against it. Nature being subjected to the law of grace, might be disposed to obey reluctantly; hence the amplitude of the command. But what purpose was to be answered by this devotion of the slave? The Apostle answers, "that the name of God and his doctrine (of subordination to the law-making power) be not blasphemed," as they certainly would by a contrary course on the part of the servant, for the most obvious reason in the world; while the sword would have been drawn against the gospel, and a war of extermination waged against its propagators, in every province of the Roman Empire, for there was slavery in all; and so it would be now.

But, says the caviler, these directions are given to Christian slaves whose masters did not acknowledge the authority of Christ to govern them; and are therefore defective as proof, that he approves of one Christian man holding another in bondage. Very well, we will see. In the next verse, (1 Timothy vi: 2,) he says, "and they that have believing masters, let them not despise them, because they are brethren, but rather do them service, because they are faithful and beloved, partakers of the benefit." Here is a great change; instead of a command to a believing slave to render to a believing master *all honor,* and thereby making that believing master in *honor* equal to an unbelieving master, here is rather an exhortation to the slave *not to despise him, because he is a believer.* Now, I ask, why the circumstance of a master becoming a believer in Christ, should become the cause of his believing slave despising him while that slave was supposed to acquiesce in the duty of rendering all honor to that master before he became a believer? I answer, *precisely,* and *only, because* there were *abolition teachers* among them, who *taught otherwise,* and consented not to wholesome words, *even the words of our Lord Jesus Christ.*—Timothy vii: 3; and "to the doctrine which is according to godliness," taught in the 8th verse, viz: having food and raiment, servants should therewith be content; for the pronoun us, in the 8th verse of this connection, means *especially* the *servants he was instructing,* as well as Christians in general. These men taught, that godliness abolished slavery, that it gave the title of freedom to the slave, and that so soon as a man professed to be subject to Christ, and refused to liberate his slaves, he was a hypocrite, and deserved not the countenance of any who bore the Christian name....

Such were the bitter fruits which abolition sentiments produced in the Apostolic day, and such precisely are the fruits they produce now.

Now, I say, here is the case made out, which certainly would call forth the command from Christ, to abolish slavery, if he ever intended to abolish it. Both the servant and the master were one in Christ Jesus....

It is taken for granted, on all hands pretty generally, that Jesus Christ has at least been silent, or that he has not personally spoken on the subject of slavery. Once for all, I deny it. Paul, after stating that a slave was to honor an unbelieving master, in the 1st verse of the 6th chapter, says, in the 2d verse, that to a believing master, he is the rather to do service, because he who partakes of the benefit is his brother. He then says, if any man teach otherwise, (as all abolitionists then did, and now do,) and consent not to wholesome words, "even the words of our Lord Jesus Christ." Now, if our Lord Jesus Christ uttered such words, how dare we say he has been silent? If he has been silent, how dare the Apostle say these are the words of our Lord Jesus Christ, if the Lord Jesus Christ never spoke them? Where, or when, or on what occasion he spoke them, we are not informed; but certain it is, that Paul has borne false witness, or that Jesus Christ has uttered the words that impose an obligation on servants, who are abject slaves, to render service with good-will from the heart, to believing masters, and to account their unbelieving masters as worthy of all honor, that the name of God and his doctrine be not blasphemed. Jesus Christ revealed to Paul the doctrine which Paul has settled throughout the Gentile world, (and by consequence, the Jewish world also,) on the subject of slavery, so far as it affects his kingdom. As we have seen, it is clear and full.

From the great importance of the subject, involving the personal liberty of half the human race at that time, and a large portion of them at all times since, it is not to be wondered at, that Paul would carry the question to the Saviour, and plead for a decisive expression of his will, that would forever do away the necessity of inferring any thing by reasoning from the premises laid down in the former dispensation....

The Scriptures we have adduced from the New Testament, to prove the recognition of hereditary slavery by the Saviour, as a lawful relation in the sight of God, lost much of their force from the use of a word by the translators, which by time, has lost much of its original meaning; that is, the word *servant*. Dr. Johnson, in his Dictionary, says: "Servant is one of the few words, which by time has acquired a softer signification than its original, knave, degenerated into cheat. While *servant*, which signified originally, a person preserved from death by the conqueror, and reserved for slavery, signifies only an obedient attendant." Now, all history will prove that the servants in the New Testament addressed by the apostles, in their letters to the several churches throughout the Roman Empire, were such as were preserved from death by the conqueror, and taken into slavery. This was their condition, and it is a fact well known to all men acquainted with history. Had the word which designates their condition, in our translation, lost none of its original meaning, a common man could not have fallen into a mistake as to the condition indicated. But to waive this fact we are furnished with all the evidence that can be desired. The Saviour appeared in an age of learning—the enslaved condition of half the Roman Empire, at the time, is a fact embodied with all the historical records—the constitution God gave the Jews, was in harmony with the Roman regulations on the subject of slavery. In this state of things, Jesus ordered his gospel to be preached in all the world, and to every creature. It was done as he directed; and masters and servants, and persons in all conditions, were brought by the gospel to obey the Saviour. Churches were constituted. We have examined the letters written to the churches, composed of these materials. The result is, that each member is furnished with a law to regulate the duties of his civil station—from the highest to the lowest.

... [W]hen God entered into covenant with Abraham, it was with him as a slaveholder; ... when he took his posterity by the hand in Egypt, five hundred years afterward to confirm the promise made to Abraham, it was done with them as slaveholders; ... when he gave them a constitution of government, he gave them the right to perpetuate hereditary slavery; and ... he did not for the fifteen hundred years of their national existence, express disapprobation toward the institution.

We have also shown from authentic history that the institution of slavery existed in every family, and in every province of the Roman Empire, at the time the gospel was published to them.

We have also shown from the New Testament, that all the churches are recognized as composed of masters and servants; and that they are instructed by Christ how to discharge their relative duties; and finally that in reference to the question which was then started, whether Christianity did not abolish the institution, or the right of one Christian to hold another Christian in bondage, we have shown, that "the words of our Lord Jesus Christ" are, that so far from this being the case, it adds to the obligation of the servant to render service with good-will to his master, and that gospel fellowship is not to be entertained with persons who will not consent to it!

I propose ... to show that the institution of slavery is full of mercy. I shall say but a few words on this subject. Authentic history warrants this conclusion, that for a long period of time, it was this institution alone which furnished a motive for sparing the prisoner's life. The chances of war, when the earth was filled with small tribes of men, who had a passion for it, brought to decision, almost daily, conflicts, where nothing but this institution interposed an inducement to save the vanquished. The same was true in the enlarged schemes of conquest, which brought the four great universal empires of the Scriptures to the zenith of their power.

The same is true in the history of Africa, as far back as we can trace it. It is only sober truth to say, that the institution of slavery has saved from the sword more lives, including their increase, than all the souls who now inhabit this globe....

Under the gospel, it has brought within the range of gospel influence, millions of Ham's descendants among ourselves, who but for this institution, would have sunk down to eternal ruin; knowing not God, and strangers to the gospel. In their bondage here on earth, they have been much better provided for, and great multitudes of them have been made the freemen of the Lord Jesus Christ, and left this world rejoicing in hope of the glory of God. The elements of an empire, which I hope will lead Ethiopia very soon to stretch out her hands to God, is the fruit of the institution here. An officious meddling with the institution, from feeling and sentiments unknown to the Bible, may lead to the extermination of the slave race among us, who, taken as a whole, are utterly unprepared for a higher civil state; but benefit them, it cannot. Their condition, *as a class,* is now better than that of any other equal number of laborers on earth, and is daily improving.

If the Bible is allowed to awaken the spirit, and control the philanthropy which works their good, the day is not far distant when the highest wishes of saints will be gratified, in having conferred on them all that the spirit of good-will can bestow. This spirit which was kindling into life, has received a great check among us of late, by that trait which the Apostle Peter reproves and shames in his officious countrymen, when he says: "But let none of you suffer as a murderer, or as a thief, or as an evil doer, or as a busy-body in other men's matters." Our citizens have been murdered—our property has been stolen, (if the receiver is as bad as the thief,)—our lives have been put in jeopardy—our characters traduced—and attempts made to force political slavery upon us in the place of domestic, by strangers who have no right to meddle with our matters. Instead of meditating generous things to our slaves, as a return for gospel subordination, we have to put on our armor to suppress a rebellious spirit, engendered by "false doctrine," propagated by men "of corrupt minds, and destitute of the truth," who teach them that the gain of freedom to the slave, is the only proof of godliness in the master. From such, Paul says we must withdraw ourselves; and if we fail to do it, and to rebuke them with all the authority which "the words of our Lord Jesus Christ" confer, we shall be wanting in duty to them, to ourselves, and to the world.

Thornton Stringfellow.

SOURCE:

Thornton Stringfellow. "The Bible Argument: Or, Slavery in the Light of Divine Revelation," in *Cotton is King, and Pro-Slavery Arguments: Comprising the Writings of Hammond, Harper, Christy, Stringfellow, Hodge, Bledsoe and Cartwright, on This Important Subject,* edited by E. N. Elliott (Augusta, Ga.: Pritchard, Abbott & Loomis, 1860), pp. 462–492.

Document 5: RELIGIOUS INSTRUCTION OF THE NEGROES

Charles Colcock Jones was the Old South's leading advocate of the domestic mission to the slaves. He dedicated most of his adult life to preaching to the slaves. Early in his life, in private letters to his future wife, he often expressed unease over the morality of slavery, specifically citing "abuses" such as the failure to give slaves religious instruction, the splitting up of slave families through sales, and state laws against slave literacy. Instead of becoming an abolitionist, Jones returned to his home to lead an effort to reform slavery up to "Bible standards," in which the rights of the slaves as moral beings created in God's image were secured. When Georgia seceded, he pledged his support to the Confederacy. Like many ministers, he hoped that an independent republic based on slavery would be able to "purify" the system of its sins.

When his denomination, the Old School Presbyterians, split into Southern and Northern wings, he was selected to give the inaugural address in December 1861 before the new Presbyterian Church in the Confederate States of America. In his address, Jones reminded his audience that the South's providential mission was to bring Christianity to the slaves. When reading the address, pay special attention to Jones's justification for giving the slaves religious instruction. The address is an excellent example of the "paternalistic" rhetoric of the Old South, which assumed that, although spiritually equal, God assigned black slaves an inferior status in this life.

An Address delivered before the
General Assembly of the Presbyterian Church,
at Augusta, Ga.,
December 10, 1861.
by Rev. C. C. Jones, D. D.
Published by Order of the General Assembly.
Richmond: Presbyterian Committee of Publication.

Our social constitution as a nation is uncommon. Over all our land, from the Chesapeake on the North to the Rio Grande on the South, and from the Atlantic ocean to the Ohio and Missouri rivers, there is dispersed and settled in intimate connection with the whites, the *negroes of Africa;* the two varieties forming our population, in the proportion of one negro to every three or four whites; and the relation between the two is that of master and slave....

The negroes were introduced for service, and have been held to service ever since; and, although recognized and protected in law as persons, neither in the condition of slaves nor of free negroes have they ever been admitted to the rights and privileges of citizenship....

With few and insignificant exceptions, (nearly all of which occurred in the early days of our colonies, and grew out of peculiar circumstances,) no laboring class in any country has remained throughout its existence more quiet, obedient, and peacefully associated with their superiors than our negro population, which is an interesting feature in their history worthy of remembrance....

They are inhabiters of one common earth with us; they are one of the varieties of our race–a variety produced by the power and in the inscrutable wisdom of God; but when, and how, and where, lies back of all the traditions and records of men. These sons of Ham are black in the first hieroglyphics; they are black in the first pages of history, and continue to be black. They share our physical nature, and are bone of our bone, and flesh of our flesh; they share our intellectual and spiritual nature; each body of them covers an immortal soul, whom God our Father loves, for whom Christ our Saviour died, and unto whom everlasting happiness or misery shall be meted in the final day. They are not the cattle upon a thousand hills, nor the fowls upon the mountains, brute beasts, goods and chattels to be taken and worn out and destroyed in our use; but they are men, created in the image of God, to be acknowledged and cared for spiritually by us, as we acknowledge and care for the other varieties of the race, our own Caucasian, or the Indian, or the Mongol. Shall we reach the Bread of Life over their heads to far distant nations, and leave them to die eternal deaths before our eyes?

What is their social connection with us? They are not enemies but friends; they are not foreigners, but our nearest neighbors; they are not hired servants, but servants belonging to us in law and gospel; born in our house, and bought with our money; not people whom we seldom see, and whom we seldom hear, but people who are never out of the light of our eyes nor the hearing of our ears. They are our constant and inseparable associates; whither we go, they go; where we dwell, they dwell; where we die and are buried, there they die and are buried; and more than all, our God is their God.

... My brethren, are these people nothing to us? Have we no gratitude, no friendship, no kind feelings for all they have done for us and for ours? Have we no heart to feel, no hand to help, no smiles to give, no tears to shed on their behalf, no wish in your inmost soul that they may know what you prize above all price, your precious Saviour, and go with you to glory, too?

What is their *value as an integral part of our population,* to *ourselves,* to our *country,* and to the *world* itself? To *ourselves* they are the source in large measure of our living, and comprise our wealth, in Scripture our "money.".. They labor for us in summer's sun and in winter's cold; to the fruit of their labor we owe our education, our food, our clothing, and our dwellings, and a thousand comforts of life that crowd our happy homes; and through the fruit of their labor we are enabled to support the Gospel, and enjoy all the priceless means of grace. Brethren, what could we do without this people? how live, how support our families? And have they no claims upon us? Are they nothing more than creatures of profit and pleasure? Are the advantages and blessings of that close connection between us in the household to be all on one side? Has our Master in heaven so ordained it? ... And what is *their value to our country and to the world?* They constitute the great bulk of our agricultural population, and the immense returns of our soil come from their patient labors; labors which furnished three-fourths of the exports of the old United States, and brought three-fourths of the revenue into the national treasury. They were the mainspring, the mighty power that set and kept in motion, year after year, the unexampled and ever increasing wealth and prosperity of the whole country....

But, brethren, to bring our subject to a point. *Why have the negroes been sent into our country at all?* For what purpose? To be our servants, our support and source of wealth and comfort? to develop the vast agricultural resources of our land? to stimulate the industry and enterprise, and add to the support, and comfort, and prosperity of the nation and of the world? No doubt He who sees the end from the beginning included all these benevolent results in assigning them their settlement here. But is this all? Who, my brethren, can assert, who can believe, that nothing is more to be seen in the Divine purposes? Does our Heavenly Father ever forget the spiritual interests of men? Beyond these worldly purposes, there was the purpose (and we say there was the purpose, for we see it fulfilled and fulfilling,) of advancing the civilization and salvation of the negroes, through the Gospel of His Son. He permitted, in His inscrutable providence, men, in their insatiable avarice, at immense sacrifices and sufferings, to collect and bring the negroes from their native continent to ours, and overruled it with all its evils for good, by precipitating a nation of imbruted, enslaved, and wretched heathen into the very lap of Christianity. In this strange work, the command to the Church, "Go ye into all the world, and preach the Gospel to every creature," is stayed; nay, turned backward, and the Lord has caused the heathen to come to us, and learn our language, and manners and customs, and live with us, that they might more easily, and speedily, and constantly hear of the Saviour's love, and believe and live; and it has been overruled to this blessed end. Since their coming, Ethiopia has stretched out her hands to God, yea, to the Saviour on the cross, and thousands and tens of thousands have been going lo! . . .

Has the Church from the beginning *recognized this good purpose of God, and fulfilled her duty to the negroes?* Partially only. And this is evident from their moral and religious condition, and from the little, comparatively speaking, that we are doing for them. . . . The negroes have been termed the heathen of our land, but the universal absence among them of all forms of idolatry, and the adoption of the Christian religion as their religion, prove that they are not a Heathen people. . . . While not heathen, they are in the mass a degraded people in their morality; and this you know from your own long and close observation of them in all the relations which they bear to their owners, and to each other, and to the Church of God, as well as I do; and they are also in the mass an ignorant and weak people in their religion, and with this fact also you are as well acquainted as I am. . . . And yet it amazes one after all to know the extent to which the knowledge of the way of salvation is diffused among them. . . . [O]ne reason why the knowledge of religion is so diffused among them, and professors are found almost everywhere is, that they preach the Gospel to each other—*the poor preach the Gospel to the poor;* so that to your surprise, in visiting districts supplied only at long intervals with preaching, you discover here and there people who profess to believe on the Lord Jesus Christ. . . . Why is this? No man need wonder that knows the power of the love of Christ in the heart of man. When you felt the power of that love in your soul, and embraced Christ as the One altogether lovely, did not your soul go out in longings that your dear family, and friends, and neighbors, and in short the whole world, might know the precious Saviour too? . . . Religion is the same in the black man that it is in you. He has felt his sins as you have, he has seen the Lord by faith as you have, he has rejoiced in hope of escape from the wrath to come through Him as you have; and, fired with love as you have been, he has gone forth into the prayer-meeting, and into the family, and into the highways and hedges, and tried to call sinners to repentance, and to compel them to come into the Gospel-feast, and this has been the work of godly women as well as of godly men.—Nor have they neglected to instruct their own children by times, and bring them up in the nurture and admonition of the Lord, and make their families Christian families. . . .

The negroes now need as a class faithful, and continued and universal religious instruction, and the grand practical question is, *how shall we as a Church communicate it to them?*

That instruction casts itself into two departments: first, *private* and then *public*. *Private instruction* is that which is communicated by *owners*. If you plead the patriarchal relation, then should you discharge your duty as a patriarch, not only "commanding your children," but your "household also after you," and they shall keep the way of the Lord to do justice and judgment, that the Lord may bring upon you that which He has promised to His faithful people. You are responsible for both children and servants.—Gather, therefore, your servants about your house to family worship, night and morning; read the Scriptures; explain them if you will; sing praises to God, and pour out your prayers before Him. Your servants will receive instruction and blessing. "But I cannot get them to attend; at least they attend very irregularly." And pray whose fault is it? If you are not able to govern your servants, you ought not to own them. Why do you not *make* them attend, as you do your children? Lay it down as a rule, permanent and not to be violated, that when, as the head of your family, you ring your bell for family worship, . . . all work of every kind throughout the house stops, and every one comes into prayers. And let the same rule obtain for morning worship, immediately before your breakfast is brought in. You will enforce this just rule but a short time before no one in your family will be conscious of its existence, and your servants, with the rest, will be ready, and take their places, morning and evening, with quietness and regularity. . . .

Next must follow plantation prayers and instruction. A comfortable room or chapel should be provided and consecrated for the purpose, where your people may assemble for worship two or three or more evenings in the week, as they may arrange among themselves; and where you, as head of your household, may meet them one or more evenings in the week for religious instruction, even if you do not carry that instruction beyond reading the

Scriptures, and singing and praying with them; only be you regular and fervent in doing so. In this room or chapel marriages may be solemnized, and funeral services performed.... And here also you may invite any kind, wayfaring minister to preach a sermon to your family and people, when he tarries a night with you....

Establish, in addition, that indispensable aid to plantation instruction, the plantation Sunday-school for the children and youth, and for all adults who choose to connect themselves with it. Assemble the school every Sabbath afternoon or evening, and as frequently in the weeks as you please to do so; conduct it on the infant school plan, questioning and instructing all together from the Scriptures and catechisms; or avail yourself of the help of your good wife, who will always second your efforts; perhaps she will prefer to take the charge of the school, and relieve you altogether; or you may put it under the care of your pious daughter or son. Experience proves plantation Sabbath-schools to be of great and lasting value, for they exert a happy influence upon the active piety of the owner and of his family; they civilize the children and youth, and they christianize them, and save their souls....

To crown all your private instruction, exhibit a consistent Christian example before your people, and govern and conduct all the operations and affairs of your plantation on Christian principles; converse with them as occasion offers on the momentous interests of their souls; secure the Sabbath to them as the day of sacred rest, given to them by the Lord; protect them in person, in family, and in their interests, from the wicked and profligate; be righteous and just in rewards and punishments; correct them for sins against God as well as against yourself, as you do your children, and save their souls from destruction....

For the public religious instruction of the negroes, we *rely in the first place* mainly, if not almost entirely, upon our *settled pastors and stated supplies*. Upon them the great burden of the work now falls, and will ever fall; by them the work must be done, or the spiritual wants of the negroes remain unsupplied....

Let it be repeated again and again: The pastors, the pastors are the laborers in this field. It cannot, it ought not to be otherwise, from the very composition of our churches and congregations. They are identified in composition with those of the Old and New Testaments, embracing husbands and wives, parents and children, masters and servants, and he who accepts a pastoral charge, accepts whites and blacks together. Husbands and masters call him, but call him for their wives, their children and servants, as well as for themselves; and the pastor who expends his labors among the whites, to the entire or almost total neglect of the blacks, is but *half* a pastor, and is laying up trouble and remorse for the day when he gives account of the souls committed to his care.... What is the matter with such a minister? Has he no eyes to see, no ears to hear, no mind to comprehend, no heart to feel?... [W]hat are we to think of the white part of that minister's charge, who permitted, and it may be required him to act so? who, in their selfishness and deadness to duty, devoured the Bread of Life from their servants all their days, and cast to them only now and then the crumbs that fell from their tables....

Our pastors should use their best judgment, and distribute their labors between the whites and blacks in just proportion, preaching one part of the Sabbath to the whites and the other part to the blacks, should they require so much of separate effort for their instruction; and preach on the plantations, in paying pastoral visits in country charges. Give notice to the master on what evening you will be with him, and that you will preach or lecture for his family and household. Right gladly will he welcome you: the family and plantation will be all astir, "our minister is coming to preach for us this evening!"... You will... go away a happier Christian and a more blest minister, we shall bid farewell to years of experience and observation in this field of labor. Of great value are those plantation meetings; they carry religion home to the people, and demonstrate your interest in them....

And, finally, the pastor should so preach the Word as not only to bring it within the comprehension of the negroes, but also to add to their knowledge and keep them improving therein. "But I cannot make them understand me. I have no talent for this sort of labor." If this sad confession be true, then you are deficient in one of the essential qualifications of a Scriptural bishop, "aptness to teach." Did it never occur to you that the difficulty may lie nearer yourself than your weak-minded auditors? If a man wishes to know how well he understands a subject, let him attempt to make it plain and simple. You may lack a clear understanding of the history, the doctrine, or the duty of the Word which you preach, and consequently fail in enlightening the ignorant. How many sermons are laboriously prepared and written, and, after all, are listened to but by a handful of men, the preacher shooting clear over the heads of the bulk of the people.... Much of our preaching does not reach our congregations. How can any people be sanctified by the Truth, unless you put them in possession of the Truth? Why bend the bow and put your arrow on the string if you shoot above and beyond the mark? Learn from the great Teacher who came from God, for He is our example. "The common people heard him gladly," "all the people were very attentive," they hung upon His lips "to hear Him." Look into His discourses, His parables, into His expositions. You see the truth He would convey to the minds of His hearers, as clearly as you can see any object through a transparent atmosphere....

We depend, in the second place, for the public instruction of the negroes upon missionaries.... He may not use all his accomplishments in the same form and to the same extent, yet he will require them all. You need wise men, and men of knowledge, and men who continually grow in wisdom and knowledge, to teach, and guide, and govern masses of ignorant men and women and children, and for reasons so obvious that I must be excused for not mentioning them.... [I]t will not be long ere the sheep will learn to know his voice, and they will follow him; they will follow him into the house of prayer upon the plantation, into the house of God upon the Sabbath day, into the Sunday school and prayer-meeting, and into the inquiry meetings; they will follow his good example, and receive the Word with all readiness of mind at his mouth; and many will believe upon the Lord through his instrumentality, and be his crown of rejoicing in that day.... He will be happy with the people, and the people will be happy with him; as much so as weak, sinful, and partially sanctified ministers and people can be in this world. Whenever he meets them he speaks kind words, and receives kind words in return. He is not ashamed of them, and they are glad in him; and when he rides along the road, and they are at work in the field, he flings over the fence among them a cheerful "good morning; good morning to you all."...

The importance of the instruction of the negroes under our present circumstances cannot be too highly estimated. Is it too much to say that the stability and welfare of both Church and State depend largely upon it? My brethren, the eyes of the civilized world are upon us. There are but two other nations besides our own that hold in their bosoms the institution of slavery. Ponder that fact and the responsibilities involved in it. None can come in from abroad to retrieve us. The negroes of the Confederate States are thrown entirely upon the care of the churches of our Lord within those States. The Christian world outside look to us to do our duty, and, more than that, *God our Saviour looks to us to do our duty.* You feel the weighty responsibility; you say by the help of God we must meet it, and meet it in the very *birthday* of our existence as the Presbyterian Church in the Confederate States of America. Then let the Presbyterian Church in the Confederate States awake and pray for the baptism of the Holy Spirit, and put on her strength; ministers, elders and members, awake, gird up your loins and quit yourselves like men. Our brethren of other denominations will awake and act also; so that we shall emulate each other's zeal, and there shall be action and re-action in all the Zion of God, and higher and higher shall rise our zeal in so good a cause, and greater and greater become our labors, until our whole population shall be evangelized, and our whole land be filled with the glory of the Lord.

Source:

Charles Colcock Jones. *Religious Instruction of the Negroes: An Address Delivered before the General Assembly of the Presbyterian Church, at Augusta, Georgia, December 10, 1861* (Richmond: Presbyterian Committee of Publication, 1862).

Document 6: "The Battle Hymn of the Republic"

Julia Ward Howe (1819–1910), abolitionist, author, and social reformer, is best remembered today as the author of "The Battle Hymn of the Republic." Julia Ward was born into a wealthy Episcopal family in New York, and she married the antislavery advocate and reformer Samuel Gridley Howe, most famous for his work with the blind. In the 1850s Julia Ward Howe became increasingly active as a radical abolitionist, writing plays and poems dedicated to antislavery. When the Civil War began, Howe and her husband supported the U.S. Sanitary Commission, a private organization composed mostly of antislavery Unitarians. Its mission was to improve the living conditions of soldiers suffering from disease and poor diet.

The couple visited President Abraham Lincoln and inspected a Union army camp in December 1861. While visiting the camp Julia Ward Howe heard the soldiers singing "John Brown's Body," a very popular marching song celebrating his sacrifice for freedom: "John Brown's body lies a-moldering in the grave / but his soul goes marching on." Inspired by the song, Howe wrote the "Battle Hymn" later that night. It was first published in The Atlantic Monthly *in February*

1862, and it quickly became the North's most famous wartime song. The song is an excellent example of how the Union cause became identified with a moral crusade for freedom expressed in religious language and symbols. How does the "Battle Hymn" compare to Lincoln's Second Inaugural Address? Consider the religious language and symbols used to explore the meaning of both the war and freedom.

Mine eyes have seen the glory of the coming of the Lord:

He is trampling out the vintage where the grapes of wrath are stored;

He hath loosed the fateful lightning of His terrible swift sword:

    His truth is marching on.

I have seen Him in the watch-fires of a hundred circling camps;

They have builded Him an altar in the evening dews and damps;

I can read His righteous sentence by the dim and flaring lamps:

    His day is marching on.

I have read a fiery gospel writ in burnished rows of steel:

"As ye deal with my contemners, so with you my grace shall deal:

Let the Hero, born of woman, crush the serpent with his heel,

    Since God is marching on."

He has sounded forth the trumpet that shall never call retreat;

He is sifting out the hearts of men before His judgment-seat:

Oh, be swift, my soul, to answer Him! be jubilant, my feet!

    Our God is marching on.

In the beauty of the lilies Christ was born across the sea,

With a glory in his bosom that transfigures you and me:

As he died to make men holy, let us die to make men free,

    While God is marching on.

SOURCE:

Julia Ward Howe. "Battle Hymn of the Republic," *Atlantic Monthly*, 9 (February 1862): 10.

Document 7: THE TWENTY-NINTH ANNIVERSARY OF THE AMERICAN ANTI-SLAVERY SOCIETY

The American Anti-Slavery Society, founded by William Lloyd Garrison in 1833, was one of the most active and engaged abolitionist organizations in the country. By 1840, its membership was nearly two hundred thousand, with approximately two thousand auxiliary societies. Most members came from religious and philanthropic backgrounds, and the group had a large number of members from the free black community. Many antislavery speakers, as well as former slaves, made impassioned speeches at meetings, further rousing abolitionist sentiment.

On May 12, 1863, the group celebrated its twenty-ninth year in existence. In the course of the meeting, members celebrated various successes, including the U.S. government's prevention of the return of fugitive slaves by the army and the antislave-trade treaty with Great Britain. William Wells Brown, a former slave, spoke at the meeting, advocating autonomy and independence for all African Americans, upon gaining their freedom; he made this speech in response to Garrison's own, "What shall be done with the slave, if emancipated?" All of the members, of course, strongly advocated the end of slavery, but debates arose as to a timeline for its end; some favored immediate abolition, while others took a more conservative view, believing that the end of slavery, while necessary, may be a long time in coming.

Overall, the group was hopeful, as the U.S. government was finally not only speaking out against slavery—it was making real progress toward the institution's abolition. To commemorate this meeting of the American Anti-Slavery Society, pamphlets were printed and disseminated, one of which is reproduced below.

SOURCE:

"Twenty-ninth Anniversary of the American Anti-Slavery Society, Tuesday, May 12, 1863." Library of Congress, Performing Arts Encyclopedia <http://memory.loc.gov/diglib/ihas/loc.rhc.as.113990/default.html> [accessed February 2, 2009].

Hymn list for the anniversary celebration of the abolitionist society founded by William Lloyd Garrison

Document 8: **ABRAHAM LINCOLN'S SECOND INAUGURAL ADDRESS**

Both sides in the Civil War trumpeted in sermons, tracts, songs, and political speeches declaring that God was on their side, that each nation was fulfilling God's will as his chosen people. With hundreds of thousands of casualties, leaders on both sides increasingly justified the bloodshed through religious terms of sacrifice and redemption. In particular, many abolitionists believed that the nation was suffering for the sin of slavery. In the heat of war, the combatants espoused a form of "civil religion" in which service for the nation was viewed as a religious duty. An interesting contrast to this rhetoric is President Abraham Lincoln's Second Inaugural Address, widely considered by historians as one of the greatest speeches in American history. Throughout the war, Lincoln wrestled with the meaning of the war. As early as 1862, Lincoln composed a private "Meditation on the Divine Will." In it, he mused "Both [sides] may be, and one must be wrong. . . . In the present civil war, it is quite possible that God's purpose is something different from the purpose of either side." Lincoln was wrestling with what contemporaries called providence, the working of God's will in human history to fulfill his purpose. In the war, both sides increasingly believed they were God's chosen instruments. In November 1864, Lincoln won reelection over former Union general George B. McClellan, and on March 4, 1865, he delivered his address. How does his address compare with Julia Ward Howe's "Battle Hymn" or with Charles C. Jones's speech?

Second Inaugural Address

March 4, 1965

Fellow-countrymen: At this second appearing to take the oath of the presidential office, there is less occasion for an extended address than there was at the first. Then a statement, somewhat in detail, of a course to be pursued, seemed fitting and proper. Now, at the expiration of four years, during which public declarations have been constantly called forth on every point and phase of the great contest which still absorbs the attention and engrosses the energies of the nation, little that is new could be presented. The progress of our arms, upon which all else chiefly depends, is as well known to the public as to myself; and it is, I trust, reasonably satisfactory and encouraging to all. With high hope for the future, no prediction in regard to it is ventured.

On the occasion corresponding to this four years ago, all thoughts were anxiously directed to an impending civil war. All dreaded it—all sought to avert it. While the inaugural address was being delivered from this place, devoted altogether to saving the Union without war, insurgent agents were in the city seeking to destroy it without war—seeking to dissolve the Union, and divide effects, by negotiation. Both parties deprecated war; but one of them would make war rather than let the nation survive; and the other would accept war rather than let it perish. And the war came.

One-eighth of the whole population were colored slaves, not distributed generally over the Union, but localized in the Southern part of it. These slaves constituted a peculiar and powerful interest. All knew that this interest was, somehow, the cause of the war. To strengthen, perpetuate, and extend this interest was the object for which the insurgents would rend the Union, even by war; while the government claimed no right to do more than to restrict the territorial enlargement of it.

Neither party expected for the war the magnitude or the duration which it has already attained. Neither anticipated that the cause of the conflict might cease with, or even before, the conflict itself should cease. Each looked for an easier triumph, and a result less fundamental and astounding. Both read the same Bible, and pray to the same God; and each invokes his aid against the other. It may seem strange that any men should dare to ask a just God's assistance in wringing their bread from the sweat of other men's faces; but let us judge not, that we be not judged. The prayers of both could not be answered—that of neither has been answered fully.

The Almighty has his own purposes. "Woe unto the world because of offenses! for it must needs be that offenses come; but woe to that man by whom the offense cometh." If we shall suppose that American slavery is one of those offenses which, in the providence of God, must needs come, but which having continued through his appointed time, he now wills to remove, and that he gives to both North and South this terrible war, as the woe due to those by whom the offense came, shall we discern therein any departure from those divine attributes which the believers in a living God always ascribe to him? Fondly do we hope—fervently do we pray—that this mighty scourge of war may speedily pass away. Yet, if God wills that it continue until all the wealth piled by the bondsman's two hundred and fifty years of unrequited toil shall be sunk, and until every drop of blood drawn with the lash shall be paid by another drawn with the sword, as was said three thousand years ago, so still it must be said, "The judgments of the Lord are true and righteous altogether."

With malice toward none; with charity for all; with firmness in the right, as God gives us to see the right, let us strive on to finish the work we are in; to bind up the nation's wounds; to care for him who shall have borne the battle and for his widow and his orphan—to do all which may achieve and cherish a just and lasting peace among ourselves and with all nations.

SOURCE:

Abraham Lincoln. "Second Inaugural Address," in *Complete Works of Abraham Lincoln*, edited by John G. Nicolay and John Hay, volume 11 (New York: Tandy, 1905), pp. 44–47.

Document 9: "Ecclesiastical Equality of Negroes"

Robert L. Dabney (1820–1898) was one of the leaders of the Southern "Old School" Presbyterians who were instrumental in defending slavery as a Christian institution before the war. Dabney, along with Charles Colcock Jones, sought to reform slavery, and he insisted that slaves had the right to religious instruction. Dabney was one of the antebellum South's leading theologians, and from 1853 to 1859 was a professor at Union Theological Seminary in Virginia. When Virginia seceded he joined the Confederate army as a chaplain and later was General "Stonewall" Jackson's chief of staff. After the war, Dabney became increasingly bitter over the South's defeat. In 1867 he wrote A Defence of Virginia, *and* Through Her the South.

In 1867 the Presbyterian Church in Virginia faced, along with white churches throughout the South, a mass exodus of black members. In conferences and denominational publications, whites debated over whether to grant black members equal standing, including ordaining black ministers with equal rights and privileges with white pastors. In the annual meeting on November 9, 1867, Dabney made a popular speech vehemently opposing any steps toward granting "ecclesiastical equality." In the speech Dabney asserted many of the themes of the "Lost Cause" ideology. Most notably, Dabney asserted that any grants of equality in the church would open Southern society to widespread amalgamation, or racial intermarriage. Readers should compare Dabney's speech with that of Charles Colcock Jones. Why was there such a wide discrepancy between the two addresses, both by Presbyterian ministers committed to the religious instruction of blacks before the war?

Thoughtful men see in this pit of tyranny and oppression, to the edge of which the negro and his allies now urge us, "below the lowest depth a lower deep still opening wide." It is a result which, we well know, the astute architects of our ruin clearly foresee and intend, and for the procuring of which they provide, when they impose the political equality of the negro, with a cunning inspired by their own master, the devil. They know mankind in its weakness and baseness. They have measured accurately the degrading effects of subjugation of poverty, of grinding oppression, of despair, upon a people once chivalrous. They know that where the ruling mob is there must be the demagogue, even as the vulture comes where the carcass is, and they know the bottomless subserviency of the demagogue. They understand the ever-increasing assumption of the negro's character, growing by its indulgence. Hence the safe calculation that, when once political equality is confirmed to the blacks, every influence will tend towards that other consummation, *social equality*, which they will be so keen to demand, and their demagogues so ready to grant as the price of their votes. Why, sir, the negroes recently elected in my own section to represent in the pretended convention, districts once graced by Henry and Randolph are already impudently demanding it. He must be "innocent" indeed who does not see whither all this tends, as it is designed by our oppressors to terminate. It is (shall I pronounce the abhorred word?) to *amalgamation!* Yes, sir, those tyrants know that if they can mix the race of Washington and Lee and Jackson with this base herd which they brought from the fens of Africa, if they can taint the blood which hallowed the plains of Manassas with this sordid stream, the adulterous current will never again swell a Virginian's heart with a throb noble enough to make a despot tremble. But they will then have, for all time, a race supple and grovelling enough for all the purposes of oppression. We have before our eyes, in Mexico, the proof and illustration of the satanic wisdom of their plan. There we saw a splendid colonial empire first blighted by abolition, then a frantic spirit of levelling, declaring the equality of the colored races with the Spaniard, and last, the mixture of the Castilian blood—the grandest of all the Gothic—resulting in the mongrel rabble which is now the shame and plague of that wretched land....

And if it shall appear that this Africanizing of our church is not duty, then how wretchedly untimely is the policy of fixing the odium of it on Presbyterianism at this time, of all others, when the whole American people are so manifestly beginning to array themselves on the issue between the white man's party and the black man's party; when this one issue is so completely absorbing all others; when the party of the white man's supremacy is gathering in such resistless might, and is so surely destined ultimately to sweep its opponent out of existence? Why attach our Presbyterianism to a doomed cause, to a type of opinion predestined to be exploded, and to leave, for all time, naught behind it but a savor of *odium* and abhorrence, cleaving for generations to all who have affiliated with it?

Let it be thoroughly considered how far this view must lead us, if squarely followed. Its advocates have much to say about "following our principles consistently without regarding popular inclinations." The attitude they assume is one of a calm superiority to such feelings. They have "risen above these mere prejudices of caste, as things unworthy of Christians." They deprecate my allusion to the practical consequences of their doctrine, as an unseemly appeal to the passions of a dead controversy, and the pride of a social order which has passed away, never to return. When I beseech them not to pervert and overstrain ecclesiastical principles in a manner not only needless, but positively erroneous, so as to make Christ's church virtually a tool for the propagation of the political heresies of negro suffrage and amalgamation, they reply with a grand dignity, that the church is a spiritual kingdom, and does not concern herself *pro* or *con* with secular results. To my common sense, the application thus given to a truth most valuable in its place, is virtually this: that if the church has an opportunity, without going an inch out of her spiritual sphere, and indeed, by the very fidelity with which she adheres to it, to give valuable support to earthly interests the most fundamental and precious, oh! then she has perverted her character; she is meddling with secular questions! But if she misunderstands and perverts her own spiritual character, to corrupt at once her own government and peace, and to give, under a spiritual pretext, most direct assistance to the vilest factionists in their assaults upon the dearest rights and interests of the community, it is all perfectly spiritual and legitimate!

Now then, gentlemen, come with me, and let us see whither this iron consistency in which you boast will lead us. You say that if a negro appears to have a scriptural call and qualification, you have no option, but must make him your own co-presbyter and ecclesiastical equal. Thus at once he becomes a joint ruler over white churches; he must sit, and speak, and vote among you. I shall not permit you to use the quiet hypocrisy of those Yankees whom you permit so imperiously to dictate your action in this matter; who after making a negro in pretense their co-presbyter and equal, give him a tacit but imperative hint to take himself off to the colored gallery, and thence witness the presbyterial proceedings as a very humble spectator. This will not do in your case; you are thoroughly consistent. So you must have this negro of yours reviewing and censuring the records of white sessions, and sitting to judge appeals brought before you by white parties, possibly by white ladies!

But this is a small part. After all the negro exodus from our communion, there are still churches which have a large majority of black communicants. After you have ordained your negro, one of these churches may regularly elect him pastor. Constitutionally, the white minority cannot here resist the will of the majority, when regularly exercised. Suppose the former come to you for remedy? Can you tell them to take dismissions and join a white church elsewhere? Distance may forbid. Besides, you will be bound by that jewel, consistency, to tell them that such a solution of their trouble would be wholly out of the question. You made race and color no obstacle to putting this negro equal to yourselves; how can you encourage these white members in making them a pretext to rend a church roll? Consistency will require you to say to them, "Remain and submit." So there you have a black pastor to white families, clothed with official title to ask their experimental, heart secrets; to visit their sick beds; to celebrate baptisms, marriages and funerals over their children! And this, on your principle, is no Utopian picture, but what may become a literal fact in a month after you execute your plan.

Now, is any one so fond as to believe still that this can be honestly, squarely done, and yet social equality can be denied? Do you tell me that after you have admitted this negro thus to your debates, your votes, your pulpits, your sick and dying bods, your weddings and funerals, you will still exclude him from your parlors and tables? *Credat Judæus Apella!* I tell you, sir, this doctrine, if it does not mean nothing, or if it does not mean Yankee hypocrisy, means ultimately, *amalgamation*. What more emphatic evidence did ever a traveler bring back to us of the utter confusion of bloods in Spanish America, than to tell us that he saw black priests to white people? But now, when the negro is grasping political equality, when he is no longer an inferior and in servitude, when his temper is assuming and impudent in many cases, when in many sections he out-numbers the whites, it becomes both church and civil society to guard this danger with tenfold as much jealousy as when they were our servants....

They quote for us also such passages as these: that in Christ "there is neither Greek nor Jew, circumcision nor uncircumcision, Barbarian, Scythian, bond nor free; but Christ is all in all." Hence they jump to the inference, that not only the blessings of redemption, but the privileges of church office and rule, are common to all believers, irrespective of caste, class, or condition. I shall show, sir, beyond all cavil, that there is a vast and an unbridged chasm between this premise and this conclusion. The argument is, that because the blessings of redemption are common to all classes and races of true believers, therefore it follows, of course, that every privilege and grade of church power must be made common to them. But the answer is, that several Bible instances themselves show that this consequence does not follow. None here will dispute that the Old Testament church had a gospel; nor will any deny that its saving blessings were common to *all believing Hebrews*, though not to all Gentiles. But lo! the priesthood, the clerical function of the day, was expressly limited to the tribe of Levi! In Galatians iii. 28—a passage parallel to the one quoted against me—St. Paul says: "There is neither Jew nor Greek; there is neither bond nor free; there is neither male nor female; for ye are all one in Christ Jesus." Blessed doctrine! Yet the same apostle says, "I suffer not a woman to teach;" thus excluding from official privilege, on grounds of class, one-half of the whole Christian world, which he had just declared to be "all one in Christ Jesus." So you see, gentlemen, that the apostle Paul evidently did not believe in your argument. Miss Antoinette Brown and Mrs. Abby Kelly were precisely with you; but the apostle was not. Again, the apostle, in the Epistles to Timothy and Titus, rules that no convert who was implicated, before his conversion, in polygamy, must be ordained a presbyter; for so the best expositors view 1 Timothy iii. 2, and Titus i. 6. Here is another exclusion on grounds of class. Surely no one will argue that these husbands of more than one wife were excluded because they *had been* sinners. Had not the apostle himself been a murderer? Or on the grounds that they were still living in sin; for this would also have excluded them from the *church*. It is an exclusion *on grounds of class,* and independent of the question of their faith and repentence. Thus we have three instances, confirmed by inspiration itself, showing that the supposed consequence does not hold, and that it is not true that all distinctions of class are abolished as to church office, because they are abolished as to church membership....

SOURCE:

Robert Lewis Dabney. "Ecclesiastical Equality of Negroes, Speech Delivered in the Synod of Virginia, Nov. 9, 1867," in *Discussions: Evangelical and Theological,* volume 2 (London: Banner of Truth Trust, 1967), pp. 199–210.

Document 10: **ARMY LIFE IN A BLACK REGIMENT**

Thomas Wentworth Higginson (1823–1911), abolitionist, author, and soldier, studied at Harvard Divinity School and became a Unitarian minister. Higginson became a radical abolitionist, participating in an attempt to rescue a captured runaway slave from a Boston jail in 1854. He later joined the secret group of supporters that helped to finance John Brown's raid on Harpers Ferry. A member of the Union army, Higginson was appointed colonel of the First South Carolina Volunteers in November 1862, the first regiment of former slaves to be recruited into the federal army. His regiment was composed mostly of newly freed slaves from the South Carolina low country.

After the war Higginson recorded his experiences and also contributed to the preservation of African American spirituals by copying the songs he heard around the campfire and on the march. In his 1882 memoirs he remarked "not since Cromwell's time have we seen so religious an army." Before the end of the war more than 186,000 African Americans served in the Union military. The spirituals recorded here give a glimpse into the worldview of former slaves fighting for their freedom. Particularly interesting is "My Army Cross Over," drawing upon the slave's favorite biblical image of freedom, the Exodus of the chosen people out of bondage, with Pharaoh's army destroyed by the wrath of God. Throughout the war, slaves greeted Union armies as deliverers sent by God—and they greeted those most joyfully who were former slaves.

Negro Spirituals.

I. Hold Your Light.

"Hold your light, Brudder Robert,—
 Hold your light,
Hold your light on Canaan's shore.

"What make ole Satan for follow me so?
Satan ain't got notin' for do wid me.
 Hold your light,
 Hold your light,
Hold your light on Canaan's shore."

 This would be sung for half an hour at a time, perhaps each person present being named in turn. It seemed the simplest primitive type of "spiritual." The next in popularity was almost as elementary, and, like this, named successively each one of the circle. It was, however, much more resounding and convivial in its music.

II. Bound to Go.

"Jordan River, I'm bound to go,
 Bound to go, bound to go,—
Jordan River, I'm bound to go,
 And bid 'em fare ye well.

"My Brudder Robert, I'm bound to go,
 Bound to go," &c.

"My Sister Lucy, I'm bound to go,
 Bound to go," &c.

 Sometimes it was "tink 'em" (think them) "fare ye well." The *ye* was so detached that I thought at first it was "very" or "vary well."
 Another picturesque song, which seemed immensely popular, was at first very bewildering to me. I could not make out the first words of the chorus, and called it the "Romandàr," being reminded of some Romaic song which I had formerly heard. That association quite fell in with the Orientalism of the new tent-life.

III. Room in There.

"O, my mudder is gone! my mudder is gone!
My mudder is gone into heaven, my Lord!
 I can't stay behind!
Dere's room in dar, room in dar,
Room in dar, in de heaven, my Lord!
 I can't stay behind!
Can't stay behind, my dear,
 I can't stay behind!

"O, my fader is gone!" &c.

"O, de angels are gone!" &c.

O, I'se been on de road! I 'se been on de road!
"O, I'se been on de road into heaven, my Lord!
 I can't stay behind!
O, room in dar, room in dar,
Room in dar, in de heaven, my Lord!
 I can't stay behind!"

 By this time every man within hearing, from oldest to youngest, would be wriggling and shuffling, as if through some magic piper's bewitchment; for even those who at first affected contemptuous indifference would be drawn into the vortex erelong.
 Next to these in popularity ranked a class of songs belonging emphatically to the Church Militant, and available for camp purposes with very little strain upon their symbolism. This, for instance, had a true companion-in-arms heartiness about it, not impaired by the feminine invocation at the end.

IV. Hail Mary.

"One more valiant soldier here,
 One more valiant soldier here,
One more valiant soldier here,
 To help me bear de cross.
O hail, Mary, hail!
 Hail, Mary, hail!
Hail, Mary, hail!
 To help me bear de cross."

 I fancied that the original reading might have been "soul," instead of "soldier,"—with some other syllable inserted to fill out the metre, —and that the "Hail, Mary," might denote a Roman Catholic origin, as I had several men from St. Augustine who held in a dim way to that faith. It was a very ringing song, though not so grandly jubilant as the next, which was really impressive as the singers pealed it out, when marching or rowing or embarking.

V. My Army Cross Over.

"My army cross over,
My army cross over,
O, Pharaoh's army drownded!
My army cross over.

"We'll cross de mighty river,
    My army cross over;
We'll cross de river Jordan,
    My army cross over;
We'll cross de danger water,
    My army cross over;
We'll cross de mighty Myo,
    My army cross over. (*Thrice.*)
    O, Pharaoh's army drownded!
My army cross over."

I could get no explanation of the "mighty Myo" except that one of the old men thought it meant the river of death. Perhaps it is an African word. In the Cameroon dialect, "Mawa" signifies "to die."

The next also has a military ring about it, and the first line is well matched by the music. The rest is conglomerate, and one or two lines show a more Northern origin. "Done" is a Virginia shibboleth, quite distinct from the "been" which replaces it in South Carolina. Yet one of their best choruses, without any fixed words, was, "De bell done ringing," for which, in proper South Carolina dialect, would have been substituted, "De bell been a-ring." This refrain may have gone South with our army.

VI. Ride In, Kind Saviour.

"Ride in, kind Saviour!
    No man can hinder me.
O, Jesus is a mighty man!
    No man, &c.
We're marching through Virginny fields.
    No man, &c.
O, Satan is a busy man,
    No man, &c.
And he has his sword and shield,
    No man, &c.
O, old Secesh done come and gone!
    No man can hinder me."

Sometimes they substituted "hinder *we*," which was more spicy to the ear, and more in keeping with the usual head-over-heels arrangement of their pronouns.

Almost all their songs were thoroughly religious in their tone, however quaint their expression, and were in a minor key, both as to words and music. The attitude is always the same, and, as a commentary on the life of the race, is infinitely pathetic. Nothing but patience for this life,—nothing but triumph in the next. Sometimes the present predominates, sometimes the future; but the combination is always implied. In the following, for instance, we hear simply the patience.

VII. This World Almost Done.

"Brudder, keep your lamp trimmin' and a-burnin,'
    Keep your lamp trimmin' and a-burnin',
Keep your lamp trimmin' and a-burnin',
    For dis world most done.
So keep your lamp, &c.
    Dis world most done."

But in the next, the final reward of patience is proclaimed as plaintively.

VIII. I Want to Go Home.

"Dere's no rain to wet you,
    O, yes, I want to go home.
Dere's no sun to burn you,
    O, yes, I want to go home;
O, push along, believers,
    O, yes, &c.
Dere's no hard trials,
    O, yes, &c.
Dere's no whips a-crackin',
    O, yes, &c.
My brudder on de wayside,
    O, yes, &c.
O, push along, my brudder,
    O, yes, &c.
Where dere's no stormy weather,
    O, yes, &c.
Dere's no tribulation,
    O, yes, &c."

This next was a boat-song, and timed well with the tug of the oar.

IX. THE COMING DAY.

"I want to go to Canaan,

I want to go to Canaan,

I want to go to Canaan,

To meet 'em at de comin' day."

SOURCE:

Thomas Wentworth Higginson. *Army Life in a Black Regiment* (Boston: Lee & Shepard; New York: Dillingham, 1882), pp. 199–202.

BIBLIOGRAPHY

Angell, Stephen Ward. *Bishop Henry McNeal Turner and African-American Religion in the South*. Knoxville: University of Tennessee Press, 1992. Angell traces the career of the most important grass-roots organizer of Southern blacks after emancipation, emphasizing his successes in establishing the African Methodist Episcopal Church in the South and his calls for black self-help and political rights.

Burin, Eric. *Slavery and the Peculiar Solution: A History of the American Colonization Society*. Gainesville: University Press of Florida, 2005. Burin traces the development, organization, and mission of the American Colonization Society (ACS) and provides a useful discussion of the religious motivations behind colonization. The ACS presented itself as a Christian reform society dedicated to sending civilized and Christianized African Americans back to Africa to convert the continent.

Cornelius, Janet D. *Slave Missions and the Black Church in the Antebellum South*. Columbia: University of South Carolina Press, 1999. Cornelius examines the complex and often contradictory relationship between Southern white missionaries and African American slaves and discusses the "domestic mission" movement in the South, along with the emergence of black churches, including their preachers, praise houses, and schools.

De Caro, Louis A. *"Fire from the Midst of You": A Religious Life of John Brown*. New York: New York University Press, 2002. Examines Brown's role as a vengeful Old Testament prophet as well as a Christian martyr. De Caro discusses Brown's religiously inspired commitment to racial equality.

Douglass, Frederick. *My Bondage and My Freedom*. New York and Auburn: Miller, Orton & Milligan, 1855. This work is the second revised edition of Douglass's account of his experiences as a slave and his escape to freedom. His account was the most famous of the slave narratives of the time, which were used by abolitionists in their campaign to overthrow slavery. Douglass emphasizes the hypocrisy of "proslavery" Christians, who preached the Gospel to slaves while denying them literacy and breaking up families in the domestic slave trade.

Genovese, Eugene D. *A Consuming Fire: The Fall of the Confederacy in the Mind of the White Christian South*. Athens: University of Georgia Press, 1998. Genovese examines the roots of Confederate identity in the antebellum religious defense of slavery, particularly the Confederacy as a providential nation and the doomed efforts to reform slavery up to "Bible Standards."

Goodman, Paul. *Of One Blood: Abolitionism and the Origins of Racial Equality*. Berkeley: University of California Press, 1998. Goodman examines the influence of religion on abolitionists' calls for racial equality. The author focuses on the role of black abolitionists in convincing their white colleagues of the evil of slavery and the continuing struggle of white abolitionists with their own prejudices.

Hatch, Nathan O. *The Democratization of American Christianity*. New Haven: Yale University Press, 1989. A useful analysis of antebellum American religion that argues for a revolution in popular participation. In revivals, the proliferation of "populist" sects like the Baptists and Methodists, and attacks on the authority of clergymen, common people increasingly took religion into their own hands.

Howard, Victor B. *Religion and the Radical Republican Movement, 1860–1870*. Lexington: University Press of Kentucky, 1990. Howard focuses on the influence of abolitionism on the Republican Party. Radicals within the party gave priority to emancipation over saving the Union, but they also asserted that without freeing the slaves, the nation could not fulfill its role as God's chosen people.

Johnson, Curtis D. *Redeeming America: Evangelicals and the Road to the Civil War*. Chicago: I. R. Dee, 1993. An excellent overview of the impact and importance of evangelicals in antebellum American society. Johnson examines the core tenets of American evangelicalism: the centrality of the Bible; the need for conversion; America as a providential nation; living a holy, benevolent life; and the coming of the millennium. This work is good for a quick overview of antebellum reform movements, revivalism, and African American religion.

Jones, Charles Colcock. *Tenth Annual Report of the Association for the Religious Instruction of the Negroes of Liberty County, Georgia*. Savannah: The Association, 1845. Jones wrote most of the annual reports of the association he founded in 1832. He used thepublications to give instruction to white Christians on how to organize domestic missions and minister to slaves.

Lincoln, Abraham. "Second Inaugural Address, March 4, 1865." In *Complete Works of Abraham Lincoln*, Volume XI, edited by John G. Nicolay and John Hay. New York: Francis D. Tandy Company, 1905, pp. 44–47. Please see Documents section of this chapter for further information.

Loveland, Anne C. *Southern Evangelicals and the Social Order, 1800–1860.* Baton Rouge: Louisiana State University Press, 1980. Loveland analyzes the attitudes of Southern white ministers toward politics, reform movements, the religious instruction of slaves, slavery, and the sectional controversy. An excellent intellectual history of Southern white Christians.

Mathews, Donald G. "Charles Colcock Jones and the Southern Evangelical Crusade to Form a Biracial Community," *Journal of Southern History,* 41 (August 1975): 299–320. A useful account of Jones's efforts to use the "domestic mission" movement to reform slavery up to Christian standards and heal the conflicts between white masters and black slaves.

McKivigan, John R. *The War against Proslavery Religion: Abolitionism and the Northern Churches, 1830–1865.* Ithaca, N.Y.: Cornell University Press, 1984. McKivigan studies the troubled relationship between abolitionists and the mainstream Northern churches. Although abolitionists never gave up their attempts to convert Northern denominations to their cause, they became increasingly alienated from more-conservative Christians whom they denounced as "bulwarks of slavery." The author focuses on the "come-outer" sects and on the impact of antislavery on the interdenominational reform societies.

Montgomery, William E. *Under Their Own Vine and Fig Tree: The African-American Church in the South, 1865–1900.* Baton Rouge: Louisiana State University Press, 1993. Montgomery examines the establishment of independent black churches in the postwar South. He focuses on institution building and the role of prominent black leaders such as Henry McNeal Turner in creating churches that served not only as places of worship, but also as centers of communities and political participation.

Noll, Mark. *The Civil War as a Theological Crisis.* Chapel Hill: University of North Carolina Press, 2006. The author examines Abraham Lincoln's observation that both sides prayed to the same God and read the same Bible, but profoundly disagreed on its meaning. Noll examines the central role of the Bible in both defending and attacking slavery.

Raboteau, Albert J. *Slave Religion: The "Invisible Institution" in the Antebellum South.* New York: Oxford University Press, 1978. An excellent overview of the religious life of slaves, discussing the influence of African beliefs and practices, the biracial Southern churches, and the creation of a unique Afro-American Christianity. Raboteau emphasizes the role of religion in resisting the dehumanizing effects of slavery and its central place in slave communities.

Sernett, Milton C. *Black Religion and American Evangelicalism: White Protestants, Plantation Missions, and the Flowering of Negro Christianity, 1787–1865.* Metuchen, N.J.: Scarecrow Press, 1975. Sernett's work gives an excellent account of the rise of the African Methodist Episcopal Church. Sernett also covers the relationship of the white domestic missions and efforts by slaves to create their own independent religious life.

"Slavery—Slave Trade—Antislavery—Abolitionism," *The Southern Christian Advocate* (November 29, 1844). This Methodist newspaper was published in Charleston, South Carolina. Denominations established weekly newspapers in most of the major cities of the South. These papers often published articles urging the conversion of slaves and defending slavery as a Christian institution.

Smith, H. Shelton. *In His Image But . . . Racism in Southern Religion, 1780–1910.* Durham, N.C.: Duke University Press, 1972. Smith traces the growth of a conservative racial orthodoxy in Southern religion after 1800. After an initial period of criticism of slavery during the late eighteenth and early nineteenth centuries, the evangelical denominations increasingly defended slavery as a divinely sanctioned institution. Includes useful discussions of the biblical proslavery argument and the splitting of the denominations over slavery.

Snay, Mitchell. *The Gospel of Disunion: Religion and Separatism in the Antebellum South.* Cambridge: Cambridge University Press, 1993. Snay examines the use of religion by Southern ministers to "sanctify" slavery in the sectional controversy. Snay argues that religion was central in constructing a separate Southern identity against a North they increasingly saw as immoral and irreligious.

Stiles, Joseph C. Speech on the Slavery Resolutions, Delivered in the General Assembly Which Met in Detroit May Last. Washington, D.C.: Jno. T. Towers, 1850. Stiles was a Presbyterian minister from Georgia who collaborated with Charles Colcock Jones in the domestic mission to the slaves. His speech was before a hostile audience at the New School Presbyterian national conference. The New School was dominated by antislavery Northerners. Stiles emphasized the role of white Southern Christians in reforming slave codes, especially removing barbarous legal punishments.

Stout, Harry S. *Upon the Altar of the Nation: A Moral History of the Civil War.* New York: Viking, 2006. The author analyzes and critiques the religiously based nationalism on both sides of the Civil War. Stout argues both sides espoused a national religion based on martyrdom and rebirth through violence. An excellent study of wartime sermons, speeches, and propaganda.

Stowell, Daniel W. *Rebuilding Zion: The Religious Reconstruction of the South, 1863–1877.* New York: Oxford University Press, 1998. Stowell focuses on the interrelation of white Southern evangelicals, Northern white evangelicals, and the newly freed black Christians in reconstructing religion in the chaos of the postwar South. Stowell concentrates on the reorganization of Southern churches, especially the role of Northern African American churches in helping to establish independent black churches in the former Confederacy. Stowell emphasizes the building and rebuilding of churches as institutions.

Stringfellow, Thornton. "The Bible Argument; or, Slavery in the Light of Divine Revelation." In Cotton Is King and Pro-Slavery Arguments, edited by E. N. Elliott. Augusta, Georgia: Pritchard, Abbott & Loomis, 1860, pp. 461–491.

Please see Documents section of this chapter for further information.

Walters, Ronald G. *The Antislavery Appeal: American Abolitionism after 1830.* New York: Norton, 1978. An excellent overview of the worldview of abolitionists. Walters includes a chapter on abolitionism and religion, emphasizing their appeal to the spirit of the Bible, their focus on moral suasion and slaveholders as sinners in need of conversion.

Wilson, Charles Reagan. *Baptized in Blood: The Religion of the Lost Cause, 1865–1920.* Athens: University of Georgia Press, 1980. An intellectual history of the efforts by former Confederates to understand and defend the Southern cause in the wake of defeat and emancipation. Wilson emphasizes the continuity between antebellum defenses of slavery and postwar efforts to reestablish white supremacy. White Southerners created a "civil religion" that defended the Confederacy as a holy and righteous cause.

~ 10 ~

THE EMANCIPATION PROCLAMATION: SLAVERY, THE CIVIL WAR, AND ABRAHAM LINCOLN

After winning the presidential election of 1860 Abraham Lincoln grappled with a personal conflict—should he take immediate steps to end slavery or take a more pragmatic approach to ending slavery so as not to further intensify the secession crisis? Lincoln answered that question publicly on March 4, 1861, during his first inaugural address. Taking a cautious approach, Lincoln tried to allay Southerners' fears that as president he would abolish slavery. "I have no purpose," Lincoln proclaimed, "directly or indirectly, to interfere with the institution of slavery in the States where it exists. I believe I have no lawful right to do so, and I have no inclination to do so." Lincoln further stated that he would enforce the 1850 Fugitive Slave Law and that the only obstacle he would erect to slavery would be to its extension into the territories. Lincoln's calming rhetoric enraged leading abolitionists, including Massachusetts senator Charles Sumner and Frederick Douglass, who called upon Lincoln to abolish slavery immediately upon taking office. As the secession crisis destroyed the Union and placed it on an imminent path to civil war, Lincoln surmised that swift emancipation would only alienate border states and intensify the ensuing conflict. Although Lincoln held a strong moral opposition to slavery, he knew there would be myriad social and political conflicts in the struggle to end the South's "peculiar institution"—slavery. Even though Lincoln eventually emancipated the slaves, the timing and scope of his emancipation policy raises some important historical questions—was the Emancipation Proclamation issued solely as a war measure and did Lincoln have constitutional authority to end slavery through a presidential decree?

With the outbreak of the Civil War on April 12, 1861, Lincoln primarily concerned himself with ending the conflict and preserving the Union. "My paramount objective in this struggle is to save the Union," Lincoln informed Horace Greeley, the editor of the *New York Tribune*, in August 1862, "and is *not* either to save or to destroy slavery" (Basler, volume 5, p. 388). Despite his publicly cautious approach to emancipation, Lincoln believed that the eventual restoration of the Union would mean the end of slavery as Lincoln viewed it as the root cause of secession and the military conflict. The difficulty for Lincoln, however, was that four states—Kentucky, Missouri, Maryland, and Delaware—maintained their allegiance to the United States, but also preserved slavery. A pragmatic politician, Lincoln knew that he needed to be careful not to do anything to alienate those states and further destroy the Union.

Lincoln's caution in showing the border states that he would not emancipate their slaves was jeopardized by abolitionist generals John C. Frémont's and David Hunter's emancipation of slaves during the war's first year. On August 30, 1861, Frémont, commanding Union forces in Missouri, emancipated the state's slaves under the language of the First Confiscation Act, which ordered that property of Confederate sympathizers could be seized

Engraving of The First Reading of the Emancipation Proclamation before the Cabinet, *from the painting by F. B. Carpenter, circa 1866* (Library of Congress)

by the federal government. Less than a year later, in May 1862, Hunter did the same, freeing all the slaves in Georgia, Florida, and South Carolina. Fearful that these unauthorized actions might cause the border states to secede, Lincoln promptly ordered both generals to rescind the orders and return the slaves to their masters, much to the dismay of Northern abolitionists.

Although Lincoln reprimanded both Frémont and Hunter, within three months of Frémont's order Lincoln drafted a plan of gradual, compensated emancipation for the smallest slaveholding state in the union—Delaware. Lincoln, who had always been a strong proponent of gradual emancipation and colonization of former slaves in places such as Liberia, proposed that all Delaware slaves over the age of thirty-five be immediately emancipated and that the other slaves be set free when they reached that age. He promised Delaware $700,000 of federal money over a period of thirty years. Lincoln further encouraged them to speed up the process by agreeing to pay them an additional $70,000 per year for ten years if they agreed to abolish slavery completely by 1872. By March 1862 Lincoln directed Congress to "cooperate with any state which may adopt gradual abolishment of slavery, giving to such state pecuniary aid, to be used by such state in its discretion, to compensate for the inconveniences . . . produced by such change of system" (Basler, volume 5, p. 144).

While Lincoln's notion of gradual, compensated emancipation might eventually have ruined slavery, free blacks and abolitionists desired a more expedient solution. After Congress passed the Militia Act in July 1862, which in part granted Lincoln the power to emancipate any slaves who labored for the Union's cause, Lincoln took the first aggressive step in ending slavery. During a cabinet meeting on July 22, 1862, Lincoln informed his chief advisors that he planned on abolishing slavery in the areas in rebellion as a means to ending the conflict. The president explained that the thousands of slaves laboring for the Confederacy were the backbone of the Confederate war effort and needed to be eliminated as a labor source. Sensing the importance of emancipation, the majority of Lincoln's cabinet supported the idea. Edwin Stanton, Secretary of War, immediately grasped the military significance of emancipation, as it would not only weaken the Confederacy's labor supply, it would also strengthen the Union's, since emancipated slaves could perform a variety of military and supportive roles to armies in the field. Only Postmaster General Montgomery Blair, a former Democrat, criticized the measure and warned that emancipation would cause a negative political backlash and diminish popular support for the war. Although supportive, Secretary of State William Seward pointed to one problem: the Army of the Potomac—the main Union force operating in the East—had not achieved a major victory. Regardless of the many successes Union forces had in the West during the first two years of the conflict, the East was regarded as the major theater of war operations. Unless a victory could be achieved there, Lincoln's proclamation freeing the slaves in areas in rebellion would carry little weight and would appear as an act of desperation. Although he did not want to delay issuing the proclamation, Lincoln agreed to wait for the Army of the Potomac to win a battle.

Lincoln did not have to wait long for this "victory": Although the battle of Antietam, fought near Sharpsburg, Maryland, on September 17, 1862, was viewed militarily as a tactical draw, it halted General Robert E. Lee's first attempt at an invasion of the North and sent Lee's Army of Northern Virginia back into Virginia. Believing that this was perhaps the closest the Army of the Potomac would come to military success in the East, Lincoln used the opportunity to issue his preliminary Emancipation Proclamation, which stated that all slaves in areas in rebellion against the United States would be declared free on January 1, 1863.

News of Lincoln's proclamation met with mixed reactions among soldiers in the Union Army. General George B. McClellan, who, as commander of the Army of the Potomac at Antietam, had given Lincoln his victory, condemned the measure. Many Union soldiers railed against the document, stating that they did not enlist to free the slaves. Rage among some Union soldiers created mutinous scenes in some regiments. Entire units condemned the proclamation and men signed petitions stating that they refused to fight unless the proclamation was revoked. When the Army of the Potomac entered Fredericksburg, Virginia, in December 1862 they destroyed the town—some of them venting their frustration over emancipation.

Long after the war, General Joshua Lawrence Chamberlain, a veteran of the Army of the Potomac's campaigns, recalled in a speech delivered on the one-hundredth anniversary of Lincoln's birth (in 1909) that "many high officers of our army disapproved this in heart and mind, if they dared not in speech. They thought the president had no right to proclaim this intention nor power to carry it into effect" (Chamberlain, 19).

Not all Union officers and soldiers condemned Lincoln's measure. Three days after the news of the proclamation reached the Army of the Potomac, General John White Geary wrote: "The President's proclamation is the most important public document ever issued by an officer of our Government" (Blair, 56). The staunchly abolitionist general Robert H. Milroy regarded the proclamation as the most important event in human history since the birth of Jesus Christ. General Henry Halleck—who in 1862 served as Lincoln's general-in-chief—believed that emancipation was a great weapon in ending the rebellion. Halleck contended that every slave set free had the equivalent impact of removing one Confederate soldier from the battlefield.

Beyond the Union army, Northerners, too, seemed divided over emancipation. Benjamin R. Curtis—a former justice of the United States Supreme Court—argued in his pamphlet *Executive Power* that no president possessed the executive authority to abolish slavery, an institution protected by the Constitution. Robert C. Winthrop, a former Speaker of the U.S. House of Representatives, also supported Curtis's assertion that Lincoln had grossly overstepped his presidential authority. Lincoln supporters, such as New York's Charles Kirkland, argued that Lincoln had every executive authority under the "laws of war" to end slavery. "The 'lawful object' of the President at this moment," argued Kirkland, "is to preserve the Constitution by putting an end to this rebellion. In order to do this, it is necessary to deprive the rebels of their means of sustaining the rebellion—one of the most effective available of those means . . . is their slaves" (Kirkland, 10). Regardless of attitudes toward emancipation one thing was certain—it had changed the course of the conflict. *Harper's Weekly* reported in the aftermath of preliminary emancipation simply: "It marked a new phase in the conduct of the war."

Although the nation appeared divided in the autumn of 1862, Lincoln did not know how many people despised the measure until the November 1862 elections. Those who supported emancipation lost miserably: thirty-one Republican seats in Congress were replaced,

Union soldiers implementing the Emancipation Proclamation along the Mississippi River (Collection of Jonathan A. Noyalas)

and at the state level, Republicans did not fare much better. The governorships of New York and New Jersey went to Democrats, and, in Lincoln's native Illinois, Democrats won a twenty-eight-seat majority in the state legislature. Some Illinois Democrats even suggested severing their bond with the Union because of emancipation.

The interim elections signaled widespread displeasure, but Lincoln firmly believed that eliminating slavery was the only way to end the conflict. Notwithstanding his belief in the importance of emancipation, Lincoln appeared gloomy in the weeks after the preliminary proclamation was issued. News of Union soldiers leaving the ranks and Northerners lashing out at free blacks left Lincoln in a sullen mood. On September 28, 1862, Lincoln informed Vice President Hannibal Hamlin that: "This, looked soberly in the face, is not very satisfactory.... The North responds to the proclamation sufficiently in breath; but breath alone kills no rebels. I wish I could write more cheerfully" (Basler, volume 5, p. 444).

Regardless of the criticism, Lincoln's own pessimism, and Republican losses in 1862, Lincoln proceeded with emancipation and issued his final proclamation on New Year's Day, 1863. On that day free blacks gathered at the White House and praised Lincoln as the great emancipator. Celebrations took place throughout Northern cities. Yet, the jubilation that African Americans felt that day also alerted them to the stark realization that Lincoln's words meant nothing unless the Civil War ended in the Union's favor.

Lincoln's Emancipation Proclamation not only freed the slaves in areas in rebellion, but also opened the door for widespread recruitment of African Americans into the army and navy. "I further declare and make known that such persons of suitable condition," Lincoln stated in the final proclamation, "will be received into the armed service of the United States." This measure eventually opened the door for nearly two hundred thousand African Americans to serve in the war effort and to take an active role in achieving emancipation's promise.

Emancipation and its guarantee to arm African Americans sent shock waves throughout the Confederacy. Although limited numbers had served the Union's cause under the Militia Act, Confederate officials knew that emancipation would swell the Union ranks. The Confederate government felt threatened and decided to discourage African American enlistment by issuing a proclamation that stated that any African American captured on the battlefield in a Union uniform would not be treated as a prisoner of war, but rather as a slave in armed rebellion—punishable by death. The Confederate government also encouraged the execution of white officers who commanded African American troops; however, the threats did little to deter African Americans from enlisting.

While Confederate officials tried to block the effects of emancipation, some of Lincoln's abolitionist generals eagerly sought ways to make emancipation a reality. Among the first to enforce emancipation was Indiana native General Robert H. Milroy. A staunch Republican and abolitionist, Milroy occupied Winchester, Virginia, on January 1, 1863, intent on emancipating slaves in Virginia's Shenandoah Valley. To Milroy this was the perfect place to bring emancipation to the slaves, because it was home to both Senator James Mason, author of the 1850 Fugitive Slave Law, and Judge Richard Parker, who presided over John Brown's 1859 trial for Brown's raid on Harper's Ferry. Four days after he entered town Milroy issued "Freedom to Slaves!" which informed area residents that he would enforce emancipation at all costs and that anyone who stood in his way would be arrested and sent beyond Union lines. Furthermore, Milroy informed his soldiers—many of whom disliked the idea of enforcing emancipation—that if they refused to comply with his order they would be dealt with accordingly. Milroy, as had other officers in the first half of 1863, tried to convince their men that despite personal views on emancipation, it was a great weapon to bring about an end to the war. Couching the impetus for emancipation in these terms inspired Union soldiers to begin to recognize the importance of emancipation and to actively enforce it.

Although generals such as Milroy carried the message of emancipation, the Union army reached only a small part of the Confederate slave population. Slaveholders who did not have to contend with occupying armies and with the enforcement of emancipation withheld the news from their slaves. To spread the word Lincoln called on Frederick Douglass to come up with an organization to spread news of emancipation in the South and bring slaves into Union lines. Although Douglass did not necessarily view Lincoln in the most positive light prior to emancipation because of Lincoln's cautious approach to the abolition of slavery, Douglass was sympathetic with Lincoln's concerns, and he thought that infiltrating the South and bringing slaves into Union lines without proper military support was not safe. Douglass advised Lincoln that the government should use special agents to inform slaves of the proclamation and encourage each slave to plan his or her own escape independently. Lincoln approved the plan.

With emancipation enforced in a limited degree in 1863 its promise was still legally tenuous because slavery was protected under the Constitution. With uncertainty about his chances for reelection in 1864 Lincoln aggressively pressured Congress to pass the Thirteenth Amendment, formally abolishing slavery. Lincoln defeated George McClellan in the presidential election and saw Congress pass the amendment on January 31, 1865; Lincoln viewed it as another great step in breaking the morale of the Confederacy—especially if border states decided to ratify the amendment.

The amendment became law through its ratification on December 18, 1865. However, Lincoln—who had fallen victim to an assassin's bullet on April 15, 1865—did not live to see the promises of the Emancipation Proclamation solidified.

Lincoln's Emancipation Proclamation was the Civil War's greatest legacy. It eliminated an institution that had divided the nation since the founding of the American Republic. Despite the criticism Lincoln received from abolitionists in 1861 and 1862 for not aggressively implementing emancipation, and despite the criticism he received from anti-emancipationists after the autumn of 1862, Lincoln paved the way for the freedom of nearly four million slaves. Perhaps it was Lincoln's vice president, Hannibal Hamlin, in a letter to Lincoln written three days after the preliminary proclamation was issued, that best captured what Lincoln and emancipation meant to the future course of the United States: "It will stand as the great act of the age. It will prove to be wise in statesmanship as it is patriotic. It will be enthusiastically approved and sustained, and future generations will, as I do, say God bless you for this great and noble act" (Basler, volume 5, p. 444).

Jonathan Noyalas

CHRONOLOGY

1861

March 4: President Abraham Lincoln is inaugurated. During his inaugural address Lincoln informs the country that he will uphold the Fugitive Slave Law and not eliminate slavery in states where it already exists; he announces that he will prevent slavery's extension into the territories in an attempt to avoid civil war.

August 6: Congress passes the First Confiscation Act, which states that any person laboring "under the laws of any State" (that is, a slave state) for a Confederate supporter shall be discharged from their labor.

August 30: Union general John C. Frémont issues an order to liberate slaves of Confederate sympathizers in Missouri.

September 2: President Abraham Lincoln orders General Frémont to rescind his order of August 30, 1861, in an attempt to reassure border slave states that he has no plans to abolish slavery.

1862

March 6: President Lincoln recommends compensated emancipation.

April 10: Congress adopts a plan for gradual compensated emancipation.

April 16: President Lincoln signs a bill abolishing slavery in the District of Columbia.

May 9: Union general David Hunter declares that slaves in Georgia, Florida, and South Carolina are free. Lincoln soon orders Hunter to rescind the order to prevent the border states from seceding.

July 12: President Lincoln issues an appeal to the border states calling for them to accept his plan of compensated emancipation.

July 13: During a carriage ride to the funeral of one of Secretary of War Edwin M. Stanton's infant sons Lincoln announces to Secretary of State William Seward and Secretary of the Navy Gideon Welles that he intends to issue a proclamation of swift emancipation.

July 17: Congress passes the Second Confiscation Act declaring that all slaves of Confederate sympathizers are to be set free.

July 22: President Lincoln presents his cabinet with the first draft of the Emancipation Proclamation.

August 14: At a meeting at the White House, President Lincoln urges a group of African American leaders to consider colonization, since African Americans will confront hardships in every region of the country regardless of when slavery is abolished.

September 17: Union general George B. McClellan engages Confederate general Robert E. Lee at the Battle of Antietam in Maryland. Although regarded as a tactical draw, Lee's first attempt at an invasion of the North is halted and the Battle of Antietam is portrayed as a victory by the Lincoln administration.

September 22: With the "victory" at Antietam, President Lincoln issues his preliminary Emancipation Proclamation.

December 1: President Lincoln urges Congress to consider drafting amendments to the Constitution providing for compensated emancipation.

1863

January 1: President Lincoln issues his final Emancipation Proclamation. Union general Robert H. Milroy occupies Winchester, Virginia, and becomes the first to actively enforce Lincoln's measure.

1865

January 31: The Thirteenth Amendment, abolishing the institution of slavery, passes Congress.

December 18: The Thirteenth Amendment is ratified, solidifying President Lincoln's promise of emancipation.

DOCUMENTS

Document 1: AN EARLY LOOK AT SLAVERY

In the decade preceding the Civil War, Abraham Lincoln held some strong opinions about the institution of slavery. Although Lincoln morally opposed slavery he understood the difficulties in ending slavery as it was protected under the Constitution. Among Lincoln's closest friends was Joshua F. Speed, who owned scores of slaves. The two had been friends for decades preceding the Civil War, and when Lincoln came to Springfield, Illinois, in 1837, the two even shared a room. Despite their close-knit friendship, the issues of the expansion of slavery into the Kansas and Nebraska Territories strained their relationship. In the following excerpt from an August 24, 1855, letter to his friend Speed, Lincoln explains his moral opposition to slavery and why he opposes its extension.

This letter, written less than six years before he was inaugurated president, illustrates Lincoln's complex views on slavery that guided him until he decided to issue the Emancipation Proclamation.

You know I dislike slavery and you fully admit the abstract wrong of it. So far there is no cause of difference. But you say that sooner than yield your legal right to the slave, especially at the bidding of those who are not themselves interested, you would see the Union dissolved... I also acknowledge your rights and my obligations under the Constitution in regard to your slaves. I confess I hate to see the poor creatures hunted down and caught and carried back to their stripes and unrequited toil; but I bite my lips and keep quiet. In 1841, you and I had together a tedious low-water trip on a steamboat, from Louisville to St. Louis. You may remember, as I well do, that from Louisville to the mouth of the Ohio, there were on board ten or a dozen slaves shackled together with irons. That sight was a continued torment to me, and I see something like it every time I touch the Ohio or any other slave border. It is not fair for you to assume that I have no interest in a thing which has, and continually exercises, the power of making me miserable. You ought rather to appreciate how much the great body of the Northern people do crucify their feelings in order to maintain their loyalty to the Constitution and the Union. I do oppose the extension of slavery, because my judgment and feeling so prompt me, and I am under no obligations to the contrary.... In your assumption that there may be a fair decision of the slavery question in Kansas, I plainly see that you and I would differ about the Nebraska law. I look upon that enactment, not as a law, but as a violence from the beginning. It was conceived in violence. I say it was conceived in violence, because the destruction of the Missouri Compromise, under the circumstances, was nothing less than violence.... The slave-breeders and slave-traders are a small, odious, and detested class among you; and yet in politics they dictate the course of all of you, and are as completely your masters as you are the master of your own negroes. You inquire where I now stand. That is a disputed point. I think I am a Whig; but others say there are no Whigs, and that I am an Abolitionist. When I was at Washington, I voted for the Wilmot Proviso as good as forty times; and I never heard of any one attempting to unwhig me for that. I now do no more than oppose the extension of slavery.... As a nation, we began by declaring that all men are created equal. We now practically read it, all men are created equal except negroes. When the Know-nothings get control, it will read, all men are created equal except negroes, and foreigners and Catholics. When it comes to this, I shall prefer emigrating to some country where they make no pretence of loving liberty—to Russia, for instance, where despotism can be taken pure, and without the base alloy of hypocrisy. ... My kindest regards to Mrs. Speed. On the leading subject of this letter I have more of her sympathy than I have of yours; and yet let me say I am your friend for ever.

A. Lincoln

SOURCE:

Speeches and Letters of Abraham Lincoln, edited by James Bryce (Cambridge, Mass.: Dutton, 1894), pp. 36–39.

Document 2: LINCOLN'S FIRST INAUGURAL ADDRESS

When Abraham Lincoln won the presidential election of 1860, many slave owners in the Deep South believed that a Republican administration would lead to the abolition of slavery. Although the 1860 Republican platform stated that slavery would be controlled by the states, it did stipulate that a Republican president would prevent the extension of slavery into the territories. Slaveholders believed that erecting obstacles to slavery's extension served as a precursor to widespread emancipation. Al-

ready confronted with secession and the formation of a Confederate government, Lincoln used his inaugural address to reiterate that he had no intentions to disrupt the South's "peculiar institution." In the excerpt that follows from Lincoln's inaugural address delivered on March 4, 1861, Lincoln, hoping to avoid civil war, informed the South that he would not end slavery where it existed and that he would make certain the 1850 Fugitive Slave Law was enforced. Lincoln's attempt to allay Southerners' fears did not avoid war and instead brought forth criticism from many abolitionists, including Massachusetts senator Charles Sumner and Frederick Douglass.

Fellow Citizens of the United States...

Apprehension seems to exist, among the people of the Southern States, that by the accession of a Republican Administration their property and their peace and personal security are to be endangered. There has never been any reasonable cause for such apprehension. Indeed, the most ample evidence to the contrary has all the while existed and been open to their inspection. It is found in nearly all the published speeches of him who now addresses you. I do but quote from one of those speeches when I declare that "I have no purpose, directly or indirectly, to interfere with the institution of slavery in the States where it exists. I believe I have no lawful right to do so, and I have no inclination to do so." Those who nominated and elected me did so with full knowledge that I had made this and many similar declarations, and had never recanted them. And more than this, they placed in the platform for my acceptance, and as a law to themselves and to me, the clear and emphatic resolution which I now read:

Resolved, That the maintenance inviolate of the rights of the States, and especially the right of each State to order and control its own domestic institutions according to its own judgment exclusively, is essential to the balance of power on which the perfection and endurance of our political fabric depend, and we denounce the lawless invasion by armed force of the soil of any State or Territory, no matter under what pretext, as among the gravest crimes....

There is much controversy about the delivering up of fugitives from service or labor. The clause I now read is as plainly written in the Constitution as any other of its provision:

No person held to service or labor in one State, under the laws thereof, escaping into another, shall, in consequence of any law or regulation therein, be discharged from such service or labor, but shall be delivered up on claim of the property to whom such service or labor may be due.

SOURCE:

"Inaugural Address of President Abraham Lincoln," March 4, 1861, in *The Life and Public Services of Abraham Lincoln, Sixteenth President of the United States: Together with His State Papers, Including His Speeches, Addresses, Messages, Letters, and Proclamations . . .*, edited by Henry J. Raymond (New York: Derby & Miller, 1865), pp. 162–163.

Document 3: ABRAHAM LINCOLN TO JOHN C. FRÉMONT

On August 30, 1861, while Union general John C. Frémont was commanding federal forces in the border slave state of Missouri, he issued a proclamation emancipating the slaves of anyone who supported the Confederacy. Frémont based his proclamation on his interpretation of the First Confiscation Act, which allowed for federal officials (soldiers) to discharge a slave from the service of a master if that master was using a slave's labor to directly support the Confederate war effort. When President Abraham Lincoln learned of Frémont's order he was irate. Although morally opposed to slavery, Lincoln first wanted to preserve the Union and prevent any further secession. Lincoln believed that Frémont's proclamation would not only entice Missouri to secede, but might also alarm the other border states and drive them to secession. The document that follows is Lincoln's letter to Frémont.

Washington, D.C.,
September 2, 1861.
Major-General Frémont:

My Dear Sir:

Two points in your proclamation of August 30 give me some anxiety:

First, Should you shoot a man, according to the proclamation, the Confederates would very certainly shoot our best men in their hands in retaliation; and so, man for man, indefinitely. It is, therefore, my order that you allow no man to be shot under the proclamation without first having my approbation or consent.

Second. I think there is great danger that the closing paragraph, in relation to the confiscation and the liberating of slaves of traitorous owners, will alarm our Southern Union friends and turn them against us; perhaps ruin our rather fair prospect for Kentucky. Allow me, therefore, to ask that you will, as of your own motion, modify that paragraph so as to conform to the first and fourth sections of the act of Congress entitled "An act to confiscate property used for insurrectionary purposes," approved August 6, 1861, and a copy of which act I herewith send to you.

This letter is written in a spirit of caution and not of censure. I send it by special messenger, in order that it may certainly and speedily reach you.

Yours, very truly,
A. Lincoln.

Source:

President Abraham Lincoln to General John C. Frémont, September 2, 1861, in *War of the Rebellion: A Compilation of the Official Records of the Union and Confederate Armies*, compiled by the U.S. War Department (Washington, D.C.: U.S. Government Printing Office, 1880–1901), series 1, volume 3, pp. 469–470.

Confiscation Act

That if, during the present or any future insurrection against the Government of the United States, after the President of the United States shall have declared, by proclamation, that the laws of the United States are opposed, and the execution thereof obstructed, by combinations too powerful to be suppressed by the ordinary course of judicial proceedings, or by the power vested in the marshals by law, any person or person, his, here, or their agent, attorney or employee, shall purchase or acquire, sell or give, any property of whatsoever kind or description, with intent to use or employ the same, or suffer the same to be used or employed in aiding, abetting, or promoting such insurrection or resistance to the laws, or any person or person engaged therein; or if any person or person being the owner or owners of such property, shall knowingly use or employ, or consent to the use or employment of the same as aforesaid, all such property is hereby declared to be lawful subject of prize and capture wherever found; and it shall be the duty of the President of the United States to cause the same to be seized, confiscated, and condemned . . . Sec. 4. That whenever hereafter, during the present insurrection against the Government of the United States, any person claimed to be held to labor or service under the law of any State, shall be required or permitted by the person to whom such labor or service is claimed to be due, or by the lawful agent of such person, to take up arms against the United States, or shall be required or permitted by the person to whom such labor or service is claimed to be due, or his lawful agent, to work or to be employed in or upon any fort, navy yard, dock, armory, ship, entrenchment, or in any military or naval service whatsoever, against the Government and lawful authority of the United States, then, and in every such case, the person to whom such labor or service is claimed to be due shall forfeit his claim to such labor, any law of the State or of the United States to the contrary notwithstanding. And whenever thereafter the person claiming such labor or service shall seek to enforce his claim, it shall be a full and sufficient answer to such claim that the person whose service or labor is claimed had been employed in hostile service against the Government of the United States, contrary to the provisions of this act.

Source:

Confiscation Act, August 6, 1861, quoted in *Documentary Source Book of American History, 1606–1913*, edited by William MacDonald (New York: Macmillan, 1923), pp. 443–444.

Document 4: APPEAL TO THE BORDER STATES

By the summer of 1862 ardent abolitionists criticized President Abraham Lincoln for not being more aggressive in ending slavery. Before Congress broke for summer recess that year, Abraham Lincoln appealed to the border states—which had a combined slave population of approximately 425,000—to consider emancipating their slaves gradually. To further entice the border states Lincoln offered financial compensation and the possibility of colonization of former slaves in South America. Lincoln attempted to convince the border states that slavery needed to be ended in the border states in order to break the Confederacy. He argued that if the Confederacy saw border states eliminating slavery, they would realize the hopelessness of their situation and end their quest for an independent Confederacy. In the excerpt that follows from a speech Lincoln delivered to Congress on July 12, 1862, he lays out his plan for compensated emancipation and illustrates to the border states the significance of their participation in ending the war.

After the adjournment of Congress, now near, I shall have no opportunity of seeing you for several months. Believing that you of the border States hold more power for good than any other equal number of members, I feel it a duty which I cannot justifiably waive, to make this appeal to you.

I do not speak of emancipation at once, but of a decision at once to emancipate gradually. Room in South America for colonization can be obtained cheaply and in abundance, and when numbers shall be large enough to be company and encouragement for one another, the freed people will not be so reluctant to go.

I am pressed with a difficulty not yet mentioned—one which threatens division among those, who, united, are none too strong. General Hunter is an honest man. He was, and I hope still is, my friend. I valued him none the less for his agreeing with me in the general wish that all men everywhere could be free. He proclaimed all men free within certain States, and I repudiated the proclamation. He expected more good and less harm from the measure than I could believe would follow. Yet in repudiating it, I gave dissatisfaction if not offence to many whose support the country cannot afford to lose. And this is not the end of it. The pressure in this direction is still upon me, and is increasing. By conceding what I now ask, you can relieve me, and much more, can relieve the country, in this important point.

Upon these considerations I have again begged your attention to the message of March last. Before leaving the Capitol, consider and discuss it among yourselves. You are patriots and statesmen, and as such, I pray you, consider this proposition, and at the least commend it to the consideration of your States and people. As you would perpetuate popular government for the best people in the world, I beseech you that you do in no wise omit this. Our common country is in great peril, demanding the loftiest views and boldest action to bring it speedy relief. Once relieved, its form of government is saved to the world, its beloved history and cherished memories are vindicated, and its happy future fully assured and rendered inconceivably grand.

I intend no reproach or complaint when I assure you that, in my opinion, if you all had voted for the resolution in the gradual-emancipation message of last March, the war would now be substantially ended. And the plan therein proposed is yet one of the most potent and swift means of ending it. Let the States which are in rebellion see, definitely and certainly, that in no event will the States you represent ever join their proposed confederacy, and they cannot much longer maintain the contest. But you cannot divest them of their hope to ultimately have you with them, so long as you show your determination to perpetuate the institution with your own States. Beat them at elections, as you have overwhelmingly done, and, nothing daunted, they still claim you as their own. You and I know what the lever of their power is. Break that lever before their faces, and they can shake you no more for ever.

Most of you have treated me with kindness and consideration, and I trust you will not now think I improperly touch what is exclusively your own, when, for the sake of the whole country, I ask, Can you, for your States, do better than to take the course I urge? Discarding punctilio and maxims adapted to more manageable times, and looking only to the unprecedentedly stern facts of our case, can you do better in any possible event? You prefer that the constitutional relation of the States to the nation shall be practically restored without disturbance of the institution; and if this were done, my whole duty in this respect, under the Constitution and my oath of office, would be performed. But it is not done, and we are trying to accomplish it by war. The incidents of war cannot be avoided. If the war continues long, as it must if the object be not sooner attained, the institution in your States will be extinguished by mere friction and abrasion—by the mere incidents of the war. It will be gone, and you will have nothing valuable in lieu of it. Much of its value is gone already. How much better for you and for your people to take substantial compensation for that which is sure to be wholly lost in any other event? How much better to thus save the money which else we sink for ever in the war! How much better to do it while we can, lest the war ere long render us pecuniarily unable to do it! How much better for you as seller, and the nation as buyer, to sell out and buy out that without which the war could never have been, than to sink both the thing to be sold and price of it in cutting one another's throats!

SOURCE:

"Appeal to the Border States in Behalf of Compensated Emancipation," July 12, 1862, in Speeches and Letters of Abraham Lincoln, edited by James Bryce (Cambridge, Mass.: Dutton, 1894), pp. 190–192.

Document 5: A New Plan for Emancipation

The day following President Abraham Lincoln's appeal to the border states to accept compensated emancipation, July 13, 1862, Lincoln attended the funeral of Secretary of War Edwin M. Stanton's infant son. Secretary of the Navy Gideon Welles and Secretary of State William Seward accompanied Lincoln to the service. During the carriage ride to the funeral Lincoln announced to his two cabinet members that he intended to issue a proclamation of emancipation. Rather than sticking to his typical proposals of gradual and compensated emancipation, Lincoln broke with his earlier philosophy and announced to Welles and Seward that this new style of emancipation would be swift and decisive. Secretary Welles, in the following excerpt, recounts Lincoln's shocking announcement.

On Sunday, the 13th of July, 1862, President Lincoln invited me to accompany him in his carriage to the funeral of an infant child of Mr. Stanton. . . . It was on this occasion and on this ride that he first mentioned to Mr. Seward and myself the subject of emancipating the slaves by proclamation in case the Rebels did not cease to persist in their war on the Government and the Union, of which he saw no evidence. He dwelt earnestly on the gravity, importance, and delicacy of the movement, said he had given it much thought and had about come to the conclusion that it was a military necessity absolutely essential for the salvation of the Union, that we must free the slaves or be ourselves subdued, etc., etc.

This was, he said, the first occasion when he had mentioned the subject to any one, and wished us to frankly state how the proposition struck us. Mr. Seward said the subject involved consequences so vast and momentous that he should wish to bestow on it mature reflection before giving a decisive answer, but his present opinion inclined to the measure as justifiable, and perhaps he might say expedient and necessary. These were also my views. Two or three times on that ride the subject, which was of course an absorbing one for each and all, was adverted to, and before separating the President desired us to give the question special and deliberate attention, for he was earnest in the conviction that something must be done. It was a new departure for the President, for until this time, in all our previous interviews, whenever the question of emancipation or the mitigation of slavery had been in any way alluded to, he had been prompt and emphatic in denouncing any interference by the General Government with the subject. This was, I think, the sentiment of every member of the Cabinet, all of whom, including the President, considered it a local, domestic question appertaining to the States respectively, who had never parted with their authority over it. But the reverses before Richmond, and the formidable power and dimensions of the insurrection, which extended through all the Slave States, and had combined most of them in a confederacy to destroy the Union, impelled the Administration to adopt extraordinary measures to preserve the national existence. The slaves, if not armed and disciplined, were in the service of those who were, not only as field laborers and producers, but thousands of them were in attendance upon the armies in the field, employed as waiters and teamsters, and the fortifications and intrenchments were constructed by them.

Source:

Gideon Welles. *Diary of Gideon Welles: Secretary of the Navy under Lincoln and Johnson* (Boston: Houghton Mifflin, 1911), volume 1, pp. 70–71.

Document 6: Life outside the United States

Despite President Abraham Lincoln's announcement to his cabinet on July 22, 1862, that he intended to issue a swift proclamation of emancipation—freeing slaves in areas in rebellion—he still believed that the best solution to racial tension in the United States was colonization. Lincoln believed that African Americans, regardless of their status, confronted hardships in the South, but also in the North, as free blacks competed with whites in the labor market. On August 14, 1862, he urged some African American leaders to consider colonization and a fresh start in a new land. The following excerpt from Lincoln's address to the group illustrates his thoughts on the potential benefits of a life outside the United States.

Why should the people of your race leave the country? It is because you and we are different races. We have between us a broader physical difference than exists between any other two races. Whether this is right or wrong I need not discuss; but this physical difference is a great disadvantage to us both. Your race suffer greatly, many of them, by living among us, while ours suffer from your presence. This affords a reason why we should be separated. Your race is suffering, in my judgment, the greatest wrong inflicted on any people. But, even when you cease to be slaves, you are yet far remote from being placed on an equality with the white race. You are cut off from many of the advantages which the other race enjoys. The aspiration of men is to enjoy the equality with the best when free, but on this broad continent not a single man of your race is made the equal of a single man of ours. Go where you are treated the best, and the ban is still upon you. I do not propose to discuss this—but to present it as a fact with which we have to deal. I cannot alter it if I would.... I believe in its general evil effects on the white race. See our present condition—white men cutting one another's throats—none knowing how far it will extend.... But for your race among us there could not be war, although many men engaged on either side do not care for you one way or the other.... It is better for us both, therefore, to be separated.

SOURCE:

Lincoln's address to a "deputation of negroes," August 14, 1862, in *Great Debates in American History: From the Debates of the British Parliament on the Colonial Stamp Act (1764–1765) to the Debates in Congress at the Close of the Taft Administration (1912–1913)*, edited by Marion Mills Miller (New York: Current Literature, 1913), volume 6, p. 212.

Document 7: ABRAHAM LINCOLN TO HORACE GREELEY

On August 19, 1862, Horace Greeley, editor of the New York Tribune, published a letter to President Abraham Lincoln—"The Prayer of Twenty Millions." The letter lambasted Lincoln for not being more aggressive in abolishing slavery. Unbeknownst to Greeley, however, Lincoln had already announced his Emancipation Proclamation to his cabinet on July 22. Three days after Greeley's letter, Lincoln responded. In the excerpt that follows, Lincoln reiterates that his ultimate goal is to save the Union by any means possible.

Executive Mansion, Washington,
August 22, 1862
Hon. Horace Greeley:

Dear Sir:

I have just read yours of the 19th instant, addressed to myself through the New York Tribune.

If there be in it any statements or assumptions of fact which I may know to be erroneous, I do not now and here controvert them.

If there be any inferences which I may believe to be falsely drawn, I do not now and here argue against them.

If there be perceptible in it an impatient and dictatorial tone, I waive it in deference to an old friend whose heart I have always supposed to be right.

As to the policy I "seem to be pursuing," as you say, I have not meant to leave any one in doubt. I would save the Union. I would save it in the shortest way under the Constitution.

The sooner the national authority can be restored, the nearer the Union will be—the Union it was.

If there be those who would not save the Union unless they could at the same time save slavery, I do not agree with them.

If there be those would not save the Union unless they could at the same time destroy slavery, I do not agree with them.

My paramount object is to save the Union, and not either to save or to destroy slavery.

If I could save the Union without freeing any slave, I would do it—if I could save it by freeing all the slaves, I would do it—and if I could do it by freeing some and leaving others alone I would also do that.

What I do about slavery and the colored race, I do because I believe it helps save the Union; and what I forbear, I forbear because I do not believe it would help to save the Union.

I shall do less whenever I shall believe what I am doing hurts the cause, and I shall do more whenever I believe doing more will help the cause.

I shall try to correct errors when shown to be errors, and I shall adopt new views so fast as they shall appear to be true views.

I have here stated my purpose according to my views of official duty, and I intend no modification of my oft-expressed personal wish that all men everywhere could be free.

Yours, A. Lincoln

SOURCE:

Abraham Lincoln to Horace Greeley, August 22, 1862, in *The Life and Public Services of Abraham Lincoln, Sixteenth President of the United States: Together with His State Papers, Including His Speeches, Addresses, Messages, Letters, and Proclamations...*, edited by Henry J. Raymond (New York: Derby & Miller, 1865), pp. 253–254.

Document 8: The First Draft

On July 22, 1862, President Abraham Lincoln announced to his cabinet that he intended to issue the Emancipation Proclamation. Lincoln's cabinet members largely approved of the idea, except for Postmaster General Montgomery Blair. A former Democrat, Blair cautioned Lincoln that such a measure would have negative political consequences for the Republicans.

Although Union armies had achieved some success in the war's Western theater, the public regarded the East as the major theater of operations, and Secretary of State William Seward warned that a military victory in the East, against General Robert E. Lee's Army of Northern Virginia, was necessary in order to legitimize the Emancipation Proclamation.

Although regarded militarily as a tactical draw, the Battle of Antietam ended Lee's first invasion of the North and was viewed as a Union victory. Five days after the battle, on September 22, 1862, Lincoln issued his preliminary Emancipation Proclamation, which stated that all slaves in areas in rebellion against the government would be set free on New Year's Day, 1863.

Proclamation of Emancipation

I, Abraham Lincoln, President of the United States of America, and Commander-in-Chief of the army and navy thereof, do hereby proclaim and declare that hereafter, as heretofore, the war will be prosecuted for the object of practically restoring the constitutional relation between the United States and each of the States, and the people thereof, in which States that relation is or may be suspended or disturbed.

That is my purpose, upon the next meeting of Congress, to again recommend the adoption of a practical measure tendering pecuniary aid to the free acceptance or rejection of all slave States, so called, the people whereof may not then be in rebellion against the United States, and which States may then have voluntarily adopted, or thereafter may voluntarily adopt, immediate or gradual abolition of slavery within their respective limits; and that the effort to colonize persons of African descent, with their consent, upon this continent or elsewhere, with the previously obtained consent of the governments existing there, will be continued.

That on the first day of January, in the year of our Lord one thousand eight hundred and sixty-three, all persons held as slaves within any States, or designated part of a State, the people whereof shall then be in rebellion against the United States, shall be then, thenceforward, and forever free; and the Executive Government of the United States, including the military and naval authority thereof, will recognize and maintain the freedom of such person, and will do no act or acts to repress such person, and any of them, in any efforts they may make for their actual freedom.

That the Executive will, on the first day of January aforesaid, by proclamation, designate the States and parts of States, if any, in which the people thereof respectively shall be then in rebellion against the United States; and the fact that any State, or the people thereof, shall on the day be in good faith represented in Congress of the United States, by members chosen thereto at elections wherein a majority of the qualified voters of such State shall have participated, shall, in the absence of strong countervailing testimony, be deemed conclusive evidence that such State, and the people thereof, are not then in rebellion against the United States.

The attention is hereby called to an act of Congress entitled "An Act to make an additional Article of War," approved March 13th, 1862, and which act is in the words and figures following—

Be it enacted by the Senate and House of Representatives of the United States of America in Congress assembled, That hereafter the following shall be promulgated as an additional article of war for the government of the army of the United States, and shall be obeyed and observed as such—

Section 1.

All officers or persons in the military or naval service of the United States are prohibited from employing any of the forces under their respective commands for the purpose of returning fugitives from service or labor who may have escaped from any persons to whom such service or labor is claimed to be due; and any officer found guilty by court-martial of violating this article shall be dismissed from the service.

Section 2.

And be it further enacted, That this act shall take effect from and after its passage.

Also, to the ninth and tenth sections of an act entitled "An Act to Suppress Insurrection, to Punish Treason and Rebellion, to Seize and Confiscate Property of Rebels, and for other Purposes," approved July 16, 1862, and which sections are in the words and figures following—

Section 9.

And be it further enacted, That all slaves of persons who shall hereafter be engaged in rebellion against the Government of the United States, or who shall in any way give aid or comfort thereto, escaping from such persons and taking refuge within the lines of the army; and all slaves captured from such person, or deserted by them and coming under the control of the Government of the United States; and all slaves of such persons found [or] being within any place occupied by rebel forces and afterwards occupied by forces of the United States, shall be deemed captives of war, and shall be forever free of their servitude, and not again held as slaves.

Section 10.

And be it further enacted, That no slave escaping into any State, Territory, or the District of Columbia, from any other State, shall be delivered up, or in any way impeded or hindered of his liberty, except for crime, or some offence against the laws, unless the person claiming said fugitive shall first make oath that the person to whom the labor or service of such fugitive is alleged to be due is lawful owner, and has not borne arms against the United States in the present rebellion, nor in any way given aid and comfort thereto; and no person engaged in the military or naval services of the United States shall, under any pretence whatever, assume to decide on the validity of the claim of any person to the service or labor of any other person, or surrender up any such person to the claimant, on pain of being dismissed from the service.

And I do hereby enjoin upon and order all persons engaged in the military and naval service of the United States to observe, obey, and enforce, within their respective spheres of service, the act and sections above recited.

And the Executive will in due time recommend that all citizens of the United States who shall have remained loyal thereto throughout the rebellion, shall (upon the restoration of the constitutional relation between the United States and their respective States and people, if that relation shall have been suspended or disturbed) be compensated for all losses by acts of the United States, including the loss of slaves.

In witness whereof, I have hereunto set my hand and caused the seal of the United States to be affixed.

Done at the City of Washington, this twenty-second day of September, in the year of our Lord one thousand eight hundred and sixty-two, and of the Independence of the United States the eighty-seventh.

Abraham Lincoln
By the President:
William H. Seward, Secretary of State

SOURCE:

Preliminary Emancipation Proclamation, in *The Life and Public Services of Abraham Lincoln, Sixteenth President of the United States: Together with His State Papers, Including His Speeches, Addresses, Messages, Letters, and Proclamations...*, edited by Henry J. Raymond (New York: Derby & Miller, 1865), pp. 257–259.

Document 9: AN APPEAL TO MANY

On December 1, 1862, one month before the Emancipation Proclamation went into effect, President Abraham Lincoln proposed that Congress pursue Constitutional amendments that would encourage compensated emancipation. Under this plan, which he believed would appeal to slave owners and abolitionists, any state or individual slave owner who manumitted their slaves prior to January 1, 1900, would receive financial compensation from the federal government. Lincoln also urged Congress to consider legislation that would allow the federal government to colonize emancipated slaves outside of the United States; in the excerpt that follows from Lincoln's annual message he enumerates the positives of such a plan.

Doubtless some of those who are to pay, and not to receive, will object. Yet the measure is both just and economical. In a certain sense the liberation of slaves is the destruction of property—property acquired by descent or by purchase, the same as any other property. It is no less true for having been often said that the people of the South are not more responsible than are the people of the North; and when it is remembered how unhesitatingly we all use cotton and sugar and share the profits of dealing in them, it may not be quite safe to say that the South has been more responsible than the North for its continuance. If, then, for a common object this property is to be sacrificed, is it not just that it be done at a common charge?

The proposed emancipation would shorten the war, perpetuate peace, insure the increase of population, and proportionately of the wealth of the country. With these we should pay all the emancipation would cost, together with our other debt, easier than we should pay our other debt without it.

I cannot make it better known than it already is that I strongly favor colonization. And yet I wish to say there is an objection urged against free colored persons remaining in the country which is largely imaginary if not sometimes malicious.

It is insisted that their presence would injure and displace white labor and white laborers. If there ever could be a proper time for mere catch arguments, that time surely is not now. In times like the present men should utter nothing for which they would not willingly be responsible through time and eternity. Is it true, then, that colored people can displace any more white labor by being free than by remaining slaves? If they stay in their old places, they leave them open to white laborers. Logically, there is neither more nor less of it. Emancipation, even without deportation, would probably enhance the wages of white labor, and very surely would not reduce them. Thus, the customary amount of labor would still have to be performed; the freed people would surely not do more than their old proportion of it, and very probably for a time would do less, leaving an increased part to white laborers, bringing their labor into greater demand, and consequently enhancing the wages of it. With deportation, even to a limited extent, enhanced wages to white labor is mathematically certain. Labor is like any other commodity in the market—increase the demand for it and you increase the price of it. Reduce the supply of black labor by colonizing the black laborer out of the country, and by precisely so much you increase the demand for, and wages of, white labor.

But it is dreaded that the freed people will swarm forth and cover the whole land? Are they not already in the land? Will liberation make them any more numerous? Equally distributed among the whites of the whole country, and there would be but one colored to seven whites. . . . Fellow citizens, we cannot escape history. We of this Congress and this administration will be remembered in spite of ourselves. No personal significance or insignificance can spare one or another of us. The fiery trial through which we pass will light us down, in honor or dishonor, to the latest generation. WE say we are for the Union. The world will not forget that we say this. We know how to save the Union. The world knows we do know how to save it. We—even we here—hold the power and bear the responsibility. In giving freedom to the slaves we assure freedom to the free—honorable alike in what we give and what we preserve. We shall nobly save or meanly lose the last, best hope of earth. Other means may succeed; this could not fail. The way is plain, peaceful, generous, just—a way which, if followed, the world will forever applaud, and God must forever bless.

SOURCE:

President Abraham Lincoln's Annual Message, December 1, 1862, in *Great Debates in American History: From the Debates of the British Parliament on the Colonial Stamp Act (1764–1765) to the Debates in Congress at the Close of the Taft Administration (1912–1913)*, edited by Marion Mills Miller (New York: Current Literature, 1913), volume 6, pp. 220–223.

Document 10: STRATEGIC ADVANTAGES

Among President Abraham Lincoln's initial and most ardent supporters of emancipation was his secretary of war, Edwin M. Stanton, who first viewed the Emancipation Proclamation as capable of diminishing the Confederate labor supply while at the same time strengthening that of the Union, Stanton believed that as Union forces campaigned in the South, emancipated slaves would become invaluable employees of the federal government, providing all sorts of assistance—from working fields and harvesting crops, to defending fortifications. In the excerpt that follows, from Stanton's end-of-year report for 1862, he clearly outlines the many military advantages that the Emancipation Proclamation would bring to the Union war effort.

Above all it is our legitimate duty to disdain no legitimate aid that may save the lives of our gallant soldiers, diminish their labors, provide for their wants, and lessen the burdens of our people. No aphorism is more universally received than that "the sole object of a just war is to make the enemy feel the evils of his injustice, and by his sufferings amend his ways; he must, therefore, be attacked in the most accessible quarter." The power of the rebels rests upon their peculiar system of labor, which keeps laborers on their plantations to support owners who are devoting their time and strength to destroy our armies and destroy our government. Whenever that system is in hostility to the government, it is, in my opinion, the duty of those conducting the war to strike down the system and turn against the rebels the productive power that supports the insurrection. Rightly organized in the recovered territory, the laborers of the rebel States will not only aid in holding fortified positions, but there labor will, as in India, free the white soldiers from the most unwholesome exposure of the South. They will cultivate the corn and forage which will feed our cavalry and artillery horses, and save the country a portion of the enormous burden now attending their purchase and transportation from the North. . . . A population of four millions, true to the interests of the Union, with a slight assistance from the army, will, under proper regulation and government, be of the greatest assistance in holding the territory once recovered. The principal staples of the South are the products exclusively of their labor. If protected upon the lands they have heretofore cultivated, with some organization, and with support from loyal detachments of colored troops, they would not only produce much of what is needed to feed our armies and their trains, but that would forever cut off from the rebellion the resources of a country thus occupied. . . . By their assistance our armies will be able permanently to operate in and occupy the country; and in labor for the army in raising its and their own supplies, full occupation can be given them, and with this there will be neither occasion nor temptation to them to emigrate to a northern and less congenial climate. Judging by experience, no colored man will leave his home in the South if protected in that home. All possibility of competition from negro labor in the North is avoided by giving colored men protection and employment upon the soil which they have thus far cultivated, and the right to which has been vacated by the original proprietors, deeply involved in the crimes of treason and rebellion. No great territory has been permanently reduced without depriving the leaders of its people of their lands and property. . . . By striking down this system of compulsory labor, which enables the leaders of the rebellion to control the resources of the people, the rebellion would die of itself.

Under no circumstances has any disposition to servile insurrection been exhibited by the Southern colored population in any Southern States, while a strong loyalty to the federal government has been displayed on every occasion and against every discouragement.

Source:

Edwin M. Stanton. End of Year Report, 1862, quoted in George C. Gorham's *Life and Public Services of Edwin M. Stanton: with Portraits, Maps, and Facsimiles of Important Letters* (Boston: Houghton, Mifflin, 1899), volume 2, pp. 87–90.

Document 11: Dissenting Opinions

When President Abraham Lincoln issued his preliminary Emancipation Proclamation on September 22, 1862, a number of legal experts condemned his measure. Among Lincoln's detractors, who argued that he overstepped his presidential powers, was former United States Supreme Court justice Benjamin R. Curtis. Late in 1862, the former justice published Executive Power, *a pamphlet that tried to illustrate the unconstitutionality of the Emancipation Proclamation. While many agreed with Curtis, some, such as New York's Charles P. Kirkland, pointed out the flaws in Curtis's legal analysis. On December 5, 1862, Kirkland mailed Lincoln a copy of his published disputation.*

The excerpt that follows is from A Letter to the Hon. Benjamin R. Curtis, *in which Kirkland argues that Lincoln clearly was within the limits of presidential powers in a time of war. Kirkland contended that emancipating the slaves was the best way to end the rebellion as it deprived the Confederacy of its largest labor source—slaves.*

To the Honorable Benjamin R. Curtis, late Associate Justice of the Supreme Court of the United States:

Without the agricultural and domestic labor of the slaves, tens of thousands of whites, who have been and now are in the rebel army, could not have been withdrawn from the cultivation of the ground, and the various other pursuits requisite to the supply, for that whole region, of the actual necessaries of life. Without the slaves, their numerous and extensive earthworks, fortifications, and the like, their immense transportation of military stores and munitions, a vast amount of labor in camps and on marches.... could by no possibility have been accomplished.

The intent of design of the proclamation, its actual effect, if it has its *intended* operation, is to forever deprive the "enemy" of this vital, absolutely essential, and, as I have just said, *indispensable,* means of carrying on *the war.* In reason, in common sense, in national law, in the law of civilized war, what objection can exist to our using our power to attain an end so just, so lawful, and I may say so beneficent and so humane, as thus depriving our "enemy" of his means of warfare? I do not believe that you, on more mature reflection, will deny the truth of what I have just stated.

But you say, "grant that we have this power and this right, they cannot be exercised *by the President,*" and for the exercise of this power, he is charged by you with "usurpation."

A few considerations will show the fallacy, the manifest unsoundness and error of your views and arguments on this point I may, in the first place, remark that the very *title* of your pamphlet, *"Executive Power,"* is a "delusion and a snare." The case does not give rise to the investigation of the President's "executive power." The word "executive," manifestly and from the whole context of the Constitution, has reference to the *civil* power of the President, to his various civil duties as the head of the nation, in "seeing that the laws are executed"—to his duties in time of *peace,* though of course the same "executive" duties shall continue in time of war; but to them, *in that event,* are superadded others, which, in no just or proper sense, can be termed "executive," but which pertain to him *in time of war* as "Commander-in-Chief." These latter duties are provided for by the letter and by the spirit of other provisions of the Constitution, by the very nature and necessity of the case, by the first law of nature and of nations, the *law of self-preservation.* What is the meaning and intent of the constitutional direction to the President, "that he shall *preserve, protect, and defend the Constitution,"* unless in *time of war* he can do so in his capacity of "Commander-in-Chief," unless in *time of war,* he shall have the power to adopt and carry out *as to the enemy* such measures as the *laws of war* justify, and as he may deem necessary. Is the Constitution designed to *do away* these laws, and render them inapplicable to our nation—in other words, is the Constitution a *felo de se?*

It cannot be denied, that in time of war, at least, the President, while in a civil sense the "executive" is at the same time the military head of the nation—"the Commander-in-Chief"—and as such *his* "command" is necessarily co-extensive with the country.

I cannot, on this point, quote anything more true and more apposite than a paragraph of your own. *"In time of war, without any special legislation, the* (our) *Commander-in-Chief is lawfully empowered by the Constitution and laws of the United States to do whatever is necessary and sanctioned by the laws of war to accomplish the lawful objects of his command."*

This is, undoubtedly, the constitutional law of the land, and being so, it of necessity upsets and overturns all your objections to the proclamation in question. The "lawful object" of the President at this moment is to preserve the Constitution by putting an end to the rebellion. In order to do this, it is necessary to deprive the rebels of their means of sustaining the rebellion—one of the most effective and available of those means, as just shown, is their slaves; the intent and object of the proclamation are to deprive them of those means. The so depriving them "is sanctioned by the laws of war," and, consequently, this act of the President is, within your own doctrine, perfectly legal and constitutional."

SOURCE:

Charles P. Kirkland. *A Letter to the Hon. Benjamin R. Curtis, Late Judge of the Supreme Court of the United States, in Review of His Recently Published Pamphlet on the "Emancipation Proclamation" of the President* (New York: Latimer & Seymour, 1862), pp. 9–10.

Document 12: "ENSLAVING THE WHITES TO FREE THE BLACKS"

Despite the belief among President Abraham Lincoln and his cabinet that emancipation was necessary to end the rebellion, many Northerners initially opposed the idea. Among emancipation's detractors was Illinois congressman William A. Richardson, who believed that emancipation would cause a flood of African Americans into the North. Such a migration, he believed, would hurt the labor market. Furthermore, Richardson believed that under Lincoln's Emancipation Proclamation and proposed Constitutional amendments for compensated emancipation and colonization the federal government would have to shoulder the financial responsibility for caring for millions of former slaves, stressing the national treasury and the financial resources of the American taxpayer. The following excerpt is taken from Richardson's speech "Enslaving the Whites to Free the Blacks" delivered in the U.S. House of Representatives on December 8, 1862.

Sir,

it is a remarkable document. It is an extraordinary message, when we come to think of its sum and substance. To feed, clothe, buy, and colonize the negro we are to tax and mortgage the white man and his children. The white race is to be burdened to the earth for the benefit of the black race.... There has been, and still is, a great anxiety felt and expressed by our people that this negro population shall not interfere with them; that it shall not jostle them in the occupations they have heretofore pursued in the various industrial pursuits of life in the great fertile regions of the West. The President tells our people, those who supported him because they believed he and his party intended to keep the non-slaveholding States and all the Territories of the Union for the sole occupation of the white race, if you do not like my plan of disposing of this black race; if you fear from their introduction among you that their labor will be brought into competition with that of your own, all you have to do to avoid this competition is to quietly leave your present fields of labor, homes to which, perhaps, you may be attached, and the graves of your kindred, and emigrate southward, and occupy the places made vacant by the exodus of what His Excellency terms the "free Americans of African descent." That is the sum and substance of it.

But, for sake of argument, admit, if you choose, that all the plans of the President touching emancipation and colonization of the negro were to-day successfully carried out, what would it accomplish in the great work of restoring the Union? Nothing—worse than nothing.

The President recommends in his annual message three propositions to amend the Constitution of the United States. The first, second, and third are for the benefit of the negro. The people are sick and tired of this eternal talk upon the negro, and they have expressed that disgust unmistakably in the recent elections. The President's proposed amendments, as a whole, or either of them, could not receive the suffrages of a majority of the people of more than two States of this Union.... He tells us there are differences of opinion among the friends of the Union "in regard to slavery and the African race among us." He says, to all of those who differ with him, surrender your convictions and come to my plan—and he calls that compromise! Compromise! Yes, I trust in God the day is not far distant when the people of this country will compromise and save the Constitution and the Union for white people, and not for the black people. Our peoples are for no other compromise than that....

The proclamation of the 22d of September last, issued by the President, took the country by surprise, and no one of the citizens more than myself. I had fondly hoped and been anxious that the President of the United States should so conduct himself in his high office as Chief Magistrate that I could lend him my support. I have been driven, with thousands of others, into opposition to the policy contained in that proclamation, for reasons which must commend themselves to every reflecting man sincerely desirous of terminating this war and suppressing the rebellion.

Mr. Lincoln, on the 4th of March 1861, on the east portico of this Capitol, took a vow, which he said was registered in Heaven, to support the Constitution of the United States. In his inaugural address delivered on that occasion he said he had no lawful authority or inclination to interfere with the institution of slavery in the States where it exists. In his proclamation of the 22d of September last he assumes that he has the power to forever free "all persons held as slaves within any State, or designated part of a State, the people whereof shall be in rebellion against the United States," thus violating the pledge so solemnly made in his inaugural address.

If the object of the proclamation was not to aid the rebellion, its effect was. It has strengthened the rebellion by driving into their army every person of the South that it was possible to drive there. Was its intent to affect those alone in rebellion? Certainly not. The slaves of every man in a rebellious State were to be free. The loyal man owning twenty slaves and the man in the rebel army owing a like number were by that proclamation to be affected precisely the same. The object of the proclamation was to benefit the negro, not to restore the Government or preserve the Constitution. It was nothing more, nothing less. It goes a bow-shot beyond anything done by this House at the last session of Congress....

Perhaps I should not anticipate the course of the President of the United States in regard to his proclamation. I trust that he will reconsider it; that he will pause and not go forward with it. This Government cannot be restored by the sword alone. You must carry with it the olive branch. The President says we are making history. I trust we are not making such history as the incendiary who swung his lighted torch in the air to burn the temple of Diana at Ephesus, and who has left his name behind, while the name of him who reared that temple has perished from our memories. I think we may expect that, under a change of policy, the blessings of Union may yet be restored and made perpetual.

SOURCE:

William A. Richardson. "Enslaving the Whites to Free the Blacks," December 8, 1862, in *Great Debates in American History: From the Debates of the British Parliament on the Colonial Stamp Act (1764–1765) to the Debates in Congress at the Close of the Taft Administration (1912–1913)*, edited by Marion Mills Miller (New York: Current Literature, 1913), volume 6, pp. 224–227, 229.

Document 13: THE EMANCIPATION PROCLAMATION

On January 1, 1863, President Abraham Lincoln issued his Emancipation Proclamation, formally abolishing slavery in areas in rebellion against the United States. In the final draft, Lincoln singled out which areas of the country would not be included in the Emancipation Proclamation and also added two significant items to the proclamation not present in the preliminary draft: first, Lincoln stated that African Americans would be legally accepted into the service of the United States military; and second, upon recommendation of his secretary of the treasury Salmon P. Chase, Lincoln added a new conclusion wherein he invoked the "favor of Almighty God."

Whereas, on the 22d day of September, in the year of our Lord one thousand eight hundred and sixty-two, a proclamation was issued by the President of the United States, containing, among other things, the following, to wit—

That on the first day of January, in the year of our Lord one thousand eight hundred and sixty-three, all persons held as slaves within any State or designated part of a State, the people whereof shall be in rebellion against the United States, shall be then, thenceforward, and forever free; and the Executive Government of the United States, including the military and naval authority thereof, will recognize and maintain the freedom of such persons, and will do not act or acts to repress such persons, or any of them, in any efforts they may make for their actual freedom.

That the Executive will, on the first day of January aforesaid, by proclamation, designate the States and parts of States, if any, in which the people thereof respectively shall then be in rebellion against the United States; and the fact that any States, or the people thereof, shall on that day be in good faith represented in Congress of the United States, by members chosen thereto at elections wherein a majority of the qualified voters of such States shall have participated, shall, in the absence of strong countervailing testimony, be deemed conclusive evidence that such State, and the people thereof, are not then in rebellion against the United States.

Now, therefore, I, Abraham Lincoln, President of the United States, by virtue of the power in me vested as commander-in-chief of the army and navy of the United States in time of actual armed rebellion against the authority and Government of the United States, and as a fit and necessary war measure for suppressing said rebellion, do, on this first day of January, in the year of our Lord one thousand eight hundred and sixty-three, and in accordance with my purpose so to do, publicly proclaimed for the full period of one hundred eight days from the day first above mentioned, order and designate, as the States and parts of States wherein the people thereof respectively are this day in rebellion against the United States, the following, to wit:

Arkansas, Texas, Louisiana (except the parishes of St. Bernard, Plaquemines, Jefferson, St. John, St. Charles, St. James, Ascension, Assumption, Terre Bonne, Lafourche, Ste. Marie, St. Martin, and Orleans, including the City of New Orleans), Mississippi, Alabama, Florida, Georgia, South Carolina, North Carolina, and Virginia (except the forty-eight counties designated as West Virginia, and also the counties of Berkeley, Accomac, Northampton, Elizabeth City, York, Princess Anne, and Norfolk, including the cities of Norfolk and Portsmouth), and which excepted parts are for the present left precisely as if this proclamation were not issued.

And by virtue of the power and for the purpose aforesaid, I do order and declare that all persons held as slaves within said designated States and parts of States are, and henceforward shall be, free; and that the Executive Government of the United States, including the military and naval authorities thereof, will recognize and maintain the freedom of said persons.

And I hereby enjoin upon the people to be declared free to abstain from all violence, unless in necessary self-defence; and I recommend that, in all cases when allowed, they labor faithfully for reasonable wages.

And I further declare and make known that such persons, of suitable condition, will be received into the armed forces of the United States, to garrison forts, positions, stations, and other places, and to man vessels of all sorts in said service.

And upon this act, sincerely believed to be an act of justice, warranted by the Constitution upon military necessity, I invoke the considerate judgment of mankind, and the gracious favor of Almighty God.

In testimony whereof, I have hereunto set my name, and caused the seal of the United States to be affixed.

Done at the City of Washington, this first day of January, in the year of our Lord one thousand eight hundred and sixty-three, and of the independence of the United States the eighty-seventh.

Abraham Lincoln
By the President:
William H. Seward, Secretary of State

Source:

Emancipation Proclamation, in Frank B. Carpenter's *The Life and Public Services of Abraham Lincoln, Sixteenth President of the United States: Together with His State Papers, Including His Speeches, Addresses, Messages, Letters, and Proclamations . . . , and the Closing Scenes Connected with His Life and Death, to Which are Added Anecdotes and Personal Reminiscences of President Lincoln* (New York: Derby & Miller, 1865), pp. 260–261.

Document 14: Freedom to Slaves!

When President Abraham Lincoln first issued his Emancipation Proclamation many Union generals lambasted the measure. Among those, however, who ardently supported Lincoln was General Robert H. Milroy. An abolitionist from Indiana, Milroy believed that the Union war effort would succeed with emancipation not only because it weakened the Confederacy's labor supply, but also because the war now had a moral objective and would place Christianity's God on the side of the Union. Since Milroy equated emancipation with Union success he became eager to enforce Lincoln's proclamation, and on January 5, 1863, four days after Milroy had led his division into Winchester, Virginia, he issued "Freedom to Slaves!" He was the first to aggressively enact Lincoln's proclamation.

Distributed and displayed throughout the northern Shenandoah Valley, the following document informed area residents of how emancipation was going to be enforced and served to encourage Milroy's soldiers—regardless of their personal views—to actively enforce the proclamation.

Whereas, the President of the United States did, on the first day of the present month, issue his Proclamation declaring "that all persons held as Slaves in certain designated States, and parts of States, are, and henceforward shall be free," and that the Executive Government of the United States, including the Military and Naval authorities thereof, would recognize and maintain the freedom of said persons. And Whereas, the county of Frederick is included in the territory designated by the Proclamation of the President, in which the Slaves should become free, I therefore hereby notify the citizens of the city of Winchester, and of said County, of said Proclamation, and of my intention to maintain and enforce the same.

I expect all citizens to yield ready compliance with the Proclamation of the Chief Executive, and I admonish all persons disposed to resist its peaceful enforcement, that upon manifesting such disposition by acts, they will be regarded as rebels in arms against the lawful authority of the Federal government and dealt with accordingly.

All persons liberated by said Proclamation are admonished to abstain from all violence, and immediately betake themselves to useful occupations.

The officers of this command are admonished and ordered to act in accordance with said proclamation and to yield their ready co-operation in its enforcement.

R. H. Milroy
Brig. Gen'l. Commanding,

Source:

"Freedom to Slaves!" January 5, 1863, Papers of General Robert Huston Milroy, Jasper County Public Library, Rensselaer, Indiana.

Document 15: A Soldier's Opinion

News of President Abraham Lincoln's Emancipation Proclamation was met with a wide array of reactions in the Union army. In the immediate aftermath of the preliminary proclamation mutinous scenes appeared in some regiments, while Union soldiers in other regiments applauded emancipation. By mid-1863, however, the attitudes of Union soldiers toward emancipation changed as they realized the military necessity of emancipation. Among the soldiers who despised emancipation and thought it would ultimately lead to a Confederate victory was Private Thomas Crowl, who served in the Eighty-seventh Pennsylvania Volunteer Infantry. Regardless of his views toward emancipation, Crowl, stationed in Winchester, Virginia, when the Emancipation Proclamation took effect, soon found himself enforcing emancipation as part of abolitionist general Robert H. Milroy's command in Virginia's Shenandoah Valley. In the letter excerpt that follows, Crowl writes angrily about Milroy, Lincoln, and emancipation. Crowl died in a Danville, Va., prison camp on September 18, 1864.

Winchester, Virginia
Jan. 28th 1863

My Dear Sister . . .

This Nigrow freedom is, what is playing hell this is a wrong thing this will Destroy our army, we never enlisted to fight for Nigrows and that is all they are at now. . . . Old Abe Lincoln . . . is the very man that is going to Destroy our country. The nigrows in this place is that Damned sassy that a white man can hardly walk the streets and our old General says that he thinks more of the Blacks than his soldiers but if we get into Battle he will stand a good chance of getting his infernal old gray head shot off. I will stay in the army till I can get a chance then I make tracks and the war may go to hell for me. I never intend to stay here an risk my life for these damned niggers and now I will close by sending you all my best.

Source:

Thomas O. Crowl to his sister, January 28, 1863, Thomas O. Crowl Letter Collection, Historical Collections and Labor Archives, Eberly Family Special Collections Library, Pennsylvania State University, University Park, Pennsylvania.

BIBLIOGRAPHY

Basler, Roy P., ed. *The Collected Works of Abraham Lincoln*, 8 volumes. New Brunswick, N.J.: Rutgers University Press, 1953. The most comprehensive assemblage of primary documents related to President Abraham Lincoln. Volumes four and five are particularly significant as they contain large numbers of documents dealing with Lincoln's views on slavery and emancipation.

Berlin, Ira, et al. *Slaves No More: Three Essays on Emancipation and the Civil War.* Cambridge: Cambridge University Press, 1992. A compilation of three essays by some of the nation's leading scholars of the African American experience, *Slaves No More* examines slavery's destruction and how African Americans attempted to realize emancipation's promise.

Blight, David W., and Brooks D. Simpson, eds. *Union and Emancipation: Essays on Politics and Race in the Civil War Era.* Kent, Ohio: Kent State University Press, 1997. A compilation of seven essays broadly dealing with slavery and emancipation. Of particular significance are Ira Berlin's "Who Freed the Slaves? Emancipation and Its Meaning" and Brooks D. Simpson's "Quandaries of Command: Ulysses S. Grant and Black Soldiers."

Boritt, Gabor S. *Lincoln the War President: The Gettysburg Lectures.* Oxford: Oxford University Press, 1992. A compilation of seven essays related to Lincoln's presidency. Especially significant to the study of emancipation is David Brion Davis's essay "The Emancipation Moment" which examines the meaning of emancipation.

Davis, William C. *Lincoln's Men: How President Lincoln Became Father to an Army and a Nation.* New York: Free Press, 1999. Examines the attitudes of soldiers toward Lincoln. Especially important is chapter 4, "The Price of Freedom," which studies the evolving attitudes of Union soldiers toward the Emancipation Proclamation.

Donald, David Herbert. *Lincoln.* New York: Simon & Schuster, 1995. Arguably the finest single-volume biography of Lincoln, it offers detailed insight into Lincoln and offers cogent explanations for Lincoln's policies.

Franklin, John Hope. *The Emancipation Proclamation.* Garden City, N.Y.: Doubleday, 1963. The first study of the Emancipation Proclamation, it examines the long path to emancipation, reactions, and legacy.

Guelzo, Allen C. *Lincoln's Emancipation Proclamation: The End of Slavery in America.* New York: Simon & Schuster, 2004. In the finest current scholarly treatment of Lincoln's Emancipation Proclamation, Guelzo presents a complete study of emancipation, examining Lincoln's complex attitudes toward slaves, what freedom meant to slaves, and the obstacles that Lincoln had to overcome to issue his proclamation.

Holzer, Harold, Edna Greene Medford, and Frank J. Williams. *The Emancipation Proclamation: Three Views, Social, Political, and Iconographic.* Baton Rouge: Louisiana State University Press, 2006. A compilation of three essays examining the impact of the Emancipation Proclamation on the United States. Also contains the Emancipation Proclamation and a study of the depictions of emancipation in art.

Jenkins, Wilbert L. *Climbing Up to Glory: A Short History of African Americans during the Civil War and Reconstruction.* Wilmington, Del.: Scholarly Resource Books, 2002. A highly readable account of African American involvement in the Civil War and Reconstruction. Chapter 1, "Abraham Lincoln: A Reluctant Friend," is pertinent as it provides a sweeping examination of Lincoln's reasons for emancipation and the African American response to it.

Klingaman, William K. *Abraham Lincoln and the Road to Emancipation: 1861–1865.* New York: Viking, 2001. Engagingly written, Klingaman's study provides a highly readable account of emancipation and how this document altered the course of American history.

McPherson, James M. *Crossroads of Freedom: Antietam: The Battle That Changed the Course of the Civil War.* Oxford: Oxford University Press, 2002. A slim volume that examines how the Battle of Antietam—fought near Sharpsburg, Maryland, on September 17, 1862—became the impetus for the Emancipation Proclamation and subsequently became a major turning point in the American Civil War.

———. *The Negro's Civil War: How American Blacks Felt and Acted during the War for the Union.* New York: Pantheon, 1965. Written by one of the nation's foremost authorities on the Civil War, this classic study addresses the wide spectrum of the African American experience during the war. In chapters 3 and 4 McPherson addresses what emancipation meant in the North and South.

Noyalas, Jonathan A. *"My Will Is Absolute Law": A Biography of Union General Robert H. Milroy.* Jefferson, N.C.: McFarland, 2006. A full biography of the first Union general to actively enforce President Lincoln's Proclamation, it examines General Robert H. Milroy's strong beliefs in emancipation and how he enforced the policy in Virginia's lower Shenandoah Valley.

Quarles, Benjamin. *Lincoln and the Negro.* New York: Oxford University Press, 1962. Quarles examines Lincoln's evolving attitudes toward African Americans and how his changing perceptions eventually drove him to issue the Emancipation Proclamation.

Smith, John David, ed. *Black Soldiers in Blue: African American Troops in the Civil War Era.* Chapel Hill: University of North Carolina Press, 2002. A compilation of fourteen essays that examine various aspects of African American involvement in the Union war effort. The book provides valuable information on how emancipation prompted the introduction of African Americans into the military.

Striner, Richard. *Father Abraham: Lincoln's Relentless Struggle to End Slavery.* New York: Oxford University Press, 2006. A lucidly written book that argues that Lincoln always despised slavery and looked for the perfect moment to end slavery. The author closely examines early influences in Lincoln's life that made him morally oppose slavery and Lincoln's political record opposing slavery in the Illinois legislature and U.S. House of Representatives.

Trefousse, Hans L. *Lincoln's Decision for Emancipation.* Philadelphia: Lippincott, 1975. A slim volume, Trefousse's work provides a sweeping overview of the path, decisions, and controversy surrounding Lincoln's Emancipation Proclamation. The book also contains an array of primary documents and secondary articles.

APPENDIX:
The Confederate Constitution
Abraham Lincoln's Proclamation on the Wade-Davis Bill
The Wade-Davis Manifesto

APPENDIX

Appendix 1: THE CONFEDERATE CONSTITUTION

Delegates from seceding Southern states gathered in Montgomery, Alabama, on February 4, 1861, in order to draft the Constitution for the Confederate States of America. The Confederate Constitution was based on the original, the United States Constitution, albeit with various changes, additions, and deletions. It was adopted March 11, 1861. The Confederate Constitution, and all the changes it wrought, brought about the Civil War and everything that came after it—particularly the turmoil of Reconstruction.

Preamble

We, the people of the Confederate States, each State acting in its sovereign and independent character, in order to form a permanent federal government, establish justice, insure domestic tranquillity, and secure the blessings of liberty to ourselves and our posterity invoking the favor and guidance of Almighty God do ordain and establish this Constitution for the Confederate States of America.

Article 1.
Section 1.

All legislative powers herein delegated shall be vested in a Congress of the Confederate States, which shall consist of a Senate and House of Representatives.

Section 2.

(1) The House of Representatives shall be composed of members chosen every second year by the people of the several States; and the electors in each State shall be citizens of the Confederate States, and have the qualifications requisite for electors of the most numerous branch of the State Legislature; but no person of foreign birth, not a citizen of the Confederate States, shall be allowed to vote for any officer, civil or political, State or Federal.

(2) No person shall be a Representative who shall not have attained the age of twenty-five years, and be a citizen of the Confederate States, and who shall not when elected, be an inhabitant of that State in which he shall be chosen.

(3) Representatives and direct taxes shall be apportioned among the several States, which may be included within this Confederacy, according to their respective numbers, which shall be determined by adding to the whole number of free persons, including those bound to service for a term of years, and excluding Indians not taxed, three-fifths of all slaves. The actual enumeration shall be made within three years after the first meeting of the Congress of the Confederate States, and within every subsequent term of ten years, in such manner as they shall by law direct. The number of Representatives shall not exceed one for every fifty thousand, but each State shall have at least one Representative; and until such enumeration shall be made, the State of South Carolina shall be entitled to choose six; the State of Georgia ten; the State of Alabama nine; the State of Florida two; the State of Mississippi seven; the State of Louisiana six; and the State of Texas six.

(4) When vacancies happen in the representation from any State the executive authority thereof shall issue writs of election to fill such vacancies.

(5) The House of Representatives shall choose their Speaker and other officers; and shall have the sole power of impeachment; except that any judicial or other Federal officer, resident and acting solely within the limits of any State, may be impeached by a vote of two-thirds of both branches of the Legislature thereof.

Section 3.

(1) The Senate of the Confederate States shall be composed of two Senators from each State, chosen for six years by the Legislature thereof, at the regular session next immediately preceding the commencement of the term of service; and each Senator shall have one vote.

(2) Immediately after they shall be assembled, in consequence of the first election, they shall be divided as equally as may be into three classes. The seats of the Senators of the first class shall be vacated at the expiration of the second year; of the second class at the expiration of the fourth year; and of the third class at the expiration of the sixth year; so that one-third may be chosen every second year; and if vacancies happen by resignation, or other wise, during the recess of the Legislature of any State, the Executive thereof may make temporary appointments until the next meeting of the Legislature, which shall then fill such vacancies.

(3) No person shall be a Senator who shall not have attained the age of thirty years, and be a citizen of the Confederate States; and who shall not, then elected, be an inhabitant of the State for which he shall be chosen.

(4) The Vice President of the Confederate States shall be president of the Senate, but shall have no vote unless they be equally divided.

(5) The Senate shall choose their other officers; and also a president pro tempore in the absence of the Vice President, or when he shall exercise the office of President of the Confederate states.

(6) The Senate shall have the sole power to try all impeachments. When sitting for that purpose, they shall be on oath or affirmation. When the President of the Confederate States is tried, the Chief Justice shall preside; and no person shall be convicted without the concurrence of two-thirds of the members present.

(7) Judgment in cases of impeachment shall not extend further than to removal from office, and disqualification to hold any office of honor, trust, or profit under the Confederate States; but the party convicted shall, nevertheless, be liable and subject to indictment, trial, judgment, and punishment according to law.

Section 4.

(1) The times, places, and manner of holding elections for Senators and Representatives shall be prescribed in each State by the Legislature thereof, subject to the provisions of this Constitution; but the Congress may, at any time, by law, make or alter such regulations, except as to the times and places of choosing Senators.

(2) The Congress shall assemble at least once in every year; and such meeting shall be on the first Monday in December, unless they shall, by law, appoint a different day.

Section 5.

(1) Each House shall be the judge of the elections, returns, and qualifications of its own members, and a majority of each shall constitute a quorum to do business; but a smaller number may adjourn from day to day, and may be authorized to compel the attendance of absent members, in such manner and under such penalties as each House may provide.

(2) Each House may determine the rules of its proceedings, punish its members for disorderly behavior, and, with the concurrence of two-thirds of the whole number, expel a member.

(3) Each House shall keep a journal of its proceedings, and from time to time publish the same, excepting such parts as may in their judgment require secrecy; and the yeas and nays of the members of either House, on any question, shall, at the desire of one-fifth of those present, be entered on the journal.

(4) Neither House, during the session of Congress, shall, without the consent of the other, adjourn for more than three days, nor to any other place than that in which the two Houses shall be sitting.

Section 6.

(1) The Senators and Representatives shall receive a compensation for their services, to be ascertained by law, and paid out of the Treasury of the Confederate States. They shall, in all cases, except treason, felony, and breach of the peace, be privileged from arrest during their attendance at the session of their respective Houses, and in going to and returning from the same; and for any speech or debate in either House, they shall not be questioned in any other place. No Senator or Representative shall, during the time for which he was elected, be appointed to any civil office under the authority of the Confederate States, which shall have been created, or the emoluments whereof shall have been increased during such time; and no person holding any office under the Confederate States shall be a member of either House during his continuance in office. But Congress may, by law, grant to the principal officer in each of the Executive Departments a seat upon the floor of either House, with the privilege of discussing any measures appertaining to his department.

Section 7.

(1) All bills for raising revenue shall originate in the House of Representatives; but the Senate may propose or concur with amendments, as on other bills.

(2) Every bill which shall have passed both Houses, shall, before it becomes a law, be presented to the President of the Confederate States; if he approve, he shall sign it; but if not, he shall return it, with his objections, to that House in which it shall have originated, who shall enter the objections at large on their journal, and proceed to reconsider it. If, after such reconsideration, two-thirds of that House shall agree to pass the bill, it shall be sent, together with the objections, to the other House, by which it shall likewise be reconsidered, and if approved by two-thirds of that House, it shall become a law. But in all such cases, the votes of both Houses shall be determined by yeas and nays, and the names of the persons voting for and against the bill shall be entered on the journal of each House respectively. If any bill shall not be returned by the President within ten days (Sundays excepted) after it shall have been presented to him, the same shall be a law, in like manner as if he had signed it, unless the Congress, by their adjournment, prevent its return; in which case it shall not be a law. The President may approve any appropriation and disapprove any other appropriation in the same bill. In such case he shall, in signing the bill, designate the appropriations disapproved; and shall return a copy of such appropriations, with his objections, to the House in which the bill shall have originated; and the same proceedings shall then be had as in case of other bills disapproved by the President.

(3) Every order, resolution, or vote, to which the concurrence of both Houses may be necessary (except on a question of adjournment) shall be presented to the President of the Confederate States; and before the same shall take effect, shall be approved by him; or, being disapproved by him, shall be repassed by two-thirds of both Houses, according to the rules and limitations prescribed in case of a bill.

Section 8.

The Congress shall have power—

(1) To lay and collect taxes, duties, imposts, and excises for revenue, necessary to pay the debts, provide for the common defense, and carry on the Government of the Confederate States; but no bounties shall be granted from the Treasury; nor shall any duties or taxes on importations from foreign nations be laid to promote or foster any branch of industry; and all duties, imposts, and excises shall be uniform throughout the Confederate States.

(2) To borrow money on the credit of the Confederate States.

(3) To regulate commerce with foreign nations, and among the several States, and with the Indian tribes; but neither this, nor any other clause contained in the Constitution, shall ever be construed to delegate the power to Congress to appropriate money for any internal improvement intended to facilitate commerce; except for the purpose of furnishing lights, beacons, and buoys, and other aids to navigation upon the coasts, and the improvement of harbors and the removing of obstructions in river navigation; in all which cases such duties shall be laid on the navigation facilitated thereby as may be necessary to pay the costs and expenses thereof.

(4) To establish uniform laws of naturalization, and uniform laws on the subject of bankruptcies, throughout the Confederate States; but no law of Congress shall discharge any debt contracted before the passage of the same.

(5) To coin money, regulate the value thereof, and of foreign coin, and fix the standard of weights and measures.

(6) To provide for the punishment of counterfeiting the securities and current coin of the Confederate States.

(7) To establish post offices and post routes; but the expenses of the Post Office Department, after the 1st day of March in the year of our Lord eighteen hundred and sixty-three, shall be paid out of its own revenues.

(8) To promote the progress of science and useful arts, by securing for limited times to authors and inventors the exclusive right to their respective writings and discoveries.

(9) To constitute tribunals inferior to the Supreme Court.

(10) To define and punish piracies and felonies committed on the high seas, and offenses against the law of nations.

(11) To declare war, grant letters of marque and reprisal, and make rules concerning captures on land and water.

(12) To raise and support armies; but no appropriation of money to that use shall be for a longer term than two years.

(13) To provide and maintain a navy.

(14) To make rules for the government and regulation of the land and naval forces.

(15) To provide for calling forth the militia to execute the laws of the Confederate States, suppress insurrections, and repel invasions.

(16) To provide for organizing, arming, and disciplining the militia, and for governing such part of them as may be employed in the service of the Confederate States; reserving to the States, respectively, the appointment of the officers, and the authority of training the militia according to the discipline prescribed by Congress.

(17) To exercise exclusive legislation, in all cases whatsoever, over such district (not exceeding ten miles square) as may, by cession of one or more States and the acceptance of Congress, become the seat of the Government of the Confederate States; and to exercise like authority over all places purchased by the consent of the Legislature of the State in which the same shall be, for the erection of forts, magazines, arsenals, dockyards, and other needful buildings; and

(18) To make all laws which shall be necessary and proper for carrying into execution the foregoing powers, and all other powers vested by this Constitution in the Government of the Confederate States, or in any department or officer thereof.

Section 9.

(1) The importation of negroes of the African race from any foreign country other than the slaveholding States or Territories of the United States of America, is hereby forbidden; and Congress is required to pass such laws as shall effectually prevent the same.

(2) Congress shall also have power to prohibit the introduction of slaves from any State not a member of, or Territory not belonging to, this Confederacy.

(3) The privilege of the writ of habeas corpus shall not be suspended, unless when in cases of rebellion or invasion the public safety may require it.

(4) No bill of attainder, ex post facto law, or law denying or impairing the right of property in negro slaves shall be passed.

(5) No capitation or other direct tax shall be laid, unless in proportion to the census or enumeration hereinbefore directed to be taken.

(6) No tax or duty shall be laid on articles exported from any State, except by a vote of two-thirds of both Houses.

(7) No preference shall be given by any regulation of commerce or revenue to the ports of one State over those of another.

(8) No money shall be drawn from the Treasury, but in consequence of appropriations made by law; and a regular statement and account of the receipts and expenditures of all public money shall be published from time to time.

(9) Congress shall appropriate no money from the Treasury except by a vote of two-thirds of both Houses, taken by yeas and nays, unless it be asked and estimated for by some one of the heads of departments and submitted to Congress by the President; or for the purpose of paying its own expenses and contingencies; or for the payment of claims against the Confederate States, the justice of which shall have been judicially declared by a tribunal for the investigation of claims against the Government, which it is hereby made the duty of Congress to establish.

(10) All bills appropriating money shall specify in Federal currency the exact amount of each appropriation and the purposes for which it is made; and Congress shall grant no extra compensation to any public contractor, officer, agent, or servant, after such contract shall have been made or such service rendered.

(11) No title of nobility shall be granted by the Confederate States; and no person holding any office of profit or trust under them shall, without the consent of the Congress, accept of any present, emolument, office, or title of any kind whatever, from any king, prince, or foreign state.

(12) Congress shall make no law respecting an establishment of religion, or prohibiting the free exercise thereof; or abridging the freedom of speech, or of the press; or the right of the people peaceably to assemble and petition the Government for a redress of grievances.

(13) A well-regulated militia being necessary to the security of a free State, the right of the people to keep and bear arms shall not be infringed.

(14) No soldier shall, in time of peace, be quartered in any house without the consent of the owner; nor in time of war, but in a manner to be prescribed by law.

(15) The right of the people to be secure in their persons, houses, papers, and effects, against unreasonable searches and seizures, shall not be violated; and no warrants shall issue but upon probable cause, supported by oath or affirmation, and particularly describing the place to be searched and the persons or things to be seized.

(16) No person shall be held to answer for a capital or otherwise infamous crime, unless on a presentment or indictment of a grand jury, except in cases arising in the land or naval forces, or in the militia, when in actual ser-

vice in time of war or public danger; nor shall any person be subject for the same offense to be twice put in jeopardy of life or limb; nor be compelled, in any criminal case, to be a witness against himself; nor be deprived of life, liberty, or property without due process of law; nor shall private property be taken for public use, without just compensation.

(17) In all criminal prosecutions the accused shall enjoy the right to a speedy and public trial, by an impartial jury of the State and district wherein the crime shall have been committed, which district shall have been previously ascertained by law, and to be informed of the nature and cause of the accusation; to be confronted with the witnesses against him; to have compulsory process for obtaining witnesses in his favor; and to have the assistance of counsel for his defense.

(18) In suits at common law, where the value in controversy shall exceed twenty dollars, the right of trial by jury shall be preserved; and no fact so tried by a jury shall be otherwise reexamined in any court of the Confederacy, than according to the rules of common law.

(19) Excessive bail shall not be required, nor excessive fines imposed, nor cruel and unusual punishments inflicted.

(20) Every law, or resolution having the force of law, shall relate to but one subject, and that shall be expressed in the title.

Section 10.

(1) No State shall enter into any treaty, alliance, or confederation; grant letters of marque and reprisal; coin money; make anything but gold and silver coin a tender in payment of debts; pass any bill of attainder, or ex post facto law, or law impairing the obligation of contracts; or grant any title of nobility.

(2) No State shall, without the consent of the Congress, lay any imposts or duties on imports or exports, except what may be absolutely necessary for executing its inspection laws; and the net produce of all duties and imposts, laid by any State on imports, or exports, shall be for the use of the Treasury of the Confederate States; and all such laws shall be subject to the revision and control of Congress.

(3) No State shall, without the consent of Congress, lay any duty on tonnage, except on seagoing vessels, for the improvement of its rivers and harbors navigated by the said vessels; but such duties shall not conflict with any treaties of the Confederate States with foreign nations; and any surplus revenue thus derived shall, after making such improvement, be paid into the common treasury. Nor shall any State keep troops or ships of war in time of peace, enter into any agreement or compact with another State, or with a foreign power, or engage in war, unless actually invaded, or in such imminent danger as will not admit of delay. But when any river divides or flows through two or more States they may enter into compacts with each other to improve the navigation thereof.

Article II.
Section 1.

(1) The executive power shall be vested in a President of the Confederate States of America. He and the Vice President shall hold their offices for the term of six years; but the President shall not be reeligible. The President and Vice President shall be elected as follows:

(2) Each State shall appoint, in such manner as the Legislature thereof may direct, a number of electors equal to the whole number of Senators and Representatives to which the State may be entitled in the Congress; but no Senator or Representative or person holding an office of trust or profit under the Confederate States shall be appointed an elector.

(3) The electors shall meet in their respective States and vote by ballot for President and Vice President, one of whom, at least, shall not be an inhabitant of the same State with themselves; they shall name in their ballots the person voted for as President, and in distinct ballots the person voted for as Vice President, and they shall make distinct lists of all persons voted for as President, and of all persons voted for as Vice President, and of the number of votes for each, which lists they shall sign and certify, and transmit, sealed, to the seat of the Government of the Confederate States, directed to the President of the Senate; the President of the Senate shall, in the presence of the Senate and House of Representatives, open all the certificates, and the votes shall then be counted; the person having the greatest number of votes for President shall be the President, if such number be a majority of the whole number of electors appointed; and if no person have such majority, then from the persons having the highest numbers, not exceeding three, on the list of those voted for as President, the House of Representatives shall choose immediately, by ballot, the President. But in choosing the President the votes shall be taken by States, the representation from each State having one vote; a quorum for this purpose shall consist

of a member or members from two-thirds of the States, and a majority of all the States shall be necessary to a choice. And if the House of Representatives shall not choose a President, whenever the right of choice shall devolve upon them, before the 4th day of March next following, then the Vice President shall act as President, as in case of the death, or other constitutional disability of the President.

(4) The person having the greatest number of votes as Vice President shall be the Vice President, if such number be a majority of the whole number of electors appointed; and if no person have a majority, then, from the two highest numbers on the list, the Senate shall choose the Vice President; a quorum for the purpose shall consist of two-thirds of the whole number of Senators, and a majority of the whole number shall be necessary to a choice.

(5) But no person constitutionally ineligible to the office of President shall be eligible to that of Vice President of the Confederate States.

(6) The Congress may determine the time of choosing the electors, and the day on which they shall give their votes; which day shall be the same throughout the Confederate States.

(7) No person except a natural-born citizen of the Confederate States, or a citizen thereof at the time of the adoption of this Constitution, or a citizen thereof born in the United States prior to the 20th of December, 1860, shall be eligible to the office of President; neither shall any person be eligible to that office who shall not have attained the age of thirty-five years, and been fourteen years a resident within the limits of the Confederate States, as they may exist at the time of his election.

(8) In case of the removal of the President from office, or of his death, resignation, or inability to discharge the powers and duties of said office, the same shall devolve on the Vice President; and the Congress may, by law, provide for the case of removal, death, resignation, or inability, both of the President and Vice President, declaring what officer shall then act as President; and such officer shall act accordingly until the disability be removed or a President shall be elected.

(9) The President shall, at stated times, receive for his services a compensation, which shall neither be increased nor diminished during the period for which he shall have been elected; and he shall not receive within that period any other emolument from the Confederate States, or any of them.

(10) Before he enters on the execution of his office he shall take the following oath or affirmation: "I do solemnly swear (or affirm) that I will faithfully execute the Office of President of the Confederate States, and will to the best of my ability, preserve, protect and defend the Constitution thereof."

Section 2.

(1) The President shall be Commander-in-Chief of the Army and Navy of the Confederate States, and of the militia of the several States, when called into the actual service of the Confederate States; he may require the opinion, in writing, of the principal officer in each of the Executive Departments, upon any subject relating to the duties of their respective offices; and he shall have power to grant reprieves and pardons for offenses against the Confederate States, except in cases of impeachment.

(2) He shall have power, by and with the advice and consent of the Senate, to make treaties; provided two-thirds of the Senators present concur; and he shall nominate, and by and with the advice and consent of the Senate shall appoint, ambassadors, other public ministers and consuls, judges of the Supreme Court, and all other officers of the Confederate States whose appointments are not herein otherwise provided for, and which shall be established by law; but the Congress may, by law, vest the appointment of such inferior officers, as they think proper, in the President alone, in the courts of law, or in the heads of departments.

(3) The principal officer in each of the Executive Departments, and all persons connected with the diplomatic service, may be removed from office at the pleasure of the President. All other civil officers of the Executive Departments may be removed at any time by the President, or other appointing power, when their services are unnecessary, or for dishonesty, incapacity, inefficiency, misconduct, or neglect of duty; and when so removed, the removal shall be reported to the Senate, together with the reasons therefor.

(4) The President shall have power to fill all vacancies that may happen during the recess of the Senate, by granting commissions which shall expire at the end of their next session; but no person rejected by the Senate shall be reappointed to the same office during their ensuing recess.

Section 3.

(1) The President shall, from time to time, give to the Congress information of the state of the Confederacy, and recommend to their consideration such measures as he shall judge necessary and expedient; he may, on extraordinary occasions, convene both Houses, or either of them; and in case of disagreement between them, with respect to the time of adjournment, he may adjourn them

to such time as he shall think proper; he shall receive ambassadors and other public ministers; he shall take care that the laws be faithfully executed, and shall commission all the officers of the Confederate States.

Section 4.

(1) The President, Vice President, and all civil officers of the Confederate States, shall be removed from office on impeachment for and conviction of treason, bribery, or other high crimes and misdemeanors.

Article III.
Section 1.

(1) The judicial power of the Confederate States shall be vested in one Supreme Court, and in such inferior courts as the Congress may, from time to time, ordain and establish. The judges, both of the Supreme and inferior courts, shall hold their offices during good behavior, and shall, at stated times, receive for their services a compensation which shall not be diminished during their continuance in office.

Section 2.

(1) The judicial power shall extend to all cases arising under this Constitution, the laws of the Confederate States, and treaties made, or which shall be made, under their authority; to all cases affecting ambassadors, other public ministers and consuls; to all cases of admiralty and maritime jurisdiction; to controversies to which the Confederate States shall be a party; to controversies between two or more States; between a State and citizens of another State, where the State is plaintiff; between citizens claiming lands under grants of different States; and between a State or the citizens thereof, and foreign states, citizens, or subjects; but no State shall be sued by a citizen or subject of any foreign state.

(2) In all cases affecting ambassadors, other public ministers and consuls, and those in which a State shall be a party, the Supreme Court shall have original jurisdiction. In all the other cases before mentioned, the Supreme Court shall have appellate jurisdiction both as to law and fact, with such exceptions and under such regulations as the Congress shall make.

(3) The trial of all crimes, except in cases of impeachment, shall be by jury, and such trial shall be held in the State where the said crimes shall have been committed; but when not committed within any State, the trial shall be at such place or places as the Congress may by law have directed.

Section 3.

(1) Treason against the Confederate States shall consist only in levying war against them, or in adhering to their enemies, giving them aid and comfort. No person shall be convicted of treason unless on the testimony of two witnesses to the same overt act, or on confession in open court.

(2) The Congress shall have power to declare the punishment of treason; but no attainder of treason shall work corruption of blood, or forfeiture, except during the life of the person attainted.

Article IV.
Section 1.

(1) Full faith and credit shall be given in each State to the public acts, records, and judicial proceedings of every other State; and the Congress may, by general laws, prescribe the manner in which such acts, records, and proceedings shall be proved, and the effect thereof.

Section 2.

(1) The citizens of each State shall be entitled to all the privileges and immunities of citizens in the several States; and shall have the right of transit and sojourn in any State of this Confederacy, with their slaves and other property; and the right of property in said slaves shall not be thereby impaired.

(2) A person charged in any State with treason, felony, or other crime against the laws of such State, who shall flee from justice, and be found in another State, shall, on demand of the executive authority of the State from which he fled, be delivered up, to be removed to the State having jurisdiction of the crime.

(3) No slave or other person held to service or labor in any State or Territory of the Confederate States, under the laws thereof, escaping or lawfully carried into another, shall, in consequence of any law or regulation therein, be discharged from such service or labor; but shall be delivered up on claim of the party to whom such slave belongs, or to whom such service or labor may be due.

Section 3.

(1) Other States may be admitted into this Confederacy by a vote of two-thirds of the whole House of Representatives and two-thirds of the Senate, the Senate voting by States; but no new State shall be formed or erected within the jurisdiction of any other State, nor any State be formed by the junction of two or more States, or

parts of States, without the consent of the Legislatures of the States concerned, as well as of the Congress.

(2) The Congress shall have power to dispose of and make all needful rules and regulations concerning the property of the Confederate States, including the lands thereof.

(3) The Confederate States may acquire new territory; and Congress shall have power to legislate and provide governments for the inhabitants of all territory belonging to the Confederate States, lying without the limits of the several Sates; and may permit them, at such times, and in such manner as it may by law provide, to form States to be admitted into the Confederacy. In all such territory the institution of negro slavery, as it now exists in the Confederate States, shall be recognized and protected by Congress and by the Territorial government; and the inhabitants of the several Confederate States and Territories shall have the right to take to such Territory any slaves lawfully held by them in any of the States or Territories of the Confederate States.

(4) The Confederate States shall guarantee to every State that now is, or hereafter may become, a member of this Confederacy, a republican form of government; and shall protect each of them against invasion; and (on application of the Legislature or of the Executive when the Legislature is not in session) against domestic violence.

Article V.
Section 1.

(1) Upon the demand of any three States, legally assembled in their several conventions, the Congress shall summon a convention of all the States, to take into consideration such amendments to the Constitution as the said States shall concur in suggesting at the time when the said demand is made; and should any of the proposed amendments to the Constitution be agreed on by the said convention, voting by States, and the same be ratified by the Legislatures of two-thirds of the several States, or by conventions in two-thirds thereof, as the one or the other mode of ratification may be proposed by the general convention, they shall thenceforward form a part of this Constitution. But no State shall, without its consent, be deprived of its equal representation in the Senate.

Article VI.

1. The Government established by this Constitution is the successor of the Provisional Government of the Confederate States of America, and all the laws passed by the latter shall continue in force until the same shall be repealed or modified; and all the officers appointed by the same shall remain in office until their successors are appointed and qualified, or the offices abolished.

2. All debts contracted and engagements entered into before the adoption of this Constitution shall be as valid against the Confederate States under this Constitution, as under the Provisional Government.

3. This Constitution, and the laws of the Confederate States made in pursuance thereof, and all treaties made, or which shall be made, under the authority of the Confederate States, shall be the supreme law of the land; and the judges in every State shall be bound thereby, anything in the constitution or laws of any State to the contrary notwithstanding.

4. The Senators and Representatives before mentioned, and the members of the several State Legislatures, and all executive and judicial officers, both of the Confederate States and of the several States, shall be bound by oath or affirmation to support this Constitution; but no religious test shall ever be required as a qualification to any office or public trust under the Confederate States.

5. The enumeration, in the Constitution, of certain rights shall not be construed to deny or disparage others retained by the people of the several States.

6. The powers not delegated to the Confederate States by the Constitution, nor prohibited by it to the States, are reserved to the States, respectively, or to the people thereof.

Article VII.

1. The ratification of the conventions of five States shall be sufficient for the establishment of this Constitution between the States so ratifying the same.

2. When five States shall have ratified this Constitution, in the manner before specified, the Congress under the Provisional Constitution shall prescribe the time for holding the election of President and Vice President; and for the meeting of the Electoral College; and for counting the votes, and inaugurating the President. They shall, also, prescribe the time for holding the first election of members of Congress under this Constitution, and the time for assembling the same. Until the assembling of such Congress, the Congress under the Provisional Constitution shall continue to exercise the legislative powers granted them; not extending beyond the time limited by the Constitution of the Provisional Government.

Adopted unanimously by the Congress of the Confederate States of South Carolina, Georgia, Florida, Alabama, Mississippi, Louisiana, and Texas, sitting in convention at the capitol, the city of Montgomery, Ala., on the eleventh day of March, in the year eighteen hundred and Sixty-one.

Howell Cobb, President of the Congress.

Source:

Constitution of the Confederate States. The Avalon Project at Yale Law School http://avalon.law.yale.edu/19th_century/csa_csa.asp [accessed February 18, 2009].

Appendix 2: **Abraham Lincoln's Proclamation on the Wade-Davis Bill**

In 1863, Abraham Lincoln proposed the 10 Percent Plan, in which 10 percent of all white males in each Confederate state had to take a loyalty oath, in order for their state to be readmitted into the Union. The states also had to recognize permanent freedom for all former slaves.

Whereas, at the late Session, Congress passed a Bill, "To guarantee to certain States, whose governments have been usurped or overthrown, a republican form of Government," a copy of which is hereunto annexed:

And whereas, the said Bill was presented to the President of the United States, for his approval, less than one hour before the *sine die* adjournment of said Session, and was not signed by him:

And whereas, the said Bill contains, among other things, a plan for restoring the States in rebellion to their proper practical relation in the Union, which plan express the sense of Congress upon that subject, and which plan it is now thought fit to lay before the people for their consideration:

Now, therefore, I, Abraham Lincoln, President of the United States, do proclaim, declare, and make known, that, while I am, (as I was in December last, when by proclamation I propounded a plan for restoration) unprepared, by a formal approval of this Bill, to be inflexibly committed to any single plan of restoration; and, while I am also unprepared to declare, that the free-state constitutions and governments, already adopted and installed in Arkansas and Louisiana, shall be set aside and held for nought, thereby repelling and discouraging the loyal citizens who have set up the same, as to further effort; or to declare a constitutional competency in Congress to abolish slavery in States, but am at the same time sincerely hoping and expecting that a constitutional amendment, abolishing slavery throughout the nation, may be adopted, nevertheless, I am fully satisfied with the system for restoration contained in the Bill, as one very proper plan for the loyal people of any State choosing to adopt it; and that I am, and at all times shall be, prepared to give the Executive aid and assistance to any such people, so soon as the military resistance to the United States shall have been suppressed in any such State, and the people thereof shall have sufficiently returned to their obedience to the Constitution and the laws of the United States,—in which cases, military Governors will be appointed, with directions to proceed according to the Bill.

Source:

"Abraham Lincoln, Proclamation on the Wade-Davis Bill," in *Great Issues in American History, Volume 2: 1864–1957,* edited by Richard Hofstadter (New York: Vintage, 1958), pp. 8–10.

Appendix 3: **The Wade-Davis Manifesto**

In general, a great majority of Congressional Republican supporters of the Wade-Davis Bill were infuriated by Abraham Lincoln's veto. In retaliation, they published a vitriolic response to Lincoln's proclamation; the manifesto, which was originally published in the New York Tribune *on August 5, 1864, is published below. However, in the end, the public perception of the statement's authors, Senator Benjamin F. Wade and Representative Henry Winter Davis, suffered more than that of Lincoln. Many readers found the statements made in the* New York Tribune *to be in poor taste and hastily considered.*

We have read without surprise, but not without indignation, the Proclamation of the President of the 8th of July. . . .

The President, by preventing this bill from becoming a law, holds the electoral votes of the Rebel States at the dictation of his personal ambition.

If those votes turn the balance in his favor, is it to be supposed that his competitor, defeated by such means, will acquiesce?

If the Rebel majority assert their supremacy in those States, and send votes which elect and enemy of the Government, will we not repel his claims?

And is not that civil war for the Presidency, inaugurated by the votes of the Rebel States?

Seriously impressed with these dangers, Congress, *"the proper constitutional authority,"* formally declared that there are no State Governments in the Rebel States, and provided for their erection at a proper time; and both the Senate and the House of Representatives rejected the Senators and Representatives chosen under the authority of what the President calls the Free Constitution and Government of Arkansas.

The President's proclamation *"holds for naught"* this judgment, and discards the authority of the Supreme Court, and strides headlong toward the anarchy his Proclamation of the 8th of December inaugurated.

If electors for President be allowed to be chosen in either of those States, a sinister light will be cast on the motives which induced the President to "hold for naught" the will of Congress rather than his Government in Louisiana and Arkansas.

That judgment of Congress which the President defies was the exercise of an authority exclusively vested in Congress by the Constitution to determine what is the established Government in a State, and in its own nature and by the highest judicial authority binding on all other departments of the Government....

A more studied outrage on the legislative authority of the people has never been perpetrated.

Congress passed a bill; the President refused to approve it, and then by proclamation puts as much of it in force as he sees fit, and proposes to execute those parts by officers unknown to the laws of the United States and not subject to the confirmation of the Senate!

The bill directed the appointment of Provisional Governors by and with the advice and consent of the Senate.

The President, after defeating the law, proposes to appoint without law, and without the advice and consent of the Senate, *Military* Governors for the Rebel States!

He has already exercised this dictatorial usurpation in Louisiana, and he defeated the bill to prevent its limitation....

The President has greatly presumed on the forbearance which the supporters of his Administration have so long practiced, in view of the arduous conflict in which we are engaged, and the reckless ferocity of our political opponents.

But he must understand that our support is of a cause and not of a man; that the authority of Congress is paramount and must be respected; that the whole body of the Union men of Congress will not submit to be impeached by him of rash and unconstitutional legislation; and if he wishes our support, he must confine himself to his executive duties—to obey and execute, not make the laws—to suppress by arms armed Rebellion, and leave political reorganization to Congress.

If the supporters of the Government fail to insist on this, they become responsible for the usurpations which they fail to rebuke, and are justly liable to the indignation of the people whose rights and security, committed to their keeping, they sacrifice.

Let them consider the remedy for these usurpations, and, having found it, fearlessly execute it.

Source:

"The Wade-Davis Manifesto," in *Great Issues in American History, Volume 2: 1864–1957,* edited by Richard Hofstadter (New York: Vintage, 1958), pp. 10–12.

BIOGRAPHIES

JAMES BLACK (1823–1893)
Temperance activist and leader

One of the founders of the Prohibition Party, James Black ran as its presidential candidate in the election of 1872. Raised in Lancaster, Pennsylvania, Black committed himself to abstinence from alcohol at the age of sixteen, after a night of carousing with other day laborers. He went on to become a member of the Washingtonians, and then a leader of the Sons of Temperance. In 1865 he was instrumental in founding the National Temperance Society and Publication House, one of the most important national organizations for publishing temperance tracts and lectures. In this endeavor he worked closely with Neal Dow, who had achieved fame from the Maine Law; and with Edward Delavan, a wealthy philanthropist who financed the publications of the society. While Black represented the radical wing of temperance activism, his energy continued the advance of political activism on the matter of prohibition.

Laura A. Cruse

Sources:

John Kobler. *Ardent Spirits: The Rise and Fall of Prohibition* (New York: Putnam, 1973).

Mark Edward Lender. *Dictionary of American Temperance Biography: From Temperance Reform to Alcohol Research, the 1600s to the 1980s* (Westport, Conn.: Greenwood Press, 1984).

JOHN BROWN (1800–1859)
Radical abolitionist

John Brown came to symbolize the sectional division over slavery: in the North, many viewed him as a saint, while he was reviled in the South as a murderer and fanatic. Born in Connecticut to an old but poverty-stricken New England family, for most of his life Brown was economically unsuccessful, going through a series of failed businesses. Brown built and sold several tanneries, herded sheep, speculated in land, and farmed. He was deeply religious, and he studied the Bible intensely. One of his most notable characteristics was a complete absence of prejudice against African Americans. His commitment to racial equality was based on his firm belief that all races were created in the image of God and were equal in his eyes.

Brown sought out the company of blacks and for two years he lived in a freedmen's community in North Elba, New York, on land donated by noted abolitionist Gerrit Smith. He actively participated in the Underground Railroad and helped organize a self-protection league for blacks to resist recapture by white Southerners. As he became increasingly dissatisfied with "moral suasion" he started to plan violent resistance to slavery, convinced that slave owners were too depraved ever to voluntarily abandon slavery. Brown increasingly saw himself in the role of an avenging Old Testament prophet.

When Brown led the raid on Harpers Ferry, he was badly wounded, captured, and tried for treason against the state of Virginia. Brown consciously scripted his trial to present himself as a Christian martyr, and in the North, mass meetings celebrated and mourned him as a martyr to freedom. Further alienating the sections, Brown was typically considered in the South to represent the threat of radical abolitionism. He was hung in Charleston, Virginia, on December 2, 1859.

Christopher Luse

Sources:

Louis A. De Caro. *"Fire from the Midst of You": A Religious Life of John Brown* (New York: New York University Press, 2002).

David S. Reynolds. *John Brown, Abolitionist: The Man Who Killed Slavery, Sparked the Civil War, and Seeded Civil Rights* (New York: Knopf, 2005).

JOHN C. CALHOUN (1782–1850)
Statesman

As the leading statesman representing the South, John C. Calhoun influenced later politicians who dominated the Civil War and Reconstruction eras with Calhoun's advocacy of states' rights and the constitutional protection of slavery. Born in the South Carolina upcountry, Calhoun earned a degree from Yale College (now University) and studied law at Tapping Reeve Law School in Litchfield, Connecticut. Returning to South Carolina to practice law, he was elected to the U.S. House of Representatives in 1810 where he served with Henry Clay of Kentucky, the Speaker of the House.

Like Clay, Calhoun was a "war hawk," advocating war with Great Britain as tensions between the two nations increased in the first decade of the nineteenth century. Calhoun served as secretary of war under President James Monroe with reform-minded effectiveness reflecting his early nationalism. Calhoun withdrew his presidential candidacy in the election of 1824, opting for the vice-presidential nomination; he won and served under John Quincy Adams. In 1828, believing that the leading contender for president, Andrew Jackson, would not survive his first term, Calhoun sought and won the vice presidency a second time. Calhoun was the only vice president to serve under two different presidents. By 1830 his nationalism began to transform into the support of states' rights. He supported nullification—essentially the right of individual states to ignore federal laws that they find unconstitutional—and maintained an interest in the continued existence of slavery. Calhoun led the 1833 effort for South Carolina's secession from the Union, but compromise was reached before drastic events occurred. Calhoun continued to agitate for constitutional protections for slaveholders and Southern rights until his death in 1850.

James K. Bryant II

Source:

Irving H. Bartlett. *John C. Calhoun: A Biography* (New York: Norton, 1993).

HENRY CLAY (1777–1852) *Statesman*

Known as the "The Great Pacificator" and "The Great Compromiser," Henry Clay was one of the most important and influential statesmen in antebellum America. Although born in Hanover County, Virginia, Clay identified himself as a "Westerner" when he moved to Lexington, Kentucky, to set up his legal practice. His ambition and charisma earned him a seat in the Kentucky state legislature and very soon a seat in the U.S. House of Representatives, where he had the distinction of being elected Speaker of the House in his first term. He served in several congressional terms. Clay, as a leading "war hawk," ardently supported the American war effort against Great Britain during the War of 1812. At war's end, Clay developed internal improvement policies that encouraged and protected domestic manufacturing from foreign competition and provided government subsidies for building national roads and canals. These efforts, called the "American System" by Clay, formed the basis of his unsuccessful presidential bid in 1824. By 1832, the rivalry between President Andrew Jackson and Clay ended in the latter's second presidential defeat. Nevertheless, Clay countered Jackson's policies by the establishment of the Whig Party, ushering in a new era in American politics. Clay was indispensable to the nation with his ability to successfully negotiate and facilitate the "Second Missouri Compromise" in 1821, the Nullification Crisis in 1833, and his resolutions for what would become the Compromise of 1850. Although a lifetime slaveholder, Clay supported the colonization of emancipated American slaves in Liberia. "It has been my invariable rule to do all for the Union," Clay told an audience in 1844, "If any man wants the key of my heart, let him take the key of the Union, and that is the key to my heart."

James K. Bryant II

Sources:

Abraham Lincoln. "Eulogy on Henry Clay, July 6, 1852," in *Abraham Lincoln, Slavery, and the Civil War: Selected Writings and Speeches*, edited by Michael P. Johnson (New York: Bedford/St. Martin's Press, 2001), pp. 39–42.

Robert V. Remini. *Henry Clay: Statesman for the Union* (New York: Norton, 1991).

BENJAMIN CURTIS (1809–1874)
Supreme Court justice

One of the greatest lawyers of nineteenth-century America, Benjamin Curtis received national fame for the dissent he wrote in the Dred Scott case. Curtis was born in Watertown, Massachusetts, in 1809. After graduating from both Harvard College (1829) and Harvard Law School (1832), he quickly established himself as a leading figure in the Massachusetts bar. A conservative Whig, Curtis was a critic of the abolitionists. Early in his career, he represented a Louisiana woman seeking to retain ownership of a slave. Pleased with Curtis's backing of the Fugitive Slave Law, President Millard Fillmore selected him to serve on the Supreme Court in 1851.

Curtis's conservative credentials made his dissent in the Dred Scott case (1857) all the more compelling. Drawing on vast historical evidence and numerous legal precedents, he defended the legality of the Missouri Compromise line and showed that blacks held citizenship in several states at the time of the Constitution's adoption. In a violation of Court protocol, Chief Justice Taney withheld publication of his final majority opinion in the Dred Scott case in order to respond more effectively to Curtis's dissent. This conduct led to an acrimonious correspondence between the two men. Curtis resigned from the Court partly because of financial concerns, but also largely as a result of Taney's conduct and final ruling in the Scott case. During the Civil War, Curtis became a vocal critic of Lincoln's muscular use of executive authority. After the war, he served as a leading attorney in President Andrew Johnson's impeachment trial in the Senate. Biographer Stuart Streichler credits Curtis with swaying several key Republicans to acquit Johnson. More importantly, Streichler contends, Curtis's arguments cemented the notion that Congress should not impeach a president because of political or policy reasons, but should treat impeachment as a strictly judicial matter.

Francis MacDonnell

SOURCES:

Richard Leach. "Benjamin Robbins Curtis: Judicial Misfit," *New England Quarterly*, 25 (1952): 507–523.

Stuart Streichler. *Justice Curtis in the Civil War Era: At the Crossroads of American Constitutionalism* (Charlottesville: University of Virginia Press, 2005).

WILLIAM EARL DODGE (1805–1883)
Businessman, temperance activist

William Earl Dodge was a successful businessman, active and influential in politics before and after the Civil War. He acquired a large fortune by founding Phelps, Dodge, and Company, which traded in copper and other resources. Dodge played an active role in reform movements, serving as director of the American Temperance Union from 1865 to 1883. Through his political and business connections, he was able to tie together temperance interests with the Freedmen's Bureau and work for multiple reforms. His other reform activities included helping to found the Young Men's Christian Association and the U.S. Indian Commission. Dodge's commitment to the Temperance Movement reflected the interest of the wealthier classes in cultivating sobriety in the working class because sobriety would improve worker productivity.

Laura A. Cruse

SOURCES:

Richard Lowitt. *A Merchant Prince of the Nineteenth Century, William E. Dodge* (New York: Columbia University Press, 1954).

John J. Rumbarger. *Profits, Power, and Prohibition: Alcohol Reform and the Industrializing of America, 1800–1930* (Albany: State University of New York, 1989).

STEPHEN ARNOLD DOUGLAS (1813–1861)
U.S. senator

"I have become a *Western* man," Stephen A. Douglas wrote in late 1833, "have imbibed Western feelings, principles and interests and have selected Illinois as the favorite place of my adoption." Known as "The Little Giant" more for his focused ambition than his small stature that supported a prominent head and broad shoulders, Douglas remains an enigma for many scholars of the sectional crisis of the 1850s. Born in Brandon, Vermont, he later moved to Canandaigua, New York. Leaving New York for Illinois, he quickly became licensed to practice law. Elected to the Illinois state legislature, Douglas held several state positions until in 1841 he became an associate justice to the Illinois Supreme Court at the age of twenty-seven. His election to the U.S. House of Representatives as a Democrat began his steady rise as a presidential contender.

Douglas, in his first term in the U.S. Senate, secured early political support from both Northern and Southern Democrats for his skillful management and guidance in the passage of the specific pieces of legislation that comprised Henry Clay's resolutions that became the Compromise of 1850. As the author of the Kansas-Nebraska Act of 1854 in the attempt to promote westward expansion, Douglas gained tremendous support from Southern Democrats and Southern Whigs with the de facto repeal of the 1820 Missouri Compromise restricting slavery in the northern portion of the Louisiana Purchase Territory. This significant piece of legislation increased sectional tensions throughout the 1850s. It also reshaped the political landscape of the country by destroying the rival Whig Party and splitting the Douglas's Democrats along sectional lines. Although Douglas defeated Republican Party candidate Abraham Lincoln for reelection to the Senate in 1858, Lincoln dashed his presidential hopes two years later by winning the 1860 election.

James K. Bryant II

SOURCE:

Robert W. Johannsen. *Stephen A. Douglas* (New York: Oxford University Press, 1973; Champaign: University of Illinois Press, 1997).

FREDERICK DOUGLASS (1817–1895)
Abolitionist

Frederick Douglass was born Frederick Augustus Washington Bailey in Talbot County, Maryland, in 1817. When his master, Aaron Anthony, died in 1826, Bailey went to live with a new master, Thomas Auld, of Baltimore. Auld's wife, Sophia, was a religious woman and taught Bailey to read the Bible. After learning to read, Bailey continued to read the Bible on his own, later graduating to antislavery literature. Growing ever more dissatisfied with his existence as a slave, Bailey first attempted to escape his Baltimore master in 1836 but failed. Two years later, on September 3, 1838, he succeeded, fleeing to New York City with Anna Murray, a free black woman from Baltimore. A few weeks after their arrival in the city, they were married by Reverend James Pennington, another former slave.

Following their marriage, the couple moved to New Bedford, Massachusetts, and chose a new surname: Douglass. Frederick Douglass became a licensed minister in the African Methodist Episcopal Zion Church, where, as a vocal member of the abolitionist movement, he frequently spoke out against slavery and colonization. Throughout the 1840s he traveled across New England, speaking at local and national conventions about his life, journey, and convictions. His abolitionist efforts attracted the attention of sympathizer William Lloyd Garrison; through Garrison, Douglass became a frequent lecturer for the Massachusetts Anti-Slavery Society. He also traveled to England and Scotland; while there, British antislavery activists "purchased" his freedom for him and filed manumission papers in Baltimore so that he would no longer be subject to fugitive slave recapture.

Upon his return from Europe, he and his family moved to Rochester, New York.

In addition to Douglass's extensive travel to promote the abolition of slavery, as well as his many public speaking engagements, he also published his *Narrative of the Life of Frederick Douglass, an American Slave* in 1845 and founded *The North Star,* an abolitionist newspaper based in Rochester, New York, in 1847. He published a more complete autobiography, *My Bondage and My Freedom,* in 1855.

Douglass supported Abraham Lincoln's campaign for the presidency of the United States, although he later disagreed with him concerning Lincoln's stance on colonization. While Douglass criticized Lincoln's preliminary Emancipation Proclamation, he praised the final version of it. During the American Civil War, Douglass strongly urged emancipation as a war measure and called for the recruitment of African American soldiers, which he believed would not only prove their abilities to fight as well as white men in battle, but also strengthen the case for emancipation.

After the end of the Civil War, Douglass continued his efforts toward equality for all. He called for passage of the Fifteenth Amendment and edited the *New National Era,* based in Washington, D.C. Furthermore, he held a number of posts, including president of the Freedmen's Savings Bank and minister-resident and consul general to Haiti. He continued to deliver speeches across the nation, particularly against lynching, in the 1890s.

Christopher M. Curtis, Christopher Luse, Brian Craig Miller, Jonathan A. Noyalas, and Zoe Trodd

SOURCES:

David W. Blight. *Frederick Douglass' Civil War: Keeping Faith in Jubilee* (Baton Rouge: Louisiana State University Press, 1991).

Frederick Douglass. *Narrative of the Life of Frederick Douglass, an American Slave,* edited, with an introduction, by David W. Blight (Boston: Bedford/St. Martin's Press, 2003).

Philip Foner. *Frederick Douglass: A Biography* (New York: Citadel, 1964).

Waldo E. Martin. *The Mind of Frederick Douglass* (Chapel Hill: University of North Carolina Press, 1984).

William S. McFeely. *Frederick Douglass* (New York: Norton, 1995).

NEAL DOW (1804–1897)
Supporter of prohibition

Neal Dow was a powerful proponent of prohibition legislation in the antebellum period. After he was elected mayor of Portland, Maine, he authored and pushed for the passage of the Maine Law, which acted as a model for other antebellum prohibition laws. A financial embarrassment in 1857 sullied Dow's reputation, but he remained prominent enough that when he applied as a volunteer for the Union forces at the beginning of the Civil War, he was made a colonel. He served with the Thirteenth Maine Volunteer Infantry, and his efforts to help his soldiers resist intemperance earned the unit the title of the "Temperance Regiment." Dow was captured by Confederates, but he was exchanged as a prisoner of war. After the war ended, Dow resumed his temperance activities, eventually receiving the nomination for presidential candidate of the Prohibition Party in 1880. Even in old age, Dow remained a vocal and powerful force for the temperance cause.

Laura A. Cruse

SOURCES:

Frank L. Byrne. *Prophet of Prohibition: Neal Dow and His Crusade* (Madison: State Historical Society of Wisconsin, 1961).

Neal Dow. *The Reminiscences of Neal Dow* (Portland, Maine: Evening Express Publishing Company, 1898).

NATHAN BEDFORD FORREST (1821–1877)
Lieutenant general in the Confederate army, grand wizard of the Ku Klux Klan

Nathan Bedford Forrest was born in Bedford County, Tennessee. Though he received little formal education, Forrest became one of the richest men in the American South. He invested in businesses, owned several plantations, and operated a slave-trading company that was headquartered in Memphis. Because he made most of his money from the slave trade, Forrest was a strong advocate of states' rights and slavery. It was no surprise that he supported the Confederacy once the Civil War erupted.

At the outbreak of the Civil War, Forrest raised a cavalry battalion in the Confederate army. As a young lieutenant colonel, he first distinguished himself in battle at Fort Donelson, where he ordered his men to charge a Union artillery battery, and then he led them in an assault that broke through the lines of Union forces that had laid siege to the fort. Forrest earned the rank of lieutenant general before the end of the war, and he fought in many of the key battles of the war. Throughout the war, Forrest became noted for his use of guerilla tactics as applied to a mobile cavalry deployment. He was a master of using mobile cavalry units to destroy Union lines of communication and to outflank opposing commanders in the field. Forrest also gained the reputation of being a war criminal following the Battle of Fort Pillow where his troops stormed the Union fortification, killing black Union soldiers as they attempted to surrender.

Forrest became interested in the Ku Klux Klan (KKK) when he learned that the secret society opposed Unionists sympathizers (carpetbaggers and scalawags) and supported the restoration of prewar political leadership in the Southern states. His active support of the terrorist organization eventually led to his nomination and election in 1867 as the KKK's first grand wizard, the national leader of the Klan. Forrest eventually distanced himself from the Klan, but not before the organization had effectively destroyed Republican rule in the Southern states, a process known as Redemption.

Kenneth Howell

SOURCE:

Brian Steel Wills. *A Battle from the Start: The Life of Nathan Bedford Forrest* (New York: HarperCollins, 1992).

WILLIAM LLOYD GARRISON (1805–1879)
Abolitionist

William Lloyd Garrison was one of the most prominent abolitionists and social reformers of the nineteenth century. He was loosely associated with the American Colonization Society's efforts to relocate slaves to the west coast of Africa but later denounced the operations of the group, citing their actions as efforts to minimize the influence of free blacks in the United States in order to support slavery. As a young journalist, Garrison was an outspoken member of the antislavery movement, serving as coeditor of the *Genius of Universal Emancipation*, a Quaker newspaper in which he regularly reported details of the atrocities of slavery, including various brutal acts and murders. He later founded the *Liberator*, his own weekly abolitionist journal, and became a founding member of several abolitionist societies, including the New England Anti-Slavery Society, the American Anti-Slavery Society, and the Friends of Universal Reform.

Garrison denounced all war and physical conflict as evil and inhuman; he held all people of color in high regard, believing that everyone deserves all of a nation's rights and freedoms. Garrison held close ties with Frederick Douglass for much of his life, but Garrison's views on the Constitution caused a rift in their relationship and placed his life in danger on a number of occasions. He was known to refer to the Constitution as a "covenant with death and an agreement with Hell," a view that was considered extreme at the time. His extreme views also included support for a Convention of the Free States as an alternative to preserving the Union after the Civil War. In addition to his support for civil rights, Garrison was a strong advocate for women's suffrage and was a frequent contributor to journals and news columns in support of feminist issues. In 1874, he was considered for the senate seat vacated by the death of Charles Sumner but declined the opportunity, citing his opposition to government service. He died in 1879 of kidney disease.

Laura A. Cruse

Sources:

Archibald H. Grimke. *William Lloyd Garrison* (New York: Negro Universities Press, 1969).

Henry Mayer. *All on Fire: William Lloyd Garrison and the Abolition of Slavery* (New York: St. Martin's Press, 1998).

ULYSSES S. GRANT (1822–1885)
Eighteenth president of the United States

Born in Point Pleasant, Ohio, Ulysses S. Grant graduated from the U.S. Military Academy at West Point, New York. Commissioned as a second lieutenant after his 1843 graduation, Grant served with the Fourth U.S. Infantry during the Mexican War (1846–1848), receiving two brevet promotions for gallantry in battle. Grant resigned from the army in 1854, but was unsuccessful in civilian life; he eventually found himself as a clerk in a leather-goods store operated by his father and brother in Galena, Illinois. When the Civil War began, Grant was appointed a colonel under the administration of President Abraham Lincoln, and soon after that, he was appointed a brigadier general of Illinois volunteer troops.

By 1862 Grant had proved himself as a top-rated general in the war's western theater, when he forced the surrenders of Forts Donaldson and Henry in Tennessee and defeated Confederate troops at the Battle of Shiloh. In 1863 he led the capture of Vicksburg, Mississippi, and lifted the Confederate siege at Chattanooga. Lincoln appointed Grant as general in chief of all U.S. armies in 1864. In April 1865, General Grant accepted the surrender of Robert E. Lee, the premier general of the Confederacy, effectively ending the four-year war.

Grant remained in command of the army and reluctantly served as interim secretary of war for a brief period under President Andrew Johnson, but he refused to accept permanent appointment to the president's cabinet. As a result of Grant's refusal, Republicans in Congress looked to him as their champion in the executive branch. Grant became the Republican candidate for president and was elected in 1868. He was reelected in 1872.

Grant was considered by many to be a weak chief executive whose terms in office were challenged by the controversies surrounding the end of the Civil War and the impeachment of his predecessor, Andrew Johnson. Grant's tolerance for corruption damaged his reputation as commander in chief; however, his presidency was not entirely flawed. His commitment to peace within the borders of the United States and preserving the Union was evident through his efforts in protecting the civil rights of the freed slaves and providing amnesty for the former Confederates. A strong advocate for voting rights for blacks and against violence by the Ku Klux Klan, Grant placed military troops throughout the South to maintain order and enforce the Constitution. Despite the challenges to his leadership, he was instrumental in the timely ratification of the Fifteenth Amendment, the Enforcement Acts, and the Civil Rights Act of 1875. He also signed the law creating the fifteen-member Electoral Commission to rule on the disputed electoral votes of the Hayes-Tilden election in 1877. In an effort to reduce the potential for violence surrounding the electoral crisis, he quickly and quietly increased the military presence in the nation's capital until the unrest was settled after the public inaugural of Rutherford B. Hayes. Grant remained an outspoken critic of Hayes's Southern policy and the suppression of freedoms and civil rights for black Americans.

Denied a third presidential term in 1880, Grant went into an investment business that went bankrupt in 1884. Diagnosed with throat cancer, Grant composed his *Personal Memoirs* to provide future funds for his wife and children. It was completed a few days before his death on July 23, 1885, and is considered by scholars as among the best American autobiographies ever written.

Cedric Adderley and James K. Bryant II

Sources:

Josiah Bunting. *Ulysses S. Grant* (New York: Times Books, 2004).

Ulysses S. Grant. *Personal Memoirs of Ulysses S. Grant* (New York: Webster, 1885; New York: Cosimo, 2007).

William S. McFeely. *Grant: A Biography* (New York: Norton, 2002).

Geoffrey Perrett. *Ulysses S. Grant: Soldier and President* (New York: Random House, 1997).

Frank J. Scaturro. *President Grant Reconsidered* (Lanham, Md.: University Press of America, 1998).

Jean Edward Smith. *Grant* (New York: Simon & Schuster, 2001).

CHARLES COLCOCK JONES (1804–1863)
Presbyterian minister

Born in Liberty County, Georgia, into a wealthy slave-owning family, Charles Colcock Jones was most noted as a leader of the Southern "domestic missions" to the slaves. The "domestic missions" were private organizations of Southern white Christians dedicated to converting and ministering to slaves neglected by the regular churches. Educated at Andover and Princeton Theological Seminaries, Jones joined the First Presbyterian Church of Savannah as pastor in 1831. In 1832 he returned home to found the Association for the Religious Instruction of the Negroes in Liberty County, Georgia, recruiting other leading ministers and planters. Jones served as professor of church history and polity at Columbia (South Carolina) Theological Seminary from 1835 to 1838 and from 1847 to 1850. In 1853 he was appointed secretary of the board of domestic missions of the Presbyterian Church. Jones was the author of numerous articles and works promoting the religious instruction of slaves, including *Religious Instruction for Negroes in the Southern States* (1837) and *Suggestions on the Instruction of Negroes in the South* (1855).

Jones wrote the most popular catechism for the oral instruction of slaves. The catechism went through many editions and was also used for instructing white children in foreign missions. Jones suffered ill health throughout the 1850s, but he made the key address at the founding of the Presbyterian Church in the Confederate States of America, where he urged the reform of slavery. Widely known as the "Apostle to the Blacks," Jones demonstrated through his actions the complexity of the relationship between white, Southern Christianity and slavery.

Sincerely committed to the conversion of slaves, Jones made concessions to Southern racism in order to gain access to slaves (including agreeing to give only oral instruction and emphasizing that Christian slaves would be more content and obedient). Many historians cite Jones as an example of how Southern white evangelicals transferred their qualms over the morality of slavery into efforts to Christianize African Americans.

Christopher Luse

SOURCES:

Erskine Clarke. *Dwelling Place: A Plantation Epic* (New Haven: Yale University Press, 2005).

Donald G. Mathews. "Charles Colcock Jones and the Southern Evangelical Crusade to Form a Biracial Community," *Journal of Southern History*, 41 (August 1975): 299–320.

ABRAHAM LINCOLN (1809–1865)
Sixteenth president of the United States

Born in Hodgenville, Kentucky, on February 12, 1809, Abraham Lincoln spent his boyhood in Indiana, where he strived to educate himself. He moved to New Salem, Illinois, at the age of twenty-one and found himself involved in a variety of tasks—storekeeper, postmaster, and militia captain in the Black Hawk War.

By 1832 Lincoln had asserted himself locally and had won a seat in the Illinois legislature where he served four terms. During his time in the legislature he taught himself law and made his first public expression of his views on slavery. When the Illinois legislature proposed a resolution to reassert slavery's constitutionality and condemn abolitionism, Lincoln voted against the measure. In 1842 he married Mary Todd; the couple had four sons, three of whom died in their youth. In 1844 he formed a law partnership with William H. Herndon, emerging as one of the most respected legal minds in Illinois.

Lincoln catapulted into national politics in 1847, winning a seat in the U.S. House of Representatives. He took with him to Congress a hatred for slavery, largely fueled by his experience aboard a ship on the Ohio River in 1841, where he had seen a dozen slaves shackled together for sale in the South. Morally opposed to slavery, Lincoln contemplated a bill to abolish slavery in Washington, D.C.; however, he soon realized the obstacles to abolition and backed down. His negative views on slavery and the Mexican War cut his tenure in the House of Representatives to one term.

In 1856 he joined the Republican Party; he went on to become its presidential candidate in 1860. On November 6, 1860, he was elected the sixteenth president of the United States of America; he was inaugurated on March 4, 1861. In an attempt to hold the Union together, Lincoln tried to allay Southerners' fears about slavery by informing them in his inaugural address that he would not abolish slavery where it existed, but that he would oppose its extension into the territories. On April 12,

1861, a little more than a month after he officially took office, Confederate forces attacked Fort Sumter, starting the Civil War. Lincoln was staunchly committed to the preservation of the Union and raised an army to do so. Until August 1862, he spoke of the preservation of the Union as his sole aim; however, he came to recognize the termination of slavery as both a needed act of justice and a necessary war measure. On January 1, 1863, Lincoln's Emancipation Proclamation freed slaves in Confederate areas not under Union control, leaving slavery in the border states intact.

A noted orator, Lincoln's famous speeches include the Gettysburg Address, his second inaugural address, and his debates with Stephen A. Douglas. In the first presidential assassination in American history, John Wilkes Booth shot Lincoln on April 14, 1865, at Ford's Theatre. Lincoln died the next morning.

Brian Craig Miller, Jonathan Noyalas, and Christina Proenza-Coles

SOURCES:

Brian R. Dirck, ed. *Lincoln Emancipated: The President and the Politics of Race* (De Kalb: Northern Illinois University Press, 2007).

David Herbert Donald. *Lincoln* (New York: Simon & Schuster, 1996).

Don E. Fehrenba. *Abraham Lincoln: Speeches and Writings 1832–1858* (New York: Routledge, 1997).

James M. McPherson. *Abraham Lincoln and the Second American Revolution* (New York: Oxford University Press, 1991).

Richard Striner. *Father Abraham: Lincoln's Relentless Struggle to End Slavery* (Oxford: Oxford University Press, 2006).

ROBERT H. MILROY (1816–1890)
First general to enforce Lincoln's Emancipation Proclamation

Known to his men as the "Gray Eagle," Robert H. Milroy confronted many difficulties in gaining a commission, and after an unexciting stint as a company officer in the Mexican War he turned his attention to a legal career. Milroy became a successful lawyer and judge prior to the Civil War.

During the Civil War, Milroy became colonel of the Ninth Indiana Infantry; he was later promoted to brigadier general. Milroy surmised that the Union setbacks—such as their catastrophic defeat at the Second Battle of Bull Run in August 1862—were caused by the Lincoln administration's apparent unwillingness to emancipate the slaves. A devout Presbyterian, Milroy argued that God would not allow the Union to achieve victory in the East until the institution of slavery was abolished.

Lincoln issued the preliminary Emancipation Proclamation, and on January 1, 1863, Milroy marched his division of nearly seven thousand troops into Winchester, Virginia. Milroy viewed Winchester as the perfect place to enforce emancipation as it was the hometown of Senator James Mason, author of the 1850 Fugitive Slave Law, and Judge Richard Parker, who had presided over John Brown's trial in 1859.

Following a loss at the Second Battle of Winchester, Milroy was placed under arrest for the Union debacle. Although exonerated by a court of inquiry, he never received a major field command after Winchester. However, as an occupation commander near Tullahoma, Tennessee, in the war's final year Milroy continued to do what he could to alleviate the suffering of former slaves.

After the war Milroy was appointed superintendant of Indian Affairs in Washington Territory. When the post was abolished in 1875, he retired.

Jonathan Noyalas

SOURCE:

Jonathan A. Noyalas. *"My Will Is Absolute Law": A Biography of Union General Robert H. Milroy* (Jefferson, N.C.: McFarland, 2006).

WENDELL PHILLIPS (1811–1884)
Abolitionist

Wendell Phillips was a social reformer and abolitionist who dedicated his life to protecting the civil rights and constitutional freedoms of African Americans, women, and Native Americans. He was a product of Boston's Beacon Street and a graduate of Harvard University and Harvard Law School. An altercation with an angry proslavery mob influenced him to denounce his privileged background and dedicate his life to the abolitionist movement. He abandoned a promising law career and refused to vote or involve himself in any political activities sanctioned by the U.S. Constitution until the slaves were granted full emancipation. He was an active member of the American Anti-Slavery Society, where he maintained a close relationship with fellow abolitionist and founder of the society, William Lloyd Garrison. Along with Frederick Douglass, he became a respected leader and a core member of the Radical Republican party. After the ratification of the Fifteenth Amendment, Phillips added the causes of women's suffrage and Native American rights to his political agenda but remained an outspoken advocate for black Americans. He argued fervently that the Fifteenth Amendment also granted citizenship to the American Indians. He was committed to the Labor Movement, and he was an active member of the Labor Reform Party, running unsuccessfully for governor of Massachusetts as a candidate in 1870.

Cedric Adderley

SOURCES:

Elbert Hubbard. *Little Journeys to the Homes of Eminent Orators: Wendell Phillips* (Aurora, N.Y.: Roycrofters, 1903).

James Brewer Stewart. *Wendell Phillips: Liberty's Hero* (Baton Rouge: Louisiana State University Press, 1986).

JAMES K. POLK (1795–1849)
Eleventh president of the United States

Arguably the only U.S. president to fulfill all of his campaign promises, James K. Polk had three main objectives: 1.) settlement of the Oregon boundary dispute with Great Britain; 2.) the acquisition of California; and 3.) the acquisition of the New Mexico Territory (including the present-day states of New Mexico, Arizona, Nevada, and Utah). Born in North Carolina, Polk established himself in Tennessee. He was elected to the U.S. House of Representatives and later served as speaker. A protégé of Jackson's, Polk was often referred to as "Young Hickory" in a play on words to Jackson's sobriquet "Old Hickory." He also served a term as governor of Tennessee. In 1844, Polk became the Democratic Party nominee for president, pitting him against the Whig nominee, Henry Clay. When Polk won the election he became the first "dark horse" or unknown candidate to win the presidency.

Not wishing to have a third war with Great Britain, Polk successfully negotiated a treaty in 1846 that established the Oregon Territory (present-day states of Oregon, Washington, and parts of Idaho) border with Canada at the 49th parallel. Polk sent John Slidell as his emissary to negotiate payment to Mexico for California and New Mexico; that was turned down. After the U.S. troops he stationed between the Nueces River and the Rio Grande in Texas were attacked, Polk asked Congress for a declaration of war against Mexico. In less than two years, Polk successfully managed to achieve military victory over Mexico and to expand the United States by a fourth of its size. Polk, as a slaveholder, believed that the Constitution guaranteed slaveholders' rights in taking slaves into the territories, but he advocated the extension of the Missouri Compromise Line of 1820 to ease the growing sectional tensions. Polk died less than three months after leaving office.

James K. Bryant II

SOURCES:

Thomas M. Leonard. *James K. Polk: A Clear and Unquestionable Destiny* (Lanham, Md.: Rowman & Littlefield, 2000).

John Siegenthaler. *James Polk, 1845–1849* (New York: Time Books, 2004).

ROBERT BARNWELL RHETT (1800–1876)
Southern secessionist

Regarded as the father of secession in the South, Robert Barnwell Rhett was born in Beaufort, South Carolina, in 1800. Raised mainly by his grandmother, Elizabeth Barnwell Gough, Rhett picked up the rudiments of education largely from her. He attended Beaufort College and studied law with his cousin Thomas Grimke, the brother of Sarah and Angelina Grimke—two of the nation's leading abolitionists.

At age twenty-six Rhett went to the South Carolina legislature. As a young lawmaker he had already begun to wonder about the merits of secession. During the tariff controversy of 1828 he actively supported John C. Calhoun's doctrine of nullification. As the years wore on, however, Rhett became more radical and broke with Calhoun, who favored compromise with the federal government over issues related to slavery. Secession, Rhett believed, was the only viable method to protect the South's peculiar institution. Rhett argued that compromise would only weaken slavery and spell its eventual demise.

During the compromises of the 1850s, Rhett heated up his secessionist rhetoric and after the Republican Party Platform of 1856 stated it opposed slavery's extension into the territories, Rhett clamored for immediate secession. In 1857, along with his son, Rhett became full owner of the *Charleston* (S.C.) *Mercury*—a newspaper devoted to secession's cause. As editor he continually reminded South Carolinians what would happen if abolitionists ruled the South. In an attempt to raise paranoia throughout the slaveholding states Rhett argued that abolitionists would invade the South and incite massive insurrection. When abolitionist John Brown raided Harpers Ferry in October 1859, Rhett appeared to be a prophet, and people began to listen more intently to Rhett's ideas.

After Abraham Lincoln won the presidential election in 1860, Rhett became the leading fire-eater, urging the South to act immediately and secede. That was the only way, in his view, that slavery could be protected. He labored intensely to secure South Carolina's secession and to allay fears that secession did not mean war. Rhett then urged fellow South Carolina secessionists to organize a meeting of the seceded states to form a Confederacy. Despite his prominent role in bringing about secession he was shut out of the Confederate government. Many at the Montgomery convention regarded him as too radical to serve in the infant government. Throughout the Civil War, Rhett focused his attention on criticizing Jefferson Davis.

Jonathan Noyalas

SOURCES:

William C. Davis. *Rhett: The Turbulent Life and Times of a Fire-Eater* (Columbia: University of South Carolina Press, 2001).

———, ed. *A Fire-Eater Remembers: The Confederate Memoir of Robert Barnwell Rhett* (Columbia: University of South Carolina Press, 2000).

FRANKLIN B. SANBORN (1831–1917)
Abolitionist

Sanborn was a member of the Secret Six—a committee that funded John Brown's abolitionist activities and consisted of Sanborn, Samuel Gridley Howe, Thomas Wentworth Higginson, Theodore Parker, Gerrit Smith, and George Luther Stearns. Sanborn's contact with Brown came through his work as secretary of the Massachusetts Kansas Commission, and he provided money and arms for Brown's activities in Kansas.

Brown met with Sanborn in January 1857, as he began his fund-raising campaign for the Harpers Ferry raid. Sanborn invited Higginson to come to Boston and meet Brown, and also introduced him to Parker. During 1857, as Brown toured New England, New York, and Pennsylvania trying to raise money, Sanborn saw him often, and arranged for Brown to make a plea directly to the Massachusetts legislature for financial support.

Sanborn went on to produce a volume of Brown's letters, published in 1885, and wrote two articles that detailed Brown's relationship with his Massachusetts supporters: "John Brown in Massachusetts" (April 1872), and "John Brown and His Friends" (July 1872). He also produced biographies of several Transcendentalists and some editions of the works of Henry David Thoreau.

Zoe Trodd

SOURCE:

Edward J. Renehan Jr. *The Secret Six: The True Tale of the Men Who Conspired with John Brown* (New York: Crown, 1995).

DRED SCOTT (? –1858) *Litigant*

Much remains obscure about Dred Scott, the principal figure in one of America's most consequential legal cases. Like other Americans of the period, his life involved constant uprooting and relocation. Born to slave parents in Virginia sometime around the turn of the century, Scott moved with his owner Peter Blow to Alabama in 1818 and to St. Louis, Missouri, in 1830. Prior to December 1833, Dr. John Emerson purchased Scott. While serving as a surgeon in the U.S. Army, Emerson brought Scott with him for extended stays in the free state of Illinois and to Fort Snelling in the Wisconsin Territory. (The latter post was in territory subject to the Missouri Compromise line's prohibition on slavery.) While living at Fort Snelling, Scott married Harriet Robinson. The couple had four children, only two of whom survived childhood. Scott's prolonged residence in a free state and in free territory gave him a strong legal case to seek freedom. In 1846, three years after Emerson's death, Scott filed suit. Throughout eleven years of litigation, the Scotts received financial and legal backing from several white supporters, especially members of the Blow family. Immediately after the adverse ruling in the Supreme Court, Taylor Blow acquired ownership of Scott and his family, and on May 26, 1857, he manumitted all of them.

Reliable assessments of Scott's character are hard to come by. Historian Walter Ehrlich writes that the antislavery press depicted Scott as a man of intelligence and character, while proslavery papers tended to portray him as unlettered and stupid. At the very least, one can conclude that something about Dred Scott inspired a considerable number of people to exert themselves on behalf of him and his family. He died on September 17, 1858, as a result of consumption (or so his contemporaries believed).

Francis MacDonnell

SOURCES:

Walter Ehrlich. *They Have No Rights: Dred Scott's Struggle for Freedom* (Westport, Conn.: Greenwood Press, 1979).
Vincent C. Hopkins. *Dred Scott's Case* (New York: Fordham University Press, 1951).

PHILIP H. SHERIDAN (1831–1888)
Union general

Although Philip Sheridan received little formal education, he earned an appointment to the U.S. Military Academy. After graduating in 1853, Sheridan served on the frontier in the Oregon Territory until the outbreak of the Civil War.

In 1861, Sheridan was redeployed to the western theater of the Civil War where he demonstrated his skills as an effective operational combat commander. He gained distinction as an infantry commander in several important military engagements. In 1864, General Ulysses S. Grant selected Sheridan to lead the cavalry corps of the Army of the Potomac in the eastern theater, where he helped defeat Confederate cavalry units operating in the Shenandoah Valley.

Following the war, Sheridan served as the military governor of the Fifth Military District (Texas and Louisiana) that Congress created with the Reconstruction Acts of March 1867. During his tenure as military governor, Sheridan insisted on basic civil rights for African Americans and sought to protect white Unionists residing in his jurisdiction. The general's determination to enforce Congressional Reconstruction policies placed him at odds with President Andrew Johnson, who eventually reassigned him to a post on the Great Plains in 1867, where he directed campaigns in the Plains Indian Wars.

Kenneth Howell

SOURCES:

Joseph G. Dawson III. *Army Generals and Reconstruction* (Baton Rouge: Louisiana State University Press, 1982).
Paul Andrew Hutton. *Phil Sheridan and His Army* (Lincoln: University of Nebraska Press, 1985).
Roy Morris, Jr. *Sheridan: The Life and Wars of General Phil Sheridan* (New York: Crown, 1992).

ROBERT SMALLS (1839–1915)
Union navy captain, U.S. congressman

Robert Smalls was born to an enslaved mother in Beaufort, South Carolina, on April 5, 1839. At the age of twelve Smalls went to Charleston to hire himself out. When the Civil War broke out, Smalls worked as a deckhand and then pilot for the Confederate steamer the *Planter*. On May 13, 1862, while the white captain and crew were ashore, Smalls, with twelve other slaves, commandeered the *Planter* from Charleston harbor and delivered its supplies, and their families, to the Union. The *Planter* became a Union gunboat with Smalls, ultimately, as her captain, the first African American to captain a ship for the U.S. Navy.

After the war Smalls returned to Beaufort; with the congressional award he received for the delivery of the *Planter* he purchased the home in which he and his mother had been slaves. Smalls was a delegate in the state constitutional convention and served in the S.C. House of Representatives and state senate. An effective Republican leader, Smalls worked for the development of public education in the state. Smalls went on to serve five terms as a U.S. congressman, during which time he sponsored the Civil Rights Act, advocated the integration of the armed forces, and promoted women's suffrage. He also petitioned Congress for relief for his former master and for a pension for the widow of David Hunter; Hunter was a Union general who had endeavored to free and arm slaves early in the war.

Smalls's political success was increasingly challenged by the hostile white-supremacist climate of post-Reconstruction South Carolina. In an act of political persecution, Smalls was found guilty of accepting a bribe in 1877; he was pardoned two years later. In 1890 Smalls began his almost twenty-year service as the U.S. customs collector in Beaufort, where he died on February 23, 1915.

Christina Proenza-Coles

SOURCES:

Edward A. Miller. *Gullah Statesman: Robert Smalls from Slavery to Congress, 1839–1915* (Columbia: University of South Carolina Press, 1995).
Dorothy Sterling. *Captain of the Planter: The Story of Robert Smalls* (New York: Doubleday, 1958).
Okin Edet Uya. *From Slavery to Public Service: Robert Smalls, 1839–1915* (New York: Oxford University Press, 1971).

EDWIN M. STANTON (1814–1869)
Secretary of War

Despite a rudimentary childhood education, Edwin M. Stanton entered Kenyon College in 1832 to pursue a career in law. When financial shortcomings forced Stanton to leave the college after two years, Stanton persevered through private study, and in 1836 he passed the bar. As the secession crisis tore the nation apart in late 1860, Stanton found himself at the epicenter as U.S. attorney general under President James Buchanan.

In January 1862 President Abraham Lincoln appointed Stanton secretary of war, to replace Simon Cameron. After Congress confirmed the appointment in mid January, Stanton urged Lincoln to be aggressive in ending the rebellion. Among the greatest weapons the South had, in Stanton's eyes, were its slaves. Since he believed they were a valuable military asset, he took every opportunity prior to emancipation to weaken the slave system, including allowing Union commanders to use runaway slaves as laborers for the army. He even contemplated a plan in the spring of 1862 to use African Americans to garrison fortifications in the South.

Lincoln issued his preliminary Emancipation Proclamation on September 22, 1862, and Stanton countered the proclamation's detractors by arguing that emancipation would not only deprive the Confederacy of its most valuable resource, but that it would also bring a new labor force to the Union cause and swell the ranks of the army and navy. Following the death of President Lincoln on April 15, 1865, Stanton kept his cabinet post under President Andrew Johnson. However, because of their differing views on postwar Reconstruction, Stanton resigned his position in late May 1868. In 1869 President Ulysses S. Grant nominated Stanton for the U.S. Supreme Court. Stanton passed away before taking the oath of office.

Jonathan Noyalas

Source:

Benjamin P. Thomas and Harold M. Hyman. *Stanton: The Life and Times of Lincoln's Secretary of War* (New York: Knopf, 1962).

ALEXANDER H. STEPHENS (1812–1883)
Unionist advocate and Confederate vice president

Alexander H. Stephens graduated from Franklin College in 1832 as valedictorian, and two years later he passed the Georgia bar. His political career began in 1837 when he won a seat in the Georgia assembly. After serving in the state legislature for six years, Stephens was elected to the U.S. House of Representatives. During his tenure in the House, which lasted until 1859, Stephens urged restraint and compromise. Although he owned thirty-four slaves Stephens did not believe that slavery should expand into the territories.

As issues over slavery threatened national stability in the 1850s, Stephens constantly urged compromise. Even during the presidential election year of 1860 he worked for the election of Illinois senator Stephen Douglas—the Northern Democratic candidate—instead of for John C. Breckinridge (the Southern Democrat). Following the election of Abraham Lincoln—who had been an old friend of Stephens's—he again urged restraint on the secession issue. He tried to convince fellow Georgians that disunion would mean the end of slavery. Stephens believed that the Constitution offered the best safeguards to slavery. Only if the new Republican administration tried to force its will on the South then should it, in Stephens's view, secede. Despite his cautious tone Georgia seceded on January 19, 1861. Stephens signed his state's secession ordinance. Although he did not agree with the measure, he vowed not to abandon his state during the crisis.

On February 9, 1861, the Confederate convention in Montgomery elected Stephens the provisional vice president of the Confederacy. Although the second highest ranking member of the newly minted Confederate government, he played no significant role; after he disagreed with President Jefferson Davis's policies, including conscription, Davis shut Stephens out of the government. Stephens only performed two official duties as vice president—attending the Virginia secession convention in 1861 and the Hampton Roads Conference in 1865. Stephens spent most of his time making certain that wounded Confederate soldiers were being cared for properly.

At the end of the Civil War, federal authorities arrested Stephens. Paroled in October 1865, Georgia elected him to the U.S. Senate. When he tried to assume his Senate seat in 1866, Radical Republicans refused to seat the former Confederate official. He eventually returned to the Senate in 1872. In the war's aftermath, Stephens wrote a number of books, including his two-volume *A Constitutional View of the War between the States*. Elected as Georgia's governor in 1882, he died only several months into his term.

Jonathan Noyalas

SOURCES:

William C. Davis. *The Union that Shaped the Confederacy: Robert Toombs and Alexander H. Stephens* (Lawrence: University Press of Kansas, 2001).

Thomas E. Schatt. *Alexander H. Stephens of Georgia: A Biography* (Baton Rouge: Louisiana State University Press, 1988).

ELIZA DANIEL STEWART (1816–1908)
Advocate of prohibition

Eliza Stewart was one of the most persevering leaders of the Women's Crusade during the winter of 1873–1874, in which women marched on saloons in an attempt to persuade owners to stop selling alcohol. She had been a Methodist schoolteacher in Ohio until the Civil War. During the war she volunteered with Soldiers' Aid Societies and the U.S. Sanitary Commission. Once the war ended, she became a leading temperance activist. During the Women's Crusade, Stewart led groups of women in prayer meetings either in or in front of saloons and other drinking establishments in an effort to get the establishments to close. Although the effects of the Crusade were short-lived, most saloon operators gave in to the demands of the women. In 1873 she founded the Women's Temperance League of Osborne, which later became the first local chapter of the Women's Christian Temperance Union. In 1876 she traveled through England, where she helped establish the British Women's Temperance Association, and in 1895 she gave the opening address at the World's WCTU convention in London.

Laura A. Cruse

SOURCES:

Eliza Daniel Stewart. *Memories of the Crusade* (Columbus, Ohio: Hubbard, 1888).

"Eliza D. Stewart," *Ohio History Central*, July 1, 2005 <http://www.ohiohistorycentral.org/entry.php?rec=358>.

HARRIET BEECHER STOWE (1811–1896)
Abolitionist and novelist

Harriet Beecher Stowe was born into a prominent evangelical family. Her father, Lyman Beecher, was a famous Congregationalist minister noted for his efforts in various reform societies, including temperance and domestic missions. Her brother Henry Ward Beecher later became one of the North's most popular preachers. In 1832 her family moved to Cincinnati; it was while Harriet Beecher lived there that she encountered slavery firsthand in nearby Kentucky. In 1836 she married clergyman and abolitionist Calvin Stowe, with whom she had seven children. During this period Stowe began her career as an author, writing essays and fiction for various magazines as well as novels focusing on romance and domestic life.

In 1850 the passing of the Fugitive Slave Law by Congress (which strengthened the legal ability of slave owners to recover runaways to the North) inspired Stowe to use her writing talent to combat slavery. What later became *Uncle Tom's Cabin* was serialized in the abolitionist periodical *The National Era* in 1851. The novel was published in 1852 to immediate success. In the United States it sold three hundred thousand copies in one year, an unprecedented number. It sold even better in England. By 1854 it had been translated into sixty languages. The novel was credited with recruiting thousands of people to the antislavery cause. Critics agree that the source of its power was Stowe's portrayal of how slavery destroyed slave families and corrupted religious life. In 1853 Stowe wrote *The Key to Uncle Tom's Cabin*, citing her sources for the atrocities in the novel. Stowe continued to write novels, including another antislavery work, *Dred, A Tale of the Great Dismal Swamp*, but she never duplicated her earlier success. She remained a prominent writer and reformer for the duration of her life.

Christopher Luse

SOURCES:

Thomas F. Gossett. *Uncle Tom's Cabin and American Culture* (Dallas: Southern Methodist University Press, 1985).

Joan D. Hedrick. *Harriet Beecher Stowe: A Life* (New York: Oxford University Press, 1994).

ROGER BROOKE TANEY (1777–1864)
Chief justice of the United States

Roger Taney served as chief justice of the United States from 1836 to 1864, longer than any other figure save John Marshall. Taney grew up in a prosperous slaveholding family in a tobacco-growing region of southern Maryland. In private life, he freed his own slaves, but in matters of public policy he proved a stalwart defender of the property rights of slave owners. Before his confirmation as chief justice of the United States on March 15, 1836, Taney devotedly served the Jackson White House as attorney general, interim secretary of war, and secretary of the treasury. Had

Taney died before rendering the Dred Scott decision (March 6, 1857), his historical reputation as a judge would no doubt have been largely positive. In a series of cases relating to economic matters, he guided the Court in a way that tended to emphasize states' rights over those of the national government, and the rights of communities over those of individual investors and property owners. Though modifying the direction of the Court under John Marshall, he did so in a pragmatic way that reassured many Whigs who had been initially skeptical of Taney. His majority opinion in the Dred Scott case reflected his vision of the Constitution as a proslavery document. Taney ruled that neither federal lawmakers nor territorial legislators could ban the expansion of slavery into the territories. He also held that the Constitution permanently denied citizenship rights to blacks.

As the Civil War approached, Taney believed the Southern states were justified in their secession from the Union, and he thought a peaceful separation of the two regions was in the best interest of all involved. In spite of his sympathies for the Southern cause, he retained his position on the Supreme Court and ineffectually endeavored to thwart Abraham Lincoln's policies regarding the draft, crackdowns on civil liberties, and the exercise of presidential authority. His most famous fight with the Lincoln administration came at the start of the war in the case of *Ex-parte Merryman*. Justice Taney, acting in his capacity as a federal circuit-court judge, ordered John Merryman released when the Lincoln administration refused to offer a writ of habeas corpus. Military officials suspected Merryman of engaging in acts of sabotage against telegraph lines and railroad bridges in Maryland, and with support from the president, the army simply ignored Taney's command. Upon Taney's death in October 1864, Lincoln appointed former secretary of treasury Salmon P. Chase as chief justice.

Francis MacDonnell

SOURCES:

Don Fehrenbacher. "Roger B. Taney and the Sectional Conflict," *Journal of Southern History*, 43 (November 1977): 555–566.
Walker Lewis. *Without Fear or Favor: A Biography of Chief Justice Roger Brooke Taney* (Boston: Houghton Mifflin, 1965).
James F. Simon. *Lincoln and Chief Justice Taney: Slavery, Secession and the President's War Powers* (New York: Simon & Schuster, 2006).
Carl B. Swisher. *Roger B. Taney* (New York: Macmillan, 1935).

HARRIET TUBMAN (1822–1914)
Underground Railroad conductor, Union spy

Harriet Tubman was born into slavery in Dorchester County, Maryland, around 1822. In her teens Tubman successfully fled her plantation and found work in Philadelphia. She returned several times to Maryland to help her relatives escape slavery, and she continued to return to the South to conduct other slaves along the Underground Railroad to the northern United States and Canada (to escape the jurisdiction of the Fugitive Slave Act of 1850). Tubman devised several tactics to make these extremely dangerous efforts successful. In her twenties, Tubman returned to slave territory nineteen times to aid fugitives, and ultimately, she helped to bring three hundred people to freedom. Tubman's extraordinary missions garnered the young, illiterate, formerly enslaved black woman international recognition as well as the appellation "Moses."

In the North, Tubman joined other abolitionists in antislavery meetings and she pledged to help John Brown recruit former slaves for his attack on Harpers Ferry. When the Civil War broke out, Tubman's extensive experience with clandestine travel between the North and the South in perilous conditions made her an outstanding spy, scout, and courier for the Union, whom she also served as a nurse and a cook. Tubman became the first American woman to lead a military raid when she guided Union general James Montgomery's Second South Carolina all-black unit, comprised of about three hundred men, in a successful raid of the Combahee River, liberating nearly eight hundred slaves and capturing or destroying Confederate property and stores. After the war she settled with her parents and other family in Auburn, New York, where she lived for some fifty years as a community activist and suffragist until her death in 1913 at age ninety-one.

Christina Proenza-Coles

SOURCES:

David W. Blight. *Passages to Freedom: The Underground Railroad in History and Memory* (Washington D.C.: Smithsonian Books, 2004).
Sarah H. Bradford. *Harriet, The Moses of Her People* (Bedford, Maine: Applewood Books, 1993 [1886]).

ST. GEORGE TUCKER (1752–1827)
Judge, law professor, emancipationist

St. George Tucker was one of the most influential members of the Virginia bar during the Early National period.

He was born in Bermuda but came to Virginia in 1772 to study law under George Wythe at the College of William and Mary. His legal career was interrupted, however, by the American Revolution; Tucker became a smuggler of goods between Virginia and Bermuda. In 1778 he married the wealthy widow Frances Bland Randolph, who had inherited three plantations and hundreds of slaves from her first husband, John Randolph. The marriage thus made St. George Tucker a slaveholder. Despite this fact, Tucker argued for the gradual emancipation of Virginia's slaves. In 1796, he published a pamphlet—*A Dissertation on Slavery: With a Proposal for the Gradual Abolition of It, in the State of Virginia*—that emphasized the incongruity between slavery and republican liberty. He also reaffirmed the view expressed by Lord Mansfield in the *Somerset* case, which held that slavery was repugnant to the common law.

In 1788 Tucker was appointed as judge to one of the newly formed district courts in Virginia. Two years later, when Wythe resigned his professorship at William and Mary, Tucker was named to the position. He taught there for the next fourteen years and shaped the law curriculum that trained a generation of Virginia lawyers. The curriculum was based largely upon Sir William Blackstone's *Commentaries on the Laws of England,* and, in conjunction with his lectures Tucker began preparing an American edition of the *Commentaries* that offered description and analysis explaining where Virginia law and precedent deviated from the English standard. Tucker's edition of Blackstone appeared in 1802, and it remained an influential text for legal training throughout the early decades of nineteenth-century America. Tucker resigned from William and Mary in 1804 and served on Virginia's Court of Appeals until 1811. Two years later, President James Madison appointed him as a federal judge and he served there for another twelve years.

Christopher M. Curtis

Source:

Charles T. Cullen. *St. George Tucker and Law in Virginia, 1772–1804* (New York: Garland, 1987).

HENRY McNEAL TURNER (1834–1915)
Bishop of the African Methodist Episcopal Church, political organizer

Henry McNeal Turner was born to free parents in Newberry Courthouse, South Carolina. Turner managed to obtain a rudimentary education, despite laws and customs against educating blacks. After receiving a preacher's license in 1853 from the Methodist Episcopal Church, South, Turner traveled as an itinerant preacher throughout the South. In 1858 he moved to St. Louis, Missouri, and joined the African Methodist Episcopal (AME) Church, later serving as a pastor in Baltimore, Maryland, and Washington, D.C.

While in Washington, Turner became friends with many of the leading antislavery Republicans, including Charles Sumner and Thaddeus Stevens. In 1863 Turner helped recruit soldiers for the First Regiment of U.S. Colored Troops and was appointed the first black chaplain by Abraham Lincoln. After the war, Turner worked with the Freedmen's Bureau in Georgia. He concentrated on organizing new congregations for the AME throughout Georgia, and he was hugely successful in convincing thousands of former slaves to leave the predominantly white Southern Methodists and join the AME.

After 1867 Turner was instrumental in organizing the Georgia Republican Party, and he served in the state house of representatives; however, in 1868, the majority of white legislators expelled all black officeholders. Turner delivered an eloquent speech protesting this injustice on the floor of the legislature, but to no avail. This proved to be a crucial event for Turner, who increasingly became despondent of ever overcoming entrenched white racism. Turner was reelected to the legislature in 1870 but was denied his seat through fraud.

Turner moved to Savannah to serve as pastor of St. Phillip's AME Church. In 1880 he was elected bishop. In the late nineteenth century Turner emerged as the most prominent advocate of black migration to Africa, organizing the International Migration Society. Between 1891 and 1898 Turner traveled four times to Africa. He helped send two ships to Liberia in 1895–1896, but many people returned complaining of disease and hardship. Turner was a major advocate of "race pride," celebrating the history and accomplishments of African Americans and urging fellow blacks to create their own institutions.

Christopher Luse

Sources:

Stephen Ward Angell. *Bishop Henry McNeal Turner and African-American Religion in the South* (Knoxville: University of Tennessee Press, 1992).

Edwin S. Redkey, ed. *Respect Black: The Writings and Speeches of Henry McNeal Turner* (New York: Arno, 1971).

DANIEL WEBSTER (1782–1852) Statesman

Perhaps one of the greatest orators of his day, Daniel Webster was a versatile political and legal actor in the first half of nineteenth-century America. Born in Salisbury, New Hampshire, Webster established a successful legal practice that led to his election to the U.S. House of Representatives as a last generation Federalist. Unlike his contemporaries Henry Clay and John C. Calhoun, Webster opposed the War of 1812 and its negative impact on New England shipping and trade. He also argued major cases before the U.S. Supreme Court, winning landmark decisions in *Dartmouth College v. Woodward* (1819) and *McCulloch v. Maryland* (1819), making him one of the nation's most celebrated attorneys. By the 1820s, Webster was elected to the U.S. House of Representatives from Massachusetts and soon after to the U.S. Senate where his debates with his senatorial colleagues gained legendary status. His 1830 reply to Senator Robert Y. Hayne of South Carolina on the legality of nullification and secession serves as an example of one of his most memorable phrases, "Liberty *and* Union, now and forever, one and inseparable."

Webster served President John Tyler as secretary of state, negotiating the Webster-Ashburton Treaty to settle the boundary disputes in the northeast between the United States and Canada. He failed in his attempts to gain the Whig nomination for president although his name was submitted as a potential contender. His final major speech in the Senate, in support of Henry Clay's Compromise resolutions in 1850, garnered enthusiastic support from Southerners and from those supporting sectional compromise at the expense of Northern "Free Soilers" and abolitionists. Webster's death in 1852 marked the last of the great Jacksonian era politicians who inherited the leadership of the Founding Fathers and kept sectional tensions from erupting into civil war.

James K. Bryant II

Source:

Robert V. Remini. *Daniel Webster: The Man and His Time* (New York: Norton, 1997).

JOHN GREENLEAF WHITTIER (1807–1892) Abolitionist, poet

John Greenleaf Whittier's first published poem, "The Exile's Departure," appeared in 1826 in the *Newburyport Free Press*, where the abolitionist William Lloyd Garrison was editor. Encouraged by Garrison, Whittier wrote for a series of abolitionist newspapers and magazines, and published numerous poems and essays on slavery and abolition, including his 1833 pamphlet "Justice and Expedience," which urged immediate abolition and attacked the American Colonization Society.

Whittier was mobbed and stoned in Concord, New Hampshire, in 1835, and began work for the American Anti-Slavery Society in 1836. In May 1838, during his tenure as editor of the *Pennsylvania Freeman,* he was burned out of his offices in Philadelphia's Pennsylvania Hall by an antiabolitionist mob. The following year he helped found the antislavery Liberty Party, and pushed for bills to get trial-by-jury for runaway slaves.

Some abolitionists felt that Whittier had failed to express the requisite level of unequivocal support for John Brown in his poem "Brown of Osawatomie." Garrison launched a semijovial attack, identifying ambivalence toward Brown in Whittier's poem and demanding more respect and appreciation on Brown's behalf. In a public letter he referenced several of Whittier's poems that seemed to endorse violence, and queried the shift toward pacifism in "Brown of Osawatomie." Indignant, Whittier replied in his own public letter to *The Liberator* that he abhorred slavery as a state of war, but that he opposed forcible means to end it.

Zoe Trodd

Source:

Edward Wagenknecht. *John Greenleaf Whittier: A Portrait in Paradox* (New York: Oxford University Press, 1967).

WILLIAM WILBERFORCE (1759–1833) Abolitionist, member of Parliament

William Wilberforce was one of the leading architects of the British abolitionist movement. He was born in Hull, where his father was a wealthy merchant. After the death of his father in 1767, Wilberforce was sent to live with his uncle and aunt, who were committed Methodists. He attended Cambridge University and developed a lifelong friendship there with William Pitt the Younger, who would later go on to become British prime minister. Wilberforce himself was elected to Parliament in 1780 and, as an independent Tory, opposed the administration of Lord North, Frederick North. When his friend Pitt became prime minister in 1783, Wilberforce supported his friend's government.

In 1784 Wilberforce underwent a profound conversion and embraced evangelical Christianity. He joined the Clapham Sect, a group of Anglican evangelicals who were dedicated to social reform. Wilberforce committed himself to using his political office to reform British society. In 1787 he joined an ecumenical group committed to abolishing the Atlantic slave trade and agreed to lead the parliamentary campaign for the Society for Effectuating the Abolition of the Slave Trade. He introduced the subject in Parliament during a speech in May 1789 but did not propose legislation until two years later. Initially, he met staunch opposition from the powerful sugar lobby, which was dominated by proslavery West Indian planters. Wilberforce was persistent, though, and over the next two decades he continued to advocate abolition of the slave trade. In 1807 he published *A Letter on the Abolition of the Slave Trade*, which summarized the evidentiary findings of two decades of research on the slave trade that he had compiled with Thomas Clarkson. The essay, along with a changing political and military situation wrought by the Napoleonic Wars, encouraged Parliament to abolish British participation in the trade that year.

Wilberforce involved himself in other reform efforts but returned to the problem of slavery in 1823 when he called for the complete abolition of slavery in the British Empire. He took an active role in the early days of this movement, but ill health forced him to resign from Parliament the following year. He died in July 1833, a few days after the House of Commons passed the Abolition of Slavery Act.

Christopher Curtis

SOURCES:

Christopher Leslie Brown. *Moral Capital: Foundations of British Abolitionism* (Chapel Hill: University of North Carolina Press, 2006).

Eric Metaxas. *Amazing Grace: William Wilberforce and the Heroic Campaign to End Slavery* (New York: HarperSanFrancisco, 2007).

James Walvin. *Black Ivory: Slavery in the British Empire*, second edition (Oxford: Blackwell, 2001).

FRANCES WILLARD (1839–1898)
Supporter of prohibition

After graduating from the North Western Women's Female College, Frances Willard began a career as a teacher. Her success led her eventually to become president of the Evanston College for Ladies, and when that school was absorbed by Northwestern University, she was named as the dean of the Women's College. She and the president of Northwestern disagreed over the direction of the Women's College in 1874, when the Women's Crusade was at its height; Willard left the school and joined a national organization, the Women's Christian Temperance Union (WCTU), as its corresponding secretary. When the WCTU was formed in the wake of the Women's Crusade, Willard took an active role in the new organization. Her force of personality and her strength of vision propelled her to become its next president, a position she held until her death. Willard's motto, "Do Everything," became the mission of the WCTU during her lifetime, and she attacked social ills as interrelated. Willard's leadership caused the WCTU to join women's activism for temperance with a cry for women's rights to political participation through the power to vote, joining women's suffrage to the cause of temperance.

Laura A. Cruse

SOURCES:

Anna Gordon. *The Beautiful Life of Frances E. Willard* (Chicago: Woman's Temperance Publishing Association, 1898).

Frances Elizabeth Willard. *Glimpses of Fifty Years* (Chicago: Woman's Temperance Publication Association, 1889).

WILLIAM LOWNDES YANCEY
(1814–1863) *Alabama secessionist*

William Lowndes Yancey's early life offered no indication that he would emerge as one of slavery's and secession's strongest advocates. Educated in the northeastern United States, William Yancey attended Williams College in Massachusetts, before moving in 1833 to Greenville, South Carolina, where Yancey studied law with one of the South's most ardent unionists, Benjamin Perry.

By the late 1830s, Yancey moved to Alabama, where he began his career as one of the South's planter elite. However, the Panic of 1837—which pushed down cotton prices—and the murdering of his slaves by a neighbor's overseer in 1839 forced Yancey to abandon all notions of running a lucrative cotton plantation. So, he turned his attention to political matters—the cause of slavery and secession.

In 1841 he was elected to the Alabama legislature and three years later he was elected to the U.S. House of Representatives. Yancey's tenure in the House ended before his first term expired. After a passionate speech that called for widespread protection of slavery in the territories, Yancey found himself in a duel to uphold his position and defend his honor. The event forced him to resign, ending his short stint in Washington.

Despite his leaving public office, Yancey continued from the late 1840s until the outbreak of the Civil War to push for unity among the slaveholding South. In 1848 he drafted the Alabama Platform, which called for the federal government to guarantee states' rights and slavery. Ten years later he formed the League of United Southerners, which promoted secession. Two years after he formed a prosecession association Yancey pushed for the Democratic Party and its presidential nominee to support the Alabama Platform. When the convention refused, Yancey led a contingent out of the meeting. Eventually, this led to a split in the Democratic Party with Stephen Douglas being the choice of Northern Democrats and John C. Breckinridge being the preference for Democrats in the South. Ultimately, the split within the Democratic Party helped solidify Abraham Lincoln's election.

After Lincoln's victory, Yancey, Alabama's leading secessionist, called for immediate secession in Alabama. Although he wrote the state's ordinance of secession, after Alabama seceded, Yancey was not chosen as a delegate to the Confederate convention in Montgomery because he was viewed as too radical to aid in forming a cohesive government. Yancey held aspirations of becoming the Confederacy's first president, but he was not considered. Confederate president Jefferson Davis appointed Yancey as an emissary to Europe to secure support for the Confederacy; however, he quit the post in March 1862 to assume a seat in the Confederate Senate. He spent his time in the Senate trying to limit Davis's power, especially when Davis's policies threatened state sovereignty.

Jonathan Noyalas

Source:

Eric H. Walther. *William Lowndes Yancey and the Coming of Civil War* (Chapel Hill: University of North Carolina Press, 2006).

GENERAL BIBLIOGRAPHY

Abels, Jules. *Man on Fire: John Brown and the Cause of Liberty.* New York: Macmillan, 1971.

Abraham Lincoln, edited by Roy P. Basler, 9 volumes. New Brunswick, N.J.: Rutgers University Press, 1953–1955; Ann Arbor: University of Michigan Digital Library Production Services <http://quod.lib.umich.edu/cgi/t/text/text-idx?c=lincoln;cc=lincoln;view=text;idno=lincoln2;rgn=div1;node=lincoln2%3A438> [accessed January 16, 2008].

Abrahamson, James L. *The Men of Secession and Civil War: 1859–1861.* Wilmington, Del.: Scholarly Resources, 2000.

Allen, Austin. *Origins of the Dred Scott Case: Jacksonian Jurisprudence and the Supreme Court, 1837–1857.* Athens: University of Georgia Press, 2006.

Anderson, Osborne P. *A Voice from Harpers Ferry.* Boston: Printed for the author, 1861.

Angell, Stephen Ward. *Bishop Henry McNeal Turner and African-American Religion in the South.* Knoxville: University of Tennessee Press, 1992.

Aptheker, Herbert. *Abolitionism: A Revolutionary Movement.* Boston: Twayne, 1989.

Barney, William L. *The Secessionist Impulse: Alabama and Mississippi in 1860.* Princeton, N.J.: Princeton University Press, 1974.

Bartlett, Irving H. *John C. Calhoun: A Biography.* New York: Norton, 1993.

Basler, Roy P., ed. *The Collected Works of Abraham Lincoln,* 8 volumes. New Brunswick, N.J.: Rutgers University Press, 1953.

Benét, Stephen Vincent. *John Brown's Body.* New York: Farrar & Rinehart, 1928.

Berlin, Ira, Reidy, Joseph, and Rowland, Leslie S. *Freedom's Soldiers: The Black Military Experience in the Civil War.* Cambridge: Cambridge University Press, 1998.

———, et al. *Slaves No More: Three Essays on Emancipation and the Civil War.* Cambridge: Cambridge University Press, 1992.

Bestor, Arthur. "The American Civil War as a Constitutional Crisis," *American Historical Review,* 69 (January 1964): 327–352.

Blight, David W. "John Brown: Triumphant Failure," *American Prospect,* vol. 11 (March 13, 2000): 44–45.

——— and Brooks D. Simpson, eds. *Union and Emancipation: Essays on Politics and Race in the Civil War Era.* Kent, Ohio: Kent State University Press, 1997.

Blocker, Jack S. *American Temperance Movements: Cycles of Reform.* Boston: Twayne, 1989.

Boritt, Gabor S. *Lincoln the War President: The Gettysburg Lectures.* Oxford: Oxford University Press, 1992.

Boyer, Richard. *The Legend of John Brown.* New York: Knopf, 1973.

Brown, Christopher Leslie. *Moral Capital: Foundations of British Abolitionism.* Chapel Hill: University of North Carolina Press, 2006.

Burin, Eric. *Slavery and the Peculiar Solution: A History of the American Colonization Society.* Gainesville: University Press of Florida, 2005.

Burkhardt, George S. *Confederate Rage, Yankee Wrath: No Quarter in the Civil War.* Carbondale: Southern Illinois University Press, 2007.

Burns, Eric. *The Spirits of America: A Social History of Alcohol.* Philadelphia: Temple University Press, 2004.

Burton, William L. *Melting Pot Soldiers: The Union's Ethnic Regiments.* Ames: Iowa State University Press, 1988.

Cain, William E., ed. *William Lloyd Garrison and the Fight against Slavery: Selections from* The Liberator. New York: Bedford/St. Martin's Press, 1994.

Carey, Anthony Gene. *Parties, Slavery, and the Union in Antebellum Georgia.* Athens: University of Georgia Press, 1997.

Carter, Samuel, III. *The Final Fortress: The Campaign for Vicksburg, 1862–1863.* New York: St. Martin's Press, 1980.

Carton, Evan. *Patriotic Treason: John Brown and the Soul of America.* New York: Free Press, 2006.

Catton, Bruce. *Grant Takes Command*. Boston: Little, Brown, 1969.

———. *A Stillness at Appomattox*. Garden City, N.Y.: Doubleday, 1953– .

Channing, Steven A. *Crisis of Fear: Secession in South Carolina*. New York: Simon & Schuster, 1970.

Cornelius, Janet D. *Slave Missions and the Black Church in the Antebellum South*. Columbia: University of South Carolina Press, 1999.

Cornish, Dudley Taylor. *The Sable Arm: Negro Troops in the Union Army, 1861–1865*. New York: Longmans, Green, 1956.

Crofts, Daniel W. *Reluctant Confederates: Upper South Unionists in the Secession Crisis*. Chapel Hill: University of North Carolina Press, 1989.

Davis, David Brion. *The Problem of Slavery in the Age of Revolution, 1770–1823*. Ithaca, N.Y.: Cornell University Press, 1975.

———. *The Problem of Slavery in Western Culture*. New York: Oxford University Press, 1966.

Davis, William C. *"A Government of Our Own": The Making of the Confederacy*. Baton Rouge: Louisiana State University Press, 1994.

———. *Lincoln's Men: How President Lincoln Became Father to an Army and a Nation*. New York: Free Press, 1999.

———. *Rhett: The Turbulent Life and Times of a Fire-Eater*. Columbia: University of South Carolina Press, 2001.

——— and Robertson, James I., Jr., eds. *Virginia at War: 1861*. Lexington: University Press of Kentucky, 2005.

DeCaro, Louis A. *Fire from the Midst of You: A Religious Life of John Brown*. New York: New York University Press, 2002.

Donald, David Herbert. *Lincoln*. New York: Simon & Schuster, 1995.

———, ed. *Why the North Won the Civil War*. Baton Rouge: Louisiana State University Press, 1960.

Douglass, Frederick. "John Brown, Speech Delivered at Storer College, Harpers Ferry, West Virginia, May 30, 1881," in *Frederick Douglass: Selected Speeches and Writings*, edited by Philip S. Foner and Yuval Taylor. Chicago: Lawrence Hill Books, 1999, pp. 633–649.

———. *The Life and Times of Frederick Douglass*, in *Douglass Autobiographies*. New York: Library of America, 1996 [1881].

———. *My Bondage and My Freedom*. New York and Auburn: Miller, Orton & Milligan, 1855. This work is the second revised edition of Douglass's account of his experiences as a slave and his escape to freedom. His account was the most famous of the slave narratives of the time, which were used by abolitionists in their campaign to overthrow slavery. Douglass emphasizes the hypocrisy of "proslavery" Christians, who preached the Gospel to slaves while denying them literacy and breaking up families in the domestic slave trade.

Eaton, Clement. *The Freedom-of-Thought Struggle in the Old South*, revised edition. New York: Harper & Row, 1964.

Ehrlich, Walter. *They Have No Rights: Dred Scott's Struggle for Freedom*. Westport, Conn.: Greenwood Press, 1979.

Ericson, David F. *Debate over Slavery: Antislavery and Proslavery Liberalism in Antebellum America*. New York: New York University Press, 2000.

Escott, Paul D. *After Secession: Jefferson Davis and the Failure of Confederate Nationalism*. Baton Rouge: Louisiana State University Press, 1978.

Faust, Drew Gilpin. *The Ideology of Slavery: Proslavery Thought in the Antebellum South, 1830–1860*. Baton Rouge: Louisiana State University Press, 1981.

Fehrenbacher, Don. *The Dred Scott Case: Its Significance in American Law and Politics*. New York: Oxford University Press, 1978.

———. "Roger B. Taney and the Sectional Conflict," *Journal of Southern History*, 43 (November 1977): 555–566.

———. *Slavery, Law, and Politics: The Dred Scott Case in Historical Perspective*, abridged edition. New York: Oxford University Press, 1981.

Fellman, Michael. *Inside War: The Guerrilla Conflict in Missouri During the American Civil War*. New York: Oxford University Press, 1989.

Filler, Louis. *Crusade against Slavery: Friends, Foes, and Reforms, 1820–1860*. Algonac, Mich.: Reference Publications, 1986.

Finkelman, Paul. Dred Scott v. Sandford: *A Brief History with Documents*. Boston: Bedford/St. Martin's Press, 1997.

———, ed. *Defending Slavery: Proslavery Thought in the Old South*. New York: Bedford/St. Martin's Press, 2003.

Foote, Shelby. *The Civil War: A Narrative*, 3 volumes. New York: Random House, 1958–1974.

Forbes, Ella. *African American Women during the Civil War*. New York: Garland, 1998.

Forbes, Robert Pierce. *The Missouri Compromise and Its Aftermath: Slavery and the Meaning of America*. Chapel Hill: University of North Carolina Press, 2007.

Fowler, William M., Jr. *Under Two Flags: The American Navy in the Civil War*. New York: Norton, 1990.

Fox-Genovese, Elizabeth, and Genovese, Eugene. *The Mind of the Master Class: History and Faith in the Southern Slaveholders' Worldview*. New York: Cambridge University Press, 2005.

Franklin, John Hope. *The Emancipation Proclamation*. Garden City, N.Y.: Doubleday, 1963.

Freehling, William W. *The Road to Disunion*, volume 1, *Secessionists at Bay, 1776–1854*. New York: Oxford University Press, 1990.

———. *The Road to Disunion*, volume 2. *Secessionists Triumphant, 1854–1861*. Oxford: Oxford University Press, 1990.

——— and Simpson, Craig M. eds. *Secession Debated: Georgia's Showdown in 1860*. New York: Oxford University Press, 1992.

Freeman, Douglas Southall. *Lee's Lieutenants: A Study in Command*, 3 volumes. New York: Scribners, 1942–1944.

———. *R. E. Lee: A Biography*, 4 volumes. New York: Scribners, 1934–1935.

Furnas, J. C. *The Road to Harpers Ferry*. New York: Sloane, 1959.

Geary, James W. *We Need Men: The Union Draft in the Civil War*. De Kalb: Northern Illinois University Press, 1991.

Genovese, Eugene D. *A Consuming Fire: The Fall of the Confederacy in the Mind of the White Christian South*. Athens: University of Georgia Press, 1998.

Glatthaar, Joseph T. *Forged in Battle: The Civil War Alliance of Black Soldiers and White Officers*. New York: Free Press, 1990.

Goodman, Paul. *Of One Blood: Abolitionism and the Origins of Racial Equality*. Berkeley: University of California Press, 1998.

Graber, Marc. *Dred Scott and the Problem of Constitutional Evil*. Cambridge: Cambridge University Press, 2006.

Griffith, Paddy. *Battle Tactics of the Civil War*. New Haven, Conn.: Yale University Press, 1989.

Guelzo, Allen C. *Lincoln's Emancipation Proclamation: The End of Slavery in America*. New York: Simon & Schuster, 2004.

Gunderson, Robert Gray. *Old Gentlemen's Convention: The Washington Peace Conference of 1861*. Madison: University of Wisconsin Press, 1961.

Gusfield, Joseph R. *Symbolic Crusade*. Urbana: University of Illinois Press, 1963.

Harrold, Stanley. *The Abolitionists & the South, 1831–1861*. Lexington: University Press of Kentucky, 1995.

Hatch, Nathan O. *The Democratization of American Christianity*. New Haven: Yale University Press, 1989.

Higginson, Thomas Wentworth. *Army Life in a Black Regiment*. Boston: Houghton, Mifflin, 1910.

Holzer, Harold, Medford, Edna Greene, and Williams, Frank J. *The Emancipation Proclamation: Three Views, Social, Political, and Iconographic*. Baton Rouge: Louisiana State University Press, 2006.

Howard, Victor B. *Religion and the Radical Republican Movement, 1860–1870*. Lexington: University Press of Kentucky, 1990.

Hyman, Harold, and Wiecek, William. *Equal Justice under Law: Constitutional Development 1835–1875*. New York: Harper & Row, 1982.

Jeffrey, Julie Roy. *The Great Silent Army of Abolitionism: Ordinary Women in the Antislavery Movement*. Chapel Hill: University of North Carolina Press, 1998.

Jenkins, Wilbert L. *Climbing Up to Glory: A Short History of African Americans during the Civil War and Reconstruction*. Wilmington, Del.: Scholarly Resource Books, 2002.

Jenkins, William Sumner. *The Pro-Slavery Argument in the Old South*. Chapel Hill: University of North Carolina Press, 1935.

Johnson, Curtis D. *Redeeming America: Evangelicals and the Road to the Civil War*. Chicago: I. R. Dee, 1993.

Johnson, Michael P. *Toward a Patriarchal Republic: The Secession of Georgia*. Baton Rouge: Louisiana State University Press, 1977.

Jones, Charles Colcock. *Tenth Annual Report of the Association for the Religious Instruction of the Negroes of Liberty County, Georgia*. Savannah: The Association, 1845. Jones wrote most of the annual reports of the association he founded in 1832. He used the publications to give instruction to white Christians on how to organize domestic missions and minister to slaves.

Keller, Allan. *Thunder at Harpers Ferry*. Englewood Cliffs, N.J.: Prentice-Hall, 1958.

Key, V. O., Jr. *Politics, Parties, and Pressure Groups*, fifth edition. New York: Crowell, 1964.

Klingaman, William K. *Abraham Lincoln and the Road to Emancipation: 1861–1865*. New York: Viking, 2001.

Knoles, George Harmon, ed. *The Crisis of the Union 1860–1861*. Baton Rouge: Louisiana State University Press, 1965.

Kraditor, Aileen S. *Means and Ends in American Abolitionism: Garrison and His Critics on Strategy and Tactics, 1834–1850*. New York: Vintage, 1969.

Krout, John Allen. *The Origins of Prohibition*. New York: Russell & Russell, 1925.

Lerner, Gerda. *The Grimke Sisters from South Carolina: Pioneers for Women's Rights and Abolition*. Chapel Hill: University of North Carolina Press, 1967.

Lincoln, Abraham. "Second Inaugural Address, March 4, 1865." In *Complete Works of Abraham Lincoln*, Volume XI, edited by John G. Nicolay and John Hay. New York: Francis D. Tandy Company, 1905, pp. 44–47. Please see Documents section of this chapter for further information.

———. "Speech at Springfield, Illinois," June 26, 1857, in *Collected Works of*

Lincoln-Douglas Debates, "Second Debate at Freeport Illinois, August, 1858" <http://www.nps.gov/archive/liho/debate2.htm> [accessed July 7, 2007].

Link, William A. *Roots of Secession: Slavery and Politics in Antebellum Virginia*. Chapel Hill: University of North Carolina Press, 2003.

Lipset, Seymour M. "Religion and Politics in the American Past and Present," in *Religion and Social Conflict*, edited by Robert Lee and Martin E. Marty. New York: Oxford University Press, 1964.

Loveland, Anne C. *Southern Evangelicals and the Social Order, 1800–1860*. Baton Rouge: Louisiana State University Press, 1980.

Malin, James C. *John Brown and the Legend of Fifty-Six*. Philadelphia: American Philosophical Society, 1942.

Mathews, Donald G. "Charles Colcock Jones and the Southern Evangelical Crusade to Form a Biracial Community," *Journal of Southern History*, 41 (August 1975): 299–320.

McKivigan, John R. *The War against Proslavery Religion: Abolitionism and the Northern Churches, 1830–1865*. Ithaca, N.Y.: Cornell University Press, 1984.

———, ed. *History of the American Abolitionist Movement*, 5 volumes. New York: Routledge, 1999.

——— and Snay, Mitchell, eds. *Religion and the Antebellum Debate over Slavery*. Athens: University of Georgia Press, 1998.

McPherson, James M. *Crossroads of Freedom: Antietam: The Battle That Changed the Course of the Civil War*. Oxford: Oxford University Press, 2002.

———. *The Negro's Civil War: How American Blacks Felt and Acted during the War for the Union*. New York: Pantheon, 1965.

Miller, William Lee. *Arguing about Slavery: John Quincy Adams and the Great Battle in the United States Congress.* New York: Knopf, 1998.

Montgomery, William E. *Under Their Own Vine and Fig Tree: The African-American Church in the South, 1865–1900.* Baton Rouge: Louisiana State University Press, 1993.

Morrison, Michael A. *Slavery and the American West: The Eclipse of Manifest Destiny and the Coming of the Civil War.* Chapel Hill: University of North Carolina Press, 1997.

Nevins, Allan. *Ordeal of the Union*, volume 1, *Fruits of Manifest Destiny, 1847–1852*. New York: Macmillan, 1992 [1947].

———. *Ordeal of the Union*, volume 2, *A House Dividing, 1852–1857*. New York: Macmillan, 1992 [1947].

———. *The War for the Union*, 4 volumes. New York: Scribners, 1959–1971.

Noll, Mark. *The Civil War as a Theological Crisis.* Chapel Hill: University of North Carolina Press, 2006.

Noyalas, Jonathan A. *"My Will Is Absolute Law": A Biography of Union General Robert H. Milroy.* Jefferson, N.C.: McFarland, 2006.

Nudelman, Franny. *John Brown's Body: Slavery, Violence, and the Culture of War.* Chapel Hill: University of North Carolina Press, 2004.

Oates, Stephen B. *To Purge This Land with Blood: A Biography of John Brown.* New York: Harper & Row, 1970.

———. *With Malice Toward None: The Life of Abraham Lincoln.* New York: Harper & Row, 1977.

Pegram, Thomas R. *Battling Demon Rum: The Struggle for a Dry America, 1800–1933.* Chicago: Ivan R. Dee, 1998.

Persico, Joseph E. *My Enemy, My Brother: Men and Days of Gettysburg.* New York: Viking, 1977.

Peterson, Merrill D. *The Great Triumvirate: Webster, Clay, and Calhoun.* New York: Oxford University Press, 1987.

Potter, David. *The Impending Crisis: 1848–1861.* New York: Harper & Row, 1976.

Quarles, Benjamin. *Allies for Freedom: Blacks and John Brown.* New York: Oxford University Press, 1974.

———. *Black Abolitionists.* New York: Da Capo, 1991.

———. *Lincoln and the Negro.* New York: Oxford University Press, 1962.

Raboteau, Albert J. *Slave Religion: The "Invisible Institution" in the Antebellum South.* New York: Oxford University Press, 1978.

Ramold, Steven J. *Slaves, Sailors, Citizens: African Americans in the Union Navy.* De Kalb: Northern Illinois University Press, 2002.

Ramsdell, Charles W. *Behind the Lines in the Southern Confederacy.* Baton Rouge: Louisiana State University Press, 1944.

Redpath, James, ed. *Echoes of Harpers Ferry.* New York: Arno, 1969 [1860].

Remini, Robert V. *Daniel Webster: The Man and His Time.* New York: Norton, 1994.

———. *Henry Clay: Statesman for the Union.* New York: Norton, 1991.

Reynolds, David S. *John Brown, Abolitionist: The Man Who Killed Slavery, Sparked the Civil War, and Seeded Civil Rights.* New York: Knopf, 2005.

Reynolds, Donald E. *Editors Make War: Southern Newspapers in the Secession Crisis.* Nashville: Vanderbilt University Press, 1970.

Risley, Ford. *The Civil War: Primary Documents on Events from 1860–1865.* Westport, Conn.: Greenwood Press, 2004.

Rorabaugh, W. J. *The Alcoholic Republic: An American Tradition.* New York: Oxford University Press, 1979.

Rossbach, Jeffrey S. *Ambivalent Conspirators: John Brown, the Secret Six, and a Theory of Slave Violence.* Philadelphia: University of Pennsylvania Press, 1982.

Royster, Charles. *The Destructive War: William Tecumseh Sherman, Stonewall Jackson, and the Americans.* New York: Knopf, 1991.

Rumbarger, John J. *Profits, Power, and Prohibition: Alcohol Reform and the Industrializing of America, 1800–1930.* Albany: State University of New York Press, 1989.

Sanborn, Franklin B. *Recollections of Seventy Years.* Boston: R. G. Badger, 1909.

———, ed. *The Life and Letters of John Brown, Liberator of Kansas, and Martyr of Virginia.* Boston: Roberts, 1885.

Scott v. Sandford. Supreme Court Collection, Cornell University Law School <http://www.law.cornell.edu/supct/html/historics/USSC_CR_0060_0393_ZO.html> [accessed January 16, 2008].

Sears, Stephen W. *Landscape Turned Red: The Battle of Antietam.* New Haven, Conn.: Ticknor & Fields, 1983.

Sernett, Milton C. *Black Religion and American Evangelicalism: White Protestants, Plantation Missions, and the Flowering of Negro Christianity, 1787–1865.* Metuchen, N.J.: Scarecrow Press, 1975.

Shaffer, Donald R. *After the Glory: The Struggles of Black Civil War Veterans.* Lawrence: University Press of Kansas, 2004.

Simon, James F. *Lincoln and Chief Justice Taney: Slavery, Secession and the President's War Powers.* New York: Simon & Schuster, 2006.

"Slavery—Slave Trade—Antislavery—Abolitionism," *The Southern Christian Advocate* (November 29, 1844). This Methodist newspaper was published in Charleston, South Carolina. Denominations established weekly newspapers in most of the major cities of the South. These papers often published articles urging the conversion of slaves and defending slavery as a Christian institution.

Smith, H. Shelton. *In His Image But . . . Racism in Southern Religion, 1780–1910.* Durham, N.C.: Duke University Press, 1972.

Smith, John David, ed. *Black Soldiers in Blue: African American Troops in the Civil War Era.* Chapel Hill: University of North Carolina Press, 2002.

Snay, Mitchell. *The Gospel of Disunion: Religion and Separatism in the Antebellum South.* Cambridge: Cambridge University Press, 1993.

Stampp, Kenneth. *America in 1857: A Nation on the Brink.* New York: Oxford University Press, 1990.

———. *And the War Came: The North and the Secession Crisis, 1860–1861.* Baton Rouge: Louisiana State University Press, 1950.

Stauffer, John. *The Black Hearts of Men: Radical Abolitionists and the Transformation of Race.* Cambridge, Mass.: Harvard University Press, 2002.

Stavis, Barrie. *John Brown: The Sword and the Word.* South Brunswick, N.J.: A. S. Barnes, 1970.

Stephens, Alexander H. *A Constitutional View of the Late War Between the States; Its Causes, Character, Conduct and Results,* 2 volumes. Philadelphia: National Publishing, 1870.

Stewart, James Brewer. *Holy Warriors: The Abolitionists and American Slavery.* New York: Hill & Wang, 1976.

Stiles, Joseph C. *Speech on the Slavery Resolutions, Delivered in the General Assembly Which Met in Detroit May Last.* Washington, D.C.: Jno. T. Towers, 1850. Stiles was a Presbyterian minister from Georgia who collaborated with Charles Colcock Jones in the domestic mission to the slaves. His speech was before a hostile audience at the New School Presbyterian national conference. The New School was dominated by antislavery Northerners. Stiles emphasized the role of white Southern Christians in reforming slave codes, especially removing barbarous legal punishments.

Stokes, Anson Phelps, and Pfeffer, Leo. *Church and State in the United States,* revised edition. New York: Harper, 1950.

Stout, Harry S. *Upon the Altar of the Nation: A Moral History of the Civil War.* New York: Viking, 2006.

Stowell, Daniel W. *Rebuilding Zion: The Religious Reconstruction of the South, 1863–1877.* New York: Oxford University Press, 1998.

Streichler, Stuart. *Justice Curtis in the Civil War Era: At the Crossroads of American Constitutionalism.* Charlottesville: University of Virginia Press, 2005.

Striner, Richard. *Father Abraham: Lincoln's Relentless Struggle to End Slavery.* New York: Oxford University Press, 2006.

Stringfellow, Thornton. "The Bible Argument; or, Slavery in the Light of Divine Revelation." In *Cotton Is King and Pro-Slavery Arguments,* edited by E. N. Elliott. Augusta, Georgia: Pritchard, Abbott & Loomis, 1860, pp. 461–491. Please see Documents section of this chapter for further information.

Sunstein, Cass. "*Dred Scott v. Sandford* and Its Legacy," in *Great Cases in Constitutional Law,* edited by Robert P. George. Princeton, N.J.: Princeton University Press, 2000.

Swisher, Carl. *History of the Supreme Court: The Taney Period,* volume 5. New York: Macmillan, 1974.

Szymanski, Ann-Marie E. *Pathways to Prohibition: Radicals, Moderates, and Social Movement Outcomes.* Durham, N.C.: Duke University Press, 2003.

Taylor, Susie King. *A Black Woman's Civil War Memoirs: Reminiscences of My Life in Camp with the 33rd U.S. Colored Troops, Late 1st South Carolina Volunteers.* New York: Markus Weiner, 1988 [1902].

Tise, Larry E. *Proslavery: A History of the Defense of Slavery in America, 1701–1840.* Athens: University of Georgia Press, 1987.

Touchstone, Blake. "Planters and Slave Religion in the Deep South," in *Masters and Slaves in the House of the Lord: Race and Religion in the American South, 1740–1870,* edited by John Boles. Lexington: University Press of Kentucky, 1988, pp. 99–126.

Trefousse, Hans L. *Lincoln's Decision for Emancipation.* Philadelphia: Lippincott, 1975.

Villard, Oswald Garrison. *John Brown, 1800–1859: A Biography Fifty Years After.* Boston: Houghton Mifflin, 1910.

Walker, David. *Appeal to the Coloured Citizens of the World,* edited by Peter P. Hinks. University Park: Pennsylvania State University Press, 2000 [1829].

Walters, Ronald G. *The Antislavery Appeal: American Abolitionism after 1830.* New York: Norton, 1978.

Walther, Eric H. *William Lowndes Yancey and the Coming of Civil War.* Chapel Hill: University of North Carolina Press, 2006.

Warren, Robert Penn. *John Brown: The Making of a Martyr.* New York: Payson & Clarke, 1929.

Wiebe, Robert H. *The Opening of American Society, from the Adoption of the Constitution to the Eve of Disunion.* New York: Knopf, 1984.

Wiecek, William. "Slavery and Abolition before the United States Supreme Court, 1820–1860," *Journal of American History,* 65 (June 1978): 34–59.

Wilson, Charles Reagan. *Baptized in Blood: The Religion of the Lost Cause, 1865–1920.* Athens: University of Georgia Press, 1980.

Wilson, Hill Peebles. *John Brown, Soldier of Fortune: A Critique.* Lawrence, Kans.: Wilson, 1913.

Wise, Stephen R. *Lifeline of the Confederacy: Blockade Running During the War.* Columbia: University of South Carolina Press, 1988.

Wolf, Eva Sheppard. *Race and Liberty in the New Nation: Emancipation in Virginia from the Revolution to Nat Turner's Rebellion.* Baton Rouge: Louisiana State University Press, 2006.

Zilversmit, Arthur. *Lincoln on Black and White: A Documentary History.* Malabar, Fla.: Krieger, 1971.

INDEX

~ A ~

abolitionism 1–8, 186–190, 246, 319, 322–323, 327, 331, 334
    criticism of 321
    religious basis of 258
abolitionist movement 68
Abolition of Slavery Act (Great Britain) 5, 335
Adams, John Quincy 7, 320
Africa 1, 323, 333
African Americans 6, 40, 117, 319, 329–330, 333
    Christianization of 325
    colonization of 295
    fear of northern migration by 301
    labor hardships 295
    military participation 163–168
    recruitment into military 288
    religion 248
    soldiers 279
    women in military 167
African Methodist Episcopal (AME) Church 250, 333
African Methodist Episcopal Zion Church 322
African slave trade 41
Alabama 5, 92–94, 102, 165, 234, 335
    Mobile 145
    Montgomery 94, 328, 330, 336
    Wetumpka 92
Alabama Platform 336
alcohol 218, 221, 226
alcoholism 219
Alexander, E. Porter 138
Alton Observer 6
American Anti-Slavery Society (AAS) 6, 68, 246, 259, 323, 326, 334
American Colonization Society (ACS) 5, 258, 323, 334
American Freedmen's Inquiry Commission 177
American Museum 221
American Revolution 4, 11, 14, 48, 218, 333
    blacks in 163
American System 67, 320
American Temperance Society 219
American Temperance Union 219, 321
Anaconda Plan 117
Anderson, Robert 95, 190
Andover Theological Seminary 325

Andrew, James O. 247
Anglican 335
Anglo-African Magazine 215
Anthony, Aaron 322
Antietam Creek 133
antislavery literature 68
Appalachian Mountains 188
Appeal 6
Appeal to the Coloured Citizens of the World 19, 189
Appomattox Courthouse 118, 161, 167
Arizona 327
Arkansas 5, 95, 102, 125, 165
    Poison Spring 166
Army, U.S. 328
    prohibitions against African Americans 163
Army of Northern Virginia 116–118, 121, 137, 145, 161, 287, 297
Army of Occupation and Reconstruction 168
Army of the Potomac 115, 118, 121, 137, 145, 287, 329
Arthur (English king) 188
Articles of Confederation 43
Association for the Religious Instruction of the Negroes 325
Atlantic Monthly, The 273
Atlantic slave trade 3–5, 15, 335
Augusta, Alexander T. 165
Auld, Sophia 322
Auld, Thomas 322

~ B ~

Baptist Church 7
"Baptist" slave revolt (Jamaica) 5
Baptists 219, 234, 246–247, 262
Barnum, P. T. 221
"Battle Hymn of the Republic, The" 273
Battles
    Antietam 115, 117, 121, 133, 287, 297
    Bull Run, First, 115
    Bull Run, Second 115, 326
    Chancellorsville 115
    Cold Harbor 118, 145
    Crater, of the 167
    Fort Pillow 166, 323
    Fort Wagner 166

Fredericksburg 115
Gettysburg 117, 137
Island Mound 165
Milliken's Bend 165
New Market Heights 167
Palmito Ranch 167
Petersburg 118, 166
Poison Spring 166
Port Hudson 165, 178
Second Winchester 326
Seven Pines 117
Shiloh 116, 125, 324
Spotsylvania Courthouse 118, 145
Vicksburg 117, 138, 145, 324
Wilderness 118, 145
Beaufort College 327
Beecher, Henry Ward 331
Beecher, Lyman 331
beer 223
Benezet, Anthony 2
Bermuda 333
Bible 247, 319, 322
Bill of Rights 43
Birney, James G. 6, 69
Black, James 224, 319
Black Hawk War 325
Blackstone, William 2, 5, 7, 333
Blair, Montgomery 287, 297
Bleeding Kansas 8
Blight, David W. 186
blockade of Southern coastline 115
Blow, Peter 328
Blow, Taylor 328
Bonaparte, Napoleon 3, 117
Book of Exodus 249
Book of Philemon 247–248
Booth, John Wilkes 326
Border Ruffians 187
border states 165
Boston, John 174
Boston Commonwealth 179
Boston Traveler 207
Bower, Ellen 168
Breckinridge, John C. 330, 336
Brief Examination of Scripture Testimony on the Institution of Slavery, A 262
British Navy 3
British Women's Temperance Association 331
Brown, Augustus C. 143
Brown, Frederick 193
Brown, John 8, 186–188, 190, 193–195, 197, 203, 206–207, 209, 214–215, 249, 279, 289, 319, 326, 328, 332, 334
Brown, Joseph E. 92
Brown, Martha McClellan 224
Brown, Mary 208
Brown, Peter 188
Brown, William Wells 6, 194
Browning, Orville H. 172
Brown, John, Jr. 187
"Brown of Osawatomie" 334
"Brown of Osawatomie" (poem, Whittier) 188, 215
Buchanan, James 61, 94, 98, 100, 330

Bureau for Colored Troops 165
Burns, Anthony 194
Burnside, Ambrose 115
Bush, George W. 51
Butler, Benjamin 164

~ C ~

Calhoun, John C. 68–70, 74, 80, 320, 327, 334
California 7, 43, 50, 69–70, 75, 172, 327
Cambridge University 334
Cameron, Simon 164, 172, 330
Canada 177, 327, 332, 334
    Ontario 188, 197
Capers, William 248
Caribbean 4–5, 177
Carney, William H. 166
Carson League 221
Cary, Mary Ann Shadd 167
Cass, Lewis 69
Catholic Temperance Pledge 226
Chamberlain, Joshua Lawrence 287
Charleston (S.C.) Mercury 327
Charlottesville (Va.) Review 122
Chase, Salmon P. 175, 303, 332
Chestnut, James 93
Child, Lydia Maria 6, 215
Christianity 2, 188, 246, 248, 250, 269, 304, 334
citizenship
    definition of 43
    denial to African Americans 40
"Civil Disobedience" 7
civil rights 324
Civil Rights Act (1875) 324, 329
Clapham Sect 335
Clarkson, Thomas 3, 335
Clay, Henry 50, 66–70, 75–76, 84, 89, 320–321, 327, 334
"Coloured Citizens of the World" 6
Columbia Theological Seminary 325
Combahee River 179, 332
Commentaries on the Laws of England 3, 333
Committee of Thirteen 94
Committee of Thirty-Three 94
Common Property Doctrine 69, 74
Commonwealth of Massachusetts v. Jennison 14
Compromise of 1850 7, 50, 70, 76, 320–321, 334
Confederacy 1, 92, 116, 269, 289, 292, 294, 323–324, 328, 330, 336
    defeat of 250
    enlistment of slaves 167
    slaves laboring for 287
    use of slaves for war effort 164
Confederate Army 121
Confederate Presbyterian Church 249
Confederate States of America 70, 94
Confederate White House 168
Congregationalist Church 219, 331
Congress 6, 15, 40, 43, 46, 69–70, 98, 163, 167, 186, 286, 298, 331
Congressional Medal of Honor 166, 168
Congressional Reconstruction 329

Connecticut 4, 319
  Litchfield 320
Conscience Whigs 6
Constitution 41–43, 45, 48–49, 66, 68–69, 94, 97, 221, 287, 289, 291, 324, 326, 330, 332
Constitution, U.S. 40
Constitutional Convention 4
Constitutional View of the War between the States, A 330
Continental Congress
  slave trade 4
Convention of the Free States 324
Conway, Moncure 188
Copperheads 137
Corps D'Afrique 165
cotton 116
Court of the King's Bench 3
Crittenden, John J. 94–95, 106
Crowl, Thomas 305
Cuba 168
Cumberland River 125
Curry, Jabez L. M. 92
Curtis, Benjamin 42–43, 45, 56, 320
Curtis, Benjamin R. 287, 300
Cushing, William 14

~ D ~

Dabney, Robert L. 277
Dartmouth College v. Woodward 334
Davis, Jefferson 94, 102, 165, 167, 328, 330, 336
  spy in household 168
Davis, Reuben 102
Declaration of Independence 14, 24, 40, 94, 246, 252
Declaration of the Rights of Man 3
Defence of Virginia, and Through Her the South, A 277
Delavan, Edward 319
Delaware 115, 285
Democratic Party 6, 41, 68–69, 89, 186, 288, 321, 327, 336
  Copperheads 137
Democratic Review 68
Department of the South 165
Department of the West 164
Dew, Thomas Roderick 7, 15
discrimination 43
Dissertation on Slavery: With a Proposal for the Gradual Abolition of It, in the State of Virginia, A 333
District of Columbia 68, 70
Dodge, William Earl 321
Dodson, Jacob 172
Douglas, Stephen A. 41, 43, 45, 61, 63, 70, 76, 89, 321, 330, 336
Douglass, Frederick 6, 24, 171, 187, 189–190, 197, 215, 247, 249, 285, 289, 292, 322–323, 327
Douglass' Monthly 171
Dow, Neal 221, 319, 322
Doyle, Mr. 195
Draft Riots 183
Dred, A Tale of the Great Dismal Swamp 331
Dred Scott and the Problem of Constitutional Evil 45
Drunkard, The 221
Dyson, Mary 167

~ E ~

Egypt 249
Ehrlich, Walter 328
Eighth New York Cavalry 167
Eighty-seventh Pennsylvania Volunteer Infantry 305
Electoral Commission 324
Ellis, John 92, 95
Emancipation Proclamation 42, 117, 164–165, 167, 223, 249, 285–289, 291, 297–299, 301, 303, 305, 322, 326, 330
Emerson, John 41, 328
Emerson, Ralph Waldo 188, 249
Enfield Model 1853 116
Enforcement Acts 324
England 45, 137, 322, 331
  cotton imports 116
  Hull 334
English common law 3
Enlightenment 2
Enrollment Act of Conscription 183
"Enslaving the Whites to Free the Blacks" 302
Episcopalian 273
Equiano, Olaudah 3
Ericsson, John 132
Estates General 3
Evangelicals 246
Evanston College for Ladies 335
Executive Power 287, 300
"Exile's Departure, The" 334
Ex-parte Merryman 332

~ F ~

Faulkner, Charles James 203
Federalist Party 334
Fehrenbacher, Don 42
Felton, Rebecca Latimer 94
feminism 324
Fifteenth Amendment 322, 324, 327
Fifth Amendment 41, 43, 51
Fifth Massachusetts Cavalry 167
Fifth Military District 329
Fifty-fourth Massachusetts Volunteer Infantry 166, 171, 182
Fillmore, Millard 70, 321
Finley, Robert 5
First Confiscation Act 164, 285, 292
First Kansas Colored Volunteer Infantry 165–166
First Mississippi Volunteers of African Descent 165
First Presbyterian Church (Savannah, Ga.) 325
First South Carolina Volunteer Infantry 184
First South Carolina Volunteers 165, 168, 279
Fitzhugh, George 7, 15, 28, 35
Florida 4, 92–94, 102, 165, 175, 286
force bill 68
Ford's Theatre 326
Forrest, Nathan Bedford 117, 323
Fort Armstrong 42
Fort Donaldson 324
Fort Donelson 323
Fort Henry 324
"Fort Hill Address" 68
Fort Monroe 164, 177

Fort Pillow 166, 323
Fort Snelling 42, 328
Fort Sumter 95, 109, 163, 168, 190, 326
Fort Wagner 166
Founding Fathers 40, 43–45
    views on slavery 45
Fourteenth Amendment 43
Fourth New York Heavy Artillery 143
France 3, 137
    cotton imports 116
Franklin, Benjamin 4
Franklin College 330
Frederick Douglass' Paper 207
Free-Soil Party 6
Free-Staters 187
Freedmen's Bureau 321, 333
Freedmen's Savings Bank 322
Freedom Journal 19
"Freedom to Slaves!" 304
Free Soilers 334
Free Soil Movement 69, 74
Free Soil Party 221
Frémont, John C. 164, 172, 285, 292
French Revolution 3
Friends of Universal Reform 323
Fugitive Slave Act 7, 164, 221, 332
Fugitive Slave Law 41–42, 70, 75, 93, 97, 104, 186, 189, 194, 285, 289, 292, 321, 326, 331

~ G ~

Gag Rule 6
Garibaldi, Giuseppe 188
Garnet, Henry Highland 189
Garrett, Thomas M. 227
Garrison, William Lloyd 5–6, 21, 188, 219, 246, 258, 322–323, 327, 334
Geary, John White 287
Genius of Universal Emancipation, The 6, 323
Georgia 4, 92–94, 97, 102, 108, 118, 155, 175, 247–248, 269, 286, 330, 333
    Atlanta 118, 145
    Liberty 325
    Savannah 118, 184, 333
    St. Mary's 177
Georgia Republican Party 333
Germany 223
Gettysburg Address 24, 326
Gist, William H. 92
Gooding, James Henry 182
Gough, Elizabeth Barnwell 327
Graber, Marc 45
gradual emancipation 258
Grand Lodge of the Good Templars 224
Grant, Ulysses S. 117–118, 125, 145, 155, 161, 165, 167, 324, 329–330
Great Britain 5, 15, 68, 320, 327
    antislavery movement in 2
Greeley, Horace 285, 296
Greene, S. Dana 132
Grimke, Angelina 327
Grimke, Sarah 327
Grimke, Thomas 327

Grovenor, Gurdon 142
Guadeloupe 3
guerrilla fighting 142

~ H ~

Haiti 3, 322
Hale, John Parker 100
Halleck, Henry 287
Halpine, Charles C. 175
Hamlin, Hannibal 288–289
Hammond, James Henry 7
Hampton Roads Conference 330
Hancock, John 4
Hargrave, Francis 3
Harpers Ferry 186–190, 289
Harper's Weekly 188, 287
Harris, James 195
Harrison, William Henry 68
Harvard University 320, 326
    Divinity School 279
    Law School 320, 326
Hayes, Rutherford B. 324
Hayes-Tilden election 324
Hayne, Robert Y. 334
Herndon, William H. 325
Higginson, Thomas Wentworth 165, 279, 328
Holmes, George Frederick 8, 27
Hooker, Joseph 115
House of Commons 3, 335
House of Representatives 7, 41, 66, 68–69, 94, 97, 102, 219, 287, 302, 320–321, 325, 327, 330, 334–335
Hovenden, Thomas 188
Howard Committee Report 195
Howe, Julia Ward 273
Howe, Samuel Gridley 273, 328
Hunter, Andrew 203
Hunter, David 165, 175, 184, 285, 329

~ I ~

Idaho 327
Illinois 5, 41, 43, 45, 66, 70, 76, 89, 173, 288, 301, 321, 328, 330
    Alton 6
    Chicago 89
    Fort Armstrong 42
    Galena 324
    New Salem 325
    Springfield 291
Illinois Supreme Court 321
Illinois Weekly Mirror 190
immigration 223
Independent, The 194
Independent Order of Good Templars 224
Indiana 43, 325
Internal Revenue Act (1862) 223
International Migration Society 333
Iowa 43
Ireland 219
    immigrants from 223
ironclad vessels 132
Ironsides 188
Israel 249

~ J ~

Jackson, Andrew 61, 67–68, 320, 327
Jackson, Thomas J. "Stonewall" 103, 277
Jacksonian period 45
Jamaica 3, 5, 45
Jefferson, Thomas 4, 14, 67–68
Jennison, Nathaniel 14
Jesus Christ 247, 259
Joan of Arc 188
"John Brown's Body" (song) 190, 273
"John Brown and His Friends" 328
"John Brown and the Colored Child" (poem) 215
"John Brown in Massachusetts" 328
John Brown Meeting the Slave Mother and Her Child (painting) 188
Johnson, Andrew 321, 324, 329–330
Johnson, Samuel 4
Johnston, Albert Sidney 125
Johnston, Joseph E. 117
Jones, Charles Colcock 248–249, 262, 269, 277, 325
"Justice and Expedience" 334
Justinian 3, 7

~ K ~

Kansas 8, 45, 70, 89, 165, 187, 291, 328
    guerrillas in 117, 142
    Lawrence 142, 187
    Pottawatomie 195
    Pottawatomie Creek 187
Kansas-Nebraska Act 43, 50, 61, 66, 89, 321
Kansas-Nebraska Bill 187
Kendall, Amos 68
Kentucky 75, 94, 106, 115, 125, 142, 173, 285, 320, 331
    Hodgenville 325
    Lexington 320
Kentucky Anti-Slavery Society 6
Kenyon College 330
Key to Uncle Tom's Cabin, The 331
King, Preston 73
Kirkland, Charles P. 287, 300
Ku Klux Klan 323–324

~ L ~

Lafayette, Marquis de 188
Lager Beer Riot 223
Lane, James H. 165
Laurens, Henry 4
Law, E. M. 145
Law of Moses 247
Lawrence massacre 142
Lay, Benjamin 2
League of Gileadites 194
League of United Southerners 92, 336
Lee, Henry "Light-Horse Harry" 124
Lee, Robert E. 116, 118, 124, 133, 137, 145, 167, 186, 203, 287, 297, 324
    surrender of 118, 161
Letter on the Abolition of the Slave Trade, A 335
Letter to the Hon. Benjamin R. Curtis, A 300
Lewis, Asahel H. 208
Lewis, Dio 224
Lewis, Maria 167
Liberator, The 6, 258, 323, 334
Liberia 5, 286, 320, 333
Liberty Party 6, 69, 334
Lincoln 95
Lincoln, Abraham 24, 35, 40, 61, 63, 92–94, 97–98, 102–103, 109, 117, 121–122, 163–164, 167–168, 171–172, 180, 186, 246, 249, 273, 285–289, 291, 293, 295, 298–300, 305, 321–322, 324–325, 328, 330, 332–333, 336
    inaugural address 112
    Second Inaugural Address 276
Lincoln, Mary (Todd) 313
Lincoln-Douglas debates 63
Longfellow, Henry Wadsworth 188
Longstreet, James 137
Lost Cause 250, 277
Louisiana 42, 92, 94, 102, 165, 178, 321, 329
    Milliken's Bend 165
    Port Hudson 165, 178
Louisiana Native Guards 165
Louisiana Purchase 6, 40, 89, 321
L'Ouverture, Tousint, 3
Lovejoy, Elijah 6
Lundy, Benjamin 6
Luther, Martin 188
lynching 322

~ M ~

Madison, James 68, 333
Maine 66
    Portland 221, 323
Maine Laws 221, 223, 228, 319, 323
Manifest Destiny 68
Mansfield, Lord 45, 333
manumission 48
Marietta Register 173
Marshall, Charles 161
Marshall, John 331
Maryland 48, 115, 117, 174, 285, 331
    Baltimore 322, 333
    Dorchester County 332
    Sharpsburg 133, 287
    Talbot County 322
Mason, George 4
Mason, James M. 80, 93, 97, 289, 326
Mason, James Murray 203
Massachusetts 6, 14, 56, 66, 84, 221, 285, 334–335
    Boston 6, 19, 279, 326
    New Bedford 322
    Springfield 194
    Watertown 320
Massachusetts Anti-Slavery Society 322
Massachusetts Indian Commission 327
Massachusetts Kansas Commission 328
Massachusetts Supreme Court 4, 14
Mathew, Theobald 219
Mayflower (ship) 188
McClellan, George B. 115, 121, 276, 287, 289
McCulloch v. Maryland 334
McDowell, Irvin 115
McLean, John 42

McLean, Wilmer 161
Meade, George 116, 118, 145
"Mediation on the Divine Will" 276
medical knowledge 117
Mercer, Charles Fenton 5
Merrick, Caroline 243
Merrimac, USS (ship) 132
Merryman, John 332
Methodist Church 7
Methodist Episcopal Church 247
Methodist Episcopal Church, South 333
Methodists 219, 246–247
Mexican-American War 69
Mexican Cession 69
Mexican War 7, 23, 324–326
Mexico 7, 68–69, 73–74, 327
    outlaws slavery 68
Michigan 43, 69
Middle Passage 3
Militia Act 165, 286, 289
Milroy, Robert H. 287, 289, 304–305, 326
Milton, John 188
Minnesota 42
Mississippi 5, 92–94, 102, 117, 125, 165, 167, 172
    Vicksburg 138, 324
Missouri 5, 41–42, 56, 70, 115, 125, 165, 172, 285
    guerrillas in 117, 142
    Island Mound 165
    St. Louis 328, 333
    statehood 66
Missouri Compromises 6, 40, 42–43, 45, 50, 56, 66, 69–70, 94, 106, 321, 328
Missouri Compromise Line 69, 74, 327
Missouri Supreme Court 41–42
Missouri Territory 66
Monitor, USS (ironclad) 132
Monroe, James 320
Montgomery, James 179, 332
Moore, Andrew B. 92
Moore, Thomas 92
Moses 188, 209
Murphy, Francis 241
Murray, James M. 75
Murray, John (Lord Dunmore) 4
Murray, William (Mansfield, Earl of) 3
muzzle-loading weapons 116
"My Army Cross Over" 279
My Bondage and My Freedom 322

~ N ~

Napoleonic Wars 335
Narrative of the Life of Frederick Douglass, an American Slave 24, 322
National Assembly (France) 3
National Era, The 331
National Sons of Temperance 224
National Temperance Society
    and Publication House 224, 242, 319
Native American rights 327
Nativists 218, 223
natural-law theory of slavery 7

naval blockade 144
Navy, U.S. 329
    black sailors in 167
Nebraska 70, 291
Nelson, Samuel 42, 45
Nevada 327
Newburyport Free Press 334
New England 70, 188, 219, 322, 328, 334
New England Anti-Slavery Society 323
Newhall, Fales Henry 188
New Hampshire 100
    Concord 334
    Salisbury 334
New Jersey 5, 288
Newman, William P. 189
New Mexico 43, 50, 69–70, 327
New National Era 322
New Testament 247
New York 4, 42, 66, 224, 246, 273, 287–288, 328
    Auburn 332
    Canandaigua 321
    New York City 42, 183, 322
    North Elba 319
    Rochester 187, 322
    Syracuse 187
    West Point 324
New York City Draft Riots 183
New York Herald 170, 175
New York Herald Tribune 215
New York Times, The 183, 241
New York Tribune 207, 285, 296
Nichols, George Ward 160
Ninth Indiana Infantry 326
Noble, Thomas Satterwhite 188
North 68, 221
    advantages over South 115
North, Frederick (Lord North) 334
North Carolina 6, 92, 95, 102, 118, 327
    Wilmington 19
Northern Democrats 70
North Star, The 189, 207, 322
Northwestern University 335
Northwest Ordinance 50
Northwest Territory
    slavery banned in 43
Nova Scotia 4
Nueces River 327
nullification 68, 327, 334
Nullification Crisis 320
Nullification Proclamation 68

~ O ~

O'Sullivan, John 68
Oakey, Daniel 155
Ohio 43, 173, 208, 331
    Cincinnati 331
    laws on slavery 42
    Mount Pleasant 6
    Point Pleasant 324
Ohio River 325
Old Testament 247, 249

Onesimus 247
Order of Retaliation 182
Oregon 327, 329

~ P ~

Pacific Ocean 69, 74
pacifism 2
Panic of 1837 335
Panic of 1839 193
Parker, Richard 206, 289, 326
Parker, Theodore 328
Parliament 3, 5, 15, 335
Paul, Saint 188, 209, 247
Pennington, James 322
Pennsylvania 4, 7, 11, 69, 190, 218, 328
    Chambersburg 207
    Gettysburg 117, 137
    Lancaster 319
    Philadelphia 4, 332, 334
    Pittsburgh 190
    Quakers 2
Pennsylvania Act for the Gradual Abolition of Slavery 11
Pennsylvania Freeman 334
Pennsylvania Hall 334
Perry, Benjamin 335
Perry, Governor Madison S. 93
Perry, Milton 92
Personal Memoirs (Grant) 324
Peter, Saint 209
Petersburg-Richmond campaigns 167
Pettus, John 92
Phelps, Dodge, and Company 321
Phillips, Wendell 6, 188, 215, 326
Pickett, George 137
Pierce, Franklin 61
Pitt, William (the Younger) 334
Plains Indian Wars 329
Planter (ship) 167, 329
Polk 69
Polk, James K. 69, 73–74, 327
Pope, John 115
popular sovereignty 70
Postal Service, U.S. 19
Potomac River 137
Potter, David 40
Prayer of Twenty Millions, The 296
Presbyterian Church 5, 247–248, 277, 325–326
Presbyterian Church in the
    Confederate States of America 269, 325
Presbyterians 219, 269
Princeton Theological Seminary 325
prohibition 319
Prohibition Party 224, 319, 323
proslavery ideology 2, 7–8, 15, 35
Puritans 188

~ Q ~

Quakers 2–3
Quantrill, William C. 142

~ R ~

Rachael (slave) 42
Rachael v. Walker 42
racism 163, 250
Radical Political Abolitionists 187–188
Radical Reconstruction 250
Radical Republican 327, 330
Randolph, Frances Bland 333
Randolph, John 333
Randolph, Peter 256
Ransom, Louis 188
Raymond, Henry 172
Reconstruction 224, 241, 320, 330
Reconstruction Acts 329
Reign of Terror 3
Religious Instruction for Negroes in the Southern States 325
Representation of the injustice and the dangerous tendency of admitting the least claim of private property in the persons of men, A 3
Republican Party 41, 45, 56, 90, 92, 94, 109, 186, 224, 291, 322, 324–325, 327, 330
"Resistance to Civil Government" 23
Revels, Hiram 250
Revolutionary War 177
Rhett, Robert Barnwell 92–93, 102, 327
Rhode Island 4
Richardson, William A. 301
Richmond Daily Dispatch 180
Right Worthy Grand Lodge of the World 224
Rio Grande 69, 327
Rochester Ladies' Anti-Slavery Society 24
Roman Empire 247
Rush, Benjamin 218
Russell, Thomas 207

~ S ~

"Sambo's Right to Be Kilt" (song) 175
Sanborn, Franklin B. 187, 328
Sandford, John A. 42
Scotland 322
Scott, Dred 8, 40–46, 70, 320, 328, 332
Scott, Harriet (Robinson)
Scott, William 42, 173
Scott, Winfield 95, 117, 124
Scott v. Sandford 40–46, 70, 74
Scriptural and Statistical Views in Favor of Slavery 262
secession 327, 330, 334–335
Second American Party System 67
Second Confiscation Act 165
Second Great Awakening 219, 246
Second Massachusetts Volunteers 155
Second Missouri Compromise 320
Second South Carolina Volunteers 167, 179, 332
Secret Six 328
Seddon, James A. 137
Senate 66, 76, 84, 94, 97, 102, 322, 330, 334
"Seventh of March" 70
Seventy-ninth Infantry Regiment 165
Seven Years' War (1756-1763) 2
Seward, William H. 95, 109, 287, 295, 297

Sharp, Granville 3
Shaw, Robert Gould 166
Shenandoah Valley 145, 289, 329
Sheridan, Philip 329
Sherman, William T. 118, 155, 160, 195
Shotwell, Randolph A. 124
Sierra Leone 5
    Freetown 4
slave marriages 249
slave owners
    rights 43
slave preachers 256
slave revolts 189
slavery 1–5, 11, 14, 23, 27, 35, 40–43, 66, 68–70, 73–74, 84, 89, 94, 97, 103–104, 106, 108, 163, 186, 219, 269, 277, 291, 319–321, 323, 325, 327–328, 330, 333, 335
    abolishment 285–289
    in territories 43–44
    outlawed in North 46
    religious defense of 246
slave trade 1, 3, 5, 15, 41, 68, 323, 335
Slidell, John 327
Smalls, Robert 167, 329
Smedes, William 172
Smith, Gerrit 319, 328
Smith, James McCune 190, 215
Smith, Joshua B. 189
social reform 335
Society for Effectuating the Abolition of the Slave Trade 3, 335
Society of Friends (Quakers) 2
Sociology for the South 7, 28
Soldiers' Aid Societies 331
Somerset, James 3, 45
Somerset Ruling 3, 45, 333
Sons of Temperance 219, 221, 227, 319
South 1, 5–6, 15, 19, 42, 48, 92, 94, 221, 224, 227, 320, 323–324, 327, 336
    exports 116
South America
    colonization of former slaves in 293
South Carolina 4, 7, 68, 74, 80, 92–94, 102–103, 106, 118, 175, 177, 248, 279, 286, 320, 334
    Beaufort 327, 329
    Charleston 68, 95, 109, 144, 167, 329
    Columbia 118, 160, 325
    Fort Wagner 166
    Greenville 335
    House of Representatives 68, 329
    Newberry Courthouse 333
    Port Royal 165
"South Carolina Exposition and Protest" 68
Southern Baptist Convention's Domestic Mission Board 262
Southern coastline 115
Southern Manifesto 102
Southwest Ordinance 43
Spain 68
Spanish American War 168
Spartacus 188
Speed, Joshua F. 291
Springfield Model 1861 116
St. Domingue 3
Stanton, Edwin M. 287, 295, 299–330
states' rights 320

Stearns, George Luther 328
Stephens, Alexander H. 92, 94, 96–97, 108, 330
Steuart, Charles 3
Stevenburg Baptist Church 262
Stevens, Thaddeus 333
Stewart, "Mother" Eliza Daniel 224, 331
Stono Slave Rebellion 4
Stowe, Calvin 331
Stowe, Harriet Beecher 7, 27, 252, 331
Strader v. Graham 42
Streichler, Stuart 321
strict constructionists 51
Stringfellow, Thornton 248, 262
Strunke, Elias 178
Stuart, J. E. B. 203
sugar lobby 335
Suggestions on the Instruction of Negroes in the South 325
Sumner, Charles 285, 324, 333
Supreme Court 8, 40–42, 45, 51, 70, 287, 321, 328, 330, 332, 334

~ T ~

Tallmadge, James, Jr. 66, 73
Taney, Roger B. 40–43, 45–46, 51, 61, 70, 321, 331
Tappan, Arthur 6
Tappan, Lewis 6
Tapping Reeve Law School 320
Taylor, Susie King 168, 184
Taylor, Zachary 69, 70, 219
Tell, William 188
temperance 22, 323
Temperance Movement 218–225, 321
Temple of Honor 237
Temple of Templars 224
Ten Islands Baptist Association of Alabama 234
Tennessee 43, 69, 95, 118, 125, 155, 324, 327
    Bedford County 323
    Fort Pillow 166
    Memphis 323
    Pittsburg Landing 125
    Tullahoma 326
Ten Nights in a Barroom 221
Texas 7, 68, 70, 94, 102, 327, 329
    Palmito Ranch 167
    San Antonio 68
Third Party System 224
Thirteenth Amendment 1, 289
Thirteenth Maine Volunteer Infantry 323
Thomas, Jesse 66
Thompson, David L. 134
Thompson, Henry 187
Thoreau, Henry David 7, 23, 328
three-fifths Clause 41, 68
Toombs, Robert 97
Transcendentalists 328
Treaty of Guadalupe-Hidalgo 69
Trowbridge, Charles Taylor 184
Tubman, Harriet 167, 179, 332
Tucker, Nathaniel Beverley 7
Tucker, St. George 5, 7, 332
Turner, Henry McNeal 250, 333
Turner, Nat 7, 189, 215
Tyler, John 68, 334

~ U ~

Uncle Tom's Cabin 7, 27, 252, 331
Underground Railroad 319, 332
Union Army 121, 273, 279, 287
Union Theological Seminary 277
Unitarians 273, 279
United Friends of Temperance 224
United States Brewers' Association 223
United States Colored Troops 165
United States Indian Commission 321
United States League of Gileadites 186
United States Military Academy 324
United States Sanitary Commission 331
Upper Canada 5
U.S. Army 41
U.S. Colored Cavalry 167
U.S. Colored Troops 165, 333
U.S. Military Academy 329
U.S. Sanitary Commission 273
Utah 43, 50, 70, 172, 327

~ V ~

Vallandigham, Clement L. 203
Vermont 4
    Brandon 321
Virginia 4, 7, 35, 48, 75, 80, 93–95, 145, 155, 167, 188, 190, 256, 277, 287, 328, 330, 332
    Appomattox Courthouse 161
    Charles Town 186, 203, 206
    Culpeper County 262
    Danville 305
    Fauquier County 262
    Fredericksburg 287
    Hampton Roads 132
    Hanover County 320
    Harpers Ferry 8, 186, 188, 190, 203, 206–207, 249, 279, 289, 319, 328, 332
    manumission law 5
    Petersburg 166
    Richmond 118, 124, 167–168
    Rockbridge County 94, 103
    Shenandoah Valley 103
    Southampton 189, 215
    Winchester 289, 304–305, 326
Virginia, CSS (ironclad) 132
Virginia and Kentucky Resolutions 68

~ W ~

Walker, David 6, 19, 189
Walker, Isaac P. 219
Walker, Quock 4, 14
War Department 165, 167
warhawk 320
War of 1812 117, 177, 320, 334
    blacks in 163
Washington, D.C. 93, 95, 102, 133, 219, 322, 325, 327, 333, 336
Washington, George 4, 145, 188, 215, 218
Washingtonians, The 219, 319
Washington Peace Conference 95
weaponry 116
Webster, Daniel 70, 84, 334
Webster-Ashburton Treaty 334
Weigley, Russell F. 117
Weld, Theodore 6
Welles, Gideon 167, 295
Wells, Robert W. 42
West Africa 5
West Indies 2, 219
Whig Party 42, 45, 56, 68–69, 89, 320–322, 327, 332, 334
Whiskey Rebellion 218
White House 288
white supremacy 170
Whittier, John Greenleaf 188, 215, 334
Wiebe, Robert 223
Wilberforce, William 3, 5, 15, 334
Wilder, C. B. 177
Wilkinson, Mr. 195
Willard, Frances 224, 243, 335
William and Mary, College of 7, 333
Williams College 335
Wilmot, David 7, 69, 73–74
Wilmot Proviso 7, 69
Wilson, Harry 223
Wisconsin 42–43, 70, 219, 328
Wisconsin Territory 45
Wise, Henry 203
Wittenmyer, Annie 224
Woman's Crusade 224
Women's Christian Temperance Union (WCTU) 224, 243, 331, 335
Women's Crusade 331, 335
women's rights 6, 224, 335
women's suffrage 22, 324, 327, 335
Women's Temperance League of Osborne 331
"Words of Advice" (Brown) 187, 194
World Temperance Convention (1846) 219
Wylie Street A.M.E. Church 190

~ Y ~

Yale College 320
Yancey, William Lowndes 92, 335
Young Men's Christian Association 321

~ Z ~

Zouaves 134